Economics, Finance and Law on MNEs

ECONOMICS, FINANCE AND LAW ON MNES

GEORGIOS I. ZEKOS

Nova Science Publishers, Inc.
New York

For permission to use material from this book please contact us:
Telephone 631-231-7269; Fax 631-231-8175
Web Site: http://www.novapublishers.com

Library of Congress Cataloging-in-Publication Data

Zekos, Georgios I.
Economics, finance and law on MNEs / Georgios I. Zekos (author).
p. cm.
Introduction -- Introduction to MNEs -- Definition of MNEs -- Issues of MNEs -- Evolution of modern MNEs -- The eclectic paradigm (OLI) -- MNEs and the law -- Legal forms of MNEs -- The role of legal factors -- MNE and codes -- MNEs, national and international law -- States and international law -- The CSR and human rights obligations of private corporations presently under international law -- MNEs and The Norms Chapter -- MNE and integration -- Integration -- MNE and regional integration -- The Impact of MNEs -- Location of MNE -- MNE and home states -- Expansion of MNE -- MNE and subsidiaries -- Multinationals and embeddedness -- Multinationals and social responsibility -- MNE and FDI -- Multinationals and taxation -- Entrance of MNE and training of the workforce -- MNE and performance -- MNE and manufacturing systems -- Transfer of technology -- Transfer of prises -- Planning and multinationals -- Management of MNE -- The management of international R&D -- Codification of knowledge flows by MNE -- The Role of FDI -- FDI -- FDI and Development -- FDI and Competition -- FDI and Productivity -- FDI and Labour -- Information Technology and FDI -- EU AND FDI -- Globalisation, MNE and finance -- Globalisation -- Globalisation and integration -- The evolvement of FDI, MNE and globalization -- Globalisation and FDI -- Globalisation and development -- Globalisation, law and economy -- Globalisation and marketing -- Financial globalization -- MNE, law and finance -- Monetary policy and financial markets -- Globalisation and finance -- Finance and dollarization -- Finance and EU -- digital economy, MNE and e-commerce -- Digital economy -- E-commerce -- E-commerce and Internet -- Logistics in globalisation and e-commerce -- E-commerce and industrial distributors -- Characteristics of digital economy -- Digital economy and globalisation -- Conclusions.
ISBN-13: 978-1-60021-831-6 (hardcover)
ISBN-10: 1-60021-831-8 (hardcover)
1. International business enterprises. 2. International business enterprises--Finance. 3. International business enterprises--Law and legislation. I. Title. II. Title: Economics, finance and law on multinational enterprises.
HD2755.5.Z45 2007
338.8'8--dc22 2007025524

Published by Nova Science Publishers, Inc. ✦New York

To the memory of my Father

Ioannis Zekos

CONTENTS

INTRODUCTION

Global capitalism was seen an essentially unstable system and a new set of global financial institutions emerged in the mid 1940s, known as the Bretton Woods Institutions. The United Nations (UN) created, mainly to function as a forum for debate. Financial institutions were needed for stabilizing currencies and enabling capital investment in underdeveloped regions. As a response to this, the so-called Bretton Woods institutions came into being, all in order to promote the new global concern. It could be said that the creation of the Bretton Woods system has eroded the sovereignty of states to impose exchange control regimes at will. The International Monetary Fund (IMF) was created to be responsible for keeping currencies stable and facilitate trade. Since money is power, and money must be regulated transnationally in a global economy, state power itself is being regulated at the multilateral level by the institutions that manage capital flows, specifically the IMF. The problem is situations in which the political element of international financial regulation allows the interests of powerful capital-owning classes, multinational enterprises, and capital-rich countries to overcome the interests of the rest of the world in the structure of international financial policy. The World Bank' mission is to facilitate capital investments in underdeveloped regions and open them for development. WTO is another trade body of independent legal identity with its goal to abolish barriers to free movement of goods and capital serving the global corporations with legislative and judicial powers for additional economic globalization. Moreover, the role of the World Bank was to provide long term financing for economic reconstruction and development. In early 20th century globalisation, there were not global financial institutions designed at stabilizing the world economy, financing development, setting global rules for international trade in goods and services, and provide a political forum to settle disputes among states such as the United Nations.

The company is best understood as a 'living' entity and its direction in the marketplace – in other words, its capacity to learn and adapt to competitive pressures – is steered by a multifaceted community of social actors, who are enrolled in a complex web of relations with other institutional and governmental elites, and so on. Companies are now in an enduring state of emergency and must consequently be prepared for regular learning and adaptation. Cyberspace is a global network of computers linked by high-speed data lines and wireless systems. Moreover, the Internet is not a net in the physical or communicational sense but an open virtual network based on a common transmission protocol. The growth in the use of the Internet has been one of the most interesting technological and political developments of the late twentieth century. The Internet is joining the assault on sovereignty and will, perhaps more than any of the other globalisation forces contribute to relegating sovereignty and its traditional trappings to the residue heap of history. Cyberspace can strengthen national and global governance. International relations are influenced by domestic political phenomena and the interaction of non-state actors across borders. Hence, cyberspace joins a long historical heritage of new information technologies threatening to upset the existing nature of politics within nation-states. The Internet as we know it embodies a key underlying technical idea, namely that of open architecture networking. In an open-architecture network, the individual networks may be independently designed and developed and each may have its own unique interface, which it may offer to users and/or other providers, including other Internet providers. Each network can be designed in accordance with the specific environment and user requirements of that network. A major shift occurred as a result of the increase in scale of the Internet and its associated management issues[1].

Is international economy less open and integrated than the regime that prevailed from 1870 to 1914? The modern concepts of direct investment on the one hand involving some notion of managerial control from abroad and portfolio investment on the other –involving the acquisition of securities issued by foreign institutions so as to claim returns without any associated control or management participation- were only developed in the early 1960s at the same time as the term MNE was itself introduced. Firms may serve foreign markets by exporting goods or by turning into MNE opening production plants in different states and provide markets with local production. International production has surpassed exports as the principal means of delivering goods and services to foreign markets[2]. The United Nations[3] define MNEs as "enterprises which own or control production or service facilities outside the country in which they are based". Multinational corporations are defined as "enterprises that have a network of wholly or partially (jointly with one or more foreign partners) owned producing, marketing or R&D affiliates located in a number of countries"[4]. In the period 1945-73 the dominant factor driving the world economy was growth in international trade. From the early 1980s starts the growth of FDI. International short-term financial flows have expanded rapidly since the abandonment of fixed exchange rates and capital controls in the 1970s. After the collapse of the Bretton Woods agreement in 1970 there is not an adequate control mechanism in place to prevent volatility to exchange rates and interest rates and in accordance with M. Miller[5] there is a need for the establishment of global governance. The American economy persisted to grow at a high rate in the 1990s. It could be said that MNEs are the agents responsible for FDI. Is FDIs distribution socially and geographically uneven on a world scale?

Is capitalism the engine of globalisation? Capitalism is a structure of production where economic activity is oriented to the accumulation of surplus and tends to exploit all possible resources. Capitalism has spurred globalisation by the way of firms pursuing global markets as means to increase their sales and higher production runs to supply global markets bringing significant economies of scale and thereby raising profit margins. On the one hand,

---

[1]G Zekos, MNEs and Human Rights in International Law and Globalization, 2006 The ICFAI journal of International Business Law, issue October p7 www.icfaipress.org .G Zekos, State Cyberspace Jurisdiction and Personal Cyberspace Jurisdiction in Cyber Crimes and Cyber Torts, 2006 ICFAI Journal of Cyber Law, May 06, p 9 *www.icfaipress.org*

[2] UNCTAD 2000, World Investment Report 2000, New York.

[3] United Nations, Multinational Corporation in World Development, United Nations, New York, 1973, p. 23.

[4] Phatak, A. 1989. International dimensions of management. Massachusetts: PWS-Kent Publishing Company.

[5] M.Miller, Where is globalisation taking us? , 1995 Futures 125-144.

Capitalism is a system in which persons are free to choose which goals to chase. On the other hand, Capitalism, the system that maximizes human freedom, cannot guarantee a moral society. It could be argued that if communities are liberally chosen, the results are a sense of joint ownership, a concurrence of concern, and a feel of belonging. Moreover, the cooperative nature of the corporation illustrates that capitalism is far from the radical individualism that critics have claimed it to be. MNE originate in the capitalistic developed economies. Edward W. Younkins[6] says that "Capitalism, the best system for wealth creation, permits individuals to spend less time on physical concerns thus giving them the time to turn to higher level pursuits of happiness such as religious pursuits, education, love, creative and fulfilling work, character development, and community building". Has capitalism achieved these ideals? A market is a place where goods are displayed and offered for sale. The buyers and sellers in a market choose what sales to perform by deliberating in the light of the alternatives that the market offers to them. Consequently the complete outcome of being in a large marketplace is not evident from physical facts such as goods crossing docks in cargo containers. The full effect includes the consequences of prices being influenced by the possible accessibility of alternatives not in fact chosen. The most favourable economic strategy for a nation is to exploit its comparative advantages as effectively as possible and the most effective way to do this is through the free operation of factor and product markets and open competition among firms. Neoclassical theory implies that free mobility of products and factors of production across national boundaries will maximize efficiency and all economic players will concentrate in what they do best, both within nations and between nations. Productive efficiency is achieved by the utilization of comparative advantages as companies are forced by competition in the market to use the most competent production techniques available. Comparative advantage is conferred by a nation's natural endowment of factors of production. On the one hand, countries that have abundant labour, relative to capital, will specialize in the production of intensive-intensive goods rather than the production of capital-intensive goods. On the other hand, countries endowed with natural resources will produce resource-intensive goods.

Do market forces determine which technology will be used? Is it the technology that is used which dictates that the market must be moulded to fit technology's requirements? Nowadays companies can transfer advanced technology to countries with low labour costs, and concurrently exploit the advantages of cheap capital in capital-rich countries. As a consequence of enhanced global mobility, a new capitalist world economy has emerged and key feature is a massive migration of capital from the industrialized countries to low-cost production sites in the third world. The cause of the globalisation of production is market forces and property rights. The advent of mass production technology brings with it the desire and the need to manage the market and to stabilize demand[7]. Multinational enterprises play vital role in promoting and shaping the patterns of economic development, and this responsibility is affected by means of their foreign direct investment decisions. MNEs are

---

[6] Edward W. Younkins, Capitalism, Commerce and the Corporation, 2002 American Law Review Thur June 13, 2002.

[7] Lester Thurow, The Future of Capitalism. New York: W. Morrow, 1996. p. 115. "The `globalization' topic arises from a cluster of empirical data which show how in many branches and areas of activity, there is a small number of relevant firms operating and there are no national boundaries to competition. So in sectors like finances, telecommunications, aerospace, semiconductors etc. there exists real world-wide competition among a reduced number of firms."

required to assess the requests of international integration of production within the enterprise, with that of the need to respond to local surroundings. MNEs operate to capitalize on the production of income and access to the capital markets.

Ghoshal & Bartlett[8] characterize MNEs as a group of geographically dispersed and goal-disparate organizations. Managing global operations for a company are more difficult as it has to face different cultures, values, rules, and shifting degrees of business, political, and economical uncertainties. Worldwide operating companies are faced with far more uncertainty, both internally and externally, than their domestic counterparts[9]. The largest 200 MNEs are estimated to account for 27.5% of world economic activity[10]. Inflows of foreign capital - whether in the form of FDI or portfolio capital - will raise the marginal product of labour and reduce the marginal product of capital in the host country. The multinationals' R&D and technology is profoundly concentrated to a few home countries, unlike MNE investment, production, and employment that are more broadly spread across both industrialized and developing economies. Technology is an essentially abstract concept, and therefore difficult to observe and evaluate. MNEs control technology supplies by virtue of their ownership of proprietary technologies, but they also account for a considerable share of the demand, via their foreign affiliates. The intra-firm character of the technology transfers that take place through trade in capital equipment and other products is less apparent, but still noticeable. A considerable share of the exports and imports of the major home countries flow between MNE parents and affiliates and closely tied to FDI. Exports from the MNE's home country may be adequate to prompt reverse engineering that is frequently recognized as one of the main sources of involuntary technology dissemination. Hence, foreign direct investment may promote economic development by contributing to productivity growth and exports in their host countries. Lower trade barriers tend to nudge out low-productivity plants while enabling the highly productive to sell more abroad. Aggregate productivity rises as employment shifts from low productivity plants driven out by import competition to high productivity plants turning toward export markets. Multinational enterprises have grown relative to the world economy and now account for at least 20 per cent of world production and 70 per cent of world trade. MNEs are vital to global trade with a third of world trade estimated to be intra-firm trade between branches of MNEs generating international transfer of technology.

Is globalisation a further step of capitalism and its new form worldwide? Globalisation affects economies include expanded trade in merchandise and services, product and technology licensing, greater international portfolio investment, and FDI. Globalisation[11] is generally defined as the "denationalisation of clusters of political, economic, and social

---

[8] Ghoshal, S., & Bartlett, C. 1990. The multinational corporation as an inter-organizational network. Academy of Management Review, 15 (4): 603–625.

[9] Zubair M. Mohamed, An integrated production-distribution model for a multinational company operating under varying exchange rates, Int. J. Production Economics 58 (1999) 81-92

[10] SARAH ANDERSON & JOHN CAVANAGH, TOP 200: THE RISE OF CORPORATE GLOBAL POWER 9 (2000), at *http://www.ips-dc.org/reports/top200.htm.*

[11] Jost Delbrück, Globalization of Law, Politics, and Markets-Implications for Domestic Law—A European Perspective, 1 IND. J. GLOBAL LEGAL STUD. 9, 10-11 (1993). David P. Fidler, The Globalization of Public Health: Emerging Infectious Diseases and International Relations, 5 IND. J. GLOBAL LEGAL STUD. 11, 14 (1997); Gordon R. Walker & Mark A. Fox, Globalization: An Analytical Framework, 3 IND. J. GLOBAL LEGAL STUD. 375, 380 (1996); Jonathan Fried, Globalization and International Law—Some Thoughts for States and Citizens, 23 QUEEN'S L.J. 259, 267 (1997).

activities" that destabilize the ability of the sovereign State to control activities on its territory, due to the rising need to find solutions for universal problems, like the pollution of the environment, on an international level. In connection with these processes, non-State actors, like Green peace or Amnesty International, become global "pressure groups" that act on behalf of the public interest. Globalisation is a complex, forceful legal and social process that take place within an integrated whole without regard to geographical boundaries. Globalisation thus differs from international activities, which arise between and among States, and it differs from multinational activities that occur in more than one nation-State. This does not mean that countries are not involved in the sociolegal dynamics that those transboundary process trigger. In a sense, the movements triggered by global processes promote greater economic interdependence among countries. Globalisation can be traced back to the depression preceding World War II and globalisation at that time included spreading of the capitalist economic system as a means of getting access to extended markets. The first step was to create sufficient export surplus to maintain full employment in the capitalist world and secondly establishing a globalized economy where the planet would be united in peace and wealth. Is it possible to halt or reverse globalisation? The following analysis will present author's view. The idea of interdependence among quite separate and distinct countries is a very important part of talks on globalisation and a significant side of today's global political economy. Is globalisation synonymous with Americanisation? Globalisation, however, is generally used descriptively but with the clear implication that since no force can change it, all had better get on board[12]. Globalisation, boosted by the acceptance of market-oriented economic policies in developing countries and transition economies, is being accompanied by extensive financial volatility characterized by currency crisis of high frequency and intensity, upsetting large developing and transition economies. Is globalisation a further step of capitalism and its new form worldwide? Has globalisation brought forward the emergence of digital economy? At present time the emerging digital economy works in tandem with the traditional forms of economy including the partly use of e-commerce and its technology. Globalisation tends to reward creative and technically skilled workers and to place its largest pressures on lower-skilled workers. Hence, globalisation affects economies include expanded trade in merchandise and services, product and technology licensing, greater international portfolio investment, and FDI. Globalisation is a dynamic and multidimensional process and so resources that used to be national are becoming internationally mobile, while national economies are growing more and more interdependent. The globalisation of trade in goods and services has opened up new and more and more vast markets and so financial markets have triggered sharp growth in investment portfolios and large movements of short-term capital, with borrowers and investors interacting through a more and more unified market. The globalisation of technology stems from the speed with which innovations are propagated, with international networks linking to public and private research centres, as well as from converging standards involving not only foreign direct investment and relocation but also joint ventures, co-operation agreements and strategic alliances. In a globalized economy, distances and national boundaries have diminished as obstacles to economic transactions. Globalization[13] has encouraged the formation of mega-

[12] Gregory Shaffer, Globalization and Social Protection: The Impact of EU and International Rules in the Ratcheting Up of U.S. Privacy Standards, 25 YALE J. INT'L L. 1, 70-88 (2000).

[13] Stiglitz, J. E. 2003. Globalization and its Discontents. New York: W. W. Norton & Co.

sized firms as competitors vie for global market share and global strategies depend on achieving economies of scale dictating that companies be large in order to compete successfully and to seek ever-increasing sources of cost advantages in world markets. With globalization, there is an increase in the number of strategic alliances not captured in formal merger and acquisition arrangements. Globalization creates financial markets that are in effect democratized and so money move more easily across borders, and money markets are more and more integrated. The democratization of information, facilitated by globalization and cyberspace, makes information available quickly and inexpensively to a vast number of stakeholders, so that the acts of companies are directly made part of the public record. Trade flows and incentives favouring advanced economies encourage lax enforcement of positive social norms on the part of developing country governments competing for scarce investment money, and offer environments in which MNEs and their agents act opportunistically.

It is extensively believed that exchange rate changes affect the value of firms with foreign operations. Currency fluctuations can have a spectacular impact on the performance of firms with international activities by affecting the relative prices of domestic and foreign goods and the value of foreign currency denominated fixed assets and liabilities. Will the effect of exchange rate changes on a firm's stock price be insignificant because multinational firms are utilizing various hedging instruments including forwards, futures, options and swaps? Firms with extensive exchange exposure and large-scale economy of using hedging are more likely to use currency derivatives. Exchange rate changes affect the values of MNEs disturbing both the prices and quantities of the inputs and outputs of multinational firms, which leads to competitive advantages or disadvantages in the global marketplace. The currency composition of foreign debt stocks can be deemed to be an effective tool for foreign debt portfolio management. Exchange rate movements affect the stock return volatility and market risk of firms and so implications for the decisions of investors in relation to portfolio risk management. Therefore, if the market risk of the firm increases, then investors demand higher returns for holding the firm's shares. The Asian crisis of 1997 has created a crisis of the concept of globalisation, understood as a set of ideas promoting unregulated free flow of capital, further global integration and further reduction of the influence of governments on economic policy making. It seems that the world financial system has failed to provide both adequate warning signals as well as solutions once the Asian crisis developed. Foreign debt management has become a key element of fiscal policymaking in terms of exchange and interest rate variability and volatility in capital flows. When governments are the key foreign dept managers, they should avoid asset and liability structures that are likely to increase portfolio management costs. The foreign dept managers must have the ability to adjust the currency composition of foreign dept portfolios in line with exchange rate movements because the currency composition of foreign debt stocks can be deemed to be an effective tool for foreign debt portfolio management. It could be argued that globalisation is beneficial providing new investment and financing opportunities. Liberalisation policies should be accompanied by strengthened prudential regulation to prevent maturity mismatches. Companies that do not participate in international markets are likely increasing their short term financing liabilities.

A company's financial strength affects its capacity to engage in foreign direct investment (FDI). The increase or decrease technology and capital flows by the MNE's are dependent on the belief about the enforcement of current and future restrictions. Integrating financial markets is in itself not a guarantee that a perfectly competitive market will be established.

Market integration alone cannot assure lowest possible prices and the expected subsequent dynamic economic growth effects. Financial strategies such as pursuing globally recognized accounting and disclosure, listing and selling the firm's equity on prestigious foreign equity exchanges, and the implementation of cross-border debt/equity swaps aimed at enhancing a firm's financial strength. The capacity of a company to develop its competitive advantage through FDI depends on discovering product, locational or financial market imperfections that encourage FDI. Some FDI is motivated by imperfections in the foreign exchange markets. The tendency of companies to own foreign income-generating assets may be influenced by financial and exchange rate variables. MNEs must expand and hold on to their present access to foreign investors.

Aim of the analysis is the investigation of matters of law and economics regarding MNEs, the influence of cyberspace and globalisation upon MNEs and finance. The globalisation of finance and the emergence of e-finance are new elements on the investigation of the financial acceleration. MNEs and FDI are factors having their own impact upon the present financial development around the globe. The interrelation of law, economics and finance will be part of the current analysis as well.

Chapter I

INTRODUCTION TO MNES

1.1 DEFINITION OF MNES

A multinational was defined as a firm that had production facilities in a number of countries, a definition that became standard in the initial international management literature[1]. Llilienthal defined MNEs as "corporations...which have their home in one country but which operate and live under the laws and customs of their countries as well"[2]. Economists define as multinational enterprise any company, which "owns, controls and manages income generating assets in more than one country"[3]. This definition distinguishes between an enterprise that engage in direct investment, which gives the enterprise not only a functional stake in the foreign venture but also managerial control, and one that engages in portfolio investment, which gives the interesting enterprise only a financial stake in the foreign venture without any managerial control. Hence, the MNE is a company that engages in direct investment outside its home country.

Can an e-MNE be defined as a firm that has facilities in a number of countries and its management achieved via cyberspace? According to Egelhoff "New theory should confront and climb over the back of old theory, not bypass or ignore old theory".[4] So, an e-MNE can be defined as a virtual enterprise that has production facilities in various countries concerning tangible goods and an advanced network dealing with intangible goods and services achieved its management via cyberspace by humans or some actions be made by electronic agents such as electronic contracts and automated sales. Of course, the programming of the electronic agents in order to deal with electronic transactions is made by the humans. Advancement in technology in order machines to think logically and make some decisions based on electronic software inserted by humans is expected in the near future but total transformation in order machines to decide on behalf of humans is far away in the very distant future. Therefore, an e-MNE can control and manage income generating assets in more than one country by the

---

[1] Ghoshal, S. and C. A. Bartlett. 'The Multinational Corporation as an International Network', Academy of Management Review, 15 (4), 1990, pp. 603-625.

[2] D Fieldhouse "The multinationals: A critique of a concept" at p 10 Multinational Enterprise in Historical Perspective 1986 Cambridge University Press.

[3] J Dunning "Multinational Enterprises and the Global Economy" 1992 Addison Wesley p 3-4. N Hood, S young "The Economics of the Multinational Enterprise" 1979 Longman p 3

[4] William G. Egelhoff, Organizational equilibrium and organizational change: two different perspectives of the multinational enterprise, Journal of International Management 5 (1999) 15–33, p32.

means of a network spread around the world and an electronic base located in a single building or place. An e-MNE can be engaged in direct investment outside its home country either on traditional plant or on electronic networks selling globally intangible goods and services.

Can simple on-line stores be regarded as e-MNEs? Are all on-line stores potential e-MNEs? It cannot be denied the development of a simple on-line store into an e-MNE if it manages to expand its service all around the world and be established as a global electronic provider[5]. The example of Amazon.com could be considered as a new form of an e-MNE. Traditional MNEs can be transformed into e-MNEs or develop in parallel electronic subsidiaries as well.

In accordance with Chandler[6] the first growth strategy was volume expansion creating a need for an administrative office; next strategy was geographic dispersion resulting in multiple field units and the third strategy, vertical integration, led to a functional organization. Finally, companies grew by product diversification, experienced administrative problems within the functional structure and converted to the M-form, the multidivisional structure, to regain profitability. It could be said that first structure[7] follows strategy, second strategies and structures develop in certain sequential stages and third organizations do not change their structures until provoked by inefficiencies. Product diversification, let to administrative problems within the functional structure that not only converted companies to the M-form but also to the multidivisional structure in order to regain profitability. A MNE as a whole is conceptualised as having the capability to combine or integrate the knowledge generated at the subsidiary level through the intra firm transfer of such knowledge (international interdependence). So, a MNE can be seen as an integrated network in which ties between nodes of the network serve as conduits for such intangibles as knowledge and expertise, as well as such tangibles as products and components[8].

Although host government policies may set the playing field, the rules of the game remain the same. The implication is that host governments, through policy decisions, can manage to some degree the influence of foreign companies on their economies. FDI decisions should fit with the MNEs' worldwide strategy, taking into account other aspects of the firm's activities. A global firm likely will have operations in multiple countries, but the location and role of each of these operations will be determined largely by the resource characteristics of the host county[9].

---

5 "Ford and Oracle To Create Multi-Billion-Dollar Business-to-Business Internet Venture," Ford Motor Company Press Release, 2 Nov. 1999 (http://www.ford.com/)."General Motors Joins Forces With Commerce One to Move into Business-to-Business E-Commerce with Innovative Internet Purchasing Enterprise," General Motors Press Release, 2 Nov. 1999 (*http://www.gm.com/*).

6 Chandler, A. D. Strategy and Structure: Chapters in the History of the Industrial Enterprise, M.I.T. Press, Cambridge, Mass., 1962. Stopford and Wells concluded: "We found that a close tie between strategy and structure exists regardless of what industry the firm is in; managers in enterprises following similar strategies in quite different industries have developed similar organizational structures and ownership policies." (p. 5). Stopford, J. M. and L. T. Wells. Managing the Multinational Enterprise, Basic Books, New York, 1972.

7 Chandler, A. D. Strategy and Structure: Chapters in the History of the Industrial Enterprise, M.I.T. Press, Cambridge, Mass., 1962.

8 Ghoshal, S., Bartlett, C.A., 1990. The multinational corporation as an interorganizational network. Acad Manage Rev 15(4), 603–625.

9 Birkinshaw, J., 1996. How multinational subsidiary mandates are gained and lost. J Int Bus Studies 25, 467–495.

It should be taken into consideration that the use of the term enterprise is favoured over corporation as it avoids restricting the object of study to incorporated business entities and to corporate groups based on parent-subsidiary relations alone. International production can take numerous legal forms. The UN[10] has moved to distinction between multinational corporations (MNCs) and transnational corporations (TNCs) and so distinguishing between enterprises across national borders-the transnational – and those owned and controlled by entities or persons from more than one country- the multinational.

According to OECD guidelines multinational enterprises "comprise companies or other entities whose ownership is private, state or mixed, established in different countries... to share knowledge and resources with the others". This author endorses the term multinational enterprises referring to different types of multinationals and avoiding a theoretical analysis about the suitability of the terminology.

The characteristic of a MNE is the ability of one firm to control the activities of another firm located in another country. The crucial difference between a MNE and a multilocation domestic enterprise is that the former operates its assets and controls their use across national borders, whereas the latter remains within them. A MNE will organize itself into divisions whose managerial reach crosses national frontiers. Moreover, a MNE trades across borders in factor inputs as well as finished products and between affiliates of the group as well as unconnected third parties. This raises the possibility of controlling trade within a MNE to the advantage of the group as a whole and represents one of the major competitive advantages possessed by MNEs over domestic companies. Additionally, MNE export technical know-how and managerial skills but usually maintain control over that knowledge by selling it only to affiliates. So, MNE differ in their capacity to locate productive facilities across national borders, to exploit local factor inputs thereby, to trade across frontiers in factor inputs between affiliates, to exploit their know-how in foreign markets without losing control over it, and to organize their managerial structure globally according to the most suitable mix of divisional lines of authority. These factors permit MNEs to affect the international allocation of productive resources and thereby to create distinct problems in the development of economic policy in the countries where they operate. Hence, MNEs should be treated as a distinct type of business enterprise for the purposes of economic regulation. According to Franko[11] European MNEs tend to use a direct reporting or mother-daughter structure when foreign operations are somewhat small and not closely integrated. As the strategic and environmental conditions facing an MNE change, the company needs to change its structure as it moves from one state of equilibrium to another state of equilibrium. Besides, Galbraith[12], Tushman and Nadler[13], state that good organizational performance requires equilibrium between certain defined information-processing requirements associated with a firm's strategy and correspondingly defined information-processing capacities provided by a firm's

---

[10] UN Doc E/5500/addl 24 May 1974. 13 ILM 800. C Wallace "Legal control of multinational enterprise" 1983 Martinus Nijhoff p 10-13.

[11] Franko, L.G., 1976. The European multinationals: a renewed challenge to American and British big business.Greylock Publishing, Stamford, CT.

[12] Galbraith, J.R., 1973. Designing complex organizations. Addison-Wesley, Reading, MA. Galbraith, J.R., Nathanson, D.A., 1978. Strategy implementation: the role of structure and process. West Publishing Company, St. Paul, MN.

[13] Tushman, M.L., Nadler, D.A., 1978. Information processing as an integrating concept in organizational design. Acad Manage Rev 3, 613–624.

structure. If strategy changes, information-processing requirements change, then structure also must change to retain equilibrium between information- processing capacities and requirements. MNEs utilize and extend market failures in the name of shareholder wealth, rather than constituting agents of global allocative competence and so making the question of their overall social utility debatable.

Different theories have attempted to identify some kind of equilibrium between degree of centralization and certain strategic and environmental contingency variables[14]. MNEs incline to decentralize decision making as the range of its foreign operations increase and as the density of its international strategy and environment increase. A kind of internal equilibrium within an MNE's organizational design for providing adequate parent-subsidiary coordination and control exist. Additionally, MNEs need to change their strategies and organizational designs as they evolve, so that at each stage of development they maintain certain balance or equilibrium between the MNE's organizational design and its strategy and environment. A transnational strategy attempts to achieve global efficiency, local responsiveness, and worldwide learning across a company's worldwide operations. MNE's don't desert states of equilibrium unless they can no longer cope successfully with their environments[15]. So, MNE's through innovation and change seek to gain competitive advantage. Formal planning and control systems of MNE's minimize and coordinate interdependency between different cultures.

Organizing the MNE is an increasingly complex task which demands the combination of the factors that at a specific time and place play the fundamental role for the development of the production of a MNE rather than other factors that have played a role in a previous time and place of production maybe for the same MNE. Production planning decisions pertain to selection of the products and the quantities to be produced in each facility. Distribution decisions concern to determining which facility would cater to the demands of which market. MNEs need the competence to endorse stability and adaptive change under conditions of equilibrium.

MNEs have been both influential and definitive to the character, establishment and operation of the global political economy, and vital to any positive reception of the forces causing its change, the contours that mould its practices, and the mechanisms by which its constitutive realms (states and markets) submissively cooperate. MNEs have doubled in number, more than tripled in terms of the number of foreign affiliates they operate, doubled the revenues they create, and increased drastically the number of people they employ[16]. The worth of private enterprise to global economic activity has grown manifestly in the twentieth century and much of this is dominated by the commercial interests of MNEs. MNEs represent collectivities of mainly national economic interests projected into international settings because of the consistency of cost efficiencies to be derived through international production,

---

[14] Garnier, G.H., 1982. Context and decision making autonomy in the foreign affiliates of U.S. multinational corporations. Acad Manage J 25 (4), 893–908. Gates, S.R., Egelhoff, W.G., 1986. Centralization in headquarters subsidiary relationships. J Int Business Stud 17, 71–92. Gemmill, G., Smith, C., 1985. A dissipative structure model of organization transformation. Hum Relations 38(8), 751–766.

[15] Romanelli, E., Tushman, M.L., 1994. Organizational transformation as punctuated equilibrium: an empirical test. Acad Manage J 37 (5), 1141–1166.

[16] UNCTAD (United Nations Conference on Trade and Development), 2003. World Investment Report 2003: FDI Policies for Development: National and International Perspectives, (New York and Geneva: United Nations).

procurement and outsourcing practices and subsequently they are sub-state actors conducting much of their dealings at the international level.

To the extent MNE activities are regional rather than global, corporate strategies that are based on MNEs widespread global character must be brought into line with the regional character of its activities. To the extent the regional concentrations of MNE activities are sub-optimal then the regional concentration of MNE activity should be revisited and made to better echo the stated global strategies[17]. The sign of the influence of the foreign presence depends on a set of conditions, and that it may turn into nasty circles of technological development in the locations affected by foreign MNE activity. The procedure of technological competition between foreign and national companies generates technological spillovers in both directions all the way through the concentration in these locations of high-tech phases of production and/or R&D activities by foreign and home companies.

MNE activity is a reinforcing factor in diverging development patterns and a minimum level of technological gap must exist in order to create room for the prospect that the ``leaking out'' of technological knowledge from MNE affiliates will benefit home companies ' technological capabilities. The power of foreign MNEs to encapsulate market shares forces national companies to concentrate efforts on narrower fields of specialization. The overseas R&D of MNEs centres on limited design and development work related to local markets rather than fundamental research into new products and processes. MNEs are more interested in forming cooperative relations with their suppliers, customers and other important resident entities, creating a technological spillover between the subsidiary and these various organizations[18].

If its foreign opponent opts for exports, FDI by a company imposes a greater disadvantage on the rival because the rival sources its intermediate wholly from its local supplier. Inward FDI induces the local company to invest abroad in order to avoid the rise in the price of the local intermediate. According to Amy J.Glass and Kamal Saggi[19] "while FDI improves welfare in the host country, welfare in the source country declines. Such a result nicely highlights the tension between host and source countries." When one company does FDI into another market, the rise in the intermediate's price forces the local company to also opt for FDI over exporting.

Increases in economic insecurity from globalization produce demands for more giving social insurance that compensates workers for a riskier environment. Exposure to external risk from trade, measured by the interaction between trade openness and the standard deviation of a country's terms of trade, is correlated with increase instability. The globalization of production by MNEs gives companies greater access to foreign factors of production and accordingly greater ease of substitution away from workers in any single location[20]. FDI by MNEs increases companies' elasticity of demand for labor and accordingly

---

[17] Rugman, Alan; Verbeke, Alain. BA Perspective on Regional and Global Strategies of Multinational Enterprises,^ Journal of International Business Studies, 35, 1, 2004, pp. 3Y18.

[18] Zanfei, A. (2000) Transnational firms and the changing organisation of innovative activities, Cambridge Journal of Economics, 24, pp. 515–542.

[19] Amy J.Glass and Kamal Saggi, Exporting versus Direct Investment under Local Sourcing, Review of World Economics 2005, Vol. 141 (4) 627, p644.

[20] Burgoon, Brian. 2001. "Globalization and Welfare Compensation: Disentangling the Ties that Bind." International Organization 55(3):509–51.

more elastic labor demands raise the instability of wages and employment, all of which tends to make workers feel more insecure.

1.2 Issues of MNEs

International companies go through an initial period with comparatively autonomous foreign subsidiaries, which are tied to the parent company by loose financial links in a way similar to a holding company. If the subsidiaries grow quickly and accumulate resources, pressures to increase control emerge at the headquarters. When the foreign product diversity increases, companies take on a worldwide product division structure. Companies that expand foreign sales without increasing product diversity normally adopt an area division structure. Besides, European multinationals went directly from the parent-subsidiary structure to a global product structure[21]. In contrast to the American multinationals, the European multinationals maintained exceedingly personalized relations with their foreign subsidiaries throughout the growth and spread of their international operations. The European multinationals with the largest operations in the United States, such as Philips and Ciba, led the change from the mother-daughter form to worldwide structures. The European firms avoided the international division stage, going immediately from the mother-daughter form to a worldwide structure. This change occurred only after having achieved a great geographical spread of international production. MNEs and non-corporate entities have to create partnerships for sustainable development by establishing and working toward common goals and the likely outcomes of these partnerships are diverse by source mobilization, reform of global governance, trade and investment liberalization, strengthening of labor standards, and establishment of accepted principles for measuring and reporting on sustainability.

In accordance with Perlmutter[22] there is some degree of ethnocentricity, polycentricity or geocentricity in all firms. In ethnocentric companies, the communication process is dominated by a flow of orders and advice from the headquarters to the subsidiaries. In polycentric companies subsidiaries should adapt to the host-country conditions and establish an as local as possible identity. The subsidiaries are assigned an excessive level of autonomy, as long as profits are acceptable. In geocentric companies, the subsidiaries are neither satellites nor autonomous actors but each part makes its unique contribution with its unique competence. The geocentric company attempts to build an organization where the subsidiaries are not only good citizens but also leading exporters of the host country, contributing to benefits such as increased hard currency, new skills and advanced technology. Headquarters and subsidiaries cooperate to establish worldwide standards and performance criteria, at the same time allowing local variations. So, important forces within companies are increasing

[21] Franko, L. G. The European Multinationals: A Renewed Challenge to American and British Big Business, Greylock, Stamford, CT, 1976. "Nevertheless, at the beginning of the 1970's, the most important bonds between center and periphery in European multinational systems were still the personal relationships between presidents of parent companies and presidents of foreign ventures." (p. 187). "The contrast could not be more complete between the management practices of the Continental European multinationals using the mother-daughter form and the archetypical American multinational with job descriptions, 'bibles' of rules, and frequent use of local nationals as foreign subsidiary presidents." (p. 190)

[22] Perlmutter, H. V. 'The Tortuous Evolution of the Multinational Corporation', Columbia Journal of World Business, (Jan-Feb), 1969, pp. 9-18.

desire to use human and material resources optimally, increased awareness of qualified people of other than the home nationality and, in particular, top management's commitment to building a geocentric company. Multidomestic[23] industries are present in several countries but the competition takes place on a country-by-country basis. The competitive advantage of a company is often particular to each country. The important competitors are either home companies or multinationals competing on a country-by-country basis. For instance, global industries, such as airlines, and automobiles, consist of a number of connected domestic industries in which the companies compete against each other on a worldwide basis. Location advantages combined with agglomeration economies foster the advantages of particular localities affecting the location choices of MNEs. Agglomeration economies give rise to virtuous circles in which oast inflows engender current and future FDI flows[24].

Local content requirements (LCRs) oblige companies manufacturing a good in a country to procure a definite minimum share of intermediate inputs domestically. LCRs continue to operate in a number of guises[25]. Rules of origin are designed to aim at the less integrated manufacturing operations of foreign-owned companies in oligopolistic industries aiming to boost the competitive position of domestic final goods producers by forcing comparable procurement conditions on to foreign companies[26]. LCRs increase competition in the oligopolistic final goods industry and reduce mark-ups, by inducing FDI that did not take place under free trade due to the occurrence of scale economies. Once FDI and vertical cooperation are detached possibilities, LCRs have a broader range of consequences than in earlier times found. The danger of FDI induces domestic companies to work together in order to set intermediate goods prices and pre-empt FDI and its related increased price competition which means that vertical cooperation has a supplementary strategic implication. Since FDI by the foreign company takes market share away from the home downstream producer _through a reduction in the foreign company's marginal costs_ and reduces demand for the upstream producer's intermediate goods, home companies have an enticement to discourage FDI. According to René Belderbos, Clive Jie-a-Joen, and Leo Sleuwaegen [27] "If economies of scale are not important and if the foreign firm is relatively efficient, the imposition of the LCR induces FDI."

It has to be taken into account that the equilibrium outcome of depends on the occurrence of economies of scale in the upstream industry, the size of the domestic market, whether the foreign multinational possesses a competence advantage, and the costs of cooperation. The host country has to reduce the existing market imperfections. René Belderbos, Clive Jie-a-

---

[23] Porter, M. E. 'Changing Patterns of International Competition', California Management Review, 28, 1986, pp. 9-40. Porter says that: "A global strategy can now be defined more precisely as one in which a firm seeks to gain competitive advantage from its international presence through either concentrating configuration, coordination among dispersed activities, or both." (1986, p. 20). Prahalad, C. K. and Y. L. Doz. The Multinational Mission, The Free Press, New York, 1987. Taggart, J. H. 'Identification and Development of Strategy at Subsidiary Level'. In J. Birkinshaw and N. Hood (eds), The Multinational Corporate Evolution and Subsidiary Development. MacMillan, London, 1998, pp. 23-49.

[24] L Nahum, Economic geography at the location of TNCs:Financial and professional service FDI to the USA, 2000 Journal of International Business Studies 367.

[25] Spencer, B.J. and R.W. Jones _1992_, 'Trade and Protection in Vertically Related Markets,' Journal of international Economics, 32, pp. 31–55.

[26] Dei, F. _1990_, 'A Note on Multinational Corporations in a Model of Reciprocal Dumping,' Journal of International Economics, 29, pp. 161–171.

[27] René Belderbos, Clive Jie-a-Joen, and Leo Sleuwaegen, Local content requirements, vertical cooperation, and foreign direct investment, De Economist 150, no. 2, 2002, p175.

Joen, and Leo Sleuwaegen[28] think that "once FDI and vertical cooperation are distinct possibilities, LCRs can have a much broader range of consequences than previously found. In general, more positive consequences for domestic welfare arise because LCRs under these circumstances offset initial market imperfections: they can induce efficiency-enhancing cooperative bargaining offsetting the price distorting effect of upstream monopolistic market power, and they induce competition increasing FDI that did not occur under free trade due to the presence of scale economies." While the typical company establishing a foreign affiliate requires outside credit to finance its investments, the relationship with its key lender takes on a valuable task in the FDI process this means that companies face flawed capital markets. Companies retain their historic lending ties, and changes in banking activity and lending practices have a noteworthy impact on the borrower's relative access to credit and as a result its competence to embark on FDI[29].

Banks invest in a comparable foreign market as their customers to avoid asymmetric information problems in regard to their foreign-located borrowers, or the significant limitations on cross-border capital controls as well as search for new overseas customers which means that much of the industry-level financial service FDI flow is explained by home-country relationships later forged with the manufacturing and other non-financial companies that are investing abroad. With the presence of home-country banks abroad, foreign non-bank affiliates often are able to turn to local affiliates of home-market banks for their capital requirements[30].

Borrowing companies become aware of that banks have some advantage over other lending institutions or methods and banks get hold of this advantage through long term unofficial operations that are built on trust and the bank's reputation for expertise, creditworthiness, and access to the high quality information fundamental to cross the informational asymmetries associated with financial markets.

A bank that considers serving either national or foreign clients located in the foreign market via FDI has to have a unique ownership advantage that allows it to successfully race with local banks[31]. To that extent banks choosing to invest abroad often locate their foreign affiliates in hosts clearly integrated with the home economy. Although the degree of host-home country integration is affected by host-specific characteristics such as geographical distance, bilateral trade flows, and less restrictive host-country regulations, the strong bank-client ties forged in the home market serve as an investment motive.

To achieve competitive advantage, companies must in some way integrate its activities on a worldwide basis. International strategy is not a simple choice between global integration and local responsiveness. The possibilities of global coordination have increased considerably through modern technology. Production and R&D becomes more and more dispersed and greater need for coordinating marketing activities worldwide. Big MNEs are converging

---

[28] René Belderbos, Clive Jie-a-Joen, and Leo Sleuwaegen, Local content requirements, vertical cooperation, and foreign direct investment, De Economist 150, 155–180, 2002. p175.

[29] Klein, Michael; Peek, Joe; Rosengren, Eric. BTroubled Banks, Impaired Foreign Direct Investment: The Role of Relative Access to Credit,^ American Economic Review, 92, 2002, pp. 664Y82.

[30] Gross, Dominique; Raff, Horst; Ryan, Michael. BInter- and Intra-sectoral Linkages in Foreign Direct Investment: Evidence from Japanese Investment in Europe,^ Journal of the Japanese and International Economies, 19, 2005, pp. 110-34.

[31] Harrison, Ann; Love, Inessa; McMillan, Margaret. Global Capital Flows and Financing Constraints, Journal of Development Economics, 75, 2004, pp. 269-301.

toward a common configuration, in which more and more specialized units worldwide are linked into an integrated network enabling them to concurrently achieve strategic objectives of efficiency, responsiveness, and innovation.[32] The subsidiary units are coordinated and controlled particularly through informal mechanisms.[33] To unite the dispersed MNEs by means of cultural control, a rather monolithic culture seems to be necessary. Companies have to cope with the demands imposed by economic imperatives, such as technology, economies of scale, and global distribution. Second, competition is distorted by the intervention of host and home governments. Third, the capacity of the organization to reallocate resources and adapt to new competitive conditions is regarded as the organizational imperative.[34] Important competitive advantages were exceptional intangible assets provided to subsidiaries by their mother companies, such as new technology and know how not effortlessly available to the home companies[35]. The success of multinationals over national competitors is based on the capability to exploit common capabilities and know how and to coordinate competitive actions across boundaries.

Increasing transfer of technology and other kinds of knowledge weakened competitive advantages based on intangible assets and contributed to the appearance of strong global competitors. Facing with the new global competition, large multinational companies frequently adopted an integration strategy, by which manufacturing costs were reduced by means of specialization. Global integration means the specialization of plants across borders into an integrated multinational production and distribution network[36]. A foreign multinational is effectively behaving like a multi-plant duopolist by having production locations in both source and host countries. It pays the host government a tariff on its export, and a tax on its profits earned from on-site production at the same rate as its host competitor. Shifting of production location from source to host less developed countries (LDCs) to take advantage of lower production cost in the latter has been a standard practice of the developed countries' (DCs') MNEs. The labour cost advantage enjoyed in the past by the MNEs from their production in source location is progressively disappearing because of the inter-country factor price equalization phenomenon. To maintain or increase their market share in an environment of increasing regional integration, the MNEs are forced to engage in export as well as on-site production in host nations. A proportional profit tax reduces the marginal

[32] Forsgren, M. Managing the Internationalisation Process: The Swedish Case, Routledge, London, 1989. Forsgren, M. 'Managing the International Multi-Center Firm', European Management Journal, 8 (2), 1990, pp. 261-267. Forsgren, M. 'Book review: C. A. Bartlett, Y. Doz and G. Hedlund (eds.): Managing the Global Firm', Organization Studies, 1992, pp. 477-480. Forsgren, M. and J. Johanson (eds). Managing Networks in International Business, Gordon and Breach, Philadelphia, 1992. Forsgren, M. and T. Pedersen. 'Centres of Excellence in Multinational Companies: The Case of Denmark'. In J. Birkinshaw and N. Hood (eds), The Multinational Corporate Evolution and Subsidiary Development. MacMillan, London, 1998, pp. 141-161.

[33] Melin, L. 'Internationalization as a Strategy Process', Strategic Management Journal, 13 (Winter), 1992, pp. 99-118. Marschan, R. 'Dimensions of Less Hierarcical Structures in Multinationals'. In I. Björkman and M. Forsgren (eds), The Nature of the International Firm. Handelshøjskolans förlag, Köpenhamn, 1997, pp. 433-450.

[34] Malnight, T. W. 'Globalization of an Ethnocentric Firm: An Evolutionary Perspective', Strategic Management Journal, 16 (2), 1995, pp. 119-141.

[35] Doz, Y. Strategic management in Multinational Companies, Pergamon Press, Oxford, 1986.

[36] Porter, M. 'The Competitive Advantage of Nations', Harvard Business Review, 68 (March-April), 1990, pp. 73-93. Porter, M. E. 'Changing Patterns of International Competition', California Management Review, 28, 1986, pp. 9-40.

revenue and marginal cost of the monopolist in equal proportion, and that leaves its output and price unchanged.

The tax reduces the MNE output from on-site production, increases its export, and reduces its total sales in the host market. The increase in host firm output will increase its market share and gross profits as well. Because the host firm has also to pay the profit tax at the same rate as the MNE, its net profit will fall. To avoid tariff on their exports, foreign companies set up on-site production facilities in the host countries[37]. Instead of producing complete product ranges for every national market, the multinational manufactures in each country only part of a common product range, but for the global market. Further trade liberalization and lower growth increased the tension between national responsiveness and global integration. Strategic control is exercised by means of sub-processes of change and a collection of management tools. Companies have to understand the nature of their administrative heritage and develop capabilities that are consistent with their heritage. Moreover, the administrative heritage influences the organizational structure, capabilities and management mentalities. Top management controls the foreign subsidiaries through their personal relationships with the subsidiary managers. The multinational management mentality regards the foreign operations as a portfolio of independent businesses. Hence, each unit should adapt its strategy and operations to the local business environment.

Transnational strategy involves a grouping of aspects of product innovation, market sensitivity, and competent production which are all indispensable to obtain competitive advantage in particular industries[38]. States have to work together with each other in exchanging information on competitive conditions, the behavior of MNEs in their territories, and limiting the opportunities for MNEs to utilize various forms of leverage to take away them of tax revenue through transfer pricing[39].

Location choices of MNEs are depended on not only abundance of certain immobile assets in particular locations but also abundance of intangible assets such as culture, human capital and institutional frameworks. Links among companies, institutions and infrastructures within a geographic area give rise to various forms of localised externalities that are external to individual companies but internal to a cluster and vital for the competitive success of individual companies taking part in clusters. Intracountry differences in terms of resources provide the basis for the competitive advantages of companies. It should be taken into account that MNEs exhibit strong geographic concentration within countries attracted to clusters of economic activity in their own and in closely related activities.

The global model can be described as a centralized hub. The role of the local subsidiaries is to assemble and sell products. They are not supposed to develop new products or strategies, not even to modify existing ones. There is a tight central control of decisions, resources and information. Managers in global companies focus more on world markets than managers in multinational and international companies, but they regard them as a single integrated market where similarities are more important than differences. The International model came into use after the World wars. To these companies it was important to transfer knowledge and

[37] Krugman, P. R. (1992). Import protection as export promotion: international competition in the presence of oligopoly and economies of scale. In G. M. Grossman (Ed.), Imperfect Competition and International Trade (pp. 75–86). Cambridge, MA: The MIT Press.

[38] Bauman, Z. (1998), Globalization, Polity, London.

[39] Dunning, J. (1995), ``The global economy and regimes of national and supranational governance'', Business and the Contemporary World, Vol. 1 No. 1.

expertise to their foreign subsidiaries. The subsidiaries in international companies may adapt products and strategies to the local environment, but they are more coordinated and controlled by headquarters than subsidiaries in multinational firms. In fact managers in most global corporations by realized that they had to combine the strategic capabilities of the models. They must at the same time be responsive to local differences, be globally efficient and be able to transfer knowledge. Hence, the multinational company is decentralized, the global company is centralized and the international company is something in between the two of them. Instead of either centralizing or decentralizing assets, the transnational company makes selective centralization and decentralization. By means of specialized operations, transnationals are in a better position to take advantage of new adaptable manufacturing technologies and split up the more and more complex R&D task into focused research areas in different places.[40]

A major barrier to the flexibility a worldwide company requires today is the uniform treatment of subsidiaries. Instead of treating all subsidiaries equally, transnational managers adapt the roles and responsibilities of the subsidiaries to the strategic importance of the local environments. Subsidiaries become strategic partners whose knowledge and capabilities are fundamental to the whole corporation. To manage a MNE's network of international activities and their interdependencies, top managers have to develop an understanding of the MNE's geographically dispersed markets and operations. A MNE's organizational capability is unique and inimitable due to activities embedded in multiple national market environments separated by geographic and cultural distances distinguishable by politico-economic variation. Globalisation means that tacit knowledge of more markets and of more activities becomes necessary and so preserving knowledge of the MNEs multinational network of activities and retaining enough continuity in tacit knowledge is a major task for managers. Hence, top managers have to develop tacit knowledge of the geographically dispersed markets in which the MNE operates formulating global strategy overseeing its implementation[41]. Global governance[42] in FDI competition could work as a tool to bring under control the decision-making discretion of national governments and make them less exposed to home lobbying by special interest groups or MNEs. As the globalization of the economy progressed, MNEs were cost-effectively motivated to transfer their production bases to developing countries, such as Latin American countries and South East Asian countries, for low wage labor and less employee protection.

MNEs are leading drivers of globalization and subsequently they could be held accountable for the success or failure of sustainable development as it relates to persistent economic growth without harm to the environment and utilization of the human workforce[43] through insufficient labor standards. Globalization raises the question of what initiatives should be undertaken to create a global economy in which sustainable development is a fact rather than an inaccessible ideal. If sustainable development is to be achieved, the

---

[40] Hedlund, G. and D. Rolander. 'Action in Heterarchies: New Approaches to Managing the MNE'. In C. A. Bartlett, Y. Doz, and G. Hedlund (eds), Managing the Global Firm. Routledge, London, 1990, pp. 15-46.

[41] N Athanassiou, D Nigh, Internationalization, tacit knowledge and the top management teams of MNCs, 2000 JIBS 471.

[42] William H. Meyer & Boyka Stefanova, Human Rights, the UN Global Compact, and Global Governance, 34 Cornell Int'l L.J. 501, 504 (2001)

[43] Erin Elizabeth Macek, Scratching the Corporate Back: Why Corporations Have No Incentive to Define Human Rights, 11 MINN. J. GLOBAL TRADE 101, 102 (2002)

corporations themselves have to adopt CSR initiatives. A social responsibility policy provides value as a strategic part of a company's activities because a company that ignores social and environmental concerns in its activities will have significant profit or returns in the sort terms and be content to maintain its operations at the status quo, but its actions have the prospective to harmfully affect society and the environment which means that its future profit is diminished when the company does not take a social responsibility approach to the global business environment.

Globalization is the trend of denationalization resulting from political, economic, and non-economic forces. Globalization is the result of the operations of MNEs in the world economy introducing into the global economy technologies, trade, and investments that bring the world closer together, both economically and culturally. MNEs have gained political and economic effect, stemming from the wealth they produce and direct investment by MNEs in developing countries exceeds inflows from official aid and net lending by international banks. While MNEs are without home territories and in that way defy conformity with only a single regime, as global non-state actors they can be agents for change which means that MNEs are valuable global law and policy actors, for better or worse.

The state facilitates the process of globalization by providing for property rights and other legal regimes that promote economic development and accordingly state's role is no longer as central as it once was and, to the extent the state engages in activities that preclude globalization, they can often be avoided by multinational actors who decide to move aspects of their operations in a different place or create parallel, if not competing, legal regimes that accommodate their interests. MNEs are more powerful than the states in which they conduct business and they can generate great development, but the role of sustainability remains to be seen.

MNES make an affirmative contribution to the development of underdeveloped countries through their investments, products, and services contributing to the development of less-developed countries by providing contact to technological and management expertise, investment and employment. On the other hand, MNEs make use of the elasticity of the sustainable development concept and in fact work against sustainable development in practice and accordingly the occurrence of MNEs in a developing country creates conflicts of interest.

It has to be taken into account that as a profit-maximizing enterprise, a company does not estimate the interests of the host country in economic and social development as it conducts its business continuing to chase its self-interested objectives such as maximizing return on investment (ROI), or return on equity (ROE), gaining market share, cutting costs, or increasing long-term competitiveness. Market integration increases economic interdependence, bringing about dependence on developing countries for resources used in or for production. In addition, procurement, production, and trade are becoming global, with companies using supply chains that reach into and across numerous states, establishing subsidiaries in foreign countries, receiving investment from and investing in other states, and taking advantage of trade liberalization. The global economy calls for something more than a profit-oriented approach by enterprises because globalization increases inequalities among states with regard to labor standards and environmental regulations, decreasing the likelihood that global development is sustainable.

Globalization raises the question of what initiatives should be undertaken to cause a global economy in which sustainable development is a certainty rather than an inaccessible ideal. Globalization renders state regulation of corporate action difficult because if sustainable development is to be achieved, the corporations themselves have to embrace CSR initiatives. While MNEs conceptualize their success as related to bottom line profits and productivity, this is a short-sighted vision for the reason that MNEs should focus on long-term strategies that will sustain a global system. Sustainable development is in MNEs best interest as it will lead to long-term sustained productivity, profits, and overall success and accordingly the long term success of MNEs in the global marketplace relies on the running of successful policies that will allow for the realization of global sustainable development. Competitiveness and profitability, as the basis for long-term continued existence, are the critical fundamentals for companies accepting social responsibility and accordingly social responsibility together with economic success play a part to a company's sustainability. It is so critical to influence companies to see social responsibility as a long-term undertaking, as a strategic investment in policies such as marketing, management tools and activities[44]. The EU has framed CSR as a long-term strategy for sustainable profitability and growth for both MNEs and states. CSR requires the structure of stronger public-private partnerships in order to play a role in sustainable development and accordingly partnerships between businesses, public institutions, and civil society address global developmental challenges by delivering value for both people and the businesses involved.

Worldwide learning requires that the company make use of all possible ways to develop innovative products and processes. Organizational learning about a new host country is not a smooth and homogeneous process across companies but it is a complex process varying significantly from company to company and the variation stems from both the nature of the knowledge and the differences in company's organizational structures. The global reach of multinationals creates a large scope of opportunities by combining elements so far not combined, by utilizing the symbiotic potential in the environment.[45] It was observed that business organizations often had constant exchange relationships with a restricted number of entities in their environment, where each entity exerted considerable influence on the organization. Uninterrupted interaction and exchange develop relationships between parties connecting their resources and activities and creating a web of personal relations.[46] Hence, the effectiveness of an organization operating in a network is depended, not only on how well the direct interaction with other parties is managed, but also on how these parties manage their interactions with third parties. Organisation is not merely a group of people but a system of consensually interdependent actions of more than two persons coordinated with a view of achieving a common goal. So, it extends from unstructured cooperative activities to complex and imposing structures[47]. To an internationally experienced company, the incentive to invest abroad regularly is its existing foreign assets rather than home-based resources.

---

[44] Opinion of the Economic and Social Committee on the Green Paper: Promoting a European framework for Corporate Social Responsibility, available at http://europa.eu.int/.

[45] Perlmutter, H. V. 'The Tortuous Evolution of the Multinational Corporation', Columbia Journal of World Business, (Jan-Feb), 1969, pp. 9-18. Perlmutter, H. V. 'Building the symbiotic societal enterprise', World Futures, (19), 1984, pp.45-56.

[46] Håkanson, L. and R. Nobel. 'Foreign Research and Development in Swedish Multinationals', Research Policy, 22 , 1993, pp. 373-396. Håkansson, H. (eds). International Marketing and Purchasing of Industrial Goods: An Interaction Approach, John Wiley & Sons, Chichester, 1982. Håkansson, H. Corporate Technological Behaviour, Routledge, London, 1989. Håkansson, H. 'No Business is an Island: The Network Concept of Business Strategy', Scandinavian Journal of Management, 5 (3), 1989, pp. 187-200.

[47] A Papandreou "Essays in Economics" 1993 Libanis, Greece.

Internationalisation[48] can be seen as a way of managing strategic interdependencies in business networks. New investors have to create a position in foreign industrial networks and investments must therefore be based on home-based strengths. The management of relationships is a significant strategic issue, and one apparent strategy is to acquire other firms in the same network.

There is a strong correlation between the degree of internationalisation and the prevalence of a multi-centre structure; management and research centres exist only when the degree of internationalisation is high. An international firm can be seen as a loosely coupled political system, each part also being engaged in trade networks of interdependent companies. A subsidiary can belong to two different systems, a trade network and the owner system, and is subject to tensions between the two roles, but the longer a subsidiary has been operating in a country, the more its behaviour will be influenced by the network. In sum, a business enterprise becomes international by connecting actors in various countries.[49] By regular exchange in a business relationship, two partners can progressively learn about each other's needs and capabilities and find opportunities to reduce the cost of exchange and increase their joint productivity. The partners in a business relationship are directly tied to each other and indirectly tied to a wider network of business relationships. The explicit competitive ability of a business enterprise is based on the combined knowledge from a unique, connected set of business relationships. In this way new knowledge is created through market exchange within a set of interrelated business relationships. The internationalisation of business enterprise is a question of the degree to which the business enterprise is connecting business relationships in various countries. The possibility of controlling subsidiaries in international business enterprises is limited. It could be said that *the multinational business enterprise* has business enterprises in a number of countries without having any connecting relationships. The network important to the subsidiary comprises not only business relationships with external actors but also with the whole network including other corporate units. The degree of embeddedness reflects the intensity of knowledge exchange between the subsidiary and other corporate units and external business actors. A subsidiary with a high degree of both corporate and external embeddedness can be of particular strategic importance to the MNE[50].

---

48 Forsgren, M. 'Managing the International Multi-Center Firm', European Management Journal, 8 (2), 1990, pp. 261-267. "An industrial network consists of units which are functionally linked via transactions of physical resources and/or knowledge, or appear in the same purchasing or sales market. Each unit often has its specific function in this system and frequently obtains components from other units therein." (p 264). Forsgren, M. 'Book review: C. A. Bartlett, Y. Doz and G. Hedlund (eds.): Managing the Global Firm', Organization Studies, , 1992, pp. 477-480. Forsgren, M. and J. Johanson (eds). Managing Networks in International Business, Gordon and Breach, Philadelphia, 1992. Forsgren, M. and T. Pedersen. 'Centres of Excellence in Multinational Companies: The Case of Denmark'. In J. Birkinshaw and N. Hood (eds), The Multinational Corporate Evolution and Subsidiary Development. MacMillan, London, 1998, pp. 141-161.

49 Andersson, U. and J. Johanson. 'International Business Enterprise'. In I. Björkman and M. Forsgren (eds), The Nature of the International Firm. Handelshøjskolans förlag, Köpenhamn, 1997, pp. 33-49.

50 Birkinshaw, J. 'Foreign-Owned Subsidiaries and Regional Development: The Case of Sweden'. In J. Birkinshaw and N. Hood (eds), The Multinational Corporate Evolution and Subsidiary Development. MacMillan, London, 1998, pp. 268-298. Birkinshaw, J. and N. Hood. 'Introduction and Overview'. In J. Birkinshaw and N. Hood (eds), The Multinational Corporate Evolution and Subsidiary Development. MacMillan, London, 1998, pp. 1-19. Birkinshaw, J. M. and N. Hood. 'An Empirical Study of Development Processes in Foreign Owned Subsidiaries in Canada and Scotland', Management International Review, 37 (4), 1997, pp. 339-364. Birkinshaw, J. M. and A. J. Morrison. 'Configurations

The world product mandate subsidiary provides the highest level of value-added, typically having R&D, manufacturing and management activities for an entire business or division.

The tendency of a MNE to adjust its organisational structure in undoubtedly differentiated stages has long been linked[51] to expanding involvement in international business. While much innovation is created at headquarters, especially in the "inter-national" firm, subsidiaries may become significant strategic partners in this and much other competitive activity. Knowledge is developed mutually and shared around the network. MNE performance is dependent on subsidiaries, not just on their existence and organisational orientation, but also on their status, characteristics and behavioural patterns. The ethnocentric MNE uses the home country culture as its dominant behavioural mode, and these are the values that drive communications, motivation, and attitude towards performance. Polycentric MNEs take the opposite approach, and attempt to encompass the host nation culture wherever subsidiaries are set up[52]. Geocentric orientation is the eventual stage, where an attempt is made to develop a truly international mode of management behaviour. The basis of sustainable competitive advantage is to achieve and preserve a better performance level than industry competitors. The nature of the strategic management process varies in MNE subsidiaries from simple and informal to complex and formal. The level of risk may be managed at a subsidiary level by adjusting the range of products sold, their nature and relatedness, the number of overseas markets entered, and so on. Risk may be managed in operations by adjusting the level of manufacturing technology in use[53], or in R&D by adjusting new product development portfolios[54].

Horizontal MNEs can be characterized as multi-plant companies that produce analogous goods and services in various countries. The establishment of horizontal multinationals is determined by a trade-off between economies of scale and trade costs and accordingly if trade costs were non-existing there would only be single-plant companies serving all markets from one location wholly utilizing economies of scale. Vertical multinationals are multi-plant companies that geographically break production into stages with a mixture of factor intensities economizing on factor price differences between countries. Vertical multinationals arise due to differences in comparative factor endowments between countries. Trade costs are impediments to the founding of MNEs and as opposed to the implications of horizontal models, trade and vertical multinationals' activities are complements. Trade costs have effects on horizontal and vertical multinationals; rising trade costs favour horizontal multinationals' activities but shape negatively activities of vertical multinationals. According

of Strategy and Structure in Subsidiaries of Multinational Corporations', Journal of International Business Studies, 26 (4), 1995, pp. 729-753.

[51] Stopford, J., & Wells, L. T. Jr (1972). Managing the multinational enterprise. New York: Basic Books.

[52] D'Cruz, J. R. (1986). Strategic management of subsidiaries. In H. Etemad and S. Dulude, Managing the multinational subsidiary. London: Croom Helm.

[53] Young, S., Hood, N., & Dunlop, S. (1988). Global strategies, multinational subsidiary roles and economic impact in Scotland. Regional Studies, 22(6), 487

[54] Taggart, J. H. (1997). Autonomy and procedural justice: a framework for evaluating subsidiary strategy. Journal of International Business Studies, 28(1), 51–76. Taggart, J. H. (1997). An evaluation of the integration–responsiveness framework: MNE manufacturing subsidiaries in the UK. Management International Review, 37(4), 295–318. Taggart, J. H., & Blaxter, T. J. (1992). Strategy in pharmaceutical R&D: a development portfolio risk matrix. R&D Management, 22(3), 241–254.

to Ingo Geishecker and Holger Görg[55] "We find a significant positive effect of endowment differences on manufacturing FDI, thus our results are strongly supportive of a vertical FDI component within manufacturing. However, for service FDI our estimation results only give support to horizontal FDI."

1.3 Evolution of Modern MNEs

Companies invested overseas so as to gain higher profits from a comparative advantage owned by them.[56] The firms had to organize an integrated international operation so as to retain control over their advantage and to avoid the uncertainties of operating at arm's length in an open market. MNEs possess competitive advantage in goods markets, through their ability to differentiate branded products, in factor markets through their possession of superior management skills and large-scale production in their possession of patents and trade secrets, in the economies of scale employed in production and their access to capital[57]. The location specific advantages model assumes that countries will specialize in the production of goods that require a high input of factors with which they are especially well endowed and that such goods will be exported in exchange for others requiring inputs of factors with which the country concerned is endowed. The choice of entry modes depends on different types of factors such as firm-specific factors, industry specific and country-specific factors. The assumptions of the model that capital and labour are immobile and the market is perfectly competitive are not realistic. Of course different countries enjoy different endowments of productive resources. Firms are not equally endowed with competitive assets, or with knowledge of global markets. The transition from trade to investment explained by reference to the transaction costs associated with the arm's length sales as compared to the long term savings in cost that can be achieved through going multinational. According to professor Vernon's[58] theory as the life cycle of the product nears its end, the only way to remain competitive is to reduce production costs by moving in low cost production areas in less developed countries. The concept of internalisation was developed in the 1930s by Coase[59] to explain the growth of domestic multiplant firms. Where a company encounters high transaction costs in procuring supplies and distributing final products through the open market, it may reduce those costs by carrying out such transactions within the firm by internalising those transactions. In other words it is achieved a vertically integrated hierarchy of the company or a horizontally integrated firm through merger or takeover. According to Buckley and Casson[60] an integrated MNE will generate flows of goods associated with production between affiliates across borders. Transborder flows of intermediate products will take place including semi-processed material and knowledge and expertise embodied in parents, R&D, labour training, management and financial activities. The MNE will undertake

[55] Ingo Geishecker and Holger Görg, The vertical investment controversy: Re-estimating the knowledge-capital model for different types of FDI, Research Paper 2005/03, p14.

[56] S Hymer "The international operations of national firms" 1976 MIT Press. J Dunning "Explaining international production" 1988 Unwin Hyman.

[57] C Kindleberger "American business abroad: Six lectures on direct investment" 1969 Yale University press.

[58] R Vernon "Sovereignty at Bay" 1973 Pelican

[59] R Coase " The nature of the firm" 1937 Economica 386

[60] P Buckley, M Casson "The future of the multinational enterprise" 1976 Macmillan.

such transfers so as to avoid the costs and inefficiencies of effecting such transactions at arm's length with outside suppliers and distributors and so to protect its "firm-specific" advantage in productive knowledge. The maintaining of the profitability of controlling and co-ordinating R&D across borders is at the heart of the successful and expanding MNE. The MNEs advantage is not located merely in the possession of a unique asset but in the process of creating and exploiting that asset through the internalisation of the relevant factor markets.

What is the unique asset of a MNE in digital economy? What is the unique asset of an e-MNE in digital economy? In both occasions the possibility of a MNE or an e-MNE to utilize its unique asset that can be a traditionally unique asset such as know-how or in general advanced technology or a network of electronic services and goods combined with tangible assets through the internationalisation of the relevant factor markets is the key element of a company being a multinational. Multinationality was a product of the internalisation of intermediate product markets in multistage production processes especially in industries such as mineral and oil. The stimulation of demand for high technology goods by governments and high income consumers have increased preferences for novelty and continued improvements in product quality and so shift towards the internalisation of markets in knowledge. The "eclectic paradigm" does not offer a single explanation of international production through MNEs. Professor Dunning's paradigm rests on the acceptance that the various theories cannot offer a complete explanation but they identify relevant and interrelated phenomena, which can lead towards a better understanding of the causes of international production by MNEs. Hence, the "eclectic paradigm" is based on the complementary nature of theories based on firm or ownership-specific, location-specific and internalisation factors, referred to as O, L and I factors.

1.4 The Eclectic Paradigm (OLI)

For years, the eclectic (OLI, Ownership, Location and Internalisation.) paradigm has remained the leading analytical framework for accommodating a range of operationally testable economic theories of the determinants of foreign direct investment (fdi) and the foreign activities of MNEs.[61] The specific construction of the OLI parameters facing any particular company, and the response of the company to that construction, is contextual.

---

[61] Caves, R. E. (1971). Industrial corporations: the industrial economics of foreign investment. Economica, 38, 1–27. Caves, R. E. (1974). Causes of direct investment: foreign firms shares in Canadian and United Kingdom manufacturing industries. Review of Economics and Statistics, 56, 272–293. Caves, R. E. (1982). Multinational firms and economic analysis. (1st ed). Cambridge: Cambridge University Press. Caves, R. E. (1996). Multinational firms and economic analysis. (2nd ed). Cambridge: Cambridge University Press. Dunning, J. H. (1977). Trade, location of economic activity and the MNE: A search for an eclectic approach. In B. Ohlin, P. O. Hesselborn, & P. M. Wijkman, The international allocation of economic activity (pp. 395–418). London: Macmillan. Dunning, J. H. (1980). Towards an eclectic theory of international production: some empirical tests. Journal of International Business Studies, 11 (1), 9–31. Dunning, J. H. (1988). Explaining international production. London: Unwin Hyman. Dunning, J. H. (1993). Multinational enterprises and the global economy. Wokingham, Berkshire: Addison Wesley. Dunning, J. H. (1995). Reappraising the eclectic paradigm in the age of alliance capitalism. Journal of International Business Studies, 26, 461–491. Dunning, J. H. (1996). The geographical sources of competitiveness of firms: the results of a new survey. Transnational Corporations, 5 (3), 1–30. Dunning, J. H. (1997). Technology and the changing boundaries of firms and governments In OECD, Industrial competitiveness and the global economy (pp. 53–68), Paris: OECD.

Economic and political features of the country or region of the investing firms, and of the country or region, the industry and the nature of the value added activity and the characteristics of the individual investing firms, including their objectives and strategies in pursuing these objectives will be reflected in the construction of the specific OLI. It is designed to satisfy a particular foreign market, or set of foreign markets, to gain access to natural resources, to promote a more efficient division of labour or specialization of an existing portfolio of foreign and domestic assets by MNEs, and to protect or augment the existing O specific advantages of the investing firms and/or to reduce those of their competitors. It could be said that some sectors are expected to cause more fdi than others because the features of the former create supplementary O advantages, or because their locational needs favour production outside their home countries, or because the net profit of internalising cross-border intermediate product markets is greater. The eclectic paradigm is embedded in a number of various economic and business theories and taken independently, none of these offer a complete explanation of the growth and decline of MNE business activity.

The pattern of foreign owned production will depend on the challenges and opportunities offered by dissimilar kinds of value added activity. Besides, the introduction of electronic commerce is not only heralding the end of the geography of some financial and information markets, but is revolutionizing the organization of intra-firm production and trade[62]. Can the changing character and boundaries of the O specific advantages of companies be satisfactorily incorporated into the eclectic paradigm? Key characteristic of the last years has been the escalating importance of fdi based on the possession of, or need to acquire, dynamic O advantages. Exchange rates affecting the extent, geography and timing of fdi together with an optimum locational portfolio of assets are a competitive advantage in their own right.[63] The logistics of the sitting of corporate activities, and the competitive advantages of nations or regions in a global economy must be taken into consideration. Companies need to take account not only of the presence and cost of traditional factor endowments, of transport costs,

Dunning, J. H. (1999). Globalization and the theory of MNE activity. In N. Hood, & S. Young, The globalization of multinational enterprise activity (pp. 21–54). London: Macmillan.

62 Graham, E. M. (1998). Market structure and the multinational enterprise: a game-theoretic approach. Journal of International Business Studies, 29 (1), 67–84. Kuemmerle, W. (1999). The drivers of foreign direct investment into research and development: an empirical investigation. Journal of International Business Studies, 30 (1), 1–24. Liu, S. X. (1998). Foreign direct investment and the multinational enterprise. A re-examination using signaling theory. Westport, Conn: Greenwood Publishing.

63 Rangan, S. (1998). Do multinationals operate flexibly? Theory and evidence. Journal of InternationalBusiness Studies, 29 (2), 217–238. Enright, M. J. (1998). Regional clusters and firm strategy. In A. D. Chandler Jr., P. Hagstrom, & O. Solvell, The dynamic firm (pp. 315–343). Oxford: Oxford University Press. Enright, M. J. (1999). The globalization of competition and the localization of competitive advantage. In N. Hood, & S. Young, The globalization of multinational enterprise activity and economic development (pp. 303–331). London: Macmillan. Rugman, A. M. (1979). International diversification and the multinational enterprise. Lexington (MA): Lexington Books. Rugman, A. M. (1982). New theories of the multinational enterprise. London: Croom Helm. Rugman, A. M. (1996). The theory of multinational enterprises: the selected scientific papers of Alan A. M. Rugman, Vol. 1. Cheltenham: Edward Elgar. Rugman, A. M., & Verbeke, A. (1998). Multinational enterprises and public policy. Journal of International Business Studies, 29 (1), 115–136.

but also of distance related transaction costs, knowledge accumulation and interactive learning, technological standards and the increasing dispersion of created assets[64].

The nature of a country or region's comparative advantage based on its possession of a unique set of immobile natural resources is now geared to its ability to offer created assets including the presence of native companies with which foreign MNEs might form alliances to complement their own core competencies.[65] The competitiveness of corporations is becoming more and more fashioned by the institutional framework within which they operate[66]. States and sub-national authorities should provide the fitting economic and social infrastructure, both for their own firms to generate the O specific assets consistent with the demands of the global economy and for foreign investors to engage in the kind of value adding activities which advances the forceful comparative advantage of the immobile assets within their jurisdiction[67]. It could be said that the locational choice of firms becomes an additional strategic variable because whatever thing can be brought from a space (real or cyberspace) is no longer a competitive advantage[68]. There is an increasing role of innovation in the contemporary global economy, and the need of companies to tap into, and exploit, resources and capabilities outside their home countries, means an extension of the boundaries of a company. Additionally, the development of a range of inter-firm coalitions is resulting in de facto internalisation, but without equity ownership. In general, strategic partnerships now being formed cannot be construed as arms length transactions as the participants have a continuing knowledge sharing relationship with each other. Have the emergence of new explanations of MNE activity (such as the growth of corporate networks and cross-border strategic alliances) added to, rather than subtracted from, the robustness of the paradigm? Dunning states that "dynamizing the eclectic paradigm, and recognizing the interdependence of the OLI components not only adds value of its original conception, but helps point the way to improving a variety of the individual theories it embraces"[69].

This author thinks that the insertion of the new energetic characteristics and factors of the global production, and trade together with the features of the digital economy within the combination of the substance of the terms Ownership, Location (the new dimension of location as founded upon and shaped by the impact of the use of cyberspace and e-logistics not only in the whole production line and marketing of MNEs but also the regional and international consumption and demand) and Globalisation-globalisation leads to a better understanding of the way the MNEs move their production around the world and maybe to a

---

[64] Solvell, O., & Zander, I. (1998). International diversification of knowledge: isolating mechanisms and the role of the MNE. In A. D. Chandler Jr., P. Hagstrom, & O. Solvell, The dynamic firm (pp. 402– 416). Oxford: Oxford University Press.

[65] UN (1998). World investment report 1997, transnational corporations: trends and determinants. Geneva and New York: UN. Vernon, R. (1966). International investment and international trade in the product cycle. Quarterly Journal of Economics, 80, 190–207.Venables, A. J. (1998). The assessment: trade and location. Oxford Review of Economic Policy, 14 (2), 1–6.

[66] Doremus, P. N., Keller, W. W., Pauly, L. W., & Reich, S. (1998). The myth of the global corporation. Princeton: Princeton University Press.

[67] Dunning, J. H. (1998). Location and the multinational enterprise: a neglected factor. Journal of International Business Studies, 29 (1), 45–66.

[68] Porter, M. E. (1994). The role of location in competition. Journal of Economics of Business, 1 (1), 35–39. Porter, M. E. (1996). Competitive advantage, agglomerative economies and regional policy. International Regional Science Review, 19 (1/2), 85–94.

[69] John H. Dunning, The eclectic paradigm as an envelope for economic and business theories of MNE activity, International Business Review 9 (2000) 163–190 at p183.

better and effective allocation of the resources. Tactical asset-acquiring FDI is to expand access to assets that protect or improve the acquiring firm's competitive advantages or reduce the competitive advantages of its rivals. In accordance with the eclectic paradigm, companies engage in FDI not to exploit existing ownership (O) advantages, but to acquire such advantages, which, when deployed with their existing O advantages, help maintain or advance their global competitive positions. According to Porter[70]— a firm's competitive advantages are basically a function of its national economic environment— whether or not the attributes of this environment are owned by the firm or available to it.

According to Rugman[71] and Dunning[72], the deepening structural integration of the world economy, and the rapidly increasing of alliance capitalism are widening the geographical scope for creating competitive advantages, and that any attempt to identify the geographical sources must include countries with which the home country firms have the most dealings, by way of trade, foreign direct investment and non-equity cooperative ventures. Multinational enterprises tend to source productive assets abroad. Hence, the transfer of technology and management practices, are coupled with a sensible level of stability, owing to the specificity of the locational assets sourced by MNEs. Companies in high technology sectors would be less dependent on created assets, but more depended on natural assets found abroad[73]. Multinationals are sourcing assets through mergers and acquisitions or by way of strategic alliances that are similar to those they already possess abroad. In line John H. Dunning and Sarianna M. Lundan stay that "while size and multinationality are related to the sourcing of foreign assets via fdi, technological intensity (along with multinationality) is positively linked to the use of cooperative alliances".[74]

MNEs are driven in a straight line by company-to-company contracting in a global scale in an era of multiplying global inter-company relations that offer more possibilities for companies to be drawn into the global/new/digital economy by globalization. It has emerged internationalization by MNEs from newly developed economies but they do not have the OLI advantages to start with and that is why they have to internationalize in order to take over the resources needed building their advantages cumulatively. The materialization of international production networks has promoted a closer amalgamation of the process of capacity build up and consequently internationalization scheme intertwined with technological and good

---

[70] Porter, M. E. (1990). The competitive advantage of nations. New York: The Free Press.

[71] Rugman, A. M. (Ed.). (1993). [Special Edition on Michael Porter's Diamond of Competitive Advantage].Management International Review, 33(2). Rugman, A. M., van den Broeck, J., & Verbeke, A. (Eds.). (1995). Beyond the diamond: research in global strategic management (Vol. 5). Greenwich, Conn.: JAI Press.

[72] Dunning, J. H. (1993). Multinational enterprises and the global economy. Wokingham, Berkshire: Addison Wesley. Dunning, J. H. (1993). Internationalizing Porter's diamond [special issue]. Management International Review, 33(2), 7–15. Dunning, J. H. (1995). Reappraising the eclectic paradigm in the age of alliance capitalism. Journal of International Business Studies, 26(3), 461–491. Dunning, J. H. (1996). The geographical sources of competitiveness of firms: some results of a new survey. Transnational Corporations, 5(3), 1–29. Dunning, J. H. (Ed.). (1997). Governments, globalization and international business. Oxford: Oxford University Press. Dunning, J. H., & Wymbs, C. (1997). The geographical sourcing of technology based assets by multi-national enterprises. Rutgers University, Mimeo.

[73] Cantwell, J. A., & Piscitello, L. (1997). The emergence of corporate international networks for the accumulation of dispersed technological competencies. Discussion Papers in International Investment and Management No. 238, The University of Reading.

[74] John H. Dunning, Sarianna M. Lundan, The geographical sources of competitiveness of multinational enterprises: an econometric analysis, International Business Review 7 (1998) 115–133, p131.

diversification plans. MNEs success based on their capacity to treat global competition as a prospect to build capacities, move into more gainful industry fields, and implement strategies that turn late arrival position into a foundation of competitive advantage. Late arrival MNEs from developing countries are pursuing strategies that make possible to draw level with established MNEs, all the way through leveraging off their latecomer advantages and tactical partnerships with market leaders[75]. According to Federico Bonaglia, Andrea Goldstein and John A. Mathews[76] "Although OECD-based MNEs retain the lead in production and innovation activities, countries and firms from the periphery are increasingly involved in production of appliances, and not merely of their components. Moreover, demand growth is much higher in emerging markets than in industrialized countries. Leaders in the white goods industry have prospered by achieving economies of scale, better control of distribution channels and rather simple innovation. Facing declining prices, they are re-strategizing, investing heavily in R&D and innovation. Still, in other markets that have traditionally been domestic-oriented, like steel and cement, the peripheral firms are demonstrating how advantages can be secured through globalized operations and service". International expansion and cross border integration is more expensive *across* regional blocks. Products, knowledge, people and capital run without problems between countries within the same region than between regions because not only of geographical proximity but also, as a result of policy-driven regional integration within the EU, NAFTA, and ASEAN.

New economy becomes interconnected putting pressures on companies to internationalize in order to boost their competitiveness. Globalization is being driven not just by the established MNEs introducing e-MNEs functions, but also by new MNEs from the periphery taking over competitive space from incumbents because of their capacity to take advantage of the linkages offered by globalization and build on a culture of continual cross-border learning and value-addition.

---

[75] Mathews, J.A. (2006). Dragon multinationals: New players in 21st century globalization. *Asia Pacific Journal of Management, 23*: 5-27. Buckley, P., & Ghauri, P.N. (2004). Globalisation, economic geography and the strategy of multinational enterprises. *Journal of International Business Studies, 35*: 81-98.

[76] Federico Bonaglia, Andrea Goldstein and John A. Mathews, Accelerated internationalization by emerging markets' multinationals: The case of the white goods sector, *www.ssrn.com* p25-26.

Chapter 2

MNEs AND THE LAW

2.1 LEGAL FORMS OF MNEs

A MNE is a corporation that owns or licenses its business activities both at home and in host countries. There are three major entry strategies for a MNE entering a foreign market: FDI, JV and Licensing. MNEs have outgrown the simple managerial structure of the entrepreneurial corporation. Technological know-how is an intangible asset and the risk of disseminating the know-how is very high if the MNE grants a licence to a foreign enterprise to use its know-how to manufacture or market a product. Corporate growth demands a greater specialization and division of labour within the firm. A major rationalization may take place with a reorganisation of the company along divisional lines of control based on managerial functions, products and areas of operation. The principal lines of control will differ according to the type of firm and the kinds of markets in which it operates. A firm may start with an export department, which is then superseded by an international division responsible for all the company's overseas activities, including exports and direct investment, which in its turn may be replaced by a global divisionalization of the firm[1]. Based on the type of good involved, a company can locate, extract, process, transport and distribute raw materials, product or service in different places and so will organise around global functional divisions[2]. Moreover, divisional structures represent the most effective communication system between the decision-making centres of a company and the market in which it operates.

In response a MNE decentralises its organisation by balancing firstly the international integration of production within the enterprise and the responsiveness of individual affiliates to the needs of the national economies within which they operate and secondly a shift of emphasis away from a hierarchical, vertical control structure, to a network of cooperative and lateral relationships. So, R&D need not remain tied to the parent company and certain divisional head offices could be relocated outside the home country. The head office is transformed from that of the ultimate policy maker to that of coordinator and identifier of new business opportunity and the organiser of task force networks within the enterprise. The enterprise is subject to greater organisational flexibility and the organisational' boundaries

---

[1] M Brooke, H Remmers, The strategy of the Multinational Enterprise, 1978, Pitman.
[2] C Bartelt, S Choshal, Managing across borders: The transnational solution, 1989, Century Business.

between individual companies themselves are obscure and an increased number of strategic alliances are formed. Is there a trend towards networking and hierarchy? Each enterprise will determine the degree of centralisation/decentralisation required in accordance with its perception of the most cost-effective and efficient strategy. Decisions, regarding personnel, labour relations or sales promotion, confined to the affiliate on a decentralised basis. Hence, the actual degree of control exercised by a parent over its affiliates will vary in accordance with a significant range of factors. MNE are divided into those based on contract, equity based corporate groups, joint ventures between independent firms, informal alliances, publicly owned MNEs and supranational forms of international business. The legally binding contract offers various options in control of the subsidiary in the host state, ranging from simple one-off export sales to complex and permanent international consortia. It could be argued that controlled contractual relations form a kind of a multinational enterprise. A producer in the home state can enter into a distribution agreement with a distributor in the host state. In this occasion may involve the transfer of intellectual property rights- trademarks and know-how- so that the seller can maintain the identity and quality of the product. For instance, the establishment of a distribution franchise is another form of distribution agreement but in this case we have the transfer of a complete business format in return for the capital contribution needed to establish the outlet from the franchisee. Under a franchise, the franchiser seeks to expand its products and image abroad in a uniform business format, which helps to develop its presence as an international business. Production agreements are another form of allowing a local manufacturer to produce the product in the host state by transferring patented technology and know-how to the local manufacturer. The local manufacturer is bound to use the technology in a manner that protects the licensor's competitive advantage in the technology. The most advanced contractual form of MNE is the international consortium and the legal form may take that of an incorporated joint venture company or partnership. In order to finish a large scale construction or engineering projects requiring the skills and resources of firms from more than one country. A common form of a MNE is that of a closely controlled group of companies linked by shares held by the parent company and its intermediate holding companies. The Anglo-American "pyramid group" is a type of structure that consists of a parent company which owns and controls a network of wholly or majority owned subsidiaries, which may themselves be intermediate holding companies for sub-groups of closely held subsidiaries[3]. The creation of transnational mergers is another structure representing a border between corporate groups headed by one parent and joint ventures between independent companies. The integration of national companies across borders into larger companies offering new economies of scale and scope is a well-established phenomenon in Europe. A twin holding company is created and located in each home state based on joint share holding by the founding parent companies and transferring the operating activities to subsidiaries. The aim of the merger is the achievement of greater economies of scale and scope than the founding companies could achieve by themselves. The result is the international divisionalization of an enterprise and the creation of new trasnational management structures.

Fiscal barriers to transnational mergers may have distorting effects on international competition, preventing the development of efficient transnational groups. For instance, the

[3] G Osunbor, The agent-only subsidiary company and the control of multinational groups, 1989 ICLQ 377.

council directive 90/434/EEC[4] of 23 July 1990 regulates the common system of taxation applicable to mergers. In different member states the development of transnational mergers in Europe is influenced by the industrial and competition policies of the EU. A new set of guidelines[5] and two block exemption regulations-2658/2000 and 2659/2000[6]-provide a general economic approach to the assessment of horizontal cooperation agreements. Besides, the Japanese Keiretsu is characterised by small intra-group cross-shareholdings coupled with strong coordinated management organised around inter-company management conferences and the control over satellite companies of the Keiretsu is exercised by means of managerial coordination. There is an allowance for substantial external shareholdings in the group companies[7]. The main aim of integrated international business is the maintenance of global competitiveness through increased international equity-based network can offer advantages in relation to the limitation of liability and the manipulation of earnings flows across borders through transfer pricing transactions.

Joint venture is any agreement or undertaking between two independent firms and involves the cooperation of two or more otherwise independent parent undertakings, which are linked in the pursuit of a common commercial, financial or technical activity[8]. In other words, there is a creation of new enterprise capability in terms of new productive capacity, new technology, new products or entities into new markets. The joint venture involves shared control by the parent undertakings and treated as an associated undertaking for accounting purposes. Joint venture may be established between affiliates belonging to the same group and the agreement is subject to the requirements of the law governing the joint venture[9]. JVs provide parent companies with a major tool for pursuing multiple objectives and are both cooperative and concentrative in nature at the same time[10]. One of the key benefits of research joint ventures (RJVs) is that they avoid duplication of research activities, so reducing the social cost of achieving any specific level of R&D output. Moreover, RJVs assist firms reap scale economies in R&D. However, when firms embark on independent R&D, competitive pressures prompt firms to invest forcefully in their own R&D in order to get advantage over their rivals so that even if they are not able to acquire the cost benefits associated with joint ventures, the level of technological advancement achieved might be more than what would have resulted from a RJV. When companies set up research joint ventures they spend or commit R&D resources cooperatively so as to maximize the combined profits they will derive as future competitors in the product market. The input of an individual firm to a joint venture is frequently not just a monetary contribution but it involves sharing of human capital, accumulated knowledge embedded in firm-specific factors, and access to information and activities within its own R&D division. If the scale of complementarity is very low then competitive RJVs lead to lower technological output relative to independent research. Nejat

[4] 1990 OJ L 225/1.
[5] EC Commission's Guidelines OJ 2001 C3/2.
[6] OJ 2000 L 304/3,7.
[7] K Miyashita, D Russel , Keiretsu: Inside the hidden Japanese conglomerates, 1994, McGraw-Hill.
[8] E Herzfeld, Joint Ventures, 1989, Jordans.
[9] F Fine, Mergers and Joint Ventures in Europe: The law and policy of the EEC, 1992 Graham and Trotman.
[10] L Nouvel,the new European treatment of JV, 2002 IBLJ 511.

Anbarci, Robert Lemke and Santanu Roy [11] state "if the degree of complementarity is moderate (not too high or too low), competitive RJVs lead to higher technological improvement, profits and social welfare when spillovers are *low*. If spillovers are high, independent R&D performs better in terms of technological improvement though RJVs are still likely to lead to higher social welfare".

Cooperative activity has become an important element of strategic behaviour, and with growing globalisation, many alliances are being formed across national boundaries, with the attendant challenges of surmounting linguistic and other cultural barriers providing new perspectives on the partnering skills needed for success in international joint ventures (IJVs). Collaboration entails not just trust and reciprocity but also the elimination of opportunism (where one or more of the elements of a JV act in their own self interest to the detriment of the others) and mutual forbearance (a level of tolerance of partner's shortcomings). Subsequently, effective partnering skills need to give emphasis to the joint interests whilst minimising real or potential conflict, and JV managers will seek to lessen conflict between the parents given the possible damage such conflicts can inflict upon the JV. The parent managers must be able to develop a transparent understanding of each other's main objectives: objectives that are hidden from a partner may generate major disappointments or misunderstandings when attempts are made to accomplish them. Those establishing the IJV must have the skills to develop a common view of a *valid* enterprise and the partnering skills are fundamentally about leveraging the resources and capabilities in a synergistic mix that will produce benefits for both sides.

As mentioned above, three types of firms exist in each country: purely domestic firms, which have headquarters and plants that produce only at home for local or export markets; the horizontal MNEs, which have headquarters at home and production plants both at home and abroad that produce the same goods; and the vertical MNEs, which fragment various stages of production by having headquarters at home and production plants in various foreign countries that manufacture various intermediate or final goods. Vertical MNEs will naturally export components to foreign affiliates and re-export to the home (or other) markets the goods produced abroad but horizontal MNEs are prevalent in the OECD area, somewhat reflecting the growing correspondence in factor costs and endowments among member countries. Moreover, MNE-based trade includes arms-length trade, which are shipments between a division of a MNE and unaffiliated buyers/suppliers and other countries and intra-firm trade, which are internal shipments between a MNE parent and its foreign affiliates. Vertical MNEs fragment the production process across countries to take advantage of factor price differentials by locating unskilled-labor intensive parts of the process in low wage countries. Horizontal MNEs replicate the entire production process in multiple countries and so avoiding tariff and transport costs. Ownership advantage in exploiting foreign markets, locational considerations (tariffs, transport costs etc) and internationalization over an arms-legth transactions are ingredients of a MNE.

The smaller companies are exporting and data show that from their foreign investment locations smaller companies have a higher export trend than larger companies. Company characteristics have a worth mentioning influence in determining both total foreign

[11] Nejat Anbarci, Robert Lemke , Santanu Roy, Inter-firm complementarities in R&D: a re-examination of the relative performance of joint ventures, International Journal of Industrial Organization 20 (2002) 191–213, p208.

investment flows and their allocation across competing locations. For instance, technologically sophisticated Japanese companies are under less competitive threat than other Japanese companies and accordingly have less need to move production closer to customers or seek cheaper locations[12]. Large size, low R&D, and high export intensity combine to advocate that Japanese foreign investors take advantage of their access to marketing channels for international trade and their superior factory-level production techniques. Companies that export a larger share of their output from their subsidiary in the host country incline to import a larger share of their inputs and exports from host countries depend upon the accessibility of a pool of trained manpower, in particular technicians and supervisors.

International joint ventures are unstable in nature and their instability is higher in developing countries as compared to developed because of the shift in government policies in developing countries during the process of liberalisation. Especially, Uday Bhanu Sinha [13] held that "the joint venture is formed in response to government restriction on foreign equity holdings in the first period. However, the joint venture becomes unstable in the second period, when the government removes the foreign equity restriction". Moreover, governments in developing countries allow the formation of joint ventures with particular restrictions on the foreign equity holdings in the earlier stages of liberalisation, but they later open up the economy entirely and allow the foreign firms to set up wholly owned subsidiaries[14]. Alessandra Casella and James E. Rauch [15]think that "Group ties increase aggregate trade and income, but hurt the anonymous market because they deprive it disproportionately of the group's more productive members". So, International joint ventures enable MNEs to obtain a number of competitive advantages, such as fast pooling of critical resources, reduced investment risk and beneficial host country business networks. However, these joint ventures often make it difficult for firms to maintain their ownership advantage. Due to the market imperfections that normally exist in developing economies, MNEs that select a wholly-owned investment vehicle can create an internal market to reduce transaction costs in such activities as production coordination, market exploitation and technology protection. Hence, foreign firms are more likely to choose a joint venture investment vehicle when local market conditions are uncertain so that they can obtain greater security and protection. Moreover, foreign electronics firms seek to set up wholly-owned businesses to avoid sharing their success with other parties. A firm can achieve marketing efficiency and effectiveness regardless of the type of ownership. A firm wholly-owned by a foreign firm may still lose money if it does not adopt an appropriate and effective strategy. Joint ventures are plagued with numerous problems, one of which is the difficulty of technology protection. For instance, a Chinese partner in a joint venture may not live up to the expectations of foreign firms. Moreover, if joint ventures do not lead to desirable local connections, this form of investment becomes much less attractive. Finally, the transaction cost of setting up a wholly-owned firm is much lower than that of negotiating for a joint venture in China. While it may

---

[12] Susmita Dasgupta, Ashoka Mody, and Sarbajit Sinha, Japanese Multinationals in Asia: capabilities and motivations, The World Bank, working paper 1634.

[13] Uday Bhanu Sinha, International joint venture, licensing and buy-out under asymmetric information, Journal of Development Economics. Vol. 66, 2001, 127–151, p127.

[14] Beamish, P.W., 1985. The characteristics of joint ventures in developed and developing countries. Columbia Journal of World Business, 13–19, Fall.

[15] Alessandra Casella, James E. Rauch, Anonymous market and group ties in international trade, Journal of International Economics 1 (2001), *www.elsevier.com/ locate / econbase* .

take years to set up a joint venture, it often needs only a few weeks to establish a wholly-owned business. When China began to open up two decades ago, low technology and labour-intensive strategies might really have helped increase firms' market share. However, as the labour cost becomes increasingly expensive and the market for low-end products becomes saturated, the same labour-intensive strategy may now be less desirable. Valuable partnering skills need to give emphasis to the joint interests whilst minimising real or potential conflict, and JV managers will seek to lessen conflict between the parents given the potential damage such conflicts can inflict upon the JV[16]. Even if there may be no immediate benefit from the *JV* formed currently, the local companies may go for a *JV* anticipating that there may be some long-term benefits, predominantly when the foreign partner brings a new technology in the near future[17]. A MNE is indifferent between selling the new technology to an outsider or to the *JV* if it can extract the same surplus from these channels but the new technology helps a MNE to extract more payoffs from the *JV*, the local partner can always outbid any outside competitor by offering a higher price to the MNE.

A prominent characteristic of developing countries is the relative instability of their policies and in the initial stage of liberalization an economy, which is liberalizing its policy towards foreign equity participation in the local market faces strong opposition from various pressure groups. If a government cannot fully commit its future (liberalization) policy, and if there is a possibility of new entrants in the future market, the existing company finds it strategic advantage to write a *JV* contract with a MNE which is expected to bring superior technologies in the future[18]. The need to compete in new and often distant markets has led to a wave of mergers and acquisitions, which have enabled enterprises to concentrate in core competencies that guarantee international competitive advantages in particular areas. Besides, MNEs have greater economic wealth than some states and they may be able to use their position of comparative power over states to play nations and communities off against each other in an effort to receive the most advantageous benefits.

The choice between the various legal forms depends on the degree of integration required for the realization of the alliance's objects and on the regulatory burdens associated with each form. A trasnational merger will be chosen where the parent firms wish fully to integrate their business operations and to ensure the benefits of limited liability. The contractual form will be set up for a specific commercial aim, which does not involve a high level of integration between the parties. Moreover, the contractual form is not used in case of joint production of a specific product or the joint provision of a service where the level of integration and risk may be higher. Publicly owned MNEs can arise first when a state-owned enterprise adopts a strategy of international expansion and second when an existing MNE is nationalised. The

---

[16] Peter J. Buckley, Keith W. Glaister, Rumy Husan, International joint ventures: partnering skills and cross cultural issues, Long Range Planning (2002). www.lrpjournal.com Jack E. Brown, "Technology Joint Ventures to Set Standards or Define Interfaces," 61 Antitrust L.J. 921, 932 (1993) ("there is increasing awareness of a heightened need for joint ventures to develop new products in the most effective manner by drawing on the different skills and areas of competence possessed by different companies. . . . Cooperation-particularly with respect to interface standards and similar issues-may represent the logical way to further research and development objectives in this area").

[17] Das, S. P., 1998, 'On the Choice of International Joint Venture: The Role of Policy Moral Hazard', Journal of Policy Reform 2: 135 – 150. Das, S. P., 1999, 'Direct Foreign Investment versus Licensing', Review of Development Economics 3: 86 – 97.

[18] Dasgupta, S. and Z. Tao, 1998, 'Contractual Incompleteness and the Optimality of Equity Joint Ventures', Journal of Economic Behavior And Organization 37: 391-413.

legal structures of publicly owned MNEs are depended on the degree of control that the state wishes to exercise over the enterprise. The position of the state as principal shareholder makes the enterprise dependent on grants from the state. The applicable control system depends on the objectives of the enterprise. The state may be a useful partner where the private sector is virtually non-existent or where it provides insufficient capital for the expansion of a business. The European Economic Interest Grouping (EEIG), which is introduced by regulation 2137/85[19], is a supranational form of business association that will facilitate cross-border cooperation between business entities operating within the EU. The EEIG is disqualified from certain commercial activities and it is not to be used as a management or holding company for the members and cannot be used for large scale manufacturing operations because it cannot employ more than 500 persons.

Mergers[20] that create new corporations by combining previously separate companies operating in the same or similar businesses have become increasingly common. Internal decision making processes tend to be exceedingly politicised in mergers, as reflected in such things as the managers ' status and departures. Decision makers in large corporate organisations do not form a coherent whole; somewhat, they are separated according to their national, professional, and ethnic backgrounds and by their various positions in the corporate system. Mergers create a new corporate management in charge of developing the new corporation[21]. If the vertically merged firm becomes a MNE horizontally, by setting up a branch and producing the final production in another country, then outsourcing reduces the union wage, raises profits and the MNE can move production between branches in the two countries. This mobility advantage enables the MNE to vary to a degree against possible union strikes and thus improve its bargaining position in negotiations. Unionisation in vertically related markets creates multinational conglomerates. According to Laixun Zhao [22]"Vertical integration always subjects the profits of the whole firm to labour–management bargaining, which puts the firm at a disadvantage, while going multinational horizontally always gives the firm mobility, enabling the MNE to play off the labour unions". Companies subcontracting an expanding set of activities, ranging from product design to assembly, from research and development to marketing, distribution, and after-sales service becoming "virtual" manufacturers, owning designs for many products but making almost nothing themselves. A company can establish a bilateral relationship and having the partner undertake relationship-specific investments so that it becomes able to produce goods or services that match the company's specific needs[23]. Companies in many countries are sub-contracting abroad an expanding range of activities, from product design and the production of intermediate inputs to assembly, marketing, and after-sales service and engaging in ever more foreign investment. Each producer needs a specialized component to serve as an input into the

---

[19] Council Regulation 2137/85 of 25 July 1985 OJ 1985 L 199/1.

[20] Olié,R.(1996).European transnational mergers. Maastricht:Proeschrift Rijskuniversiteit Limburg.

[21] Eero Vaara, Role-bound actors in corporate combinations: a sociopolitical perspective on post-merger change processes, Scand.J.Mgmt.17 (2001) 481-509

[22] Laixun Zhao, Unionization, vertical markets, and the outsourcing of multinationals, Journal of International Economics 55 (2001) 187–202,p 201.

[23] Gene M. Grossman and Elhanan Helpman, Outsourcing in a Global Economy 2002, Harvard Institute of Economic, Research Discussion Paper Number 1966

production of its final goods. According[24] to Arijit Mukherjee and Udo Broll if there is asymmetric information concerning the foreign company's cost of production or the production technology then, the foreign firm may prefer to do direct investment rather than export.

Do (semi) cooperative industrial ownership structures, such as the Japanese keiretsu system, yield their members advantages in exploiting opportunities for FDI? Members of keiretsu and chaebol hold ownership shares in each other, obtain repeated financing from associated member banks, and participate on joint committees. It is argued that information effect is of greater importance than the direct incentive effects induced by overlapping ownership structures and overlapping ownership structures do not matter, but their main effect is through the incentives to create and share information relevant to the costs of undertaking FDI[25]. The process of liberalization in the developing countries allows the multinational to do FDI and so the MNE can choose exports or setting up a subsidiary to carry out the production abroad. FDI helps the MNEs to produce their products with lower cost compared to export avoiding costs like transportation costs and/or tariffs. Fixed cost associated with FDI reduces foreign company's net profit from FDI compared to export and under complete information the foreign company always prefers trade than direct investment[26]. Thus, it could be argued that direct investment may help the multinational to signal the true cost of production to the international markets. Consequently, signaling cost advantages through the observable action of FDI explains an economic reason for becoming a multinational enterprise in international segmented markets.

Individual companies in poor protection countries are able to take measures to make better the quality of protection for their investors, and markets respond optimistically to such efforts. Investor protection affects a country’s welfare through its impact on investment by foreign companies. To the extent poor shareholder and creditor protection hinders home companies’ abilities to raise capital or poor shareholder protection facilitates sub-optimal investment behavior, foreign multinationals that do not operate under such constraints will take comparative advantages. That's why, national company activity is indeed lower in countries with poor investor protection, but increased foreign multinational activity might fill this empty space.

Cross-border investment contributes significantly to a country’s economic development and accordingly if weak investor protection attracts real investment by foreign multinationals, this investment provides another path by which harmful outcomes are mitigated. Changes in cross-border activities over time have impact on the relation between investor protection and financial development. On the other hand, cross-border acquisitions affect the value of the target company’s industry, and the valuation effects seem to be different with investor protection. Multinational companies arise because they benefit from comparative advantages that prevail over the costs of doing business abroad. Companies from countries with strong shareholder rights and strong rule of law make more value enhancing cross-border investment

[24] Arijit Mukherjee Udo Broll, 2001, Export and direct investment as a signal in global markets, keele Working Paper

[25] Bruce Blonigen, Christopher J. Ellis, and Dietrich Fausten. Industrial Groupings and Strategic FDI: Theory and Evidence. November 2000, p25.

[26] Marjit, S. and A. Mukherjee, 2001, ‘Technology transfer under asymmetric information: the role of equity participation’, Journal of Institutional and Theoretical Economics, 157: 282– 300.

decisions. Profitable projects are untouched by home companies in countries with weaker shareholder and creditor protection for the reason that access to capital is more constrained or costly and accordingly large multinationals enjoying access to both external impartiality and debt have a comparative advantage[27].

Poor investor protection results in constrained or more costly access to capital and accordingly financing constraints are noticeably greater in nations with poor protection for investors. Companies in weak shareholder protection countries pay out less in dividends, hold excess cash, and manage earnings more antagonistically and accordingly control-block votes are more valuable when shareholder protection is weak suggesting that controlling shareholders can take out private benefits[28]. Companies over invest in low growth industries and under invest in high growth industries in weak investor protection environments[29]. Returns are negative to cross-border acquisitions by bidders from states with weak shareholder rights, but they are positive for acquisitions by bidders from countries with strong shareholder rights and subsequently cross-border targets are from countries with weaker shareholder protection than the acquirers[30].

Agency conflicts between management and shareholders are higher for larger, established companies generating large free cash flows available for optional spending. The size of a country's private credit market is related to the scale of protection it provides for creditors and access increases after creditor protection is improved. Stronger protection for creditors prevents managers from making value-increasing investment decisions and subsequently managers make decisions to decrease firm risk. Comparative advantages associated with creditor protection stem from home companies' difficulty in obtaining debt financing when creditor protection is weak[31]. Weak protection of both shareholders and creditors appears to magnetize foreign investment.

Foreign direct investment in the form of mergers and acquisitions (M&A) is a successful way of competing in a tough global environment[32]. Vasco Rodrigues [33] has shown that "merger occurrence is determined by the interplay of the initial number of firms in the industry, the expected competitive intensity, and the possibility of economizing on fixed costs through merger". After the merging process is concluded, the owner of every independent firm decides its managerial inducement for his manager. In fact Miguel Gonzalez-Maestre and Javier Lopez-Cunat [34] state, "The incentive for merger, under delegation, is considerably

[27] Rossi, S., and P. Volpin. "Cross-Country Determinants of Mergers and Acquisitions." Journal of Financial Economics 74 (2004), 277-304.

[28] Wurgler, J. "Financial Markets and the Allocation of Capital." Journal of Financial Economics 58 (2000), 187-214.

[29] Love, I. "Financial Development and Financing Constraints: International Evidence from the Structural Investment Model." Review of Financial Studies 16 (2003), 765-791.

[30] Lins, K. V., D. Strickland, and M. Zenner. "Do Non-U.S. Firms Issue Equity on U.S. Stock Exchanges to Relax Capital Constraints." Journal of Financial and Quantitative Analysis 40 (2005), 109-133.

[31] Nenova, T. "The Value of Corporate Voting Rights and Control: A Cross-Country Analysis." Journal of Financial Economics 68 (2003), 325-351.

[32] Claudio D. Milman, James P. D'Mello, Bulent Aybar, Harvey Arbela´ez, A note using mergers and acquisitions to gain competitive advantage in the United States in the case of Latin American MNEs, International Review of Financial Analysis10 (2001) 323–332

[33] Vasco Rodrigues, Endogenous mergers and market structure, International Journal of Industrial Organization 19 (2001) 1245–1261,p1245.

[34] Miguel Gonzalez-Maestre, Javier Lopez-Cunat, Delegation and mergers in oligopoly International Journal of Industrial Organization 19 (2001) 1263–1279, p1263.

increased with respect to the setting without delegation. In fact, we prove that the level of welfare in the setting with delegation is, in some cases, lower than the corresponding level under non delegation". If companies compete in a homogeneous product market, mergers will be unprofitable to the merging firms. Martin J. Conyon, Sourafel Girma, Steve Thompson, and Peter W. Wright [35] found that "the *absolute* number of employees falls substantially, along with output, in the hostile merger case alone. This appears to be the consequence of a high level of post-merger divestment that distinguishes hostile transactions". Does cross-border M&As increase the productive capacity? Despite the warm attitude towards inward Foreign Direct Investment (FDI) among investment liberalizing countries, concerns are raised about the influence of cross-border mergers and acquisitions (M&As) on development[36]. Domestic assets are more efficiently used when transferred from domestic to foreign ownership, since MNEs are corporations with strong firm-specific assets in terms of technology, know-how of marketing and organization. One of the major functions of FDI is to transfer assets from less efficient to more efficient owners and managers[37]. MNEs operating in more than 20 countries have twice the exposure of MNEs who operate in one country having one subsidiary and exposed to exchange rate fluctuations which means that exposure is a function of foreign operations[38]. Moreover, Henrik Horn and Lars Persson [39] stated, "in concentrated markets, mergers are conducive to market structures with large *industry* profits, and thus points to a potential conflict between private and social incentives. It is shown how mergers may be undertaken in order to pre-empt other possible, and socially more desirable, mergers".

Does technological change lead to infinite economies of scale, such that large firms always have lower costs and higher profits than smaller firms? Only the large, oligopolistic firms can finance a satisfactory R&D program leading to new technological discoveries to maintain or increase market share that means that a good number of the large enterprises become ever larger over time, both in absolute and relative terms. Besides, the information technology perspective offers some valuable and perhaps valid reasons for declining establishment size. Frederic L. Pryor [40] shows that "average establishment size has decreased since the late 1960s, that the number of establishments per enterprise has levelled off since the early 1980s, and that the average size of enterprises reveals an undulating pattern with a sharp upturn at the end of the century due to the impact of the merger wave". International M&A are not only quantitatively valuable, but in policy making they are often viewed in a different way than those involving national firms only and so governments sometimes allow or encourage mergers between domestic firms that have adverse effects on domestic

[35] Martin J. Conyon, Sourafel Girma, Steve Thompson, Peter W. Wright, Do hostile mergers destroy jobs? Journal of Economic Behavior & Organization Vol. 45 (2001) 427–440, p427.

[36] Markusen, J. R., 1995, The Boundaries of Multinational Enterprises and the Theory of International Trade, Journal of Economic Perspective 9, 169-189. Horn, H. and L. Persson, 2001, "Endogenous Mergers in Concentrated Markets," International Journal Of Industrial Organization, Vol. 19, 1213-1244. Kamien, M. I. and Zang, I., 1990, "The Limits of Monopolization Through Acquisition," Quarterly Journal of Economics, 2, 465-99.

[37] Lipsey, R. E., 2000, Interpreting developed countries' foreign direct investmens, NBER Working Paper 7810.

[38] G Allayannis, J Ihrig, 2001, Markups and Exposure, Review of Financial studies, 14, No3 p805-835.

[39] Henrik Horn, Lars Persson, Endogenous mergers in concentrated markets, International Journal of Industrial Organization 19 (2001) 1213–1244, p1213.

consumers, with the aim of promoting international competitiveness[41]. Steffen Ziss [42] considers that "the profitability of merger in oligopoly is significantly enhanced if firms delegate the output decision to an agent and then motivate the latter using strategic rent shifting contracts". Besides, anti-competitive mergers benefit competitors more than the merging firms. Companies can uphold collusive prices if they think that undercutting their rivals would trigger a price war and consequently harm future profits the potential short-term gain from a deviation can then be outweighed by the long-run losses from the price war[43]. The present merger wave is the dominance of horizontal amalgamations, whereby firms in the same industry are combined. The merging process derives into the long-term energy-absorbing processes of technological integration. If there is a positive effect on share prices at the time of a merger announcement, the gains accumulate to the target 's shareholders. Most acquisitions either have no value consequences or the consequences for the stockholders of the acquiring firms are negative[44].

As discussed earlier, cultural differences in JVs can prejudice information flow and organizational learning and lead to misunderstanding and mistrust leading to instability and poor performance. Cultural difference could be defined at the national level and at the partner level. Especially, MNEs doing business abroad face additional costs arising from unfamiliarity of the local environment (cultural, legal, political and economic differences), and from the need to coordinate activities across geographic distances. Thus, a company is expected to incur fewer costs and enhance shareholder value if the JV is located in its home country than if it is located abroad[45]. Strategic alliances have taken increasing importance as a means to control competitive forces and to enter into activities involving risks too high to be taken as individual ventures and the joint venture (JV) is one of the most frequently used contractual forms in strategic alliances. JV composition can condition the development of the relationship since it affects members' behaviour and, accordingly, the dynamics of the collaboration process and the correct composition is an indispensable condition for attaining the goals set by the alliance providing a good joint working relationship allowing for the development of synergies and cooperative partner behaviour[46]. Besides alliance composition, governance structure -the hierarchical chart of the relationship- plays a significant role in the success of the relationship and the important question in terms of governance structure is

---

40 Frederic L. Pryor, Will most of us be working for giant enterprises by 2028?, Journal of Economic Behavior & Organization Vol. 44 (2001) 363–382, p363.

41 Henrik Horn, Lars Persson, The equilibrium ownership of an international oligopoly, Journal of International Economics 53 (2001) 307–333.

42 Steffen Ziss, Horizontal mergers and delegation, International Journal of Industrial Organization19 (2001) 471–492, p471.

43 Olivier Compt, Frederic H H Jenny, Patrick Rey, Capacity constraints, mergers and collusion, European Economic Review 46 (2002) 1-29. Hema A. Krishnan, Daewoo Park, The impact of work force reduction on subsequent performance in major mergers and acquisitions: An exploratory study, Journal of Business Research 55 (2002) 285– 292.

44 Horn, H., & Persson, L. (1999). The equilibrium ownership of an international oligopoly London: Centre for Economic Policy Research.

45 Sangphet Hanvanich, Stewart R. Miller, Malika Richards, S. Tamar Cavusgil , An event study of the effects of partner and location cultural differences in joint ventures, International Business Review 12 (2003) 1–16

46 Sarkar, M., Echambadi, R., Cavusgil, S., & Aulakh, P. (2001). The influence of complementarity, compatibility, and relationship capital on alliance performance. Journal of the Academy of Marketing Science, 29(4), 358–373.

autonomy—greater autonomy means greater hierarchical control[47]. In some JVs, managers from the parent organizations are very active in determining the strategic direction taken by the relationship, whereas in others, the JV management team is able to make its own choices with unimportant intervention from the parent firms. Autonomy and JV composition cannot be dealt with independently, as only a balance between these two factors will render optimum levels of performance.

Taking into account that knowledge is regarded as a crucial ingredient in competitive success and the integration of global markets intensifies competition, companies must allocate more attention to ways of acquiring the knowledge resources that they need and with continuously shifting technologies, products and processes, competitive advantage rests on the ability of a company to learn and circulate accumulated knowledge through-out the organization. The ability to learn is doubtless the most essential intangible asset that a company can possess[48]. The methods used by companies to exploit knowledge and improve organisational efficiency has to be done through more efficient use of skills in order to achieve the outcome of raising productivity or retaining or enhancing competitiveness[49]. Although IJVs present a vehicle for learning and while alliances create value there is prevalent recognition of the complexity inherent in this process of value creation evidenced by the high failure rate for IJVs and the low level of satisfaction with IJV performance, particularly in developed countries.[50] JVs can be used as a medium for organisational and inter-organisational learning. Certain technology or other types of know-how, of the other partner are the object of learning from a partner which learning motive is strong in alliances where the companies desire to discover new opportunities or to acquire new capabilities[51]. Alliances are often the best way for companies to swiftly acquire and deploy new skills and knowledge can be used jointly and combined across various functions. While managing an alliance with a partner is itself a great learning experience, especially if the partner is a foreign company, the significant thing is to learn how a JV works, the problems that arise and the possibilities that exist for organising, guiding and developing in different areas. Collaboration enhances organizational learning through the accumulation of experience and knowledge about how to manage alliances that can be used later in the design and management of other collaborations. Absorptive capacity is a characteristic of a company that is required and shaped over many years and is not likely to change during the course of a particular alliance relationship depending on a company's prior preparation and requires

---

[47] Stuart, T. (2000). Interorganizational alliances and the performance of firms: a study of growth and innovation rates in a high-technology industry. Strategic Management Journal, 21, 791–811.

[48] Child, J., & Faulkner, D. (1998). Strategies of co-operation: Managing alliances, networks, and joint ventures. Oxford: Oxford University Press.

[49] Keith W. Glaister , Rumy Husan, Peter J. Buckley, Learning to manage international joint ventures, International Business Review 12 (2003) 83–108

[50] Beamish, P. W., & Delios, A. (1997). Improving joint venture performance through congruent measures of success. In P. W. Beamish, & J. P. Killing (Eds.), Co-operative strategies: European perspectives (pp. 103–127) p108.

[51] Nti, K. O., & Kumar, R. (2000). Differential learning in alliances. In D. Faulkner, & M. de Rond (Eds.), Co-operative strategy: Economic, business and organizational issues (pp. 119–134). Oxford: Oxford University Press. Lyles, M. A., & Salk, J. E. (1997). Knowledge acquisition from foreign parents in international joint ventures. In P. W. Beamish, & J. P. Killing (Eds.), Cooperative strategies: European perspectives (pp. 325–355). San Francisco, CA: The New Lexington Press.

continuous and sustained investment[52]. Thus, companies learn to create more value as they accumulate experience in joint venturing.

It is a task for MNEs to establish a reliable front-end financial target in international joint venture (IJV) negotiations with emerging economic countries (EECs). IJV effort tends to enhance revenues and/or decrease costs, as compared with totally owned foreign subsidiaries however this weight alone is not enough to rationalize the IJV investment, or endorse the financial target that an MNE aims at because there is a need to forecast the total value that the IJV can engender by identifying the prospective benefits and costs that an MNE has when engaging in the potential IJV[53].

A MNE needs to take into consideration the prospect cost of the investment establishing a full assessment of the total value that could be generated by the IJV itself[54]. When the relationship between the excess value and financial target is ascertained, a MNE can determine its front-end target for the IJV with assertion. R&D and/or marketing JVs facilitate vertical integration which increases the social intricacy of companies' resource deployments and the pursuit of R&D and/or marketing JVs create entry barriers. That's why it shifts the weight of competition onto rivals and renders parents' JV-based rents less exposed to competitive imitation[55]. Nevertheless, vertical integration increases the inter-connectedness among transactions and hence raises organizational costs. Competitive advantage are obtained more effectively depending on the type of partner (firms; state-owned enterprises) with whom companies enter into JVs. Various JV motivations driving individual partners lead to conflicting behaviors, including opportunistic conduct by each partner that would at last compromise the venture's capacity to succeed. Nevertheless, parents with previous JV experience may be able to offset some of the negative effects of such conduct.

2.2 The Role of Legal Factors

A MNE should possess some unique competitive advantage, which is capable of international exploitation. Large size may be important to successful innovation because of high research and development costs, which can only be borne by a larger enterprise. Firm size is closely connected to the protection of technological advantage. A system of patent law ensures the protection of the firm's competitive advantages by granting to the firm a monopoly for the exploitation of that advantage for a specified period of time. Patent rights[56] will complement the MNEs protection of its innovation through the market power it enjoys as a result of its integrated international network and from the difficulty of re-creating advanced

---

52 Cohen, W. M., & Levinthal, D. A. (1990). Absorptive capacity: a new perspective on learning and innovation. Administrative Science Quarterly, 35, 128–152.

53 Johnson, Jean L., John B. Cullen, Tomoaki Sakano and JamesW. Bronson (April 2001) "Drivers and outcomes of parent company intervention in IJV management: A cross-cultural comparison." Journal of Business Research, Vol. 52, No. 1, pp.35-49.

54 Lee, Don Y. (May 2001) "Power, conflict, and satisfaction in IJV supplier – Chinese distributor channels." Journal of Business Research, Vol. 52, No. 2, pp.149-160.

55 Robson, M., Leonidou, L., & Katsikeas, C. (2002). Factors influencing international joint venture performance: Theoretical perspectives, assessment, and future directions. Management International Review, 42(4): 385–418.

56 S Magee "Information and the multinational corporation: An appropriability theory of direct investmen" in J Bhagwati The New International Economic Order 1977 MIT Press p 317.

industrial technology. Cyberspace has brought a revolution into the protection of intellectual property of MNEs. Patent law is not used to protect the MNEs advantages because in certain countries the technology transfer laws, which establish controls over the manner in which the foreign firm may sell and apply its technology in the host state. The major capital exporting states insist on the legal protection of intellectual property rights owned by their MNEs. For instance, patent protection played a crucial role in encouraging direct investments in France, England, and Germany[57]. Legal conditions that permit the growth of large corporations can be seen as instruments in the growth of MNEs[58].

While the existence of the corporate legal form has been a necessary element in the growth of large corporate groups, it is not a sufficient element. It could be said that economic factors have been the primary stimulants to the development of large corporations. Legal factors have influenced the form that enterprises would take but not causing their evolution. It is worth noting that cartels and mergers have been complementary and not alternative strategies for the expansion of MNEs. Antitrust consideration acts as decisive factor in the growth of large national and MNEs. A firm may have to go multinational so as to coordinate and neutralize the threat posed by its competitor's decision to go multinational. Going multinational is a defensive behaviour and a response to competitive attac coming from the firm that goes multinational first.[59] Certain companies invest abroad not to achieve economies of scale and production but to diversify investment and to reduce risk.[60] The possession of access to raw materials and the extractive technology may not be a permanent source of advantage. The possession of raw materials by a firm should be accompanied by specific asset conditioned by locational factors, including home and host state legal regulation, and technological factors. The role of legal factors as elements in the MNE host state bargaining process should not be overlooked. The ability of a MNE to take advantage of differences in regulatory environments between states is seen as one of its internalisation advantages.

The long run political or other costs of internalisation may eventually make it prohibitively expressive especially where host nations adopt discriminatory policies towards MNEs. Moreover, firms become multinational in order to take advantage of lower labour costs that result from the firm's enhanced ability to "Divide and rule" but producing in various countries firms divide their workforce, thereby reduce labour's bargaining power and consequently obtain lower labour costs[61]. The ability to reduce labour costs may be at least a contributory reason for the existence of some multinationals.[62] The advantage enjoyed by the MNEs over domestic companies as an exploiter of labour will depend to a significant degree on the legal conditions regarding labour relations that are imposed on it by host countries. Countries may differ in the extent to which their laws will preserve the corporate advantage of MNEs over labour. So, legal factors may assist in the preservation of the MNEs advantages in this field. Traditional notions of territorial sovereignty are not up to the job because they

---

[57] J Dunning "Changes in the level and structure of international production: The last one hundred years" in M Casson The growth of international business 1983 Allen & Unwin.

[58] L Hannah "Merger, cartels and concentration: Legal factors in US and European experiences" in N Horn and J Jkocka Law and The Formation of Big Enterprises 1979 Cottingen.

[59] F Knickerbacker "Oligopolistic reaction and the multinational enterprise" 1973 Harvard University Press. K Cowling, R Sugdan "Trasnational monopoly capitalism" 1978 Wheatsheaf Books.

[60] R Kopits "Multinational coglomerate diversification" 1979 Econ Int 99

[61] K Cowling, R Sugden , Transnational monopoly capitalism, 1987, Wheatsheaf Books.

[62] N Pitelis, R Sugden, The nature of the transnational firm, 1991, Routledge.

fail to recognize the economic reality of MNEs in the globalized economy. Transnational Companies are not recognized as international legal entities, although international law does grant them a privileged international status. MNEs have a private legal identity granted by the countries where their headquarters are. As far as international public legal identity is concerned it cannot be conceived for MNEs despite their current economic weight because it would mean they were equivalent to States. The transnational group does not, in itself, possess an identity which can be distinguished from each of the entities that make it up, so that it can only be obliged to answer for its acts in a fragmented way, so that it benefits from the opposing interests of the States in which it operates. The transfer of prohibited or regulated activities in one State to countries with fewer regulations allows them to escape their responsibilities. In principle it is not illegal to take advantage of the disparities neither between states nor of the differences caused by the unequal development between different countries. Transfer of industries or other very dangerous activities, as well as their transfer to countries with cheap labour and lower social protection levels in order to make production costs cheaper are examples of abuses committed by MNEs. Does the power of MNEs erode that of States? MNEs are not the most important vehicles for capital, because transnational capital does not necessarily use MNEs as it has many other ways in which it can flow. All damage is not to be attributable to MNEs because the volatility of capital produces damaging effects, such as is the case with pension funds, which are invested in risky operations in the very short term and can have catastrophic results if the system undergoes a crisis. MNEs wield very great power, but it is perhaps erroneous to believe that they have more power than the State, because they are dependent on it for growth.

In the internationalization of competition law, sovereign countries are not the only actors; there are also forces such as the EC, North American Free Trade Agreement (NAFTA), the WTO, the OECD and MNEs, which have gained escalating importance in the internationalization of competition law. Countries and MNEs stand in absolute contrast in the process of internationalization of competition law. A country is expected to protect the public interest, and for long it was regarded as the only method for public participation and control in the shaping of society and the legal, economic and political orders within. Above and beyond, MNEs exist to promote their self-interests. In fact, there has been an unprecedented transfer of sovereignty from countries to MNEs which means that instead of keeping sovereignty in the 'upwards' reservoirs of countries, it is being transferred downwards and placed into the system of business power. MNEs escape or get round the laws of countries, and subsequently democratic control which means that with an increased process of globalisation, MNEs can make use of their personnel and corporate structure to drain know-how away from one country to another.

MNEs choose to operate in jurisdictions with lax competition law enforcement and accordingly they will be able to avoid jurisdictions where competition law is firmly or genuinely enforced. MNEs exercise power in a thoughtful functional sense directly because they play a role in enhancing the economic wealth of countries, in particular developed ones. On the other hand, the lobbying capacity of MNEs affords them the opportunity to gain political power and have an influence in the decision making process at government level within countries. Moreover, MNEs are a variable in determining the extent to which competition law is internationalized and have played a part in the developing of the competition laws of countries however such laws contain provisions that limit their freedom of action, in particular when competition in the market place is expected to be distorted.

The involvement of more than one competition authority and the reaching of inconsistent results by those authorities in a particular transaction may lead to international conflicts between the countries concerned which can be damaging to MNEs, who are anxious about the application of more than one home competition laws to their transactions. MNEs are concerned about the costs in time and money incurred when their operations are subjected to review by numerous home competition authorities. Furthermore, conflicting results drag MNEs into diplomatic disputes between countries, where it is typical for industrial policy considerations and other considerations to overrule competition policy considerations. The ability of MNEs to affect their legal environment through contractual arrangements, lobbying of home and host states and IEOs, and the development of substantive norms of international business law are complex and imperative matters, which has to be taken into account.

It is by no means easy to forecast what the influence of any legal system on any individual will be, and so to which MNEs it should appeal[63]. Therefore, MNE preferences may not be internally uniform which means that a MNE's customers, competitors, shareholders and lenders all have an influence upon its preferences, which may in turn affect MNE's locational decisions. MNEs like all economic decision makers operate within the confines of bounded rationality and so MNEs may in fact be unable to find and/or analyse the information critical to make such a prediction.

2.3 MNE and Codes

Without an existing mechanism for global enforcement of rules and laws there is no uncomplicated practical alternative for making realistic improvements in the contemporary climate of injurious corporate conduct which means that global governance absent global government is unsuccessful in bringing about required change.

A decisive factor to the successful creation, implementation, assessment and spreading of efficient codes of conduct is the establishment of clear and sound principles that are associated not only with the needs and mental picture of the author company, but also with the needs and vision of the affected stakeholders. A company's successful implementation of a code of conduct is dependent on the kind of the internal organizational dynamics and internal due processes, together with a top management team and corporate culture committed to enacting socially responsible behavior. Effective codes are those that go together with existing laws and regulations, satisfy concerns produced as a result of vacuums created by weak laws and regulations, and show consideration for home industry, region, country norms and values and accordingly successful codes must have an influence beyond just the words, by improving conditions in calculable ways. The behavior of MNEs is affected by the proper operating environment, both in terms of the industry sector of which they are members, and of the host country environment that is home to their overseas operations and these twin conditions assist to decide the capacity of companies to act in a way that would meet or exceed social hope of its stakeholders, as the nature of norms represented in home societies and competitive environments are enabling of good behavior and delimiting. Local environments that have not developed the fitting social infrastructure or rule of law to go

63 A. Perry (2000), 'Effective Legal Systems and Foreign Direct Investment: In Search of the Evidence' 49 ICLQ 779–799.

along with investment are less clear and prone to corruption as well, exacerbating the dilemma.

Voluntary[64] codes of conduct at the company level are flawed in the main with respect to transparency and accountability attributed to a disregard of the pervasiveness with which codes exist within the organizational processes and routines institutionalized in the company prior to the code's creation[65].

What are the OECD Guidelines for Multinational Enterprises? The Guidelines are recommendations addressed by governments to multinational enterprises operating in or from adhering countries. The OECD Guidelines for Multinational Enterprises are one of the world's leading corporate responsibility instruments and are becoming a principal international benchmark for corporate responsibility containing voluntary principles and standards for responsible business conduct in such areas as human rights, environment, anti-corruption, taxation, labour relations, and consumer protection intending to support the positive contributions multinational enterprises can make to economic, environmental and social progress[66]. The Guidelines are relevant for both multinational and domestic enterprises. So, the guidelines lay down standards for the activities of MNEs and their observance is voluntary and not legally enforceable. Every state has the right to prescribe the conditions under which MNE operate within its national jurisdiction subject to international law, the international agreements to which it subscribes and they are not a substitute for national laws to which MNEs are subject. The United Nations Code of Conduct (the 1976 OECD Guidelines on Multinational Enterprises) failed to materialize. Can multinationals be left to implement codes of conduct unilaterally? The multinationals were seen as prospective agents of their home countries, acting against the interests of the host countries in which they established or took over subsidiaries. MNEs are occasionally considered more centered in a specific state than are transnational corporations. They were assumed to use a high level of control over the actions of these subsidiaries. In the 1980s, there was small actual action for implementing or strengthening the performance of the principles of the OECD and ILO instruments concerned. Most countries were far more interested in obtaining multinational investment than in controlling it. Technological and structural developments, combined with changes in the way in which global sourcing and distribution is done, have weakened and eliminated the naming of the management of a global enterprise with a given home country. The global company is not based on confrontation and power struggles between socio-economic and political blocks. The enforcement of any given principles has to be compatible with the way in which today's market is structured and functions. The opening up of the global economy has intensified global competition, and reactions by consumers and public opinion to un-ethical production have become an important economic factor. Moreover, working and living conditions in countries where global companies do their sourcing have become increasingly transparent. Besides, short of refusing to purchase when in doubt, multinational and national producers do not control their suppliers. Additionally, countries, which have ratified the eight fundamental Labour Conventions, have the constitutional obligation not only to ensure their implementation but also to report every second year. *The*

---

[64] Sethi, S. P. 2003. Setting Global Standards: Guidelines for Creating Codes of Conduct in Multinational Corporations. Hoboken, N.J.: John Wiley & Sons, Inc.

[65] Windsor, D. 2004. "The Development of International Business Norms." Business Ethics Quarterly 14(4): 729-54.

[66] OECD Policy Brief: The OECD Guidelines for Multinational Enterprises, June 2003.

Declaration on Fundamental Principles and Rights at Work and its Follow-up were adopted by the International Labour Conference in June 1998, which does not duplicate but rather complements the regular standards supervisory mechanism. The OECD Guidelines for Multinational Enterprises and the ILO Tripartite Declaration on Multinational Enterprises and Social Policy remain parallel. The ILO assists governments, the business sector and trade unions in identifying problems related to the observance of core labour standards.

They describe general criteria covering a range of multinational activities without defining the term MNE. The sharing of knowledge among companies or other entities does not in itself indicate that such companies constitute a MNE. Majority ownership is not the exclusive form of linkage between companies in different countries allowing significant influence over the activities of each other. All entities are expected to co-operate and assist in observing the guidelines without the guide lines being a model of co-operate decision making or indicating the way parent companies communicate with their affiliated entities. The guidelines cannot supersede or substitute the national laws governing corporate liability. MNE should co-operate with the local community and there is a need for a certain amount of integration of the various entities of a MNE into the economic context of the countries in which they operate. The guidelines encourage greater transparency of the enterprise as a whole through the publication of information sufficient to improve public understanding. The management of a MNE should provide facilities to employee representatives to assist in developing effective collective agreements. The sensitivity of certain business decisions is such that it is difficult for management to give employee representative's early notice of specific changes. Management has a range of possibilities from which to choose to enable meaningful negotiations or consultations between management and employee representatives. Moreover, SA8000 was developed in 1997 and was put together by an advisory board convened by Social Accountability International (SAI). SA8000 was developed more to empower the supplier-side of the equation to enable the supplier organisations to gain recognition for their efforts in the area of social accountability. Invariably, because of the "political" situation, the nature of press allegations and the need for multinational enterprises to manage their risks, SA8000 has become a tool for multinational enterprises to further improve their own social accountability performance and that of their supplier base. This is not necessarily wrong, but, to repeat, SA8000 was developed to respond to supplier needs rather than those of multinational enterprises.

Over the years, not only SA8000, but also a number of different company codes and other international instruments have been developed. Clearly these have had a major influence on the way that NGOs, unions, workers and corporations actually view their responsibilities in the social accountability arena. The reality of the situation is that the aspirations of the international instruments are a long way away from where companies are operating today. Do all codes delineating standards remain mainly words? Yet the gap between the words and the actions is still large. To achieve sustainability, information and dialogue from all actors in society is needed. In systems of democratic governance, it is the government that it is to take on the responsibility of ensuring society wide implementation and it is government that in the face of uncertainty is to make a decision. Governments need to display a certain amount of policy coherence, especially related to linking the codes they sign up to. Sultana Bashir & Nick Mabey[67] consider the need for clarification of the scope and applicability of the OECD Guidelines on Multinational Enterprises outside the OECD territory, explain the role of the Contact Point and the actions to be taken when investigating alleged breaches of the Guidelines, consent to sanctions and other measures available to the Contact Point to address proven breaches of the Guidelines, build on mechanisms for non-OECD citizens or groups to invoke the Guidelines effectively, work out mechanisms for mediation of disputes between key stakeholders, incorporate mandatory safeguards against pressure from MNEs to lobby for the drop of social and environmental standards, embrace mandatory provisions regarding minimum legal, environmental and social standards to be observed that could be linked to existing BITs such as abiding by existing standards specified by law in the country of investment[68].

MNEs contribute to the GNP of the countries in which they do business by the foreign investment that they provide. However, the contribution via taxation is reduced through fiscal incentives to attract foreign direct investment. MNE activity draws workers from the developing world into the complex course of cross-border production. Furthermore, MNEs create backward and forward linkages with local industry, predominantly to the extent that they draw on locally-produced goods in their production processes. There may also be transfer of technology and expertise[69]and contribution flows through the workers. Individual company codes of corporate conduct issued by head offices of MNEs and containing vague assertions that local labor standards will be respected. Do the self-regulatory measures leave un-answered the question of who will mediate and regulate relations between MNEs and workers? These codes incline not to refer to freedom of association and the right to bargain collectively, even as it may be recognized locally. Indeed, they do not normally refer to the ILO Declaration on Fundamental Principles and Rights at Work,[70] or to the specific fundamental labor standards that embody those principles and rights. According to Adelle Blackett[71] "the tendency of these codes to overlook the pluralistic foundations of labor regulation, and their extension of unilateral management power over particular places, is problematic…they reinforce certain problematic asymmetries and entrench limited state regulatory action…The United Nation's effort must be informed, however, by a thicker theoretical understanding of what it means to create a fluid site for cosmopolitan democratic participation that accounts for the specificity of labor regulation in particular places." It could be said that codes of corporate conduct are regulatory links that connect workplace conditions to the global production chain. Labor law provide worker protection and worker agency

---

[67] Sultana Bashir & Nick Mabey, Can the OECD MNE guidelines promote responsible corporate behaviour? An analysis of p&o's proposed port in Dahanu, India, A WWF-UK Research Paper, November 1998.

[68] OECD (1999), Background Papers for the Review of the Guidelines for Multinational Enterprises, Committee on Investment and for Multinational Enterprises, OECD, Paris, 1999.

[69] See ILO Governing Body, Subcommittee on Multinational Enterprises, GB.280/MNE/1/1, 280th Session, Geneva, Mar.2001 (PartI) at 76, 124, available at *http://www.ilo.org/public/english/standards/relm/gb/obcs/gb280/mne-1-1.htm*. The Realization of Economic, Social and Cultural Rights: The Relationship between the enjoyment of human rights, in particular, international labor and trade union rights, and the working methods and activities of transnational corporations, E/CN.4/Sub.2/1995/11 (July 24, 1995), at 49, available at http://www.unhdnr.ch/huridocda/

[70] ILO, 1998 Declaration of Fundamental Principles and Rights at Work and its Follow-Up, 37 I.L.M. 1233 (adopted June 18, 1998), at *http://www.ilo.org/public/english/standards/ decl/declaration/text /index.htm*

[71] Adelle Blackett, Global Governance, Legal Pluralism and the Decentered State: A Labor Law Critique of Codes of Corporate Conduct, 8 IND. J. GLOBAL LEGAL STUD. 401 at 412

through democratic participation.[72] Through collective action, independent workers' representatives negotiate the relationship between workers and management and the collective bargaining relationship must respect certain basic balances between management and worker rights.

The 2000 Review of the Guidelines recommends observance of the Guidelines by enterprises wherever they operate, and not only in the OECD area. In other words, t*he OECD Guidelines for Multinational Enterprises* provide a set of recommendations for worldwide responsible corporate behaviour consistent with existing legislation and both complement and reinforce efforts by the private sector to define and implement responsible business conduct. These voluntary Guidelines – specifically aimed at the behaviour of Multinational Enterprises – provide a government- backed set of principals and standards of good corporate behaviour and help to level the playing field between competitors in the international market place. In their efforts to increase knowledge of the Guidelines, National Contact Points will co-operate with a broad range of organisations and individuals, including, as appropriate, the business community, employee organisations, other non-governmental organisations, and the interested public. The National Contact Point -- often a government office -- is responsible for encouraging observance of the Guidelines in its national context. The effectiveness of the National Contact Point is a crucial factor in determining how influential the Guidelines are in each national context. All National Contact Points should function in a visible, accessible, transparent and accountable manner. The Guidelines are a comprehensive, multilaterally endorsed code of conduct for multinational enterprises. They provide voluntary principles and standards for responsible business conduct, in a variety of areas including employment and industrial relations, human rights, environment, information disclosure, competition, taxation, and science and technology. Moreover, the Guidelines establish principles covering a broad range of issues in business ethics including information disclosure, corruption, and consumer interests. Protection against corporate ethical abuses is afforded all the way through principles and through laws or regulations. Societies diverge in their accent on either normative controls or legal and regulatory controls to vary behavior. Normative approaches rely on agreed upon societal principles to direct corporate behavior, and the founding of trust between corporations and affected stakeholders serves as security that rights and rights on both sides are properly executed. The imposition of rules in a norm-based society is met with antagonism, while the hope that principles and norms will inadequately control corporate excess is met with skepticism in otherwise rule-bound societies.

Governments have committed themselves to promoting their observance and effective implementation. They aim to promote the positive contributions multinationals can make to economic, environmental and social progress. The Guidelines are not aimed at introducing differences in treatment between multinational enterprises and national enterprises, but reproduce good practice for all. Additionally, the Guidelines are designed to avert misunderstandings and build an atmosphere of confidence and predictability between business, labour, governments and society as a whole. They are supported by business and labour organisations, as well as several non-governmental organisations. Their non-binding nature, however, does not imply less commitment by adhering governments to encourage their observance. Although they are addressed to enterprises, the Guidelines need the support of the business community, labour representatives and non-governmental organisations in

[72] Harry W. Arthurs, Labor Law Without the State?, 46 U. Tor. L. J. 1, 3 (1996).

order to be effective. Moreover, the Declaration on International Investment and Multinational Enterprises promotes a comprehensive, interlinked and balanced approach for governments' treatment of foreign direct investment and for enterprises' activities in adhering countries. The goal of the governments adhering to the Guidelines is to promote the optimistic contributions that multinational enterprises can make to economic, environmental and social progress and to minimise the difficulties to which their different operations may give rise. The recent review enabled the OECD to respond to the need for a thorough consideration of the Guidelines and to ensure their continued relevance and effectiveness in the rapidly changing global economy. Public concerns about the impact of deepening globalisation on home and host societies meant that the most recent review was conducted in a different economic environment. Many features of the Guidelines have been maintained – performance by firms is still voluntary; the institutional structure of the follow-up procedures is largely unchanged; and the Guidelines remain an integral part of the OECD Declaration. All internationally recognised core labour standards are now covered by the Guidelines. Enterprises must raise their environmental performance, through such measures as improved internal environmental management, stronger disclosure of environmental information, and better contingency planning for environmental impacts. Additionally, a recommendation on human rights has been introduced. Moreover, new chapters on combating corruption and on consumer interests have also been added. The National Contact Points will continue to embark on promotional activities, handle investigations on the Guidelines, and discuss matters covered by them, including implementation in specific instances. Thus, the National Contact Point is accountable for encouraging adherence of the Guidelines in its national context and for ensuring that the Guidelines are well known and understood by the national business community and by other interested parties. Additionally, each National Contact Point will submit an annual report of its activities to the OECD Committee on International Investment and Multinational Enterprises (CIME). The CIME is the OECD body responsible for managing the functioning of the Guidelines, and it is estimated to take steps to improve their effectiveness issuing clarifications on the application of the Guidelines in specific circumstances.

The CIME will continue to offer clarifications of the meaning of the Guidelines, as necessary, in particular instances and in response to requirements or queries from adhering governments, business or labour representatives. The non-binding nature of the Guidelines precludes the CIME from acting as a judicial or quasi-judicial body. The revised Guidelines make apparent that the recommendations represent good practice wherever enterprises operate, not just within the OECD area. The individual circumstances of individual host countries need to be taken into consideration and that the implementation procedures need to be adapted to the difficulties that arise for National Contact Points when looking into matters covered by the Guidelines in non-adhering countries. After making an preliminary assessment of whether the issues raised deserve further examination, the National Contact Point will offer its advice to help the parties involved to resolve the issues. Where no agreement can be reached on the issues raised, the National Contact Point will then issue a statement or make recommendations as appropriate. If a party is uncertain about the Guidelines' applicability in a particular context, that party should approach the National Contact Point. The purpose of the clarification is to provide additional information about whether and how the Guidelines apply to a particular business situation. The CIME regularly consults with the Business and Industry Advisory Committee (BIAC) and the Trade Union Advisory Committee (TUAC) on matters relating to the Guidelines and on other issues concerning international investment and multinational enterprises. BIAC and TUAC are accredited to the OECD as official advisory bodies and have as their members business and labour federations in each of the adhering countries. If an enterprise is directly concerned, the National Contact Point should contact the enterprise to notify it that an issue related to the Guidelines has been raised. It might be proper for the National Contact Point to make contact with other National Contact Points if the issue under consideration concerns more than one adhering country. Keeping in mind the international character of the Guidelines and the need to avoid conflicting national interpretations, where there is any doubt or where there are divergent views, the matter should be brought to the attention of the CIME before the NCP gives a final answer. The clarification is not a judgement on the behaviour of an individual enterprise and so clarifications that arise in connection with individual companies do not refer to them by name. National Contact Points are expected to respond to enquiries from governments of non-adhering countries. National Contact Points may take steps to develop an understanding of the issues at stake, for instance through contacts with the management of the company in the home country or with officials in the non-adhering country.

As mentioned above, issues dealt with in the recently revised Guidelines include: disclosure and transparency (updated to encourage social and environmental accountability), employment (now covering all internationally recognised core labour standards), and environment (encouraging MNEs to raise their environmental performance through improved internal environmental management and better contingency planning for environmental impacts). The OECD Principles of Corporate Governance are intended to assist Member and non-Member governments in their efforts to assess and improve the legal, institutional and regulatory framework for corporate governance in their countries and to provide guidance and suggestions for stock exchanges, investors, corporations, and other parties that have a role in the procedure of developing good corporate governance. Corporate governance provides the makeup through which the objectives of the company are set, and the means of attaining those objectives and monitoring performance are determined. The corporate governance framework depends on the legal, regulatory, and institutional environment constituting only part of the larger economic context in which companies operate including macroeconomic policies and the degree of competition in product and factor markets. The Principles concentrate on governance problems that result from the parting of ownership and control. International flows of capital permit firms to access financing from a much larger pool of investors. Even if corporations do not rely first and foremost on foreign sources of capital, obedience to good corporate governance practices will help develop the confidence of domestic investors, may reduce the cost of capital, and eventually induce more stable sources of financing. The Principles are non-binding and do not aim at detailed prescriptions for national legislation but they can be used by policy makers, as they develop their legal and regulatory frameworks for corporate governance, and by market participants as they develop their own practices. Governments have an imperative responsibility for shaping an effective regulatory framework to allow markets to function efficiently and to respond to expectations of shareholders and other stakeholders. It is up to governments and market participants to decide how to apply these Principles in developing their own frameworks for corporate governance, taking into consideration the costs and benefits of regulation. It should be taken into account that the Global Compact at the United Nations and the OECD Guidelines are complementary. The

OECD Guidelines for Multinational Enterprises (MNEs)[73] aim is to ensure that MNEs operate in harmony with the policies of the countries where they operate. Moreover, internationally agreed guidelines can help to prevent misunderstandings and build an atmosphere of confidence and predictability between business, labour and governments. The Guidelines address the MNEs from OECD countries encouraging the positive contributions of MNEs. Enterprises should take full account of countries' general objectives, co-operate with local community and business interests and abstain from bribery and inappropriate political activities. Transparency and accountability towards the range of stakeholders in business – including employees, customers, suppliers, shareholders, local communities, society at large and the environment – are both a *standard* that is expected, and a *mechanism* for securing compliance with codes of conduct designed to meet society's expectations.[74] The objective OECD Global Forum on International Investment is to improve the investment climate for domestic and foreign enterprises, support the positive contribution which multinational enterprises can make to economic and social progress and minimise and resolve difficulties, which might arise from their operations.

The Global Reporting Initiative (GRI)[75] is a long-term, multi-stakeholder, international undertaking whose mission is to develop and disseminate globally applicable sustainability reporting guidelines for voluntary use by organisations reporting on the economic, environmental, and social dimensions of their activities, products and services. The GRI was convened by the Coalition for Environmentally Responsible Economies (CERES) and the United Nations Environment Programme (UNEP). The *Guidelines* provide a framework for reporting that promotes comparability between reporting organisations while recognising the practical considerations of collecting and presenting information across diverse reporting organisations. Application of the GRI *Guidelines* is voluntary intending to support and supplement existing initiatives and agreements, predominantly those international treaties and conventions that represent universal norms and practices.

2.4 MNEs, National and International Law

MNEs[76] operate across national borders, beyond the constraints of any one nation's national law and so their actions are regularly viewed as beyond the reach of any law eluding national legal systems. Additionally, MNEs have been accused for forced labor, and support of armed conflicts in pursuit of their corporate interests[77]. Moreover, MNEs assume powers

[73] *www.oecd.org*

[74] Ann M. Florini, Does the Invisible Hand Need a Transparent Glove? The Politics of Transparency. Paper prepared for the Annual World Bank Conference on Development Economics, Washington D.C., April 28-30 1999. Available at *www.worldbank.org/research/abcde/papers.html*

[75] *www.globalreporting.org*

[76] "multinational corporations include transnational enterprises, however legally organized, that "engage in FDI [foreign direct investment] and that own or control value adding activity outside their national boundaries." John H. Dunning, *Towards a New Paradigm of Development: Implications for the Determinants of International Business Activity*, 15(1) TRANSNAT'L CORPS. 173 & N. 1 (2006).

[77] HUMAN RIGHTS WATCH, SUDAN, OIL AND HUMAN RIGHTS 48 (2003), available at http://www.hrw.org/reports/2003/sudan1103 / (asserting that exploitation of oil by foreign companies has increased human rights abuses and made oil into "the main objective and a principle cause of [Sudan's] war."). Craig Forcese, Deterring "Militarized Commerce": The Prospect of Liability for "Privatized" Human Rights Abuses, 31 OTTAWA L. REV. 171 (2000). Doe v. Unocal Corp., 963 F.

resembling those of states and many of these MNE activities have been the source of substantial allegations of human rights abuses[78].

On the one hand, national law systems have made a range of changes meant to make it easier to control MNEs[79]. A state exercises its power only within the territory it controls[80].

On the other hand, there is a failure of states to monitor and implement compliance with what substantive normative framework[81] has been enacted and is supposed to be binding within the territory of the enacting state[82].

Supp. 880 (C.D. Cal. 1997); Doe v. Unocal Corp., 110 F. Supp. 2d 1294 (C.D. Cal. 2000), aff'd in part, rev'd in part by Doe v. Unocal Corp., 2002 WL 31063976 (9th Cir. Sept. 18, 2002), vacated by Doe v. Unocal Corp., 2003 WL 359787 (9th Cir. Feb. 14, 2003) (granting en banc review) OECD, MULTINATIONAL ENTERPRISES IN SITUATIONS OF VIOLENT CONFLICT AND WIDESPREAD HUMAN RIGHTS ABUSES 11 (2002), available at *http://www.oecd.org/dataoecd/46/31/2757771.pdf* David Kinley, Human Rights, Globalization and the Rule of Law: Friends, Foes or Family?, 7 UCLA J. INT'L L. & FOREIGN AFF. 239 (2002). Wiwa v. Royal Dutch Petroleum Co., 226 F.3d 88 (2d Cir. 2000); Wiwa v. Royal Dutch Petroleum Co., 2002 U.S. Dist. LEXIS 3293 (S.D.N.Y. 2002) (finding that plaintiffs' allegations that Shell participated in deportation, forced exile and torture of the Ogoni people in Nigeria, as part of a widespread attack, satisfied a claim for crimes against humanity under the Alien Tort Claims Act); Bowoto v. Chevron, 312 F. Supp.2d 1229 (N.D. Cal. 2004) (refusing to dismiss allegations that Nigerian plaintiffs suffered gross human rights abuses at Chevron's behest, and with the company's support, cooperation and financial assistance). Jordan J. Paust, Human Rights Responsibilities of Private Corporations, 35 VAND. J. TRANSNAT'L L. 801, 803 (2002).

78 Chris Jochnick, Confronting the Impunity of Non-state Actors: New Fields for the Promotion of Human Rights, 21 HUM. RTS. Q. 56 (1999) (describing Texaco's activities in Ecuador's Amazonian region as "a state unto itself.");Maria McFarland Sanchez-Moreno & Tracy Higgins, No Recourse: Transnational Corporations and the Protection of Economic, Social and Cultural Rights in Bolivia, 27 FORDHAM L. REV. 1663 (2004) (documenting the various state functions assumed by TNEs in Bolivia.); Jim Lobe, Papua Killings Could Set Back U.S. Plans, ASIA TIMES, Sept. 18, 2002, available at http://atimes01.atimes.com/atimes/Southeast_Asia/DI18Ae04.html (noting that the military in Papua "has often acted as partners or agents for foreign companies"). Final Report of the Panel of Experts on the Illegal Exploitation of Natural Resources and Other Forms of Wealth of the Democratic Republic of the Congo, U.N. SCOR, U.N. Doc. S/2002/1146 (2002) (concluding that the drive to control natural resources was a major motive of the war). Presbyterian Church of Sudan v. Talisman Energy, Inc., 244 F. Supp. 2d 289 (S.D.N.Y. 2003) (rejecting defendant's contention that corporations cannot violate international law in light of plaintiffs' allegations of corporate participation in war crimes, torture, enslavement and genocide in conjunction with Sudanese oil production);

79 Yves Delazay, *Regionalism, Globalization and Professional Society, in* REGIONALISM AND GLOBAL ECONOMIC INTEGRATION: EUROPE, ASIA, AND THE AMERICAS, 197, 198 (William D. Coleman & Geoffrey R. D. Underhill, eds., London: Routledge, 1998).

80 Jeremy E. Eizenstadt, John Edward Porter, and Jeremy Weinstein, *Rebuilding Weak States*, Foreign Affairs (Jan./Feb. 2005) ("the gravest danger to the nation lies in the weakness of other countries--the kind of weakness that has allowed opium production to skyrocket in Afghanistan, the small arms trade to flourish throughout Central Asia, and al Qaeda to exploit Somalia and Pakistan as staging grounds for attacks"); Martin j. Hillenbrand, Power and morals, 134-188 (New York: Columbia University Press, 1949). Ian Ayres and John Braithwaite, Responsive Regulation: transcending the deregulation debate 3-19 (New York: Oxford, 1992)

81 "Legal systems and legal services have become commodities in international trade, as legal experience is transferred from one country to another. It is now possible to get an economic advantage in international trade by ensuring that your trading partner's legal system is more like your legal system than like that of your competitors." Philip Alcott, The health of nations: society and law beyond the state 60 (Cambridge University Press, 2002).

82 Michael Johnston, *The Definitions Debate: Old Conflicts in New Guises, in* The Political Economy of Ccorruption 11 (Arvind K. Jain, ed., New York: Routledge, 2001).

Corporate entities[83] are significant institutions in domestic law and have a key and broad role in the international arena. MNEs have argued against any legal responsibility to abide by the *jus cogens* norms enshrined in the Universal Declaration. It could be said that there is no international law mechanism for calling the corporation itself to account and so a background of impunity surrounds MNE activities[84]. Steven R. Ratner[85] argues that the international community has to step into this legal vacuum and make clear that MNEs are held to the same *jus cogens* norms as are individuals and states. However, business entities are subject to criminal liability for actions or omissions taken by agents acting on the corporation's behalf[86]. It has to be taken into account that the final version of the Rome Statute granted the ICC[87] jurisdiction over only natural persons and ICC jurisdiction does not extend to legal persons.

Soft law instruments such as the United Nation's Global Compact, the ILO Declaration, OECD's Guidelines for Multinational Enterprises and the recent UN Norms on the Responsibilities of Transnational Corporations and Other Business Enterprises with Regard to Human Rights highlight the varied roles MNEs and other legal persons can play in war crimes and human rights abuses[88]. Private codes amount to little more than vague statements of principles and they do not include complaint mechanism, and provide no grounds for legal redress[89]. The MNE does not have a concrete presence in international law but it appears in many different forms and contexts. On the other hand, MNEs are already treated as actors with rights under some international regimes and responsibilities under others such as in

---

[83] Barcelona Traction, Light and Power Company, Ltd. (Belg. v. Spain), 1970 I.C.J. 3, 33 (Feb. 1970)

[84] Iwanowa v. Ford, 67 F. Supp. 2d 424, 445 (D.N.J. 1999) ("No logical reason exists for allowing private individuals and corporations to escape liability for universally condemned violations of international law merely because they were not acting under color of law"). Presbyterian Church of Sudan v. Talisman Energy, Inc., 244 F. Supp. 2d 289, 308 (S.D.N.Y. 2003). "'the law of nations simply does not encompass principles of corporate liability.'" E.T. Mitchell, A Theory of Corporate Will, 56 ETHICS 96, 103 (1946) (postulating that the corporation itself can foresee the legal consequences of action, and therefore plan accordingly, more readily than can individuals).

[85] Steven R. Ratner, Corporations and Human Rights: A Theory of Legal Responsibility, 111 YALE L.J. 443 (2001).

[86] Theodor Meron, Is International Law Moving Towards Criminalization?, 9 EUR. J. INT'L L. 18, 20 (1998).

[87] Rome Statute of the International Criminal Court, U.N. Doc. A/CONF.183/9 (July 17, 1998), reprinted in 37 I.L.M. 999 (1998) art. 25(1) ("The court shall have jurisdiction over natural persons pursuant to this Statute.").

[88] "The Global Compact is not a regulatory instrument –it does not "police", enforce or measure the behavior or actions of companies." The Global Compact, What is the Global Compact, at http://www.unglobalcompact.org/Portal/ International Labour Organization, ILO Declaration on Fundamental Principles and Rights at Work (June 1998), *http://www.ilo.org/dyn/declaris/declarationweb .aboutdeclarationhome?var_language=EN* OECD Guidelines for Multinational Enterprises (2000), *http://www.oecd.org/dataoecd/56/36/1922428.pdf* Norms on the Responsibilities of Transnational Corporations and Other Business Enterprises with Regard to Human Rights, U.N. ESCOR Sub-Commission on the Promotion and Protection of Human Rights, 55th Sess., Agenda Item 4, U.N. Doc. E/CN.4/Sub.2/2003/12/Rev.2 (2003). Curtis j. Milhaupt & Mark d. West, Economic organizations and corporate governance in japan: the impact of formal and informal rules 1 (Oxford University Press, 2004) (but note the caution, "But law interacts with other, less formal institutions, such as markets, codes of best practice, social norms, and shared beliefs about how the world works." Id).

[89] Todd Weiler, Balancing Human Rights and Investor Protection: A New Approach for a Different Legal Order, 27 B.C. INT'L & COMP. L. REV. 429 (2004). Oren Perez, *Reflections On An Environmental Struggle: P&O, Dahanu, And The Regulation Of Multinational Enterprises*, 15 GEO. INT'L ENVTL. L. REV. 1, 25 (2002).

article 2(14) of the Basel Convention[90] defines "person" for purposes of its criminal prohibitions as "any natural or legal person." The MNE's role in international law is defined by reference to its ties to a specific state. The legal personality of the MNE was confirmed in the Barcelona case[91] as analogous to that of a national of a state giving rise to state responsibility for conduct of a MNE in the state's own territory. An object of international law such as a MNE possesses only derivative legal personality. MNEs have been characterized as individual nationals of states rather than as independent entities. The international regulations efforts affirm rather than challenge the assumption that it is a state's prerogative to deal with MNEs through its national legal systems. The power of recognition of other entities as subject of international law is one of the prerogatives of states. The UN[92] has been recognised as a subject of international law by merely confirming the international legal status already conferred upon the UN by states.

State sovereignty remains the international frame of reference. Paul Streeten[93] has pointed out that globalization can come "from above," in the form of MNEs, international capital flows, and world markets, or it can come "from below," reflecting the concerns of individuals and groups throughout the world. Globalization is changing the nature of global social relations, intensifying the obsolescence of the "society of states" model, and demanding an important change in the social theory of international law towards a global society of persons. It could be said that globalization requires changes into the context of international law in order to deal with global public law phenomena such as having many states concurrently involved in disputes, and expand the domain of justice from the national into the global, as the basic normative criterion for international law. The reassessment of the substance of international legal doctrines and institutions such as boundaries, sovereignty, legitimacy, citizenship, and the territorial control of resources, the international law can be re-establishment into the international law of a global society. Furthermore, it has to be taken into consideration the fact of the development of cyberspace and the cyber-territory where not only many commercial electronic transactions take place affecting simultaneously many jurisdictions but also there is an extensive transfer of political and social views and ideas changing the global arena and so creating the cyber-society circumventing any notion of real world sovereignty and territory.

The dominant contemporary basis of international law has been the "society of states" model. International law is a social space in which states are the subjects and it exists to order a community in which states are the members. States in international society are viewed as autonomous sources of moral ends, immune from external interference. Thus, international law is the law of the states being the main persons in international law. The main doctrines of non-intervention, self-determination and state responsibility treat the state as the key locus of autonomy, self-realization, and rights, and are framed principally in view of the interests and needs of territorial states. International harms to individuals are understood within a framework of harm to a state's rights. In other words, all entities with any personality

---

[90] Basel Convention on the Control of Transboundary Movements of Hazardous Wastes and their Disposal, available at http://www.basel.int/text/con-e.htm OECD Convention on Combating Bribery of Foreign Public Officials in International Business Transactions, art. II, available at *http://www.oecd.org/document/21/0,2340,en_2649_34859_2017813_1_1_1_1,00.html*

[91] Barcelona Traction, Light and Power Company, Ltd. (Belg. v. Spain), 1970 I.C.J. 3, 33 (Feb. 1970)

[92] The Reparations case [1949] ICJ 174.

[93] Paul Streeten, Globalization and its Impact on Development Co-operation, 42 Dev. 11, 11 (1999).

(international organizations and natural persons themselves) gain their personhood, and the extent of their legal rights in international law, from grants flowing from the primary persons of international law, states. Human rights, international economic law, and the emergence of international civil society, make the "society of states" model gradually more deficient normatively. Additionally, it is observed a lack of democratic participation and legitimacy, lack of distributive justice, lack of basic welfare rights and security.

The fundamental moral status of individual persons is the basis to reconfigure international law[94]. Justice is an asset within political communities[95], not between them and so the possibility of global justice needs the existence of global political communities which have not shaped until know. On the other hand, there is a development of cyber communities which can be divided into cyber-economic communities and cyber-political communities. Globalization is altering the character of global social relations, and creating the basis for both society and community at the global level and so globalization is lifting relationships out of the firmly territorial into the "global" and cyber-territorial[96]. Globalization requires a deep re-examination of social regulation and governance at the global level, leading to a system in which states will still have a paramount role, but there is a need to attribute international legal personality to other entities as well which act simultaneously in many states. It must be taken into consideration that in globalization, people are more and more competing for the same resources on a global scale in a shared territory which is the planet "ΓH" and so the heart of any new global regulation and attribution of international legal personality to other non-states actors such as MNEs has to protect its existence from any destruction caused by overexploitation. Moreover, globalization brought a capacity to efficiently respond to the needs and concerns of others beyond our boundaries, through the transnational mobilization of information, power, capital, or public opinion which means that state's policies and political and consumer choices, are influencing the life prospects of others in direct and spectacular ways[97].

Is there a need to move from the public law of inter-state relations, to the public law of a global community of persons? Is there a need for global institutions to be modeled upon a sort of world states? Territorial boundaries now serve as the structure on which we hang a range of concepts of distributive justice such as citizenship and the territorial control of resources, which overwhelmingly influence the life prospects of all affected individuals. Citizenship illustrates how the current "society of states" model of international law permits territorial boundaries to function at the global level as one of the main obstacles to delivery of a global basic package. Global public law needs to deal with distributive issues both between and within states. Globalization means that the problem of inequality is a vital problem of global social relations, in the same way it is a central problem of justice at the national level. It is argued that the answer to the question of business enterprise responsibility could be found in

---

[94] Charles Beitz, "Cosmopolitan Liberalism and the State System," in Political Restructuring in Europe (BROWN ED. 1994) (surveying contemporary cosmopolitanism).

[95] Heba Shams, "Law in the Context of 'Globalisation:' A Framework of Analysis," 35 INT'L LAWYER 1589 (2001).

[96] GLOBAL TRANSFORMATIONS (HELD, ET AL. EDS 1999) (reviewing evolution of meta-state institutions).

[97] Dirk Messner, "World Society – Structures and Trends," in GLOBAL TRENDS & GLOBAL GOVERNANCE 24 (KENNEDY, ET AL. EDS. 2002).

a transnational system and according to Professor Steven Ratner[98], ''any answer not depending exclusively on diverse and possibly parochial national visions of human rights and enterprise responsibility must come from international law.''

The relationship between the international system and MNEs represents a fundamental challenge to the international legal order premised on the centrality of states[99]. It has to be remembered that the corporation is private property, owned by its shareholders and its rationale is to maximize the wealth of the owners and the role of the directors is to facilitate the owners' financial interests[100]. As mentioned earlier professor Berle[101] stated that ''all powers granted to a corporation or to the management of a corporation. . . are necessarily and at all times exercisable only for the ratable benefit of all the shareholders as their interest appears.''

The corporation as a legal person separate from its owners is a Western institution. A corporation is a legal fiction that serves as a nexus for a mass of contracts which various individuals have voluntarily entered into for their mutual benefit[102]. A corporation is an artificial person, with many of the legal rights of a biological one. Limited liability statutes came to shield individual shareholders from personal lawsuits for wrongs by corporations whose shares they own. Moreover, the corporation operates as a legal construct only with governmental approval and government's granting of the corporation's juridical personality is seen as warranted by the state's desire to promote social welfare and so corporations are beneficial to society. It is argued that the proper purpose of the corporation includes advancing the general welfare through providing opportunities for meaningful employment, satisfying consumer desires, and contributing to community life[103]. To that extent as mentioned above professor Dodd[104] argued that managerial powers were held in trust for the entire community and not just for shareholders: ''public opinion, which ultimately makes law, has made and is today making substantial strides in the direction of a view of the business

98 Steven R. Ratner, Corporations and Human Rights: A Theory of Legal Responsibility, 111 YALE L.J. 443, 446 (2001) at 448.

99 Simon Chesterman, Oil and Water: Regulating the Behavior of Multinational Corporations through Law, 36 NYU J. INT'L L. & POL. 307, 307 (2004). Elliot J. Schrage, Judging Corporate Accountability in the Global Economy, 42 COLUM. J. TRANSNAT'L L. 153 (2003); Henry Hansmann & Reinier Kraakman, The End of History for Corporate Law, 89 GEO. L.J. 439, 441 n.5 (2001) (''. . . corporationsFwhether ''concessions'' or contractsFshould be regulated when it is in the public interest to do so.'').

100 See Milton Friedman, The Social Responsibility of Business is to Increase its Profits, NY TIMES MAG., Sep. 13, 1970, at 122–26 ''there is one and only one social responsibility of business to use its resources and engage in activities designed to increase its profits so long as it stays within the rules of the game, which is to say, engages in open and free competition without deception and fraud.''. Daniel J. H. Greenwood, Fictional Shareholders: For Whom Are Corporate Managers Trustees, Revisited, 69 S. CAL. L.REV. 1021, 1023 (1996) (''All but the communitarians agree that virtually the sole task of corporate law is to ensure that managers act as agents for the shareholder owners.'');

101 Adolph A. Berle, Corporate Powers as Powers in Trust, 44 HARV. L. REV. 1049, 1049 (1931).

102 Daniel R. Fischel, The Corporate Governance Movement, 35 VAND. L. REV. 1259, 1273 (1982). Stewart J. Schwab & Randall S. Thomas, Realigning Corporate Governance: Shareholder Activism by Labor Unions, 96 MICH. L. REV. 1018, 1076 (1998) (discussing the controversy over whether fund managers have the power to consider other values beyond shareholder wealth maximization, given the Interpretative Bulletin).

103 William T. Allen, Our Schizophrenic Conception of the Business Corporation, 14 CARDOZO L. REV. 261, 264 (1992).

104 E. Merrick Dodd, Jr., For Whom Are Corporate Managers Trustees?, 45 HARV. L. REV. 1145, 1148 (1932).

corporation as an economic institution which has a social service as well as a profit-making function . . . .'' It has to be taken into consideration that pursuing social welfare best serves shareholder interests[105] as well.

A company pursuing profit and do 'good works' at the same time is unlikely to do neither very well[106]. A company's corporate social responsibility confirmation has an impact on the bottom line through its effect on the company's ''reputational capital,'' and so reputation-goodwill brings firm market value[107]. Corporate behaviour turns out to be unavoidably linked to product image and consequently a company's social identity is as important as its brand identity. Corporate actions taken relative to the social environment have straight effects on the economic well-being of the organization through their impact on the organizational members[108]. It could be said that financial performance either precedes or is simultaneous with social performance[109]. The shareholder wealth is decreased when companies act in a socially irresponsible or illegal manner but when enterprises act in a socially responsible and law-abiding manner increase shareholder wealth[110]. So, the objective of corporate law is to maximize share value[111] and any social responsibility is complementary and valuable as long as contributes to the wealth of the profits of the shareholders. Corporate social responsibility is an initiative that has been touted as a prospective remedy for the harms of globalization that encumber the realization of sustainable development--that is, inequities in wealth, environmental degradation, and unfair labor practices that are established by globalization.

---

[105] Margaret M. Blair & Lynn A. Stout, A Team Production Theory of Corporate Law, 85VA. L. REV. 247, 250–51 (1999) (arguing that ''corporate assets belong not to shareholders but to the corporation,'' that shareholders, executives, employees, creditors and the local community all ''have an interest in [the] enterprise's success,'' and that, accordingly, the job of the corporation's ''internal hierarchy'' is to ''coordinate the activities of the team members, allocate the resulting production, and mediate disputes among team members over that allocation''); G. Mitu Gulati et al., Connected Contracts, 47 UCLA L. REV. 887, 895 (2000) (calling attention to ''the cooperation, conflict, competition, and compromise among equity investors, lenders, managers, workers, suppliers, customers, and all others who contribute to an economic endeavor''); Marleen A. O'Connor, The Human Capital Era: Reconceptualizing Corporate Law to Facilitate Labor-Management Cooperation, 78 CORNELL L. REV. 899, 936–65 (1993) (arguing that corporate law should be changed to encourage employee representation on the board of directors and should encourage standing to sue); Lawrence E. Mitchell, A Theoretical and Practical Framework for Enforcing Corporate Constituency Statutes, 70 TEX. L. REV. 579, 630–43 (1992) (arguing that courts should modify corporate law to grant stakeholders standing to sue directors when harmed by corporate action).

[106] B. J. McCabe, Are Corporations Socially Responsible? Is Corporate Social Responsibility Desirable?, 4 BOND L. REV. 1, 20 (1992).

[107] Charles J. Fombrun et al., Opportunity Platforms and Safety Nets: Corporate Citizenship and Reputational Risk, 105 BUS. & SOC'Y REV. 85 (2000).

[108] Christine M. Riordan et al., Corporate Image: Employee Reactions and Implications for Managing Corporate Social Performance, 16 J. BUS. ETHICS 401, 410 (1997).

[109] Lee E. Preston & Douglas P. O'Bannon, The Corporate Social-Financial Performance Relationship: A Typology and Analysis, 36 BUS. & SOC'Y 419, 428 (1997).

[110] Jeff Frooman, Socially Irresponsible and Illegal Behavior and Shareholder Wealth: A Meta-Analysis of Event Studies, 36 BUS. & SOC'Y 221, 221 (1997). George W. Dent, Jr., Proxy Regulation in Search of a Propose: A Reply to Professor Ryan, 23 GA. L. REV. 815, 823 (1989) (proposing that shareholders be required to post a bond that could be recovered if respectable voting support is achieved).

[111] Roberta Romano, Less is More: Making Institutional Investor Activism a Valuable Mechanism of Corporate Governance, 18 YALE J. ON REG. 174 186 n.30 (2001) (''Social responsibility proposals are not a focus of this article because they are not advanced in order to improve corporate performance and are consequently, not compatible with the objective of U.S. corporate law, which is to maximize share value.'').

The more and more globalised nature of business and the new Economy, a knowledge-based, technology-driven environment that has, among other things, affected a raise in stakeholders' access to information[112]. A conglomerate is not just a self-centered profit-making unit, but the company and its actions are also integral to the economy, society, and environment in which they take place. A social responsibility policy provides value as a tactical part of a company's daily activities.

Policies of privatization, liberalization and deregulation have been pursued not only through national states, but also through a host of supra-state agencies, sub-state bodies and private regulatory mechanisms. Globalization has broken the near-monopoly that centralized, sovereign, territorial, national government held on governance in the world prior to the 1960s. The growth of supra-state rules and institutions has occurred with globalization. Several of the largest and most influential supra-state mechanisms—such as, the IFIs, NAFTA, the WTO and the OECD—have become key channels for the furtherance of neoliberal policies. Predominantly remarkable is the fact that certain powerful states have actively promoted neoliberalism, both within their own jurisdictions and abroad. Supra-territorial spaces have opened up new sectors like digital information, telecommunications and electronic finance where major additional surplus accumulation can be achieved. Capitalist interests tend to choose a laissez-faire approach to the global arena, just as in any other geographical context[113]. The accelerated globalization in the late twentieth century presented capital with a key prospect to resurrect free markets. Specifically, the contemporary growth of global spaces has given capital greater mobility and power relative to the other partners in the statist social contract of the twentieth century government and labour[114]. Thus, trans-border corporate structures and trans-world commodity flows have significantly unleashed capital from territorial constraints. States have turned out to be more accommodating to business relative to labour, perceiving that enterprises could move between jurisdictions, while workers remain territorially confined. Cyberspace and global telecommunications have opened potential to extend offshore arrangements to other sectors such as electronic commerce and so competition from offshore sites has encouraged greater privatization, liberalization and deregulation at onshore locations by governments that wish to persuade capital to stay. Nevertheless, globalization has provided capital with enhanced means to limit or evade territorially bound regulatory constraints, and large stores of assets have moved to trans-world spaces with possibilities for enhanced private accumulation in view. It has to be taken into consideration that capitalists have in recent years adopted voluntary self- regulatory codes of corporate conduct, in the name of social and environmental responsibility.

Globalisation is about a transformation of basic institutions and it's not just dominated by economic forces, and much more closely connected with communication affecting the state and nations. On the one hand, globalisation takes certain powers away from the nation and so nations are not as much in command of their economic futures as they used to be. On the other hand, the nation state is still a vital power in the world. Moreover, nation states remain more important than their principal power rivals in the global system, the large corporations because corporations have legal personality which cannot suffocate human personality from a

---

[112] Elisa Westfield, Globalization, Governance, and Multinational Enterprise Responsibility: Corporate Codes of Conduct in the 21st Century, 42 VA. J. INT'L L. 1075, 1082 (2002)

[113] Sklair, L. 2002. Globalization: Capitalism and Its Alternatives. Oxford University Press, Oxford.

[114] Standing, G. 1999. Global Labour Flexibility: Seeking Redistributive Justice. Macmillan, Basingstoke.

certain level downwards and states and governments supposed to be the safeguards of human personality from any abuses. MNEs are not as powerful as nations, certainly not as powerful as the larger nations and the reasons are that nations still have territory, whereas companies don't. Nations still have access to military power and control the means of violence, whereas corporations, if they ever do, only do so very indirectly. It is questionable the fact that governments might be dependent to the economic power of a MNE because the governing political party might be elected using the finance of some economic interests which might coincide to those of a MNE. Nations are still largely responsible for establishing frameworks of law, and those frameworks of law considerably affect what corporations can do in the world.

Economic and industrial globalization has increased international competition and given rise to the need for an increasingly integrated and evolving legal system. With the emergence of the global marketplace, governments have promoted global competition through the increase in international trade, while developing legal systems to make certain industrial competitiveness. Since corporations can now easily move to alternate forums with fewer protections if workers demand too much, labor's bargaining power vis-à-vis employers has diminished[115]. It has to be taken into account that the global environment encourages countries to deregulate labor law in a "race-to-the-bottom" to attract multinational corporations and foreign investment. There is a race-to-the-bottom for governments to attract MNEs by having less regulation and a race-to-the-bottom among MNEs to search for lower production costs.

2.5 States and International Law

Law helps to define the role of an individual in society and the relations with others that make sense[116]. Formal legal rules are often related to the formation of legal consciousness which includes the ways in which individuals deploy, transform, or subvert official legal understandings. Moreover, law is constantly shaped and reshaped by the ways it is used, even as law's constitutive power constrains patterns of usage[117]. Law is not just a set of legal rules, treaties, or international standards, but a numerous of local social and institutional interactions exerting remarkable influence on how justice is in reality administered. It has to be taken into account that while national authorities are the key actors in the regulatory arena, regulation is more and more an international affair[118]. Nation-state sovereignty may be affected by norms

[115] Katherine Van Wezel Stone, Labor and the Global Economy: Four Approaches to Transnational Labor Regulation, 16 MICH. J. INT'L L. 987, 989 (1995). "A number of scholars have noted that the global economy diminishes the regulatory capability of the nation-state and thus calls into question conventional views of sovereignty."

[116] David M. Trubeck, Where the Action Is: Critical Legal Studies and Empiricism, 36 STAN. L. REV. 575, 604 (1984)

[117] Davina Cooper, Local Government Legal Consciousness in the Shadow of Juridification. 22 J. L. SOC'Y 506 (1995).

[118] Paul B. Stephan, The Futility of Unification and Harmonization in International Commercial Law, 39 VA. J. INT'L L. 743, 744 (1999) (arguing that international harmonization efforts are often the product of rent-seeking by various industry groups). Anne-Marie Slaughter, Global Government Networks, Global Information Agencies, and Disaggregated Democracy, 24 MICH. J. INT'L L. 1041, 1046–48 (2003). Wolfgang H. Reinicke, The Other World Wide Web: Global Public Policy Networks, FOREIGN POL'Y, Winter 1999/2000, at 44–45 ("Global public policy networks have emerged over the last

articulated, disseminated, and enforced transnationally or internationally[119]. Sovereignty is a domestic concept, related only to the source of legitimate authority within a state. International law principles of state sovereignty have never provided authoritative checks on the behavior of nation-states. International law norms, including norms about inviolate nation-state sovereignty, are essentially a set of tools serving the instrumental aims of the powerful.

Under international law, sovereignty protects the state against foreign interference[120]. Under municipal law, sovereignty expresses the state's supreme power and so its supremacy over all other societal spheres. Globalization increases the interaction between the same spheres of different nations, going beyond the phenomenon of the interdependence of states leading to a partial fusion of once separate national realms, especially the fusion of national economies into a single world economy. Moreover, strengthened transnational bonds and partial fusions have led to a 'de-nationalization', which is manifested in various ways.

Nation states shaped by a variety of forces, including the norms and institutions of international law itself. The state is embedded in a wider institutional environment, and governmental and non-governmental actors similarly are part of the feedback circle that both constructs and responds to non-national norms. International and transnational activity in both public and private international law curtailed the prerogatives of nation-states[121]but nation-state sovereignty once again in its rightful place at the core of the international order[122]. Nation-states sovereignty may well become diffused in order to accommodate various

decade, experimenting with new ways to gather knowledge and disseminate information on specific issues."). Lori M. Wallach, Accountable Governance in the Era of Globalization: The WTO, NAFTA and International Harmonization of Standards, 50 U. KAN. L. REV. 823, 825 (2002) ("Expansive international rules strongly enforced through international dispute resolution bodies have significant implications for the laws and policies domestic governments may establish, as well as for the processes domestic governments use to make policy."). Ernst-Ulrich Petersmann, Theories of Justice, Human Rights and the Constitution of International Markets, 37 LOY. L.A. L. REV. 407, 455 (2003) ("[T]he increasing 'global justice campaigns' by non-governmental organizations (NGOs) which influence international rule-making ever more actively (e.g., on the International Criminal Court, environmental agreements, WTO negotiations), illustrate the emergence of a new international 'civil society.'"). Celia Wasserstein Fassberg, Lex Mercatoria—Hoist with Its Own Petard?, 5 CHI. J. INT'L L. 67 (2004) (arguing that the modern revival of lex mercatoria departs significantly from the historical conception).

119 Steve Charnovitz, WTO Cosmopolitics, 34 N.Y.U. J. INT'L L. & POL'Y 299, 306–07 (2002) (arguing that the "orthopolitics" model of the sovereign state system is of declining relevance for World Trade Organization policy analysis and should be replaced by a "cosmopolitics" of direct participation by nonstate actors). Peter J. Spiro, Globalization and the Foreign Affairs Constitution, 63 OHIO ST. L.J. 649, 667–73 (2002) (arguing that the decentralization of governmental structures and activity is undermining sovereignty and the state system); Ruti G. Teitel, Humanity's Law: Rule of Law for the New Global Politics, 35 CORNELL INT'L L.J. 355, 363–65 (2002) (arguing that international institutions are increasingly the source of norms previously supplied by states).

120 The S.S. 'Lotus' (Fr. v. Tur.), 1927 PCIJ, (ser. A) No. 10, 18. 'International law governs the relations between independent States. The rules binding upon States emanate from their own free will as expressed in conventions or by usages . . . in order to regulate the relations between these co-existing independent communities or with a view to the achievement of common aims. Restrictions upon the independence of States cannot therefore be presumed':

121 Ryan Goodman & Derek Jinks, Toward an Institutional Theory of Sovereignty, 55 STAN. L. REV. 1749, 1752 (2003).

122 Dominique Moïsi, Early Winners and Losers in a Time of War, FIN. TIMES (U.S. ed.), Nov. 19, 2001, at 15 ("In the post-cold-war global age, the state's legitimacy and competence appeared to be waning. Caught between the emergence of civil society and the growing power of transnational corporations, the

international, transnational, or non-territorial norms[123]. Even when a treaty's language establishes obligations of private parties means that international law requires the states-parties to recognize the obligations set forth in the treaty[124]. Actually the Convention simply obligates the states-parties, when resolving disputes coming within its scope, to apply the Convention's substantive rules of liability and so the Convention does not "impose" liability on an air carrier. Only a state can violate the Convention or incur international responsibility for a breach. In other words, the Warsaw Convention is understood to be addressed to the courts of the states-parties, imposing on them the obligation to resolve disputes in accordance with the treaty's provisions and private parties incur such obligations by virtue of whatever domestic laws give domestic legal force to the rights and obligations contemplated by the treaty.

The primary obligations Treaties impose are obligations of states, such as the obligation to take steps to forbid specific private conduct or to give effect to specified liabilities. Even though the treaties contemplate the imposition of obligations on non-state actors, they do not themselves directly impose international legal obligations on such entities which means that the treaties regulate private parties indirectly rather than directly[125]. Under the classic model, a treaty is never self-executing under international law with respect to the obligations of private parties and so such obligations are never imposed by the treaty itself, only by the domestic legal provision--be it statutory or constitutional--that gives the treaty domestic legal force.

International law is law by, of, and for the nation states. No international sovereign legislature or executive exists, nor is any international court armed with both general and compulsory jurisdiction and so both the creation of, and compliance with, international law are mainly dependent on nation-states[126]. Mechanisms for enforcing international law independent of the nation-state are weak because the international field lacks the requisite mechanisms to express sovereignty. As Professor Laurence Helfer and Professor Anne-Marie Slaughter explained in Toward a Theory of Effective Supranational Adjudication, "the problem is relatively straightforward. International tribunals lack a direct coercion mechanism to compel either appearance or compliance[127]." The value of a particular court rests on its

---

state appeared to be fighting a rearguard battle. Now, with security a priority, it is back with a vengeance.").

[123] Hannah L. Buxbaum, Conflict of Economic Laws: From Sovereignty to Substance, 42 VA. J. INT'L L. 931, 942–54 (2002) (discussing ways in which "regulatory power traditionally enjoyed by sovereign states has shifted" to the supranational level, to private actors, and to "informal networks constituted among sub state-level agencies in different countries");

[124] The Warsaw Convention provides, inter alia, that "a carrier shall be liable for damage sustained by a passenger" in certain circumstances. The U.S. Supreme Court recently understood those words to "impose liability on an air carrier" under the circumstances stated. Convention on Combating Bribery of Foreign Public Officials in International Business Transactions, Dec. 17, 1997, arts. 1-2, 4, 37 I.L.M. 1, 4-5. Convention on the Elimination of All Forms of Racial Discrimination, Sept. 28, 1966, art. 2(1)(d), 660 U.N.T.S. 195, 218. Convention for the Unification of Certain Rules Relating to International Transportation by Air ("Warsaw Convention"), Oct. 12, 1929, art. 17, 49 Stat. 3000, 137 L.N.T.S. 11, 23. Olympic Airways v. Husain, 540 U.S. 644, 646, 655-57 (2004).

[125] Foster v. Nielson, 27 U.S. 253, 314 (1829),

[126] Louise Arbour, Genesis of International Criminal Justice: From an Impossible Marriage of Law to the Promising End of Impunity, 1 MCGILL INT'L R. 8 (2000). "the establishment of an effective international criminal jurisdiction is therefore fundamental both to the effectiveness of international law and to world peace."

[127] Laurence R. Helfer, Anne-Marie Slaughter, Toward a Theory of Effective Supranational Adjudication, 107 YALE L. J. 273, 285 (1997)

power to compel a party to a dispute to defend against a plaintiff's complaint and to comply with the resulting judgment. It is worth mentioning that international courts often do not have the required sovereignty to directly compel such actions, the effectiveness of adjudication often depends on an international or supranational tribunal's ability to persuade national government institutions, directly and through pressure from private litigants, to use their power on its behalf and so this uncertain position is above all problematic in situations where international law seeks to protect individuals and not nation-states. Human rights abuses cannot expect a nation-state to protect against because many times the nation-state is complicit in the abuse. It could be said that the founding of an effective international criminal jurisdiction is primary to the effectiveness of international law.

Multinational treaties[128] are the key vehicles through which most international law is enacted but the classical model of international law perceives treaties as contracts between or among nations, not individuals and so treaties only confer legally enforceable rights upon states. Individuals cannot sue to enforce a treaty and can only receive protection from a treaty to the extent that a nation-state will enforce its obligations[129]. If a state party fails to complain about a treaty violation that they had bargained for, it serves as evidence that the state party did not in reality intend to bargain for such a right.

There is a need for balance between national sovereignty and the creation of internationally uniform standards and so harmonization can take place with international methods of coercion. The ILO is an example of an organization that encourages harmonization but is armed with only minimal methods of coercion. Moreover, The ILO encourages harmonization by adopting uniform standards in conventions, while allowing nations to adopt and ratify these standards on a voluntary basis[130] but since nation-states that do not wish to approve these uniform standards are under no obligation to do so. Cross-border monitoring occurs when a transnational treaty requires each member nation to enforce the nation's own laws but cross-border monitoring requires multilateral implementation, which means the treaty's member nations have some power to enforce the laws of each individual nation. While public international law has had difficulty creating coercion mechanisms to enforce entire regimes, private international law has been far more successful in protecting individuals' rights through contract. Besides, U.S. unilateralism, with its characteristic resistance to international treaties, including those agreed upon by other nations, is categorically not new[131]. Through their participation in the European Union, many European

128 Robert Anderson, "Ascertained in a Different Way": The Treaty Power at the Crossroads of Contract, Compact, and Constitution, 69 GEO. WASH. L. REV. 189, 243 (2001).

129 Donald C. Dowling, From Social Charter to the Social Action Program 1995-1997: European Union Employment Law Comes Alive, 29 CORNELL INT. L. J. 47 (1996).

130 Lisa G. Baltazar, Comment, Government Sanctions and Private Initiatives: Striking a New Balance for U.S. Enforcement of Internationally-Recognized Workers' Rights, 29 COLUM. HUM. RTS. L. REV. 687, 699 (1998). Robert Howse, The World Trade Organization and the Protection of Workers' Rights, 3 J. SMALL & EMERGING BUS. L. 131, 133 (1999). Andrew Guzman, Labor, Trade and Legitimacy, 91 CAL. L. REV. 885 (2003).

131 JED RUBENFELD, UNILATERALISM AND CONSTITUTIONALISM, 2004 NEW YORK UNIVERSITY LAW REVIEW 1971 at 2028 "*If we cannot restrain ourselves, we will leave the world nowhere to appeal—but heaven.*"(Stress added). Harlan Grant Cohen, The American Challenge to International Law: A Tentative Framework for Debate, 28 YALE J. INT'L L. 551, 559 (2003). Jules Lobel & Michael Ratner, Bypass sing the Security Council: Ambiguous Authorizations to Use Force, Cease-Fires and the Iraqi Inspection Regime, 93 AM. J. INT'L L. 124, 139–41 (1999). Cara Drinan, Note, Article 36 of the Vienna Convention on Consular Relations: Private Enforcement in American

states today have surrendered prerogatives and trappings of national sovereignty long considered unchallengeable[132].

International law enjoys a kind of higher-law status throughout much of Europe and in other parts of the world today. International law is higher than local law procedurally, in that its norms and tribunals stand above their national counterparts within the legal hierarchy and so it is higher than national law substantively, in that it derives from a higher source of authority and serves higher purposes. On the one hand, international law has never quite achieved higher-law status in America; it almost has lower-law status. In the American constitutional perspective, law gains no special authority by virtue of being international law, and courts obtain no special legitimacy by virtue of being international courts. On the other hand, the European commitment to international law rests on the idea that international law is superior to national law and in any other case international law could not accomplish its essential objective, which is to check national sovereignty, including national popular sovereignty.

International law generally places duties on states and, more recently, individuals. MNEs are creatures of national law and they varied in status, ranging from some that are entirely private (including individual investors) to others that are effectively controlled by the government. European companies became the primary agents for the economic exploitation of the colonial territory and so that support gave enterprises and individuals access to the wealth of the colonies on particularly favorable terms[133].

Alongside the decolonization process occur another change in international law—the elaboration of a body of international human rights law that placed direct duties on states toward their own people. States and other actors came to see the relationship between a state and its inhabitants as governed by a set of human rights norms. Host states and MNEs adjusted their economic and legal relationship through economic development agreements providing in great detail the rights enjoyed by the host state and the duties of the foreign investor, in particular, with respect to payments by the former to the latter[134]. It has to be taken into account that the right to nationalize is subject only to compensation by the state taking into account its applicable laws and regulations and all circumstances that the state considers pertinent with no reference to international law. As the political and economic

Courts After LaGrand, 54 STAN. L. REV. 1303, 1307–10 (2002) (describing how American courts have continued to ignore ICJ's final holding in LaGrand case).

132 Rosa Maria F. Egea, The Common Foreign and Security Policy of the European Union: A Historical Perspective, 7 COLUM. J. EUR. L. 41, 45–49 (2001). Thomas M. Franck, Clan and Superclan: Loyalty, Identity, and Community in Law and Practice, 90 AM. J. INT'L L. 359, 369 (1996) (describing phenomenon of certain states in Europe "scrambling to surrender chunks of their precious sovereignty to the European Union, which manages migration for its member governments, as well as credit policies, trade, competition policy and aspects of foreign relations"). Case 6/64, Costa v. ENEL, 1964 E.C.R. 585, 593. "By creating a Community of unlimited duration, having its own institutions . . . and, more particularly, real powers . . . , the Member States have limited their sovereignty rights . . . and have thus created a body of law which binds both their nationals and themselves."

133 Antony Anghie, Finding the Peripheries: Sovereignty and Colonialism in Nineteenth-Century International Law, 40 HARV. INT'L L.J. 1 (1999) (demonstrating the incorporation of colonialism within legal doctrine).

134 Rudolf Dolzer, New Foundations of the Law of Expropriation of Alien Property, 75 AM. J. INT'L L. 553 (1991) (proposing the balancing of interests of host states and investors); Burns H. Weston, The Charter of Economic Rights and Duties of States and the Deprivation of Foreign-Owned Wealth, 75 AM. J. INT'L L. 437 (1981) (endorsing the thrust of General Assembly resolutions from the 1970s).

power of many host states increased, these states demanded and achieved renegotiation of the agreements with MNEs to increase their share of the wealth generated by the investment[135]. Moreover, host states sought to rein in the power of MNEs by drafting a multinational code of conduct for transnational corporations[136]. The Code emphasized the need for foreign investors to follow host country law, go along with host country economic policies, and avoid interference in the host country's domestic political affairs. Thus, the overall effect of the decolonization period with respect to corporate-host state relations was to underline the rights of states and the duties of MNEs.

Nowadays host states have adjusted national laws to make them more attractive to MNEs, handed over tracts of land to de facto control by corporations, or merely turned a blind eye to violations of national law[137]. Consequently, MNEs are powerful global actors that some states lack the resources or will to control and so states in order to gain investments may go as far as soliciting corporations to work together in impinging human rights which means that reliance on state duties is inadequate. International human rights law primarily contemplates two sets of actors who may be held liable for abuses—states, through the concept of state -mainly civil-responsibility, and individuals, through the concept of individual -mainly criminal-responsibility. On the one hand, states are duty-holders for the full range of human rights, whether defined in treaties or customary law. On the other hand, individual responsibility applies to a far smaller range of abuses, mainly characterized by the seriousness of their physical or spiritual assault on the individual.

It is worth mentioning that the failure of state responsibility stems primarily from trends in modern international affairs confirming that MNEs may have as much or more power over individuals as governments. Susan Strange[138] emphasizes the need to conceptualize power beyond political power to incorporate economic power and as a result concludes that markets matter more than states. MNEs have wielded considerable power over their employees but governments have to enforce their own laws as well as to protect the human rights of their citizens[139]. Many less developed states welcome foreign investment and so some governments have neither the interest nor the resources to monitor corporate behavior, either with respect to the MNEs' employees or with respect to the broader community.

As MNEs have become more international, they have also become ever more independent of government control and so MNEs have headquarters in one state, shareholders in others, and global operations. If the host state fails to regulate the acts of the company, other states, including the state of the corporation's nationality, may choose to abstain from

---

135 Samuel K.B. Asante, Restructuring Transnational Mineral Agreements, 73 AM. J. INT'L L. 335, 341-49 (1979) (reviewing the host states' practice of gaining control through joint ventures);

136 Hans W. Baade, The Legal Effects of Codes of Conduct for Multinational Enterprises, in 1 LEGAL PROBLEMS OF CODES OF CONDUCT FOR MULTINATIONAL ENTERPRISES 3 (Norbert Horn ed., 1980) (demonstrating how codes might produce binding norms under domestic and international law). Kenneth J. Vandevelde, The Political Economy of a Bilateral Investment Treaty, 92 AM. J. INT'L L. 621 (1998) (evaluating BITs as vehicles for promoting economic liberalism).

137 Eyal Benvenisti, Exit and Voice in the Age of Globalization, 98 MICH. L. REV. 167 (1999) (analyzing the problem as one of a global " prisoner's dilemma"); Jeffrey L. Dunoff & Joel P. Trachtman, Economic Analysis of International Law, 24 YALE J. INT'L L. 1, 54-55 (1999) (endorsing an economic analysis of the race to the bottom). Michael W. Gordon, Of Aspirations and Operations: The Governance of Multilateral Enterprises by Third World Nations, 16 U. MIAMI INTER-AM. L. REV. 301, 325-40 (1984).

138 SUSAN STRANGE, THE RETREAT OF THE STATE 47 (1996).

139 Gregory H. Fox, Strengthening the State, 7 IND. J. GLOBAL LEGAL STUD. 35 (1999).

regulation based on the extraterritorial nature of the acts at issue[140]. Moreover, MNEs shift activities to states with fewer regulatory burdens, including human rights regulations. On the other hand, recognition of duties on MNEs under international law could support home states to regulate this conduct or authorize others to do so; at the same time, it would suggest a baseline standard of conduct for MNEs themselves that could be monitored by interested constituencies.

It is worth mentioning that some multinational enterprises are themselves recognizing the limits of duties on states and for instance Unocal has stated publicly that "human rights are not just a matter for governments[141]." The call for corporate responsibility parallels the evolution of the existing corpus of law beyond state liability to cover individual responsibility, under which individuals are criminally responsible for serious human rights abuses[142]. It is argued that there is need to place obligations on entities such as MNEs that have the resources to violate human rights and whose conduct cannot appropriately be policed by the state where they function. Steven R. Ratner[143] argues that "If international law provided for a regime whereby the corporations had duties themselves and incurred some penalty for violations of them, it would place the incentives on the party with the greatest ability and interest in addressing corporate conduct."

States have accepted the idea of duties of non-state actors through the corpus of international criminal law on human rights atrocities. The notion of corporate duties represents a departure from the emphasis on the state as duty-holder and seeks to justify that new direction. The European Court of Justice has held that provisions of the Treaty of Rome (the EU's founding document) that prohibit states from discriminating based on nationality and require equal pay for equal work apply directly to private entities[144]. German courts had developed the notion of third-party (or horizontal) effect (*Drittwirkung*), holding that some German constitutional rights affect private legal relationships[145].

Is there a need for reconceptualization of international law to govern private behaviour? The emergence of new fragmented centres of power, such as trade unions, and MNEs means that the definition of the public sphere has had to be adapted to include these new bodies and

---

[140] Peter J. Spiro, New Players on the International Stage, 2 HOFSTRA L. & POL'Y SYMP. 19, 28-30 (1997).

[141] Human Rights and Unocal: Our Position, at *http://www.unocal.com/responsibility/humanrights /hr1.htm*

[142] David Wippman, Atrocities, Deterrence, and the Limits of International Justice, 23 FORDHAM INT'L L.J. 473 (1999); M. Cherif Bassiouni, An Appraisal of the Growth and Developing Trends of International Criminal Law, 45 REVUE INTERNATIONALE DE DROIT PÉNAL 405, 405-06 (1974).

[143] Steven R. Ratner, Corporations and Human Rights: A Theory of Legal Responsibility, 2001 The Yale Law Journal 443 at 465 A. Yasmine Rassam, Contemporary Forms of Slavery and the Evolution of the Prohibition of Slavery and the Slave Trade Under Customary International Law, 39 VA. J. INT'L L. 303, 329-42 (1999) (showing the evolution of international law on slave trade to cover a broad array of practices).

[144] Case 36/74, Walrave v. Association Union Cycliste Internationale, 1974 E.C.R. 1405; Case 43/75, Defrenne v. Société Anonyme Belge de Navigation Aérienne Sabena, 1976 E.C.R. 455. Gavin Phillipson, The Human Rights Act, "Horizontal Effect" and the Common Law: A Bang or a Whimper?, 62 MOD.L. REV. 824 (1999) (opining that the legislation is unlikely to have a major effect in private litigation), Dawn Oliver, The Human Rights Act and Public Law/Private Law Divides, 4 EUR. HUM. RTS. L. REV. 343 (2000) (stating that significant impacts are possible).

[145] Lüth Case, BverfGE 7, 198 (1958), translated in Donald p. Kommers, The constitutional jurisprudence of the federal republic of Germany 361 (2d ed. 1997); B.S. MARKESINIS, The Applicability of Human Rights as Between Individuals Under German Constitutional Law, in 2 ALWAYS ON THE SAME PATH 175 (2001) (reviewing and endorsing trends in case law);

activities[146]. It could be said that in light of the increase in corporate power and of the associated inadequacy of state responsibility, the law needs to respond to abuses that do not implicate the state directly and so to apply to activities by MNEs. It should be taken into account that everything that a corporation does that might affect the welfare of those in the corporation's sphere of operations is a human rights abuse.

I has to be taken into consideration that while international law works from the starting point that states should be held responsible for human rights abuses, and only then acknowledges the need for duties on others, corporate liability has worked from the opposite position—that of national civil and criminal law holding individuals accountable—to make a case for corporate liability. Corporations act as organizations and are not purely the sum of individuals working for them and because they have autonomy of action, including the capacity to change their policies, they can be held responsible for the outcomes resulting from these policies[147]. International law has already effectively recognized duties of corporations and international law doctrine poses no considerable impediment to recognition of duties beyond those of states. Private persons cannot be liable under international law because only states are full subjects of international law with legal personality because only states can enjoy the full range of legal rights and duties and make claims for violations of rights. Non-state entities may enjoy forms of international personality and for instance personality enjoyed by corporations in light of treaties allowing victims of human rights to sue states in regional courts or permitting foreign investors to sue states in the International Centre for the Settlement of Investment Disputes[148]. Moreover, actors other than states have duties under international law but control mechanisms are central because law cannot exist without them[149].

As discussed earlier, conventions and their wording make clear that they do recognize duties on enterprises regarding their employees[150]. It has to be taken into account that most

---

146 Evert Albert Alkema, The Third-Party Applicability or "Drittwirkung" of the European Convention on Human Rights, in PROTECTING HUMAN RIGHTS: THE EUROPEAN DIMENSION 33, 33-36 (Franz Matscher & Herbert Petzold eds., 2d ed. 1990). Jean Rivero, La protection des Droits de l'Homme dans les rapports entre personnes privées, in 3 RENÉ CASSIN AMICORUM DISCIPULORUMQUE LIBER 311 (1971).

147 Brent Fisse & John Braithwaite, The Allocation of Responsibility for Corporate Crime: Individualism, Collectivism and Accountability, 11 SYDNEY L. REV. 468, 483-88 (1988). Peter A. French, Collective and Corporate Responsibility 156-63 (1984) (endorsing the idea of " reactive fault" based on a corporation's failure to institute procedures to prevent the repetition of a harmful act); Celia Wells, Corporations and Criminal Responsibility 143-46 (1993) (discussing liability based on aggregating the responsibility of certain officers and considering internal decision making structures); see also J.E. Parkinson, Corporate Power And Responsibility 358-59 (1993) (focusing on criminal liability, but arguing that the mens rea of a corporation should be replaced by the concept of defective decision making); V.S. Khanna, Corporate Liability Standards: When Should Corporations Be Held Criminally Liable?, 37 AM. CRIM. L. REV. 1239 (2000) (calling for a mixed liability regime).

148 Wolfgang Friedmann, The Changing Structure Of International Law 223 (1964) (calling for " a limited ad hoc subjectivity" for MNEs).

149 Carlos S. Nino, The Duty To Punish Past Abuses of Human Rights Put into Context: The Case of Argentina, 100 YALE L.J. 2619, 2621 (1991) (" [A] necessary criterion for the validity of any norm of . . . positive international law . . . is the willingness of . . . states and international bodies . . . to enforce it.").

150 Convention Concerning the Application of the Principles of the Right To Organise and To Bargain Collectively, adopted July 1, 1949, art. 1, http://ilolex.ilo.ch:1567/english/convdisp2.htm The 1981 Occupational Safety and Health Convention contains six articles specifically obligating employers to attain certain standards Convention Concerning Occupational Safety and Health and the Working

states view labor rights as a subset of human rights and, especially, of economic and social rights and so the rights of employees create duties for corporations representing a move towards an acceptance by states that the rights of the citizenry can create other duties for corporations[151]. Treaties related to environment impose an international standard of liability on the corporation[152] but the treaties provide for implementation by national courts and so confusing the existence of responsibility with the mode of implementing it. On the one hand, international law does not itself impose liability on the corporations because the mechanism for enforcement is through a private lawsuit in one or more states. On the other hand, the use of national courts to implement the liability does not detract from the law's imposition of individual responsibility[153]. Moreover, states have developed international law creating binding obligations on corporations with respect to discrete economic activities[154]. While adhering to the orthodox distinction between duties of governments under international law and duties of enterprises under national law, the treaty nevertheless makes clear that the responsibility of businesses is recognized and may be regulated by international law[155].

Both the Treaty Establishing the European Community (i.e., the 1957 Treaty of Rome, as amended) and the binding decisions of the European Council and Commission have created a vast body of legal obligations which apply directly to corporate entities[156]. Direct effect is

---

Environment, adopted June 22, 1981, http://ilolex.ilo.ch:1567/english/convdisp2.htm ; see, e.g., id. art. 16(1) ("Employers shall be required to ensure that, so far as is reasonably practicable, the workplaces, machinery, equipment and processes under their control are safe and without risk to health.").

151 Virginia A. Leary, The Paradox of Workers' Rights as Human Rights, in Human Rights, Labor Rights, And International Trade 22 (Lance A. Compa & Stephen F. Diamond eds., 1996). Philip Alston & Gerard Quinn, The Nature and Scope of States Parties' Obligations Under the International Covenant on Economic, Social and Cultural Rights, 9 HUM. RTS. Q. 156 (1987) (providing an overview of perceptions on economic, social, and cultural rights and discussing states parties' obligations).

152 Paris Convention on Third Party Liability in the Field of Nuclear Energy, done July 29, 1960, 956 U.N.T.S. 251. Brussels Convention on the Liability of Operators of Nuclear Ships, done May 25, 1962, reprinted in 57 AM. J. INT'L L. 268 (1963). Vienna Convention on Civil Liability for Nuclear Damage, done May 21, 1963, 1063 U.N.T.S. 265. International Convention on Civil Liability for Oil Pollution Damage, done Nov. 29, 1969, 26 U.S.T. 765, 973 U.N.T.S. 3 Brussels Convention Relating to Civil Liability in the Field of Maritime Carriage of Nuclear Material, done Dec. 17, 1971, 974 U.N.T.S. 255. Convention on Civil Liability for Oil Pollution Damage Resulting from Exploration for and Exploitation of Seabed Mineral Resources, done Dec. 17, 1976, 16 I.L.M. 1450.

153 Bruno Simma & Andreas L. Paulus, The Responsibility of Individuals for Human Rights Abuses in Internal Conflicts: A Positivist View, 93 AM. J. INT'L L. 302, 308 (1999) (distinguishing between delicta juris gentium and direct international responsibility, where the former applies to crimes in which states are authorized or required to prosecute and the latter to a smaller category of crimes).

154 Convention on Combating Bribery of Foreign Public Officials in International Business Transactions, Dec. 17, 1997, http://www.oecd.org/daf/nocorruption/20nov1e.htm

155 David A. Gantz, Globalizing Sanctions Against Foreign Bribery: The Emergence of a New International Legal Consensus, 18 J. INT'L L. & BUS. 457 (1998). Report of the Committee on Economic, Social, and Cultural Rights, U.N. ESCOR, Supp. No. 2, at 102, 106, U.N. Doc. E/2000/22 (2000) ("While only States are parties to the Covenant and are thus ultimately accountable for compliance with it, all members of society—individuals, families, local communities, non-governmental organizations, civil society organizations, as well as the private business sector—have responsibilities in the realization of the right to adequate food.").

156 Treaty Establishing the European Community, Nov. 10, 1997, art. 81, O.J. (C 340) 3 (1997)(Article 81 of the Treaty forbids anticompetitive behavior.) Case 26/62, Van Gend en Loos v. Nederlandse Administratie Der Belastingen, 1963 E.C.R. 3, 12 (" [T]his Treaty is more than an agreement which merely creates mutual obligations between the contracting states . . . . [T]he Community constitutes a new legal order of international law for the benefit of which the states have limited their sovereign rights, albeit within limited fields, and the subjects of which comprise not only Member States but also

now a cornerstone of the EU legal system. Thus, the European Community law provides both direct rights and duties on corporations and so states can conclude treaties providing for direct corporate responsibility and implement those treaties successfully.

Governments have recognized duties of corporations through a number of significant soft law instruments[157]. If states and international organizations can accept rights and duties of corporations in some areas, there is no theoretical bar to recognizing duties more broadly, including duties in the human rights area. The doctrine of state responsibility has recognized that the government can act through a variety of actors in breaching its international obligations and international decision-makers estimate the connections between these actors and the government to establish whether the state has violated international law[158]. The ties between the government and the MNE play a key role in determining the obligations of the corporation and if an enterprise has close ties to the government, it has prima facie a greater set of obligations in the area of human rights[159]. The rules of state responsibility that make the state liable for the acts of some private actors has to provide for the responsibility of those private actors because the state is responsible for certain acts of private actors and those actors can also be held responsible for that same conduct under international law.

When a private entity acts on behalf of the state, it is as liable as the state for violations of human rights[160]. International decision-makers have recognized a variety of ways in which private entities can become agents of the state[161]. International law accepts notions of complicity, whereby one entity engages in otherwise lawful conduct that serves to aid other entities in violating norms[162]. A state can be responsible for the acts of another state, based on

their nationals. . . . Community law therefore not only imposes obligations on individuals but is also intended to confer upon them rights which become part of their legal heritage.") J.H.H. Weiler, The Transformation of Europe, 100 YALE L.J. 2403, 2413-15 (1991) (describing the direct effect as key to the "constitutionalization" of EU law).

[157] Declaration Adopted by the Governing Body of the International Labour Office at Its 204th Session (Nov. 1977), *http://www.ilo.org/public/english/standards/norm/sources/mne.htm*

[158] Military and Paramilitary Activities (Nicar. v. U.S.), 1986 I.C.J. 14 (June 27); Loizidou v. Turkey, 310 Eur. Ct. H.R. (ser. A) (1995).

[159] Costello-Roberts v. United Kingdom, 247 Eur. Ct. H.R. (ser. A) 50, 58 (1993) (holding that a state cannot "absolve itself from responsibility by delegating its obligations to private bodies").

[160] Jones v. Alfred H. Mayer Co., 392 U.S. 409, 420-44 (1968) (holding that 42 U.S.C. § 1982, which bans racial discrimination in real property transactions, was a proper exercise of congressional power under the Thirteenth Amendment). Gallagher v. "Neil Young Freedom Concert," 49 F.3d 1442, 1447 (10th Cir. 1995) (" In order to establish state action, a plaintiff must demonstrate that the alleged deprivation of constitutional rights was 'caused by exercise of some right or privilege created by the State or by a rule of conduct imposed by the State or by a person for whom the State is responsible.'" (quoting Lugar v. Edmonson Oil Co., 457 U.S. 922, 937 (1982))), George v. Pac.-CSC Work Furlough, 91 F.3d 1227, 1230 (9th Cir. 1996) (" 'If a private actor is functioning as the government, that private actor becomes the state for purposes of state action.'" (quoting Gorenc v. Salt River Project Agric. Improvement & Power Dist., 869 F.2d 503, 508 (9th Cir.1989))). Doe v. Unocal Corp., 110 F. Supp. 2d 1294, 1307 (C.D. Cal. 2000), aff'd, 248 F.3d 915 (9th Cir. 2001) (" In order to establish proximate cause, a plaintiff must prove that the private individuals exercised control over the government official's decision to commit the section 1983 violation."); Ireland v. United Kingdom, 25 Eur. Ct. H.R. (ser. A) at 64 (1978) (holding that a state is " strictly liable" for the conduct of subordinates).

[161] Military and Paramilitary Activities (Nicar. v. U.S.), 1986 I.C.J. at 64-65. Loizidou v. Turkey, 310 Eur. Ct. H.R. (ser. A) at 23-24 (1995). Prosecutor v. Tadic, Case No. IT-94-I-A, para. 137 (Int'l Crim. Trib. for Former Yugoslavia Appeals Chamber July 15, 1999), *http://www.un.org/icty/tadic/appeal /judgement/index.htm*

[162] Jackson v. Metro. Edison Co., 419 U.S. 345, 352-53 (1974) (recognizing state action where a private entity exercises powers traditionally reserved to the state, but finding that the defendant did not do so);

a variety of tests involving its cooperation[163]. If a business essentially contributes to a violation of human rights by the government with knowledge of that activity, it should be held responsible as a matter of international law and so a business has a duty not to form such complicit relationships with governments.

Has the end of the nation state arrived as a result of globalization? Only states can undertake the needed work to ensure that international norms to which they have bound themselves in international fora which produce norms that by their very nature are generalizable across a variety of jurisdictions are respected in their territories. Only states have the knowledge essential to regulate industries operating within their territories incorporating firms, whether as subsidiaries of multinationals or national firms. The enforcement of norms relating to corporate social responsibility constitutes a valuable part of the development of the state alongside the development of the market. The development of state capacity has to occur in tandem with the development of the market, it becomes more likely that the weakness of the former will jeopardize the latter. If the state shows itself to be unsuccessful in controlling market actors, then the state may come under attack. Presently, in the global context, the State influence on private actors is more indirect, more distant, so that the doctrine of State action has only a limited scope of application[164].

With nation-states the law governing the global system was entirely international and international law emphasized bilateral and multilateral treaties between and among states, the activities of the United Nations, the pronouncements of international tribunals, and the norms that states had obeyed for long enough that such norms could be deemed customary. Law was seen as a sole function of state sovereignty. The rise of a conception of international human rights in the post-World War II era transformed individuals into international law stakeholders, possessing their own entitlements against the state[165]. International law derived mainly from state practice[166]but private individuals and non-governmental organizations

---

Beanal v. Freeport-McMoRan, Inc., 969 F. Supp. 362 (E.D. La. 1997) (dismissing claims because of the plaintiff's failure to allege sufficient ties between actual abuses by the government and Freeport), aff'd, 197 F.3d 161 (5th Cir. 1999). John E. Noyes & Brian D. Smith, State Responsibility and the Principle of Joint and Several Liability, 13 YALE J. INT'L L. 225 (1988) (reviewing situations of multiple state responsibility for breaches of international law); cf. James Crawford, Third Report on State Responsibility, U.N. GAOR, Int'l Law Comm'n, 52d Sess., paras. 267-278, U.N. Doc. A/CN.4/507/Add.2 (2000) (recognizing each state's responsibility in the case of joint action, but not equating this principle with common-law joint and several liability).

[163] G.A. Res. 3314, U.N. GAOR, 29th Sess., Supp. No. 31, at 142-43, U.N. Doc. A/9631 (1974) (holding that " the action of a State in allowing its territory, which it has placed at the disposal of another State, to be used by that other State for perpetrating an act of aggression against a third State" constitutes illegal aggression); Harold Hongju Koh, Bringing International Law Home, 35 HOUS. L. REV. 623 (1998) (suggesting that nations obey international law when they internalize norms).

[164] G.W. Anderson,'Social Democracy and the Limits of Rights Constitutionalism' (2004) 17 The Canadian Journal of Law & Jurisprudence 31;

[165] Louis Henkin, Human Rights and State "Sovereignty," 25 GA. J. INT'L & COMP. L. 31, 33 (1995–1996) ("At mid-century, the international system began a slow, hesitant move from state values towards human values.").

[166] Joel R. Paul, Holding Multinational Corporations Responsible Under International Law, 24 HASTINGS INT'L & COMP. L. REV. 285, 285–86 (2001). Susan Bibler Coutin et al., In the Mirror: The Legitimation Work of Globalization, 27 LAW & SOC. INQUIRY 801 (2002). Thomas Buergenthal, The Advisory Practice of the Inter-American Human Rights Court, 79 AM. J. INT'L L. 1, 20 (1985) ("A legal system developed over centuries to regulate relations between states must make considerable conceptual adjustments to accommodate the extension of its normative reach to individuals."). Austin Sarat & Jonathan Simon, Beyond Legal Realism?: Cultural Analysis, Cultural Studies, and the Situation

acting both internationally and nationally are contributing to the materialization of new international norms which confer greater rights and obligations on private individuals and firms, shifting the focus of international law. International law is merely a product of states pursuing their interests on the international stage and that international legal norms, consequently, cannot pull states towards conformity contrary to their interests. International legal norms will not always determine nation-state behaviour[167].

As mentioned earlier, MNEs elude national regulation because they operate in multiple jurisdictions. MNEs take advantage of the complexity of political and legal systems to create a world of their own and so accommodating the conduct of their operations to many legal systems but are not in any real sense subject to any of them[168]. Voluntary CSR initiatives seek to create an international regulatory framework that applies directly to MNEs, thereby bypassing the state. The centre of gravity of fundamental rights lies still in the national constitutions and so their structural effect on the whole legal order is similarly limited to the nation states with few spillover effects on transnational relations. Principally, MNEs regulate whole areas of life through private governance regimes of their own to a higher degree than their national counterparts do. Primary rights segregate from politics areas of autonomy allotted either to social institutions or to persons as social constructs.

Global companies nowadays are legal fictions that act as a center for the coordination of contractual relations, from supply chains and distribution channels to financial arrangements and licensing agreements where their legal and headquarters locales regularly bear little relation to the places where their goods and services are produced or delivered. Globalization is accompanied both by a race for lowest production costs and increasing demands for corporate social responsibility. Global CSR implies that MNEs will be held responsible for actions beyond the firm's boundaries and beyond their local community to contain suppliers, distributors, alliance partners, and even sovereign nations in which they do business. Corporations are established powerful social institutions with enormous potential as levers of public policy. Additionally, MNEs provide a mechanism for the spread of standards around the world, both within their own corporate boundaries and among their suppliers and other contractors[169].Globalization in production and sales has been accompanied by globalization in regulatory jurisdiction, as firms adjust their legal homes for tax and other benefits. MNEs locate their nominal headquarters or subsidiaries outside the country for tax purposes, while a few multinationals have split their jurisdictional loyalties so many ways as to erase any semblance of national identity. Moreover, MNEs in the 21st century face a number of colliding forces in product markets, capital markets, and in the polities where they operate

of Legal Scholarship, 13 YALE J. L. & HUMAN. 3, 19 (2001) ("Law is part of the everyday world, contributing powerfully to the apparently stable, taken-for-granted quality of that world and to the generally shared sense that as things are, so must they be.").

[167] Susan S. Silbey, Making a Place for Cultural Analyses of Law, 17 LAW & SOC. INQUIRY 39, 41 (1992) (arguing that "law is a part of the cultural processes that actively contribute in the composition of social relations"). Mark C. Suchman & Lauren B. Edelman, Legal Rational Myths: The New Institutionalism and the Law & Society Tradition, 21 LAW & SOC. INQUIRY 903, 907 (1996) ("Law and Society scholarship depicts the law as a culturally and structurally embedded social institution.").

[168] Cynthia Day Wallace, The Multinational Enterprise And Legal Control: Host State Sovereignty In An Era Of Economic Globalization 11 (2002) Pall A. Davidsson, Legal Enforcement of Corporate Social Responsibility within the EU, 8 COLUM. J. EUR. L. 529 (2002)(stating that economic power of MNEs often surpasses that of states).

and so product market competition, along with lowered trade barriers and advances in ICTs, have led to the expansion of global supply chains, sourcing high value-added steps to advanced economies and outsourcing low value-added steps to developing economies with lower wages and labor standards.

It could be argued that the new international sovereignty in globalisation involves nation-state participation in a wide range of international and trans-governmental regimes, networks, and institutions, all of which have become indispensable for governments to accomplish what they once could do on their own within a defined territory. The escalation of MNEs activity has renewed interest in the feudal idea of *lex mercatoria* and other plural forms of law that operate outside the nation-state system[170].

It is worth mentioning here that NGOs more and more formulate global standards of corporate behaviour and the "codes of conduct" have appeared most notably with regard to human rights, environmental protection, and fair labor standards[171]. NGOs could be seen as interest groups focused on specific issues. NGOs' role is to scrutinize local bureaucratic actors and apply various forms of pressure.

2.6 The CSR and Human Rights Obligations of Private Corporations presently under International Law

As mentioned above, the primary rules of international law are addressed to states (and state officials), not non-state actors. Under the secondary rules of international law, only states acquire responsibility for breaching the primary rules of international law. Individuals have rights under international law.

CSR is a term that refers to a mixture of initiatives ranging from voluntary codes of conduct to programs whereby companies can undergo external audits to verify the adequacy of their practices in a range of areas of social concern. CSR measures should supplement and not supplant state regulation[172]. International law nowadays imposes important obligations directly on private corporations representing a considerable exception to the classical

[169] Kristensen, P.H. and J. Zeitlin, 2005, Local Players in Global Games: The Strategic Constitution of a Multinational Corporation, New York: Oxford University Press.

[170] Richard Epstein, The Empirical And Theoretical Underpinnings of the Law Merchant, 5 CHI. J. INT'L L. 1 (2004).

[171] Peter J. Spiro, New Global Potentates: Nongovernmental Organizations and the "Unregulated" Marketplace, 18 CARDOZO L. REV. 957, 959 (1996) (detailing how interest groups, even "[w]here stymied by national regulators[,] . . . can accomplish equivalent results by commanding consumer preferences, which in turn works to constrain corporate or state behavior"). Peter L. Lindseth, Democratic Legitimacy and the Administrative Character of Supranationalism: The Example of the European Community, 99 COLUM. L. REV. 628, 633 (1999) (noting that such a deficit occurs whenever normative power is transferred to "agents that are not electorally responsible in any direct sense to the 'people' whose 'sovereignty,' or at least some portion of it, the agents are said to exercise").

[172] Michael Santoro, Beyond Codes of Conduct and Marketing: An Organizational Integrity Approach to Global Labor Practices, 25 HUM. RTS. Q. 406 (2003). "At the turn of the century, multinational corporations (MNCs) have learned—often the hard way as a result of embarrassing exposes—that their bottom line can suffer when they fail to live up to public expectations about honoring human rights in third world countries. Among other things, global marketing firms are being asked to provide transparent assurance that their suppliers in third world nations avoid the use of child labor and honor workers rights to acceptable living wages, overtime pay, safe and healthy working conditions and free association."

position. The secondary rules of international law recognize that "the conduct of a person or group of persons" may give rise to international responsibility "if the person or group of persons is in fact exercising elements of the governmental authority in the absence or default of the official authorities and in circumstances such as to call for the exercise of those elements of authority.[173]" While definitions of CSR vary, the term in general refers to actions taken by firms with respect to their employees, communities and the environment going beyond what is legally required of a firm. CSR can create a conflict between different shareholders and insiders personally benefit from the fact that they are associated with firms that have a high CSR rating. Additionally, CSR has as its theoretical base the notion that the responsibility of a corporation extends beyond the traditional Anglo-American objective of providing financial returns to its shareholders. Multinationals take CSR issues into account in selecting suppliers and business partners[174]. It is argued that social responsibility of business is to increase its profits[175].

Managers and directors of corporations are legally required to advance the interests of shareholders within the constraints of the law. If international law imposes obligations on

---

173 Draft Articles on Responsibility of States for Internationally Wrongful Acts, U.N. GAOR, 56th Sess., Supp. No. 10, art. 9., U.N. Doc. A/56/10 (2001)

174 Ethical Corporation Magazine, "Study Reveals Corporate Social Responsibility a Major Factor in Overseas Investment and Purchasing," Press Release of January 20, 2004 www.cswire.com/article/cgi/2410.html_ Christian Aid, Behind the Mask: The Real Face of Corporate Social Responsibility (Jan. 21, 2004), *www.chrsitianaid.org.uk/indepth/0401csr/csr_behindthemask.pdf*

175 Adolph A. Berle, Corporate Powers as Powers in Trust, 44 HARV. L. REV. 1049, 1061 (1931) (stating directors' powers one held in trust for the shareholders as the only beneficiaries of the corporation); Merrick Dodd, For Whom Are Corporate Managers Trustees, 45 HARV. L. REV.1145, 1147-48 (1932) (stating Berle does not think that shareholder profit maximization is the only purpose that corporations exist); Adolph A. Berle, For Whom Are Corporate Managers Trustees: A Note, 45 HARV. L. REV. 1365 (1932) (stating profit maximization is not the only purpose of a corporation). Bernard Black & Reinier Kraakman, A Self-Enforcing Model of Corporate Law, 109 HARV. L. REV. 1911, 1921 (1996) (arguing that principal goal of corporate law is to maximize shareholder wealth); Henry Hansmann & Reinier Kraakman, The End of History for Corporate Law, 89 GEO. L.J. 439, 441, 449-51 (2001) (stating that shareholder primacy is likely to dominate future development of corporate law); Michael Bradley et al., The Purposes and Accountability of the Corporation in Contemporary Society: Corporate Governance at a Crossroads, 62 LAW & CONTEMP. PROBS. 9, 11 (1999) (examining how the changing dynamic of business organizations impacts and influences the relationship between corporate governance and its constituents); Daniel J.H. Greenwood, Fictional Shareholders: For Whom Are Corporate Managers Trustees, Revisited,69 S. CAL. L. REV. 1021, 1023 (1996) ("All but the communitarians agree that virtually the sole task of corporate law is to ensure that managers act as agents for the shareholder owners."); Roberta Romano, The Political Economy of Takeover Statutes, 73 VA. L. REV. 111, 113 (1987) (asserting that core goal of corporate law is to maximize equity share prices); John C. Coffee, Jr., Unstable Coalitions: Corporate Governance as a Multi-Player Game, 78 GEO. L.J. 1495, 1496 (1990) (discussing role of stakeholders in firm). Margaret M. Blair & Lynn A. Stout, A Team Production Theory of Corporate Law, 85 VA. L. REV. 247, 310-11 (1999) (positing that where shareholders are widely dispersed, shareholders' voting rights are practically meaningless, given collective action problems, shareholders' rational apathy, and the power top managers exercise in nominating the candidates for the board and in otherwise shaping the voting agenda); David Millon, Theories of the Corporation, 1990 DUKE L.J. 201, 261-62 (praising case law that reaffirms directors' discretion to consider non shareholder interests); Lawrence E. Mitchell, A Theoretical and Practical Framework for Enforcing Corporate Constituency Statutes, 70 TEX. L. REV. 579, 630-43 (1992) (arguing that courts should modify corporate law to grant stakeholders standing to sue directors when the former are harmed b y corporate action); Marleen A. O'Connor, The Human Capital Era: Reconceptualizing Corporate Law to Facilitate Labor-Management Cooperation, 78 CORNELL L. REV. 899, 936-65 (1993) (arguing that corporate law should be changed to encourage employee representation on the board and standing to sue);

corporations only indirectly, then managers and directors need concern themselves only with the domestic laws of the states in which they operate[176]. Managers have no duty under corporate law to abide by directly-applicable norms of international law not backed by enforcement sanctions, except insofar as the risk of creation of such sanctions in the future makes it unprofitable to disregard such rules[177]. If international law directly imposes obligations on corporations the corporation will be subject to enforcement action by international institution, either in existence or created after the fact[178].

International legal norms that impose obligations on corporations are in fact of the indirect variety and do not conflict with the classic position. For instance, reference is made to the European concept of *Drittwirkung*[179], under which particular provisions of the European Convention of Human Rights (ECHR) are understood to contemplate "horizontal effect," meaning that they apply as between private parties but the European authorities show that the state has the obligation in these circumstances to take steps to ensure that private parties act in certain ways towards other private parties. It affirmed the responsibility of the state for its failure to prevent or punish private conduct that infringed human rights, but it did not hold that private individuals who inflict such injuries are guilty of violating the Convention[180].

The recognition of an obligation on the part of states to impose obligations on private parties, including corporations, would not be a conceptual departure from the classic model. The international community has established mechanisms to adjudicate non-state actors' international responsibilities in the context of international criminal law. Hence, if an international mechanism is established for enforcing an international norm against a non-state actor, then it may be said that the international norm applies directly to non-state actors[181]. A rule of international law imposing obligations directly on people and non-state actors, not backed by an international enforcement mechanism, could later become enforceable, for instance, through the successive creation of an international tribunal with the power to impose criminal penalties, as occurred with the establishment of the International Criminal Tribunals for the Former Yugoslavia and Rwanda[182].

---

[176] Sosa v. Alvarez-Machain, 124 S. Ct. 2739 (2004). Frank H. Easterbrook & Daniel R. Fischel, Antitrust Suits by Targets of Tender Offers, 80 Mich. L. Rev. 1155, 1177 n.57 (1980) ("Managers not only may but also should violate the rules when it is profitable to do so.").

[177] Cynthia Williams, Corporate Compliance with the Law in the Era of Efficiency, 76 N.C. L. Rev. 1265, 1270 (1998).

[178] Bruno Simma & Andreas L. Paulus, The Responsibility of Individuals for Human Rights Abuses in Internal Conflicts: A Positivist View, 93 Am. J. Int'l L. 302, 308-11 (noting that provisions that "allow for trial at both the national and the international levels... establish [] the truly international legal character of the crime," whereas provisions that "merely refer to the obligation of the parties either to try or to extradite alleged criminals... do not qualify... as crimes of a truly international character"

[179] Evert Albert Alkema, The Third-Party Applicability or "Drittwirkung" of the European Convention on Human Rights, in Protecting Human Rights: The European Dimension 33, 37-38 (Franz Matscher & Herbert Petzold eds., 1988).

[180] Kent Greenfield, Ultra Vires Lives! A Stakeholder Analysis of Corporate Illegality (With Notes on How Corporate Law Could Reinforce International Law), 87 Va. L. Rev. 1279, 1375 n.290 (2001); Velásquez-Rodriguez Case, Inter-Am. C.H.R. 35, O.A.S./ser./ L/V/III19, doc.13 (1988).

[181] Beth Stephens, The Amorality of Profit: Transnational Corporations and Human Rights, 20 Berkeley J. Int'l L. 45, 76 (2002).

[182] Statute of the International Criminal Tribunal for Rwanda, art. 7, S.C. Res. 955, U.N. Doc. S/RES/955 (1994), available at *http:// www.ictr.org/ENGLISH/basicdocs/statute.html* (adopted November 8, 1994 and establishing temporal jurisdiction over all specified crimes occurring after January 1, 1994); Statute

It should be taken into account that the Declaration does not as such have binding force, and that the language in question appears in the preamble of that instrument and so many of the rights set forth in the Declaration are thought to have attained the force of customary international law, but even supporters of imposing international human rights obligations on corporations acknowledge that this portion of the preamble has not itself attained such force[183]. Besides, Article 16 of the Norms, which provides that "transnational corporations . . . shall be subject to periodic monitoring and verification by United nations, other international and national mechanisms already in existence or yet to be created," is a robust indication that the Norms were intended to be directly applicable to private corporations. Some of the human rights that the Norms set forth as directly applicable to corporations are generally recognized as directly applicable to private individuals under existing international law. For instance, the Norms provide that "transnational corporations and other business entities shall not engage in . . . war crimes, crimes against humanity, genocide, torture, forced disappearance, forced or compulsory labour, hostage taking, extrajudicial, summary or arbitrary executions, other violations of humanitarian law or other international crimes against the human person as defined by international law[184].'The Norms go noticeably further than existing international law in imposing human rights obligations on private corporations requiring private corporations to respect some rights that, under existing international law, are either not broadly recognized, unprotected from private infringement, or intended to be protected from private infringement through the national laws of the states-parties but very few human rights norms apply directly to non-state actors under international law as it exists today[185]. Furthermore, international law has in some way recognized duties upon corporations by

---

of the International Criminal Tribunal for the Former Yugoslavia, art. 8, S.C. Res. 827, U.N. Doc. S/RES/827 (1993) (adopted May, 25, 1993 and establishing temporal jurisdiction over all specified crimes occurring after January 1, 1991). If the legal norms for which these tribunals have the power to impose penalties were not directly operative on individuals at the time the violations occurred, there would be a problem under the principle of nulla poena sine lege previa. On the other hand, the Rome Statute establishing the International Criminal Court defines the crimes for which prosecutions are possible and authorizes prosecutions only for crimes committed after the entry into force of the treaty. Rome Statute of the International Criminal Court, July 17, 1998, art. 11, U.N. Doc. A/CONF.183/9, 37 I.L.M. 999, available at *http://www.un.org/law/icc/statute/romefra.htm*

[183] Universal Declaration of Human Rights, G.A. Res. 217A (III), U.N. GAOR, 3d Sess., at 71, U.N. Doc. A/810 (1948), Jordan Paust, Human Rights Responsibilities of Private Corporations, 35 Vand. J. Transnat'l L. 801, 810-11 (2002). Surya Deva, Human Rights Violations by Multinational Corporations and International Law: Where from Here?, 19 Conn. J. Int'l L. 1, 13 (2003); Louis Henkin, The Universal Declaration at 50 and the Challenge of Global Markets, 25 Brook. J. Int'l L. 17, 25 (1999). International Council on Human Rights Policy, Beyond Voluntarism: Human Rights and the Developing International Obligations of Companies 61 (2002), available at *http://www.ichrp.org/ac/excerpts/41.pdf* (stating that the preamble to the UDHR has at best "indirect legal effect").

[184] Unocal, 110 F. Supp. 2d at 1310 (holding that international law prohibits complicity in state violations of human rights norms, but defining complicity more narrowly than "benefiting from").Unocal, 110 F. Supp. 2d at 1307-09 (finding that norms against forced labor are directly applicable). Presbytarian Church of Sudan v. Talisman Energy, Inc., 244 F. Supp.2d 289 (S.D.N.Y. 2003) (Declaration of James Crawford and Declaration of Christopher Greenwood). The conclusion that the primary norms do apply to corporations as well as private individuals derives some support from the decision of the U.S. Military Tribunal in Nuremburg stating that certain violations had been "committed by Farben." Int'l L. Rep. (1948), at 675.

[185] Doe v. Unocal, 395 F. 3d 932, 945 (9th Cir. 2002) (Forced labor is "among the 'handful of crimes... to which the law of nations attributes individual liability,' such that state action is not required"

prescribing international labor law, environmental law, anti-corruption law, and economic sanctions.

Is the development of a corpus of law that would recognize obligations on businesses to protect human rights the right solution? States have human rights obligations toward all persons on their territory stemming from the fact that governmental control and jurisdiction is determined on a territorial basis. Besides, MNEs do not exercise such a geographically fixed form of jurisdiction. MNEs operate in different localities and different countries. Each state can regulate the human rights abuses that take place on its territory even by foreign-based MNEs as well as the activities of MNEs headquartered on the territory even if the abuses take place overseas. States could promote uniformity of regulation of MNEs for activities with human rights implications through a multilateral instrument recognizing certain obligations upon corporations. MNEs activities that harm the environment, violate labor and human rights, and corrupt state actors and institutions remain problems in all market economies.

Can international law move in the direction of generally extending human rights obligations of states to private corporations? It is argued that international law could move in the direction of extending human rights obligations of states to private corporations to the extent such obligations are subject to application to non-state actors. Consequently, private corporations would have no duties with respect to functions classically performed only by governments, such as the granting of fair trials, but all other norms would be extended to private corporations within the sphere of their activities.

MNEs have become powerful enough to use major pressure on many governments but some times the presence of MNEs is optimistically correlated with both civil liberties and political freedoms in developing countries[186]. On the one hand, state conduct contributing probably to some private interests sometimes significantly impinges upon human rights and so this has sufficed to justify the imposition of human rights obligations on states. On the other hand, the fact that MNEs are powerful and their behavior is sometimes detrimental to human rights is essential but not sufficient conditions for concluding that international law should directly impose human rights obligations on private corporations. It is argued that the imposition of international law obligations on corporations either should be a matter of unconcern to states, whose own powers and responsibilities would not be affected by such a progress, or should be welcomed by states, whose own international legal burdens would be lightened if responsibilities were imposed on corporations[187].

It has to be taken into account that states still hold a monopoly of international law-making but it seems that exercise this power mainly on behalf of the economic interests which supply them with the power of money and that is the reason for their hesitance to endorse the Norms. States occasionally favor adhering to international human rights norms in order to entrench the norms and in consequence tie the hands of successors whom they may

---

186 William H. Meyer, Human Rights and MNCs: Theory versus Quantitative Analysis, 18 Hum. Rts. Q. 368, 392 (1996). Jackie Smith, Melissa Bolyard & Anna Ippolito, Human Rights and the Global Economy:A Response to Meyer, 21 Hum. Rts. Q. 207 (1999) (disputing Meyer's methodology and findings).

187 In re Agent Orange Product Liability Litig., 2005 WL 729177 *39-40 (E.D.N.Y. 2005) (Declaration of Kenneth Howard Anderson Jr.). (Anderson considers that imposition of obligations on corporations would be unwelcome from the standpoint of controlling behavior because it fragments responsibility for such behavior, dilutes accountability, and lets states ethically off the hook. If that were the case one would expect states--who still hold a monopoly of international law-making--to welcome the direct imposition of obligations on corporations. Their reaction to the Norms suggests that they are hesitant to move in this direction.)

not trust[188]. The imposition of direct obligations on MNEs, backed by an effective international mechanism to enforce those obligations, would correspond to a major disempowering of states. The articulation of norms that would regulate corporations would clearly diminish state sovereignty in the sense that states would no longer be permitted to impose conflicting regulations.

The fact that international law makes states and only states responsible for violations gives states effective control over compliance with these obligations. A shift to a model of private party liability accompanied by effective international enforcement mechanisms would remove the power of states to determine whether and when such international legal norms will be obeyed. A transformation has occurred in Europe, where under the doctrines of Direct Effect and Supremacy, the European Union has created legal obligations that trump conflicting municipal laws and apply directly to individuals and so with acceptance by the European Court of Justice and the EU member states, these doctrines are now the cornerstones of the EU's legal system, rendering the legal relationship between member states comparable to that between federal states[189].

International legal norms addressed to non-state actors are far less likely to be observed in the absence of effective enforcement mechanisms. Under international law a state's breach of one obligation justifies an injured state's breach of its own legal obligations toward the violating state the violating state would have to weigh in the analysis its vulnerability to countermeasures. Breach of a rule of international law will affect the state's reputation for keeping its promises. A state's reputation for breaching international obligations could be expected to deter other states from entering into potentially beneficial treaties with it. Violations of international legal norms lead over time to the weakening of the rule, and ultimately to its passing. Private individuals are typically regulated by municipal legal systems, and coercion is a universal feature of such systems.

2.7 MNEs and the Norms

MNEs having massive budgets and driven basically by profit, use the smallest number of workers possible, move from jurisdiction to jurisdiction with relative ease, importe labour to the disadvantage of local labour, and do not always take into account the social needs of the countries in which they are operating.

The *Norms* show the extent to which the issue of corporate social responsibility is no longer confined to charitable giving, or understood in the context of shareholder welfare maximization but pointing up the way in which the transnational realities of corporate operation have affected assumptions of regulatory home, away from the state and toward transnational or international institutions. The subject of corporate responsibility exceeds the narrow focus on economic norms such as directors' duties to shareholders, exposure obligations to regulatory authority or employee relations. Corporate regulation is no longer a

---

[188] Stacie Jonas, The Ripple Effect of the Pinochet Case, 11 Hum. Rts. Brief 36, 36 (2004) (describing several advances in the application of human rights law after Pinochet left power, such as a vast increase in the number of cases brought and a reinterpretation of amnesty law). Paul Schiff Berman, The Globalization of Jurisdiction, 151 U. Pa. L. Rev. 311, 527 (2002) (discussing increased human rights enforcement in Argentina).

[189] J. H. H. Weiler, The Transformation of Europe, 100 Yale L.J. 2403, 2413-16 (1991).

matter limited to the traditional fields of "corporate" or "economic" law and policy; it is now also a creature of social policy. Thus, the *Norms* regard corporate law as an object of international law assuming preemption, and the supremacy of international law, even an international law of private contract, over state regulation.

According to 1995 Report[190] MNEs use their great influence - control on the flow of transnational capital- to play governments and communities off one another in order to maximize profits and achieve the lowest labor, consumer and environmental costs achievable. Globalization increases locational mobility of MNE's and their monopolistic and oligopolistic tendencies have increased the bargaining power of MNE's and have been associate with a loss of decision-making capacity by States, in particular in developing countries showing a trade liberalization and the dismantling of locally protective legislation resulting in a reduction of the competence of national government to establish the required conditions for the realization of economic, social and cultural rights. Decisions regarding location are driven by MNEs' policy perspective rather than definite spatial considerations, competitive industry clusters provide specific inducements for MNEs that distort the lines between behaviour in line with strategic policy as against spatial considerations. Technological reserve gives way to technological co-operation under these conditions which suggests that decisions about location are pre-determined by virtue of cluster location and so government policy plays a considerable role in influencing initial investment decisions by creating favourable conditions that facilitate cluster formation.

MNE profit-maximizing behavior affects the allocation of high and low skill work on a worldwide basis in a way that penalizes developing states and so the methods of work of MNEs have implications for the effective enjoyment of a number of human rights. The universal strategies of MNEs intensify existing regional and international inequalities by sharpening the polarization between low-wage assembly work and high-skilled activities and in fact maximizing profit rather than promoting equality and improving human well-being.

While markets are an economically effective means of governing transactions, market failures occur to the extent there is incomplete or asymmetrical information that might promote opportunism. A perfect market would rely on key norms of reciprocity to exercise transactions assuming full and accurate information, but in reality markets fail and globalization has done little to ease the bounded rationality of our information searches, given the increase of available information made feasible by technological advances[191]. Not all parties to a transaction have equal access to information, regardless its growing democratization and those with access are often unable to digest all the needed information in a timeframe suitable to exploit instantaneous opportunities. With market failure and attendant increases in transaction costs, bureaucracies intervene to successfully and efficiently audit and monitor the legitimacy of transactions. While most MNEs and their subsidiaries do respect local laws, there are many who do not, mainly where laws are weakly enforced. The

---

[190] ECOSOC, Sub-Comm'n on Prevention of Discrimination & Prot. of Minorities, The Realization of Economic, Social and Cultural Rights: The Relationship Between the Enjoyment of Human Rights, in Particular, International Labour and Trade Union Rights, and the Working Methods and Activities of Transnational Corporations, U.N. Doc. E/CN.4/Sub.2/1995/11 (July 24, 1995)

[191] Dowell, G., S. Hart, and B. Yeung, 2000. "Do Corporate Global Environmental Standards Create or Destroy Market Value?" Management Science 46(8): 1059-74. David Kinley, Justine Nolan and Natalie Zerial, The politics of corporate social responsibility: Reflections on the United Nations Human Rights Norms for Corporations, 2007 Legal Studies Research Paper No. 07/10, (2007) 25 C&SLJ 30.

globalization trend does necessitate integrative solutions that engender a degree of trust among allied communities to the social contract with the desired outcome being an improvement in the efficiency of governance worldwide.

According to 1996[192] Report MNEs' social role is not the passive, voluntary, and permissive social role of corporations expressed in the Berle-Dodd debate, or in the American cases but the maximization of corporate operations from maximization of shareholder wealth to maximization of corporate input to economic and social development.

The globalization of economic activities by MNEs brought an increasing volutaty responsibility of MNEs towards society but emerging and current international rules do not recognize MNEs' social activities and accordingly cannot regulate and promote MNEs' social responsibility. Even if each MNE subsidiary is subject to its host country's regulations, the MNE as a whole is not fully accountable to any single country. Thus, international, rather than national, regulatory frameworks are required to suitably control MNE activity across borders. The absence of a uniform regulatory system allows abuse by powerful private economic interests able to utilize differences in economic power and social organization among the states hosting their operations.

The activities of MNEs influence many aspects of life, including work, health, food, economics, environment, trade and transfer of technology and so international community has, since the 1970s, sought a comprehensive, multilateral and universal framework to regulate their conduct without a success on an obligatory basis until know[193].

It could be argued that there is a need for the development of an international legal machinery to mediate, adjust, and diminish national and international conflicts facilitating the imposition of operative governmental controls over the activities of MNEs encouraging the harmonious development of international economic relations.

According to 1998[194] Report MNEs are vehicles for the transfer of wealth from poorer to richer states and from workers to investors and there is a need of correction at a level of political governance at least as powerful and extensive as the MNEs to be regulated. MNEs play a key part in international economic life and are in position to obstruct moves towards the respect for and protection of social policies and human rights. Globalization will lead to the establishment of more wealthy and powerful MNEs but also even greater numbers of poor people and so international law must adapt in order to deal with the problem arising from their operation. The 1998 Sub-Commission Report specifies that MNEs "are of course organizations whose *raison d'etre* is to make a profit" but there is a need for the implementation of a universal democratic principle of governance in international standards.

---

192 ECOSOC, Sub-Comm'n on Prevention of Discrimination and Prot. of Minorities, The Impact of the Activities and Working Methods of Transnational Corporations on the Full Employment of all Human Rights, in Particular Economic, Social, and Cultural Rights and the Right to Development, Bearing in Mind Existing International Guidelines, Rules and Standards Relating to the Subject Matter, U.N. Doc. E/CN.4/Sub.2/1996/12 (July 2, 1996)

193 René Reich-Graefe, Changing Paradigms: The Liability of Corporate Groups in Germany, 37 Conn. L. Rev. 785 (2005).

194 ECOSOC, Sub-Comm'n on Prevention of Discrimination & Prot. of Minorities, Working Document: The Realization of Economic, Social and Cultural Rights: The Question of Transnational Corporations, ¶ 16, U.N. Doc. E/CN.4/Sub.2/1998/6 (June 10, 1998)

The *Norms* seek a supra-national basis for regulating corporations after the failure of attempts through other organs of the United Nations. Moreover, the *Norms*[195] provide a basis for imposing, at an international level, a public law oriented constituency model on corporate organization and so serve as the basis for using corporations against states that are unenthusiastic or unable to implement emerging international law norms, whether or not technically binding as "law," within their territories. The General Provisions contribute the foundations for the development of a system of international law implemented through the private law of contract requiring the incorporation of its provisions into all MNEs contracts and include monitoring/disclosure obligations with respect to *Norms* compliance. In other words, the *Norms* utilize the flexibility of private law making to maximize the effectiveness of its implementation without the interference of state actors. MNEs are prohibited from doing business with any natural or other legal persons unless these also "follow these or substantially similar Norms[196]." This author considers that it is time to bring some criteria in order MNEs to become state actors with rights and liabilities. MNEs can have a second legal personality other than of a corporation that of a *functional state actor* for international law purposes and the specific matters of human rights, crimes against humanity and environment protection.

The *Norms* monitor the activities of MNEs at the international level by creating a web of reporting and observing involving states, international actors, and elements of civil society. Monitoring and implementation of the *Norms* have need of "amplification and interpretation of intergovernmental, regional, national and local standards with regard to the conduct of transnational corporations[197]". The *Norms* broadly define "transnational corporation" to include an "economic entity operating in more than one country or a cluster of economic entities operating in two or more countries – whatever their legal form, whether in their home country or country of activity, and whether taken individually or collectively[198]." The legal definition overrides national law regarding the legal autonomy of corporations related to each other through share ownership embracing the idea of enterprise liability as the basis for the imposition of the substantive rules of the *Norms* and so States that have not adopted enterprise liability as a basis for corporate liability either have to ignore their own statutes or to harmonize them with the *Norms*. The general liability provision of Paragraph 18 obligates MNEs to provide "prompt, effective and adequate reparation to those persons, entities and communities that have been adversely affected by failures to comply with these Norms" and because there is no recognition and reference to the distinct legal personalities of the corporations that together constitute the MNE piercing the corporate veil for all litigation involving an allegation of breach of its provisions.

A savings clause ensures that MNEs and other business enterprises will pursue the course of conduct that is the most protective of human rights and in fact the *Norms* declare adherence

[195] ECOSOC, Sub-Comm'n on the Promotion and Prot. of Human Rights, Report of the United Nations High Commissioner on Human Rights on the Responsibilities of Transnational Corporations and Related Business Enterprises With Regards to Human Rights, ¶ 52(d), U.N. Doc. E/CN.4/2005/91 (Feb. 15, 2005) Frank Bottomley, From Contractualism to Constitutionalism: A Framework for Corporate Governance, 19 Sydney L. Rev. 277, 313 (1997) (discussing corporate constitutionalism as a replacement for the dominant contractual paradigm because it allows "contemplation of companies as governance systems.").

[196] Norms ¶ 15.

[197] Commentary, ¶ 16 cmt. (a).

[198] Norms, ¶ 20.

to the principle that states remain the primary font of regulation in the areas the *Norms* cover[199].

There is definition of stakeholder which includes all actors such as consumer groups, customers, governments, nongovernmental organizations, public and private lending institutions, suppliers, and trade associations affected by an economic enterprise as understood in the economic or socio-political sense abandoning the shareholder model of governance and imposing a stakeholder model for purposes of corporate governance. By radically broadening the actors who are, indirectly but effectively, given governance rights *within* any corporation required to adhere to the *Norms,* there is broadening on core issues of domestic corporate law—fiduciary duty, rights to control the corporation, rights to participate in corporate decision making, exit rights, and the like—all of which have traditionally been tied to shareholder primacy, the core assumption of corporate law. In other words we have displacement of the shareholder model for a stakeholder model by incorporating public law social responsibility as a core norm of MNE corporate governance compliance which for this author changes the substance of a MNEs going against nature of MNEs and their fundamental role as corporations.

The *Norms* bring a modification of corporate governance beyond recognition from a private economic entity not only mostly and also above all obliged to its investors and to the maximization of entity wealth, to a public social, political, and economic entity which is not a MNEs with the internationally accepted form, obliged to the political communities in which it operates as well as to the international communities from which regulation arises, and to the maximization of the public welfare and this is a form of corporate regulation outside the reach of current corporate law .

Norms introduce a range of public law duties that MNEs should undertake as a matter of private law between MNEs and the whole web of actors with whom the MNE does business or otherwise operates. MNEs in their present form are in a position to influence the economies of most countries and are beyond the regulatory capacity of any one of them. Furthermore, MNEs, by their very wealth and power, have the means to produce wealth without constraining profits for their shareholders and so by their behavior contribute to new standards on human rights. Hence, MNEs should not be detached from either human rights issues or the general obligation to contribute to the development and progress of humankind, since rights are universal, indivisible, interdependent and interrelated.

MNEs are expected to incorporate into their contracts and respect generally recognized responsibilities and norms contained in United Nations treaties and other international instruments. On the other hand, many of the rights guaranteed by the *Norms* either have no formal binding or legal effect as international law, or are derived from conventions or treaties that have not been ratified by all of the state parties within which MNEs would have to operate. Many countries have not ratified all the principal human rights instruments and there is a need for a reference to customary international law. The *Norms* not only repeat the key responsibility of States with respect to human rights, but also proclaims that in their

[199] This declaration implicates both the nationality and territorial principles of state power to regulate under international law. The territorial principle provides that states exercise jurisdiction over all natural and juridical persons present within their borders. The nationality principle provides that states exercise jurisdiction over their nationals, wherever they may be. The nationality principle limit a state's jurisdiction (even within its territory) based on the nationality of the persons or entities against whom jurisdiction might be asserted.

individual spheres of activity and influence MNEs have the same obligations as States with respect to human rights.

MNEs must show due diligence that do not contribute to or benefit from human rights abuses and the failure of due diligence may result in MNE liability for underlying human rights abuses. It is stated that the establishment of a web of private human rights norms through private contract "may not be used by States as an excuse for failing to take action to protect human rights, for example, through the enforcement of existing laws[200]." In fact, MNEs are obligated to ensure equality of opportunity and equal treatment for all workers and labor standards are to be based on both national (host country) and international norms.

As mentioned above, the appropriate provisions of the Norms shall be incorporated into the contract and at least those provisions should be made available upon request to stakeholders in order to guarantee compliance which means that parties to the MNE's contracts enforce compliance under the national law of contract and so Stakeholders will enforce these obligations opening the MNE to review by and accountability to a surprisingly large number of actors, in addition to holders of capital interests debt or equity in the corporation. It could be said that this broad accountability of MNEs for matters outside that interests of the holders of capital interests makes MNEs an unworkable form of corporation.

It seems that it is imposed on MNEs a certain obligation to negotiate with states to induce them to design and execute national action programs to "eliminate the worst forms of child labor consistent with ILO Convention No. 182" and so there is de facto recognition of the power of MNEs as public law actors[201]. It could be argued that it is created an obligation in a non-state actor to negotiate national legislation with a nation-state in accordance with international norms memorialized in an international convention. The Norms impose international law standards domestically through the private law of MNE contracts. Thus, the *Norms* seek to harmonize, at an international level, worker unionization rights as defined by and subject to international norms developed through the International Labor Organization causing a problem both in those jurisdictions that have not ratified international labor conventions, and in those states whose political or judicial branches interpret domestic rights to unionize differently from that evolving under international standards[202]. It questionable how a MNE can honour the labor obligations of the *Norms* in countries that have not ratified the underlying international standards without also violating the *Norms*' vital obligation that MNEs respect the national sovereignty of the countries in which they operate.

MNEs are required to acknowledge and respect not only the international and domestic law of the host state, but also additional policy goals and objectives such as the rule of law, the public interest, development of social, economic, and cultural policies including transparency, accountability, and prohibition of corruption and the authority of the host state[203]. Thus, the *Norms* introduce a new principle of corporate governance according which

---

200 ECOSOC, Sub-Comm'n on the Promotion and Prot. Of Human Rights, Commentary on the Norms on the Responsibilities of Transnational Corporations and Other Business Enterprises with Regard to Human Rights, U.N. Doc. E/CN.4/Sub.2/2003/38/Rev.2 (Aug. 26, 2003), ¶ 1 cmt. (b).

201 Commentary, ¶ 6 cmt. (d).

202 Iliana Christodoulou-Varotsi and Dmitri A. Pentsov, Labor Standards on Cypriot Ships: Myth and Reality, 37 Vand. J. Transat'l L. 647 (2004). Philip R. Seckman, Invigorating Enforcement Mechanisms of the International Labor Organization in Pursuit of U.S. Labor Objectives, 32 Denv. J. Int'l L. & Pol'y. 675, 686–89 (2004).

203 Norms, ¶ 10.

corporate activity has to be directed to the encouragement of social progress and development, rather than shareholder wealth maximization. It is imposed a certain duty on MNEs to ensure that goods and services provided are not used to abuse human rights. It seems to be imposed on MNEs an obligation to implement social and economic welfare policies in a development context, perhaps in place of or in coordination with the state. Hence, the *Norms* shift from a shareholder maximization model to a public law model imposing on MNEs a key obligation to serve the political community in which they function according to international standards. There is an intention to permit the Human Rights Commission to develop its own financial reporting rules for MNEs, focusing on the human rights obligations of these entities. Moreover, MNEs shall respect and contribute to economic, social, political, and civil rights and the right to development adding significant constraints on MNE activity outside the context of current corporate law.

The *Norms* contemplate that consumer protection standards are to be harmonized in accordance with international standards, with MNEs as agents of the international legal order through private ordering where countries resist adoption of international standards. MNEs are charged with an affirmative obligation to contribute to the goal of sustainable development and the *Commentary* adopts a broad liability standard for environmental damage[204]. It could be said that the *Norms* attempt to make great changes to both the internal norms of corporate governance[205] and in general to the structure of international law. The *Norms* make an obvious and comprehensive advance over existing voluntary standards for regulating business behaviour. The obligations imposed upon MNEs are beyond the competence of international law. *Norms* impose upon MNEs legal obligations that have not been adopted by some or all of the countries in which MNEs may operate and it could be said that it is attempted to shift traditional subjects of state responsibility onto private economic entities, providing a convenient means through which states avoid their own obligations to those for whom they might be responsible. Under the *Norms,* MNEs within the restrictions of their resources and capabilities shall support social progress and development by expanding economic opportunities— predominantly in developing countries and so making clear that all decisions of the MNE have to take into account input from stakeholders[206]. Consequently, MNEs have an obligation to contribute to the fulfilment of economic, social, and cultural rights of the people in whose political territory the MNE operates.

Substituting a public for a private law basis for corporate governance alters not only the focus of regulation, but also the division of power over the corporate entity. If everyone is a stakeholder, and everyone has an "ownership" interest in the corporation without contributing to the capital by being a shareholder, then not only the focus of governance shifts but also it introduced another foundation to the substance of ownership and so we will have shareholders and stakeholders in a corporation probably having a different kind of ownership upon a corporation. In other words, the direction of corporate activity, as well as the objects to which these organizations are directed, changes. On the one hand, under the laws of most of the industrialized countries, the object of a corporation is to increase the capital of its shareholders, within the limits of its resources and capabilities and to that extent shareholders

---

[204] Commentary, ¶ 14 cmt. (b).

[205] Carolin F. Hillemanns, UN Norms on the Responsibilities of Transnational Corporations and Other Business Enterprises With Regard to Human Rights, 4 German L.J. 1065 (2003) (describing the Norms and their effects on corporate governance discourse).

[206] Commentary, ¶ 10 cmt. (a). ¶ 16 cmt. (i).

maintain ultimate control of the corporate governance machinery and the duty of those appointed by them flows wholly to shareholders[207]. On the other hand, under the *Norms*, shareholder (capital ownership) interests are equated with those of other stakeholders (social ownership) and so the board of directors will have to balance the interests of different actors whose interests in the corporation, direct or indirect, appear now to form a part of the board's fiduciary obligation. As a matter of the national law of most states, the autonomous legal personality of a corporation matters is established and most states have developed very strong public policies in favor of legal autonomy. At the same time, practically all states have rules for imposing liability on shareholders or related corporations under circumstances in which such "piercing of the veil" of autonomy is warranted[208]. To the extent that limited liability is waived, a shareholder's contract rights are affected[209].

It could be argued that the *Norms* can serve as a vehicle for creating customary international law through the cumulative changes in corporate behavior brought about through the *Norms* and so as customary international law, the *Norms*, would preempt state corporate law to the extent they were inconsistent. The *Norms* seek a radical transformation of the *de jure* function of MNEs and so MNEs are no longer understood as entities whose rationale is limited to the economic sphere and whose activities must be regulated to make certain that they engage only in economic activities. Instead, the *Norms* understand MNEs as entities with social, cultural, civil, and political purposes on par with economic purposes and so the *de facto* assertion of power by MNEs is used as the basis for extending their *de jure* authority into areas typically reserved for state power alone. To that extent MNEs interfere with the political, social, cultural, and economic life of the countries in which they operate and so MNEs are treated as virtual state actors for purposes of many normative requirements which means that a MNE becomes a state within a state. Therefore, if MNEs act as states then there is no need for the state's existence as a second state in the MNE-state and so all the current states could be substituted by MNEs-states.

The *Norms* transform the corporation from an entity whose first purpose is to maximize profits as purely economic creature into an entity whose principal purposes are encompassed in the great human rights treaty framework of the United Nations. Thus, the *Norms*, through private law, compel a significant array of functions once monopolized by public bodies. In the end, then, the MNE derives a direct relationship to international law on an order comparable to that enjoyed by states. To that extent, MNEs become key human rights and political actors. There is a change on MNEs' character from private enterprises of limited objective to public actors with positive political obligations exceeding that of the states in

---

[207] Thomas Lee Hazen, Silencing the Shareholders' Voice, 80 N.C. L. Rev. 1897, 1900 (2002) (Shareholders are the owners of the corporate enterprise. As the risk takers, they stand to gain from the success of the business. Simultaneously, they stand to lose their investment if the enterprise fails. Due to the shareholders' stake in the business, corporate law has vested ultimate control of the corporation in the shareholders.)

[208] Robert B. Thompson, Piercing the Veil Within Corporate Groups: Corporate Shareholders as Mere Investors, 13 Conn. J. Int'l L. 379 (1999). Stephen Bainbridge, Abolishing Veil Piercing, 26 J. Corp. L. 479, 506–14 (2001). Ian Ramsey & David Noakes, Piercing the Corporate Veil in Australia, 19 Company & Securities L.J. 250 (2001).

[209] Henry Hansmann & Reiner Kraakman, Toward Unlimited Shareholder Liability for Corporate Torts, 100 Yale. L.J. 1879, 1919–20 (1991) (advocating elimination of limited liability protection for shareholders in tort claims against the corporation). Einer Elhauge, Sacrificing Corporate Profits in the public Interest, 80 N.Y.U. L. Rev. 733, 840–58 (2005).

which they operate. According to Larry Catá Backer[210] "The breadth of the public, and inherently political, obligations of TNCs is immense: TNCs must "encourage social progress and development," adopt and internalize specific labor policies in their global operations, and "contribute to [the] realization" of such rights as "the rights to development, adequate food and drinking water, the highest attainable standard of physical and mental health, adequate housing, privacy, education, freedom of thought, conscience, and religion and freedom of opinion and expression, and shall refrain from actions which obstruct or impede the realization of those rights."" In fact, MNEs attributed with obligations, parallel to those of other public law actors, to abstain from any action which supports, solicits, or encourages States or any other entities to abuse human rights, or to renounce the production of weapons that have been declared illegal under international law regardless of the relationship of that law to the position of the host or home country[211].

Do MNEs become competitor to state power and states no longer have a monopoly of power under international law? It is attempted a direct imposition on MNEs a private law entity of human rights and other international obligations expanding the meaning of applicable international law to include soft law—laws that states have never recognized as binding. The *Norms* seek to impose responsibility for the enforcement of international law norms straight on MNEs all the way through the imposition of a binding set of rules and establishing a direct connection between international law norms, non-state actors, and individuals without any mediating role for the state itself. Hence, the status of MNEs is transformed from objects to subjects of international law representing a fundamental change from the status quo, shifting regulatory authority from states to non-state actors. It could be said that there is a creation of a new category of international law subject that of the MNE and in effect ranking below that of the nation-state. The annoyance of binding norms on MNEs will constitute a major departure from the current framework of international law altering states' monopoly of control over decisions to adopt and implement international norms within their territories[212]. It is worth mentioning that in the European Union human rights obligations

---

210 Larry Catá Backer, Multinational Corporations, Transnational Law: The United Nations' Norms On The Responsibilities Of Transnational Corporations As A Harbinger Of Corporate Social Responsibility In International Law, 2005 Columbia Human Rights Law Review 101 at 177.

211 Norms, ¶ 11, Commentary, ¶ 3 cmt. (b). Hon. Delissa A. Ridgeway & Mariya A. Talib, Globalization And Development—Free Trade, Foreign Aid, Investment And The Rule Of Law, 33 Cal. Western Int'l L.J. 325, 332 (2003). Yoshiro Miwa, Corporate Social Responsibility: Dangerous and Harmful, Though Maybe Not Irrelevant, 84 Cornell L. Rev. 1227, 1250–53 (1999) (criticizing the conflation of corporate and state regulation in Japan before the Second World War and its relation to Marxist views of the relation of the state and corporation).

212 United Kingdom of Great Britain and Northern Ireland, The Responsibilities of Transnational Corporations and Related Business Enterprises With Regard to Human Rights, ¶ 3, *http://www.ohchr.org/english/issues/globalization/business/contributions.htm* "The primary responsibility for the promotion and protection of human rights lies with States. . . . The international community could have an important role supporting these efforts, but creating and upholding the framework remains the responsibility of a State." Austl. Permanent Mission to the U.N., Comments by Australia in Respect of the Report Requested from the Office of the High Commissioner for Human Rights by the Commission on Human Rights in its Decision 2004/116 of 20 April 2004 on Existing Initiatives and Standards Relating to the Responsibility of Transnational Corporations and Related Business Enterprises With Regard to Human Rights, at 2 (Sept. 8, 2004), *http://www.ohchr.org/english/issues/globalization/business/contributions.htm* "legal responsibility for the implementation of international human rights standards rests primarily with those States who are a party to the standards."

and responsibility are allocated to corporations, but the legal obligations rest with the States. In general regardless the globalisation effects worldwide, every state continues to have the central responsibility for its own sustainable development, and for ensuring protection of human rights. Of course MNEs take part in dialogue sponsored by states and international actors, between government and business representatives, the trade unions and NGOs.

It could be argued that establishing duties and obligations for MNEs, which are non-State actors, goes well beyond the current state of international law as well as international legal process circumventing all recognized law making processes by compelling international obligations on entities that have neither accepted them nor played a part in their creation[213]. Hence, MNEs will have the authority to internationalize their transactions through their contractual relations and so the *Norms* do not remake international law but merely extend it but there is the prospective to shrink the force of state monopoly on lawmaking, even within a state's territory. MNEs can be used as a method of forcing, within the territory of any state, implementation of a host of international laws, some or all of which might have been lawfully rejected by the state itself. Changing responsibility for the implementation of human rights standards to MNEs could make it easier for states to evade their principal responsibility for ensuring respect for human rights.

Can private law be used to effect public policy? Claire Cutler[214] considers that private law is a basis for effecting public policy and rejecting the idea of the neutrality of private law. The employment of MNEs as a substitute for or addition to the state in the implementation of human rights norms is a momentous event within any theory of international law and governance. The operation of international human rights norms through private contract to expand drastically the scope of international norms means the introduction of new standards of international custom through contract. MNEs conduct their activities according to the ordinances, laws and regulations in force in the country, in the same way as do other national enterprises. The Preamble of Norms reaffirms "that transnational corporations and other business enterprises . . . have, inter alia, human rights obligations and responsibilities and that these human rights norms will contribute to the making and development of international law as to those responsibilities and obligations." Hence, Non-state actors such as principally MNEs could serve as a vehicle for the adoption of behavior models on which soft and then hard law can be based and so the *Norms* provide a basis for the building of consensus necessary for the adoption of hard international law[215].

The Norms would compel MNEs to adhere to treaties to which governments of countries in which they operate might not be parties, and which might not be enforced through national laws. Norms sought to privatize monitoring and enforcement of international standards through MNEs. Norms empower organizations not accountable to any democratically

---

[213] Fleur Johns, The Invisibility of the Transnational Corporation, 19 Melb. U. L. Rev. 893, 905–06 (1994).

[214] Claire Cutler, Global Capitalism and Liberal Myths: Dispute Settlement in Private International Trade Relations, 24 J. Int'l Stud. 377 (1995)

[215] U.N. Comm'n on Transnat'l Corps., Transnational Corporations: Certain Modalities for Implementation of a Code of Conduct in Relation to its Possible Legal Nature, ¶ 8, U.N. Doc. E/C.10/AC.2/9 (Dec. 22, 1978). "A Code of Conduct on transnational corporations, whether in legally binding or non-binding form, represents an effort to formulate expectations which Governments collectively feel justified to hold with regard to the conduct of transnational corporations." Id. Such a code "becomes thereby a 'source' of law for national authorities as well as for the international corporations themselves."

controlled community[216] to serve as a sort of Praetorian Guard of a system of voluntary monitoring and disclosure[217]. The MNE, rather than the state, is charged with the implementation of the *Norms* by incorporating the *Norms* in all of its contractual relations. States are accountable to their political community and are subjects of international law, all the way through which they are legitimated and serve to reinforce principles of democratic organization and the rule of law. Thus, the Norms use MNEs as a means of end-running states, and in the process create the basis for the expression of customary international law principles that will apply to states.

---

[216] Oren Perez, Normative Creativity and Global Legal Pluralism: Reflections on the Democratic Critique of Transnational Law, 10 Ind. J. Global L. Stud. 25, 43 (2003) ("Most of these organizations are not governed in a democratic fashion. It is not clear why they should be treated as true representatives of the public.").

[217] Isabella D. Bunn, Global Advocacy For Corporate Accountability: Transatlantic Perspectives From The NGO Community, 19 Am. U. Int'l L. Rev. 1265 (2004).

Chapter 3

MNE AND INTEGRATION

3.1 INTEGRATION

Integration means the removal or reduction of intra- bloc price discrimination that is a feature of segmented markets in the presence of imperfect competition.[1] Integration provides expanded opportunities for countries to engage in inter-industry specialization within a bloc, in accordance with comparative advantage, so bringing about a rationalization of its production. Rationalization brings forward an improvement of resources allocation and homogenous products produced by companies that lack market power and acquire few or no transaction costs. Integration affects the international location of industrial activities but imperfect integration creates regional winners and losers. Growth can be a powerful destabilising force but the interregional learning spilovers are a stabilising force[2]. The increase in intra-bloc trade in manufactures is centred on the interaction of scale economies and product differentiation.[3] A considerable part of the trade that is carried on between industrial countries and among, EU and EFTA results from arbitrary specialization drive by scale economies and product differentiation.[4]

Liberalization and regional market integration means that the gains from trade stem solely from increased competition in the presence of scale economies and product differentiation rather than from comparative advantage as such. Integration increases effective market size giving rise to more competition. Larger market size encourages longer production runs and so reductions in cost. Trade expansion enables more products to be produced profitably so generating welfare gains from increased product diversity.

Integration permits companies to engage in more plant specialization thus reducing the number of products produced in a given plant with attendant cost reductions. Product differentiation means that firms have varying degrees of market power in each of their markets. Market power and price-cost margins are directly related to market share. A reduction in trade barriers means a reduction in real trade costs between the members of an economic grouping should be beneficial for all countries involved since each country will

---

[1] P Robson "The economics of international integration" 1998 Routledge.

[2] R Bildwin, R Forslid, The core-periphery model and endogenous growth: stabilising and destabilizing integration, 2000 Economica 307.

[3] A Dixit, V Norman "Theory of international trade" 1980 Cambridge University Press.

[4] E Helpman, P Krugman " Market structure and foreign trade" 1985 MIT Press.

gain in its export markets. The interaction between scale economies and transportation costs gives rise to linkages between firms and labour/customers or between the firms themselves via their demand for intermediate products. It could be said that integration in the form of reductions in trade costs can yield agglomeration and under certain circumstances increased inequality in real incomes. The tendency for concentration of industrial activity may be weaker when we allow firms to set up production plants both at home and abroad. As the firms' get more options with regards to the location decision, the tendency for economic activity to agglomerate is weakened. When the firm can choose to locate different types of activities in different locations, there may be a tendency for certain types of activities to agglomerate. The introduction of horizontal multi-region firms weakens agglomeration tendencies and it does so to a greater extent the higher the degree of multiplant economies of scale. Firms that choose to operate in more than one location rarely are purely horizontal or purely vertical in nature. Horizontal firms have a home country in which they incur the main part of their fixed costs. The presence of multiplant economies of scale would tend to spread out production. Horizontal multi-region firms are generally stabilising in the sense that they decrease the range of trade costs for which the core-periphery outcome occurs. Besides, the introduction of vertical multi-region firms can be said to lead to more agglomeration. Activities such as R&D and corporate management clearly seem to be more geographically concentrated than production activities in general. [5] The level of coordination and integration in MNEs is affected by the length of time the acquired affiliate has been part of the parent corporation and the process of corporate coordination and integration tends to spread out over time, with business linkages becoming stronger as an effect of steady processes of organisational adjustment. Coordination and integration build upon interactive learning and past experiences. Liberalization and increasing cross-border economic activity associated with globalisation are unalterable and accordingly have changed the 'rules of the game' which means that MNEs have to follow.

Foreign affiliates gradually and successfully learn from their business environments. Moreover, the coordination and integration process evolves over time strengthening the business linkages as a result of gradual organisational adjustments and interactive learning processes. Besides, a marked cultural distance between two countries has a negative effect on the establishment of foreign affiliates. The integration of technology between companies constantly involves the transfer of technical skills that are dependent and embedded in individuals and teams. The transfer of technology comes up against differences in values, norms, beliefs and other taken-for-granted ways of behaviour that direct individuals towards their definite objectives. The integration of the technology of acquired affiliates in MNEs tends to be greater, the larger the affiliates while smaller affiliates tend to be less integrated[6]. The attractiveness of FDI is to promote the integration of the global economy via capital mobility, technology and the transfer of management expertise[7].

---

[5] Baldwin R. and A. J. Venables (1996) "Regional Economic Integration". In Handbook of International Trade, Vol. III. Amsterdam: North-Holland.

[6] Papanastassiou,M.(1999).Technology and production strategies of multinational enterprise (MNE) subsidiaries in Europe. International Business Review, 8, 213. Dunning,J.H.(1997). Alliance capitalism and global business. London: Routledge.

[7] Georgiou, G.C., Weinhold, S., 1992. Japanese direct investment in the US. The World Economy 15, 761-778.

Network-based conceptions of the multinational have associated international growth and maturity with upgraded capabilities of foreign subsidiaries, enhanced horizontal communication across national borders, as well as the systematic utilization of knowledge from several organizational bases. Increasingly, the focus has shifted from the strategic benefits of utilizing emerging resources in individual foreign subsidiaries towards advantages associated with the continuous integration and sharing of knowledge within the multinational network. Moreover, international integration and sharing of knowledge requires significant commitments to foreign markets. The integration and sharing of knowledge is expected to result in considerably enhanced product offerings and completely new combinations of existing technologies. International duplication of technological capabilities can more and more be used as a unique advantage from multinationality. Traditional center–periphery relationships are disappearing in the MNE. Interdependence and integration initially involved cross-flows of materials and components, and is eventually suggested to provide a unique opportunity to integrate knowledge and re-combine technologies on an international basis[8].

The multinational enterprise has become increasingly able to utilize internationally dispersed technological capabilities to its advantage. So, the multinational enterprise can gain exclusive advantages from the international exchange of technological knowledge both across and within individual technologies. Globalisation and integration at the regional level is an irreversible trend. Besides, Marxist tradition argues that economic integration is a resolution to cope with contradictions of the capitalist world[9]. Expansion of markets is due from developments in science, in technology and its application in communication and transportation as the major cause that brought economic integration. The globalization of economic activity, which emerged as a latest incident, has provided incentives for restructuring the international operations of companies in several ways. Food MNEs in Europe pursued a competitive strategy analogous to those of established and sophisticated MNEs in other manufacturing sectors such as electronics and pharmaceuticals. The establishment of a multinational network of operations would involve taking into account the unique advantages of smaller countries.

Changes in socio-economic backgrounds increased market size and interdependence among countries, which resulted in the formation of major economic blocs[10]. Trade expands when transaction costs are insignificant compared to gains from international transactions. Participation into economic integration is determined by national interests and defined by the position of a country in the international system[11] while national interests are defined by domestic politics[12]. National politics is a reflection of domestic industrial and economic interests. If nongovernmental organizations (NGOs) or interests in international arena are established, monopolistic position of the government will be reduced. In fact, all countries and most industries are affected by globalisation either in a single or a number of

[8] Andersson, U., Forsgren, M., 1996. Subsidiary embeddedness and control in the multinational corporation. Int. Business Rev. 5(5), 487–508.

[9] Cocks, P.: Towards a Marxist Theory of European Integration, International Organization, Winter, 1980.

[10] Keohane, R., and Nye, J.: Power and Interdependence: World Politics in Transition. Little Brown & Company, Boston, 1977. Geoffreey, G.: The Transition to Economic and Monetary Union, in B. Eichengreen and J. Frieden, eds., Forging an Integrated Europe. The University of Michigan Press, Ann Arbor, MI, 1998.

[11] Waltz, K.: Theory of International Politics, Addison-Wesley, Reading, MA, 1979.

[12] Bulmer, S.: Domestic Politics and European Community Policy Making, Journal of Common Market Studies 21 (1983).

macroeconomic indicators. According to Junmo Kim [13] "each country and each industry in different groups would feature divergent performance outcomes". A greater interaction across countries by intensifying international knowledge spillovers may radically alter the dynamics of convergence across countries and, within countries, across regions.

An innovation contributes to a local economy, employing people who spend their money in the neighbourhood. Ideas travel further or faster than they would if confined to market dealings. Inventions generate noteworthy social benefits beyond those captured in a market transaction. Innovators capture only some percentage of the social value of their inventions. The social importance of innovations far exceeds the personal value. It is worth mentioning that spillovers[14]subsidy third parties including competitors and prospective competitors. Employees get hold of knowledge about innovative products and processes that they can put to use in another place[15]. Spillovers drive extra innovation and fields with noteworthy spillovers experience more and faster innovation than fields with smaller number spillovers[16]. In fact spillovers promote greater innovation. Companies in electronics and biotechnology/nanotechnology increase rather than decrease their R&D investment in the face of momentous intra-industry spillovers[17]. In innovation spillovers cannot be ignored. Regardless of the fact that spillovers do not always interfere with incentives to invest, they are taken into consideration in order to decide about the location of the company dealing with high quality of technology. If countries originally have various levels of productivity in the high-tech sector, their comparative performance depends on the intensity of knowledge spillovers. If these are low, the high-tech sector expands faster in the initially more productive country. The intensification of knowledge spillovers, due to more cross-country interaction, extensively alters the growth paths and knowledge spillovers bring convergence across regions that can competitively produce the high-tech goods. Specialization causes divergence in per capita income, because endogenous productivity improvements affect primarily the production of the high-tech sector and because after integration countries by and large specialize in the sector in which they have a comparative advantage. The speed of economic integration has increased and goods flow more easily across the globe than they used to do due to a combination of technological progress, which has lowered transport costs, and improvements in trade related service sectors, and trade liberalisation measures that certainly have been quite extensive[18]. Globalisation is not a panacea for development and the macroeconomic policies must be right as well as the institutions supporting the economy because excessive corruption, poor policies or poorly implemented policies will negate the

[13] Junmo Kim, Economic Integration of Major Industrialized Areas: An Empirical Tracking of the Continued Trend, Technological Forecasting and Social Change 67, 187–202 (2001), p201.

[14] Brett M. Frischmann & Mark A. Lemley SPILLOVERS, 2007 COLUMBIA LAW REVIEW 257

[15] Holger G¨org & Alexander Hijzen, Multinational Enterprises and Spillovers, *in* Globalisation and Productivity Growth 92, 92–93 (Holger G¨ org et al. eds., 2005) (noting ways in which spillovers to competitors occur)

[16] Dietmar Harhoff, R&D Spillovers, Technological Proximity, and Productivity Growth—Evidence from German Panel Data, 52 Schmalenbach Bus. Rev. 238, 258 (2000) ("High-technology firms react more sensitively to spillovers in terms of their R&D spending, and their direct marginal productivity gain from spillovers (in excess to the effect from enhanced R&D spending) is considerably larger than the respective gain for less technology-oriented firms.").

[17] Zoltan J. Acs et al., The Knowledge Spillover Theory of Entrepreneurship 23 (Ctr. for Econ. Policy Research, Discussion Paper No. 5326, 2005).

[18] Arne Bigsten and Dick Durevall, Is Globalisation Good for Africa? 2002 Working Papers in Economics no 67 Göteborg University

effect of attempts to open up and integrate in the world economy. Economic success in a globalised world is dependent on policies that respect the constraints imposed by markets[19].

According to Sanjaya Lall and Rajneesh Narula[20] "MNEs and FDI may well lead to an increase in productivity and exports, but they do not necessarily result in increased competitiveness of the domestic sector or increased industrial capacity, which ultimately determines economic growth in the long run. FDI per se does not provide growth opportunities unless a domestic industrial sector exists which has the necessary technological capacity to profit from the externalities from MNE activity. This is well illustrated by the inability of many Asian countries that have relied on a passive FDI-dependent strategy to upgrade their industrial development." The rapid spreading out of trade in services has been accompanied by fast-growing trade in intermediate inputs. There is a growing division of production, in which MNEs play a key role. Technological alteration, such as computer-aided design and computer-aided manufacturing, contributed to division of production. Additionally technological changes contributed to growing outsourcing within and across national borders. An organized relationship exists between the characteristics of business companies and their taking part in foreign trade and investment. According to Elhanan Helpman[21] "there is heterogeneity as a result of productivity differences across firms within industries, because some firms happen to be luckier than others. Second, there is heterogeneity in organizational form. The two are related, however, because differences in productivity induce different choices for the organization of production and distribution. In this theory, trade and FDI patterns are jointly determined with organizational structures, such as sourcing and integration strategies."

The classification of FDI into vertical and horizontal forms has become less important in practice for the reason that large multinationals invest in low-cost countries to start export platforms from which they serve other countries around the world, and the sizeable flows of FDI across developed countries cannot be classified as horizontal FDI[22]. Productivity spillover effects take place from capital and technology flows from the foreign MNEs, providing an important vehicle by which the local economy and home companies can profit from FDI. Spillovers take place when home companies develop their competence by working directly or indirectly with MNEs. For this reason, spillovers can take the form of both horizontal spillovers when home companies benefit from the presence of foreign companies in their sector and vertical spillovers which refer to productivity spillovers taking place due to linkages between foreign companies and their home suppliers.

MNEs help to advance quality standards and provide access to foreign markets, as well as to highly skilled labour. MNEs act as vital catalysts for new business establishment in the IT

---

[19] Coe, D., Helpman, E., Hoffmaister, A. (1999), "North-South R&D Spillovers", Economic Journal 107. Esfahani, H.S. (2000), "Institutions and Government Controls", Journal of Development Economics 63:197-329. Rodrik, D. (2000), "Institutions for High-Quality Growth: What they are and How They Acquire Them", NBER Working Paper No 7540, Cambridge Mass. Subramanian, A., Tamirisa, N. (2001), "Africa's Trade Revisited", IMF Working Paper WP/01/33, Washington DC.

[20] Sanjaya Lall and Rajneesh Narula, Foreign Direct Investment and its Role in Economic Development: Do We Need a New Agenda? The European Journal of Development Research, Vol.16, No.3, Autumn 2004, pp.447–464, p 461.

[21] Elhanan Helpman, TRADE, FDI, AND THE ORGANIZATION OF FIRMS, NBER Working Paper 12091 p41.

[22] Eaton, Jonathan, Samuel Kortum and Francis Kramarz (2004), "Dissecting Trade: Firms, Industries, and Export Destination," American Economic Review (Papers and Proceedings) 94, pp. 150-154.

sector[23]. The education acquired from dealing with a large MNE offers the prospect for developing an improved working relationship; learning about distribution of networks, payment cycles and doing business internationally[24]. It has to be taken into account that there is a visible lack of willingness on the part of MNEs to engage energetically with the home business and community sectors. MNEs provide at best only medium and low support for local suppliers, education programmes and local community initiatives.

A central source of the MNE's energetic institutional superiority arises from its competence to pull out rents from other major stakeholders such as states and workers through increasing bargaining power all the way through globalization over these groups. Regulation is the tool applied by governments to imperfect markets in order to reproduce price and output that would otherwise take place under competitive conditions and the original remit of regulation was the supervision and control of economic activities in order to put right market failure[25]. Regulation has evolved into a means of enabling politicians to reshuffle monopoly profits in line with perceptions of "fair" price whereas avoiding the call for transparency and accountability that accompanies acts of taxation/subsidization[26]. The allocation of benefits between the MNE and the host country is dependent on the result of negotiations, which are biased in favour of the stronger negotiator, which tends to be the MNE[27].

International and home initiatives have introduced a more competitive global environment across all sectors and accordingly all economies are exposed to irresponsible, profit motivated, behaviour of international business and needs to be protected. FDI plays a momentous role in the move of CEE economies and in order to maximize the advantages of inward investment it is decisive for the governments of these countries to estimate the character of such investment. Home industries in CEE countries have to be restructured to make certain that they are competitive to develop the spillovers from the primary investment. Home companies should be encouraged to reach considerable degrees of independence from their foreign partner in order to achieve the maximum possible gain from the inward investment. Neither the laissez-faire recipe, consisting in the removal of constraints to the free working of market forces on an international scale, nor the acceptance of wholly defensive policies in opposition to globalization, are adequate for the reason that it is not realistic to interrupt the process, create the appropriate institutions, and then restart the process in a way that is more hospitable with the development of the industrial systems involved.

---

23 Cope, J. (2003), "Entrepreneurial learning and critical reflections: discontinuous events as triggers for 'higher-level' learning", Management Learning, Vol. 34 No. 4, pp. 429-50.

24 Blomstro¨ m, M. and Kokko, A. (1998), "Multinational corporations and spillovers", Journal of Economic Surveys, Vol. 12 No. 3, pp. 247-77.

25 Annett, A. (2001), "Social fractionalization, political instability, and the size of government", IMF Staff Papers, Vol. 48 No. 3.

26 Calzolari, G. (2001), "The theory and practice of regulation with multinational enterprises", Journal of Regulatory Economics, Vol. 2, pp. 191-211.

27 Littlechild, S. (2000), Privatisation, Competition and Regulation, The Institute of Economic Affairs, London.

3.2 MNE and Regional Integration

MNEs have the capacity to bypass the market, which is relied upon to determine the effects of integration on resource allocation. Regional and corporate integration both seek to overcome forms of market failure. Concerning regional integration the primary motivation is to reduce the allocative and efficiency costs of market distortions induced by national policies. MNE avoid the transaction costs of using markets to organize particular activities by internalising intermediate product markets. In other words, the enterprise can reduce the allocative and efficiency costs of distortions produced by public policies in the context of its global operations. The operation of MNEs involves intra-firm trade and the creation of internal markets for goods and factors.

A MNEs ownership links, which generate economies in transaction costs and benefits from co-ordination, do not themselves significantly affect the locational distribution of its physical production activities or the scale of its plants. The international location of production should not impede the attainment of the pattern indicated by considerations of regional cost minimization[28]. Patterns of oligopolistic rivalry among MNEs do affect their investment decisions. MNEs seek to preserve a balance of interest vis-à-vis their rivals, it appears that their investment in production facilitates may not serve to minimize the costs of production. In situation of oligopoly it is difficult if not impossible to make a priori predictions about the impact of MNEs in the context of integration. Predictions of the effects of the trade policy on the behaviour of MNEs in oligopolistic situations are sensitive to the assumptions and a multiplicity of outcomes is possible.

How a decision on FDI on the part of a MNE is affected by integration? Dunning argues that the propensity of a firm to undertake foreign production depends on the combination of the following three factors: 1. Its ownership- specific advantages in the form of proprietary intangible assets vis-à-vis its actual or potential rivals. 2. Its locational advantages in the foreign market. 3. Internationalisation opportunities that derive essentially from market failure. FDI will be the chosen option only if the firm can exploit all the advantages at the same time. Integration brings changes that enhance the locational advantages of production inside the regionally integrated area vis-a vis third countries for both domestic and foreign MNEs, giving rise to increased FDI altering the relative competitiveness of countries within the bloc and so affecting both the intra-bloc location of inward FDI and that of intra-bloc FDI itself. Kindleberger[29] refers to investment creation and investment diversion characterising the response of foreign MNEs to regional economic integration. Investment creation is the expanded FDI that is generated by trade diversion. It should be taken into account that new plants established inside the common market by outsiders to serve the market that would otherwise be cut off by tariffs and non-tariff barriers. Trade creation provides opportunities for a reorganization of production within the common market to take advantage of scale economies and specialization. Investment diversion describes the effects of trade creation on already established foreign MNEs.

---

[28] J Buckley, M Casson "The future of the multinational enterprise" 1976 Macmillan. R Caves "Multinational Enterprise and Economic Analysis", 1982, Cambridge University Press. F Kindleberger "European Integration and the national corporation" 1966 Columbia Journal of World Business 65.

[29] C Kindleberger, 1970, The international corporation, MIT Press.

What are the effects of economic integration with the strategic responses of enterprises that are engaged in international production? Yanopoulos identifies four types of investment responses: defensive import-substituting investment; reorganization investment; rationalized investment and offensive import-substituting investment. Each of these responses represents different strategic responses to economic integration[30]. Defensive import-substituting investment represents a company's attempt to maintain its market share in the bloc by shifting from a trade-based to an investment' based strategy. Re-organisation investment encourages a reallocation of activity according to competitive advantage. The elimination of trade barriers within a bloc should reduce production costs inside the area making it a more attractive place for international sourcing by MNEs. Rationalised investment is a response to international differences in production costs. The effects of integration on efficiency growth and innovation give rise to offensive import-substituting investment or export-oriented investment to take advantage of new markets. Thus, rationalised and reorganization investment encourage trade. Finally, each of the different strategies has an effect on the level of FDI into the country or region as well as on the intra-bloc distribution of investment. In the early stages of operating in host environments, MNE competitive advantage is based on factors such as superior technology and products, which produce direct social as well as proprietary benefits, or positive-sum effects. Nevertheless, once competitive advantage is achieved, MNEs tend to modify their emphasis to protecting their market positions through the exercise of market power and bargaining leverage which keep on to create proprietary benefits but can have negative social consequences.

What is the impact of inward FDI undertaken for the purpose of sourcing domestic technology? The extent and character of a MNEs investment responses to integration depends not only on the impact of integration on OLI advantages that rest on efficiency considerations but significantly on its impact on those that are related to strategic behaviour proper. Cost, demand and production data are factors that have to be taken into consideration in predicting ex ante the effects of integration or in ex post evaluation. The goals and policies of regional blocs and activities of MNEs are interactive and dynamic and concerned not merely with economic efficiency and growth but also with political and cultural aims.[31] Thus, economic goals of regional economic integration are the generation of static efficiency gains by rationalization and to promote dynamic efficiency and growth and international competitiveness by improving technological and entrepreneurial capacity. The economic characteristics of the bloc and its economic weight are important since they determine its attractiveness as a location for trans-border investment and so the bargaining power of the bloc. The distribution of the gains from rationalization-induced FDI inflows between group and non-group actors may need to be addressed if they have implications for the distribution of rents and for the dynamic competitive efficiency of the bloc. Limiting inward investment undertaken for technology sourcing may have a favourable effect on growth.[32] Specific policy intervention is needed in order to balance the ability of MNEs to circumvent through internalisation the constraints of macroeconomic, financial or other policies. MNEs as such have never been subjected to policy regulation. Offensive asset seeking investment and investment motivated by rationalization can both be expected to increase. As mentioned above, apart from mergers and acquisitions, an important element of the response of MNEs to

[30] G Yanopoulos "FDI and European Integration" 1990 Journal of Common Market Studies 235.

[31] M Panic "The Impact of multinationals on national economic polisy" Multinationals and Europe 1991 Routledge p 204-22.

[32] D Neven, G Siotis "FDI in the European Community: Some policy Issues" 1993 Oxford Review of Economic Policy 72.

integration was their resort to cross-border strategic alliances as affording a more flexible, less costly, risk-reducing alternative. The decrease of trade and capital transfer barriers, the new potential offered by information technologies, the reduction of transport costs, the improved infrastructure and educational standards in many countries of the world make possible a high mobility of capital and investments permitting MNEs to generate supply chains on a global basis or reallocate resources within a short period of time. Capital seeks out the cheapest offers of factors of production and so MNEs are slowly distancing themselves from the regulatory limits of individual countries, without a sufficient legal system being established at a universal level.

Chapter 4

The Impact of MNEs

4.1 Location of MNE

Economic activities are unevenly distributed across space. The location of production firmly depends on the contrast between centripetal-local supply, home-market size- and centrifugal -immobile factors include land and natural resources, but, in an international setting, even people, the lack of international labour migration, spatially-dispersed factors create dispersed markets encouraging firms to establish the production near their customers-forces which in turn determines whether a country/region can experience industrial agglomeration[1]. As long as trade costs remain high, entrepreneurs organize production in various countries/regions in order to service detached local markets but as economic integration is intensified companies tend to agglomerate[2].

Economic integration, factor mobility, and rapid developments in transportation and communications technologies perform essential part in MNEs expansion policies. The location of MNE investments is bit by bit becoming the most central organizational consideration of the MNE. For regional economics, the foremost question is to understand and foretell the MNE's decisions concerning its desired spatial composition of activities requiring the development of a sound location theory of the MNE. The management analysis of MNE location behavior provides critical challenges as to how economic geographers and provincial scientists judge the predicament of industrial location.

For the MNE the magnetism of some locations lies in the fact that they can provide the MNE with important assets in the form of good infrastructure, both physical such as transport and communication links and human such as well trained work force and an efficient labor market. Country level differences in labor market institutions result in free trade location patterns that are unfavorable for home interests, compared to a state of affairs with fixed company locations inducing home governments to make use of import tariffs as a means to influence companies' private location decisions and to expand home interests compared to

---

[1] Davis, D.R. and D.E. Weinstein, 1999, 'Economic Geography and Regional Production Structure: an Empirical Investigation', European Economic Review, Vol. 43.

[2] Amiti, M., 1998, 'New Trade Theories and Industrial Location in the EU: a Survey of Evidence', Oxford Review of Economic Policy, Vol. 14, N° 2.

free trade. According to David Collie and Hylke Vandenbussche[3] "the presence of unions in the domestic country is what drives the domestic government to use optimal trade policy. The reason is that if a domestic firm decides to move abroad to serve the domestic market from a distance, this decision results in the loss of domestic jobs and wages. Only when the repatriated profits from moving abroad are large enough to compensate the domestic country for the loss in union rent, the home government will not intervene. But in many cases moving abroad, while profitable for the domestic firm involved, reduces welfare for the domestic country as a whole. In that case, an import tariff used by the home government to dissuade its firm from moving abroad raises home welfare."

Cluster may be defined as a geographic concentration of competitive companies in the same industry that either has close supplier-customer relationships with other industries in the county, use common technologies, or share a specific labor group that provides companies with a competitive lead over the same industry in other places.

The potential contributions of FDI to both promoting the levels of, and shaping the patterns of, home and provincial economic development, are becoming ever more important. The policy responses of regional and home authorities to FDI development opportunities are becoming an ever more fundamental determinant of economic outcomes.

MNEs operate in a tentative environment in which it has to constantly tackle the "market versus hierarchy" dilemma. A MNE has to decide whether to synchronize multifaceted production and supply activities largely via market mechanisms or via an internally planned organizational and decision-making system. A consideration of the organizational formation of the MNE under a mixture of conditions, and the relationship between the organizational structure of the MNE, the information "internalization" behavior of the MNE, and the location behavior of the MNE have to be taken into account in deciding the location. All location decisions for MNEs are organizational and informational decisions, and the MNE as a matter of fact has to make organizational decisions in tandem with location decisions. In order to analyze the MNE location problem, it is required to bear in mind both the organizational and locational choices together[4]. The location decision is a multifaceted one, since it subsumes within it decisions regarding the mode of entry whether the FDI is implemented through an acquisition or a greenfield' investment or joint venture and the industry of entry whether the FDI occurs in the central line of business of the parent MNE or represents a diversification away from this business.

Companies primarily establish themselves in a foreign market through exporting which is an entry strategy representing a low risk entry mode but it offers modest control mechanism if market conditions change. Greenfield investment by setting up a new plant or the acquisition of an established company in the foreign market represents favorable foreign direct investment alternatives. There exists an apparent global trend of cross-border M&A as a preferred market entry strategy driving the expansion in foreign direct investment. Foreign direct investment in form of greenfield' investment becomes appealing for companies to spread out in underdeveloped countries. Companies with sound organizational skills choose takeovers, while companies with sound technological skills favor greenfield operations. Takeovers turn out to be more common because of increasing instability and uncertainty.

[3] David Collie and Hylke Vandenbussche, Can Import Tariffs Deter Outward FDI?, Open economies review 16: 341–362, 2005,p 360.

[4] Porter, M.E. 1998. Clusters and the new economics of competition. Harvard Business Review 76(6): 77-90.

Greenfield investments are principally attracted by interregional distribution of local manufacturing. A company's dedication to invest into a new market is associated with costs which cannot be recovered once the project is initiated. FDI decisions are investment decisions under uncertainty and are the first commitment of subsequent expansion. A MNE permits the transfer of resources and activities internationally. The option of entry mode not only depends on the linked extra costs but also on the uncertainty surrounding the venture. According to Bernard Michael Gilroy and Elmar Lukas[5] "foreign direct investment may emerge as the initially preferred strategy given low levels of uncertainty".

MNEs operated by predominantly creating new products and processes in their home markets and then afterward adapted these for use in foreign markets. The MNE grows large in its home markets ahead of turning to international activity beginning with exports. There is rising growth in the amount of FDI, which can be described as "export platform", where a MNE exports most of its production so that the home market in the host country is of no meaning to its location decision. The export-platform FDI (EPFDI) has a home country point of reference -output exported back to the home country-, a third-country direction -output exported to destinations other than the home country- or a global course -output exported to home and third countries. The international division of production associated with globalization /new technologies and the promotion of this nature of investment by particular economies as part of their economic development strategies are the elements for the increasing importance of EPFDI.

As the volume of foreign sales grows, the MNE responds by increasing the scale of its conduct in the foreign market, in due course replacing exports with home value making like manufacture. This change is accompanied by the MNE moving to take control of activities in the foreign market by, for instance, the setting up of wholly owned subsidiaries. The MNE as a network enterprise is perceived to be uniquely positioned to bring together the activities of various subsidiaries in a manner which gives it forceful advantages. Whereas the traditional subsidiary exploited the technological advantages of its parent MNE, more and more modern subsidiaries now acquire competencies of their own that can be leveraged to advantage right the way through the total MNE network. This implies that competencies created in one location can be used in another, subsequently that there may be a multi-directional current of information and goods between more or less self-ruling subsidiaries. MNEs have to adopt more high-level means of coordination so as to persistently sustain their home and global knowledge advantage.

A company going transnational must own a pack of "intangible assets" such as technology, product differentiation, management know-how, marketing and selling skills. These resources, which exist on account of market imperfections and entry barriers, capitulate a rent to the company competent of meeting the cost of "foreignness" associated with overseas production and present an edge over home and third-country companies in particular markets. It has to be taken into account that the cost of "foreignness" includes the cost involved in collecting information on foreign market surroundings such as consumer preferences and competitors, regulations and other institutional frameworks underlying the

[5] Bernard Michael Gilroy, Elmar Lukas, The choice between greenfield investment and cross-border acquisition: A real option approach, The Quarterly Review of Economics and Finance 46 (2006) 447–465 p 460.

market. Furthermore, it includes the extra cost of managing an enterprise from a distance rather than locally.

By the multinational firms' ability to relocate activities to countries with lower wages, the home countries may become more exposed to factor price adjustment in terms of falling relative wages. Relocations across locations may thus have significant impact on the overall welfare and income distribution of the countries in which the multinational firms operate. There is a complementary relationship between employment in the domestic and foreign parts of the firm as well. Even in the case where a firm locates a production plant abroad simply to supply a foreign market from a foreign subsidiary, some complementary activities such as headquarter activities will be undertaken at home. How different types of activity are dispersed within firms, and the role of multinational corporations MNEs in shifting the geographical division of labour? A firm with production units in several locations that only seeks to minimise production costs will choose to produce wherever it is least costly to do so. If there is a relocation of production, this is likely to affect production costs in units not directly affected by this relocation. Thus, if the foreign plants serve the parent firm with components that are assembled at home, costs will increase in the parent firm as well, which in turn has a negative effect on product demand. If the parent firm instead exports components to the foreign plants, demand for components will decrease, with a similarly negative effect on labour demand in the home firm. Higher trade costs associated with trade with low-income countries offset the potential gains from lower production costs so that the extent of vertical decomposition is larger between affiliates in different high-income locations than between affiliates in high-and low-income locations.[6] Hence, employment in different parts of a firm seems to be linked through a relationship of complementarity rather than substitution. The motives for establishing R&D units abroad are very much driven by learning from technological excellence and lead markets and dynamic interactions between R&D, marketing and advanced manufacturing. The attractiveness of the European Union will be more and more determined by 'dynamic efficiency', the ability to support learning processes in complex system innovations, and the interaction of specific institutions firms. The process of internationalisation in research, product development and market introduction has been accompanied by a more and more selective focus on a very few R&D locations and the concentration of innovation activities at so-called first-class centers. The intensification of global competition increases the importance of the role of regional conditions. The efficiency and effectiveness of administrative processes in policy-making and the establishment of lateral structures and coordination mechanisms between the different policy areas are becoming decisive factors for the 'absorptive capacity'. The absorptive capacities of large and above all small enterprises, as well as of public R&D institutions within the Community are decisive for innovativeness and competitiveness. [7]

---

[6] Blomström, M., G. Fors and R. E. Lipsey (1997), "Foreign Direct Investment and Employment: Home Country Experience in the United States and Sweden", Economic Journal, 107, 1787-1797. Braunerhjelm, P. and K. Ekholm (eds.) (1998) The Geography of Multinational Firms, Boston: Kluwer Academic Publishers. Feenstra, R. C and G. H. Hanson (1996), "Globalization, Outsourcing, and Wage Inequality", American Economic Review, 86, 240-245. Markusen, J. R (1995), "The Boundaries of Multinational Enterprises and the Theory of International Trade", Journal of Economic Perspectives, 9, 169-189.

[7] Cantwell, J.A., 1995. The globalization of technology: what re-mains of the product cycle model?. Cambridge Journal of Economics 19, 155–174. Archibugi, D., Michie, J., 1995. The globalization of technology: a new taxonomy. Cambridge Journal of Economics 19, 121–140. OECD, 1998.

What is the impact of MNEs on the location and characteristics of innovatory capabilities across national boundaries within Europe? According to industry structure view[8] a company's performance is primarily determined by the structural conditions of the industry in which the company competes, while the resource-based view of the firm[9] argues that the resources and capabilities of the individual companies are the main determinant of firm performance. The role of country conditions as a determinant of firm performance is particularly important to MNEs[10]. Selecting country markets for entry and investment and evaluating the performance of their country subsidiaries are two basic problems that MNEs face. The structural conditions of the industry determine the management of firms within the industry, which in turn determines firm performance. Market position and resources and capabilities are the most important determinants of performance, which implies that intra-industry differences in firm performance exist. Corporate effects add to business unit performance by providing economies associated with resource sharing, and by the capability to transfer rent-creating resources among the business units[11]. A MNE's capacity of picking the right countries for entry and investment should lead to significant competitive advantage, which means that strategic choice at the corporate level is very important for corporate performance. MNEs may pursue various strategies towards the international organisation of their technological activity.

Geographical proximity is important to the extent to which various lines of innovative activity influence one another, because of the existence of knowledge spillovers that are geographically bounded[12]. Innovation is expected to concentrate geographically in areas that provide agglomeration economies that increase and smooth the progress of the innovation process. Countries that hold concentrations of innovative inputs in some field of production will develop a comparative advantage in the industries in question. Moreover, leading countries or regions in any field or international centres of excellence in research and innovation incline to maintain their position over time. The transmission of information about production costs becomes crucial where there is strategic interaction between the companies of different countries. In case information about costs is incomplete, the location of a plant will be chosen not only for its impact on actual production costs, but also for its impact on the perception of costs as held by foreign rivals[13]. So, the informational role of plant location decision is a vital element in understanding the behaviour of a MNE.

Transparency and accountability towards the range of stakeholders in business – including employees, customers, suppliers, shareholders, local communities, society at large and the environment – are both a standard that is expected, and a mechanism for securing

---

Globalization of Industrial R&D: Policy Implications. Working Group on Innovation and Technology Policy, June 1998. Reger, G., 1999. How R&D is coordinated in Japanese and European multinationals. R&D Management 29 1, 1999.

8 Porter, M.E., 1980. Competitive Strategy. Free Press: New York.

9 Wernerfelt, B., 1984. A resource-based view of the firm. Strategic Management Journal 5, 171–180.

10 Petra Christmann , Diana Day , George S. Yip, The relative influence of country conditions, industry structure, and business strategy on multinational corporation subsidiary performance, Journal of International Management 5 (1999) 241–265.

11 Collis, D.J., Montgomery, C.A., 1998. Creating corporate advantage. Harvard Business Review 76, 70–83.

12 Feldman, M.P., 1993. An examination of the geography of innovation. Industrial and Corporate Change 2 3, 451–470.

13 K. Bagwell, R Staiger, Informational aspects of fopreign direct investment and the multinational firm, 2003 Japan and the World Economy 1-20.

compliance with codes of conduct designed to meet society's expectations.[14] Direct inward investment by MNEs has long been regarded as bringing significant net benefits to industrialised economies. As mentioned above, MNE manages to control the activities, roles and strategies of its foreign subsidiaries but this control aspect cannot be taken for granted, especially in complex, competitive industries with rapidly changing business environments. The affiliate that becomes over-embedded in its national environment may be viewed as 'captive' by HQ and thus loses authority within the organisation and may be cut off from future developments or flows of strategic resources and knowledge. The degree of autonomy is related to MNE philosophy and perceptions of the local environment. MNE. Higher levels of local decision-making power facilitated the formation of locally-developed innovations and their diffusion through-out the international network. In addition, local autonomy did not in any way impede the acceptance of parent company innovations. The more rapidly growing and more worldwide integrated the MNE, the less may be the autonomy granted to the subsidiary. Increased decision-making power does not only emerge from aggressive bargaining with the parent but also local autonomy may be increasingly encouraged by escalating the capability of local R&D and the quantity of local materials that go into the subsidiary's product. High-autonomy firms are much more export-oriented and carry out notably more complex R&D locally.[15] Important location-specific advantages motivating foreign direct investment (FDI) are these days related to the foreign- located created assets, such as technological know-how, that MNEs believe are necessary to complement their own "specific competencies.[16] To generate international competitive advantages through local technological linkages, MNEs need to manage their international units in a coordinated and integrated manner. Hence, this allows MNEs to combine geographically restricted resources and capabilities and to help expand international economies of scale and scope. Less hierarchical MNE networks have emerged, where flows of components, products, resources, and information runs vertically between parent- firms and their affiliates, as well as horizontally between sister affiliates in different countries. Affiliates increasingly operate as product line- regional-or functional headquarters[17].

---

[14] Ann M. Florini, Does the Invisible Hand Need a Transparent Glove? The Politics of Transparency. Paper prepared for the Annual World Bank Conference on Development Economics, Washington D.C., April 28-30 1999. Available at www.worldbank.org/research/abcde/papers.html

[15] Aylmer, R.J. (1970) Who makes marketing decisions in the multinational firm? Journal of Marketing Oct., 25–39. Bartlett, C. and Ghoshal, S. (1986) Tap your subsidiaries for global reach. Harvard Business Review Nov–Dec., 87–94. Birkinshaw, J.M. and Morrison, A.J. (1995) Configurations of strategy and structure in subsidiaries of multinational corporations. Journal of International Business Studies 26, 729–754. Doz, Y.L. (1986) Strategic Management in Multinational Companies. Pergamon Press, Oxford. Garnier, G.H. (1982) Context and decision making autonomy in the foreign affiliates of U.S. multinational corporations. Academy of Management Journal 25, 893–908. Gates, S.R. and Egelhoff, W.G. (1986) Centralization in headquarters – subsidiary relationships. Journal of International Business Studies Summer, 71–92. Kim, W.C. and Mauborgne, R.A. (1991) Implementing global strategies: the role of procedural justice. Strategic Management Journal 12, 125–143. Porter, M.E. (1990) Competitive Advantage of Nations. Free Press, New York. Taggart, J.H. (1997) An evaluation of the integration responsiveness framework: MNE manufacturing subsidiaries in the UK. Management International Review 37, 295–318. Young, S., Hood, N. and Dunlop, S. (1988) Global strategies, multinational subsidiary roles and economic impact in Scotland. Regional Studies 22, 487–497.

[16] Gassman,O.,&Von Zedtwitz,M.(1998).Organization of industrial R&D on a global scale .R &D Management ,28 (3),147 .

[17] UNCTAD.(1993).World Investment Report. Transnational corporations and integrated international production .New York: United Nations.

Increased freedom of trade and the emergence of many strong new MNEs let to an intensified and globalised competitiveness in the market place for existing standardised products and so have had a crucial influence on the strategic evolution of MNEs. The value of acquiring inputs into the creative process of a MNE from several locations is recognised. Various countries demonstrate their uniqueness as sources of original technology and significant market trends. As a result, a new kind of subsidiary has emerged which helps the MNE to tap into, and activate, these disseminated knowledge sources, as part of the group's wider creative programmes. Subsidiaries are expected to contribute to the growth of the core of knowledge available to the MNE and, more directly, to a significant and individualised extension of the group's product range. A subsidiary's ability to increase value-added based scope around its own technology can take it through an increased autonomy[18]. The emergence of the technological-creativity-based independence at the subsidiary level provides enormous potentials for MNEs. Localised R&D is expected to be a crucial element in the ways that creative subsidiaries assert their individualised position within the group's technological scope. Additionally, collaborative R&D arrangements with independent local enterprises provide an equally relevant, but externalised, means of benefiting from the host-country's knowledge heritage and research scope[19].

The distinctive technological capability of an individual subsidiary should be seen as an expression of the location-specific advantages of the host country as implemented, within the existing technological course of the MNE's overall operations[20]. The subsidiaries' view of their own progress will remain within the probable expected scope of the group. May the MNE group's overall technological trajectory be widened or reformulated, according to the ideas and capacities of individual subsidiaries? MNE central management should determine the development of the group within the framework of the independent evolutionary scope of its key creative subsidiaries. A subsidiary may take responsibility for the creation of a product that derives from an idea, which either emerges within the subsidiary itself, or is acquired from elsewhere in the group. If the global market for a product becomes exceptionally large and dispersed, the forces that lead to overseas production normally in MNEs may point towards the implementation of some decentralised supply.

Moreover, if full development of a product idea needs enhancement of the technological background through more applied research work, which exceeds the scope of the R&D resources possessed by the subsidiary itself, this may be subcontracted to another laboratory in the MNE group. Centrally organised R&D in the MNE group initially derives the outlines of an important new product concept[21]. Then, the most effective application of this new

[18] White, R. E., & Poynter, J. A. (1990). Organisation for world-wide advantage. In C. A. Bartlett, Y. Doz, & G. Hedlund, Managing the global firm (pp. 95–113). London: Routledge. Hedlund, G. (1993). Assumptions of hierarchy and heterarchy, with applications to the management of the multinational corporation. In S. Ghoshal, & D. E. Westney, Organisation theory and the multinational corporation (pp. 211–236). New York: St. Martin's Press. Hedlund, G., & Rolander, D. (1990). Action in heterarchies—new approaches to managing the MNE. In C. A. Bartlett, Y. Doz, & G. Hedlund, Managing the global firm (pp. 15–46). London: Routledge.

[19] Papanastassiou, M., & Pearce, R. D. (1994). The internationalisation of research and development by Japanese enterprises. R&D Management, 24(2), 155–165.

[20] Robert Pearce, The evolution of technology in multinational enterprises: the role of creative subsidiaries, International Business Review 8 (1999) 125–148.

[21] Taggart, J. H. (1996). Multinational manufacturing subsidiaries in Scotland: strategic role and economic impact. International Business Review, 5(5), 447–468. Taggart, J. H. (1997). US MNE affiliates in the

product concept requires that it be innovated promptly in each major national/regional market, and also in ways, which fully respond to the market needs and production conditions of each of these distinctive environments.

4.2 MNE and Home States

Services attract the largest share of direct investment outflows, though when measured against the GDP size of sector, manufacturing still remains the most important recipient. Additionally, the OECD code of conduct on MNEs represents a change in the attitude against MNE as antagonists to the national states and brings together the legitimate goals of both business and government in the conduct of FDI. The distribution of manufacturing FDI shows that it is increasingly being directed towards sophisticated manufacturing with high value added, like electronics and chemicals and away from investment in low value-added labour intensive industries like textiles clothing and food processing. Horizontally integrated focused investment strategies are increasingly the order of the day. MNE rely upon their "home base" as the center for their economic activities. Joint ventures, partnerships and strategic alliances are involved in interdependent international networks of business activity. Is it an advantage of the dominance of home country business activity over the activities of a MNE? The dominance of home country business activity is an advantage rather than a constraint on company overall performance. International businesses are largely confined to their home territory in terms of their overall business activity and remain nationally embedded.[22] Capital mobility and free trade will provoke a shift of manufacturing investment from the high-wage rich industrial countries to law-wage developing countries. Will this reduce employment in the rich countries? It will accelerate de-industrialisation without compensating advantages for them and at the same time will not bring the benefits of prosperity to the mass of workers in the developing countries. Wages will be hold down in third world and education will produce skilled and cheap labour forces. MNEs will use low-wage production to penetrate the domestic markets of the rich countries. Protectionism intensified the political economic competition of the major industrial powers, strengthening tendencies towards authoritarianism and imperialism in the weaker of them. Strategies of compensating for domestic economic crisis by political expansion were the direct result of a failure in the international economy.

It should be taken into account that FDI to the developing world is even in periods of peak flow, a tiny portion of the capital stock of the developed world. Since 1990 the net flow of investment has reduced the advanced countries' capital stock by 0,5 percent.[23] In both the advanced and developing countries alike the adoption of flexible manufacturing strategies will act against giving priority to low cost workers, who will enjoy competitive advantage only in unskilled handwork or in repetitive mass production where specialized and dedicated machinery can compensate for labour skill. The problem inhibiting further coordination at present is the divergent interests that still characterize an international economy where,

UK: a special relationship? In P. J. Buckley, M. Chapman, J. Clegg, & A. R. Cross, The Organisation of International Business. Proceedings of the Annual Conference of the UK Chapter of Academy of International Business. Leeds: C.I.B.U.L.

[22] R Reich " The work of nations " 1992, New York, Vintage.

[23] P Krugan "Does Third world growth hurt first world prosperity?" 1994 Harvard Business Review 113-121.

despite the claims of the globalisation effects, the major nation states of the developed countries and increasingly the emerging trading blocs are the dominant players.

Even though MNEs are strategic actors playing a role in the development of all of dimensions such as foreign direct investments, financial flows, national and supra-national governance of such processes, it may be very valuable to separate international production from other aspects of globalization because multinationals donate to powerful lobbying which repeatedly have a negative influence on political decisions at the national and supra-national levels. While the flows of inward and outward foreign direct investments correspond to a limited share of the gross world product -less than 5 per cent, as compared with the 40 per cent represented by the sum of import/export-, it is true that, in the last decade, they have grown at a rate more than double that of world trade[24]. MNEs engage in sizeable intra- and inter-company trade, and about a third of world trade is undertaken by MNEs whereas the contribution of MNEs to global production and commercialisation of goods and services appears to be even greater if one considers total sales of foreign affiliates, which have grown three times as fast as exports of foreign affiliates and even faster as compared to world trade. Moreover, MNEs are the unquestionable leaders in high technology production, as witnessed by the fact that more than one third of the top 100 multinational companies classified by the World Investment Report function in the electronics and chemical-pharmaceutical industries.

There is a great deal of increased uncertainty in the international economy relative to the stability of the period between 1950-1972. The political role of government is central in the new forms of economic management. National governments can still compensate for the effects of internationalisation and for the continued volatility of the financial markets, even if they cannot unilaterally control those effects or prevent that volatility. States are communities of fate, which tie together actors who share certain common interests in the success or failure of their national economies. Markets may or may not be international, but wealth and economic prosperity are still essentially national phenomena. National policy can provide certain key inputs to economic performance that cannot be bought or traded on the market. Markets need to be embedded in social relations. National governments remain a crucial element in the economic success of their societies.[25] The modern state is the possession of the monopoly of the means of violence within a given territory. Do governance and territory pull apart? Different agencies will control aspects of governance and some important activities will be ungoverned. The rise of the modern state, as a territorially specific and politically dominant power is depended on international agreements. States were perceived as the primary political communities, with the capacity to determine the status of and to make rules for any activity that fell within contemporary understandings of the scope of legitimate authority. Democratic sovereignty includes citizens and binds them through a common membership that is denied to others. It is worth mentioning that the nation state has ceased to be an effective economic manager. The state can only provide those social and public services international capital deems essential and at the lowest possible overhead cost. The EU represents an arena of potential stabilization for the international economy and fit its member countries. A more active practice of international management requires that the blocs will

---

[24] UNCTAD (2002), World Investment Report 2001: TNCs and Export Competitiveness, United Nations, Geneva.

[25] W Hutton "The state we're in" 1995 London. S Huntington "The clash of civilizations" 1993 Foreign Affairs Vol. 72 No3 P 22-49.

form into coherent managerial entities themselves. The gap between the potential for extended governance and the perception and policies of the major actors remains substantial. For instance, environmental concerns can better be addressed by diverting the revenue of growing and prosperous international economy than a stagnant one, which would be a real danger if widespread protectionism ensued. Protection of specific actors over definable periods may be justifiable at times, and this would be less damaging for sale individual economies in a world where trading blocks took responsibility for deciding that a relationship between them evolve. While national governments may no longer be "sovereign" economic regulators in the traditional sense, they remain political communities with extensive powers to influence and to sustain economic actors within their territories. Besides, the centralization of EU policy is promoting the increasing importance of effective regional government. Regional governments are more able to assess the needs of industry because they possess more localized information. Hence, regional government must be seen as a crucial component of national economic management.[26] Between blocs and within blocs there will be fundamental differences on the ability to respond to competitive pressures and changing international conjunctures.

Flexible forms of production can cope with shifting and volatile patterns of international demand. The new production strategies and the increasing importance of regional economies are a direct response to the internationalisation of markets in manufacturing goods and the complex and changing patterns of demand bought about by servicing diverse markets in a period of volatile trading conditions and uncertain growth.[27] Trade blocs represent a vital intermediate level between general institutionalised governance mechanisms for the world economy as a whole. The triad of the EU, Japan and NAFTA dominates the world's economy and it is likely to account for a majority share of the world manufacturing output, world trade and FDI. The triad could effectively control the direction of the world economy. In fact, the EU creates a common legal framework that enables all economic actors to operate with a measure of certainty throughout Europe. The new globalised economy allows companies and markets to allocate the factors of production to greatest advantage, and without the distortions of state intervention. As stated earlier, States have less exclusive control over the economic and social process within their territories and they are less able to maintain national distinctiveness and cultural homogeneity. There is a difference between a strictly global economy and a highly internationalised economy in which most companies trade from their bases in distinct national economies. A world economy with a high and growing degree of international trade and investment is not necessarily a globalized economy. Multinational enterprises are aware that consumption patterns and attitudes towards local and international brands have changed and that these changes need to be tracked constantly in the various markets[28]. Holger Gorg and Eric Strobl [29] "find that the presence of multinational companies has had a positive effect on the entry of indigenous firms". Moreover, Keith Head and John

[26] C Sabel "Flexible specialization and the Re-emergence of regional economies" in Hirst P Reversing Industrial Decline 1989 Oxford.

[27] Lloyd P "Regionalization and World Trade" 1992 OECD Economic Studies No 18 p 7-43.

[28] Thomas Tsu Wee Tan, Tan Jee Lui, Globalization and trends in international marketing research in Asia, Journal of Business Research 55 (2002) 799– 804

[29] Holger Gorg, Eric Strobl, Multinational companies and indigenous development: An empirical analysis, European Economic Review 46 (2002) 1305 –1322, p1320.

Ries [30] found that "The positive effect of FDI on domestic skill intensity, however, diminishes as investment shifts towards high-income countries. Increases in affiliate employment in low-income countries also raise a firm's reliance on finished goods purchases, suggesting that overseas employment affects domestic skill intensity because imports of final goods from foreign affiliates displace domestic production".

National governments compete to attract investments from MNEs, principally from enterprises that may generate positive spillover effects for national companies. Especially, multinationals are vital in industries characterized by a high value of intangible assets, a large share of professional and technical workers in their work force, and products that are new or technically complex. Companies benefit from spillovers from MNEs using more advanced technology. Movement of highly skilled staff from MNEs to domestic firms, national companies learning superior production techniques from MNEs (demonstration effect), and competition from MNEs forcing domestic rivals to update production technologies to become more productive are the main channels for spillovers. Productivity spillovers affect domestic firms with moderate technology gaps vis-a-vis foreign companies with at least some capability of being able to make use of spillover effects. National companies in the different countries where an MNE is localized differ with respect to characteristics that affect the magnitudes of spillover effects and productivity spillovers are higher in developed than in developing countries. It is characteristic that according to Krugman[31] 'knowledge flows . . . leave no paper trail by which they may be measured and tracked'. Foreign direct investments have been rapidly increasing and effective tax rates are central factors for determining the localisation decisions of MNEs[32].

4.3 Expansion of MNE

Market penetration decisions should align geographic concentration and market entry channel options with specific business strategies, goals, and objectives. Market expansion should be driven by a clear set of goals and objectives and a set of strategic directions for creating competitive advantage[33]. Product differentiation in particular industries does present some competitive advantage on outward-investing companies[34].

MNEs need to align their product or market focus based on strategic directions, the geographic focus of expansion, and the modes of entry into new markets[35]. International

[30] Keith Head, John Ries, Offshore production and skill upgrading by Japanese manufacturing firms, Journal of International Economics 58 (2002) 81–105

[31] Krugman, P.R., 1991. Geography and Trade. MIT Press, Cambridge, MA. p. 53

[32] Devereux, M.P., Freeman, H., 1995. The impact of tax on foreign direct investment: Empirical evidence and the implications for tax integration schemes. International Tax and Public Finance 2, 85–106.

[33] Fuchs, P.H., Mifflin, K.E., Miller, D. and Whitney, J.O. (2000) Strategic integration: competing in the age of capabilities. California Management Review 42, 118–147.Pennings, J.M. (1993) Executive reward systems: a cross-national comparison. Journal of Management Studies 30,261–280. Rondinelli, D.A. and Black, S.S. (2000) Multinational strategic alliances and acquisitions in Central and Eastern Europe: partnerships in privatization. Academy of Management Executive 14,85–98.

[34] Kumar, N. & Pradhan, J.P. (2003) Export Competitiveness in the Knowledge-based Industries: A Firm-level Analysis of Indian Manufacturing, RIS Discussion Paper, No. RIS-DP ~ 43/2003, New Delhi.

[35] Buckley, P.J. and Casson, M.C. (1998) Models of the multinational enterprise. Journal of International Business Studies 29,21–44.Buckley and Casson contend that global business expansion in many MNEs is driven by a dynamic agenda that is shaped by (1) uncertainty and market volatility; (2) flexibility and

expansion decisions are influenced by the aptitude of MNEs to discover locations for foreign direct investment based on their underlying strategic thrust[36]. Firms seeking to expand internationally must assess country market factors, develop an entry strategy, and then organize themselves properly to compete in those countries that have favourable market conditions. A company's abilities to organize separate activities that add value for customers depend on its power to align the diverse components of its value chain such as firm infrastructure, human resource management, technology development, and procurement. [37] Financing, human resource development and information technology become fundamental functions for the triumph of MNEs as they expand internationally[38]. Managerial alignment involves adjusting management practices to the cultural characteristics of the countries in which a firm operates. Cultural differences among countries are so momentous that management methods are entirely culture-bound.[39]

The geographical distribution of research investments is a much more recent phenomenon than the physical distribution of production aimed at achieving reduction in manufacturing and/or shipment costs[40]. Until recently, many companies, even if engaged in multinational manufacturing and marketing of their products, made use of centralized research facilities, conveniently located in order to get the best possible access to external knowledge sources, such as leading universities, public research centers, and competitors' spillovers. The advantage of carrying on R&D activities in many countries may therefore, under appropriate conditions, stem from the opportunity of capturing spillovers in a given place, being able to sell a customized product in another, and enjoying some public financial support in still another one. The higher R&D becomes, the better direct subsidies to R&D work as an attraction factor. [41]The geographical dispersion of technological capabilities is becoming an important addition to the overall internationalisation of the MNE. The internationalisation of advanced technological capabilities has been associated with improved elasticity and the formation of new innovation processes within the MNE.

Flexibility and the integration of internationally dispersed technological capabilities are thus presented as important ways of gaining power from internationally dispersed resources, and have been added to the established list of sequential advantages from multinationality. The growth and international expansion of technological capabilities in the MNE is intimately associated with accumulating international experience and escalating commitments to foreign

---

the value of real options; (3) the potential for cooperation through joint ventures and business networks; (4) entrepreneurship, managerial competence and corporate culture; and (5) organizational change, including the empowerment of subsidiaries and employees.

[36] Dunning, J.H. (1998) Location and the multinational enterprise: a neglected factor. Journal of International Business Studies 29,45–66.

[37] Chen, H. International performance of multinationals: a hybrid model. 1999 Journal of World Business 34, 157–170. Chen found that the market performance of MNEs depends on close alignment of marketing strategies and entry modes with corporate financial and physical resources.

[38] Bartlett, C.A. and Ghoshal, S. (1998) Managing Across Borders: The Transnational Solution. Harvard Business School Press, Boston.

[39] Pil, F.J. and MacDuffie, J.P. (1999) What makes transplants thrive?: managing the transfer of 'best practice' at Japanese auto plants in North America. Journal of World Business 34, 372–391.

[40] Levitt, T.: The Globalization of Markets, Harvard Business Review May–June, 92–102 (1983). Howells, J.: The Internationalization of R&Dand the Development of Global Research Networks, Regional Studies 24 (6), 495–512 (1990).

[41] Menzler-Hokkanen, I.: Multinational Enterprises and Technology Transfer, International Journal of Technology Management 10, 293–310 (1995).

markets[42], reinforced by the centrifugal forces which over time enhance technological activity among foreign units of the established multinational. The use of foreign acquisitions as a means of foreign entry and expansion has added 'instant embedded-ness' in local markets, introducing sophisticated technological resources that are predominantly responsive to local suppliers, buyers and related firms.[43]. The evolution of foreign technological capabilities depends on market conditions at the critical time of foreign expansion and firm-specific events like unexpected merger and acquisition opportunities. Additional influencing factors include management attitudes towards internationalisation, strategy and dispersion of technological capabilities[44], as well as the amount of operational and technological freedom granted to foreign affiliates[45]. Duplication of capabilities can allow for international knowledge exchange and the transfer of research projects within the multinational network. International diversification of technological capabilities is normally recognized as an increasingly important component of the multinational network.

On the prospect that foreign MNEs will increase employment, exports, or tax revenue, or that the knowledge brought by the foreign companies may spill over to the host country's national companies, governments across the world have lowered various entry barriers and opened up new sectors to foreign investment providing a mixture of forms of investment incentives to support foreign owned companies to invest in their jurisdiction including fiscal incentives such as lower taxes for foreign investors, financial incentives such as grants and preferential loans to MNEs, as well as measures like market preferences, infrastructure, and occasionally even monopoly rights. Global trade liberalization has made it easier for MNEs to set up international production networks, so that a larger share of output is shipped to international customers or affiliated companies in other countries rather than sold to local customers reducing the influence of market size and allowed smaller countries to compete for investments that would inevitably have been directed to the major markets some decades ago[46]. Regional integration has similar effects, allowing MNEs to supply all or several member states from a single location within the region and so incentives have also become more and more vital for national policymakers who are trying to support local production, employment, and welfare[47].

The effects of incentives are expected to be particularly strong in the competition for FDI within regions or even countries, when the primary investment decision has been taken and

---

[42] Johanson, J., Vahlne, J.-E., 1990. The mechanism of internationalization. International Marketing Review 7 4 , 11–24.

[43] Andersson, U., Johanson, J., Vahlne, J.-E., 1997. Organic acquisitions in the internationalization process of the business firm. Management International Review 37, 67–84. Zander, I., 1998. The evolution of technological capabilities in the multinational corporation—dispersion, duplication and potential advantages from multinationality. Research Policy 27, 17–35.

[44] Patel, P., Pavitt, K., 1997. The technological competencies of the world's largest firms: complex and path-dependent, but not much variety. Research Policy 26, 141–156.

[45] Behrman, J.N., Fischer, W.A., 1979. The coordination of foreign R&D activities by transnational corporations. Journal of Inter national Business Studies 10 3, 28–35. Behrman, J.N., Fischer, W.A., 1980. Overseas R&D of Transnational Companies. Oelgeschlager, Gunn and Hain Publishers, Cambridge, MA.

[46] Kathuria, V. (2000), Productivity Spillovers from Technology Transfer to Indian Manufacturing Firms, Journal of International Development, Vol. 12, pp. 343-369.

[47] Easson, A. (2001), Tax Incentives for Foreign Direct Investment Part 1: Recent Trends and Countertrends, Bulletin for International Fiscal Documentation, Vol. 55, 266-274, p272 "decisions that would not have been influenced by a mere two-year tax holiday may well be swayed by a 10-year holiday".

the investor is choosing between alternative locations in a given region. It should be taken into account that countries provide generous incentives without noteworthy inflows, because some other country has offered a more attractive investment package[48]. It is worth mentioning that when most countries compete aggressively for FDI, it is difficult for any individual country to stay out of bidding contests, which successfully shift profits from the host country to MNEs[49]. As a result, there is a trend to overbid and the subsidies may very well surpass the level of spillover benefits, with welfare losses accordingly. According to Magnus Blomström & Ari Kokko [50]"good governance in the area of FDI policy is to consider the investment incentive packages as part of the country's overall industrial policy, and make any incentives available on equal terms to all investors, foreign as well as local. The incentives should focus in particular on those activities that create the strongest potential for spillovers, including linkages between foreign and local firms, education, training, and R&D." Hence, by increasing the local supply of human capital and up to date infrastructure and by improving other essentials for economic growth, a country does not only become a more attractive site for MNEs, but there is increased possibility that its private sector benefits from the foreign participation through spillover benefits.

4.4 MNE and Subsidiaries

Subsidiaries within a MNE are not just the long-arm of the headquarters and they diverge in terms of history, contexts, capabilities and organizational roles. Subsidiaries are part of a MNE, which has its own objectives in establishing them, but the subsidiaries themselves have their own objectives that do not automatically coincide with the objectives of the MNE. Subsidiaries in the MNE have a strategic role in the organization that goes beyond the usual role of exploiting the parent company's firm-specific advantages. It is suggested that the performance of foreign subsidiaries is superior to that of domestic firms because of their possessions of firm-specific advantages in the MNE[51]. Tangible and intangible assets are deployed beneficially abroad after being developed domestically[52]. Subsidiaries are embedded in two different business networks: the corporate network consisting of relationships within the MNE and the external network comprised of relationships in the subsidiary's home market. The market performance is the performance in the market-place where the subsidiary competes with all other companies, while the organizational performance is the performance in the political process inside the MNE, where the subsidiary aims to affect strategic decisions

---

[48] Swenson, D.L. (1998), The Effect of U.S. State Tax and Investment Promotion Policy on the Distribution of Inward Investmentln, in R.E. Baldwin, R.E. Lipsey, and J.D. Richardson, eds., Geography and Ownership as Bases for Economic Accounting, Chicago: University of Chicago Press.

[49] Barros. P.P. and L. Cabral (2000), Competing for Foreign Direct Investment, Review of International Economics, Vol. 8, 360-371.

[50] Magnus Blomström & Ari Kokko, The Economics Of Foreign Direct Investment Incentives , Working Paper 168 January 2003, p21.

[51] Caves, R. E. (1982). Multinational enterprise and economic analysis. Cambridge: Cambridge University Press. March, J. G., & Sutton, R. I. (1997). Organizational performance as a dependent variable. Organization Science, 8 (6), 698–706. Nahapiet, J., & Ghoshal, S. (1998). Social capital, intellectual capital, and the organizational advantage. Academy of Management Review, 23 (2), 242–266.

[52] Dunning, J. H. (1988). The eclectic paradigm of international production: a restatement and some possible extensions. Journal of International Business Studies, 19 (2), 1–31.

of relevance to the subsidiary. A firm has exchanges with counterparts in its business network, but some exchanges are more embedded than others are in terms of mutual adaptation, trust and relation-specific investments. The more a certain relationship with a customer, supplier or some other counterpart has developed into a close relationship, the higher the possibility of a firm to gain new knowledge through exchange with this counterpart. Activity links between firms related to technology are influential factors behind the firms' capacity to absorb new technology from each other. The technological embeddedness of a subsidiary is crucial for its ability to acquire external knowledge about new technology.[53] A subsidiary's access to relationships with particular counterparts is significant for its absorptive capacity and, subsequently, for its performance in the market-place. There is a casual link between technology embeddedness and organizational performance, with the MNEs dependence on the focused subsidiary's resources, rather than its market performance, as an intermediate variable. The corporate headquarters' evaluation of the contribution of a subsidiary to the MNE's competitive advantage must include an analysis of the subsidiary's business relationships, and especially those, which are characterized by a high degree of embeddedness.[54]

The changes in the affairs between MNE subsidiaries and their parent network have been driven largely by the changes in the institutional and market environments in which MNEs work together with the changes in the ICTs which have primary afforded such modifications leading to alterations in the MNE arrange of decision-making and means of coordination. There is an increased call for strategic decision-making at the subsidiary level with the result that subsidiaries are now more profoundly involved at a much earlier stage in the MNE's innovation process requiring an increased level of collaboration between headquarters and subsidiaries[55].

It has to be taken into consideration that the competence-development path of the overseas subsidiary is not unavoidably in keeping with the former objectives of the home country parent organization leading to internal organizational tensions and conflicts. Competence will not always strengthen the subsidiary's rank within the MNE, and it could in reality hinder it in some cases[56]. The MNE is a network and the loosening of the conventional hierarchical formation and increased subsidiary responsibility has made many MNEs more like political coalitions with the result that the MNE is not mechanistically focused on value maximization. While the parent company and its headquarters want to preserve the degree of advantages of hierarchical organization while gaining home knowledge through autonomous

---

[53] Halinen, A., & Tormroos, J.-A . (1998). The role of embeddedness in the evolution of business networks. Scandinavian Journal of Management, 14 (3), 187–205. Kumar, R., & Nti, K. O. (1998). Differential learning and interaction in alliance dynamics: a process and outcome discrepancy model. Organization Science, 9 (3), 356–367.

[54] Andersson, U., Forsgren, M. (2000). In search of centre of excellence: network embeddedness and subsidiary roles in multinational corporations. Management International Review, 40 (4). Forsgren, M., & Pedersen, T. (1998). Centres of excellence in multinational companies: the case of Denmark. In J. Birkinshaw, & N. Hood, Multinational corporate evolution and subsidiary development. London: Macmillan.

[55] Hitt, M.A., B.W. Keats, and S.M. DeMarie. 1998. Navigating the new competitive landscape: Building strategic flexibility and competitive advantage in the 21st century. Academy of Management Executive 12(4): 22-42.

[56] Forsgren, M., and T. Pedersen. 2000. Subsidiary influence and corporate learning: Centers of excellence in Danish foreign-owned firms, in U. Holm and T. Pedersen (Eds.), The emergence and impact of MNE centers of excellence. London: Macmillan, pp. 68-78.

subsidiaries, in fact attempting to complete both objectives is remarkably difficult. Subsidiaries embedded in leading technological centers of competence are sources of impending competitive advantage that in reality remain unrealized due to the inside political structure of the MNE. The gain of the MNE's geographically dispersed network is a tremendous undertaking. An MNE must control a hierarchy of objectives in order to adopt some priority benchmarks for decision-making so as to take advantage of the chances of success.

The international diversification of earnings should enable MNEs to sustain a higher level of debt than domestic corporations (DCs), without increasing their default risk[57]. However, MNEs have both a lower debt ratio and a higher agency cost of debt than DCs[58]. Each multinational is unique with its own separate foreign subsidiary network structure. The relationship between the debt policy and the degree of multinationality depend on the strategy of diversification. The effect of agency costs and international environmental factors such as foreign exchange risk and political risk on the debt policy of an MNE could differ with its diversification strategy. Industrially diversified firms have higher debt ratios due to risk reduction and the mixture of international and product diversification decreases the operating risk of MNEs. International diversification does not appear to inferior earnings unpredictability. The international environmental factors of foreign exchange risk and political risk are certainly related to the debt ratio of MNEs.[59] Moreover, MNEs[60] with a high level of international and product diversification face lower levels of default risk.

When establishing new plants overseas, MNEs are offered substantial investment incentives by host countries. Competition for FDI plays a positive role by facilitating efficiency-enhancing location decisions that would not be made if subsidies were banned and exerting a technological spillover. Allowing subsidies makes the MNE to switch location and invest where it generates the highest welfare gains benefiting the poorer one. By inducing the MNE to switch from exports to FDI, subsidies intensify competition in the market beneficial for consumers whereas it is detrimental for local companies[61]. It should be taken into consideration that unfettered capital flows do not automatically increase growth but such cross-border investment is deleterious to expansion under certain conditions[62].

---

[57] Eiteman, David K., Stonehill, Arthur I., Moffett, Michael H., 1998 (eighth edition). Multinational Business Finance, Addison-Wesley, Massachusetts.

[58] Chen, Charles J.P., Cheng, Anges C.S., He, Jia, Kim, Jawon, 1997. An investigation of the relationship between international activities and capital structure. Journal of International Business Studies 28(3), 563–577. He, Jia, Ng, Lilian K., 1998. The foreign exchange exposure of japanese multinational corporations. Journal of Finance 53(2), 733–753.

[59] Sambharya Rakesh B., 1995. The Combined Effect of international diversification and product diversification strategies on the performance of U.S.-based multinational corporations. Management International Review 35(3), 197–218.

[60] Allen Linda, Pantzalis Christos, 1996. Valuation of the flexibility of multinational corporations. Journal of International Business Studies 27(4), 633–653. Shapiro, Alan C., 1996 (fifth edition). Multinational Financial Management. Prentice–Hall, New Jersey. Wright, Francis W., Madura, Jeff, Wiant, Kenneth J., 1997. The differential effects of agency costs on multinational corporations, Working Paper, Florida Atlantic University, April.

[61] Head,K.,Ries,J.,Swenson,D.,1999.Attracting foreign manufacturing: Investment promotion and agglomeration. Regional Science and Urban Economics 29,197 –218. UNCTAD,2001.World Investment Report: Promoting Linkages. United Nations, New York and Geneve.

[62] Durham,J.B.,2000.Extreme bound analysis of emerging stock market anomalies: Nothing is robust. Journal of Portfolio Management 26,95 –103. Durham,J.B.,2001.Sensitivity analyses of anomalies in developed stock markets. Journal of Banking and Finance 25,1503 –1541.

Competition globally is more and more knowledge-based and driven by a complex matrix of price and innovation factors. The global strategies of foreign investors outline that matrix and the benefits it generates for recipients at different moments in time and across industrial sectors.

The arrangement of factors makes the determined attraction of foreign investment and its use for strategic purposes a far more important, though highly uncertain endeavour, in particular if measured against long-term, dynamic development goals. The focus of strategies for the draw of FDI was on 'production' and in that context employment and output were key indicators of success. Some countries sought to magnetize MNEs with an export orientation[63]. The leading position of foreign companies in 'strategic' sectors, their influence on the capacity of home companies to compete and the high cost of technology transfer through the MNE led to a period in which more unconfirmed policies towards foreign direct investment were introduced and companies in important sectors were nationalised. Even though developing countries are more and more 'open for business', their appealing prospective is nowhere near as great as that of their competitors in the industrialised world. The failure to race in attracting foreign investment is matched by the complications most developing countries face in using foreign investment advantageously for innovation.

MNEs located R&D in their subsidiaries abroad primarily for the purposes of the adaptation of products developed in their home countries to local tastes or customer needs, and the adaptation of processes to local resource availabilities and production conditions. Competitively stronger MNEs locate R&D abroad, and have a greater variance in the levels of R&D across their subsidiaries, with R&D becoming concentrated in sites where local conditions are most conducive to technology creation[64]. Transnational activity is fuelled in part by the basic economics of comparative advantage and in part by the growing realization that strategic alliances can better meet the needs of global products and customers. Operating transnationally brings to the firm the benefits of access to novel markets and raw materials and the opportunity to incorporate and develop knowledge derived from the best possible operations world-wide. Information technology (IT) makes globalisation possible by providing a co-ordination mechanism for geographically dispersed activities. Information technology reshapes individual organizations into global co-operatives by providing a coalition mechanism. The focus of management in MNEs is global integration and local responsiveness: how best to meet local demand while capitalizing on world-wide competitive advantages[65]. Local customer needs, market conditions, and governmental regulations provide incentives to firms to develop local-bound host country particular advantages. Strategic alliances are the interdependencies that exist among global organizations. The process of alliance formation is encouraged by rising competition, accelerating technological change, the

[63] Wong, Poh-Kam, 2001, 'The Role of the State in Singapore's Industrial Development', in Poh-Kam Wong and Chee-Yuen Ng (eds.), Industrial Policy, Innovation and Economic Growth, Singapore: University of Singapore Press, pp.503–79.

[64] Cantwell, J.A. and Kosmopoulou, E. 2000, What determines the internationalisation of corporate technology? University of Reading Discussion Papers in International Investment and Management, 284. Cantwell, J.A. and Mudambi, R. 2000. The location of MNE R&D activity: The role of investment incentives, Management International Review, 40(Spl Issue 1), pp.127-148

[65] P. Hagstrom, New information systems and the changing structure of multinational corporations, in: Managing the Global Firm, Routledge, Chapman & Hall, London, UK, 1990, pp. 164-185. J. Karimi, B.R. Konsynski, Globalization and information management strategies, Journal of Management Information Systems 7 (4), 1991, pp. 7-26.

need for information, and the realization that alliances portray opportunities that might otherwise be unavailable. A parent-child corporation creates structural units in the form of marketing and/or manufacturing subsidiaries in one or more countries. A global firm is one whose competitive position in one country is drastically affected by its position in other countries. The global firm targets the international market without distinguishing national or political boundaries. In global companies, decision-making is fairly decentralized. So, Firms, which are more dispersed with autonomous subsidiary units, follow a decentralized management philosophy, which is also reflected in the design of their information systems. Transnational strategy outperforms other tactical postures escalating operating elasticity which in turn prompts foreign subsidiaries to act in response advantageously to the business potential of the global marketplace.

The dual imperatives of local responsiveness and global integration are becoming more fundamental for the continued existence and growth of MNEs and accordingly MNEs are turning to the transnational strategy combining global market power and superior internal competence, local sensitivity and differentiation, and global innovation and diffusion. Transnational corporations experiment with ways of selectively shifting the roles and tasks of their foreign subsidiaries to echo the differences in external environments and internal capabilities and as a result within the transnational corporations, subsidiaries became competent of pursuing different strategic roles with their managerial discretion to maintain the overall corporate orientation[66].

In satisfying the problematical challenges of pursuing global integration and efficiency, home sensitivity and differentiation, and worldwide innovation and differentiation, foreign subsidiaries of a transnational corporation take on varying strategic roles apt for its institutional framework and internal capabilities. A headquarters–subsidiary relationship context is comprised of the following factors: the locus of strategic control, the character of dependency and interdependency, the occurrence of common values, the locus of decision-making, and the focal point of strategy. Different headquarters–subsidiary relationship contexts generate varying governance issues for the MNE headquarters and accordingly firm-level corporate governance in MNEs should be utterly tailored for each foreign subsidiary. Corporate governance of MNEs resides at two different levels—headquarters (parent) and subsidiaries. Parent-level corporate governance is concerned about how the parent company's rights, tasks, management, and power are distributed and monitored.

Foreign subsidiaries that are wholly or partially owned by MNEs deal with their shareholders and other home stakeholders while they are accountable for the parent company's welfare[67]. Foreign subsidiaries act as intermediaries to meet a host country's legal and political wants and/or to echo a parent company's strategic considerations. The transfer of corporate governance practices through cross-border mergers increases company value in those states where corporate governance is poor.

MNEs have to deal with more demanding global shareholders and stakeholder groups seeking more detectable explanations for important strategic decisions and global operations

---

[66] O'Donnell, S.W., 2000. Managing foreign subsidiaries: agents of headquarters, or an interdependent network? Strategic Management. J. 21, 525– 548.

[67] Luo, Y., 2004. Corporate governance and accountability in multinational enterprises: concepts and agenda. J. Internat. Manag. 11, 1–18.

through the network of dynamic foreign subsidiaries[68]. Separation of ownership and control leads to self-interested behaviors by the agent and accordingly both shareholders and managers are depicted as efficacy maximizers.

The agent will follow his or her own interests, which may depart from the principal's interests and solely, managers, by virtue of their firm-specific knowledge and managerial capability, are believed to gain an advantage over shareholders who are removed from the company process. It is possible that agency problems could be aggravated if it becomes more complicated for the principal to monitor and judge what the agent is doing and has done for the principal. The extent of complexity to which the principal faces in monitoring and judging whether the agent has behaved accurately is an important factor in determining the level of agency problems. The headquarters–foreign subsidiary relationship in MNEs is considered such a principal–agent structure as the headquarters designate decision-making authorities and tasks to foreign subsidiaries. The extents of trouble to which the principal headquarters face in the observation and verification process are dependent upon the strategic roles of foreign subsidiaries. Foreign subsidiaries transmit various levels of agency problems to the headquarters depending on the strategic role they are undertaking such as specific contributors, home implementers, and world mandates.

Momentous differences exist in the headquarters–subsidiary relationship contexts across foreign subsidiaries within the same MNE, owing to shifting native environments and unique organizational capabilities and accordingly it is vital to grasp that even for the same MNE, a symmetrical treatment of corporate governance for all its foreign subsidiaries will be improper. Corporate governance of foreign subsidiaries within the same MNE needs to be tailored for each subsidiary and accordingly a differentiated fit is a key contingency requirement in order to accomplish desired organizational outcomes because the headquarters–subsidiary relationships within the same MNE vary comprehensively from subsidiary to subsidiary.

As a particular contributor, a foreign subsidiary is dependent on the headquarters and especially co-dependent with other subsidiaries within the same MNE and subsequently the conduct and outputs of foreign subsidiaries must be evident within the coordinated network system for the reason that strategic responsibilities and strategic management are in the sphere of headquarters, and foreign subsidiaries have to apply strategies dictated from headquarters, the locus of decision-making and planning are shifted away from the managers of foreign subsidiaries to the headquarters. Consequently, decision-making is centralized at headquarters to make sure an integrated comeback to global competition. The capability or competency to be aware of and create home awareness resides within each country location and accordingly the actions and outputs of a home implementer become less detectable and confirmable than those of a specialized contributor or a world mandate, which makes the headquarters–subsidiary relationship subject to upcoming problems of unfavourable selection and moral hazard in parallel.

Since strategic responsibilities and strategic control are in the sphere of each foreign subsidiary, the locus of decision-making is shifted away from the managers of headquarters to those of subsidiaries and accordingly decision-making is decentralized at each foreign subsidiary to make sure speedy and home context-sensitive responses. A home implementer

---

[68] Luo, Y., Zhao, H., 2004. Corporate link and competitive strategy in multinational enterprises: a perspective from subsidiaries seeking host market penetration. J. Internat. Manag. 10, 77– 105.

is offered distinctly more opportunities for managerial discretion, and in turn subsidiary managers are less constrained in decision-making. Strategic responsibilities to guarantee the overall corporate goals are centralized and coordinated universally at the headquarters but strategic monitor is dispersed among varied central foreign subsidiaries throughout the organization rather than centralized. To that extent a foreign subsidiary as a world mandate is less dependent on the headquarters but interdependent with other subsidiaries within the same MNE to execute its international mandates[69].

Although the subsidiary as a world mandate takes a vital role in pursuing a transnational strategy, it remains a part of an co-dependent network system and accordingly while the locus of decision-making is shifted to the subsidiary, the interdependency with other subsidiaries as well as with headquarters makes the subsidiary still remain and act within the overall parameters of the MNE as a whole[70]. The fact that the subsidiary is responsible for strategic decisions with regard to the products or services does not imply full amount of subsidiary autonomy. The existence of shared common values and beliefs between headquarters and subsidiaries makes it more expected that a world mandate subsidiary will use their native knowledge and assets to chase the interests of the MNE as a whole and not just their own adherent interests[71].

Not all foreign subsidiaries will contribute the resources needed to maintain the national competitiveness of their host nation. One of the mechanisms MNE managers have used to meet the challenges of implementing a coordinated global strategy is the differentiation of the strategic roles assigned to the various foreign subsidiaries of a single firm. Some subsidiaries may be given the authority to make strategic and operating decisions unconventionally; whereas, others may be implementers of headquarters-developed strategic decisions. One strategic role that a foreign subsidiary can be given is that of a world or global product mandate. The corporate expertise for the product or product line resides in the subsidiary, with the subsidiary managing the R&D, production, and marketing activities on a global basis. Thus, strategic and operational activities are centralized and co-ordinated worldwide, but the critical point or focus of decision-making is at the subsidiary level, not at headquarters. Within a multinational that gives some of its subsidiaries a global mandate role, the responsibilities for global decision-making are dispersed throughout the organization, with the responsibility for the set of value activities for different products or product lines being centralized at different subsidiary locations. Decisions regarding R&D, production, and marketing are made at the subsidiary level, although operational activities may occur at other locations. So, subsidiaries may develop, produce, and market their products for use on a global basis. They do not merely market internationally a product that was originally developed for the local market, but rather, they take the lead in developing a product intended for worldwide sale from its inception. The higher level of strategic decision-making helps develop the expertise and managerial capabilities of the middle- and upper-level managers at the subsidiary. The level of technology used in the processes performed at the foreign

---

69 Klapper, L.F., Love, I., 2003. Corporate governance, investor protection, and performance in emerging markets. J. Corp. Financ. 195, 1 –26.

70 Gillies, J., Dickinson, M., 1999. The governance of transnational firms: some preliminary hypotheses. Corp. Gov. 7, 237– 247.

71 Gupta, A.K., Govindarajan, V., 2000. Knowledge flows within multinational corporations. Strateg. Manage. J. 21, 473– 496.

subsidiary is an-other important factor in the degree to which the subsidiary can contribute to the host nation's competitiveness.

An industrialized nation's technological resources and skills will be enhanced to a greater extent by firms investing in such knowledge-based industries as electronics, pharmaceuticals, and biotechnology, which employ a high level of technology and knowledge-based skills, than by those investing in low-tech, intensive-intensive industries. Foreign subsidiaries can be an important channel for the transfer of high-tech knowledge through the demonstration and application of advanced product and process technologies and innovative managerial techniques. Training provides a mechanism for transferring product and process technology and for building the technical and managerial skills of the subsidiary's local workforce. Information can be transferred more effectively through formal training programs, but the transfer of know-how is facilitated through less formal means. Moreover, the information component of product and process technology can be communicated quite easily through formal training programs. The teaching of know-how requires frequent interaction within small groups, which facilitates the sharing of experiences and the building of a common stock of knowledge.[72] Both formal training programs and informal interactions among employees are important in the transfer of information and know-how from the foreign subsidiary to the workforce of the host country.

Another characteristic of a foreign subsidiary that can enable it to contribute to the skill of the workforce and innovative capability of its host country is international interdependence. International interdependence refers to the degree to which the activities and outcomes of the foreign subsidiary affect or are affected by the activities and outcomes of headquarters or other foreign subsidiaries of the MNE. A global organization links its competitive position across its various country locations and reacts to or initiates changes in the competitive environment in international as well as domestic markets. Sources of competitive advantage for the multinational can include international scale and scope economies and advantages that result from operating in a specific country location. Furthermore, international interdependence has become more and more important as multinationals need to capitalize on knowledge and capabilities acquired in one market in order to compete successfully in other international markets. Any subsidiary that is dependent on another subsidiary will ensure that the other subsidiary on which it is dependent has the resources and capabilities that are necessary for the two of them to perform their interdependent roles. Thus, an interdependent network of subsidiaries is expected to exhibit a level of inter-unit cooperation and resource transfer that is not exhibited or necessary at low levels of interdependence.

As a subsidiary experiences a greater amount of international interdependence, it is more likely to be a receiver as well as a supplier of intra-MNE flows of explicit and tacit knowledge. Subsidiaries that are an integral part of an interdependent MNE network will have access to the knowledge and skills of the other units of the MNE with which they are interdependent. In particular, such foreign subsidiaries will have greater access to the skills and knowledge required to perform their organizational function successfully, escalating their aptitude to contribute to their host countries those resources that enhance the country's national competitiveness. From the investing firm's perspective, an environment conducive to

[72] Jones, C., Hesterly, W.S., Borgatti, S.P., 1997. A general theory of network governance: exchange conditions and social mechanisms. Acad Manage Rev 22, 911–945.

innovation is highly desirable, because of the fact that the innovation' process is influenced by the environment where it takes place. Foreign subsidiaries should take initiative as a means of tapping into new opportunities as they arise around the world.[73] It could be said that activities of exploitation end to 'drive out' activities of exploration or creation[74]. There are disparate forces at various levels and locations within the organization that suppress subsidiary initiatives with the result that many efforts probably do not come to fruition. Initiative is a discrete, proactive undertaking that advances a new way for the enterprise to use or expand its resources. Subsidiary initiative merely refers to any initiative that occurs outside the home country of the MNE. If an initiative is to lead eventually to a new business activity for the corporation it seems logical that it needs to gain resource allocation, market approval and organizational legitimacy. Success is more than just a matter of resource allocation. The initiative process is driven to a large degree by the relative power of the subsidiary unit vis-a`-vis the corporate headquarters. Power is typically associated with influence over people's behaviour and decision outcomes. [75] Structural power in a corporation is eventually a legally granted authority. The need for innovation became more and more crucial as the knowledge intensity of production dramatically increased in the last quarter of the twentieth century and innovation-based competition diffused speedily around the world.

Investments not only in R& D but also in other intangibles such as software, engineering, design, training, marketing and management plays a superior part in the production of goods and services. Sustainability of comparative advantage based solely on the existence of location-specific raw materials or cheap labour began to erode and competitive advantages changed quickly. Importing foreign technology and creating it locally are not alternatives but corresponding, most developing countries have not kept up in building the knowledge-based capabilities needed to compete.

Learning through reverse engineering, national content requirements and procurement rules that had proved so functional in earlier catch-up strategies were ever more compromised by efforts to embrace standardized global rules governing trade, investment and intellectual property. The need to strengthen knowledge and information flows by building linkages within the national innovation system and with partners abroad became clear and such changes gave rise to an upward interest in the application of an innovation system frame to development planning and policy-making. A system of innovation is a network of economic agents, together with the institutions and policies that affect their inventive behaviour and functioning. Actor competences, habits and practices with respect to linkages, investment and learning are momentous in determining the character and comprehensiveness of their

[73] Bartlett, C.A., & Ghoshal, S. (1986). Tap your subsidiaries for global reach. Harvard Business Review, 64(6), 87–94.

[74] Hedlund, G. (1986). The hypermodern MNE: a heterarchy? Human Resource Management, 25, 9–36. Hedlund, G., & Ridderstråle, J. (1992). Towards the N-Form corporation: exploitation and creation in the MNE. IIB Working Paper, RP 92/15. March, J. G. (1991). Exploration and exploitation in organizational learning. Organization Science, 2(1), 71–87.

[75] Pfeffer, J. (1981). Power in organizations. Marshfield, MA: Pitman. Pfeffer, J. (1992). Managing with power: Politics and influence in organizations. Boston, MA: Harvard Business School Press. Pfeffer argues that it is "a force sufficient to change the probability of an individual's behavior from what it would have been in the absence of the force", Galbraith, J. K. (1983). The anatomy of power. Boston: Houghton Mifflin. Galbraith outlines power as "the possibility of imposing one's will on the behavior of others", and March, J. G. (1995). A primer on decision making: How decisions happen. New York: The Free Press. March describes it as "the capability to get what you want or to fulfill your identity".

interactions[76]. While it is essential to have a synopsis of the 'national' system of innovation, subdivision specificity in industrial structure and technological terms and the individual routine and practices of actors in that sector are key elements in shaping policy dynamics and policy impacts.

FDI has become the most key source of external financing for many states. FDI can accelerate host countries' growth by contributing to home sources of capital, transferring and developing technology and expertise. The utmost contribution that FDI can make to expansion is less the capital, than the knowledge that it brings and the part it plays in networking and interacting within the native system. Government's vision, its capacity to set FDI within the context of the country's development goals and target the right MNEs are central. By merely attracting a MNE to locate within the geographical confines of a specific country does not lead to an assured flow of knowledge.

MNE affiliates are parts of an enormously diverse network and their conduct is shaped by other institutional referents and strategies but innovative policy-making has a role to perform in reshaping the parameters within which the decisions of foreign affiliates are made. The capacity of native companies to understand and use new information and knowledge is rendered more difficult and the overall benefits of FDI crucially depend upon host country policies. In a developing country context along with strategic targeting, matching policies aimed at strengthening the linkages and knowledge flows that maintain a course of innovation will be needed which is a basis for cluster escalation and for the progressive transformation of a cluster of co-located actors into an innovation system.

Economic development through the stages can be associated with improvements to location-specific advantages, rising inward FDI and, from stage three onwards, rising outward FDI by local companies, that ultimately results in a positive net investment situation. FDI activity is influenced by the formation of the economy, and at once influences its development. The impact of FDI is translated into two main areas of impact at the level of the company the influence on the affiliate itself, and then the impact on local companies via linkages. According to Joanna Scott-Kennel[77] "inward FDI can be associated with indirect, but positive, impacts on local industry, where foreign affiliates engage in linkages with local firms. This is particularly apparent for collaborative linkages, and linkages that involve the transfer of product-related technologies, research and development, economies of scale, distribution systems and inputs. There are also spillovers from the parent–affiliate transfer of human resources, skills, training, information, experience and expertise. This lends support to previous research that reports a positive interplay between inward foreign direct investment and local capability building."

The subsidiary's external network is an asset from which power can be derived, if it consists of relationships that can only be accessed through the subsidiary. Managers develop informal procedures to help them evaluate and choose between the multitudes of initiatives that they are asked to lend their support to. Creation-oriented activities offer less definite and more remote returns on investment, they threaten existing power bases within the corporation, and they challenge institutionalised routines and behaviours. The MNE is repeatedly

---

[76] Mytelka, Lynn K., 2000, 'Local Systems of Innovation in a Globalized World Economy', Industry and Innovation, Vol.77, No.1, pp.15–32 (June).

[77] JOANNA SCOTT-KENNEL, Foreign Direct Investment: A Catalyst for Local Firm Development?, The European Journal of Development Research, Vol.16, No.3, Autumn 2004, pp.624–652, p 647

modelled as a network of semi-autonomous subsidiary units in various sovereign jurisdictions[78]. Moreover, traditionally most MNEs gave their foreign subsidiaries exploitational roles, frequently marketing and selling of the corporation's products in the foreign market. Subsidiary initiatives have to be pursued with the objective of changing the charter of the subsidiary unit.

MNEs like many other large organizations often function as internal markets, so that the 'customer' for a product produced by one subsidiary unit may well be another subsidiary unit within the boundaries of the enterprise[79]. Subsidiaries within a MNE are not just the long-arm of the headquarters and they differ in terms of contexts, capabilities and organizational roles. Thus, subsidiaries operate as independent actors in the market-place where they establish relationships with counterparts like suppliers and customers, but they are also dependent on the strategic decisions within the MNE when it comes to allocation of resources inside the MNE. Subsidiary performance is conceptualised as the performance of a subsidiary in its own market-place as well as its performance within the MNE in terms of its influence on the MNE's strategic decision-making. Subsidiaries follow various strategies and obtain changed roles in the MNE. Is the performance of foreign subsidiaries superior to that of domestic firms because of their possessions of firm-specific advantages in the MNE? Subsidiaries seek to perform well in both the local market-place and the corporate network. Economic transactions between two actors (parent company-subsidiary) are more or less embedded in a social and cultural context with mutual adaptation of the partners' perspectives, interests and resources occurring over time. Activity links between companies related to technology are decisive factors behind the firms' capacity to absorb new technology from each other[80]. The technological embeddedness of a subsidiary is vital for its capability to get hold of external knowledge about new technology. Hence, technology development is a key resource of economic growth and competitive advantage. According[81] to Ulf Andersson, Mats Forsgren and Torben Pedersen "An important task for management will be to handle the possible trade-off between the flexibility connected to arms-length relationships and learning connected to embeddedness in relationships". The success of global business depends, to a considerable degree, on the quality of a multinational's human resources and on how successfully these critical resources are managed and developed.

Control and coordination of subsidiary units is an important issue for MNEs because MNEs competitive capability depends on the fact that subsidiaries' actions support their parent corporations' global strategies, and that relevant knowledge developed in one unit is promptly diffused to and implemented in other units[82]. The feedback-seeking behaviour

---

[78] Forsgren, M., & Johanson, J. (1992). Managing networks in international business. Philadelphia: Gordon & Breach. Galbraith, J. (1982). Designing the innovating organization. Organizational Dynamics, Winter, 5–25. Galbraith, J. K. (1983). The anatomy of power. Boston: Houghton Mifflin.

[79] Rothwell, R. (1977). The characteristics of succesful innovators and technically progressive firms. R&D Management, 7(3).

[80] Kumar, R., & Nti, K. O. (1998). Differential learning and interaction in alliance dynamics: a process and outcóme discrepancy model. Organization Science, 9 (3), 356–367. Lane, P. J., & Lubatkin, M. (1998). Relative absorptive capacity and interorganizational learning. Strategic Management Journal, 19, 461–478.

[81] Ulf Andersson, Mats Forsgren, Torben Pedersen, Subsidiary performance in multinational corporations: the importance of technology embeddedness, International Business Review 10 (2001) 3–23, p19.

[82] O'Donnell, S. W. (2000). Managing foreign subsidiaries: agents of headquarters or an independent network? Strategic Management Journal, 21, 525–548. Andersson, U., & Forsgren, M. (2000). In search

(FSB) of subsidiary top managers is an especially important instance for self-regulatory behaviour of the MNE's subsidiaries. The more FSB there is in an organisation, the larger is the number of organizational members who constantly do their best to improve their performance[83]. Monitoring and inquiry (direct or indirect) are two strategies of feedback[84]. Feedback obtained through inquiry is easier to interpret (and hence to act upon) than feedback obtained through monitoring, but may also entail greater effort and face loss costs and the obtained feedback usually more obscure. Feedback seeking through monitoring is more common when subsidiary top managers communicated with parent company executives more often. Moreover, participation in corporate socialisation mechanisms increased commitment to the realisation of shared corporate goals, consequently heightening the value of feedback on how those goals were being attained[85]. Furthermore, manager's feedback seeking inclination is motivated by high level of intra-corporate social interaction, trust, and shared vision. The structural dimension of social capital has a positive impact on managerial FSB in MNEs. According to Wilhelm Barner-Rasmussen [86]"Feedback-seeking through monitoring and through inquiry share important determinants; both are influenced by trust, the extent to which subsidiary top managers' bonus depend on their own unit's performance, and top managers' tenure in the subsidiary."

When MNEs enter foreign countries via acquisition of previously independent companies, they take over the acquired companies' routines of operation and culture imposing their own procedures only to a limited degree. By contrast, when MNEs make new investments, they are able to mould the new affiliates, often replicating key features of the parent company in them and the level of coordination and control exercised by MNEs is considerably higher and home-country influences are transferred to the affiliates[87]. The conduct of affiliates is formed by the contrasting pressures of the external host environment and the internal pressure of the MNEs mainly the parent firm and so affiliates established from scratch follow the routines and standard operating procedures of the parent companies more closely than acquired firms, while acquisitions exhibit external isomorphism with the external host environment in which they have been operating formerly as independent companies carrying more of the characteristics of the parent company, which, in turn, mirrors the conditions of the home country, than affiliates established via acquisitions of an existing company. Headquarters' control over newly establishments is stronger, and the levels of shared value and communication between the headquarters and the affiliates are higher than between establishments via acquisitions[88]. Home affiliates and, to a lesser extent, home

of centres of excellence: network embeddedness and subsidiary roles in multinaitonal corporations. Management International Review, 40(4), 329–350.

83 Gupta, A. K., Govindarajan, V., & Malhotra, A. (1999). Feedback-seeking behaviour within multinational corporations. Strategic Management Journal, 20, 205–222.

84 Ashford, S. J., & Cummings, L. L. (1983). Feedback as an individual resource: personal strategies of creating information. Organization Behaviour and Human Performance, 32, 370–398.

85 Sully de Luque, M. F., & Sommer, S. M. (2000). The impact of culture on feedback-seeking behavior: an integrated model and propositions. Academy of Management Review, 25(4), 829–849.

86 Wilhelm Barner-Rasmussen, Determinants of the feedback-seeking behaviour of subsidiary top managers in multinational corporations, International Business Review 12 (2003) 41–60, p57.

87 Harzing, A.W., 2002. Acquisitions versus greenfield investments: international strategy and management of entry modes. Strateg. Manage. J. 23, 211–227.

88 Zeile, W.J., 1998. Imported inputs and the domestic content of production by foreign-owned manufacturing affiliates in the United States. In: Baldwin, R.E., Lipsey, R.E., Richardson, J.D. (Eds.),

companies are benefiting from resources contributed by MNEs. The whole affirmative relationship between parent–affiliate and affiliate–home company linkages is tempered by the extent of linkage formation. The quality, rather than just the quantity, of foreign–home relationship must be of concern of companies looking to compete internationally. Home companies must be in the point to leverage their exchanges with subsidiaries of overseas MNEs and gain from inflows of foreign resources. In developing nations the benefits of FDI are not always imminent due to large technology 'gaps' but developed countries have much to profit from FDI, because of the complementarities between home and foreign resources.

The effect of the transfer of resources associated with inward FDI is crucial at the level of the company in two discrete areas, first for the affiliate, these resources have a say to competitiveness, productivity and output and second the resident company, they can contribute to capabilities and advancement. It is critical for policy-makers to take this broader vision; to prevent underestimating the size of the impact of FDI, and to better aim at the types of FDI that are more likely to forward longer-term linkages in the resident economy.

Companies internationalise predominantly through an extension of the boundaries of their ownership across national borders. Equity agreements are associated with greater access to resources in foreign countries, enabling MNEs to build their advantages on these resources to a greater degree than non-equity arrangements, thus weakening the impact of the home country depending largely on the nature of the competitive advantages of the firm and its proprietary assets. Companies are reluctant to transfer proprietary knowledge to non-equity partners to prevent 'leakage' of competitive devices and new technology to outsiders. Full ownership signifies larger commitment to the host environment and it is more likely when companies have long-term plans for a particular market[89]. There is a close association between the level of control exercised by the headquarters and the influence of local resources on the characteristics of affiliates. Moreover, in transfers from Europe to China there is a change in the form of ownership towards the wholly foreign owned enterprise, in order to structure and manage the organisation and its functions, and ultimately as a way of dealing with the detailed level of knowledge and technology[90].

Foreign activities give MNEs access to resources available in various countries and by using these resources develop and sustain their competitive position. The more MNEs are operating abroad, the more they extend their advantages separately of the resources of their home countries and accordingly, the advantages of MNEs with more intense international activity are less related to particular conditions in their home country than the advantages of MNEs with more moderate international activity developing new capabilities and augmenting existing capabilities through their experience in foreign countries. A company's capabilities and strategies are molded by its investment and market activities reflecting the conditions in the host country to a better degree over time and host country experience contributes to the development of distinctive capabilities by the affiliates and over time becoming more independent and to a greater degree build up their own capabilities independently of the MNE, based on the resources of host countries. Hence, the power of home-country resources

Geography and Ownership as Bases for Economic Accounting. University of Chicago Press, Chicago, IL, pp. 205–234.

[89] Park, S.H., Chen, R., Gallagher, S., 2002. Firm resources as moderators of relationship between market growth and strategic alliances in semiconductor start-ups. Acad. Manage. J. 45 (3), 527–545.

[90] Peter Bruun, David Bennett Transfer of Technology to China: A Scandinavian and European Perspective, European Management Journal Vol. 20, No. 1, pp. 98–106, 2002

for the international competitiveness of MNEs diminishes as MNEs increase their international activity[91]. The link between nationality and competitiveness is influenced by the changing strategies of companies in international competition[92]. MNEs investing in countries at levels of development higher than their home countries are subjective to the conditions available there more than MNEs investing in countries at lower levels of development. According to Lilach Nachum [93]"It is likely that when MNEs implement higher value-added activities (e.g., R&D) in the home country and transfer overseas lower value-added activities, home countries would influence their competitiveness to a greater degree than when the geographic configuration of their value-added activity differs."

Developing country companies have ownership-advantages over developed country companies for the reason that of their competence to build distinctive proprietary resources by minor innovations such as adaptation and upgrading diverse from innovation in developed country companies. The intangible assets of developing country companies are based on a lower stage of research, technology and skills but can generate ownership advantages over developed country companies.

Many developing countries have accumulated a worth mentioning level of technological capabilities all the way through large-scale public and private investment in skills, information and technological efforts. Their technological development is not limited to the introduction of foreign technology and their adaptation to native conditions for the reason that the prompt growth of high-technology exports from developing countries over the last two decades indicates that their companies are improving competitiveness in many knowledge-based fields.

Even though many advanced developing country companies have shown greater than ever sophistication in their firm-specific assets, there still exist momentous differences in the quality and scale of innovations undertaken by these companies as compared with developed country enterprises[94]. Developing country outward-investing companies differ from developed country MNEs in company size, technology, skills, brand names and access to information as regards global markets.

It is not enough to monitor shifts in brand perception or market share but it is far more important to possess a holistic understanding of the total operating environment (including political and economic issues) and have better appreciation of the competitors' plans and activities. Marketing research should not just be conducted in response to one apparent market threat or opportunity, but rather on an ongoing basis in order to achieve a sustainable advantage. Additionally, Marketing intelligence is providing management with the facts, information, and insights it needs to make the best, most efficient business decisions dependent on the company's strategy, but it also shapes the strategy of companies and it a

---

[91] Nachum, L., 1999. The Origins of the International Competitiveness of Firms: The Impact of Location and Ownership in Professional Service Industries. Edward Elgar, Aldershot.

[92] Delios, A., Beamish, P.W., 2001. Survival and profitability: the role of experience and intangible assets in foreign subsidiary performance. Acad. Manage. J. 44 (5), 1028–1038.

[93] Lilach Nachum, Does nationality of ownership make any difference and, if so, under what circumstances? Professional service MNEs in global competition, Journal of International Management 9 (2003) 1–32, p28.

[94] Magnus Blomström & Ari Kokko, The Economics of Foreign Direct Investment Incentives (Nat'l Bureau of Econ. Research, Working Paper No. 9489, 2003), available at http://www.nber.org/papers/w9489.

responsibility of top management[95]. Different MNE subsidiaries experience varying degrees of costs of doing business abroad (LOF-the liability of foreignness) in respective host countries. The international business environment (IBE) is an amorphous aggregate of several elements that differ along geographical, social, political and economic dimensions. The effect of the global meta-environment that shapes and affects the host country's policies and the effect of multilateral trade agreements or regional economic blocks, the subsidiary's ability to leverage the parent MNE's worldwide strength, experience, R&D and perhaps its brand equity should be taken into account[96]. Until now, the MNE had to contend only with the host country's environment in which its subsidiary was embedded. Nevertheless, with ever-increasing global integration, the MNE's value chain activities are spread over many more countries and they now have to contend with multiple host country environments subject to complex interactions amongst various IBE elements[97]. MNEs have to constantly adapt to growing environmental complexity and uncertainty while still exhibiting some degree of consistency amongst its numerous globally dispersed units[98]. Thus, for MNEs, scanning and interpretation of the IBE is linked with strategy formulation and implementation processes and so it is indispensable for the MNE to continuously reappraise and modify its strategy in order to remain always in sync with the rapidly changing IBE. Additionally, MNEs with superior skills at reading the IBE reduce their LOF and instead enjoy a competitive advantage over rival MNEs and even local companies. While the local companies might enjoy certain inherent advantages, being on their home territory, MNEs can offset those by leveraging their global links through improved skills in exploiting the IBE embedded in the MNEs' employees and assimilated into company routines or employing joint ventures, networks, localization and demanding matching resource commitments. According to Len J. Trevino, Robert Grosse [99] "The firms demonstrate increased propensity for FDI when they are more technology intensive, when their managers have more international experience, and when they are more profitable, controlling for firm size, financial leverage, prior global expansion, and home-country currency variation."

The delegation of strategic roles to overseas units is imperative if potential key resources are to be swiftly identified and accessed by MNEs. Local autonomy is not sufficient for the effective mobilization of dispersed knowledge within MNEs and important is the role of regional levels of management in identifying the strategic potential of knowledge resources contained in local units in extracting this knowledge from its local context and in diffusing it to the MNE units. There is a need for linkages between knowledge embedded in locally conducted activities and innovation exploited at the global level by the MNE. Hence, MNE

[95] Thomas Tsu Wee Tan, Tan Jee Lui, Globalization and trends in international marketing research in Asia, Journal of Business Research 55 (2002) 799– 804

[96] Spar, D., 2001. National policies and domestic policies. In: Rugman, A., Brewer, T. (Eds.), The Oxford Handbook of International Business. Oxford Univ. Press, Oxford.

[97] Brewer, T.L., Young, S., 2001. The multilateral regime for FDI: institutions and their implication for business strategy. In: Rugman, A., Brewer, T. (Eds.), The Oxford Handbook of International Business. Oxford Univ. Press, Oxford.

[98] Zaheer, S., Mosakowski, E., 1997. The dynamics of the liability of foreignness: a global study of survival in financial services. Strategic Manage. J. 18 (6), 439–464.

[99] Len J. Trevino, Robert Grosse, An analysis of firm-specific resources and foreign direct investment in the United States International Business Review 11 (2002) 431–452

regional offices mediate between knowledge generation at the local level and knowledge application at the global level[100].

International trade in intermediate goods and capital equipment are key sources of technology diffusion and accordingly economic development. The use of foreign intermediate goods in final output production gives enterprises way in to new technology in embodied form and trade in specific inputs enhance growth by facilitating learning about the products and replication of the technologies developed in other countries[101]. Moreover, economic growth can be enhanced through export-oriented policies and the highest payback arising from export promoting policies are increased real output all the way through an increase in demand for country's output via exports, raise of specialization in the production of export goods which enhance the productivity level and general skill levels, and loosening of foreign exchange constraints which in turn can make it easier to import inputs and tolerate output expansion.

Governments around the world take part in international competition for FDI, not least by offering subsidies to multinational companies and developing countries are seeking FDI in order to add-on home savings and encourage catching-up processes. FDI contributes to dynamic productivity and income growth in host states. FDI induces divergence, rather than convergence, not only because host countries not have absorptive capacity, but also for the reason that multinational companies supply not as much of technology to developing countries.

The motivations underlying FDI fluctuate across fields and manufacturing industries. Resource seeking FDI in the primary sector often takes place in economic enclaves with fragile linkages to the resident economy. FDI-related technology transfers and spillovers to the native economy would be required in poor countries to restrict largely wide productivity gaps. The foremost challenge facing policymakers in developing countries is not to invite FDI, but to expand the native conditions required to gain from the perceived distinctive advantages of FDI. The absorptive capability of host states in making use of superior technologies applied by foreign direct investors is essential in this regard and resident companies are far behind the technological frontier to get hold of opportunities for technological and managerial imitation. Human capital formation, institution building and native enterprise development help elevate the velocity of absorption of technological and managerial innovations accessible worldwide. The technological gap has to be narrowed if not it makes little sense to enter into the antagonistic international competition for FDI by offering fiscal incentives and utter subsidies, in order to attract FDI in technically advanced operations.

Home market oriented MNEs create affirmative spillovers through forward linkages for both home exporters and non-exporters[102]. Moreover, home exporters profit from backward linkages with export oriented multinationals, but experience reductions in productivity due to backward linkages with home market oriented multinationals. For instance, the export

---

[100] K Asakawa, M Lehrer, Managing local knowledge assets globally: The role of regional innovation relays, 2003 Journal of World Business 31.

[101] Frances Ruane and Ali Uğur, Export Platform FDI and Dualistic Development, IIIS Discussion Paper No. 28

[102] Driffield, Nigel, Max Munday and Annette Roberts (2002), "Foreign direct investment, transactions linkages, and the performance of the domestic sector", International Journal of the Economics of Business, Vol. 9, pp. 335-351.

behaviour of foreign companies is determined tremendously by strategic considerations involving the gap in costs, productivity and market size between the UK and foreign countries[103]. According to Holger Görg and Alexander Hijzen[104] "First, spillovers depend on the market orientation of FDI, with export oriented FDI being more likely to generate positive spillovers, while domestic market oriented FDI seems to crowd out domestic firms and reduce their productivity. Second, the export orientation of domestic firms matters, in general, exporters appear to benefit most from spillovers."

4.5 Multinationals and Embeddedness

The multinational corporation can be considered to be a system of interdependent units with flows of knowledge, products and capital between them in different countries[105]. Ghoshal and Bartlett[106] have stated different attributes of a MNE in terms of the characteristics of the networks within which the different subsidiaries are embedded using a resource dependence perspective. The subsidiaries are dependent on specific resources for their operations. The environment and its resources are defined as resource areas rather than specific relationships.[107] Moreover, network theory recognises that critical resources are linked to the subsidiaries' specific exchange relationships with customers, suppliers and other counterparts[108]. Hence, network theory introduces a more specific description of the critical resources and recognises that for each unit, the most important resource is the web of specific relationships in which it is embedded[109]. The notion of embeddedness in a business network setting includes different types of embeddedness, for instance technological, social or political embeddedness[110]. When the subsidiaries are embedded in business network structures, the ability of headquarters to make a correct evaluation of the behaviour and

[103] Porter, M. and Ketels, C. H. M., (2003) "UK Competitiveness: moving to the next stage" DTI Economic Papers No. 3.

[104] Holger Görg and Alexander Hijzen, Multinationals and Productivity Spillovers, Research Paper 2004/41, p19.

[105] Bartlett, Cristopher A. and Sumantra Ghoshal. 1989. Managing across borders. The transnational solution. Harvard Business School Press, Boston. Gupta, Anil K. and Govindarajan, V. 1991. Knowledge flows and the structure of control within multinational corporations. Academy of Management Review, 16(4): 768-792.

[106] Ghoshal, Sumantra and Christopher A. Bartlett. 1990. The multinational corporation as an interorganizational network. Academy of Management Review, 15(4): 603- 625. Pfeffer, Jeffrey and Gerald R. Salancik. 1978. The external control of organizations. A resource dependence perspective. Harper & Row, New York.

[107] Larsson, Anders. 1985. Structure and change: Power in transnational enterprise. Acta Universitatis Upsaliensis, Stockholm: GOTAB. Forsgren, Mats. 1989. Managing the Internationalization Process: The Swedish Case.Routledge, London.

[108] Snehota, Ivan. 1990. Notes on a Theory of Business Enterprise. Department of Business Studies, Uppsala University. Håkansson, Håkan and Jan Johanson 1993. The Network as a Governance Structure: Interfirm Cooperation Beyond Markets and Hierarchies. In G. Grabher. Editor. The Embedded Firm, Routledge, London.

[109] Grabher Gernot. 1993. Rediscovering the Social in the Economics of Interfirm Relations. In G. Grabher, editor. The Embedded Firm. Routledge, London. p. 4 "Embeddedness' refers to the fact that economic action and outcomes, like all social action and outcomes, are affected by actors' dyadic relations and by the structure of the overall network of relations."

[110] Halinen, A., & Tornroos, J.-A . (1998). The role of embeddedness in the evolution of business networks. Scandinavian Journal of Management, 14 (3), 187–205.

performance of the subsidiaries diminishes because headquarters lacks knowledge of the subsidiaries' specific operating environments.[111] Therefore, when trying to control the subsidiaries' behaviour, top management must compete with the subsidiaries' exchange partners' influence. Different attributes of an MNE can be explained by the characteristics of the networks within which the different subsidiaries are embedded. It could be argued that the behaviour of collectives, for instance companies, divisions and subsidiaries, is also constrained by their embeddedness in ongoing relationships.[112] Moreover, the affect from the surrounding system of business relationships, that is to say, from the network, on the subsidiaries' development and behaviour is expected to have consequences for headquarters' ability to control and integrate the subsidiaries. Within the network perspective, relationships are considered to form complex patterns of technical, economic and social interdependence. Interrelationships between firms and the actual interdependence and adaptation can take different forms. Tangible interrelationships arise from the opportunity to share activities in the same value chain, while intangible interrelationships involve the transfer of management know-how among separate value chains[113]. In fact, customers' customers, complementary suppliers, suppliers' suppliers that soundly influences the subsidiary's direct relationships will also add to its embeddedness. The more important such indirect relationships are to the subsidiary, the tighter the structure of the network and thereby the more embedded the subsidiary is. Hence, integration of foreign subsidiaries is not principally a question of designing the organisation in such a way as to achieve adequate levels of co-operation between the units. So, it is a matter of trying to promote flexibility and economies of scope and scale among units embedded in different business networks, which are not actually suited to integration.

MNEs belong to multiple business networks. These networks are first of all sets of exchange relationships in which the subsidiaries are embedded. On the one hand, exchange partners have some influence over the subsidiaries through adaptation and interdependence. On the other hand, the more embedded the subsidiaries are in their networks, the greater the chance there is that the headquarters' ability to control the subsidiaries' behaviour has been curtailed. Moreover, resources controlled by one subsidiary and needed by other subsidiaries in the MNE may allow the subsidiary to affect strategic behaviour if resource dependence so dictates.[114] There is a need to find the right balance between global integration and local adaptation because local capabilities in the different subsidiaries are vital resources that should be employed on a global scale to achieve competitive advantage. Direct contacts, planning procedures, liaison roles, teams and matrix structures are administrative devices enhancing information exchange and co-operation in the company that can be related to integration[115]. Hence, the more of these devices, the stronger is the integration. The closeness

[111] Holm, Ulf, Jan Johanson and Peter Thilenius. 1995. HQ Knowledge of Subsidiary Network Contexts in the MNE. International Studies of Management and Organization. 25(1-2): 97 – 119.

[112] Cook, Karen. 1977. Exchange and Power in Networks of Interorganizational Relations. Sociological Quarterly. 18: 62 – 82.

[113] Porter, Michael E. 1985. Competitive Advantage: Creating and Sustaining Superior Performance. Free Press, New York.

[114] Kallinikos, Jannis. 1984. Control and Influence Relationships in Multinational Corporations: The subsidiary's viewpoint. Acta Universitatis Upsaliensis, Studia Oeconomiae Negotiorum, Liber, Stockholm.

[115] Galbraith, Jay R. and D. A.Nathanson. 1978. Strategy Implementation: The Role of Structure and Process. West Publishing Company, Minnesota.

of the headquarters and the subunits together with the actual flows of goods and services between the subsidiary and the rest of the company measure the degree of integration. In fact, it is the actual outcome of integrative efforts that is reflected in the flows between the subsidiary and the rest of the MNE. On the one hand, corporate embeddedness shows how deeply a subsidiary is involved in its business relationships with other internal units. On the other hand, the subsidiary is embedded in specific business relationships with counterparts outside the MNE called as external embeddedness.

As mentioned above, headquarters' control becomes more difficult because, rather than being a single entity facing a homogeneous environment, the MNE is composed of a set of differentiated structures and processes, each of which existing in one of the subunits of the organisation.[116] Dependence is not only an important source of control, but also a useful tool for examining the management of the MNE[117]. Headquarters use different control mechanisms in order to integrate their subsidiaries according to the overall strategy of the company. It should be taken into account that subsidiaries are embedded in business networks that include other actors inside and outside the MNE and the subsidiary's role in the network is formed in interaction with these actors rather than through any specific decision by headquarters.[118] Furthermore, the subsidiary's strategic role assigned by headquarters does not have to match with its role in the network and its strategic identity in the network is based on business relationships developed over a long time. The conflict between the corporate role and the resource control related to the business network can be considerable and may also be interpreted in a different way by subsidiary and headquarters. Hence, the latter's role is supposed to be the implementation of a common strategy, in which every entity has its own special position within the MNE. For instance, co-ordinating the different subsidiaries' R&D activities in order to avoid the duplication of investments and to reach large-scale economy in production and development is the main concern of the headquarters of a MNE. The ability to integrate R&D is assumed to be one of the most critical competitive forces among the main competitors in the industry. If we consider that headquarters task is above all planning, co-ordinating and controlling, this can always be challenged by the influence of actors in the network, irrespective of whether these actors are corporate or external. So, it is the degree of embeddedness that counts not the organisational border. The existence of personal relationships and "shared values" between headquarters and subsidiary management are crucial factors for headquarters to be able to exert control[119]. Headquarters will control operationally interdependent subsidiaries through different integrative mechanisms while operationally independent subsidiaries will experience a higher degree of autonomy.[120]As

---

[116] Rosenzweig, Philip. M. and Jitendra Singh. 1991. Organizational environments and the multinational enterprise. Academy of Management Review, 16(2): 340-61. Ghoshal, Sumantra and Eleanor D. Westney. 1993. Organization Theory and the Multinational Corporation. St. Martins Press, New York.

[117] Doz, Yves and C. K. Prahalad. 1993.Managing DMNEs: A Search for a New Paradigm. In S. Ghoshal and D. E. Westney, editors. Organization Theory and the Multinational Corporation. St. Martins Press, New York. Doz, Yves and C. K. Prahalad. 1981. Headquarters Influence and Strategic Control in MNEs. Sloan Management Review. Fall.

[118] Forsgren, Mats. 1990. Managing the International Multi-centre Firm: Case studies from Sweden. European Management Journal. 8: 261 – 267.

[119] Bartlett, Cristopher A. and Sumantra Ghoshal. 1995. Changing the Role of Top Management. Harvard Business Review. May – June.

[120] Gupta, Anil K. and Govindarajan, V. 1994. Organizing for knowledge flows within MNEs. International Business Review, 4: 443-457.

mentioned above, subsidiaries seek to perform well in both the local market place *and* in the corporate network. The market performance is the performance in the market place where the subsidiary competes with all other companies, while the organizational performance is the performance in the political process inside the MNE, where the subsidiary aims to influence strategic decisions of relevance to the subsidiary. A unit's performance is dependent on its ability to obtain valuable resources from the environment.[121] Moreover, the firm's ability to recognize the value of new, external information[122], and its ability to assimilate it and apply it to a commercial end is crucial for the firm's competitive advantage.[123]

Passive learning means acquiring objective and observable facts of the other firm's capability that occurs at arms-length and only the most visible parts of another firm's knowledge can be acquired. Besides, active learning means acquiring tacit knowledge embedded in a firm's social context which is, therefore, more difficult for others to imitate[124]. An interactive relationship with the other firm is acquired in order to get such knowledge.[125] The capacity to absorb new technology is dependent on the degree of embeddedness in specific relationships of the firm's business network. So, the embeddedness of the subsidiary network is decisive for its ability to acquire external, tacit knowledge about new technology. Technological embeddedness is certainly related to the subsidiary's market performance and organizational performance reflecting the importance of the network relationships for the constant improvement of how work is done in the subsidiary. In other words market performance shows the subsidiary's ability to obtain financial resources from the environment and is itself considered by other members of the MNE to be the crucial sign of the subsidiary's ability to contribute to the MNE's economic well being. Both these factors will improve the subsidiary's possibility to be influential within the MNE. It could be said that the relationship between a subsidiary's technological embeddedness and its organizational performance is dependent on the MNE's dependence on the subsidiary[126]. The more the rest of the MNE is dependent on exchange of resources with a subsidiary, the greater the likelihood that the latter can affect the MNE's strategic decisions. The main question of managing the international corporation depends on finding the right trade of between local adaptation and integration of subsidiaries. So, a complex duty for management of the international corporation is to gather knowledge about the subsidiaries' contexts.

---

[121] Sölvell, Örjan and Ivo Zander. 1995. Organization of the dynamic multinational enterprise – The home-based and the heterarchical MNE. International Studies of Management and Organization, 25 (1-2): 17.

[122] Kumar, Rajesh. and Kofi O. Nti. 1998. Differential learning and interaction in alliance dynamics: A process and outcome discrepancy model. Organization Science, 9(3): 356-367.

[123] Dunning, John H. 1996. The geographical sources of the competitiveness of firms: some results of a new survey. Transnational Corporations, 5(3): 1-29.

[124] Lane, Peter J. and Michael Lubatkin. 1998. Relative absorptive capacity and interorganizational learning. Strategic Management Journal, 19: 461-478.

[125] Nahapiet, Janine and Sumantra Ghoshal. 1998. Social capital, intellectual capital, and the organizational advantage. Academy of Management Review, 23(2): 242-266. Cohen, Wesley and Levinthal, Daniel A. 1990. Absorptive capacity: A new perspective on learning and innovation. Administrative Science Quarterly, 35:128-152.

[126] Krackhardt, David. 1990. Assessing the political landscape: structure, cognition and power in organizations. Administrative Science Quarterly, 35: 342-369.

4.6 Multinationals and Social Responsibility

MNEs have emerged as the dominant governance institutions on earth exceeding most governments in size and power. The most successful MNEs in the global economy are adapting by continuously forming complex networking forms of relationships such as international networks and alliances[127]. Is morality in business moving from individual principles to relations between business actors? One can argue that no single organization or corporation can solve the ecological, human or social problems all by itself and the network might be the real opportunity for MNEs who want to take their responsibility in conjunction with doing business[128]. Are socially responsible activities expensive driving up prices resulting in declining demand and less profit? Consumers over time recognize the ethically aware organization, which in the end leads to superior respect by the customers and so to higher profitability for the company.

MNEs now represent many of the largest economic entities on Earth, larger than most countries, amounting to about thirteen of the fifty largest economic entities, and about forty-eight of the largest one hundred. [129] Multinational businesses have the ability to avoid or to hamper legal enforcement on certain occasions – by withdrawal or by threatening withdrawal from economically dependent nations[130]. Could particularly mobile MNEs become ungovernable entities? A MNE is mobile, however, and may successfully escape punishment – albeit at significant cost – even surviving the collapse of a national government. How the social contract might be applied to multinational enterprises[131]. Friedman[132] is an advocate of the position that executives have the exclusive responsibility of promoting egoism "within the rules of the game" in the corporate setting: ". . . there is one and only one social responsibility of business – to use its resources and engage in activities to increase its profits so long as it stays within the rules of the game, which is to say, engages in open and free competition, without deception or fraud. . . . Few trends could so thoroughly undermine the very

---

[127] Kelemen, Mihaela and Peltonen, Tuomo, 2001. Ethics, morality and the subject: the contribution of Zygmunt Bauman and Michel Foucault to 'postmodern' business ethics. Scandinavian Journal of Management, No. 17, 151-166.

[128] Osman-Gani, A. M., Ahmed, Z. U. and Sok Ling, N., 2000. Investing in Emerging Asian Markets: A study of prospects for and problems of doing business in Vietnam. Globalization, the Multinational firm and Emerging Economies, Vol. 10, 293-313. Levitt, Theodor, 1958. The dangers of social responsibility. Harvard Business Review. September-October, 41-50. p43Theodore Levitt: "Business must fight as if it were at war. And, like a good war, it should be fought gallantly, daringly, and above all, not morally." Friedman, Milton, 1962. Capitalism and Freedom. University of Chicago Press. Chicago. p133 Milton Friedman writes: "Few trends could so thoroughly undermine the very foundations of our free society as the acceptance by corporate officials of a social responsibility other than to make as much money for the stockholders as possible."

[129] Comparison of Fortune Magazine's 1999 "Global 500" Gross Corporate Revenues to 1998 Gross Domestic Products as listed by World Bank. A comparison with GNP produces similar results: corporations rank thirteen of the top fifty, and forty-seven of the top one hundred. Fortune Magazine: Global500, *http://www.fortune.com/fortune/global500.* World Bank: World Development Indicators 2000,*http://www.worldbank.org/data/databytopic/GDP.pdf,* *http://www.worldbank.org/data/databytopic/GNP.pdf,* June 12, 2000.

[130] Manuel Velasquez, "International Business Ethics: The aluminum companies in Jamaica," Business Ethics Quarterly 5, 1995, pp. 865–870.

[131] Thomas Hobbes, Leviathan (1651). Quotations from Leviathan are taken from edition of E. Curley (Indianapolis: Hackett, 1994).

[132] Milton Friedman, Capitalism and Freedom. (Chicago: University of Chicago, 1962) at 133.

foundations of our free society as the acceptance by corporate officials of a social responsibility other than to make as much money for their stockholders as possible..". It is not apparent how law can be enforced against an entity such as a MNE, which may opt to withdraw from any nation at any time. What about enforcement against e-MNE? The tangible assets of an e-MNE are subjects to enforcement under the traditional means as well. It is obvious that an e-MNE can escape punishment more easily rather than a MNE. So, enforcement of punishment regarding electronic transactions can be applicable to e-MNE transactions. The multinational may consider, and might survive, the calculated sacrifice of assets or of a corporate arm within a specific country. For enterprises that command capital, employment, and resources that represent a significant economic force within a country or region, the political threat of withdrawal may also suffice to significantly temper punishment. MNEs may, for example, press the advantages of multinational production too far. National differences in standards and wages are among their greatest advantages: enterprises can yield maximum advantage by exploiting the lax environmental standards of one government and the low wages of another. But such activity can take significant tolls on nations and on the environment. Multinational enterprises of the new economy face a difficulty in being ethical today because ethics becomes at times a question of profits. Globalization and economic libertarianism without a systematic responsibility by the global corporations creates a predatory system making hard task for ethically conscious MNEs to survive.

If artificial persons are contractors who can demand legitimacy, then they must be in a position to act, or to withhold action, as well as to reason. They must be agents who bear responsibility for their actions. Corporations have structures recognized in law, such that some stakeholders can legally press their interests against those of other stakeholders. If a corporation is structured to allow for this possibility, it is not evident that the interests of the corporation can be identified with those of any particular stakeholder, or any set of stakeholders.[133] Are corporations resident in single nations bound to the national contract? It could be argued that MNEs would have similar status in each of the nations within which they reside. So, MNEs with many arms may survive the loss of individual arms in some nations, and we should anticipate that their practical reason might entertain calculated losses that undermine the social contracts of some of their nations. Are multinational actors rationally bound to consider the opportunities available for forming trans-national social contracts? Palmer[134] considers that a multinational enterprise must act according to standards that promote global sustainability of government, labour conditions, and resources. Where a multinational to flout sustainable activity in any nation, its action would tend to destabilize the governments of all nations, promoting an outcome that cannot be in any corporation's interest, nor in the interest of any corporate owner or stakeholder. A short-term and localized strategy of non-sustainable but highly profitable exploitation might appear, at first glance, to be in the interest of a multinational enterprise, since the enterprise could withdraw from the local area after engaging in ruinous behaviour. Such a strategy, however, cannot be

[133] See "Consolidation snubs Shareholders," St. Petersburg Times, Sept. 29, 1997. (*http://www.times.spb.ru/archive/times/300-301/consoli-dation. html*); Stroh v. Millers Cove Resources Inc. (1995), 55 A.C.W.S. (3d) 87 (Ontario Gen. Div.) (*http://www.mccarthy.ca/cc7-corp.html*), December 5, 1998. Peter French, "The Corporation as a Moral Person," American Philosophical Quarterly 16 (1979), p. 210.

[134] Eric Palmer, "Social Contracts and Multinational Corporations," Knowledge Tools for a Sustainable Civilization (Toronto: IEEE, 1996).

universalised; it may work for any one company, but were other corporations to engage in similar behaviour, widespread collapse would follow. DesJardins[135] says that corporations are obliged to comply with a "moral minimum" of standards, grounded in non-egoistic ethical intuitions, rather than in egoistic practical reason. A corporation might be in a position to show that non-stable activity can nonetheless be sustained by, for example, ongoing technology implementation, or retraining of workers. Will corporate social responsibility take the place of governments assuming their responsibilities, including taking binding measures to protect the rights of workers? Trade unions consider, for example, that free collective bargaining, while essentially voluntary, is a quite effective means to protect workers. CSR concerns the impact of companies on society's needs and goals. For instance, the implementation of the OECD Guidelines requires the respect of democratic institutions and processes. Through global action for decent corporate behaviour workers obtain the respect of their right to take care of themselves. The central issue in corporate social responsibility is, therefore, trade union rights: freedom of association and the right to organise as well as the right to collective bargaining. Any code that does not include freedom of association and collective bargaining cannot even pretend to be credible. As mentioned above, the OECD Guidelines for Multinational Enterprises and the ILO Tripartite Principles on Multinational Enterprises and Social Policy featured trade union rights. The global economy requires global social dialogue. The UN Global Compact is not a code, although it is built on a foundation of fundamental principles covering labour standards, human rights, and the environment. It encourages responsibility through engagement at the global level. Good global industrial relations provide a sensible way to solve problems based on the recognition that conflict exists between workers and employers. The OECD Guidelines are rules and should be treated as expectations, not options. The common aim of the governments adhering to the Guidelines is to support the constructive contributions that MNEs can make to economic, environmental and social progress and to minimise the difficulties to which their numerous operations may give rise. Hence, governments can use the Guidelines to insist on corporate social responsibility.

A private person, natural or legal, lacks the legal personality at international law to pursue a claim in its own right. Transnational Companies are not recognized as international legal entities, although international law does grant them a privileged international status. Public international law is only implemented in their regard through state action, so that they continue to be subject only to domestic law of States. It could be said that an investment agreement between a state and a MNE is an international contract subject to international law[136]. MNEs have a private legal identity granted by the countries where their headquarters are. In order to analyse MNEs it is necessary to make a reference to its economic national links and above all political links in the sense of defence of national interests. To increase their power, large firms merge, modifying the panorama of production and marketing creating networks of companies to protect themselves against the fluidity of markets and their risks, which means solvent markets are becoming smaller, because of the intense concentration of capital in countries to which the profits of these companies flow and consequently bringing about inequality at the expense of the weaker markets. The strategy of mergers goes hand in

[135] Joe DesJardins, "Corporate Environmental Responsibility," Journal of Business Ethics 17 (1998), pp. 825–838.

[136] Texaco Arbitration 1978 ILM 1.

hand with a strategy designed to strengthen the financial capital of the firm, which invests in financial speculation. MNEs are noted for having numerous financial and productive assets in various countries and also for being able to easily handle their assets throughout the world, setting up their companies where it is most appropriate for their goals, with regard to tax burdens, salary costs, technical and scientific capacity. Easing commercial exchanges and access to money sources (banks, subsidies, stock exchanges) benefits large companies, which develop and become global. But national economies are not developed to the same level and nor is the economic power of large companies the same, nor that of States, which results in rules being imposed by the richer countries in accordance with their interests. Global companies tend to appropriate national markets, leaving those in the country the option of either surviving in unprofitable areas or of allying with the MNEs, which bring capital. It could be argued that regional groupings such as the European Union or NAFTA do not supply a valid counterweight to this process, because they apply the same liberal economic and financial rules as the WTO and the IMF, serving as an experimental area of globalisation and granting official status to global companies as principal players in economy and finance.

Currency markets are linked to the will of States. Profits are transferred and the company in the headquarters' country merely records the transactions on the books but does not actually dispose of the capital. A nationality cannot be conferred on the capital nor can it be determined by geographical means. In order for the law to be applied, there is no other solution than to apply to each company the legal provisions of the country in which it exists. As discussed earlier, multinationals are those, which have branches in different countries. International jurisdictions, which exist, are not applicable except to States, which have voluntarily submitted to them (the International Court of Justice) and to some individuals who have committed particularly serious crimes, as a consequence of decisions taken by the Security Council (the Courts relating to ex-Yugoslavia, Rwanda). Thus, MNEs are economic agents of private law and are subject in principle to rule of law and to the jurisdiction of its courts. The transnational group does not, in itself, possess an identity which can be distinguished from each of the entities that make it up, so that it can only be obliged to answer for its acts in a fragmented way, so that it benefits from the opposing interests of the States in which it operates. The transfer of prohibited or regulated activities in one State to countries with less regulation allows them to escape their responsibilities. The transfer of industries or other very dangerous activities (such as in the case of Bhopal), as well as its transfer to countries with cheap labour and lower social protection levels in order to make production costs cheaper, are examples of abuses committed by MNEs. In principle it is not illegal to take advantage of the disparities between States, nor of the differences caused by the unequal development between different countries as long as there are no violations of fundamental human rights, such as the right to health and the right to life. In each State there are legal provisions to incriminate MNEs for damage to the environment, for non respect of labour norms in effect or for any crime carried out by companies, however, very little is done to enforce these provisions.

There are various systems for defining jurisdiction[137]: a) that of the State in which the multinational has requested legal identity; b) that of the headquarters of the company or the place where decisions are taken; c) that of the State in which the company is registered. There is also an idea of control: when a company control 100% of all the shares of another company

[137] U Kohl, Eggs, jurisdiction and the Internet, 2002 ICLQ 555.

it must answer for its actions or for crimes committed by the branch. States can exercise jurisdiction on MNEs but they do not wish to do so. When the MNEs commit violations of the labour rights of workers, for example, it is the State, which is obliged to compensate them for not having exercised sufficient vigilance. It is appropriate to consider that the State is responsible, because it is always responsible for the application of norms in its territory under its jurisdiction. The acceptance of criminal liability by legal entities is linked to the liability of large corporations in cases of violation of human rights, which is demonstrated in armed conflicts and in the so-called situations of social risk or damage. The role of MNEs in the manufacturing and marketing of weapons of war and of toxic chemical products used in internal and international armed conflicts is well known. The system of criminal responsibility of legal entities should also be accompanied by individual criminal responsibility. A MNE can commit a crime of "pollution" or of monopoly, perfectly described in law, but in order to demonstrate that he is not responsible must prove a state of necessity and the elements that the judge will take into consideration cannot be "subjective", only those which are "objective". Furthermore, the regime for a multinational can be different in different States, depending on whether or not they have ratified the conventions. International labour norms take on great importance in this period of globalisation or internationalisation, which is nothing other than the internationalisation of capital, a process which has been taking place since the end of the Cold War on the basis of a hegemonic model according to which the power of the State is undermined and the power of MNEs is increased. These companies are acting in conjunction with certain organizations such as the IMF and the World Bank. MNEs have a scope, which cannot be defined by their capital or branches throughout the world, given that often they do not have production units (such as in the case of Nike), but instead they expand by using subcontractors, which often do not realize they are working for a MNE.

This new form of both centralization and at the same time dispersion of capital determines a process of accumulation which is without precedent and which creates difficulties for the application of labour norms, because a large part of the production is moved to different countries and the new working methods do not create nucleuses of presence in production in countries which were adapting to previous forms of organization of workers. This represents a challenge for trade union organizations, which try to establish alliances and create new ways in which to organize categories of workers, such as migrants, women, and the unemployed. The trade unions also fight for international labour norms to be respected and try to develop norms to regulate international capital, that is, to regulate MNEs. It is not acceptable that Codes of Conduct be optional and not mandatory. Furthermore they cannot replace national legislation or international norms. In reality they have the effect of improving the image of companies without creating obligations for them. It is necessary to have it established that such Codes of Conduct must be obligatory and there should be sanctions when they are not implemented. They should also include in their applicability not only the companies but also all subcontractors, through agreements, which create obligations between companies and their service providers. It is not valid to state that companies cannot control their subcontractors because if they can do it with regard to the goods they receive then they can also do so with regard to social aspects.

Multinational enterprises are widely accepted as an integral part of the international economy and contribute in many ways to promoting progress toward sustainable development. Sustainable development has to be viewed in light of the dichotomy between the affirmative offerings that MNEs make to the economic expansion of developing countries and the conflicts of interest brought about by their occurrence in developing countries. Sustainable development means economic escalation relieving the vast shortage of less developed countries, based on policies that keep up and expand the environmental resource base and accordingly it ensures that humanity meets the needs of the present without compromising the competence of future generations to meet their own needs[138].

The ability of MNEs to organise their operations beyond national boundaries gives rise to concerns about possible conflicts with national policies and about concentrations of economic and political power. Hence, MNEs have improved the management controls and practices they use to achieve appropriate standards of business conduct in their day to day operations. MNEs that foster reasonable codes and meaningful reporting procedures can help to defuse disruptive situations. MNEs can create conditions that socialize and empower individuals and give them the tools to interact more successfully in their society. Corporations are the primary actors in globalisation which is a process driven by market forces. Has terrorism to do with globalisation? Most of the many varieties of terrorism are responses not to global phenomena but to intensely local ones. Terrorism may hold back globalisation by increasing the costs of international trade, travel, transportation and capital flows. People need to guard against the antiglobalisation tendencies, which have previously led the world community to protectionism and war. Globalisation has improved communications and so actions of MNE in remote places can be known and disseminated throughout the world in a matter of minutes or hours which means better protection of the rights of the workers[139] and in general human rights. Incorporating human rights concerns into operations of MNE brings with it rewards[140].

4.7 MNE AND FDI

Some multinational enterprises arise to take advantage of factor price differences across countries called vertically integrated because they fragment their production process vertically across countries. Besides, some MNE arise to evade the costs of international trade called horizontally integrated because they replicate an identical production process across countries. MNE more and more follow what they call complex integration strategies establishing affiliates in some foreign countries to conserve on transport cost and establishing affiliates in others to take advantage of factor price differentials. Companies that undertake vertical (horizontal) foreign investments lower their unit costs and thereby expand their sales. Real GNP is the most essential determinant of outward FDI. Exchange rate is also one of the central factors influencing outward FDI. The outward FDI position of countries is influenced by state features and also the same types of endowments have diverse connotation for various countries[141].

Low transport costs encourage vertical FDI by making the use of low cost labor attractive while high transport costs encourage horizontal FDI by making international trade expensive.

---

138 Alex Y. Seita, Globalization and the Convergence of Values, 30 CORNELL INT'L L.J. 429, 432 (1997)

139 S Greathead "The Multinational and the "New Economy": Examining the business case for human rights" 2002 VJTL 719.

140 L Lim "Terrorism and globalisation: An international prespective" 2002 Vanderbilt J TL 703.

141 Dimitrios Kyrkilis, Pantelis Pantelidis, Macroeconomic determinants of outward foreign direct Investment, International Journal of Social Economics Vol. 30 No. 7, 2003 pp. 827-836

Whether the two foreign locations are substitutes or complements depend critically on the initial level of transport cost and the level of FDI in one country depends in part on the policies and characteristics of its neighbors, but the nature of these interdependencies varies with industry characteristics[142].

Multinational enterprises rely upon ICT to arrange worldwide their activity, spread in a variety of quasi-decentralized manufacturing and service units integrated into a network of international flows of intermediary and final products, manufactured in preferred countries according to the local systems of relative prices, globalize the brands and status of a few universal companies that sell worldwide customized varieties of a limited number of products based upon the recombination of homogeneous modules. The global integration of marketing services, distribution chains, advertising and broadcasting makes probable to take advantage of economies of density in the global markets for final products and so the lower are the unit costs and the more successful can be the investments and the higher are the competitive advantage of global players on local competitors. Reductions in transaction costs increase the scope for specialization and so efficiency in the production of knowledge itself with important cumulative effects in terms of rates of introduction of new technologies. The development of the information technology sector has been fast albeit in a context marked by the slowdown of other key sectors of the economy.

In perfect capital markets with full information FDI, debt and portfolio equity are indistinguishable but in the presence of incomplete information, these flows are dissimilar from one another[143]. In fact, developing countries with vulnerable financial institutions, and low corporate governance and accounting standards draw a higher share of their capital inflows in the form of FDI[144]. Foreign direct investors have a cutting-edge advantage over domestic investors in extracting information about the true value of the company. Hence, investors according to Assaf Razin, Efraim Sadka [145]"If they acquire a domestic firm, they can apply their superior micro-management skills in order to elicit the true value of the productivity factor. This advantage stems from their special experience and know-how in this particular industry. In this case FDI investors outbid other investors for the top productivity firms." Between 1984 and 1998 the worldwide flow of FDI increased by over 1000%, while world trade grew by 91%, and world output merely by 27%[146]. The changing trend of investments by MNEs to new destinations, however, cannot entirely be explained by the liberalization measures undertaken by governments, or its institutions, like the inward

---

142 Markusen, J., Venables, A., 2000. The theory of endowment, intra-industry and multinational trade. Journal of International Economics 52, 209–234. Slaughter, M., 2000. Production transfer within multinational enterprises and American wages. Journal of International Economics 50, 449–472. Venables, A., 1999. Fragmentation and multinationals. European Economic Review 43, 935–945.

143 Hart, O., 2000. Financial Contracting, Nancy L. Schwartz Lecture, Kellogg Graduate School of Management, Northwestern University. 'if the shareholder does something to improve the quality of management, then the benefits will be enjoyed by all shareholders. Unless the shareholder is altruistic, she will ignore this beneficial impact on other shareholders and so will under-invest in the activity of monitoring or improving management.'

144 Loungangi, P., Razin, A., 2001. Foreign direct investment: a critical view. Financial and Development 38 (2), 6–10.

145 Assaf Razin, Efraim Sadka, Gains from FDI inflows with incomplete information, Economics Letters 78 (2003) 71–77, p76.

146 WTO (1998). World Trade Organization Annual Report, 1998. New York: United Nations.

investment agencies (IIAs)[147]. The levels of development in various countries, and their governments' policies, also differentially affect FDI decisions. Escalating competitive intensity and oligopolistic rivalry induce MNEs to restructure FDI, by making new efficiency and market seeking investments into developing countries moving on a regional, rather than on an individual country basis, for agglomeration benefits[148].

Investment in foreign markets may generate economies of scale that lower costs enabling MNEs to make use of economies of scope, since technical, marketing, financial, and regulatory aspects can be treated concurrently for various products stabilizing the total demand a firm addresses over a given period because geographical regions behave as improperly related markets featured by different demand patterns. MNEs rely on monopolistic advantage to export advanced labor-saving products to developing countries in early stages of the product's life cycle, and engage in import as the product becomes more standardized. There is a simultaneous relationship involving global integration and local responsiveness. The entry mode, such as licensing, franchising, joint ventures, wholly owned subsidiaries, acquisitions, and new ventures decision, is critical success factor for MNEs' international operations an important performance measure influenced by industry-level factors, firm-level factors, and host country characteristics. MNEs diverge in their choice of entry modes due to differences in the autonomy their headquarters seek to award to local subsidiaries, diverse resource demands of these subsidiaries, and heterogeneity in perceived risk levels associated with the targeted markets explained by the sequential results of R&D activities. Foreign MNE operations are influenced by strategies of the host country's government and whereas competitive and economic forces push a foreign MNE toward global integration, the policy of a host country government may need a higher level of local responsiveness. Hence, the host government as a strategic player that can affect the strategic behavior and performance prospects of MNEs. MNEs exploit internationally accumulated tangible assets such as technological know-how, marketing ability, and effective management to outposition local firms. Additionally, MNEs are generally more experienced than local companies in competing against many different competitors and being responsive to the demands of many different customers expecting foreign MNEs to have superior internal and external capabilities relative to local companies. Accordingly, foreign MNEs will be more likely to be conceived as adaptive organizations relative to their local counterparts. The key to achieving firms' objectives lies in defining the needs and desires of the targeted customer segment and in satisfying these needs more effectively than competitors contributing to the definition of marketing strategy and competitive advantage[149]. Effective leadership requires an executive to employ a style and behaviours that match the context dependent upon the exceptional requirements of each organisation's personnel, life stage and environmental

---

147 Mudambi, R. (1999). Multinational investment attraction: principal-agent considerations. International Journal of the Economics of Business, 6(1), 65–79.

148 Deepak Sethi, Stephen Guisinger, David L. Ford Jr., Steven E. Phelan, Seeking greener pastures: a theoretical and empirical investigation into the changing trend of foreign direct investment flows in response to institutional and strategic factors, International Business Review 11 (2002) 685–705.

The study then provided empirical evidence of such a change, showing how over the 20-year period 1981–2000, the trend of US FDI has shifted from the developed countries of Western Europe, to the developing countries of Asia.

149 Caves RE. Multinational enterprise and economic analysis. New York: Cambridge Univ. Press; 1996. Fiegenbaum A, Hart S, Schendel D. Strategic reference point theory. Strateg Manage J 1996;17(3):216–36.

setting[150]. Are the characteristics that characterize leadership in traditional bricks and mortar organizations equally applicable to the e-world environment? E-leaders need to be innovative, risk-taking individuals. Technical skills are necessary for managers to solve problems, evaluate performance and direct subordinates. Global connectivity means that time and space are no longer constraints to e-organisations, which are inherently cross-border and effortlessly able to enter into alliances with several partners. Information on new competitors, products and services is instantly and worldwide available and barriers to entry are normally low and connectivity and flexibility transforms the way new companies can build networks and reach market scale in short timescales[151]. E-leaders must have a greater technical awareness of the capabilities and limitations of IT and generate shared visions of the future and a widely held set of central corporate values. Moreover, E-leaders must display less control-orientated behaviours and focus on the inspirational vision. With the onset of a financial crisis investors adjust expectations regarding growth in domestic demand, exchange rates, and cash flows for repatriation, capital may be repatriated or allocated to other markets that yield higher risk-adjusted returns. FDI is regarded as less responsive to adverse macroeconomic developments. The direct investor has an informational advantage over any creditor regarding future payoffs from the foreign project. The high returns of foreign affiliates based on access to intangible assets-technology, managerial know-how, and international marketing- explains the expansion of MNEs. Through its intra-firm markets for goods, finance and information, the Multinational enterprise overcomes the segmentation of national markets, and the financial performance of any one affiliate will be evaluated against that of all others. Foreign affiliates in emerging markets have privileged access to international capital markets and overcome impediments to external payments by means of transfer pricing.

Exports from the MNE's home country may be adequate to prompt reverse engineering that is often recognized as one of the main sources of involuntary technology dissemination[152]. A large share of both license sales and sales of technologically advanced products are directed to MNE affiliates, and FDI seems to be more important for the geographical spread of technologies than sales of technology to unrelated parties. It should be taken into consideration that a unique characteristic of direct investment is that the control and ownership of the technologies used by the affiliates stay in the MNEs' possession. The majority of channels for the dissemination of modern, advanced technology are external effects or ”spillovers” from foreign direct investment, rather than formal technology transfer arrangements[153]. Additionally, spillovers take place when the MNEs cannot reap all the productivity or efficiency benefits that follow in the host country's local firms as a result of

---

[150] Goleman, D. (2000) Leadership that gets results. Harvard Business Review 78(2), 78–90. Park, R. and Campbell, A. (2001) E-commerce in financial services: an e-agenda for the corporate parent. European Management Journal 19(4), 417–423. Carr, N. (1999) Being virtual: character and the new economy. Harvard Business Review 77(3), 181–186. Penny Horner-Long, Richard Schoenberg,, E-Business And Leadership, European Management Journal Vol. 20, No. 6, pp. 611–619, 2002

[151] Kotha, S., Rajgopal, S. and Rindova, V. (2001) Reputation building and performance: an empirical analysis of the top 50 pure Internet firms. European Management Journal 19(6), 571–586. Dussart, C. (2001) Transformative power of e-business over consumer brands. European Management Journal 19(6), 629–637.

[152] Zander, U. (1991), Exploiting a Technological Edge - Voluntary and Involuntary Dissemination of Technology, Stockholm; Institute of International Business, Stockholm School of Economics. Chapter 5.

[153] Blomström, M. (1989), Foreign Investment and Spillovers: A Study of Technology Transfer to Mexico, London; Routledge

the entry or presence of MNE affiliates. A technology that is exploited through FDI will not be licensed to the local competitors in the host country. Taking into account that the characteristics of the host country's industry and policy environment are central determinants of the net benefits of FDI, foreign direct investment promotes economic development by contributing to productivity growth and exports in their host countries but the precise kind of the relation between foreign MNEs and their host economies vary between industries and countries. Removal of trade barriers will entail more concurrent business cycles, since a higher level of trade will allow demand shocks to more easily spread across national borders[154]. According to Andrew Burke, Holger Görg and Aoife Hanley[155] "negative competition/displacement effects dominate in dynamic markets while positive knowledge spillover and linkage effects dominate in static industries... The results indicate a challenge for industrial policy in dynamic markets in terms of arriving at the right balance when trading off the direct positive effect of FDI against the negative indirect effect on the survival of new ventures. This trade-off will be influenced by the extent to which policy makers discount future benefits and costs as the negative influence on new firm survival is likely to be small in current economic terms but could be potentially enormous over a longer term horizon if a 'promising start-up' that was otherwise destined for success is snuffed out of its fledgling existence before it had a chance to develop competitive resilience".

Capital account restrictions have been lifted in many countries and activity in international financial markets has increased markedly over the last decades leading to international financial integration. According[156] to Philip R. Lane and Gian Maria Milesi-Ferretti "the aggregate returns on foreign assets and liabilities depend on the composition of the international balance sheet between equity and non-equity components...the figures show a strongly positive relation between the equity share and the average return—a larger equity share is associated with a higher return."

Capital market integration provides the opportunity for enhanced diversification as investors shift to higher risk/expected return projects because they are able to diversify their overall risk. Robert Johnson, Luc Soenen [157]considered that "increased bilateral exchange rate volatility and a higher ratio of stock market capitalization in the US relative to other countries contribute to lower comovement." Emerging markets have high average returns, low overall volatility, low exposure to world factors, and little integration[158].

Enterprises base their competitive advantages to a considerable degree on the resources and characteristics of their home countries and these resources play a momentous role in shaping their advantages than resources elsewhere because the ability of firms to access resources in foreign countries by way of foreign investment is limited. MNEs of the same national origin share many common attributes that often cut across industrial classifications

---

[154] Frankel, J., Rose, A., 1998. The endogeneity of the optimum currency area criterion. Economic Journal 108, 1009–1025.

[155] Andrew Burke, Holger Görg and Aoife Hanley, *The Impact of Foreign Direct Investment on New Firm Survival in the UK: Evidence for Static v. Dynamic Industries,* Research Paper 2007/09, p14.

[156] Philip R. Lane and Gian Maria Milesi-Ferretti, International Financial Integration, 2003, IMF Working Paper WP/03/86, p22.

[157] Robert Johnson, Luc Soenen, Economic integration and stock market comovement in the Americas, J. of Multi. Fin. Manag. 13 (2003) 85/ 100

[158] Harvey, C.R., 1993. Portfolio enhancement using emerging markets and conditioning information. In: Claessens, S., Gooptu, S. (Eds.), Portfolio Investment in Developing Countries. The World Bank, Washington, DC.

and individual firms and distinguish them from MNEs of other nationalities[159]. Companies based in countries that are comparatively well-endowed with particular resources possess initial advantages over firms of other nationalities and such advantages arise from their favourable access to national resources and their knowledge of the way in which these resources can best be utilized getting competitive advantages. Some companies exploit opportunities and adapt to the advantages and disadvantages of their home country more than others utilizing the resources of home countries building competitive strength and they can capitalise on advantages associated with these resources more than other companies can. Moreover, companies differ also in their ability to overcome home-country disadvantages by developing their own resources, autonomously of those of the home country or by drawing on resources available elsewhere. Some companies are inherently better at turning the resources in their external environment into competitive advantages. Hence, MNEs are large, superior in technology, or unique in their product line compared with their indigenous counterparts in order to overtake disadvantages arising from operation in foreign countries and from running operations in multiple markets.

Is FDI an attempt driven by the need of companies to tap into strategic resources in foreign markets and to gain access to new technologies and organisational capabilities that will provide them with strategic advantages? Companies engage in FDI to tap into strategic resources in foreign markets, to gain or find out about complementary technologies, and to harness and resourcefully deploy assets complementary to their own to make the best use of their own core competencies[160]. Companies seek to tap into sources of knowledge in foreign countries and absorb new kinds of knowledge, as long as they have already benefited from their existing knowledge and product base and have exploited them in a better way[161].

On the one hand, when investment is driven only by the intention to exploit the firm's advantages in foreign countries the advantages of MNEs mirror the conditions of their home country and foreign influences are limited, while home countries remain the most significant location affecting the advantages of MNEs. On the other hand, when companies invest to get access to certain resources and assets in foreign countries, they establish foreign operations to build or upgrade their competitive advantages based on foreign resources. Asset-seeking FDI drives investment in developed countries, where the level of knowledge is greater than in the home country and the investment of these companies in other developing countries is driven by asset exploiting motivation. Reduced risk sharing has significant effects on the cross-country correlation of consumption, in addition to affecting the cross-country correlations of other variables such as output and investment[162].

---

[159] McKendrick, D.G., 2001. Global strategy and population-level learning: the case of hard disk drive. Strateg. Manage. J. 22, 307–334. Nachum, L., 2000. FDI, the location advantages of home countries and the competitiveness of TNCs: US FDI in professional service industries. In: Aharoni, Y., Nachum, L. (Eds.), The Globalisation of Services: Some Implications for Theory and Practice. Routledge, London, pp. 75–92.

[160] Mathews, J.A., 2002. Dragon Multinational: A New Model for Global Growth. Oxford Univ. Press, Oxford. Wesson, T.J., 2001. Foreign Direct Investment and Competitive Advantage. Edward Elgar, Cheltenham.

[161] Bas, C.L., Sierra, C., 2002. Location versus home country advantages in R&D activities: some further results on multinationals' location strategies. Res. Policy 31, 589–609.

[162] Steve Ambler, Emanuela Cardia, Christian Zimmermann, International transmission of the business cycle in a multi-sector model, European Economic Review 46 (2002) 273.

Governments compete to attract foreign direct investment hoping that MNEs will bring new technologies, management skills and marketing know-how[163]. The extent of IPR protection affects the composition of inflows of foreign direct investment and a weak IPR regime deters foreign investment in high technology sectors where intellectual property rights play an important role[164]. On the one hand, a weak IPR regime increases the likelihood of imitation that makes a host country a less attractive location for foreign investors. On the other hand, strong protection shifts the preference of multinational corporations from FDI towards licensing. Investors in sectors relying heavily on protection of intellectual property are deterred by a weak IPR regime in a potential host country. The lack of IPR protection deters investors from undertaking local production and encourages them to focus on distribution of imported products[165].

The historical-cost position of U.S. direct investment abroad (USDIA) grew 10 percent in 2002, up from a 5-percent increase in 2001 but the foreign direct investment in the United States (FDIUS) decreased for the first time since at least 1946. Despite a return to positive earnings by U.S. affiliates in 2002, reinvested earnings were negative because foreign parents chose not to re-invest their share of those earnings in their affiliates[166]. Tariff-jumping FDI allows a foreign firm to evade a trade barrier by locating production within the destination market. According to Bruce A. Blonigen, KaSaundra Tomlin, Wesley W. Wilson [167]"announcements of plant expansions (and, to some extent, new plants) have significantly larger negative effects on domestic firms' profits than other types of FDI, including acquisitions and joint ventures. This makes sense because plant expansions add domestic capacity in the industry, unlike acquisitions, and are by foreign firms that have already established themselves in the domestic market, unlike joint ventures."

The cross-border capital flows accounted for by the FDI of multinationals has been rising in recent years, mainly for many developing countries for which FDI is now the largest type of capital inflow linking financial and product markets across countries via transfers of physical capital, technology, and management techniques and integration of goods and capital markets, in turn, helps integrate national labor markets. The vertical-FDI view is that multinationals arise to take advantage of international factor-price differences and companies become multinational by locating production in countries where manual-labor costs are low and headquarters in countries where skilled-labor costs are low but vertical separation of production occurs without multinationals as well[168]. The horizontal-FDI view is that multinationals arise because trade barriers make exporting costly and a company becomes multinational by building production plants at both home and abroad, each serving just that

---

[163] Primo Braga,C.,Fink,C.,2000.International transactions in intellectual property and developing countries. International Journal of Technology Management 19,35 –56.

[164] Yang,G.,Maskus,K.,2001.Intellectual property rights and licensing: An econometric investigation. Weltwirtschafliches Archiv 137,58 –79.

[165] Caves,R.E.,1996.Multinational Enterprise and Economic Analysis. Cambridge University Press, Cambridge. Primo Braga,C.,Fink,C.,2000.International transactions in intellectual property and developing countries. International Journal of Technology Management 19,35 –56.

[166] Maria Borga, Direct Investment Positions for 2002 Country and Industry Detail, July 2003SURVEY OF CURRENT BUSINESS 22

[167] Bruce A. Blonigen, KaSaundra Tomlin, Wesley W. Wilson, Tariff-jumping FDI and Domestic Firms' Profits, Draft: June 2002. p21.

[168] Feenstra, R.C. and G.H. Hanson. 2001. Global Production and Rising Inequality: A Survey of Trade and Wages. Mimeo, UC Davis and University of Michigan.

country's consumers[169]. For instance, U.S. firms supply foreign markets more through FDI and less through exports the larger is the scale of corporate operations relative to the scale of production[170]. Multinationals face a decision between production-oriented and distribution-oriented FDI[171]. It could be said that multinationals arise when scale economies in headquarter activities are strong relative to scale economies in production. UNCTAD[172] reports that from 1986 through 2000, worldwide cross-border outflows of FDI rose at an annualised rate of 26.2%, versus a rate of just 15.4% for worldwide exports of goods and services and in the second half of the 1990s this difference widened to 37.0% versus just 1.9%.

The impending drawbacks of certain types of FDI for the host countries include the deterioration of the balance of payments as profits are repatriated, the environmental impact mainly in the extractive and heavy industries, the lack of certain linkages with local communities, the social consequences of an accelerated commercialization in less developed countries, and the effects on competition in national markets. Moreover, the technologies or know-how transferred through FDI might turn out to be ill-adapted to the host country, depending on its existing state of economic development. The host country authorities need to improve economic structures, infrastructure and human capital, while at the same time putting in place environmental, social and competition safeguards sharing a responsibility for maximising the benefits of FDI for development, for instance by pursuing policies of openness to trade and technology transfer that do not unduly hold back the activities of MNEs in developing economies. The development of an effective and equitable investment incentive regime, establishing a level playing field for foreign and domestic investors is one of the most significant issues. Hence, corporate governance mechanisms facilitate the efficient functioning of capital markets and promote the efficient allocation of resources. International investment promotes growth, alter the composition and geographical distribution of economic activities, stimulate competition and make possible the international diffusion of technologies. Rodrik[173] considers that globalisation increases economic insecurity and consequently demands for a robust welfare state. The multinationalization of production is the distinguishing feature of the current phase of globalisation. According to Kenneth Scheve, Matthew J. Slaughter [174] "FDI by multinational enterprises (MNEs) may be an important factor generating worker insecurity. FDI by MNEs may increase firms' elasticity of demand

---

[169] Lipsey, R.E. 2001. Foreign Direct Investment and the Operations of Multinational Firms. Mimeo, Queens University. Markusen, J.R. 2001. Multinational Firms and the Theory of International Trade . Cambridge, MA: MIT Press. Markusen, J.R. and K. Maskus. 1999a. Multinational Firms: Reconciling Theory and Evidence. NBER Working Paper No. 7163. Markusen, J.R. and K. Maskus. 1999b. Discriminating among Alternative Theories of the Multinational Enterprise. NBER Working Paper No. 7164.

[170] Yeaple, S.R. 1999. The Determinants of U.S. Outward Foreign Direct Investment: Market Access versus Comparative Advantage. Mimeo, University of Wisconsin.

[171] Gordon H. Hanson, Raymond J. Mataloni, Jr., Matthew J. Slaughter Expansion Strategies of U.S. Multinational Firms Initial Draft: April 2001.

[172] United Nations Conference on Trade and Development. 2001. World Investment Report: Promoting Linkages. New York: United Nations.

[173] Rodrik, Dani. 1997. Has Globalization Gone Too Far? Washington, D.C.: Institute For International Economics.

[174] Kenneth Scheve, Matthew J. Slaughter, Economic Insecurity And The Globalization Of Production, Nber Working Paper 9339, p29.

for labor. More-elastic labor demands, in turn, raise the volatility of wages and employment, all of which tends to make workers feel more insecure."

The prime social benefit conferred by MNEs is measured by the profit its subsidiary accumulates because a MNE mainly appropriates rents from innovation[175]. Trade, migration of workers, and FDI are the drivers of globalisation but FDI is probably the most visible. Over the last two decades global FDI flows have grown at least twice as fast as trade[176]. MNEs are part of global production networks and, within these networks, transfer production in reaction to changes in costs. MNEs modify their labour demand more swiftly than local companies in response to shocks, but have a more inelastic demand curve relating to wages. MNEs have an inflexible demand for labour due to differences in skill structure. According to Holger Görg, Michael Henry, Eric Strobl and Frank Walsh[177] "the extent of local linkages indeed reduces the wage elasticity of labour demand for foreign owned plants. In robustness checks we find that the results hold when allowing for plant heterogeneity in terms of size and when taking account of exit".

4.8 Multinationals and Taxation

National governments lower corporate taxes as a consequence of increased globalisation. Furthermore, globalisation tends to raise labour taxes and social expenditures[178]. The principal aim behind the taxation of MNEs is to collect revenue on the undistributed profits of the company and upon the distributions of profits made to shareholders, in accordance with the rules applicable to the taxing jurisdiction concerned[179]. The advantages that accrue to multinational choice can also shade toward illegality in the area of taxation. Corporations may trade among their arms in a fashion that the OECD refers to as "at less than arm's length."[180] A transaction between two economic agents is at arm's length if prices or exchanges for products are set at full fair-market value. The arms of a multinational may trade at less than arm's length, however, allowing the company to conceal portions of the real value of supplies or of manufactured goods. By this means, a corporation may cloak traditionally taxable gains in value that unfold over various stages of manufacture. Such gains may ultimately be taxed at a different stage of trading, but the business can often declare added value where it is to its own advantage to do so, because taxes are lower in some states. Taxes may also be artificially reduced as a result of special arrangements with specific governments. By pooling taxation, multinationals may concentrate wealth in some favoured countries, once again drawing upon other countries in non-sustainable ways. Multinationals, then, are particularly well situated to gain from disparities in wages and standards across countries and also to realize gains by

---

175 Mark Christopher Casson, Multinational Enterprises: Their Private and Social Benefits and Costs, World Economy, Vol. 30, Issue 2, pp. 308-328, February 2007

176 United Nations (2004), *World Investment Report 2004*, UN: Geneva and New York.

177 Holger Görg, Michael Henry, Eric Strobl, Frank Walsh, Multinational Companies, Backward Linkages and Labour Demand Elasticities IZA DP No. 2506 p 14.

178 Lucas Bretschger, Frank Hettich, Globalisation, capital mobility and tax competition: theory and evidence for OECD countries, European Journal of Political Economy Vol. 18 (2002) 695–716

179 S Picciotto "International business taxation" 1992 Weidenfeld.

180 Organization for Economic Cooperation and Development, Declaration by the Governments of OECD Member Countries on International Investment and Multinational Enterprises. OECD Working Papers v.5, #20 (Paris: OECD, 1997), Annex I, 7, p. 9. OECD (1997), "Taxation," 2, p. 12.

disregarding arm's length rules for transactions.[181] A multinational enterprise strives to maximize its consolidated after-tax income or to minimize its global tax liability. Multinationals can defer their home-country tax liabilities on repatriated foreign dividends, in active assets, passive as-sets or both in host countries[182]. It is worth mentioning here the problems created by the electronic transactions of e-MNE concerning their taxation. Multinationals can shift profits from high-tax countries to low-tax countries by manipulating transfer prices on cross-border interplant transactions. For instance, charging a below-cost price on products and services provided by a plant in a high-tax jurisdiction to a plant in a low-tax jurisdiction reduces the profit of the former and increases the profit of the latter.[183] Furthermore, multinationals can reduce their overall taxes by reallocating their debt from a low-tax jurisdiction to a high-tax jurisdiction to take advantage of the high interest deduction in the high-tax jurisdiction. Whenever there is tax difference between home and host countries, there is a tax advantage for a multinational to shift profits from the higher tax country to the lower tax country by debt shifting (or interest payments), among other means. Besides, it is possible that a multinational will prefer debt shifting as a preferred mechanism, as it may potentially be the least costly mechanism. More specifically, debt shifting is free from: a) any audit consequences resulting from aggressive transfer pricing; and b) potential difficulty in evaluation trade-offs between tax differentials and investment choices, or high potential long run cost due to the irreversibility of investments. The extent of the debt shifting by the U.S.-based multinational would also depend on whether it faces an excess credit or an excess limitation situation.[184] The enterprise must establish transfer prices in a rational way in order to avoid any dispute. Cost-plus and sales-plus are two methods of transfer of prices. MNEs use different conduits to channel funds depending on their relative profitability to the group. Certain channels may be preferred over others because transfer price manipulations will be harder to detect. The costs of running on effective transfer pricing operation may be too great given the possibility of conflicts between central management and local profit centre managers.

A subsidiary is liable to tax on its undistributed profits and the parent is liable to tax on the profits remitted to it by its subsidiary which means a risk of double taxation when a subsidiary pays a dividend out of its profits remitted to it by its subsidiary. In order to combat

---

[181] A statement by a recent president of Standard Oil provides a telling example: We're not in the energy business. . . . We're in the business of trying to use the assets entrusted to us by our shareholders to give them the best return on the money they've invested in the company. Quoted in Fritjof Capra, The Turning Point (New York: Simon & Schuster, 1982), p. 228.

[182] Weichenrieder, Alfons J. (1996). "Anti-Tax-Avoidance Provisions and the Size of Foreign Direct Investment." International Tax and Public Finance 3, 67–81. Weichenrieder, Alfons J. (1996). "Fighting International Tax Avoidance: The Case of Germany." Fiscal Studies 17, 37–58. Weichenrieder, Alfons J. (1996). "Transfer Pricing, Double Taxation, and the Cost of Capital." Scandinavian Journal of Economics 98, 445–452. Weichenrieder, Alfons J. (1998). "Foreign Profits and Domestic Investment." Journal of Public Economics 69, 451–463.

[183] Grubert, Harry. (1997). "Another Look at the LowTaxable Income of Foreign-controlled Companies in the United States." Draft, 2/5/97, U.S. Treasury Department. Grubert, Harry, William C. Randolph, and Donald J. Rousslang. (1996). "Country and Multinational Company Responses to the Tax Reform Act of 1986." U.S. Treasury Department, Office of Tax Analysis, May 11.

[184] Slemrod, Joel B. (1995). "Tax Policy toward Foreign Direct Investment in Developing Countries in Light of Recent International Tax Changes." In Fiscal Incentives for Investment and Innovation, Anwar Shaw (ed.), Oxford University Press, pp. 289–307. Bernard, Jean-Thomas, and Robert J. Weiner. (1990). "Multinational Corporations, Transfer Prices and Taxes: Evidence from the U.S. Petroleum Industry." In Taxation in the Global Economy, Assaf Razin and Joel Slemrod (eds.). The University of Chicago Press.

international double taxation, the tax laws of most capital-exporting countries include rules for its alleviation. States may enter into bilateral tax treaties[185] which regulate the incidence of international double taxation experienced by *inter alia* firms operating in both countries. The recent examples of MNEs and scandals concerning their financial management around the world show that false accounts, over estimated profits or false financial statements are methods used by MNEs in order either to avoid taxation or to achieve better prices of their shares in the stock exchange. This is a very risky policy that shows absence of control by their directors or not observance of the duties by the directors and their interest is focused on manipulation of events rather than any economic and scientific management.

Effective tax rates are vital factors for determining the location and investment decisions of multinational enterprises. These enterprises tend to be significant in industries that are characterized by high levels of R&D relative to sales, a large share of professional and technical workers in their work force, products that are new or technically complex, and high levels of product differentiation and advertising[186]. The international nature of a MNE and the high number of interfirm transactions make it difficult for the tax authorities to observe its true income and costs. Complex technology implies obstacles for the authorities to ascertain the firm's efficiency, and thereby derive its true operating profits. Many of the inputs are not standard commodities with established market prices, making it more difficult to monitor costs or compel effective transfer pricing regulation[187]. The inherent flexibility of multinationals not only helps these firms to minimise the costs of axes and regulations in a given jurisdiction, but it also aids the multinational in pitting one government against the other as countries compete for foreign direct investments. So, a MNE may try to reduce tax payments in one country by an implicit threat of directing a larger fraction of its investment to another country[188].

Foreign direct investment by a DC's multinational in another DC has been a growing trend in the recent decades establishing the "tariff-jumping" phenomenon under growing regional integration throughout the developed world. There is an increase of the on-site production of the European and Japanese corporations (Toyota, Honda, and Nissan, or the German auto-manufacturers, such as Volkswagen and BMW) in the United States in order to avoid the existing tariffs or the threat of stiffer taxes[189]. Exclusive dependence on export from the source country plant to satisfy foreign demand, the increasing convergence of labor costs across DCs and the calls for local job protection or creation as the result of increasing regional integration forced MNEs to engage in export as well as on-site production in host nations. According to Amar K. Parai [190] "a tax cut would reduce the host firm's market share and gross profit. But it will increase the total domestic output and employment, and also the

---

185 R Park "Fiscal jurisdiction and actual basis taxation: lifting the corporate veil to tax foereign company profits" 1978 Columbia LR 1609.

186 Markusen, J.R., 1995. The boundaries of multinational enterprises and the theory of international trade. Journal of Economic Perspectives 9 (2), 169–189.

187 Osmundsen, P., Hagen, K.P., Schjelderup, G., 1998. Internationally mobile firms and tax policy. Journal of International Economics 45, 97–113.

188 Katrak, H., 1983. Multinational firms' global strategies, host country indigenisation of ownership and welfare. Journal of Development Economics 13, 331–348.

189 Conway, P., & Wang, D. (1998). Managing foreign direct investment: commitment, deterrence, and diversion. Pacific Economic Review 3, 13–31.

190 Amar K. Parai, Profit tax and tariff under international oligopoly, International Review of Economics and Finance 8 (1999) 317–326, p325.

net income of both the host and foreign firms. When the host government's ability to raise tariff is limited, it should seriously consider a corporate tax cut policy for creating more jobs and corporate earnings at home". Globalisation has implications for countries' tax systems. Taxation is based on the "territoriality principle," that is, the right to tax incomes and activities within the territory of the jurisdiction. So, globalization is expected more and more to constrain governments' choice of tax structures and tax rates, especially in smaller countries. Internationally mobile factors of production-financial capital and some highly trained segments of the labor market can avoid taxes levied in particular countries. The capacity for tax evasion by individuals and corporations has also been enhanced. Indeed, many countries have experienced an erosion of the capital income tax base. Some governments have responded to the erosion by establishing favorable tax regimes. This "tax competition" may affect the average tax level of some countries by obliging them to lower tax rates for certain taxes. To the extent that the allocation of capital will be driven by tax considerations rather than by pre-tax rates of return, the allocation of capital will be less efficient. Personal income taxes and expenditure policies related to social spending are likely to become a more important factor in labor migration[191]. Apparently, globalisation will increasingly tend to cause tax systems to converge either through tax harmonization or via tax competition across jurisdictions. In the 1990s, the impact of globalisation began to be felt more intensely as capital markets were liberalized and economies became more integrated. Many multinationals now realize that a global approach to designing and documenting transfer-pricing policies is desirable. The fast growth in world trade and especially in trade within multinationals creates problems for national tax authorities owing to the potential abuse of "transfer prices" by the multinationals, including on loans, the allocation of fixed costs, and the valuation of trademarks and patents. Electronic money will substitute for real money in individual transactions. Offshore financial centers and tax havens have gained significance as conduits for financial investments and their growth has been stimulated by the flow of digital information that allows money and knowledge to be moved without difficulty and cheaply in real time, and by the regulatory arrangements of several countries. One of the challenges from using complex financial instruments, such as derivatives, is that they can be used in tax-avoidance schemes by exploiting uncertainties and inconsistencies in their tax treatment.

A government will look to other states' taxing policies in order to modify its own tax policy and comply with MNEs' preferences and accordingly the demand of tax incentives by one state pressures other states to take up comparable incentive process in order to stay competitive[192].

Governments are unwilling to eradicate subsidies for fear that national companies may lose international competitiveness, a feature that the companies will stress through their lobby group. The escalating integration of the world economy puts more weight on this argument.

---

191 "Variously described as a new hypermobility of capital or as a scale dissonance between the organization of the political and the economic, there are new pressures being brought to bear upon agencies of the state and upon labor." Kevin R. Cox, *Introduction: Globalization and Its Politics in Question, in* Spaces Of Globalization: Reasserting The Power Of The Local 1, 2 (New York: Guilford Publications, 1997).

192 Joshua P. Rubin, Note, Take the Money and Stay: Industrial Location Incentives and Relational Contracting, 70 N.Y.U. L. Rev. 1277, 1311 (1995) ("The empirical and anecdotal evidence discussed below suggests that economic pressures driving inter-jurisdictional competition for industrial location forces localities to provide incentives against their better interests.").

Lobbying in favor of tax incentives provokes competition among countries and accordingly a race to the bottom arises due to interest group actions.

Global governance means an international system of order that embraces both "hard law" and "soft law" and which is the authority to manage, monitor or enforce a set of norms, rules and regulations of transnational extent to accomplish collectively-accepted supranational interests. The grounds behind global governance are that the global economy needs formal, worldwide rules and norms to steer governments and businesses. It could be argued that an international governance mechanism is needed to take on a number of functions in the new global economy; in particular, it must supply distinct public goods and resolve market failures[193]. Global governance can serve as a national and global efficiency-enhancing tool and accordingly implementing global governance approach prevents corruption, which is flourishing due to the lack of clearness in the provision of tax incentives by governments. Bribing reduces the prospect that MNEs will invest in the country and accordingly corruption distorts competition on the native market by favoring local companies with an advantage in bribing. According to Katariina Hakkala, Pehr-Johan Norbäck and Helena Svaleryd[194] "In any case where corruption encourages FDI through reduced marginal costs, it would be better for the country to attract more investment by abolishing costly regulations and increasing transparency to avoid the anti-competitive effect on the local market. However, such a change might prove politically difficult to implement as local officials would lose out on bribes and local firms would face increasing competition from foreign firms. Thus, not only the local officials would have a reason to oppose anti-corruption measures, but also the local firms."

Manipulation of prices by companies ensures that profits are accumulated in low-tax jurisdictions or in states with the aim of providing FDI tax incentives[195]. Dunning[196] argues that "because there is competition for MNE activity both between home and host countries, and between different host countries, the opportunities for MNEs to play one nation against another are enhanced without the establishment of supranational institutions and harmonized inter government action towards [transfer pricing measures]."

Existing tax rules were established to handle transfers of physical goods and services across borders. The growth of international trade has escalated the significance of tax revenues from cross-border business activities for the treasuries many countries. To that extent globalization, e-commerce and the escalating use of tax havens have created a fiscal crisis that threatens the security of the tax base of most industrialized nations, which are struggling to employ mechanisms and outdated tax rules to identify and collect crucial revenues. Once the value of an electronic or information good or service has been established, the marginal cost for marketing, producing and transmitting an online product approaches zero. As mentioned above, if governments are unable to successfully tax the domestic income derived by e-commerce activities, multinational enterprises will continue to shift income-producing operations to low-tax or no-tax jurisdictions. Technological developments

---

[193] John O. McGinnis & Mark L. Movsesian, Commentary, The World Trade Constitution, 114 Harv. L. Rev. 511, 514 (2000) (explaining that the WTO reflects many of the insights that inform the U.S. Constitution in promoting both free trade and accountable government).

[194] Katariina Hakkala, Pehr-Johan Norbäck and Helena Svalery, Asymmetric Effects of Corruption on FDI: Evidence from Swedish Multinational Firms, Working Paper No. 641, 2005.

[195] Julie Roin, Competition and Evasion: Another Perspective on International Tax Competition, 89 Geo. L.J. 543, 585 (2001).

[196] John H. Dunning, Multinational Enterprises and the Global Economy 523 (1993).

permit multinational enterprises to reallocate business income by to tax havens and relative low-tax jurisdictions. Moreover, the application of static residency rules for tax purposes is becoming more and more difficult in a digital economy and the absence of any multilateral consensus on how to establish the residency of a global e-commerce business and the attribution of e-commerce income continues to represent a major problem for international tax authorities which means that as long as tax authorities place emphasis on the residency of the taxpayer, we will witness a diminution of the tax base of many industrialized countries and the potential loss of tax revenues[197]. Multinational enterprises have a reason to increase the income of the enterprise in a low tax jurisdiction and reduce the enterprise's income in a relative high tax jurisdiction establishing prices for transfers of products and services prices among related entities in a manner that shifts taxable revenues beyond the jurisdiction of the authorities increased in global trade and the growth of e-commerce[198].

As multinational enterprises continue to decentralize functions, the development of telecommunications and information technology has made it easier to shelter progressively more complex transfer price transactions from tax authorities and the growth of electronic commerce presents a remarkable challenge to existing transfer pricing mechanisms because digital products and services tend to be highly integrated and intangible in nature. The current system of taxation for global business income needs reform. Bilateral tax treaties provide that a host country may tax active business income only if it can be attributed to a permanent establishment within the country but it is now possible to carry out extensive and profitable electronic commerce activities in a foreign jurisdiction without having to maintain a physical presence in the foreign country. Hence, as long as the permanent establishment concept remains the core requirement for taxation of international business income, nations will be precluded from asserting tax jurisdiction over e-commerce income. International tax rules must be improved in order to maintain a fair division of tax revenues and source country taxation finds legitimacy in the benefits theory of taxation. Fairness exists in the international tax system only in so far as tax jurisdiction and revenues are allocated among nations in a manner that conforms to prevailing views of international justice and equity. Placing a company anywhere on cyberspace makes it present, in effect, everywhere, there is no central, worldwide, technical control point, and it is difficult to assign a physical location for taxation purposes to the component parts of electronic transactions or the digital bits associated therewith. The way that information travels through cyberspace complicates matters and users of cyberspace have no control over, and customarily no specific knowledge of, the path that is travelled by the information they search for or circulate making it harder for companies doing business in cyberspace to know in which countries they are or are not subject to taxation.

Multinational enterprises maximize global after-tax profits by changing revenues to low-tax, and deductions to high-tax, jurisdictions. Not only the tax policy change but also the additional administrative compliance costs of documentation, harmfully affect company success. Even the threat of a penalty harmfully affects market valuations. An upsurge in either tax rate or stage of corruption reduces inward foreign direct investment. Corruption in a host

[197] Susan M. Lyons, International Consensus Needed in Taxation of Electronic Commerce (1997) 14 Tax Notes Int'l 1199. Reuven S. Avi-Yonah, The Rise and Fall of Arm's Length: A Study in the Evolution of U.S. International Taxation (1995) 15 Virginia Tax Rev. 89

[198] Jinyan Li, "Global Profit Split: An Evolutionary Approach to International Income Allocation" 50 Can. Tax J. (2002) 823. James D. Cigler and Susan E. Stinnett, Treasury Seeks Cybertax Answers with Electronic Commerce Discussion Paper (1997) 8 J. Int'l Tax'n 56

country reduces the prospect of an investment. A company's experience of the market reduces the negative appearance of corruption on local sales, suggesting that MNEs' bribing disadvantage relative to local company decreases with familiarity.

Global markets force governments to lower levels of capital taxation and government spending. Globalization via capital holders force states to decrease capital taxation and government spending and it is politicians in their effort to please their financiers and implement their policies who make the decision to lessen taxation and government spending. Governments provide social safety nets and other solutions to reduce the negative effects of globalization[199]. Nathan Jensen[200] consider that "for politicians, the rewards of corporate tax reductions have been greatly over-exaggerated. Politicians turning to multinationals in an effort to create jobs, facilitate technology transfer, or jump-start economic growth need to develop a different set of policy levers to attract the investments of multinationals. For academics, these results provide an alternative explanation for the lack of the race to the bottom in corporate tax rates. There is not a race to the bottom because firms do not use their feet to demand a convergence, or even a lowering, of corporate tax rates". Altering a country's corporate tax rate permits governments to take credit for new investment in the country. Corporate tax reductions lead likely to higher FDI flows. The tax difference between foreign-owned and locally-owned companies has to be substantial in order to attract inflow FDI. According to Peter Egger, Wolfgang Eggert and Hannes Winner[201] "our estimates suggest a savings effect of 594 Euros per employee or about 56 percent as compared to domestically-owned subsidiaries. For larger plants and ones in thinner markets with a strong relative importance of foreign ownership the tax savings effect is even higher. These findings are robust both in qualitative and in quantitative terms to alternative estimation procedures and other sensitivity checks". While local companies have to deal only with the national tax system, MNEs face the complicated choice of determining their general indebtedness and the distribution of their debts to the parent company and the subsidiaries across all countries in which the MNE functions. Hence, the financial composition of a MNE reflects the tax systems of all the countries where it functions. An amendment in tax policy optimally causes the MNE to adjust its capital structure in all the countries where it functions. Harry Huizinga, Luc Laeven, and Gaëtan Nicodème[202] think that"on the basis of a large sample of European firms over the 1994–2003 period, we find that a firm's leverage depends on national tax rates as well as international tax rate differences. The relationship between leverage and international tax rate differences reflects the presence of international debt-shifting. While statistically highly significant, both the "domestic" and "international" effects of taxation on leverage are rather small... Countries with relatively low rates of taxation may benefit from international debt-shifting, as local establishments of multinational firms will be less highly leveraged than they would otherwise be—resulting in a higher corporate income tax revenues". MNEs evade bilateral non-resident dividend withholding taxes by using channel

[199] Scheve, Kenneth and Matthew J. Slaughter. 2004. "Economic Insecurity and the Globalization of Production." *American Journal of Political Science* 48 (4): 662-674.

[200] Nathan Jensen, Fiscal Policy and the Firm: Do Low Corporate Tax Rates Attract Multinational Corporations? *www.ssrn.com* p27.

[201] Peter Egger, Wolfgang Eggert, Hannes Winner, Saving taxes through foreign plant ownership, 2007 cesifo working paper no. 1887, p18.

[202] *Harry Huizinga, Luc Laeven, and Gaëtan Nicodèm,e* Capital Structure and International Debt-Shifting, 2007 IMF Working Paper WP/07/39 p 16.

companies in other states. Harmonizing corporate income tax rates and introducing a harmonised tax basis for MNEs will reduce but not eradicate international debt-shifting globally.

4.9 Entrance of MNE and Training of the Workforce

Corporate headquarters' control of subunit behaviour and performance becomes a central integrating function in MNEs. Headquarters should increase control over foreign subsidiaries in order to diminish the uncertainty of their investment, since such control ensures that the behaviours originating in separate parts of the organization are like-minded and support common goals. The geographical and cultural reserve between headquarters and subsidiaries in MNE relationships increases the complexity of the underlying agency relationship[203]. Hence, varied types of control may be used by MNEs, including strategic control or informal control, in order to obtain more subjective and delicate information about the foreign subsidiaries. Multinationals are potentially important to the national vocational education and training systems in which they operate. To the extent that they develop and implement efficient and effective training and development programmes, MNEs may exert a leadership role. Comparing the role of parent companies in shaping the strategic directions of the human resources and training functions helps to establish to what extent a polycentric approach is adopted in managing the training function. Such an approach involves recognizing national differences and decentralizing control. There is evidence that many MNEs seem to transfer their established practices from their home markets to over-seas ones[204]. MNEs may allow considerable autonomy to their subsidiaries in developing and implementing training and development strategies. There is a tendency to move away from the highly centralized structures for managing training and development. This involves delegating responsibility to the individual sites and to line managers, while maintaining a corporate role for activities such as planning, co-ordination and management development. So, MNEs have the capacity to provide leadership to the sector in fostering a training culture and implementing training reforms.

FDI, the establishment or acquisition of production subsidiaries abroad by multinational enterprises MNEs, is predominantly essential because it is a source of capital and knowledge about production techniques. Emerging economies must have strong and increasing interests in attracting trade, FDI, and technological capability. MNEs have a number of ways to serve foreign markets. Companies may choose simply to export at arm's-length to an individual country or region or may decide to undertake FDI, which requires selecting where to spend and in what kind of facilities, whether to procure existing operations or construct new plants, which production techniques to pursue, and how large an equity position to take with potential local partners. Companies may prefer a joint venture with some defined share of

---

203 Eunmi Chang M. Susan Taylor, Control in Multinational Corporations (MNEs): The Case of Korean Manufacturing Subsidiaries, Journal of Management 1999, Vol. 25, No. 4, 541–565.

204 Whitley, R., "The comparative study of business systems in Europe", in Whitley, R. (Ed.), European Business Systems, Sage Publications, London, 1992, p. 277. Caligiuri, P.M. and Stroh, L.K., "Multinational corporation management strategies and inter-national human resources practices: bringing IHRM to the bottom line", The International Journal of Human Resource Management, Vol. 6 No.3, September, 1995, pp. 494-507.

input costs, technology provision, and profits or losses, in particular in unknown or regulated markets. Finally, MNEs may choose to license a technology, product, or service. Multinational enterprises may embark on horizontal FDI where the subsidiary produces products and services similar to those produced at home, or vertical FDI, in which the subsidiary produces inputs or undertakes assembly from components. Vertical FDI is more widespread among MNEs that invest in developing (low-wage) economies, while horizontal FDI tends to distinguish the investment decisions of MNEs operating across borders within the industrialized, developed nations. Horizontal subsidiaries manufacture for local or regional markets only, without exporting much output to the host country. Besides, the output of vertical subsidiaries is more likely to be exported within MNEs, both to the host country and to other countries with similar demand characteristics. FDI affects a country's exporting activity when the rationale of the FDI is to make use of host country comparative advantages and sell in other national markets. Integrating economies are more expected to yield from improving intra-regional market ease of access leading to export-oriented FDI than from tougher external trade policy, and may wish to offer investment incentives to promote FDI by outside companies.

Universal FDI flows are driven above all by cross-border mergers and acquisitions3 where premiums rewarded by acquirers are based on likely synergies and so low quality host state governance reduces synergies, in this manner picture cross-border mergers and acquisitions economically infeasible. Enhancing the tax rate on MNEs or the corruption level of host countries reduce FDI inflows. Corruption decreases the successful protection of foreign investors' intangible property. Increased corruption minimizes inward FDI and shifts the ownership arrangement towards joint ventures. According to Sviatoslav A. Moskalev [205] "around the globe FDI flows from governance-abundant to governance-poor countries, and further, that those countries whose governance improves enjoy greater FDI while those whose governance deteriorates receive less foreign investment".

Companies engaged in exporting have affirmative performance characteristics including higher productivity, larger size, and greater capital intensity. MNEs pay higher wages than national counterparts, and globally engaged companies undertake more innovation[206]. Multinationals that export are typically goods producers while more than half of multinational importers are in the wholesale and retail sector. Exporters are more productive, more capital-intensive, pay higher wages, make use of more technology and have more proficient workers than non-exporting companies even when controlling for industry and geography. There is sizeable escalation in the number of companies that export, import and trade with related parties sending a greater number of products to a larger set of more countries and trading companies are becoming more and more import and export intensive in terms of their money value of trade per worker[207].

Companies engage in FDI once they have developed monopolistic advantages, such as advanced management skills, differentiation of products and technological developments that permit them to defeat domestic competitors in international markets. FDI play a key part in improving the aptitude of the host country to respond to the opportunities offered by global

[205] Sviatoslav A. Moskalev, Governance and Foreign Direct Investment, 2007 *www.ssrn.com* p15.
[206] Antràs, Pol and Elhanan Helpman, (2004), .Global sourcing., Journal of Political Economy 112: 552-580.
[207] Bernard, Andrew B. and J. Bradford Jensen. (2004). .Exporting and Productivity in the USA.Oxford Review of Economic Policy, 2004, Vol. 20, No. 3, 343-357.

economic integration, a goal more and more recognized as one of the key aims of any development strategy and accordingly countries become more in tune with global market trends and are able to gear their exporting activity to higher demand fields. An emerging economy can expand its relative bargaining ability with foreign multinationals in the conduct of direct investment by getting better on the array of resources it has to offer[208]. As Vernon supported a company tends to become multinational at a certain stage in its growth and in certain stage of the product cycle initially expanding by means of exports. Corporations take hierarchical control of monopolistic advantages to protect them against market imperfections. Companies move from export through knowledge agreements to foreign direct investment as the firm increases its understanding of a market. Exports to foreign countries are more and more being replaced by the direct production of goods in company plants located in these nations. As discussed earlier, the forms of capital participation in international enterprises are modes in which MNEs enter the intended host country through investment. There are two basic entry modes: wholly- owned subsidiary and joint venture. Transaction costs are major determinants of MNEs' entry modes and MNEs tend to choose an entry mode that minimizes transaction costs. The greater the sociocultural distance in the host country then the lower the degree of equity participation that a MNE could aim for. Sociocultural distance creates enormous information needs and hence high information costs for intending MNEs and in an unfamiliar cultural environment MNEs have little knowledge of the local market and business practice. Consequently, MNEs find it difficult to transfer home technologies and management techniques to an unknown operating environment and this disadvantage may be avoided by forming joint ventures with local firms and turning management partially over to local partners, who generally outperform new foreign entrants.[209] Operating in a foreign culture at a distance increases business uncertainty and unpredictability. Proprietary knowledge is a core component of firms' ownership advantages and influences effectively MNEs' international production and entry modes. The proprietary nature of a product, process and the amount of marketing expertise firms possess are factors that found to be highly correlated with percent ownership[210].

Firms seek to exert more control as the technological content of the product increases and R & D expenditure to total sales is usually used to measure the intellectual proprietary content of a product or process.[211] A higher degree of control is more often employed for technically sophisticated products, which tend to have a higher proprietary content than unsophisticated products, which means that firms tend to employ a completely-controlled entry vehicle in order to protect their interest in proprietary knowledge. Newer technologies are likely to be handled by wholly owned subsidiaries, which offer high control. The products gradually lose their initial proprietary value and become mature, therefore less administrative control is

---

208 Lages, L. (2000), "A conceptual framework of the determinants of export performance: reorganizing key variables and shifting contingencies in export marketing", Journal of Global Marketing, Vol. 13 No. 3, pp. 28-52.

209 Root, F. (1987), Entry Strategies for International Markets, Lexington Books, Lexington, MA.

210 Pan, Y. (1996), ``Influences on foreign equity ownership level in joint ventures in China", Journal of International Business Studies, Vol. 27 No. 1, pp. 1-26. Buckley, P. and Casson, M. (1985), The Economic Theory of the Multinational Enterprise, Macmillan, London. Buckley, P. and Casson, M. (1996), ``An economic model of international joint venture strategy", Journal of International Business Studies (Special Issue), No. 5.

211 Anderson, E. and Gaignon, H. (1986), ``Modes of foreign entry: a transaction cost analysis and propositions", Journal of International Business Studies, Vol. 17 No. 3, pp. 1-26.

needed. On the one hand, a foreign investing firm would have a higher propensity to form joint ventures with local firms if its technology is standardized. On the other hand, if local firms hold significant proprietary assets and marketing expertise, they will either have fewer incentives to form joint ventures with foreign firms, or require more control over joint ventures.

External uncertainty is the unpredictability of the firm's environment.[212] In a highly unpredictable environment, MNEs tend to limit their equity involvement by avoiding full ownership in order to diversify the business risks. At the same time, they may want to get greater control to compensate for high risks. Country risk and the uncertainty of business environment may increase the information need and management cost for MNEs to operate fully owned subsidiaries in the host country. To minimize transaction costs and business risks, MNEs need to form joint ventures with local firms. Local partners are essential for foreign entrants since they have expertise in exploring domestic markets, managing local labour and organizing local supplies of raw materials and intermediate products. A booming economy and rapidly expanding domestic market in the host country would strengthen its attraction for foreign investment. If the host country government encourages joint ventures by using favourable policy treatments such as tax concessions, other things being equal, MNEs may have incentives to choose joint venture as an entry mode.[213] Hence, the policy orientation of the host government is one of major determinants for the ownership of foreign subsidiaries.

MNEs invested more in training compared with the local firms. Product innovation involves the extensions to the range of products while capital innovation results in changes to machines and equipment, including automation and the introduction of information technology. Work process innovation deals with changes to the way work is organized. The strongly innovative character of MNEs is evident from the fact that they introduce new technology than local firms. MNEs have a greater incidence of training and retraining of their workforce. The most important aspect of industrial training by MNEs consists not only of training provided to production workers but also to skilled workers and management staff geared towards complementing existing skills as required for the immediate performance of the MNEs. MNEs draw on the existing pool of trained candidates, sometimes depriving local firms of highly trained personnel. The presence of MNEs offering sophisticated employment opportunities could stimulate potential employees to invest in advanced training. The current trend is for the MNEs to leave product and process designs to parent companies overseas while they are only involved in the production of standardized products using relatively mature processes. [214] Structural rather than cultural determinants tend to be explanators for the

---

[212] Williamson, O. (1979), ``Transaction cost economics: the governance of contractual relations", Journal of Law and Economics, No. 22, October, pp. 233-62. Williamson, O. (1981), ``The economics of organization: the transaction cost approach", American Journal of Sociology, Vol. 87 No. 3, pp. 548-77. Williamson, O. (1985), The Economic Institutions of Capitalism: Firms, Markets, Relational Contracting, Free Press, New York, NY.

[213] Gomes-Casseres, B. (1989), ``Ownership structures of foreign subsidiaries: the theory and evidence", Journal of Economic Behavior and Organization, January, pp. 1-25. Gomes-Casseres, B. (1990), ``Firm ownership preferences and host government restrictions: an integrated Approach", Journal of International Business Studies, Vol. 21 No. 1, pp. 1-22.

[214] Cantwell, J., Technological Innovation and Multinational Corporations, Basil Blackwell, Oxford, 1989. Adnan, M.A. and Ali, A., "Technological Acquisition and Absorption via Multinational Companies: The Malaysian Experience", Journal Ekonomi Malaysia, Vols. 21, 22, 1990, pp. 151-71.

choices of multinational corporations[215]. The US firms, for example, tend to be non-unionised, while the Japanese firms tend to be unionised, albeit with single union deals.[216]

The informal socio-political component comprises non-institutional factors, such as public and local community pressure, and demands from nongovernmental organizations (NGOs) and other forms of agency. For the subsidiaries of MNEs, the external context is defined both by the local context, and the context of the MNE as a whole. This includes headquarter policies host and home country regulatory frameworks, international regulations and codes of conduct, local and international NGO demands, and media comment. A firm needs to give attention to all customers, including those within the organization.[217] An internal customer orientation is important in multinational corporations (MNEs) where internal customers may be in foreign countries and direct contact with external customers may be limited[218]. Organizational learning capacity (OLC) is an intangible resource that is deeply embedded in the fabric of an organization. Moreover, OLC influences the quality of the work of both partners in the sourcing unit and the ultimate success of the supply chain.[219] Organization is a bundle of resources and an administrative framework that links and coordinates activities of individuals and groups. The growth of an organization is limited in part by the ability of managers to coordinate and link organizational resources. Knowledge is perhaps the most imperative resource for developing a sustainable competitive advantage.[220] Knowledge and the capacity to develop knowledge are the most important resources that generate added value in the supply chain.[221] Once domestic firms break down physical and psychological boundaries and identify themselves as part of the global community, they can improve their positioning and regain competitive advantage in their home country as well as in other parts of the world. In the MNE, setting the social structure of the strategic sourcing unit is multifaceted because its members may be in different countries and thus may face special, language, and cultural barriers. The strategic sourcing unit is composed of two participants — corporate buyers and internal customers. Both buyers and customers have to find a balance between exploiting the benefits of economies of scale and adaptation to the

---

[215] Marginson, P. and Sisson, K. (1994), "The structure of transnational capital in Europe: the emerging Euro-company and its implications for industrial relations", in Hyman, R. and Ferner, A. (Eds), New Frontiers in European Industrial Relations, Blackwell, Oxford.

[216] Watanabe, S. (1993), "Growth and structural change of Japanese overseas direct investment: implications for labour and management in host economies", in Bailey, P., Parisotto, A. and Renshaw, G. (Eds), Multinationals and Employment: The Global Economy in the 1990s, ILO, Geneva.

[217] Kohli, A. K., & Jaworski, B. J. (1990, April). Market orientation: the construct, research propositions, and managerial implications. Journal of Marketing, 54, 1–18.

[218] Conduit, J., & Mavondo, F. T. (2001). How critical is internal customer orientation to market orientation? Journal of Business Research, 51, 11–24.

[219] Dyer, J. H., & Singh, H. (1998). The relational view: cooperative strategy and sources of interorganizational competitive advantage. Academy of Management Review, 23 (4), 660–679. Hult, G. T. M. (1998). Managing the international strategic sourcing function as a market-driven organizational learning system. Decision Sciences, 29 (1), 193–216.

[220] Grant, R. M. (1996). Prospering in dynamically-competitive environments: organizational capability as knowledge integration. Organization Science, 7 (4), 375–387. Grant, R. M. (1996). Toward a knowledge-based theory of the firm. Strategic Management Journal, 17, 109–122 (Winter Special Issue).

[221] Handfield, R. B., & Nichols Jr., E. L. (1999). Supply chain management. Upper Saddle River, NJ: Prentice-Hall. Hult, G. T. M., Hurley, R. F., Giunipero, L. C., & Nichols Jr., E. L. (2000). Organizational learning in global purchasing: a model and test of internal users and corporate buyers. Decision Sciences, 31 (2), 293–325.

local circumstances.[222] Hence, OLC is significantly related to customer orientation within strategic sourcing units.[223]

How that workforce is recruited, trained, challenged and involved become critical components in ultimate organizational success and reward play a major part to produce a high-performance people focused on organisational objectives. Linkages with companies in other countries through networks of business relationships help small and medium-sized businesses, which are addressing international markets to overcome hurdles of market and cultural differences. The more significant the international linkages between companies, the more that strategy formation involves negotiation, agreement and exchange between business leaders from various national cultural values and traditions requiring successful interaction between individuals from different national backgrounds, each with their own aims and goals, over complex issues generating appropriate levels of trust requires shared language, beliefs and understandings[224].

Technical progress and growth can be based on creation of entirely new knowledge, or adaptation and transfer of existing foreign technology. According to Van den Berg[225] "it is the quality of the labor force, its accumulated experience and human capital, its education system, and so on, that determines an economy's ability to create new ideas and adapt old ones". It is less costly to learn to use existing technology than to produce new technology, which means that developing countries have the potential to grow faster than developed economies for any given level of investment or R&D spending. Accordingly, improvements in education and human capital are necessary for absorbing and adapting foreign technology, and to generate sustainable long-run growth[226]. MNEs undertake a major part of the world's private R&D efforts and produce, own, and control most of the world's advanced technology leaking to the surrounding economy through external effects or spillover that raise the level of human capital in the host country and generate productivity increases in local companies. FDI not only introduces new ideas but it also strengthens the human capital base needed to adjust these ideas to the local market[227]. Economies with weaker initial conditions are expected to

---

[222] Nohria, N., & Ghoshal, S. (1994). Differentiated fit and shared values: alternatives for managing headquarters – subsidiary relations. Strategic Management Journal, 15, 491–502. Barkema, H. G., & Vermeulen, F. (1998). International expansion through start-up or acquisition: a learning perspective. Academy of Management Journal, 41 (1), 7–26. Dooley, K., Anderson, J., & Liu, X. (2000). Process quality knowledge bases. Journal of Quality Management, 4 (2), 207–224.

[223] Hurley, R. F., & Hult, G. T. M. (1998). Innovation, market orientation, and organizational learning: an integration and empirical examination. Journal of Marketing, 62 (3), 42–54. Jensen, M. C., & Meckling, W. H. (1995). Specific and general knowledge, and organizational structure. Journal of Applied Corporate Finance, 8 (2), 4–18.

[224] Bowman, C. and Daniels, K. (1995), ``The influence of functional experience on perceptions of strategic priorities", British Journal of Management, Vol. 6 No. 2, pp. 157-67. Buckley, P. and Casson, M. (1997), ``An economic model of international joint venture strategy", in Beamish, P. and Killing, J. (Eds), Cooperative Strategies, Lexington Press, San Francisco, CA, pp. 3-32.

[225] VAN DEN BERG, H. (2001), Economic Growth and Development, McGraw-Hill, Singapore, p226.

[226] GÖRG, H. and E. STROBL (2000), "Multinational Companies, Technology Spillovers, and Firm Survival: Evidence from Irish Manufacturing", GLM Research Paper 2000/18, University of Nottingham. GÖRG, H. and E. STROBL (2001), "Multinational Companies, Technology Spillovers, and Plant Survival: Evidence from Irish Manufacturing", EIJS Working Paper 131, Stockholm School of Economics. GÖRG, H. and E. STROBL (2001), "Multinational Companies and Productivity Spillovers: A Meta-Analysis", The Economic Journal 111, issue 475, pp. 723-739.

[227] Blomström, M., A. Kokko And M. Zejan (2000), Foreign Direct Investment: Firm and Host Country Strategies, Macmillan, London.

experience smaller inflows of FDI, and those foreign companies that enter are likely to use simpler technologies that contribute only marginally to local learning and skill development.

4.10 MNE AND PERFORMANCE

Is firm performance determined by the structural conditions of the industry in which the firm competes? The resources and capabilities of the individual firms are the main determinant of firm performance[228]. In a team, time is divided between production and coordination of activities with the other team members. Information technology increases the team's coordination capabilities rather than increasing the number of team members in order to increase production. The production and coordination activities are balanced in an equilibrium condition where production and the information generated by the production activity are traded off against the time it takes to deal with similar information generated by other team members[229]. Improving information technology increases team output, but affects the choice of best possible subgroup size in various ways depending on the type of information technology investment. The available computing and communication technology may determine the choice of tasks for a team or an organization. Improved information technology may allow teams and organizations to undertake tasks that require very high degrees of coordination[230].

The role of country conditions as a determinant of firm performance is important to MNEs. The structural conditions of the industry determine the conduct of firms within the industry, which in turn determines firm performance. Characteristics of the individual firm, such as its market position and its resources and capabilities are the main determinants of performance, which implies that intra-industry differences in firm performance exist. Business unit effects stem from the market position of the business relative to its competitors and from resources definite to the business unit[231]. Is firm performance determined by factors that are not controllable by firm management or factors controllable by management are more important? Country characteristics are least controllable by subsidiary management but structural characteristics of the industry within the country prejudiced by subsidiary managers

---

[228] Child, J., 1997. Strategic choice in the analysis of action, structure, organizations and environment: retrospect and prospect. Organization Studies 18, 43–76.

[229] Albanese, R., and D. D. Van Fleet, 1985. Rational Behavior in Groups: The Free-Riding Tendency. Academy of Management Journal 10(2), 244--255. DAVIS, J. H., 1969. Group Performance. Addison-Wesley, Reading, MA. Festinger, L., A. Pepitone, And T. Newcomb, 1952. Some Consequences of De-Individuation in a Group. Journal of Abnormal and Social Psychology 47, 382--389. GALBRAITH, J. K., 1967. The New Industrial State. Houghton Mifflin, Boston, MA. Gist, M. E., E. A. Locke, and S. M. Taylor, 1987. Organizational Behavior: Group Structure, Process, and Effectiveness. Journal of Management 13(2), 237--257.

[230] Hiltz, S. R., and M. Turoff, 1985. Structuring Computer-Mediated Communication Systems to Avoid Information Overload. Communications of the ACM 28(7), 680--689. Markus, M. L., and D. Robey, 1988. Information Technology and Organizational Change: Causal Structure in Theory and Research. Management Science 34(5), 583--598. Zalesny, M. D., E. Salas, and C. Prince, 1995. Conceptual and Measurement Issues in Coordination: Implications for Team Behavior and Performance. Research in Personnel and Human Resources Management 13, 81--115.

[231] Collis, D.J., Montgomery, C.A., 1998. Creating corporate advantage. Harvard Business Review 76, 70–83.

only insofar as actions by individual local subsidiaries alter industry structure[232]. While corporate characteristics are more controllable by subsidiary management as the subsidiary management may have some influence on which corporate attributes and assets get transferred into the country, strategic characteristics are mainly the direct responsibility of local subsidiary management.[233]

FDI involves the transfer to a subsidiary company abroad of a put together of equity capital and of intermediate resources, the nature of which is both tangible (machinery) and intangible (management and organization know-how). The handover is carried out under common ownership and control and under the neoclassical economic theory the export of equity capital may be somewhat explained by inter-country differences in the return to capital due to differentials of capital endowments, productivity and labor costs.

A subsidiary abroad, because it takes benefit of technology and know-how transferred as part of the FDI tie together, is able to accomplish productivity levels equivalent to the ones at home. In general marginal productivity of capital is associated with the height of interest rate, meaning that low interest rates affirm low marginal productivity of capital and the opposite. Productivity differentials exist between countries having matching factor proportions however diverse rates of technological change and accordingly speedier introduction of new technologies in one country enhance labor productivity faster than in countries with a rather average pace of technological change attract equity capital flowing out of the latter into the former aiming to take advantage of the dispersion effect the introduction of new technologies might have.

The least controllable factors will have the largest effects on subsidiary performance.[234] Country characteristics are the most imperative determinant of subsidiary performance, followed by industry structure, subsidiary strategy, and corporate characteristics which means that subsidiary performance is essentially determined by conditions outside the control of subsidiary management[235]. According to industry structure view[236] a company's performance is primarily determined by the structural conditions of the industry in which the company competes, while the resource-based view of the firm[237] argues that the resources and capabilities of the individual companies are the main determinant of firm performance. This author considers that the individual characteristics and advantages of a company must comply with the demands and structural conditions prevailing in the industry, the country and the environment where the company performs. The role of country conditions as a determinant of firm performance is particularly important to MNEs[238]. Selecting country markets for entry

---

232 Hoskisson, R.E., Hill, C.W., Kim, H., 1993. The multidivisional structure: organizational fossil or source of value? Journal of Management 19, 269–298. McGahan, A.M., Porter, M.E., 1997. How much does industry matter, really? Strategic Management Journal 8, 15–30.

233 Birkinshaw, J.M., Morrison, A.J., 1995. Configurations of strategy and structure in subsidiaries of multinational corporations. Journal of International Business Studies 26, 729–753.

234 Montgomery, C.A., Porter. M.E., 1991. Strategy: Seeking and Securing Competitive Advantage. Boston: Harvard Business School.

235 Yip, G.S., 1992. Total Global Strategy: Managing for Worldwide Competitive Advantage. Prentice Hall: Engle-wood Cliffs, NJ.

236 Porter, M.E., 1980. Competitive Strategy. Free Press: New York.

237 Wernerfelt, B., 1984. A resource-based view of the firm. Strategic Management Journal 5, 171–180.

238 Petra Christmann , Diana Day , George S. Yip, The relative influence of country conditions, industry structure, and business strategy on multinational corporation subsidiary performance, Journal of International Management 5 (1999) 241–265.

and investment and evaluating the performance of their country subsidiaries are two basic problems that MNEs face. The structural conditions of the industry determine the management of firms within the industry, which in turn determines firm performance. Market position and resources and capabilities are the most important determinants of performance, which implies that intra-industry differences in firm performance exist. Corporate effects add to business unit performance by providing economies associated with resource sharing, and by the capability to transfer rent-creating resources among the business units[239]. A MNE's capacity of picking the right countries for entry and investment should lead to significant competitive advantage, which means that strategic choice at the corporate level is very important for corporate performance.

4.11 MNE and Manufacturing Systems

As companies more and more compete with a dissimilar stock of knowledge, management of the company's knowledge base has emerged as a key challenge in maintaining sustainable competitive advantage entered a new era of knowledge management. The values and culture of an organization have a considerable influence on the learning process and how successfully a company can adapt and change.[240]

Business globalisation is leading to widespread restructuring of international manufacturing systems in MNEs. Lack of global vision and suitable strategies during the internationalisation have become main barrier to the successful management of international operations.[241] The international market is not only a sum of different national markets. International business strategy is based upon these individual markets and sets up objectives and policies independently to fulfil the specific requirements of different countries. To satisfy the growing global market, the traditional products and related development strategies are obviously not enough to satisfy companies' internationalisation. Many MNEs have sought to achieve lower cost, higher quality, faster product introduction, greater flexibility, and shorter delivery time, all at the same time, which has become a necessary requirement of global competition. Companies need to pay more attention to their internal capability building and new patterns of manufacturing system searching to create a proactive competitive influence rather than a reactive responsiveness to the new industrial environment.

New generations of communication and transportation technologies are creating the possibility for MNEs to organise their worldwide operations more effectively and efficiently. Worldwide market opportunity, new patters of competition, and reorganising potential or possibility requires a new generation of networks beyond the classical pipeline of physical transformation. The networking characteristics of the new manufacturing system must involve an extensive perspective covering geographic dispersion and interdependent

239 Collis, D.J., Montgomery, C.A., 1998. Creating corporate advantage. Harvard Business Review 76, 70–83.

240 Shan L. Pan, Dorothy E. Leidner, Bridging communities of practice with information technology in pursuit of global knowledge sharing, Journal of Strategic Information Systems 12 (2003) 71–88

241 Klassen, R.D., Whybark, D.C., 1994. Barriers to the management of international operations. J. Operat. Manage. 11.

coordination rather than the traditional focus on separated manufacturing sites. [242] International manufacturing network design is simplified into location decision and good factory design. Performance priorities, efficiency/cost, quality, dependability, and flexibility, which, in addition to three other key variables, market orientation, experience and product characteristics, play important roles in the development of international manufacturing configurations (IMC) strategies.[243] One type of IMC with specific patterns of geographic dispersed facilities and shared common infrastructure/mechanism could lead to a synergy[244]. The interdependent coordination in the networks is a determinant of network structure. [245] The coordination between future market requirements and corporate strategies influences not only the corporate organisation but also the manufacturing network and factory internal characteristics.

Manufacturing globalisation might be defined as the process of moving from independently managed businesses serving local markets to networks of businesses serving the businesses' chosen markets in a coordinated and optimised way. Manufacturing networks are the main outcome of globalisation and capability development is one of the key motivations of the process. Just as global strategy cannot be actually operated without manufacturing networking, the manufacturing system and whole business require globalised coordination and cooperation. The manufacturing competitiveness will profoundly depend upon network construction and mechanisms rather than separated factory nodes[246]. Manufacturing businesses are more and more faced with decisions involving global considerations and capability development.

A dynamic view of technological advantages emphasizes a shift of strategic and technological initiative away from the country of origin, involving a mix of exploitation of established technological capabilities as well as the foreign introduction of technologies that are new to the multinational group[247]. Initial foreign involvement reflects efforts to reduce risk and uncertainty, for example by concentrating on geographically close and familiar markets, limiting the initial investments or building flexibility into the ways in which foreign markets are penetrated. Increasing commitments involve the replacing of exports and independent agents by sales and manufacturing subsidiaries. These changes reflect ambitions to better service home customers as well as local management's aspirations to gain control over resources and operational decision-making.

---

[242] Daniels, Daniels, 1993. Global Vision: Building New Model for the Corporation of the Future. McGraw-Hill.

[243] DuBois, F.L., Toyne, B., Oliff, M.D., 1993. International manufacturing strategy of U.S. multinationals: a concept framework based on a four-industry study. J. Int. Business Stud., 2nd Quarter.

[244] Flaherty, M.T., 1989. Coordinating international manufacturing and technology. In: Porter, M.E. Ed. , Competition in Global Industries. Harvard Business School Press.

[245] Dicken says that. ''Each of these strategies has rather different implications for the internal relationships between the individual parts of the enterprise. In particular, units which are part of a vertically integrated operation tend to be locked into a much tighter network of internal interdependencies with other parts of enterprise''. Dicken, P., 1992. Global Shift: The Internationalisation of Economics Activities, 2nd ed. Paul Chapman.

[246] Baden-Fuller, C., Stopford, J., 1991. Globalisation frustrated: the case of white goods. Strategic Manage. J. 12. Sprague, L.G., 1990. Strategic analysis for global manufacturing. In: Moody, P.E. Ed. , Strategic Manufacturing: Dynamic New Direction For the 1990s. Business One Irwin.

[247] Patel, P. (1995). Localized production of technology for global markets. Cambridge Journal of Economics, 19, 141–153.

During the first stages of the internationalisation process the introduction of new technology remains the responsibility of the home country units. Most forms of foreign involvement require a certain amount of technology transfer, as even mere sales efforts require an understanding of the product and the ability to demonstrate it successfully to local customers. Operations in foreign markets over time tend to become increasingly embedded in the local business environment. Hence, increasing embeddedness in the local business environment involves the establishment of closer ties with customers and suppliers, as well as with other actors such as research organizations, universities and government institutions. Becoming embedded in the local business environment implies access to distinctive inputs for the development of new technology. Each local environment tends to display a constellation of resources which promotes technological development in some unique areas, and which only to a limited extent is transferable across national or regional boundaries. Internationalisation, enhanced resource commitments to foreign markets and increasing local embeddedness may have a long-term effect on the organization of technological capabilities in the MNE. Specifically, foreign units have been found to become less dependent on the supply of upgraded products and technology from the home country units, repeatedly developing their own unique capabilities and fields of technological expertise. [248] Some firms are using foreign locations to supply technology, which is corresponding to the technological capabilities available in the home market[249]. The exceptional capabilities of foreign units play an important role in the formation of multi-centre structures within the multinational enterprise, particularly when foreign acquisitions have added new product areas and technologies to the acquiring firm. Enhanced resource commitments to foreign markets and increasing local embeddedness are fundamentally driven by ambitions to exploit technological advantages in foreign markets and the passing of time. Moreover, availability of resources and increasing embeddedness in idiosyncratic business environments provide a platform for the discovery and exploitation of new technological opportunities, which in some cases turn out to be commercially viable in international markets.[250] Proliferation of international acquisitions has often provided 'instant embeddedness' in local business environments[251]. Foreign acquisitions are normally undertaken to improve local market positions or to restructure industries without confronting retaliation by established competitors. The acquisition of firms, whether domestic or foreign, increases the likelihood that new and more distantly related fields of technology are added to the established technology portfolio.

---

[248] Patel, P., & Pavitt, K. (1998). The wide (and increasing) spread of technological competencies in the world's largest firms: A challenge to conventional wisdom. In A. D. Chandler, P. Hagstrom & O. Solvell, The dynamic multinational firm. Oxford: Oxford University Press. Zander, I. (1997). Technological diversification in the multinational corporation—Historical trends and future prospects. Research Policy, 26, 209–227.

[249] Cantwell, J., & Randaccio, F. S. (1992). Intra-industry direct investment in the European Community: Oligopolistic rivalry and technological competition. In J. Cantwell, Multinational investment in modern Europe—Strategic interaction in the integrated community. Edward Elgar.

[250] Birkinshaw, J. (1997). Entrepreneurship in multinational corporations: The characteristics of subsidiary initiatives. Strategic Management Journal, 18(3), 207–229. Birkinshaw, J., & Hood, N. (1998). Multinational corporate evolution and subsidiary development. New York: Macmillan Press.

[251] Andersson, U., Johanson, J., & Vahlne, J.-E. (1997). Organic acquisitions in the internationalization process of the business firm. Management International Review, 37, 67–84.

Foreign subsidiaries frequently develop both higher levels of technological activity and more sophisticated operations[252]. International growth of the MNE involves increasing technological diversity on account of units located outside the country of origin. Foreign units not only represent an increasing share of all new technologies that are developed within the multinational network, but are also responsible for a disproportionate number of entries into new and more distantly related fields of technology[253].

4.12 Transfer of Technology

Are MNEs an important channel of international technology diffusion? Does the positive effect reflect technology diffusion by MNEs? The presence of MNEs increases competition in the host country and thereby leads to improved market efficiency and higher productivity. The level of human capital is crucial for a country to benefit from the technology spillovers of MNEs[254]. Higher spending by the affiliates on technology transfer corresponds to greater technology diffusion to the host country. FDI[255] can have a positive effect on per capita income growth only if the recipient country had reached a minimum human capital threshold.

Technology - broadly interpreted to include both product, process, and distribution technology, as well as management skills - is one of the proprietary assets that allow firms to become multinational and establish affiliates in foreign markets. MNEs undertake a key part of the world's private research and development (R&D) efforts and produce, own, and control most of the world's advanced commercial technology. Thus, MNEs also play a central role in the international diffusion of technology. In fact, the opportunity to get access to modern technology is one of the central host country motives for attracting inward FDI. Technology spillovers seem to be confined to a small area, so that new technology is diffused first to firms

---

[252] Barkema, H. G., Bell, J. H., & Pennings, J. M. (1996). Foreign entry, cultural barriers, and learning. Strategic Management Journal, 17, 151–166. Dunning, J. H. (1994). Multinational enterprises and the globalization of innovatory capacity. Research Policy, 23, 67–88. Johanson, J., & Mattsson, L.-G. (1988). Internationalization in industrial systems—A network approach. In N. Hood & J.-E. Vahlne, Strategies in global competition. London: Croom Helm.

[253] Mudambi, R. (1998). The role of duration in multinational investment strategies. Journal of InternationalBusiness Studies, 29(2), 239–262. Niosi, J. (1997). The globalization of Canada's R&D. Management International Review, 37(4), 387–404. Nobel, R., & Birkinshaw, J. (1998). Innovation in multinational corporations: Control and communication patterns in international R&D operations. Strategic Management Journal, 19, 479–496.

[254] Aitken, B.J., Harrison, A.E., 1999. Do domestic firms benefit from direct foreign investment? Evidence from Venezuela. American Economic Review 89, 605–618. Barro, R., Sala-i-Martin, X., 1997. Technology diffusion, convergence, and growth. Journal of Economic Growth 2, 1–26.

[255] Borensztein, E., Gregorio, J., Lee, J., 1998. How does foreign direct investment affect economic growth. Journal of International Economics 45, 115–135. Lichtenberg and van Pottelsberghe de la Potterie found that inward FDI flows did not carry knowledge spillovers among OECD countries during the period 1970–1990, while Hejazi and Safarian 1996 found significant R&D spillovers in FDI from the US to other OECD countries during the same period. Lichtenberg, F., van Pottelsberghe de la Potterie, B. 1996. International R&D spillovers: a re-examination. NBER Working Paper No. 5668, Cambridge, MA. Lichtenberg, F., van Pottelsberghe de la Potterie, B., 1998. International R&D spillovers: a comment. European Economic Review 42, 1483–1491. Hejazi, W., Safarain, E., 1996. Trade, investment and United States R&D spillovers. Working Paper No. 65, The Canadian Institute for Advanced Research.

operating close to the innovator[256]. A patent is a provisional monopoly awarded for the commercial use of an innovation. A country's stock of patents can be seen as a proxy variable for its stock of commercial knowledge. Geographic distance is more of information flow barrier for SMEs than for MNEs, since the latter are able to draw on information from their networks of foreign affiliates. Foreign investment is a significant channel for the international diffusion of technology from host to home country affiliates. Thus, FDI may have a role in the international diffusion of knowledge.

Key element of liberalisation has been greater openness to FDI as a means of acquiring technologies, skills and entrée to international markets, and of entering energetic trade and production systems internal to MNEs.

The role of the MNE as a source of capital and technology has grown over time, as other sources of capital have become scarcer or more unpredictable and technical transform has accelerated. MNEs continue to dictate the making of technology; indeed, with the rising costs and risks of innovation their magnitude has been raised with the exception of very new technology areas. MNEs supply new technologies or present new products to the country's export basket; but most developing countries do not have the organizational capabilities to employ effective selection policies, and their attempts to do so often end up scaring off MNEs altogether[257].

MNEs have become more mobile, searching the world for lower cost, more proficient production sites and for new markets. The interaction of technical transform with its need for more and higher skills and better infrastructure with superior FDI mobility has not reduced the need for resident capabilities in developing countries. FDI transfers technology to native companies by backward linkages, labour turnover, international technology spillovers and horizontal linkages. The capacity of the host economy to benefit from MNE linkages has been found to depend essentially on the relative scientific capabilities of recipient and transmitter: the greater the distance between them, the lower the strength of linkages.

MNEs build more linkages when they use intermediate goods intensively, communication costs between parent and affiliate are high and the home and host markets are somewhat parallel in terms of intermediate goods. On the other hand, affiliates established by mergers and acquisitions have stronger links with national suppliers than those established by Greenfield investment[258].

While unsatisfactory absorptive capacity tends to lead to the unproductive use of technology inflows, knowledge accumulation is much more rapid once the threshold point of absorptive aptitude is crossed. The cost of imitation increases as the follower closes the opening with the leader and the number of technologies offered for replication falls and accordingly there are diminishing returns on marginal increases in absorptive ability as companies approach the frontier of knowledge[259]. While learning and absorption take place at

---

256 Audretsch, D. B. and M. P. Feldman (1996), "R&D Spillovers and the Geography ofInnovation and Production", American Economic Review, Vol. 86, pp. 630-640.

257 Borensztein, E., De Gregorio, J. & Lee, J. -W. (1998) How does foreign direct investment affect economic growth?. Journal of International Economics, 45, pp. 115-135.

258 Dunning, J.H. and R. Narula, 2004, Multinational and Industrial Competitiveness: A New Agenda, Cheltenham: Edward Elgar.

259 Benito, G., B. Grogaard and R. Narula, 2003, 'Environmental Influences on MNE Subsidiary Roles: Economic Integration and the Nordic Countries', Journal of International Business Studies, Vol.34, pp.443–56.

the company level, the success or failure of individual companies occurs within a 'system' and accordingly there exists a broad knowledge base outside industrial enterprises; this foundation is vital to technological gathering by industry.

Technological advances and globalization create the need for inter-firm cooperation in order to stay competitive. Research and development (R&D) intensity and the level of sophistication of any specific industry are certainly correlated with the intensity and number of alliances in those industries. Technological joint ventures—those involved in R&D activity—can be critical in high-technology industries due to the dynamic rate of technological development, product complexity and the high cost of product R&D. Investments and outputs from R&D in market transactions are subject to moral hazard and adverse selection problems resulting from a company's inability to accurately monitor and assess output value[260]. Cultural relatedness and country risk factors do matter when it comes to R&D activity in biotechnology joint ventures[261].

Technology transfer is facilitated by trade contacts. Importers may benefit directly from imports of technology embodied in machinery and equipment, while exporters are probable to be influenced by contacts with foreign clients, who may demand product alterations and assist in finding technical solutions. Migration and a variety of academic and scientific contacts are very likely to facilitate knowledge flows.[262] The diffusion of knowledge is expected to be more intensive between countries with comparable industry structures. Trade contacts and outward FDI seem to facilitate technology diffusion. Additionally, outward FDI is a major channel for the diffusion of foreign technology to MNEs as well as to SMEs[263]. It should be taken into consideration that foreign affiliates are occasionally located in foreign "centers of excellence", where one purpose of the investment is to learn about foreign technology.

As mentioned above, MNEs bring with them certain amount of proprietary technology that constitutes their firm-specific advantage and allows them to compete effectively with local firms who have the superior knowledge of local markets, consumer preferences, and business practices. The entry of the MNE affiliate disturbs the existing equilibrium in the market and forces home firms to take action to protect their market shares and profits. Spillovers from FDI may occur from increased competition and labour turnover, or through demonstration, and may take place either in the foreign affiliate's own industry or among the affiliate's suppliers and customers in other industries. Spillovers may not materialize if the technology disparity between foreign and local firms is too large.

---

[260] Das, S., Sen, P., Sengupta, S., 1998. Impact of strategic alliances on firm valuation. Acad. Manage. J. 41, 27–41.

[261] Malika Richards , Donna Marie De Carolis, Joint venture research and development activity: an analysis of the international biotechnology industry, Journal of International Management 9 (2003) 33–49

[262] Enos, J. L. (1989), "Transfer of Technology", Asian-Pacific Economic Literature, Vol. 3, pp. 3-37. Griliches, Z. (1992), "The Search for R&D Spillovers", Scandinavian Journal of Economics, Vol. 94, Supplement, pp. 29-47. Jaffe, A. B., M. Trajtenberg and R. Henderson (1993), "Geographical Localization of Knowledge Spillovers As Evidenced by Patent Citations", Quarterly Journal of Economics, Vol. 108, pp. 577-98.

[263] Blomström, M. and A. Kokko (1996), "Multinational Corporations and Spillovers", CEPR Discussion Paper No. 1365, April. Braunerhjelm, P. and R. Svensson (1996), "Host Country Characteristics and Agglomeration in Foreign Direct Investment", Applied Economics, Vol. 28, pp. 833-840. Cantwell, J. (1989), Technological Innovation and Multinational Corporations, Oxford and Cambridge; Basil Blackwell.

Local participation with multinationals reveals the MNEs' proprietary knowledge and in that way facilitates spillovers. [264] If there is a risk for foreign firms to loose their intangible assets to a local partner, they may either refuse to invest or bring less advanced technologies to the affiliates. The greater the foreign control over an affiliate, the more sophisticated technologies would be transferred from the parent firm. Hence, the more technologies brought in to the affiliate, the larger is the scope for spillovers.[265] Local partners are likely to have better knowledge of local conditions regarding factor endowments and skill of employees. Such factors clearly affect the choice of technology brought in by the MNEs and thereby the degree of spillovers, since technologies suitable for local conditions will have the largest effect on host country firms. Labour productivity is positively related to capital intensity, labour skill, capacity utilization, and scale of operation. Furthermore, labour productivity is higher in establishments with foreign equity than in purely domestically owned firms and that the latter benefit from spillovers from FDI. Multinationals have a wide range of technologies to choose between when they invest abroad, and that they will adapt their technology transfer to the competitive situation and other conditions in the host economy. Local participation with multinationals reveals the MNEs proprietary knowledge and in that way facilitates technology spillovers to the domestic sector. The competitive pressure from FDI is one potentially important determinant of spillovers. Foreign entry into a market may increase competition and force domestic firms to become more efficient. The negative effects of the economy-wide distortions resulting from import substituting policies are likely to overweigh any positive spill over benefits from FDI in the protected sector. It could be said that technology spillovers are more a result of the increased competition that follows FDI than ownership sharing of the multinational affiliates.[266]

The telecommunications sector increased its capital spending sharply in the 1990s, after governments opened the market to new entrants and spurred by the introduction of marketable new technologies – notably mobile phones and Internet access services. As technological innovation made competition more and more possible in the long-distance and international telephony markets, policy makers sought to liberalise the access of new entrants. For instance, new legislation was adopted in the United States under the Telecommunications Act of 1996 and in the European Union under the Telecommunications Directive of 1997. Sector-specific National Regulatory Agencies (NRAs) were set up to complement the roles of economy-wide competition authorities[267]. The privatisation or partial privatisation of incumbent public operators; the opening of the sector to foreign ownership; price regulation for services where dominant positions prevail; and other measures such as number portability enhanced consumer choice and competition has intensified with consumers benefited from greater choice, lower prices and higher quality services. In the new markets of mobile telephony and Internet access services, the absence of pre-established market positions has

---

264 Blomström, M. and A. Kokko (1998), "Multinational Corporations and Spillovers", Journal of Economic Surveys, Vol. 12, pp. 247-277.

265 Ramachandran, V. (1993), "Technology Transfer, Firm Ownership, and Investment in Human Capital", Review of Economics and Statistics, Vol. 75, pp. 664-670. Beamish, P. W. (1988), "Multinational Joint Ventures in Developing Countries", London: Routledge.

266 Kokko, A. (1996), "Productivity Spillovers from Competition between Local Firms and Foreign Affiliates", Journal of International Development, Vol. 8, pp. 517-30. Sjöholm, F. (1997), "Technology Gap, Competition and Spillovers from Direct Foreign Investment: Evidence from Establishment Data", Working Paper No 212, Stockholm School of Economics.

267 OECD (2003), Communications Outlook 2003, Paris.

facilitated competition[268]. The liberalisation of the sector, together with the emergence of new telecommunications technologies resulted in high expectations for future revenues and earnings, boosting share prices and allowing unprecedented levels of borrowing[269].

Firm-specific assets, which include such things as marketing ability, product differentiation or Research and Development (R&D), can be seen as giving a firm a competitive edge, which enables it to expand production into foreign markets.[270] A firm may not only expand sales abroad in order to draw on its technology asset, it may also be done to gain resources to develop this asset. Implementing the technology abroad rather than at home is more costly, due to technology transfer costs. Should higher R&D intensity lead firms to choose overseas production relative to exporting? At higher transfer costs high-tech firms choose to export. R&D intensive firms may find it more profitable to avoid technology transfer costs rather than physical transport costs. High-tech or R&D-intensive firms then gain more by avoiding transfer costs of technology than by avoiding transport costs of physical units, since more complex technology demands larger resources for technology transfer. [271] Although most R&D in MNEs is still centralised or controlled by corporate headquarters, thus resulting in one-way transfers of technology from parents to their foreign-located affiliates, it has recently been shown that many affiliates are developing their own capacity to generate new technology.[272] The transfer of technology from foreign-located affiliates to their parent and sister-firms thus seems to be growing more important. The integration of localised and firm specific technological advantages is of critical importance, leading potentially to new firm explicit advantages for any MNE that has the capacity to tap into and integrate localised pools of technological skills and competencies.

The acquisition of existing companies is more and more aimed today at acquiring new or complementary technological capabilities[273]. While technological specialisation between MNE units is essential if the best use is to be made of universal competencies, the inclination to distribute technological competence geographically also works against the integration and control of company- wide R&D[274]. The international transfer of technology may thus lead to coordination problems, longer development times, and a decline in the overall productivity of

---

268 Patrick Lenain and Sam Paltridge After The Telecommunications Bubble Economics Department Working Papers NO.361 ECO/WKP(2003)15

269 Binmore, K. And P. Klemperer (2002), "The biggest auction ever: the sale of the British 3G Telecom licenses", The Economic Journal, No. 112, March.

270 Fors, G., 1997. Utilazation of R&D results in the home and foreign plants of multinationals, Journal of Industrial economics 45, 341-358.

271 Cheng, L., 1984. International competition in R&D and technological leadership, Journal of International Economics 17, 15–40. Dunning, J.H., 1977. Trade, location of economic activities and the MNE: A search for an eclectic approach, in P.-O. Hesselborn, B. Ohlin and P.-M. Wijkman, eds., The International Allocation of Economic Activity, (MacMillan, London), 395–418. Ekholm, K., 1998. Proximity advantages, scale economies and the location of production, in P. Braunerhjelm and K. Ekholm, eds, The Geography of Multinational Firms, (Kluwer Academic Publishers, Boston), 59–76.

272 Cantwell,J.(1999).From the early internationalization of corporate technology to global technology sourcing. Transnational Corporations ,8 (2),71. Pearce,R.D (1999).The evolution of technology in multinational enterprises: The role of creative subsidiaries.International Business Review ,8 ,125.

273 Dunning,J.H.(1995).Reappraising the eclectic paradigm in the age of alliance capitalism. Journal of International Business Studies ,Third Quarter,461.

274 Reger,G.(1999).How R&D is coordinated in Japanese and European multinationals. R &D Management , 29 (1),71.

the R&D process[275]. Intra- firm trade in intermediate inputs offers an important way for MNEs to break up their firm specific advantages across borders, since these inputs over and over again embody proprietary knowledge generated on the basis of R&D[276]. Much FDI these days is motivated by the investing firms' desire to complement their own firm precise advantages with technological competencies possessed by home business partners. It should be taken into consideration that corporate research and development (R&D) investment plays a role in a firm's future growth. In accordance with the Internalisation theory[277] and the Eclectic theory[278] an MNE is created whenever markets are internalised across national boundaries. A firm's location strategy is determined by the interaction of comparative advantage, barriers to trade, and regional incentives to internalise and the firm will be multinational whenever these factors make it most advantageous to locate various stages of production in different countries. Moreover, a firm's R&D investment plays a crucial role in the firm's innovation activities, representing future growth opportunities. A firm's degree of multinationality plays, at least to some extent, a role in determining the effect of R&D investment. [279] Furthermore, the possession of proprietary information is the key reason why MNEs can survive the competition of DCs in host countries. MNEs are exposed to supplementary risk including political risk and foreign exchange risk, which would not exist in a domestic market.

The traditional centralized R&D structure that was seen in the post-war years is progressively being eclipsed by the emergence of global R&D networks, the number of knowledge sources is increasing and it is essential to utilize the best to stay competitive adapting to local needs calls for local presence and multiple sites encourage the development of more ideas due to the varied international backgrounds in global networks[280]. There is a process of rationalisation and streamlining of activities in large companies leading to a concentration of activities to centres of excellence, or core centres for various activities within the company. Not only final goods production but production itself is becoming increasingly global.

A know-how advantage would enable MNEs to convert the output of R&D into a new form of production at a lower cost than DCs (mainly owing to economies of scale) and to reduce communication costs between R&D, production and marketing. Successful multinational operation is the result of many factors, together with an organization's capacity to innovate. Core competencies build either internally through R&D or externally through

---

275 De Meyer,A.(1992).Management of international R&D operations. In: Granstrand,O., Ha _ L., Sjo K S.(Eds.),Technology management and international business. Internationalization of R &D and technology. Chichester: Wiley.

276 Gray,H.P.(1993).Intra-firm trade in finished goods and services. In H.P.Gray (Ed.), Transnational corporations and international trade and payments . United Nations Library on Transnational Corporations, vol.8. London: Routledge.

277 Rugman, A.M., 1981. Inside the Multinationals: The Economics of Internal Markets. Columbia University Press, New York. Buckley, P.J., Casson, M., 1976. The Future of the Multinational Enterprise. Holmes & Meier, New York.

278 Buckley, P.J., 1989. The Multinational Enterprise: Theory and Applications. Macmillan, London.

279 Szewczyk, S.H., Tsetsekos, G.P., Zantout, Z., 1996. The valuation of corporate R&D expenditures: evidence from investment opportunities and free cash flow. Financial Management 25 (Spring), 105–110.

280 Teigland, R., C.F. Fey, and J. Birkinshaw, Knowledge dissemination in global R&D operations: An empirical study of multinationals in the high technology electronics industry. Management International Review, 2000. 40(1): p. 49-.

competitive collaborations are among the significant corporate resources, enabling firms to differentiate themselves from others and having the potential to create excess returns in a competitive environment[281]. R&D expenditure can be seen as an important measure of the level of corporate innovation activities. When a firm's international competitors are innovative, this firm must find commercial opportunities based on the competitors' new products and services and not merely emphasis on original creativity[282]. Kiyohiko Ito and Elizabeth L. Rose [283] consider that "there are different elasticities of sales performance with respect to corporate R&D expenditures and industry average R&D intensity in the United States and Japan'. MNEs operate an international intelligence system for the acquisition and collection of key proprietary knowledge relevant to R&D, and for the exploitation of the commercially applicable knowledge generated by R&D. Additionally, MNEs have a broad market environment and have affiliates located in multiple economies. The performance of these multiple economies gives rise to diversification opportunities for MNEs, which would in turn cause more stable cash flows for MNEs.[284]

There has been a shift of technological capabilities away from the country of origin[285] and dispersed capabilities are integrated within the frame of international development projects. It should be taken into account that the multinational's capacity to thoroughly assimilate new technology from foreign countries is overestimated.[286]The highest dispersion of advanced technological capabilities has been achieved by firms which over time have committed substantial resources out-side the country of origin, suggesting that the potential advantages from dispersed innovation activity come relatively late in the firm's internationalisation process. International merges and acquisitions have considerably increased the degree of overlap in the multinational network[287]. The re-organization of capabilities within the sample firms is a gradual and long-term process. There is a tension between evolutionary growth and increasing commitments to foreign markets and a preference for concentrating technological capabilities to a limited number of units. The concentration of technological capabilities to a few locations results from the costs and difficulties associated with international technology transfer and an unwillingness to disseminate technology for fear of losing control over

---

281 Prahalad, C. K., & Hamel, G. (1990). The core competence of the corporation. Harvard Business Review, May–Jun., 79–91.

282 Berger, S., Dertouzos, M. L., Lester, R. K., Solow, R. M., & Thurow, L. C. (1989). Toward a new industrial America. Scientific American, 260, 39–47.

283 Kiyohiko Ito , Elizabeth L. Rose, Innovations and geographic focus: A comparison of US and Japanese firms, International Business Review 8 (1999) 55–74, p71.

284 Lee, K.C., Kwok, C.Y., 1988. Multinational corporations vs. domestic corporations: International environmental factors and determinants of capital structure. Journal of International Business Studies 19 (Summer), 195–217.

285 Cantwell, J., 1995. The globalization of technology: what remains of the product cycle model?. Cambridge J. Econ. 19, 155–174.

286 Malmberg, A., Solvell, O., Zander, I., 1996. Spatial clustering, local accumulation of knowledge and firm competitiveness. Geografiska Ann. 78B 2, 85–97. Pearce, R.D., 1989. The Internationalization of Research and Development by Multinational Enterprises. MacMillan, London. Teece, D.J., 1977. Technology transfer by multinational firms: the resource cost of international technology transfer. Econ. J. 87, 242–261.

287 Jaffe, A.B., Trajtenberg, M., Henderson, R., 1993. Geographic localization of knowledge spillovers as evidence by patent citations. Q. J. Econ., pp. 577–598.

resources[288]. The development of a worldwide learning capability in the MNE would require deliberate efforts to transfer experiences from a few established technologies to the people involved in technologies of more recent origin. In open economies where firms are dependent on foreign markets for their survival, MNEs often play a prominent role. For instance, the majority of the Swedish[289] multinationals' R&D is undertaken at home, while most of their sales are in foreign markets. Technologies developed at home to a large extent are exploited abroad which means that the expansion in foreign sales by MNEs has enabled the firms to grow large and spend more resources on R&D. The activities of MNEs are important both for the technological development and international competitiveness of open economies.

It is common ground that possession of firm-specific advantages is generally required before a firm is able to penetrate foreign markets. Companies with higher R&D outlays have a technological advantage relative to other firms and, so, are more successful in foreign markets. Expansion of sales facilitates further R&D investments, since the created knowledge can be utilized to a higher degree. Firm-specific advantages increase the market concentration and can be derived from superior technology, human capital, or product differentiation across industries and technologies. Profitability, solidity, or cash flows are important determinants of R&D expenditures. More funds will be available to finance further R&D projects if the firm earns profits from its foreign operations. Technological opportunity and the extent a firm can appropriate the returns from its R&D expenditures influence a firm's R&D-decision. Hence, for MNEs in small countries, there is less scope to finance R&D investments by sales in the home market alone that means that foreign markets will be essential for development as well as for the financing of R&D activities[290]. Manufacturing firms from small economies have limited growth opportunities in their home markets, and so are more dependent on foreign sales.

The gradual discovery of important advantages from flexibility and cross-fertilization within the multinational network may well shift the balance towards further dispersion and duplication, although it is doubtful to enduringly resolve the tension between centrifugal and centripetal forces in the MNE. The potential advantages from internationally duplicated capabilities appear to emerge reasonably late in the internationalisation process, and do not essentially affect all firms to the same extent. [291] While the overseas R&D laboratories require autonomy to foster creativity and new idea generation, the headquarters frequently demand coordination and control of overseas R&D activities. Generally, autonomy is an important feature of the value system and incentive structure for doing good science, but disproportionate local autonomy may hinder coherent innovation strategy as a multinational. External linkages of knowledge and ideas among the scientists may endanger internal coherence as a company. The lack of balance between external and internal linkages is liable

---

[288] Forsgren, M., Holm, U., Johanson, J., 1995. Divisional headquarters go abroad—a step in the internationalization of the multinational corporation. J. Manage. Stud. 32 4, 475–491. Hedlund, G., 1986. The hypermodern MNE—a heterarchy?. Hu man Resour. Manage. 25 1 , 9–35.

[289] Gunnar Fors, Roger Svensson, R&D and foreign sales in Swedish multinationals: a simultaneous relationship?, Research Policy 31 (2002) 95–107

[290] Cohen, W.M., Klepper, S., 1996. A reprise of size and R&D. Economic Journal 106 (437), 925–951.

[291] Dunning, J.H., 1994. Multinational enterprises and the globalization of innovatory capacity. Res. Policy 23, 67–88.

to generate autonomy-control tension[292]. Moreover, the need for local autonomy depends on the extent to which the sources of global innovation is concentrated in the local country or dispersed throughout the world[293]. Hence, the extent of cluster versus dispersion in innovation source may vary across industries[294].

The inter-country pattern of location of R&D is expected to be unequal depending upon the accessibility of R&D infrastructure and resources and policy framework. The internationalisation of the R&D of firms may be motivated by the following three broad reasons: First to support their foreign production by adaptations such as adaptations of consumer goods to the local cultural environment. The second motivation for overseas R&D could be to rationalize it according to cost considerations. It may include rationalization of development of certain products and processes at an overseas R&D unit in view of economies of scope or scale. Finally, MNEs locate R&D in other countries advanced in their own fields to benefit from the localized knowledge spillovers or purely to keep track of the activities of their competitors. Although the importance of overseas R&D as a proportion of the total R&D activity of corporations has grown over time, it continues to be the least globalized of MNEs' value adding activities even in the most internationalised industries. The leading edge R&D in the core technologies of corporations is still performed in home countries while research towards customisation and foreign production support is increasingly conducted locally as affiliates become more intensely integrated into local markets. The internationalisation of the R&D activity of MNEs has increased over time particularly since the mid-1980s. Host country market size, technological resources and capability considerably affect R&D activity of US affiliates[295]. The local market orientation of affiliates and the presence of trade barriers seemed to favour affiliate R&D mainly in developing countries signifying the motivating need for doing adaptations for the local markets. Firms choose their investments in product R&D determining the degree of differentiation between their products. The equilibrium level of process R&D investment increases with the degree of product differentiation. While process R&D enlarges the price-cost margin by reducing the marginal cost of production, product R&D allows companies to charge higher prices by increasing consumer willingness to pay for their products. Product R&D increases demand for the products and the increased demand raises the equilibrium output levels and thus enhances

---

[292] Asakawa, K., 1996. External–internal linkages and overseas autonomy-control tension: The management dilemma of the Japanese R&D in Europe. IEEE Transactions on Engineering Management 42 (1), 24–32.

[293] Cantwell, J., 1995. The globalization of technology: what remains of the product cycle model? Cambridge Journal of Economics 19 (1), 155–174. Cantwell, J., Janne, O., 1999. Technological globalization and innovative centres: the role of corporate technological leadership and locational hierarchy. Research Policy 28, 119–144. Ghoshal, S., Bartlett, C., 1990. The multinational corporation as an interorganizational network. Academy of Management Review 15 (4), 603–625. Gibbons, M., Johnston, R., 1974. The roles of science in technological innovation. Research Policy 3, 220–242.

[294] Gerybadze, A., Reger, G., 1999. Globalization of R&D: recent changes in the management of innovation in transnational corporations. Research Policy 28, 251–274. Burt, R., 1992. Structural Holes: The Social Structure of Competition. Harvard, Cambridge, MA.

[295] Kumar, N., 1996. Intellectual property protection, market orientation and location of overseas R&D activities by multinational enterprises. World Development 24 4 , 673–688. Kumar, N., 1998. Multinational enterprises, regional economic integration, and export-platform production in the host countries: an empirical analysis for the US and Japanese. Weltwirtschaftliches Archiv 134 3 , 450–483. Kumar, N., 1999. Multinational Enterprises, Overseas R&D Activity and the Global Technological Order. Occasional Paper No. 56, Research and Information System for Developing Countries, New Delhi.

returns from process R&D. Moreover, process R&D increases equilibrium output levels by lowering costs of production and makes product R&D more attractive. Ping Lin and Kamal Saggi[296] consider that "firms invest more in product R&D in the presence of process R&D than in its absence. Cooperation in the two types of R&D affects R&D incentives in different ways. While cooperation in product R&D encourages both types of R&D, cooperation in process R&D has the opposite effect".

Countries abundant in low cost R&D manpower may be able to attract some R&D activity from MNEs. The scale of national technological effort also affects the location of overseas R&D of MNEs favourably. Countries possessing a considerable scale of national technological activity have better chances of attracting the R&D activity of MNE affiliates than others. Therefore, a significant proportion of R&D activity of MNEs is clearly driven by the need to follow R&D activity of leaders in their own fields[297]. Has overseas R&D played the limited role of supporting the ability of MNEs to apply their commercially established and probably centrally derived technology effectively in new market environments and production locations? Decentralised R&D becomes integral to the ways in which MNEs seek to strategically enhance fundamental dimensions of their product scope and to sustain the vitality and originality of their core science base. Retaining strategic competitiveness in the long-term needs enhancement of the fundamental core of scientific knowledge, which is available to the MNE group. According to Hirschey and Caves[298] a MNE was perceived as determining ''the location of its R&D by reconciling centripetal and centrifugal forces''. The degree of need for R&D support of overseas sales or production may depend on the market to which it expected to be sold. Sales on the host-country market may have other needs for R&D support than exports, and exports to the MNE's home country may have dissimilar need for support than those to third countries. So, R&D location in MNEs is influenced by economies of scale. Hewitt[299] states that the extent and nature of overseas R&D will depend inter alia on the stage of evolution of the firm's globalisation strategy.

MNEs are adopting new tactical approaches to the chase of global competitiveness, which involve restructuring the roles of individual subsidiaries and a reformulation of their intra-group interdependencies in order to support this new positioning. While decentralised R&D were depended on decisions within a bilateral relationship between a central parent unit and an individual subsidiary, newer perceptions underline positioning of distinctive operations within inter-dependent networks of mutually-supportive facilities. At present,

---

[296] Ping Lin, Kamal Saggi, Product differantation process R&D, and the nature of market competition, European Economic Review 46 (2002) 201-211, p210.

[297] Niosi, J. Ed. , 1999. Special Issue on Globalization of Technol ogy. Research Policy, 28 2–3. Patel, P., 1997. Localised Production of Technology for Global Markets. In: Archibugi, D., Michie, J. Eds. , Technology, Globalization and Economic Performance. Cambridge Univ. Press, Cambridge, pp. 198–214.

[298] Hirschey, R.C., Caves, R.E., 1981. Internationalisation of research and transfer of technology by multinational enterprises. Oxford Bulletin of Economics and Statistics 42, 115–130. p. 117. Archibugi, D., Michie, J., 1995. The globalisation of technology: a new taxonomy. Cambridge Journal of Economics 19, 121–140. p. 122. Archibugi, D., Michie divide 'technological globalisation' into i the global exploitation of technology, ii global technological collaboration, iii the global generation of technology.

[299] Hewitt, G., 1980. Research and development performed abroad by US manufacturing multinationals. Kyklos 33, 308–326. Hewitt, G., 1983. Research and development performed in Canada by American manufacturing multinationals. In: Rugman, A.M.Ed. , Multinationals and Technology Transfer—The Canadian Experience. Praeger, New York, pp. 36–49.

overseas R&D units often play an important role in allowing a specific subsidiary to pledge its claim to a powerful product development position within the wider creative and supply programmes of MNEs. In other words, overseas R&D play increasingly powerful roles in the creative processes themselves. The entry of the MNE affiliate disturbs the existing stability in the market and forces home firms to take action to protect their market shares and profits. The degree of local ownership in the FDI does neither seem to affect the productivity in the foreign establishment, nor the degree of spillovers to the domestic sector.[300] In accordance with Robert D. Pearce[301] "the roles and motivations of these overseas labs now reflect particularly strategic needs of these companies as they build globalised perspectives on markets and technology into their pursuit of competitiveness". Technology available to the MNE is applied commercially as efficiently as possible in all differentiated segments of the global market[302]. MNEs build specialised roles in product development or knowledge creation around individualised hi-tech and innovative competences in their decentralised operations[303].

While MNEs have traditionally operated with a centralized R&D structure, the use of dispersed constellations in R&D activities is seen to increase leading to increase challenges, due to communication and integration issues, and a co-location of development efforts is often seen as more advantageous when possible. In order to achieve competitive advantage companies must constantly create, transfer, and exploit knowledge that is more and more dispersed throughout their global operations. The traditional centralized R&D structure that was seen in the post-war years is progressively being eclipsed by the emergence of global R&D networks because the number of knowledge sources is increasing and it is essential to utilise the best to stay competitive adapting to local needs calls for local presence encouraging the development of more ideas due to the varied international backgrounds in global networks[304]. Many MNEs are both increasing the globalisation and concentrating their R&D resources.

The introduction of new ICT in the global economy parallels widening and ever escalating asymmetries among countries and even regions within countries[305]. The extent to which new technology is advanced and its consequences in terms of productivity growth however vary across regions according to their endowments and relative prices. Technology and relative prices interact with each other in assessing output levels, average costs and the

---

[300] Beamish, P.W., 1998. Multinational Joint Ventures in Developing Countries. Routledge & Kegan Paul, London. Blomstrom, M., Kokko, A., 1998. Multinational corporations and spillovers. Journal of Economic Surveys 12, 247-277.

[301] Robert D. Pearce, Decentralised R&D and strategic competitiveness: globalised approaches to generation and use of technology in multinational enterprises MNEs, Research Policy 28 1999 157–178, p 175.

[302] Pearce, R.D., Singh, S., 1992. Globalising Research and Development. Macmillan, London. Perrino, A.C., Tipping, J.W., 1989. Global management of technology. Research and Technology Management 32, 12–19.

[303] Taggart, J.H., 1996. Multinational manufacturing subsidiaries in Scotland: strategic role and economic impact. International Business Review 5, 447–468. Taggart, J.H., 1997. R&D complexity in UK subsidiaries of manufacturing multinational corporations. Technovation 17, 73–82. Zejan, M.C., 1990. R&D activities in affiliates of Swedish multi-national enterprises. Scandinavian Journal of Economics 93, 487–500.

[304] Doz, Y.L. and G. Hamel, Alliance Advantage. 1998, Boston: Harvard Business School P. Bartlett, C.A., Y. Doz, and G. Hedlund, eds. Managing the Global Firm.1990, Routledge: New York.

[305] Ruttan, V.W., 2001. Technology Growth and Development. An Induced Innovation Perspective. Oxford University Press, Oxford.

real levels of total factor productivity. Moreover, mismatching between the local system of relative factor prices and the composition of the marginal productivity of the production factors has dominant consequences on the actual effects of the introduction of a new technology[306]. Composition effects stem from the relative competence of the techniques, defined in terms of factor intensity, available for each technology, firms select in equilibrium under the joint effect of relative factors costs and output elasticities. Exclusively the introduction of biased technological changes affects both the partial productivity of each production factor and the general competence of the production process[307]. The endorsement of localized technological innovations which build up the capability and experience accumulated in learning by doing and learning by using the techniques in place, diminish the switching costs that are indispensable to adjust to the new equilibrium techniques and make the best use of the local endowments, provides major opportunities to take advantage of the new technological system and yet contrast its ranking effects[308].

The amalgamation of technical transform with the development of native contexts has implications on the progression through which knowledge is generated and diffused across national boundaries. Besides, MNEs more and more resort to applications abilities localised in host economies to match their knowledge bases and accordingly by interacting with native companies and institutions they are enabled to swiftly contextualize the offered technology to pull out economic value from it.

MNEs being interested in gaining access to local knowledge are expected to be prone to transfer valuable technology on a reciprocal basis and accordingly by getting involved in collaborative networks with native counterparts, foreign subsidiaries are more likely to generate backward and forward linkages, and to engender good organization effects in upstream and downstream local industries. Due to cooperation with local companies and institutions, MNEs get more and more embedded in host economies, match their managerial and technical practices to resident needs, subsequently increasing the appropriateness of technology being produced and transferred. Host country governments perceive the chance of attracting value added activities from abroad mostly depends on the capacity of the resident economy to supply high quality infrastructures and human capital, so driving national efforts in the path of high prospective investments[309].

The pile up of technological and technical skills requires a country to embrace a wider set of industrial policies aiming in developing training, at a company level, in the a mixture of activities of planning, production engineering, quality control and R&D[310]. Innovation provides new and unique opportunities for creating new companies and expanding old ones and accordingly their market share is enlarged and, with greater than ever returns to scale, they benefit from greater production effectiveness and a higher rate of economic expansion. Greater production proficiency enables industries to enlarge their national market share

---

306 Jorgenson, D.W., 2001. Information technology and the U.S. economy. American Economic Review 91, 1–33.

307 Antonelli, C., 2001. The Microeconomics of Technological Systems. Oxford University Press, Oxford.

308 Antonelli, C., 1995. The economics of localized technological change and industrial dynamics. Kluwer, Boston.

309 Collier, P. and Dollar, D. (2002), Globalisation, Growth and Poverty: Building an Inclusive World Economy, Oxford University Press, New York, NY.

310 Durham, B. (2004), "Absorptive capacity and the effects of foreign direct investments and equity foreign portfolio investments on economic growth", European Economic Review, Vol. 48, pp. 285-306.

through import substitution, to increase local consumption and, at the same time, to invade new foreign markets and reinforce their export share. Investment in R&D enables companies to hold a competitive edge over their competitors, at least during the first stage of the innovation transmission course.

R&D activity is a medium for innovative industrial activities, and in due course it is accountable for the growth in productivity and total revenue. Daniel Shefer and Amnon Frenkel[311] argue that "the level of export increases monotonously with firm size regardless of industrial branch or location. Nevertheless, the rate of exports among high-tech firms is substantially greater than that found among the traditional group of firms. Approximately, 50% of the variation in the firms' R&D expenditures can be explained by such variables as innovation, industrial branch affiliation, total revenue, export orientation and age of firm."

One of the principal dimensions of strategic planning refers to the level of vertical disintegration and vertical disintegration means subdividing an industry into a number of levels along the value chain, and companies at each level focus on their own speciality. Companies are characterized by a shared reliance and support in information sharing, manufacturing, logistics, and innovation and besides being supported by a concrete infrastructure, strategic investment incentives, intellectual property protection, and integrated resource development from the government they are forced by the national environment to expand their competitiveness through R&D efforts. Additionally, innovative efforts of the individual companies through value-added activities complemented by qualified human resources[312].

The hypothesis of technological innovation refers to any incremental or sweeping change in technology embodied in product and process including the transform in value activities such as service and management enabling a company to offer a greater variety of valuable, rare, matchless and differentiated products, and accordingly lead companies to higher financial performance pointing out that the profitability of new product development (NPD) is unquestionably related to the creativity of NPD. It has to be taken into consideration that modern technology effortlessly becomes obsolete and the generation of innovation requires major investment of resources and a company has to strengthen its innovative capability all the way through internal development supplemented by external network linkage.

Technical activities that convert inputs into outputs are of the essence to an organization's survival and accordingly technological innovation is critical to a company acquiring and sustaining competitive advantage and improving its functioning in a dynamic environment[313]. Especially, innovation is among the most key means through which small- and medium-sized enterprises (SMEs) contribute to increased economic dynamics in each industry.

The sustainability of strategic advantages is subject to amend due to various market forces that are economic, technological or social in nature which is even more challenging in the fast-changing information technology (IT) industry for the reason that the value chain

---

[311] Daniel Shefer, Amnon Frenkel, R&D, firm size and innovation: an empirical analysis, Technovation 25 (2005) 25–32, p31.

[312] Peter J. Sher, Phil Y. Yang , The effects of innovative capabilities and R&D clustering on firm performance: the evidence of Taiwan's semiconductor industry, Technovation 25 (2005) 33–43

[313] Zahra, S.A., Ireland, R.D., Hitt, M.A., 2000. International expansion by new venture firms: international diversity, mode of market entry, technology learning, and performance. Academy of Management Journal 43 (5), 925–950.

structure changes sporadically and alters the comparative market power and profitability of the encompassing sectors.

Global competition requires increased technology transfer across national boundaries for global marketing opportunities. MNEs home-country operations are the leading supplier of innovation for global transfer and utilization. Successful transfer and adoption of new technology in the shortest time practical is of overriding value to many companies. To that extent, the organizational capacity to take advantage of existing firm-specific capabilities and to transfer them within the MNE constitutes a key competitive plus of the MNE. The intricacy in transferring technology is predominantly pronounced in the MNE context where the parties involved come from different backgrounds that may pose language, and social constraints.

Successful technology transfer by major suppliers to their transplants to supply their overseas customers is of paramount worth and represents a key competitive advantage. In order for a MNE to continue to exist in the global market, it needs to discover and learn new ways while in tandem exploiting what it has already learned and accordingly in spite of whether a MNE is exploiting existing or exploring new knowledge, organizational learning is a vibrant progression that consists of interpreting, integrating, and institutionalizing at three levels: individual, group, and organizational.

MNEs exist not because of market malfunction in the buying and selling of knowledge, but because of their effectiveness as an organizational vehicle by which to relocate their superior knowledge across borders. Cooperation within a MNE facilitates the relocation of a set of capabilities that is easier to take place within the MNE than across organizations. MNEs focus in the internal transfer of tacit knowledge, in particular for the type of technology that is less codifiable, more multipart, and harder to teach. It is this exploitation of unique capabilities by transferring and recombining them across borders within the MNE helps it prolong its competitive advantage over their competitors. Nevertheless, it is expensive for the MNE to transfer technology that is less codifiable and harder to teach[314].

Since competition among companies is based upon their grade of divergence capabilities, a MNE's abilities to create and replicate new knowledge faster than their plagiarized and innovative competitors are of highest worth. It is decisive for MNEs to keep up their competitive lead by exploiting their existing proprietary technology worldwide and those MNEs that have transferred proprietary knowledge to their foreign subsidiaries are able to pull their competitive advantage not only in their home market, but also in various host markets.

4.13 Transfer of Prises

A transfer price is the price that a selling department, division or subsidiary of a company charges for a product or service supplied to a buying department, division, or subsidiary of the same firm. TP policies have considerable effects on performance evaluation and motivation of subsidiary managers.[315] Transfer prices are treated as a mark-up for each

[314] Yukako Sunaoshi, Masaaki Kotabe, Janet Y. Murray, How technology transfer really occurs on the factory floor: a case of a major Japanese automotive die manufacturer in the United States, Journal of World Business 40 (2005) 57–70

[315] O'Connor, W., 1997. International transfer pricing, in: Frederick, D.S.C. (Ed.), International Accounting and Finance Handbook, second ed. Wiley, New York.

product, applied on the production cost plus the shipping cost, which includes tariffs. The problem is to find sufficient transfer prices so that the global corporate goals are satisfied and the performance measures are fair for all the firm's subsidiaries and divisions[316]. The utilization of the arm's length principle, which establishes the use of transfer prices as if the involved parties did not belong to the same corporation, is extensively accepted. Most current TP policies are based on either external market prices or internal costs. Both have the advantage of being acceptable to tax authorities.[317] Many firms appear to design TP policies to take advantage of discrepancy tax structures among countries. Designing TP policies to minimize taxes legally should not be ignored by MNEs that prefer to design policies consistent with the corporate strategy and organizational structure of the company. International transfer pricing (ITP) is the monetary value attaching to goods, services and intangibles traded between units of the same group, which cross national boundaries. Headquarter services are subject to cost sharing arrangements unless the provision adds value when a mark-up is applied. MNE strategy influences the ITP process and policy. The dynamics of specific countries or regions result in ITP being adjusted which, in turn, may lead to a more fundamental reappraisal of strategy. Systems are introduced to distinguish managerial and subsidiary performance when ITP adjustments may benefit group global performance but disadvantage one subsidiary. Managerial performance and rewards are aggregated to a regional not country basis[318].

MNEs involved in manufacturing and distribution of products, commercial reality led to an emphasis on either a global marketing strategy or a global vertical integration strategy. Product transfers unavoidably involve intangible transfers, thereby imposing a dual concern on these MNEs to document and justify both ITP and royalty agreements. The dynamics of global markets imply that ITP adjustments may lead to strategic reassessment over time. There is a need for fiscal authorities and MNEs to share information on their perspectives of national tax liability and global commerciality. The transfer of price is an internal price. The internal price brings an international allocation of resources within the MNE and maximizes its global profits. The internal price defines the international location profits in pursuit of the goal of tax minimization. What is the effect of transfer pricing by a MNE on global welfare and an individual countries? Transfer pricing reduces the inefficiency caused by government intervention designed to segment national markets by arbitrating differences in tariff and tax rates and interest rates.[319] The MNE has to choose the efficient transfer price that produces an allocation of MNE resources closest to what would occur under free trade. If a MNE is the sole producer of a particular product in an integration group that is subject to a tariff in the importing country, pre-integration tax-minimizing transfer pricing has no effect on allocative efficiency, since output and price remain unaffected. However, transfer pricing makes possible an international transfer of income from the tariff revenue of the country of importation to increased monopoly profits for the producer. With integration, there is price

---

[316] Eccles, R.G., 1985. The Transfer Pricing Problem: A Theory for Practice. Lexington Books, Lexington.

[317] Mueller, G.G., Gernon, H., Meek, G.K., 1997. Accounting: An International Perspective, fourth ed. Irwin Book Team, Chicago. Stitt, I., 1995. Transfer pricing for the next century. Accountancy 116, 92-94.

[318] Elliott, J. (1998) International Transfer Pricing: A Survey of UK and Non-UK Groups. CIMA Publishing. UNCTAD (1997) World Investment Report — Transnational Corporations, Market Structure and Competition Policy: Overview. United Nations, New York and Geneva.

[319] R Aliber "Transfer pricing: A taxonomy of impacts on economic welfare" Multinationals and Transfer Pricing. Croom Helm.

convergence and a net gain in income and welfare in the bloc as a whole and so tax-avoiding transfer pricing is eliminated. The pre-integration efficiency cost of tariffs can be partly offset by the MNEs ability to determine transfer prices. Integration will result in more efficient production. If market integration is accompanied by appropriate fiscal harmonization the incentive of tax-avoiding pricing by MNEs could be eliminated. A MNEs capacity to internalise markets facilitates not only practices aimed at efficiency gains or tax minimization, but also strategic behaviour aimed at market control. Strategic responses to regional economic integration may affect the results quantitatively, but it is possible that they may affect the results qualitatively. If transfer prices are used as cross subsidizing a subsidiary in order to eliminate local competition, maintaining a position of market dominance or hindering potential competitors from entry, their manipulation must be expected to affect not only trade patterns, but also the character of industrial production, static and dynamic efficiency and the intra regional distribution of benefits from integration.

MNEs generated more or less 1/3 of the total exports in the world in 2002 and 10.7% of the world output while in 1990 this number was 6.7%[320].The globalisation with central drivers MNEs created an international system of production and allocation within the enterprises requiring transfer prices for the exchange of goods and services between subsidiaries, including the dealings with the headquarters[321]. International Transfer Pricing based on a multipart number of variables related to legal, financial and operational matters interrelated with taxation, marketing, production, and financial management. On the one hand, resident manager focus on the performance of the resident subsidiary instead of the MNEs performance and employees are concerned to their jobs and wage. On the other hand, governments' awareness goes to job creation and taxes collected from the subsidiaries located in the country. Under perfect competition, the fitting transfer price is the market price if not it should be the marginal cost of the seller division. In case that market price does not exist or the market does not exist for the product or service, the option is cost-based transfer price[322]. The transfer pricing plan is a result of energetic relations of variables related to the environment, the strategy, the type of good, the management structure, the information management systems, and the compensation system. ITP strategy is decided at the parent MNE with a partial autonomy of resident managers relating to the independence to negotiate the terms of business deals including price and the choice of the source of supplies[323].

[320] UNCTAD – United Nations Conference on Trade and Development (2003), World Investment Report 2003 – FDI Polices for Development: National and International Perspectives, New York and Geneva: United Nations.

[321] Zeile, W. J. (2003), Trade in Goods Within Multinational Companies: Survey-based Data and Findings for the United States of America, *http://www.bea.gov* (41% of the exports and 45% of the imports from USA to Europe was internal transfer between subsidiaries of multinationals).

[322] Anthony, R. N. and Govindarajan, V. (2003), *Management Control Systems*, New York: McGraw-Hill, International Edition. Garrison, R. H., Noreen, E. W. and Seal, W. (2003), Management Accounting, Cambridge: McGraw-Hill Education.

[323] Borkowski, S. C. (1996), An Analysis (Meta and Otherwise) of Multinational Transfer Pricing Research, *The International Journal of Accounting*, Vol. 31, no. 1, 39-53.(in US multinationals 61% of respondents divisional managers or business-unit managers decide the ITP or negotiate with their superiors at the parent company). Chan, K. H. and Lo, A. W. Y. (2004), The Influence of Management Perception of Environmental Variables on the Choice of International Transfer-Pricing Methods, *The International Journal of Accounting*, Vol. 39, no. 1, 93-110. (75% of MNEs subsidiaries in China had autonomy to decide the source of supplies of materials and components from related companies). By

According to João Carvalho das Neves and António Samagaio[324] "Concerning the transfer price methods we find a preference of German subsidiaries operating in Portugal for cost-based methods while American subsidiaries prefer market-based methods... 65% of the variance in the choice of transfer pricing methods and policy is explained by three factors – management of performance, treasury management and taxation and competitiveness of the subsidiary". The transfer pricing has an influence in the functioning of the subsidiary mainly on metrics such as return on investment, market share and comparative profitability to key competitors.

Multinationals offer stockholders value because they serve as a vehicle for international diversification opportunities that may otherwise not be available to investors due to capital market imperfections. Transfer pricing is regarded as the vehicle through which multinationals can swing income from high tax to low tax jurisdictions. MNEs, more so than home companies, are able to take advantage of their greater mobility by tapping low-cost sources of labor and raw materials wherever they might exist[325]. Technology transfer in the diverse forms of applied research is associated with modes or entry strategies used by a given multinational and accordingly in the chemistry industry technology transfer is highest from companies whose modes of entry do not implicate importation of finished drugs in measured quantity form.

4.14 Planning and Multinationals

Most, if not all, organizations adopt some form of planning. Planning processes need to be carefully conceived to be effective, perhaps limited in scope, and suitable for the context[326]. Moreover, planning includes the determination of the means to achieve certain ends, environmental scanning, and information gathering functions, accessing sources both internal and external to the organization. Flexibility and complexity, comprehensiveness, time horizon, internal/external orientation, top management commitment, direction, programming, and implementation-oriented are the important dimensions in planning processes[327]. Planners in MNEs must pay special attention to stakeholders in both home and host countries including producers, customers, governments, and rival firms. National cultural differences can be appropriate and useful level of analysis and should be taken into consideration during the

contrast Arpan, J.S. (1972), International Intracorporate Pricing: Non-American Systems and Views, *Journal of International Business Studies*, Vol. 3 no. 1, 1-18.(transfer prices are defined centrally)

[324] João Carvalho das Neves and António Samagaio, INTERNATIONAL TRANSFER PRICING POLICY IN US AND GERMAN SUBSIDIARIES, WORKING PAPER N. 6 /2006 p14.

[325] Saudagaran, S.M. (2001) International Accounting: A User Perspective. (Cincinnati: South-Western College Publishing).

[326] Kargar, J. (1996). Strategic planning characteristics and planning effectiveness in small mature firms. Mid-Atlantic Journal of Business, 32 (1), 19–34. Karger, D. W., & Malik, A. A. (1975). Long range planning and organizational performance. Long Range Planning, 8 (2), 60–64. Nohria, N., & Ghoshal, S. (1997). The differentiated network: Organizing multinational corporations for value creation. San Francisco, CA: Jossey-Bass.

[327] Boyd, K. K. (1991). Strategic planning and financial performance: a meta-analytical review. Journal of Management Studies, 28 (4), 353–374. Brock, D. M., & Thomas, D. C. (1998). Planning in subsidiaries of international organizations: organization structure, local responsiveness and global integration. In T. A. Scandura, & M. G. Serapio Jr, (pp.163–181). Research in international business and intercultural relations, vol. 7. Conneticut: JAI Press.

planning process[328]. The environments within which MNEs operate continue to change. Subsidiaries can gain or lose resources and autonomy, have their charter changed, and generally face unstable relations within the MNE[329]. The challenge for international managers in planning across cultures is to take account of conflicting styles, which means that the prospective for synergies may be realized while potential clashes avoided[330].

4.15 Management of MNE

MNEs undertake more affiliate activity relative to exporting the higher are transport costs and trade barriers and the lower are plant-level scale economies[331]. According to Hedlund and Ridderstrale, established theories of the MNE[332] and its management suffer from a neglect of aspects of innovation, renewal, change and new sources of competitiveness. Informal relationships between managers has become of increasing importance in managing the modern multinational[333]. Central management should retain an important position in a group, which progressively more emphasises decentralised creativity, but that the nature of its role may need to be appreciably restructured[334]. Moreover, central management in a MNE that seeks to maximise its global competitive potential through product innovation, has to recognize that it cannot itself detect all the relevant market and technological opportunities, which means that it has to rely on overseas subsidiaries to perceive such opportunities and develop the knowledge and resources to meet them. Hence, an important potentiality of the use of productive subsidiaries is to bring into play radical possibilities outside of the existing technological impetus of a MNE. A universal strategy that encompasses mandated inventive subsidiaries should provide networked roles for more dependent rationalised product subsidiaries focusing on the supply of established products. The taking up of international heterogeneity through differentiated subsidiaries should endeavour to pursue a cohesive and coherent improvement of group-level competence.

---

328 Smith, P. B., & Bond, M. H. (1999). Social psychology across cultures. Boston: Allyn & Bacon.

329 Alexander, A. (1995). Planning for planners. Long Range Planning, 28 (3), 101–104.

330 Birkinshaw, J., & Hood, N. (1998). Multinational subsidiary evolution: capability and charter change in foreign-owned subsidiary companies. Academy of Management Review, 23 (4), 773–795. Kanter, R. M., & Dretler, T. (1998). "Global strategy" and its impact on local operations: lessons from Gillette Singapore. Academy of Management Executive, 12 (4), 60–68. Xu, B., Wang, J., 1999. Capital goods trade and R&D spillovers in the OECD. Canadian Journal of Economics 32, 1179–1192.

331 Feenstra, R., Hanson, G., 1996. Globalization, outsourcing, and wage inequality. American Economic Review 1, 240–245. Feenstra, R., Hanson, G., 1996. Errata to globalization, outsourcing, and wage inequality. American Economic Review 2, 1. Feenstra, R., Hanson, G., 1997. Foreign direct investment and relative wages: evidence from Mexico's Maquiladoras. Journal of International Economics 1, 371–393.

332 Hedlund, G., Ridderstrale, J., 1997. Toward a theory of the self-renewing MNE. In: Toyne, B., Nigh, D. (Eds.), International business: an emerging vision. University of South Carolina Press, Columbia, SC, pp. 329–354.

333 Ghoshal, S., Korine, H., Szulanski, G., 1994. Interunit communication in multinational corporations. Manage Sci 40 (1), 96–110. White, R.E., Poynter, T.A., 1990. Organizing for worldwide advantage. In: Bartlett, C.A., Doz, Y.L., Hedlund, G. (Eds.), Managing the global firm. Routledge, London, pp. 95–113.

334 Birkinshaw, J. M. (1996). How multinational subsidiary mandates are gained and lost. Journal of International Business Studies, 27(3), 467–495.

Competition among MNEs has become an interdependent process. MNEs are experiment with different models of organization structure, as internal and external to the group pressures increase. Centralization of R&D capacity subsidiaries are usually involved in the production of mature and standardized goods[335]. Technology creation is not a centralized effort. Developments in the tactical positioning of R&D allow MNEs to handle successfully the different dimensions of competition, to test various forms of organization structure and to assign innovative roles to their subsidiaries. Marina Papanastassiou [336]thinks that "MNEs should thus find organizational forms that would integrate R&D managers efficiently with other departments on both group and subsidiary level as well as with other R&D departments in the group". Moreover, MNEs have been consolidating their subsidiaries to give them geographic or product range responsibilities. Decisions are normally made at headquarters and frequently involve channelling resources within a corporation. The main function of the headquarters is to run the internal capital market, which effectively re-distributes resources within the firm[337]. It should be taken into consideration that the managers of various subsidiaries are in competition with each other for resources allocated by headquarters and so they have an incentive to overstate the value of their projects. If the mandate of the subsidiary does not affect the capacity of headquarters to control its resources, then the formation of tactically independent subsidiaries with global mandates is always beneficial for MNEs. The advantages of globalisation derived from headquarters are reinforced by the advantages of strategic decision-making at the regional level. Independence may reduce MNE headquarters' control of their subsidiaries resources, reducing the efficiency of their internal capital markets. Hence, if increasing the role of a subsidiary's mandate reduces headquarters' capability to control its resources, then the advantages of subsidiary strategic independence must be offset against the reduced efficiency of the MNE's internal capital market. In other words the role of headquarters in a multi-unit Corporation is to run an internal capital market, re-distributing financial resources on the basis of its unbiased evaluation of the various units' prospects[338]. Especially, effective JV management teams do not simply happen but characterized by appropriate composition, incentives, structure, pro-cess, and group leader[339].

As MNEs seek to respond to key dimensions in the intensification of globalised competition vital strategic roles have emerged in them for international networks of R&D laboratories. Corporations are finding it indispensable to adopt global perspectives on the ways in which they apply their existing technological scope commercially and also pursue its longer-term extension through access to new scientific knowledge. MNEs must get their pioneering products into the key segments of the global market as quickly as possible in order to make the most effective use of the commercial potential of their current technology.

---

335 Papanastassiou, M., & Pearce, R. (1998). Individualism and interdependence in the technological development of MNEs: the strategic positioning of R&D in overseas subsidiaries. In J. Birkinshaw & N. Hood, Multinational corporate evolution and subsidiary development (pp. 50–75). London: MacMillan.

336 Marina Papanastassiou, Technology and production strategies of multinational enterprise (MNE) subsidiaries in Europe, International Business Review 8 (1999) 213–232.

337 Stein, J. C. (1997). Internal capital markets and the competition for corporate resources. Journal of Finance, 52(1), 111–133. Lamont, O. (1997). Cash flow and investment: evidence from internal capital markets. Journal of Finance, 52(1), 83–109.

338 Ram Mudambi, MNE internal capital markets and subsidiary strategic independence, International Business Review 8 (1999) 197–211.

339 Jiatao Li, Katherine R. Xin, Anne Tsui, Donald C. Hambrick, Building Effective International Joint Venture Leadership Teams in China, 1999,Journal of World Business / 34(1) 52

Overseas R&D labs should meet the competitive objectives of their particular position in the MNE's supply network and meet local tastes and accommodate local production conditions. The technological strategy of a MNE is not only concerned with the most advantageous application of its current knowledge to the contemporary competitive environment but there is also a need to constantly revitalise and upgrade the group's core technology, in order to provide a basis for sweeping new generations of innovative products that would seek to guarantee its commercial health into the longer-term. Through interdependent international network of research labs a MNE can bring together a strong and organized set of complementary inputs that enables it to build up its fundamental knowledge base through high-quality access to progress in scientific disciplines that are most likely to produce the technological force towards commercial innovation. Decentralised R&D in MNEs has undergone a metamorphosis, from one of offering small-scale ad hoc support to separate local operations to that of playing a vital role in global strategies that relate to both existing market competitiveness and technological evolution[340]. In-house R&D in subsidiaries is more likely to be part of a product development process[341]. Hence, decentralised R&D units provide basic and/or applied research inputs into interdependent global programmes of pre-competitive exploration.

Control has been described as the process that regulates organizational activities so that they are in accord with the organization's stated objectives. Control systems differ based on the means used to exercise control. Snell[342] suggested that the strategic context of organizations determines the level of administrative information available and subsequently the choice of the proper control system type. MNEs have to develop contextual control systems to fill the control gap created by the decline in their ability to plan the tasks of a foreign subsidiary in a formal way and contextual control as influencing foreign subsidiary activities in an informal way in the case of mature foreign subsidiaries. Moreover, MNEs look for lowering their control costs by identifying subsidiaries whose contexts suggest other forms of control or by identifying subsidiaries whose contexts propose exercise of control to a lesser extent. The internal differentiation within MNEs means different strategic contexts that include differences in knowledge flows within the MNE system, the strategic roles of foreign subsidiaries, work flow integration, environmental and cultural differences among the foreign subsidiaries, environmental complexity, and the resource level of subsidiaries in order to prescribe appropriate control systems. According[343] to Raman Muralidharan and Robert D. Hamilton "the differences in the strategic role of the foreign subsidiary over its developmental stages hold implications for staffing, designing and implementing reward systems, enforcing operating procedures, and using managerial practices". MNEs should use the identification of the developmental stages of their numerous foreign subsidiaries as a tool to measure the current and future overall control demands faced by the enterprise.

---

340 Cantwell, J., 1995. Multinational corporations and innovatory activities: towards a new, evolutionary approach. In: Molero, J. Ed., Technological Innovation, Multinational Corporations and New International Competitiveness. Harwood Academic Publishers, Luxembourg, 21–57. Howells, J., Wood, M., 1993. The Globalisation of Production and Technology. Belhaven Press, London.

341 Patel, P., 1995. Localised production of technology for global markets. Cambridge Journal of Economics 19, 141–153.

342 S. A. Snell, Control theory in strategic human resource management: the mediating effect of administrative information, Academy of Management Journal 35, 292-327 (1992).

343 Raman Muralidharan and Robert D. Hamilton III, Aligning Multinational Control Systems, Long Range Planning, Vol. 32, No. 3, pp. 352 to 361, 1999, p 358.

Technology in the advanced industrialized countries and in the developing world is widely recognized as a source of unanticipated and often seriously adverse environmental consequences. It should be taken into account that electronic commerce promises not only to radically alter the financial structure of various countries not to mention the rest of the world but also to alter the control systems applied between parent company and subsidiaries not to mention the interrelation between MNEs and E-MNEs.

Do governments pursue trade policies for the purpose of influencing FDI? Monopoly power in trade is the basis for trade agreements in a standard model[344]. The decision to engage in multinational production reflects a trade-off between the firm's desire to be close to foreign markets and the desire to concentrate production at home and take advantage of economies of scale[345]. A horizontal MNE is a company that sets up plants abroad to produce the same product that it produces at home. This is distinguished from a vertical MNE, in which divides different stages of the production process between plants in various countries[346]. Trade restrictions can induce firms to engage in multinational production that may benefit consumers in the host country as such production avoids transport costs. If transport costs are low between the neighbouring countries and high elsewhere, then the unique outcome is a preferential trade agreement between the neighbouring countries[347]. It is only through scale economies and transport costs, that tariff-jumping FDI produces welfare gains through the home market effect[348]. Foreign direct investment consists mainly of two-way flows between developed economies, in similar industries, and most of it is horizontal[349]. Even the threat of protection may induce FDI[350]. As mentioned above, the decision of a company to sell through a foreign affiliate rather than export is to a large extent affected by tariffs, transport costs, and scale economies[351]. Caves said that ''a great deal of survey and anecdotal evidence confirms the influence of tariffs on MNEs' locational decisions, not least because many trade restrictions have sought just that result''[352]. The geographical distribution of research investments is a much more recent phenomenon than the physical distribution of production

[344] Bagwell, K., Staiger, R., 1999. An economic theory of GATT. American Economic Review 89 (1), 215–248.

[345] Rodney D. Ludema, Increasing returns, multinationals and geography of preferential trade agreements, Journal of International Economics 56 (2002) 329–358.

[346] Caves, R., 1996. In: Multinational Enterprise and Economic Analysis, 2nd Edition. Cambridge University Press, New York. Smith, A., 1987. Strategic investment, multinational corporations and trade policy. European Economic Review 31, 89–96.

[347] Ludema, R.D., 1999. Why are preferential trade agreements regional-increasing returns, multinationals and the geography of free trade agreements? Georgetown University Working Paper 99-04. Maggi, G., 1999. The role of multilateral institutions in international trade cooperation. American Economic Review 89 (1), 190–214.

[348] Bagwell, K., Staiger, R., 1997. Multilateral tariff cooperation during the formation of customs unions. Journal of International Economics 42, 91–124. Bagwell, K., Staiger, R., 1997. Multilateral tariff cooperation during the formation of free trade areas. International Economic Review 38 (2), 291–320.

[349] Markusen, J.R., 1995. The boundaries of multinational enterprises and the theory of international trade. Journal of Economic Perspectives 9 (2), 169–189. Markusen, J.R., Venables, A.J., 1998. Multinational firms and the new trade theory. Journal of International Economics 46, 183–203.

[350] Blonigen, B., Feenstra, R., 1997. Protectionist threats and foreign direct investment. In: Feenstra, R. (Ed.), The Effects of US Trade Protection and Promotion Policies. University of Chicago Press, Chicago, IL, pp. 55–80.

[351] Brainard, S.L., 1997. An empirical assessment of the proximity-concentration trade-off between multinational sales and trade. American Economic Review 87 (4), 521–544.

aimed at achieving reduction in manufacturing and/or shipment costs[353]. Access to spill over sources, the local incentives, the likelihood of achieving significant cost reductions, and the need to diversify and adapt goods to local tastes and needs in order to compete profitably are determinants of R&D investment. The benefit of carrying on R&D activities in many countries stem from the chance of capturing spillovers in a given place, being able to sell a customized product in another, and enjoying some public financial support in still another one.

A company needs to know where its knowledge assets and sources are sited, and it needs to find a means of combining particular knowledge[354]. The management necessity is to move towards structures that increase knowledge combination. Successful strategies to contest knowledge ''stickiness'' will involve combinations of local and global configurations of knowledge. Knowledge characteristics have a local essence because of market conditions that are specific to geographical location, or they may be due to the localisation of individual industrial specialisations. On the one hand, the technology of knowledge transfer resides in the corporation, and may be a vital factor in releasing and combining local competencies. On the other hand, the organisational structure of a company may be a result of central management dictate, or may have evolved over time, but may well be in conflict at any given time with the needs of horizontal knowledge transfer and effective knowledge management. There is a degree of tension between the local needs of operating business units and the global requirements of each corporation as a whole, these needs are not in unavoidable opposition to one another, but instead they are jointly supportive. Knowledge is resource that can be used to create gains out of the insecurity facing the firm. Moreover, it is advanced knowledge about areas of ambiguity that enables a company to create and sustain profitable applications of physical and human resources. Primary uncertainty results both from instability outside the firm, including exogenous shocks changes in consumer's preferences and peripheral technological change, and also from endogenous change due to the firm's internal or collaborative research and development activities. Secondary uncertainty arises if managers are unable to join their knowledge in ways that are useful to the firm though unsuccessful communication or lack of access to knowledge resources. Tertiary uncertainty arises if managers choose not to expose knowledge that they hold, or if they disclose incorrect or deceptive information. Complementarity of a different kind of knowledge arises when there are interactions or externalities between the functioning of a firm in various geographical or product areas and these interactions may be complementary or negative in their influence on the outcome for a firm. A multinational enterprise engages in the synthesis and assimilation of knowledge that is at first localised and which the enterprise seeks to apply more broadly. P.J. Buckley and M.J. Carter[355] talk about "global knowledge to indicate knowledge that is generally available across the corporation, accessible to all operating subsidiaries, as well as

[352] Caves, R., 1996. In: Multinational Enterprise and Economic Analysis, 2nd Edition. Cambridge University Press, New York. p. 34.

[353] Cinthia Campi and Agostino La Bella, Analysis of the Interaction between Regional R&D Productivity and the Investment Strategies of Multinational Enterprises, Technological Forecasting and Social Change 58, 241–249 (1998).

[354] Williamson, O.E., 1996. The Mechanisms of Governance. Oxford Univ. Press, Oxford.

[355] Peter J. Buckley, Martin J. Carter, Process and structure in knowledge management practices of British and US multinational enterprises, Journal of International Management 8 (2002) 1–20, p7. At p8 " MNE subsidiaries can become 'knowledge brokers' and form distinctive competencies".

to the administrative center". The firm's deliberate knowledge exploitation strategy makes global knowledge available to all within the firm, emphasising the accessibility of knowledge rather than its location[356]. Displaying global strategic configurations by firms depends notably on the individual circumstances of the market opportunities available to the firm. Technological or marketing know-how and expansion as a multinational is chosen when internal transfer of knowledge is more efficient than the alternatives of licensing the usage of that knowledge to others or of international trade in the firm's output. It could be said that a company's global knowledge combines the first parental know-how supplemented by complementary knowledge from operational subsidiaries[357]. Can granting of strategic independence to subsidiaries limit the capacity of headquarters to control resources and may reduce the competence of the internal capital market of MNEs? Every subsidiary exists within, draws upon and contributes to the internal knowledge market of a corporation[358]. Dynamic factors suggest significant changes over time in the role of subsidiaries with a corporation. According to Hedlund and Rolander[359] hierarchy ''entails a geographical diffusion of core strategic activities and coordinating roles, a break with the notion of one uniform hierarchy of decisions as well as organisational positions, and an increased focus on normative control mechanisms''. The transfer of parental knowledge to the overseas subsidiary, the getting hold of local knowledge by the subsidiary and the combined application of these two sets of knowledge are additive concerning parental and subsidiary knowledge[360].

It is superior knowledge about areas of uncertainty that enables a company to create and sustain profitable applications of physical and human resources. Uncertainty is resulting both from volatility outside the firm, together with exogenous shocks changes in consumer's preferences and external technological change, and also from endogenous change due to the firm's internal or collaborative research and development activities[361]. Other uncertainty arises if managers are unable to merge or choose not to reveal their knowledge in ways that are beneficial to a company though ineffective communication or lack of access to knowledge resources. According to Peter J. Buckley, and Martin J. Carter [362]"conceptualisation of knowledge management should move away from thinking of unidirectional flows of

---

356 Harzing, A.-W., 1998. Integration within MNEs: from multidomestic to global and transnational firms? In: Mirza, H. (Ed.), Global Competition Strategies in the New World Economy: Multilateralism, Regionalisation and the Transnational Firm. Edward Elgar, Cheltenham.

357 Pearce, R.D., 1999. Evolution of technology in multinational enterprises: the role of creative subsidiaries. Int. Bus.Rev. 9 (2), 125–148.

358 Mudambi, R., 1999. MNE internal capital markets and subsidiary strategic independence. Int. Bus. Rev. 8 (2), 197–211.

359 Hedlund, G., Rolander, D., 1999. Action in heterarchies —new approaches to managing the MNE. In: Bartlett, C.A., Doz, Y., Hudlund, G. (Eds.), Managing the Global Firm. Routledge, London, p. 15.

360 Gupta, A.K., Govindarajan, V., 2000. Knowledge flows within multinational corporations. Strategic Manage. J. 21, 473–496. Forsgren, M., Pedersen, T., Foss, N.J., 1999. Accounting for the strengths of MNE subsidiaries: the case of foreign-owned firms in Denmark. Int. Bus. Rev. 8 (2), 181–196. Casson, M.C., 1997. Information and Organisation: A New Perspective on the Theory of the Firm. Clarendon Press, Oxford.

361 Buckley, P.J., Carter, M.J., 1999. Managing cross-border complementary knowledge: conceptual developments in the business process approach to knowledge management in multinational firms. Int. Stud. Manage. Organ. 29(1), 80–104. Buckley, P.J., Carter, M.J., 2000. Knowledge management in global technology markets: applying theory to practice. Long-Range Plann. 33 (1), 55–71.

362 Peter J. Buckley, Martin J. Carter, Process and structure in knowledge management practices of British and US multinational enterprises, Journal of International Management 8 (2002) 29–48, p47.

knowledge towards much more complex interactions". Moreover, in accordance with L.J. Trevino and R. Grosse [363]"international diversification is one means by which firms can leverage under-utilized intangible resources".

The evolvement of the concept of Human Resource Management in the mid-1980s led to the recognition that the workforce was one of the important areas of competitive advantage. A reward strategy has been put in place and so building systems of competence-based pay or incorporating the reward for improving competencies within a performance pay system has been introduced. There is the need for rewards to retain considerable flexibility and pay must become more variable which means that instead of a wage or salary being a fixed amount each week, month or year, a growing proportion should become contingent upon performance[364].

Entrepreneurship drives innovation and technical change, and for that reason generates economic growth. According to Aldrich, H., & Zimmer, C. [365]entrepreneurial activity ''can be conceptualized as a function of opportunity structures and motivated entrepreneurs with access to resources'' In fact, all human action is the result of both motivational and cognitive factors such as ability, intelligence, and skills[366]. Human motivation plays a significant role in the entrepreneurial process together with the external factors such as the status of the economy, the availability of venture capital, the actions of competitors, and government regulations. It could be argued that entrepreneurship is a creative process by rearranging resources in a new way. People differ in their willingness and abilities to act having important effects on the entrepreneurial process[367]. Scott Shane, Edwin A. Locke, Christopher J. Collins [368]consider that "entrepreneurial activity depends on the decisions that people make, suggesting that the attributes of the decision makers should influence the entrepreneurial process."

---

363 L.J. Trevino, R. Grosse, An analysis of firm-specific resources and foreign direct investment in the United States, International Business Review (2002), p18. www.elsevier.com/locate/ibusrev

364 Walsh, J. (1998), ```McJob' image first target in burger recruitment war", People Management, 22 January. Brown, D. and Armstrong, M. (1997), ``Terms of enrichment", People Management, 11 September, pp. 36-8.

365 Aldrich, H., & Zimmer, C. (1986). Entrepreneurship through social networks. In D. Sexton, & R. Smilor (Eds.), The art and science of entrepreneurship (pp. 3–23). Cambridge, MA: Ballinger p3. Kirzner, I. (1997). Entrepreneurial discovery and the competitive market process: an Austrian approach. The Journal of Economic Literature, 35, 60–85.According to Kirzner "entrepreneurial action is the process through which supply and demand are equilibrated" Shane, S., & Venkataraman, S. (2000). The promise of entrepreneurship as a field of research. Academy of Management Review, 25(1), 217–226. Shane & Venkataraman consider that "entrepreneurship is an important process by which new knowledge is converted into products and services". Zahra, S., & Dess, G. (2001). Entrepreneurship as a field of research: encouraging dialogue and debate. Academy of Management Review, 26(1), 8–11. Zahra & Dess say that "entrepreneurship has become an important vocation and we need to understand its role in the development of human and intellectual capital". Shane, S., & Venkataraman, S. (2000). The promise of entrepreneurship as a field of research. Academy of Management Review, 25(1), 217–226, p218. Shane and Venkataraman's define entrepreneurship as the process by which ''opportunities to create future goods and services are discovered, evaluated, and exploited.''

366 Locke, E. A. (2000). Motivation, cognition and action: an analysis of studies of task goals and knowledge. Applied Psychology: An International Review, 49, 408–429.

367 Zacharikis, A. (1997). Entrepreneurial entry into foreign markets: a transaction cost perspective. Entrepreneurship Theory and Practice, 21(3), 23–39.

368 Scott Shane, Edwin A. Locke, Christopher J. Collins, Entrepreneurial motivation, Human Resource Management Review 13 (2003) 257–279

Explicit and systematic knowledge[369] management (KM) methods are regarded as key approaches to expand enterprise performance, either through knowledgeable people delivering work more effectively, or through other ways of leveraging intellectual capital (IC). Workers everywhere can access the latest information on advanced concepts and methodologies, business issues, and technology. Sustained success and viability involve effective execution of internal functions and interactions with environment. So, key operational objective is to make the customer successful by customizing products and services to satisfy individual needs while at the same time implementing the enterprise goals[370]. Companies cannot die in an individual, biological sense and the common view of technological change emphasizes automation and other capital-intensive production devices transforming the nature of human interaction with work in a straightforward way but less noticeable is the transformation in work and markets created by the superabundance of newly designed technology-based products. Technological change transforms the nature of the marketplace by altering the relative cost, features and availability of products leading to rapid product introduction and so to rapid product obsolescence[371]. The need for flexibility in management thinking is causing a greater dependence on education than on on-the-job experience in the training of managers. Companies influence the behavior and values of the individual, while the company itself is constructed or composed of these same individuals[372]. Supply chain management represents a critical competency in today's global business environment. IT should be used to lower inter-organizational coordination costs without increasing transaction risk and electronic markets reduce buyer search costs[373]. Top managers of trading partners should integrate EDI with their respective internal computer systems demonstrating strong leadership in developing an appropriate organizational infrastructure and building intimate relationships with their trading partners eliminating the potential negative effects of the technical and security/legal problems. The sharing of business information is a crucial element, which binds supply chains together from end-to-end.[374] Cyberspace has created opportunities for supply-chain reconfiguration and integration driving a virtualization of supply chains, and demanding new mindsets in managing business. The development of virtual trading communities represents a structural change of marketplace where intermediaries adopt various strategies in three distinct, yet related phases of the intermediation-disintermediation- reintermediation cycle, as e-commerce innovations are implemented.[375] The growth of virtual trading communities encompasses companies in the supply chain with commercial and collaborative interests and with intention to establish new

---

369 Ruggles, R. (1998), ``The state of the notion: knowledge management in Practice'', California Management Review, Vol. 40 No. 3.

370 Hansen, M.T., Nohria, N. and Tierney, T. (1999), ``What's your strategy for managing knowledge?", Harvard Business Review, Vol. 77 No. 2, March-April, pp. 106-18.

371 Guyon, J. (1999), ``Next up for cell phones: weaving a wireless web", Fortune, Vol. 140 No. 8.

372 Terence C. Krell, Organizational longevity and technological change, Journal of Organizational Change Management, Vol. 13 No. 1, 2000, pp. 8-13.

373 Weib, G. (Ed.) (1998), Multi-Agent Systems, MIT Press, Cambridge, MA.

374 Deloitte Research (2001), Collaborative Commerce-Going Private to Get Success, e-view by Deloitte Consulting and Deloitte & Touche, New York, NY. Murillo, L. (2001), ``Supply chain management and the international dissemination of e-commerce'', Industrial Management & Data Systems, Vol. 101 No. 7, pp. 370-7.

375 Chircu, A.M. and Kauffman, R.J. (1999),``Strategies for Internet middlemen in the intermediation-disintermediation- reintermediation cycle'', Electronic Markets, Vol. 9 No. 1, pp. 109-17.

business relationships via cyberspace. Industry-specific knowledge assets embodied in virtual knowledge communities become a new source of capital. Companies should learn to identify, understand and satisfy quality standards and needs after a period of experience[376]. Trustworthiness, quality-satisfaction, value, and risks are the main four factors in relation to creating a profitable and sustainable business environment. Trust is needed in every buyer-seller relationship in order to facilitate the business transaction and advanced technologies raise a lot of uncertainties in the marketplace[377]. Technology advancements cannot breed customer confidence in using cyberspace and business strategy should be formulated such that companies are able to build trust, demonstrate quality, delivery value and control risks in their day-to-day operations. Hence, companies must instill customer confidence in the use of cyberspace channels, which is an on-going and evolving process in order to have good long-term business relations. According to May So and Domenic Sculli[378] customers "demand high quality products and a very high standard in the associated pre-sales and after-sales services. They seek satisfaction and expect a sound trust relationship with suppliers. This is especially true in the current Internet era, in which customers have a large number of choices from competing products and suppliers. With almost unlimited choices available in the marketplace, why should a customer choose a particular product, when an alternative product is just ``a click away''?". Companies should leverage the online presence into real value and profits developing an ongoing relationship with end users, a task previously handled primarily through a sales channel[379]. New forms of trading, like e-commerce, call for a robust and secure technical infrastructure, in order to be appropriately performed and be fully exploited and information systems should execute their functions whilst ensuring information protection against hazards such as unwanted or unwarranted dissemination, alteration, or loss[380].

Business rules- business policies, the business practices, and business definitions how the actual business is run - aim to influence or guide behavior and information in the organization that should be well known and treated as a valuable asset to the organization assumed in the development of information systems in a company[381]. Companies should apply business rules appropriately to transform bytes of data into useful information and so gain knowledge for making key business decisions connecting the physical and logical data implementations.

Production and operations management in manufacturing involves a whole constellation of activities including the control of materials, machines, production schedules and labour to guarantee that levels of production are in line with sales. Major developments in production management technologies since the 1970s have included gradually more complex computer-

---

[376] Roberto Gilioli Rotondaro, Defining the customer's expectations in e-business, Industrial Management &Data Systems 102/9 [2002] 476-482

[377] May W.C. So and Domenic Sculli, The role of trust, quality, value and risk in conducting e-business, Industrial Management & Data Systems 102/9 [2002] 503-512.

[378] Ibid p510.

[379] William Lightfoot and James R. Harris, The effect of the Internet in industrial channels: an industry example, Industrial Management & Data Systems 103/2 [2003] 78-84.

[380] T. Tryfonas, E. Kiountouzis and A. Poulymenakou, Embedding security practices in contemporary information systems development approaches, Information Management & Computer Security 9/4 [2001] 183-197.

[381] Gerhard Steinke and Colleen Nickolette, Business rules as the basis of an organization's information systems, Industrial Management & Data Systems 103/1 [2003] 52-63.

aided production management (CAPM)[382] systems referring to information systems, which use computers to assist in the management and control of production[383]comprising varying software and hardware blended with organizational practices in order to meet the specific needs of the adopting company a complex design and decision process which is socially shaped by a range of actors and groups both within and outside boundaries of the adopting organization and so inherently sensitive to social shaping[384]. According to Jacky Swan, Sue Newell, Maxine Robertson [385]"By codifying CAPM into a single and standard ``best practice" template (i.e. MRP2- is not ``turnkey" but has to be adapted to the necessities of the adopting organization, with many design parameters modeled and set according to local requirements-), technology suppliers are able to simplify the complex organizational design issues associated with the introduction of configurational technologies and thus make users more likely to adopt." ``Manufacturing Resources Planning" (MRP2) software suppliers offer a range of computerised modules for managing demand forecasting, purchase orders, bills of materials that can and should apparently be linked together in a closely prescribed way in order to achieve the fully integrated system.

4.16 THE MANAGEMENT OF INTERNATIONAL R&D

Technology production has usually been centralized in the host country of the MNEs[386]. Vertical integration through borders requires a somewhat higher degree of coordination and technology transfer among units. Desire to reduce the costs of communication and control, economies of scale in R&D, better synchronization between central productive facilities and R&D units, better safeguard of strategic technical knowledge, easier way in to home-country governments than to foreign ones, more experience with home than with overseas markets in the launching of new products are factors dictating centralization. There is growing decentralization of R&D based on demand-side, supply-side and environmental factors[387]. Demand-side factors embrace increasing the subsidiary's competitiveness through the transfer of technology from the parent company which requires at least some adaptive R&D capabilities in the former, subsidiary pressures to improve its status within the corporation, greater access and sensitivity to local markets, and proximity to customers. Supply-side factors comprise hiring foreign and usually scarcely mobile skilled labour, escalating the inflow of ideas from dynamic markets and monitoring development of technological fields abroad. Environment factors include a friendly regulatory legislation for intellectual property,

---

382 Fleck, J. (1994), ``Learning by trying: the implementation of configurational technology", Research Policy, Vol. 23, pp. 637-52.

383 Corke, D. (1985), A Guide to CAPM, Institute of Production Engineers, London.

384 Ciborra, C. (1997), ``Crisis and foundations: an inquiry into the nature and limits of models and methods in the IS discipline", Proceedings of the 5th European Conference on Information Systems, Cork, Ireland, pp. 1549-60.

385 Jacky Swan, Sue Newell, Maxine Robertson, The diffusion, design and social shaping of production management information systems in Europe, Information Technology & People, Vol. 13 No. 1, 2000, pp. 27-45, p36.

386 William G. Egelhoff, Organizational equilibrium and organizational change: two different perspectives of the multinational enterprise, Journal of International Management 5 (1999) 15–33.

387 Granstrand, O., Hakanson, L., Sjolander, S. Eds. , 1992. Technology Management and International Business. Wiley, Chichester.

which is key in industries such as pharmaceuticals and electronics, tax advantages, subsidies for R&D, and government pressures to develop the subsidiary's capabilities beyond the simple assembly of established products and into innovative activities. Ronstadt[388] held that US MNEs had established foreign R&D units not only to transfer and adapt their home technology to foreign markets but also developing new products for local markets. Support for local manufacturing was found to be the main activity of expatriate R&D establishments[389]. The new telecommunications technologies have triggered a virtual spatial revolution in terms of the geography of production because while the marginal cost of transmitting information may be invariant to distance, apparently the marginal cost of transmitting knowledge, and principally tacit knowledge, rises with distance[390].

Multinationals invest abroad for access to markets rather than low wages[391] and the most significant determinant seems to be access to large and prosperous markets. MNEs tend to invest for purposes of selling goods and services rather than for gaining access to low-cost labor and other resources for producing goods and services. Trade in inputs has grown much faster than trade in final goods, and he estimates that intermediates now account for 30% of world trade in manufactures[392]. In the presence of vertical specialization small changes in tariffs generate large changes in trade flows[393]. Multinationals modify the nature of their foreign operations in response to local market conditions making affiliates more oriented toward producing for local consumers and more vertically integrated in countries with higher wages, higher tariffs, and larger markets, and they make affiliates more oriented toward processing inputs imported from abroad and more vertically specialized in countries with lower wages, lower tariffs, and smaller markets[394].

Globalization has not had symmetric impacts on knowledge and information. On the one hand, globalization has made it possible to transfer information costlessly across geographic space. On the other hand, the geographic dimension of knowledge remains a local phenomenon unaffected by globalization. While the relative cost of obtaining information has been significantly reduced, the cost of obtaining knowledge remains fundamentally unchanged triggering a shift in comparative advantage.

---

388 Ronstadt, R.C., 1984. R&D abroad by US multinationals. In: Stobaugh, R., Wells, Jr., L.T. Eds. , Technology Crossing Borders. Harvard Business School Press, Boston.

389 Pearce, R.D., 1992. Factors influencing the internationalization of R&D in multinational enterprises. In: Buckley, P.J., Casson, M. Eds., Multinational Enterprises in the World Economy.Elgar, London.

390 Griliches, Zvi, 1992, "The Search for R&D Spillovers," Scandanavian Journal of Economics, 94(S), 29-47. p. 29Griliches has defined knowledge spillovers as "working on similar things and hence benefiting much from each other's research."

391 Raymond Mataloni, Jr "U.S. Multinational Companies: Operations in 2000," Survey of Current Business, December 2002, p. 112. According to BEA data: "Worldwide production, capital expenditures, and employment of U.S. MNC's remained concentrated in the United States in 2000; U.S. parents account for about three-fourths, and MOFA's for about one-fourth, of their combined gross product of $2,695.3 billion, capital expenditures of $519.6 billion, and employment of 31.2 million. These shares were essentially unchanged from 1989."

392 Feenstra, Robert C. 1998. The Integration of Trade and the Disintegration of Production. Journal of Economic Perspectives, Vol.12 (4), Fall, pp. 31-50.

393 Yi, Kei-Mu. 2002. Can Vertical Specialization Explain the Growth of World Trade? Journal of Political Economy 245.

394 Blonigen, Bruce A., Ronald B. Davies, and Keith Head. 2002. Estimating the Knowledge Capital Model of the Multinational Enterprise: Comment. NBER Working Paper No. 8929. Carr, David L., James R. Markusen, and Keith E. Maskus. 2001. Estimating the Knowledge-Capital Model of the Multinational Enterprise. American Economic Review, 91, pp. 693-708.

Large[395] MNEs have in some industries such as pharmaceuticals, computer and telecommunications equipment, created global networks of laboratories. Local marketing units and expatriate production managers have a crucial say in the ideas and the selection of R&D projects when the mission of the laboratory is designing products for foreign markets. Geographical proximity and the search for larger markets seem crucial determinants for the overseas R&D activities of firms. Jorge Niosi and Benoit Godin [396] held that "a global network of R&D labs is much more constraining, requiring higher levels of coordination and international flows of R&D personnel, budgets, technology, and initiatives from the parent company to its foreign R&D establishments". Moreover, in accordance with Paula D. Harveston, Ben L. Kedia and John D. Francis [397] "short-term orientation measures are associated with higher performance for North American and European MNEs with high dependence on foreign operations but not for Pacific Rim MNEs. However, Pacific Rim MNEs were found to focus more on achieving long-term performance goals when compared to the North American and European MNEs". Countries are barely able to influence the activities of large, oligopolistic MNEs whose businesses and internal structures are global in scale, and can without problems be shifted to new production sites decentralizing their productive and distributive capacities. Hence, countries must facilitate the access to new technologies and active inducement of foreign direct investments[398].

The international triumph of Japanese corporations, above all the largest MNEs, has been credited to competitive strategies popularly characterized as placing almost complete emphasis on attainment of sales and market share growth rather than profitability, particularly over the short term. The ability of management to follow objectives other than profitability should be further enhanced. Corporate governance systems show large differences globally, and their structure and effectiveness are determined, at least to some extent, by the strategic, cultural, political, and legal background in which they are developed and applied[399]. In accordance with J. Michael Geringer, Colette A. Frayne and David Olsen [400] "changes in governance mechanisms and their effectiveness are expected in response to changing environments over both time and space, and such a model could provide a more complete understanding of the evolving compensation–performance relationship in large corporations from Japan and other nations".

A company's internal control system must have as its standard goal the management of risks important to the fulfilment of its business objectives. E-business necessitates a flexible,

---

[395] Casson, M., Singh, S., 1993. Corporate R&D strategies: the influence of firm, industry and country factors on the decentralization of R&D. R&D Management 23 2 , 91–107.

[396] Jorge Niosi , Benoit Godin, Canadian R&D abroad management practices, Research Policy 28 1999 215–230, p230.

[397] Paula D. Harveston , Ben L. Kedia, John D. Francis, MNE's dependence on foreign operations and performance: a study of MNEs from the "Triad" regions, International Business Review 8 (1999) 293–307, p293.

[398] McKendrick, D.G., R.F. Doner, and S. Haggard (2000), From Silicon Valley to Singapore: Location and Competitive Advantage in the Hard Disk Drive Industry, Stanford University Press, Stanford.

[399] Brown, C., Nakata, Y., Reich, M., Ulman, L., 1997. Work and pay in the United States and Japan. Oxford University Press, Oxford. Prowse, S., 1995. Corporate governance in an international perspective: a survey of corporate control mechanisms among large firms in the U.S., U.K., Japan and Germany. Financial Markets, Institutions, and Instruments 4 (1), 1–63.

[400] J. Michael Geringer, Colette A. Frayne, David Olsen, Rewarding growth or profit?: Top management team compensation and governance in Japanese MNEs, Journal of International Management 4 (1998) 289–309, p305.

innovative and empowered workforce. New and existing competitors can quickly usurp current market status through delivering greater service excellence at all stages of the customer relationship. Competitive advantage is likely to be rapidly eroded, along with established stakeholder relationships, if an organization fail to minimize the risks surrounding both its decision-making and its implementation abilities. David Smith[401] considers that "many organizations are making quite fundamental strategic mistakes; mistakes that are often then repeated by others. This may be because they have failed to recognize the need to apply advanced risk management thinking to both the strategic and implementation issues surrounding the E-business imperative".

When information can be freely disseminated on the Internet, it may be most advantageous for a seller to provide lower levels of information to control the intensity of competition in the multichannel marketplace. Pricing and communication strategies are tied to the Internet's penetration in the marketplace and as the penetration increases, online and offline strategies will converge. Cyberspace fosters a loose and vast network of partners as distinct from the formal and narrow relationships in traditional business. According to Vijay Mahajan and R. Venkatesh [402]"e-business models may have to balance the divergent short- and long-term objectives". Clustered FDI[403] not only appears to attract more suppliers than dispersed FDI but also facilitates technology and knowledge spillovers more than dispersed FDI[404]. V. Owhoso, K.C. Gleason, I. Mathur, and C. Malgwi [405] found that firms that use the FDI mode of expansion do better than firms expanding using non-FDI modes of expansion.

Ownership affects technology diffusion in host economies, since the strength of foreign participation is expected to affect the inducement of parent firms to transfer intangible assets such as technology and management skills to their affiliates[406]. Thus, productivity or technological spillovers may differ according to the ownership structure. Technology transfer occurs merely by an employee traveling to an overseas affiliate and discussing technology or through a series of E-mails rather than through an explicit royalty or licensing payment that would show up in companies' financial accounting statements or foreign direct investment operations reports.

The internationalisation of industrial R&D in current years has been interpreted as the endeavour of technology-intensive companies to utilize location-specific innovation advantages in order to compete in a more and more globalized environment. International R&D does not automatically mean a globally integrated approach to R&D. According to

---

401 David Smith, E-BUSINESS STRATEGY RISK MANAGEMENT, Computer Law & Security Report Vol. 16 no. 6 2000, p394

402 Vijay Mahajan, R. Venkatesh, Marketing modeling for e-business, Intern. J. of Research in Marketing 17 2000 215–225, p224.

403 Rodney D. Ludema, Increasing returns, multinationals and geography of preferential trade agreements, Journal of International Economics 56 (2002) 329–358.

404 EDMUND R.THOMPSON, Clustering of Foreign Direct Investment and Enhanced Technology Transfer: Evidence from Hong Kong Garment Firms in China, 2002World Development Vol.30, No.5, pp.873 – 889.

405 V. Owhoso, K.C. Gleason , I. Mathur, C. Malgwi, Entering the last frontier: expansion by US multinationals to Africa, International Business Review (2002) www.elsevier.com/locate/ibusrev

406 Natalia Barbosa , Helen Louri, On the determinants of multinationals' ownership preferences: evidence from Greece and Portugal, International Journal of Industrial Organization 20 (2002) 493–515.

Maximilian von Zedtwitz and Oliver Gassmann [407] "The establishment of new R&D units is influenced by two principal factors: access and support of local markets, and access to local science and technology".

The technology and innovation policy requires a broad understanding of the interaction between long-term economic development the internationalisation-globalisation of the world economy, government intervention into economy, and microeconomics of the innovation on company level. Countries aiming to catch-up with more developed world have to prepare science and technology programs that are in tune with rapid technological development. A widening of disparities in technological capacity between more and less technologically advanced countries is a central political issue of technological development. The capability to innovate is cumulative as innovation gives birth to more innovation[408]. Many MNEs have globalised their production, but few have shifted research and development capabilities or corporate headquarters away from their traditional home bases because technology in terms of machines and blueprints has become exceptionally mobile while technological competence embodied in competent humans is still much less so.

4.17 Codification of Knowledge Flows by MNE

The management of knowledge is increasingly considered as a main source of competitive advantage for corporations. Firms enjoy a competitive advantage if they know how to expand, disseminate, and exploit organizational knowledge internally, effectively share with, transfer to, and receive knowledge from business partners[409]. Since the modern-day business environment calls upon the ability to constantly adapt and deal with new situations, events and contexts, effective knowledge creation matters more now than ever before. Nevertheless, knowledge creation and utilization are not always unified in time and space. The management of knowledge flows is important for MNEs because they operate in geographically and culturally diverse environments. Differences between regional markets require adaptation of products and operations to regional conditions. Growing global competition requires the exploitation of economies of scale on a global scale. To manage such contingencies, MNEs can derive great competitive advantage by managing knowledge flows between their subunits. Codification of organizational knowledge can greatly facilitate flows of organizational knowledge between subsidiaries. Knowledge management in MNEs involves problematical choices because the costs and benefits of codification most likely depend on the kind of knowledge to be codified, the forms of codification used, and on the strategic framework of the MNE[410]. Corporations can create expert systems, databases, flow charts, and reports on any part of their operations. The level of codification of organizational

---

407 Maximilian von Zedtwitz, Oliver Gassmann, Market versus technology drive in R&D internationalization: four different patterns of managing research and development, Research Policy 31 (2002) 569–588, p586.

408 Sigurdson Jon, & Cheng, Alfred Li-Ping 2001), Introduction Œ New Technological Landscape in Asia Pacific, Special issue of the International Journal of Technology Management, Vol. 22, No 5/6.

409 Simonin, B. L. (1999). Ambiguity and the process of knowledge transfer in strategic alliances. Strategic Management Journal, 20, 595-623.

410 Prahalad, C. K., & Hamel, G. (1990). The core competence of the corporation. Harvard Business Review, 79-91 (May-June). Prusak, L. (1996). The knowledge advantage. Strategy and Leadership, 24, 6-8 (March/April).

knowledge is not exogenous to organizations. Companies that successfully expand, disseminate and exploit knowledge internally, that protect knowledge from expropriation and imitation by competitors, and that know how to gather and distribute knowledge efficiently and resourcefully, enjoy a competitive advantage.

Firms can derive competitive advantage from pursuing multiple and non-bureaucratic forms of codification, such as intranets, shared databases, expert systems, e-mail, EDI, cyberspace and rapid prototyping technologies. Modern forms of codification provide fast and reliable access to organizational knowledge across geographical, social, and organizational boundaries. They facilitate the transfer of knowledge into and out of organizational knowledge repositories, and they tend to be further competent and appropriate than earlier forms of codification. MNEs that do not invest in codification of their knowledge impede knowledge flows, and so forego the benefits of exploiting knowledge that is generated in particular locations across the entire organization. Finally, according to Martin Schulz and Lloyd A. Jobe[411] "knowledge flows are most facilitated when technical knowledge is codified in numbers and codes, marketing and sales knowledge is codified in text and language based forms, and when strategic knowledge regarding competitors is encoded in objects and people".

Larger companies face greater uncertainty to generate knowledge that is more costly to transfer to decision makers. While minimizing total cost requires allocating some decision rights from the CEO's office to lower levels of the firm the value is increased by minimizing the total of knowledge transfer costs and control costs. Knowledge transfer costs arise because decision makers have limited mental and sensory faculties ensuring that some agents do not have knowledge in common. And so such lack of common knowledge is a barrier to communication. If knowledge relevant to decisions resides at lower levels of a company then decentralization reduces knowledge transfer costs. The cost of transferring knowledge from the CEO to lower level decision makers reduces the net benefit from decentralization resulting in less decentralization. The costs of transferring decision rights from the CEO to lower levels are control costs increasing with the specialization of knowledge. The costs of controlling unit managers are higher for companies that generate more specialized knowledge reducing the tendency for companies generating relatively more specialized knowledge to be more decentralized. Technology is the primary determinant of organization design and changes in technology convert specialized to non-specialized knowledge leading to assembly of knowledge resulting to the creation of firms and affect their organization. The degree of specialization of a company's knowledge depends on demand for product heterogeneity across customers, which can be induced by geographic dispersion of the company's operations. Knowledge of local customs, conditions, regulations and preferences is costly to gain and costly to transmit to others not familiar with the conditions. The greater the environmental uncertainties then the more specialized are the knowledge and in environmental uncertainty transfer costs are likely to be associated with expected and unexpected changes in the environment. According to Andrew A. Christie, Marc P. Joye, Ross L. Watts [412]"more decentralized firms tend to generate more specialized knowledge,

[411] Martin Schulz, Lloyd A. Jobe, Codification and tacitness as knowledge management strategies An empirical exploration, Journal of High Technology Management Research 12 (2001) 139-165, p161

[412] Andrew A. Christie, Marc P. Joye, Ross L. Watts, Decentralization of the firm: theory and evidence, Journal of Corporate Finance 9 (2003) 3 – 36, p33.

have less externalities among the firms' investments, have higher growth and greater uncertainty about the firms' returns. Decentralized firms also tend to be larger and unregulated."

FDI is a mechanism that helps a state prevailing over geographic localization of knowledge diffusion. Accordingly, a driving force behind many FDI-friendly government policies is the hope of acquiring modern technology and know-how, together with product and process technology as well as management, distribution and marketing skills. It has to be taken into account that local subsidiaries of foreign MNEs might be a channel through which domestic technology falls into the hands of foreign competitors. Knowledge outflows downgrade the competitiveness of host country companies in global markets. According to Jasjit Singh[413] "there are indeed not just knowledge inflows from foreign MNCs to host country organizations but also significant knowledge outflows back from host country organizations to foreign MNCs. In fact, on an average, MNCs appear to contribute less to host country knowledge than they gain from it. This asymmetry in knowledge flows exists not only in the aggregate but also in a large majority of the individual countries… knowledge flows from the domestic economy to MNC subsidiaries are only slightly smaller than knowledge flows even between domestic organizations, and are significantly larger than knowledge flow back from MNC subsidiaries to domestic firms. In other words, the constraints imposed by liability of foreignness appear to be rather limited as far as acquisition of technological knowledge is concerned". Knowledge flows reflect the causal patterns of personnel mobility. Knowledge transmission is constrained by geographic distance. Inter-organizational mobility of personnel is a vital determinant of cross-country differences in patterns of knowledge circulation. In fact MNEs are a vehicle that facilitates global distribution of knowledge by combining intra-company mechanisms for long-distance knowledge reassign with localized knowledge exchange with organizations in various parts of the world. MNEs have the capacity to transfer and integrate knowledge worldwide. Companies make possible interpersonal networks enabling transmission of tacit knowledge over large distances. If MNE subsidiaries are involved in cutting-edge research or innovative product expansion, high degree of knowledge spillover benefits result for the host country. A MNE subsidiary is less expected to be a source of advanced technological knowledge than it could have been if its central part were doing original R&D. MNEs control leakage of their centre technologies by leveraging their globally innovation network and complementary capabilities, which makes certain that access to knowledge from just their local subsidiary would not be very precious for a prospective competitor in the host state. Innovations resulting from mixing of knowledge across MNE subsidiaries in various locations are more valuable than those arising only from knowledge from one subsidiary.

---

[413] Jasjit Singh, Asymmetry of Knowledge Spillovers between MNCs and Host Country Firms, 2006 *www.ssrn.com* p4,32.

Chapter 5

The Role of FDI

5.1 FDI

Foreign direct investment (FDI) is the vehicle by which firms achieve their strategic objectives. A company must possess some asset such as product and process technology or management and marketing skills that can be used beneficially in the foreign affiliate in order to invest in production in foreign markets. FDI introduces competition, promotes efficiencies and corporate rationalisation, and helps to restructure the economy.

The entry of a MNE represents something more than a simple import of capital into a host country. Kindleberger[1] thinks that "for direct investment to thrive there must be some imperfection in markets for goods or factors, including among the latter technology, or some interference in competition by government or by firms, which separates markets". The multinationals' R&D and technology is profoundly concentrated to a few home countries, unlike MNE investment, production, and employment that are more extensively spread across both industrialized and developing economies. It is not obvious how MNE technology spreads across international borders and what role MNEs play in the process because "technology" is a theoretical concept, and so not easy to observe and evaluate. MNE technology can be distributed to new users through formal market transactions - transfers - or through informal, non-market mediated channels that may be voluntary or involuntary. MNEs control technology supplies by virtue of their ownership of proprietary technologies, but they account for a significant share of the demand, via their foreign affiliates. The intra-firm character of the technology transfers that take place through trade in capital apparatus and other products is less evident. A significant share of the exports and imports of the major home countries run between MNE parents and affiliates[2]. The industrialized nations have remained the major contributor as well as the major recipient of FDI though FDI flows to the developing world have more than doubled between 1990 and 1999. According to Avik Chakrabarti [3] in 1999, nearly 58% of 30 global FDI flows went to the industrial countries, 37% to developing countries, and just 5% to the transition economies of Eastern Europe.

---

[1] Kindleberger, C.P. (1969), American Business Abroad, New Haven; Yale University Press. p. 13

[2] UNCTC (1988), Transnational Corporations in World Development: Trends and Prospects, New York; United Nations Centre on Transnational Corporations. p. 91

[3] Avik Chakrabarti, A theory of the spatial distribution of foreign direct investment, International Review of Economics and Finance 12 (2002) 1–21.

FDI embodies two typical assets: 1) capital and 2) technology or a number of intangible advantages. Freedom of capital movements in the form of FDI sometimes clash with concerns about loss of national sovereignty and other possible adverse consequences involving a controlling stake by often large MNEs over which domestic governments, it is feared, have little power. Developing countries have been wary of inward FDI and even in the United States, the surge of Japanese FDI in the 1980s led to extensive concerns about excessive foreign control and undesirable effects on national security and in legislative action. Adverse economic and political effects caused by FDI on the host country include balance of payments deficits, reduced domestic research and development, diminished competition, crowding-out of domestic companies and lower employment. The benefits of inward FDI are substantial, mainly in developing countries where foreign technology and managerial expertise are sought. Restrictions on foreign ownership are the most obvious barriers to inward FDI. Prerequisites that foreign investors must show economic benefits increase the cost of entry and so discourage the inflow of foreign capital. Other formal restrictions that discourage FDI inflows include constraints on the ability of foreign nationals either to manage or to work in affiliates of foreign companies and other operational controls on these businesses stipulating that nationals or residents must form a majority of the board of directors. FDI inflows into manufacturing are approximately wholly unrestricted, aside from economy-wide measures such as screening. In fact, many countries seek to encourage foreign investment in manufacturing. Construction and hotels and restaurants are also comparatively lightly restricted. Some "sensitive sectors", remarkably telecoms, transport, electricity, and finance are regularly highly or considerably restricted. European Union has no or very limited discriminatory screening of foreign investment and screening is minor in the United States and Japan. All countries have equity restrictions, but these vary significantly concentrated in a few sensitive sectors, namely transport, telecommunications, finance and electricity. Moreover, restrictions on FDI have decreased manifestly over time for most countries. Finally, heavily restricted sectors are those that are extremely sensitive to national security or national sovereignty considerations: telecommunications, air and maritime transport, finance, public utilities, and media[4].

The internalization theory posits that foreign direct investment will boost a company's market value -comparative to its accounting value- if the company possesses firm-specific intangible assets such as superior production skills, patents, marketing advantages, managerial skills, or consumer goodwill[5]. The value of these intangible assets can be improved by escalating the size of the company's markets. A company enhances its price by expanding abroad and controlling foreign operations if the expected gains from exploiting the intangibles in a foreign market exceed the costs of operating a foreign subsidiary. Internalization, or global amalgamation of economic doings, reduces the MNE's require for undertaking innovatory activities at their affiliates. Internalization of ownership-specific assets, such as proprietary technology, brand goodwill, and managerial skills, offers important chances for benefiting from lower costs, higher quality as well as scale economies. Nevertheless, the major shortcoming of internalization lies in the decline of the learning

---

[4] Stephen S. Golub, Measures Of Restrictions On Inward Foreign Direct Investment For Oecd Countries, Economics Department Working Papers No. 357 ECO/WKP(2003)11

[5] Rugman, A.W. (1981) Inside the Multinationals: The Economics of Internal Markets. (New York: Columbia University Press).

processes and spillovers in the host economy regardless that key strategic decisions concerning innovation are not delegated to the affiliates. Clustering makes it easier to develop backward and forward linkages, to diminish transport and communication delays as well as to increase the prospective for positive externalities. According to Pradeep Kanta Ray and Shams-ur Rahman [6]"TNCs display a relatively low inclination to adapt products to suit local markets, but appear to assist the process of knowledge spillovers to local sub-contractors through activities involving business process outsourcing... TNCs are not superior to local enterprises in terms of vertical inter-firm linkages they generate with ancillary suppliers".

The capital for financing FDI can come from the host country or from global financial markets or may be raised on the local capital markets of the recipient nation. FDI may or may not be associated with a net external addition to the local capital stock. FDI can be seen as a source of investment in capital and technology or related assets, the variables capable of improving productivity and wages in a recipient economy. So, FDI is more likely to be important in industries with significant firm-specific, intangible, knowledge-based assets (KBAs). MNEs are in actual fact exporters of KBA, including technology, engineering, management, marketing, and financial services. Human capital skills are significant in generating KBAs. Moreover, multinationals sell the services of devices that protect the value of their KBAs, including patents, trademarks, trade secrets, and copyrights[7].

MNEs locate production or market activities abroad where they can benefit from market power expansion and location specific advantages. So, market expansion and cost reduction are the two advantages that MNEs pursue through FDI. While direct sales and other related activities enlarge market power, cheap labor, raw materials or other related advantages in the host country lead to cost reduction. Foreign direct investors obtain major control over the firm they invest in applying hands-on management (micro-management) standards that permit them to react in real time to changing economic environments and gain control over the firm. Foreign direct investors have a cutting-edge advantage over domestic investors in extracting information about the true value of the firm applying their superior micro-management skills in order to elicit the true value of the productivity factor. Foreign direct investors' advantage stems from their special experience and know-how in a particular industry outbidding other investors for the top productivity firms[8]. Developing countries with weak financial institutions, and low corporate governance and accounting standards catch the attention of a higher share of their capital inflows in the form of FDI[9].

Exports from the MNE's home country may be adequate to prompt reverse engineering that is often recognized as one of the main sources of involuntary technology dissemination[10]. A large share of both license sales and sales of technologically advanced products are directed

---

[6] Pradeep Kanta Ray and Shams-ur Rahman, The propensity for local innovation and interfirm linkages in transnational corporations versus local enterprises in India, *Transnational Corporations,* Vol. 15, No. 2 (August 2006) 92-93.

[7] Keith E. Maskus, The Role Of Intellectual Property Rights In Encouraging Foreign Direct Investment And Technology Transfer, 9 Duke J. of Comp. & Int'l L. 109

[8] Assaf Razin, Efraim Sadka, Gains from FDI inflows with incomplete information, Economics Letters 78 (2003) 71–77

[9] Loungangi, P., Razin, A., 2001. Foreign direct investment: a critical view. Financial and Development 38 (2), 6–10. Portes, R., Rey, H., 1999. The Determinants of Cross-Border Equity Flow: The Geography of Information, NBER Working Paper No. 7336.

[10] Zander, U. (1991), Exploiting a Technological Edge - Voluntary and Involuntary Dissemination of Technology, Stockholm; Institute of International Business, Stockholm School of Economics. Chapter 5.

to MNE affiliates, and FDI seems to be more important for the geographical spread of technologies than sales of technology to unrelated parties. It should be taken into consideration that a unique characteristic of direct investment is that the control and ownership of the technologies used by the affiliates stay in the MNEs' possession. The majority of channels for the dissemination of modern, advanced technology are external effects or "spillovers" from foreign direct investment, rather than formal technology transfer arrangements[11]. Additionally, spillovers take place when the MNEs cannot reap all the productivity or efficiency benefits that follow in the host country's local firms as a result of the entry or presence of MNE affiliates. A technology that is exploited through FDI will not be licensed to the local competitors in the host country. Taking into account that the characteristics of the host country's industry and policy environment are central determinants of the net benefits of FDI, foreign direct investment promotes economic development by contributing to productivity growth and exports in their host countries but the precise kind of the relation between foreign MNEs and their host economies vary between industries and countries. Removal of trade barriers will entail more concurrent business cycles, since a higher level of trade will allow demand shocks to more easily spread across national borders[12].

Entry levels for attracting FDI have risen, and investors are focusing on countries with strong resident capabilities. Mobile MNEs seek strong corresponding factors wherever they locate. There is no conflict over the long term between inward FDI and domestic capabilities. With the growing role of MNEs in economic life in most countries, developing country governments have removed margins on FDI inflows.

Liberalization has not always increased FDI inflows into host developing countries for the reason that the deduction of restrictions on FDI does not create the matching factors that MNEs need; it only allows them to take advantage of existing capabilities more liberally. Therefore, FDI response tends to be most forceful where local capabilities are strong when liberalisation takes place.

As mentioned above, in order to invest abroad, the conglomerate must own certain specific intangible assets whose capacity is not exhausted by production for the home market. Ownership must be exclusive and the assets must confer benefits that offset the costs of operating in an alien environment in competition with firms indigenous to the host country. In an imperfect capital market, the financial power of the multinational and its easy access to global credit and equity markets constitutes another asset, which may be decisive in capital-intensive industries. If production is to be expanded abroad rather than at home, foreign location must offer benefits that cannot be captured by export from a home base. Examples of such benefits are low labour costs, geographic advantages, favourable tax-treatment or a market protected by import restrictions or transport costs. FDI will be induced only if more profitable than the options of selling the asset or leasing or licensing it. Where the quality of a product cannot be assessed by inspection, the possibility of repeat purchases by the buyer and of a build-up of reputation by the seller offers safeguards against moral hazard. FDI is a potent ingredient in the development process, it is an acknowledged conduit for the transfer of

[11] Blomström, M. (1989), Foreign Investment and Spillovers: A Study of Technology Transfer to Mexico, London; Routledge

[12] Frankel, J., Rose, A., 1998. The endogeneity of the optimum currency area criterion. Economic Journal 108, 1009–1025.

technology and human skills, it is a purveyor of new ideas and it is a source of capital without being a panacea for the development problem but FDI is more important in promoting growth and technical change in economies open to competition from both external and internal markets[13]. Moreover, FDI responds to market forces, but if the markets are distorted its response is not the sort which would enhance the development objectives of the recipient countries. In the case of FDI, foreign companies are personally involved in the operations of the local economy, unlike in the case of trade and licensing agreements. Attracting foreign direct investment in the form of physical capital creates positive spillover effects to the local economy such as increased demand for labour. Transfer pricing and profit shifting are the most important future international tax issues for multinational corporations (61%), followed by double taxation relief and foreign tax credits (10% and 13%)[14]. Cross-border intra-firm trade prices are influenced by the profit-shifting strategies of multinationals[15]. Global sales and gross product associated with international production have increased faster the global exports and GDP -by 3.2 per cent and 4.1 per cent, correspondingly, during the period 1982-99 and around 50 per cent, is on account of intra- trade between affiliates of MNEs[16].

Additionally, in the case of the multinational enterprise, its involvement in the local economy is marked, and perceptions concerning its threat to political and economic sovereignty of nation states are heightened. Mergers and acquisitions of locally owned companies by foreign companies account for around one-third of all FDI flows to developing countries, In fact, the freedom of policy makers in developing countries is constrained by the need to accommodate the interests of big business.[17] On the other hand, multinationals pay higher wages than comparable locally owned companies in developing countries, and it is the electorate, not the multinationals, which dictate tax and expenditure policies of nation states[18]. So, the nation state should protect the interests of the public realm and policy makers must institute the sort of policies, which not only attract sufficient volumes of FDI but also promote its efficient utilisation. Countries, which have failed to institute trade and investment policies designed to create jobs and employment opportunities are also the ones, which seek low wage jobs from multinationals.

Macro economic stability including exchange rate stability, distortion free product and labour markets which allow for the play of comparative advantage in resource allocation, a stable policy frame work on FDI, and resource endowments including a threshold level of human capital are the main determinants of FDI. Fundamentally there is a need to promote the establishment of a stable policy framework and the elimination of distortions in product and labour markets, which means stability of policies leading to economic steadiness may more often than not promoting necessarily political stability. Whist the efficiency gains the MNEs generate, the technology and know-how they transfer to host countries are recognised, their operations are also viewed with suspicion because their size, the spread of their operations and their endowments of financial and human resources are seen to thwart the

---

13 Balasubramanyam, V.N. Sapsford David and Salisu Mohammed (1996) " Foreign Direct Investment and Growth in EP and IS Countries " Economic Journal, vol. 106.

14 Ernst &Young (2001), "Transfer Pricing 2001 Global Survey"

15 Clausing, Kimberly A. (2001), "Tax-Motivated Transfer Pricing and U.S. Intrafirm Trade Prices", mimeo.

16 United Nations (2000) World Investment Report, (UN New York and Geneva)

17 Noreena Hertz (2001) " decrying Wolf " (Reply to Martin Wolf) Prospect August -September 2001

18 Wolf Martin (2001) " The Infantile Leftist" (Review of Noreena Hertz's book ,The Silent Takeover) Prospect July 2001

growth of locally owned companies, undermine local consumer interests and indeed pose a threat to national sovereignty. Hence, the confront the developing countries face is one of a trade off between economic sovereignty and the fruits that FDI yields but a compact on FDI under the aegis of the WTO should generate the vital investment climate for FDI to fulfill its potential. Moreover, multilateral competition policy has a role in promoting greater international contestability of markets and the WTO is well placed to extend its remit to the development of a multilateral competition policy compact[19].

Despite extensive liberalisation over the past two decades, there is scope for further reducing policy barriers to integration of OECD markets and remaining barriers have a considerable influence on trade and FDI, with anticompetitive domestic regulations and restrictive labour market arrangements estimated to curb integration as much as explicit trade and FDI restrictions further liberalisation of trade, FDI and domestic product and labour markets on global integration could be substantial. Unreasonably restrictive product and labour-market regulations can act as barriers to trade and FDI having a significant impact on the extent of trade and activities of MNEs and the state of the domestic physical infrastructure influence countries' capacities to participate in the globalisation of economic activity. Trade, foreign direct investment and the related activity of multinational enterprises are the main channels through which global economic integration is achieved, integration improves global welfare and so the elimination of needless policy barriers to trade and investment is desirable. Trade openness increases competitive pressures and stimulates imitation, adoption and innovation, fostering productivity improvements and technical progress not mentioning that internationalisation of production increases competitive pressures in OECD markets because, in manufacturing, FDI is related to goods trade and, in non-manufacturing, commercial presence is one of the main modes of cross-border service supply. FDI as an important vehicle for technology transfer and a stimulus to innovative activity through resource reallocation, competition, trade, technology transfer is a gradually more important driver of growth[20].

Border barriers to manufactured goods trade are generally low in OECD countries, but remaining barriers continue to exert a negative influence on trade flows and free-trade areas do not have increased drastically cross-border supply of services. A number of countries still have a relatively restrictive environment in some important non-manufacturing industries, such as electricity, transport and telecoms and restrictions take the form of explicit limits on the foreign ownership of domestic firms and are estimated to curb considerably FDI stocks in protected countries. Domestic product-market regulations imposing unnecessary costs on businesses and creating barriers to entry exert a distinct negative influence on FDI and so foreign investors allocating their portfolio on the basis of expected relative returns, the countries with relatively restrictive and costly product-market regulations will tend to have lower stocks of foreign capital. Hence, product-market reforms diminishing the relative

---

[19] P. M. Smith (1999) 'A long and winding road: TRIPS and the evolution of an international competition framework', Journal of International Economic Law, 2, 435-440. D. T. Tarullo (1999) 'Competition policy for global markets', Journal of International Economic Law, 2, 445-455. I. G. Bercero and S. D. Amarasinha (2001) 'Moving the trade and competition debate forward', Journal of International Economic Law, 4, 481-506. B. Bora, P. J. Lloyd, and M. Pangestu (2000) 'Industrial policy and the WTO', World Economy, 23, 543-559.

[20] OECD (2002), Foreign Direct Investment and Development: Where Do We Stand?, Paris. OECD (2002), Foreign Direct Investment for Development -- Maximising Benefits, Minimising Costs, Paris.

restrictiveness of regulations are expected to increase the level of inward FDI in a given country. Strict employment protection legislation (EPL) and high tax wedges on labour income have an effect on the labour market in the home country in ways that curb its exports by making the reallocation of labour across companies, industries and occupations problematical. Thus, if EPL increases the risk/return ratio on foreign investment due to increased uncertainty regarding costs foreign investors are possible to choose locations where this ratio is lowest, irrespective of the potentially offsetting effect of the collective bargaining regime. Superior infrastructure conditions are significant for reducing transport and communication costs and increasing trade, particularly in some services where international transactions entail such conditions to be good in both origin and destination countries and so policies that develop infrastructure building, either by ensuring efficient public investment or encouraging private investment, can considerably increase both the bilateral and global volumes of service trade.

The upward trend in FDI flow points to a rising internationalisation of production over the 1990s. An increasing cross-country dispersion of the amount of FDI supplied and hosted relative to the size of the investor and host countries occurred and by the year 2000, the variances of the in stock and out stock as ratios to GDP among OECD countries were larger than two decades earlier[21]. FDI can be directed at affiliates of the parent company that act simply as financial intermediaries in redirecting the funds to a third country and foreign affiliates in the local market is eventually the best indicator of the actual degree of internationalisation of production in OECD countries and in most countries the presence of foreign affiliates in services is either equivalent or higher than in manufacturing. Differences in reporting conventions make cross-country comparisons problematical, the industry classification of foreign affiliates is often inconsistent with the reporting conventions of industrial statistics making impossible the relation foreign-affiliate production or employment to total production or employment in a given industry.

A company must possess an ownership advantage, such as a patent, which it wishes to exploit in foreign markets, locational considerations, such as tariffs and transport costs, dictate the supplying foreign markets by foreign production. Furthermore, a company has to prefer internalisation over an arms-length transaction which means open its own plant abroad rather than licensing its technology. When there is in existence strategic interaction between companies of various countries serving a foreign market, the transmission of information about production costs becomes vital and multinationalization can come up as a way of transmitting cost information to foreign rivals regardless that its actual costs of serving the foreign market are higher as a result. Moreover, FDI is correlated with exports to the host country market: just enough foreign direct investment would be undertaken to indicate the firm's efficient technology, and the rest of its foreign market share would be exported from the home plants. The choice of plant location will affect the firm's actual production costs to the extent that factor price differentials exist between countries, and the perception of the firm's production costs as believed by rival companies. Accordingly, in the presence of asymmetric information about costs, the role of locational considerations takes on a new

[21] Giuseppe Nicoletti, Steve Golub, Dana Hajkova, Daniel Mirza and Kwang-Yeol Yoo, Policies And International Integration: Influences On Trade And Foreign Direct Investment Economics Department Working Papers No. 359 ECO/WKP(2003)13, p16.

dimension. According to Kyle Bagwell, Robert W. Staiger[22] "the location of production facilities abroad directly informs rival firms of an entrant's production costs, and the case of firm-specific informational asymmetries where the decision to locate production facilities abroad signals the costs of the entrant".

Transnational investments are viewed in LDC's as vehicles of technology transfer even more than as purveyors of capital. Activities in which reputation is a crucial asset constitute yet another field in which FDI is likely to flow. Where standardised but labour-intensive operations can be separated from an otherwise capital- and technology-intensive process and located in labour-abundant, low-wage economies, this could be a basis for FDI. So, FDI is induced only when it is essential to avoid subcontracting these phases to local producers. For instance, Mining or plantation agriculture for export may be heavily multinationalised because of their capital-intensive technology, the transaction costs saved through forward integration with user industries and their dependence on a world-wide distribution network. Besides, the pattern of expatriate investment is determined by the specific advantages expatriates command over their competitors. Light, labour-intensive manufactures involve small commitment and offer quick returns; the immediate stance of government policy is more relevant to them than its long-term prospects. Expatriates have an advantage over domestic producers in exports because of their superior knowledge of foreign markets and technology. Capital-intensive investment particularly in infrastructure has a long gestation period and makes the investor a hostage to fortune.

The most important locational determinants of FDI are the economic factors that influence the prospects for MNEs to engage profitably in production activities. These include the size and growth of host country markets (which depend primarily on macroeconomic performance, especially the level and growth of national and per capita real income); access to regional or international markets for exports from a host country; the availability of human resources, including relatively low-cost and, especially, efficient, flexible and skilled labour; technological and innovation capabilities; natural resource endowments; and the quality of the infrastructure. A second important set of determinants relates to the environment for conducting business and economic activity in the host country. This includes political and economic stability, and efficient and encouraging policies towards industry, trade and private enterprise activity in general, whether domestic or foreign, and institutional structures for implementing them. A third set of determinants relates to the design and implementation of policies specifically related to FDI. Maintaining and increasing the level and growth of FDI flows to and within the region could, therefore, assist in the process of economic recovery in the region.

FDI is no longer flowing to the established destinations, and that its determinants and purpose have changed to new destinations and cannot wholly be explained by the liberalization measures undertaken by governments, or its institutions, like the inward investment agencies (IIAs)[23]. The levels of development in different countries, and their governments' policies, also differentially influence FDI decisions. Even with the best of incentives an IIA would fail to attract FDI if the country had poor infrastructure, and

[22] Kyle Bagwell, Robert W. Staiger Informational aspects of foreign direct investment and the multinational firm, Japan and the World Economy 466 (2002) 1–20 at 19.

[23] Mudambi, R. (1999). Multinational investment attraction: principal-agent considerations. International Journal of the Economics of Business, 6(1), 65–79. Mudambi, R. (1995). The MNE investment location decision: some empirical evidence. Managerial and Decision Economics, 16, 249–257.

political/economic instability or the country was neither a large market, nor a low-wage haven. It should be taken into account that MNEs might move to an unattractive location, even without incentives, if their rivals were entering that market. Economic benefits of foreign direct investment have fuelled the worldwide movement towards liberalization but national security concerns related to the foreign control of domestic industries regularly represent a key counterweight to this general trend. For instance, national security concerns will increasingly create opportunities for the restriction of foreign direct investment in US and the rise of transnational security threats apparent after September 11 transformed the context within which Exon-Florio[24] will operate and the evaluation of national security considerations will shift from national origin to individuals.

The theory of capital movements (portfolio investments) was the earliest explanation for FDI[25]. Unlike portfolio investments, transferring knowledge, and other intangible firm assets, to organize production abroad did not surrender ownership or control. Companies set up production facilities abroad for products that had already been standardized and matured in the home markets.[26] It should be taken into account that company's knowledge and skills comprise implied ownership advantages that take time to develop, and the MNEs, with their capacity to formulate and handle complex organizational structures, control these advantages through worldwide investments in order to sustain them. Market size and growth, barriers to trade, wages, production, transportation and other costs, political stability, psychic distance and host government's trade and taxation regulations, performance requirements, cultural distance, GDP *per capita* and infrastructure are factors affecting FDI location[27]. On the one hand, productive market, liberal host government policies, technological infrastructure, skilled labor, cultural proximity and oligopolistic rivalry caused more investments to pour in, including investments from Japan and some newly industrialized countries to Europe. On the other hand, intense competitive pressure reduced profit margins, which forced MNEs to transfer manufacturing operations to countries with lower factor costs and wages such as Asian countries contributed to the restructuring of FDI capital. While reinvested profits and some fresh investments continued into Europe in the knowledge-based and technology intensive sectors, MNEs started making *effectiveness* seeking investments into Asia. Host governments regularly allow market access only as a *quid pro quo* for obtaining capital and technology through FDI on favorable terms. MNE investments to China, India, and Indonesia, there were both, of the market seeking as well as effectiveness seeking variety. Large MNEs cannot afford to give up emerging markets to their competitors by default, and

[24] Exon-Florio Amendment to the 1988 Trade Act, Pub. L. No. 100-418, § 5021, 102 Stat. 1425 (1988) (codified at 50 U.S.C. app. § 2170. Jose E. Alvarez, Political Protectionism and United States International Investments Obligations in Conflict: The Hazards of Exon-Florio, 30 VA. J. INT'L L. 1, 56

[25] Iversen, C. (1935). Aspects of international capital movements. London and Copenhagen: Levin and Munksgaard. Aliber, R. Z. (1971). The multinational enterprise in a multi currency world. In J. H. Dunning (Ed.), The Multinational Enterprise. London: Allen and Unwin.

[26] Vernon, R. (1966). International investment and international trade in the product cycle. Quarterly Journal of Economics, 80, 190–207.

[27] Dunning, J. H. (1993). Multinational enterprises and the global economy. Reading, MA: Addison-Wesley Publishing Company. Dunning, J. H. (1995). Reappraising the eclectic paradigm in an age of alliance capitalism. Journal of International Business Studies, 26(3), 461–491. Olibe, K. O., & Crumbley, C. (1997). Determinants of US private foreign direct investments in OPEC nations: From public and non-public policy perspectives. Journal of Public Budgeting, Accounting and Financial Management, 9(2), 331–355.

so follow their rivals into the developing countries' markets. Besides, the developing countries, take various institutional measures for attracting FDI through liberalization, infrastructure improvement, human capital development and investment incentives. Not only technological advances and structure of economic development, but also new organizational forms, and new methods of organizing economic activity drive and restructure international business activity. Moreover, the host country's political and economic system, and its government's policies have always been considered essential in assessing its investment environment.

While economic growth, and technology transfer to the host country are important consequences of FDI, development of technological infrastructure and human capital are critical prerequisites, and so antecedents for FDI[28]. Moreover, while psychic distance has been pertinent so far in FDI decisions[29], its importance might gradually reduce with increasing globalization and development of new/digital economy. An open economy, good infrastructure and technological base, labor with high educational and technical skills, low wages, stable currency, investment-friendly policies, low tariffs, and taxation incentives are some other criteria contributing to the host country's attractiveness. Governments provide a trade-and-investment-friendly environment and good infrastructure. Furthermore, benefits of a geographically and culturally integrated market, common communication infrastructure, comparable trade and investment policies, reasonably barrier-less intra-regional trade, and agglomeration advantages persuade MNEs to assess prospective FDI destinations on a regional, rather than a single country basis exploiting agglomeration advantages, facilitated by regional economic integration and an international division of labor. According to *D. Sethi et al*[30] "institutional and strategic factors into theory… need to be considered in tandem to explain the change in trend of FDI flows".

Foreign expansion of MNEs leads to a sliding stress on real wages for somewhat scarce types of labor in the home country. Nevertheless, besides cost reductions, an important motive for outward foreign direct investment is market spreading out. For instance, German MNEs tend to be attracted to countries with rather plentiful supplies of skilled labor, while there is no evidence of such skill tracing for Swedish MNEs[31]. The estimated labor demand elasticities apply to marginal wage changes across locations in which MNEs own manufacturing affiliates. Investors are not only interested in learning about companies' foreign operations in general but are also interested in the source of earnings, domestic versus foreign. Although both foreign and domestic earnings are value relevant, stock returns are

---

28 Noorbakhsh, F., & Paloni, A. (2001). Human capital and FDI inflows to developing countries: New empirical evidence. World Development, 29(9), 1593–1610. Narula, R., & Wakelin, K. (1998). Technological competitiveness, trade and foreign direct investment. Structural Change and Economic Dynamics, 9, 373–387.

29 UNCTAD. (1997). World investment report 1997. New York: United Nations. United Nations. (1998). World investment report 1998. New York: United Nations.

30 Deepak Sethi, Stephen Guisinger, David L. Ford Jr., Steven E. Phelan, Seeking greener pastures: a theoretical and empirical investigation into the changing trend of foreign direct investment flows in response to institutional and strategic factors, International Business Review 11 (2002) 685–705 at 701.

31 Sascha O. Becker, Karolina Ekholm, Robert Jaeckle, Marc-Andreas Muendler, Location Choice And Employment Decisions: A Comparison Of German And Swedish Multinationals, Cesifo Working Paper NO. 1374, 2005.

more sensitive to changes in foreign earnings than to changes in domestic earnings[32]. Foreign earnings are incrementally more value-relevant than domestic earnings[33].

The inflow of FDI includes a raise in the production base, the introduction of new skills and technologies and the creation of employment. Technology disseminated through FDI by and large includes the 'entire pack-age' including experts, skills and the financial resources to exploit the technology appropriately. Foreign investors increase productivity in host countries and FDI is often a catalyst for domestic investment and technological progress. Increased competition associated with the entry of an MNE upgrades the competence and product quality in national companies, and opens up possibilities for export[34]. Foreign affiliates of MNEs have a higher labour productivity compared to local firms playing an important role in the dissemination of gains from innovations, particularly for developing countries. FDI brings tangible and intangible assets that have large impacts on development and the inflow of FDI through mergers and acquisitions bring improved corporate governance, including better organisational and managerial skills. Corporate governance mechanisms facilitate the effective functioning of capital markets and uphold the efficient allocation of resources.

Is there a transition from multinational enterprises that take advantage of labour cost differentials in different countries to global network enterprises? Global production networks lead to companies that integrate their dispersed supply, knowledge, and customer bases into global (or regional) production networks. According to Dieter Ernst and Linsu Kim [35]"network participation may provide new opportunities for effective knowledge diffusion to local firms and industrial districts in developing countries, *provided* appropriate policies and support institutions are in place that enable local suppliers to exploit the opportunities and pressures that result from network participation". On the one hand, companies engage in product or process specialisation in order to utilize international differences in locational comparative advantages and integrate them with other activities performed in another place through intra-firm trade. On the other hand, FDI and trade are flourish in different activities and industries, suggesting a discrepancy between the competitiveness of companies and their home countries.

Many companies tend to decrease their activities in countries with high labour cost and shift to places where the cost of labour is low and where the social security system is less extensive which means that advanced countries are forced to adopt similar low standards in order to remain competitive. Will globalisation force the developed countries to contract their social spending and to move towards the system with minimum social spending that is prevalent in poor countries? Paul De Grauwe and Magdalena Polan[36] consider that "social spending does not seem to hinder countries in their continuous battle for competitiveness. On

[32] Thomas, W.B. 2004. "Firm characteristics and the pricing of foreign earnings of U.S. multinational firms." Journal of International Financial Management and Accounting Vol. 15 No. 2: 145-173. Givoly, D. and C. Hayn. 2000. "The changing time-series properties of earnings, cash flows, and accruals: Has financial reporting become more conservative?" Journal of Accounting and Economics Vol. 29 No.3: 287-320.

[33] Christophe, S.E. 2002. "The value of U.S. MNC earnings changes from foreign and domestic operations." Journal of Business Vol. 75 No. 1: 67-93.

[34] Ahn, S. and Hemmings, P. (2000), " Policy Influence on Economic Growth in OECD Countries: An Evaluation of the Evidence", OECD Economics Department Working Paper, no. 246, Paris: OECD.

[35] Dieter Ernst, Linsu Kim, Global production networks, knowledge diffusion, and local capability formation, Research Policy 1419 (2002) 1–13, p12.

[36] Paul De Grauwe, Magdalena Polan, Globalisation and Social Spending, 2003 Cesifo Working Paper NO. 885 p22

the contrary, high social spending goes together with strong competitiveness." Globalisation puts pressure on countries and governments to be competitive and one way governments can increase competitiveness of the country is to improve the efficiency of government institutions which means better governance. In other words globalisation pushes governments to be more responsible to the needs of their citizens.

Foreign investment may benefit host countries through transfers of technology, stimulation of technology diffusion from new competition, and provision by foreign firms of worker training and management skill development[37]. FDI[38] results in increased host country productivity through technology transfer, but only when the initial level of host industry competition is relatively low. More technology spillovers were evident when there existed small technology gaps between the foreign investor and the host economy.[39] For instance, foreign firms locate plants in the United States to gain access to existing technologies, but also spur new technological development within those clusters with which they are involved.[40] Innovation or introduction of something entirely new and unexpected is a non-linear act of unpredictable consequences and cannot be planned. Innovation is usually expensive, risky, disturbing, destabilising and expectant with conflicts and in return, innovation creates a new, normally unknown faculty, which introduces a value diverse from the customary system of social values. The world consists of information just as it contains material and energy. According to Borisz Szanto[41] "There is a race going on between human innovative intelligence and the general regression we are witnessing, causing and participating in. The human being is in a desperate contest with him-self. Actually, this is what the problem of sustainability really means".

Favorable factors in investment take account of market size, growth rate, policies, increased interest in investment due to the good functioning of companies, and the cost of labor. FDI is prized by developing countries for the pack of assets that MNEs deploy with their investments and most of these assets are intangible in nature and are primarily inadequate in developing countries including technology, management skills, design, quality features, and brand names. Positive impacts of FDI on national investment are not assured and in some cases, total investment may enhance much less than FDI or may even fail to rise when a country experiences a raise in FDI which means that the assumption that underpins policy toward FDI in most developing countries—that a liberal policy toward MNEs is adequate to make certain positive effects—fails to be upheld by the data[42].

---

[37] Harrison, A., 1994. The role of multinationals in economic development: the benefits of FDI. Columbia J World Bus 29(4), 6–11.

[38] Chung, W., 1997. Foreign direct investment's effect on host industry mark-up and productivity in the U.S.: the influence of initial host industry competition. Paper presented at the Academy of International Business annual meeting, Monterrey, Mexico.

[39] Kokko, A., 1994. Technology, market characteristics, and spillovers. J Develop Econ 43, 279–293.

[40] Almeida, P., 1996. Knowledge sourcing by foreign multinationals: patent citation analysis in the U.S. semiconductor industry. Strat Manage J 17, 155–165. Cantwell stated that "the use of technology in new environments feeds back into fresh adaptation and (depending on the state of local scientific and technological capability) new innovation" Cantwell, J. 1989. Technological innovation and multinational corporations. Blackwell, Oxford, UK. p 9.

[41] Borisz Szanto, The paradigm of globalism, Technovation 21 (2001) 673–687, p687.

[42] Manuel R. Agosin & Roberto Machado, Foreign Investment in Developing Countries: Does it Crowd in Domestic Investment? Oxford Development Studies, Vol. 33, No. 2, June 2005

Foreign investors increase productivity in host countries and FDI is often a catalyst for domestic investment and technological progress. [43] Increased competition associated with the entry of an MNE upgrades the efficiency and product quality in national firms, and opens up possibilities for export.[44] Foreign investment plays an important role in the dissemination of gains from innovations, especially for developing countries.[45] Furthermore, foreign direct investment stimulates growth and has a larger impact than investment by domestic firms.[46] Developing countries need to have reached a certain threshold of development before being able to capture the benefits associated with FDI.[47] Vertical production processes are being *fragmented*, with discrete pieces of these processes being outsourced to countries that have advantages in providing the inputs that fragments use, whether this be unskilled workforce, capital, or cheap energy sources. The costs involved in fragmentation have declined spectacularly, including not only transportation costs, but also the costs of monitoring deliveries and coordination, the costs of delivering information, and the costs involved in dealing in arms-length transactions with foreigners.[48] An export position can be established for those products in which the country's comparative productivity is highest, even if this means that the country exports those goods to other nations in which the total level of input productivity is even higher[49]. Government regulations and taxation can affect the productivity or net returns of inputs[50]. On the one hand, investment liberalisation may lead to increased production and consumption of polluting goods or to an expansion in industrial activity. On the other hand, FDI can improve structural efficiencies and make new investments in environmental protection possible. Companies are forced to improve their managerial efficiency further. Manufacturers are trying to reduce financial and non-financial costs by reducing equipment investment, optimizing inventory control and reducing personnel costs. Companies should place more importance on the strategies to be more profitable through development of competitive products and cost reduction, strengthening the accounting/auditing capabilities so as to make their financial statements more reliable. Direct investment must improve both corporate profitability and dividend rates, in order to boost the economic benefits of the citizens in both the investor and host countries. Companies should achieve managerial efficiency optimizing their financial infrastructure. For instance, HK' manufacturing FDI in China based on sub-contracting and cross-border operations including

43 De Mello, L.R. (1999)," Foreign Direct Investment-led growth: evidence from time series and panel data" , Oxford Economic Papers 51, 133-151.

44 Markusen, J.R. And Venables, A.J. (1999), "Foreign direct investment as a catalyst for industrial development", European Economic Review, Vol. 43: 335 356.

45 Ahn, S. And Hemmings, P. (2000), " Policy Influence on Economic Growth in OECD Countries: An Evaluation of the Evidence" , OECD Economics Department Working Paper, no. 246, Paris: OECD.

46 Borensztein, E., De Gregorio, J. And Lee, L-W (1998), " How does foreign investment affect economic growth", Journal of International Economics, Vol. 45: 115-135

47 SAGGI, K. (2000), " Trade, foreign direct investment and international technology transfer: a survey" , World Bank, Washington DC.

48 Jones, R.W., 2000. Globalization and the Theory of Input Trade. MIT Press, Cambridge, MA. Jones, R.W., Kierzkowski, H., 1990. The role of services in production and international trade: a theoretical framework. In: Jones, R.W., Krueger, A. Eds., The Political Economy of International Trade. Blackwell, Oxford.

49 Donald R. Davis, Technology, unemployment, and relative wages in a global economy, European Economic Review 42 (1998) 1613-1633

50 Ronald W. Jones, Private interests and government policy in a global world, European Journal of Political Economy Vol. 16 2000 243–256

plant relocations achieved to reduce manufacturing production costs and maintain its competitive edge in the world economy. Superior networked facilities of highway system, river shipments and railway transportations, ocean and airport facilities together with communication supporting facilities capitalize agglomeration economies mobilizing FDI from HK to China. HK has acted as a service-orientated city performing service functions and regions of China mainly manufacturing operations.

MNEs continue to restructure the global economy. Global FDI outflows amounted to $779 billion. Global FDI inflows rose by 29% to $916 billion in 2005, compared to a 27% increase in 2004[51]. Inward FDI continues to expand in all sub-regions and shows an ongoing explosion in cross-border mergers and acquisitions (M&As), somewhat fuelled by funds deriving from commodity price increases. While China[52] has emerged as the largest FDI receiver among all developing countries, there has lately been a reappearance of FDI flows to Africa and Latin America, driven by scenario for better earnings in the extractive industries. FDI is more and more intended to supply global and regional markets, frequently in the perspective of international production networks, and the increase of such networks offers, in principle, new potential for developing countries and economies in transition to profit from FDI in the manufacturing sector[53]. FDI has played a vital supporting role as it helped China to integrate into a regional production network, by this means speeding up the country's technological integration into the global economy[54]. Positive monetary conditions boosted capital build up and investment, fuelled by escalating non-equilibrium profits, has been the key drivers of growth[55]. Countries located near important regional groupings gain from extra FDI through regionalization. The exclusion of intraregional tariffs supports vertically-motivated intraregional FDI. MNEs set up efficiency-seeking affiliates in various countries within a regional grouping that can deal with imports for re-export. FDI is preferred over exporting if tariffs are higher and the set costs of a new factory are lower. Agglomeration effects because of clustering of economic activities bring out an irregular spread of benefits amongst members of a grouping. MNEs focus in more productive sub-sectors within China's electronics industry. Productivity profits from FDI are noteworthy for particular but not all groups of companies in China's electronics industry which means that spillovers benefits do not flow mechanically from FDI depending probably on host country industry features and on the policy environment in which MNEs function[56].

How the labor market in the home country is affected by outward foreign direct investment (FDI)? In case that there is a big degree of complementarity between activities moved abroad and activities remaining in the home country, it is possible that the firm and the home country workers agree whether it is preferable to undertake FDI. Besides, if there is a big degree of substitutability between activities in foreign affiliates and activities in the home

---

[51] World Investment Report FDI from Developing and Transition Economies: Implications for Development United Nations New York and Geneva, 2006.

[52] *China in a Globalizing World,* UNITED NATIONS New York and Geneva 2005

[53] Trade And Development Report, 2006united Nations New York and Geneva

[54] Cheung KY and Lin P (2004). Spillover effects of FDI on innovation in China: Evidence from the provincial data. *China Economic Review*, 15:25–44. IMF (2004). Competitors will have to adjust as China continues to grow. *IMF Survey*, 31 May 2004, 153–154.

[55] Dunning JH (1998). Globalization and the new geography of foreign direct investment. *Oxford Development Studies*, 26:47–70.

[56] Peter J. Buckley, Jeremy Clegg and Chengqi Wang, Inward FDI and host country productivity: evidence from China's electronics industry, *Transnational Corporations,* Vol. 15, No. 1 (April 2006) p13.

country, it is probable that the firm gains but the workers lose from FDI. Zhao[57] states that FDI gives rise to lower wages, whereas we discover that it depends on the degree of substitutability between activities in the home country and the host country. Is a positive elasticity of substitution between parent employment and employment in foreign affiliates? Brainard and Riker[58] quote cross-elasticities of substitution between labor in parent US firms and foreign affiliates and between labors in various affiliates. A high degree of complementarity between host country activities and home country activities reduces the employment loss in the home country when a company expands activities in the host country, and, if the wage costs in the host country are adequately low, employment in the home country may actually increase. Hence, since the wage is lowest in the multinational case, the firm always prefers to be multinational. According[59] to Mette Yde Skaksen and Jan Rose Sørensen "The higher the degree of substitution between activities in the host country and the home country, the more likely it is that the trade union and the firm disagree whether the firm should become multinational". Moreover, John A. List [60] indicates that stringent environmental regulations do not have a negative impact on FDI inflows. FDI inflows rise where local capabilities are strengthened and new capabilities are created; they decline or go down where they are not.

The scenery of a foreign investment depends at the outset on the host country's technological, human resource and supplier capabilities. Foreign investments in high value-added activities, needing excessive proficiency levels, tend to be 'location-sticky'. MNEs undertake chronological investments and building of higher levels of competences in locations that grant sub-optimal returns however where they have preceding experience[61]. The creation of linkages and the internalisation of spillovers from MNE activities still depend on resident absorptive capacity. The quality of FDI spillovers depends on the capacity and proficiency of the subsidiary depending to some extent on factors internal to MNEs, including their internationalisation strategy, the part of individual affiliates in their global system and the motivation for their investment. Internal strategies interact with host country capabilities and resources.

FDI has come to play an unprecedented role as a source of management, technology, and external funding for the developing countries and economies-in-transition. When does FDI contribute most to the development process? Foreign direct investment contributes most to the development process when the affiliate is wholly owned and fully integrated into the global operations of the parent company. There is an important distinction between investors producing solely for domestic consumption in the host economy, and investors using the host country locale as a site from which to strengthen their larger competitive position in international markets. Once the parent investors commit themselves to incorporate the output

---

[57] Zhao, L., 1998. The impact of foreign direct investment on wages and employment. Oxford Economic Papers 50, 284–301. Zhao, L., 1995. Cross-hauling direct foreign investment and unionized oligopoly. European Economic Review 39, 1237–1253.

[58] Brainard, S.L., Riker, D.A., 1997. Are US multinationals exporting US jobs? NBER working paper 5958.

[59] Mette Yde Skaksen , Jan Rose Sørensen, Should trade unions appreciate foreign direct investment, Journal of International Economics 55 (2001) 379–390, p389.

[60] John A. List, US county-level determinants of inbound FDI: evidence from a two-step modified count data model, International Journal of Industrial Organization 19 (2001) 953–973

[61] Hagedoorn, J. and R. Narula, 2001, 'Evolutionary Understanding of Corporate Foreign Investment Behaviour: US Foreign Direct Investment in Europe', in R. Narula (ed.), International Trade and Investment in a Globalising World, New York: Pergamon.

from a host country into a larger strategy to meet global or regional competition -- there is evidence of a dynamic "integration effect", which provides newer technology, more rapid technological upgrading, and closer positioning along the frontier of best management practices and highest industry standards, than any other method for the host economy to acquire such benefits. There is evidence of more intensive coaching for suppliers in quality control, managerial efficiency, and marketing than any other means for firms in the local economy to gain these skills.[62]

Global operations and strategic activities of MNEs have become more and more dependent on their geographically scattered yet internally differentiated foreign subunits, whether they may be joint ventures, cooperative alliances, wholly-owned subsidiaries, branch offices, or other forms, for global expansion. Moreover, a MNE is a differentiated yet coordinated network of units that both compete and cooperate. MNEs have to manage their intra-organizational knowledge flows, internalize globally coordinated operations, and detach various subunits with unusual strategic identities and roles. To generate value, parties or units cannot act in isolation and accordingly they have to be aware of their interdependence.

Cooperation and competition coexist concurrently for the reason that subunits are enticed or enforced to collaborate but in the meantime they come across conflicts arising from competing for limited parent resources, corporate support, market expansion, power delegation, and global position. Competition is underpinned by resource or transactional interdependence in which competition and cooperation are intertwined and numerous subunits in detach locations have to deal with various issues and play diverse roles, giving rise to cooperation on some issues, projects, functions, or knowledge development and competition on other issues, projects, or markets.

MNEs engage in cross-unit transfer and sharing of knowledge that reflects their idiosyncratic competencies bolstering and sustaining a competitive advantage. Inside an MNE, competition occurs between or among unlike subunits but to expand new knowledge and to make the most of economies of scope for their business operations, these units have to cooperate with each other and learn from each other. In the meantime, they compete with each other in a number of aspects of their business operations for the reason that they are compared on the starting point of their capacity to carry out tasks or goals. Each subunit has a varying level of both cooperation and competition with equal subunits differing in their individual needs for cooperation and competition due to idiosyncrasies in their external environments and internal capabilities. This difference is furthered by the diverse strategic roles played by unconnected subunits as established by the headquarters. According to Yadong Luo[63] "Competitive pressure and product similarity may simultaneously increase both cooperation and competition. In order to maximize system gains from inter-unit coopetition, headquarters managers must establish and nourish the organizational infrastructure that coordinates coopetition. Particularly, it is important to build the intranet system, incentive system, encapsulation system, and coordination system."

---

62 Theodore H. Moran. 1998. Foreign Direct Investment and Development: The New Policy Agenda for Developing Countries and Economies in Transition. Washington, D.C.: The Institute for International Economics. Wilson Perez Nunez. 1990. Foreign Direct Investment and Industrial Development in Mexico. Paris:OECD

63 Yadong Luo, Toward coopetition within a multinational enterprise:a perspective from foreign subsidiaries, Journal of World Business 40 (2005) 71–90, p88.

MNEs have extended their presence all over the globe, conducting a large amount of actions for a multitude of purposes and they have had to administer a mixture of forces–geographic, product, market, and technology–that relate and become more multipart on a global scale. It has to be taken into account that governing these activities with intelligibility and effectiveness or accountability and growth requires a well-prepared plan that strategically plots which governance mechanisms and liability systems ought to be employed and how they should be deployed. Corporate governance, which is the set of market-based, culture-based, and discipline-based mechanisms that support self-interested executives to make decisions that get the most out of the company's value to its main stakeholders and corporate accountability, which is the set of institutional and accounting systems that add to clear exposé and open support in corporate activities, strategic decision-making, and financial information. Corporate accountability is concerned with the extent to which a company is transparent in its corporate activities and responsive to those it serves requiring not only financial reporting accountability but also strategic decision transparency. Underlying to corporate accountability is the prevalent availability of relevant, reliable, and accurate information about a company's performance, investment opportunities, governance, value, financial position and risk.

Corporate accountability interrelates to corporate governance because it affects the reliability of information needed to maintain important activities, such as the creation and existence of enforceable contracts, the monitoring of managers by the board of directors and outside investors and regulators, and the implementation of investor rights as governed by securities laws.

The intricacy a MNE faces is related to its geographic spreading for several reasons including its dependence on foreign sales and value creation inputs, the various institutional and task environments within which it operates, and increased competitive pressures for cooperation and coordination across geographically distributed operations. Operations are becoming more intricate by national adaptation requirements and foreign competition and this density in turn increases information processing and agency demands. The MNE control such demands by instituting more creative governance arrangements in terms of information acquisition and monitoring.

Foreign direct investment is most likely to be harmful -- actually damaging -- to the growth and welfare of the developing countries and the economies-in-transition when the investor is sheltered from competition in the domestic market and burdened with high domestic content, mandatory joint venture and technology-sharing requirements. Many of the most important actions that host countries can take to attract and utilise FDI in their development programs they must initiate on their own -- in particular, improving the micro- and macro-economic functioning of their economies, and strengthening commercial and judicial institutions that provide stability and dependability to all investors, domestic as well as foreign.

It could be argued that FDI will improve competitiveness and, thus, create employment and increase the welfare of the host nation.[64] This is a result of inward investment increasing

[64] Dunning, J.H., " The prospects for foreign direct investment in Central and Eastern Europe", in Buckley, P.J. and Ghauri, P.N. (Eds), The Economics of Change in Eastern and Central Europe: Its Impact on International Business, Academic Press, London, 1994. Giese, A.S., Kahley, W.J. and Riefler, R.F., "Foreign direct investment: motivating factors and economic impact", Regional Science Perspectives,

the number of entrants in the indigenous industry which forces all competitor firms in the industry to become more competitive by reducing costs and improving efficiency and quality. This should result in lower prices and more efficient levels of consumer service. Benefits may accrue from co-operation as well as competition. Much FDI activity is achieved by way of a joint venture between a foreign company and an indigenous company and this may bring advantages such as risk diversification, capital requirement reductions and lower start-up costs[65]. Indirect impact will manifest itself in the creation of spillovers and linkages – typically in suppliers and customers – whereas the dynamic impact will affect the competitive environment. Inward investment is likely to stimulate the production of global competitors in the recipient country[66].

The nature of FDI activities is now very different and the process of globalisation has made its impact on the world economy. So, FDI will play a significant role in the transition of these economies. However, in order to maximize the advantages of inward investment it is necessary for the governments of these countries to appraise critically the nature of such investment. The existing domestic industries may have to be restructured to ensure that they are sufficiently competitive to develop the spillovers from the initial investment. The use of joint ventures may well be a way of achieving additional spin-offs for the indigenous industry. This process will be encouraged if foreign-owned firms perceive that such alliances may be formulated with a minimum of bureaucratic procedure. Domestic firms should be encouraged to achieve significant degrees of strategic independence from their foreign partner in order to achieve the maximum possible benefit from the inward investment.

Multinational sales have grown tremendously in the last two decades outpacing the significant expansion of trade in manufactures[67]. While vertical FDI involves fragmentation of production across countries (a parent company invests in a production facility in another country in order to produce inputs that will be shipped back to the parent for further processing), horizontal FDI refers to investments in production facilities abroad that are designed to serve foreign customers. Growth of international specialization has been a dominant feature of the international economy. Companies service foreign buyers through a variety of channels: they can export their products to foreign customers, serve them through foreign subsidiaries by engaging in foreign direct investment, and license or contract with foreign firms to produce and sell their products. The most productive companies engage in foreign activities such as FDI[68]. Moreover, companies invest abroad when the gains from avoiding transport costs outweigh the costs of maintaining capacity in multiple markets.

Vol. 20, 1990, pp. 105- 27. Dunning, J.H., "Re-evaluating the benefits of foreign direct investment", Transnational Corporations, Vol. 3 No. 1, 1994, pp. 23-51.

65 Perlmutter, H.V. and Heenan, D.A.,."Cooperate to compete globally", Harvard Business Review, March-April, 1986, pp. 78-86.

66 United Nations Conference on Trade and Development, Division on Transnational Corporations and Investment, World Investment Report: Transnational Corporations and Competitiveness, United Nations, Geneva and New York, 1995. United Nations Conference on Trade and Development, Division on Transnational Corporations and Investment, World Investment Report: Transnational Corporations and Integrated International Production, United Nations, Geneva and New York, 1993.

67 Markusen, James R. 2002. Multinational Firms and the Theory of International Trade. MIT Press.

68 Melitz, Marc J. 2002. "The Impact of Trade on Aggregate Industry Productivity and Intra-Industry Reallocations." NBER Working Paper No. 8881.

Companies substitute FDI sales for exports when transport costs are relatively high and when plant-level returns to scale are relatively weak[69].

Low-productivity companies supply the domestic market but not foreign markets, while high-productivity companies also serve foreign markets but affiliate sales relative to exports are larger in sectors with more productivity dispersion. Foreign markets are served more by exports comparative to FDI sales when trade frictions are lower or economies of scale are higher. According to[70] Elhanan Helpman, Marc J. Melitz, and Stephen R. Yeaple "we have identified a new element, namely, within-sectoral heterogeneity, that plays an important role in the structure of foreign trade and investment." Imports from foreign affiliates of U.S.-based firms has fallen from 23.9% of total U.S. imports in 1977 to 16.3% in 1999, suggesting that foreign out-sourcing might have outpaced foreign intra-firm sourcing by U.S. firms[71].

5.2 FDI and Development

FDI has come to play an unprecedented role as a source of management, technology, and external funding for the developing countries and economies-in-transition. When does FDI contribute most to the development process? Foreign direct investment contributes most to the development process when the affiliate is wholly owned and fully integrated into the global operations of the parent company. There is an important distinction between investors producing solely for domestic consumption in the host economy, and investors using the host country locale as a site from which to strengthen their larger competitive position in international markets. Once the parent investors commit themselves to incorporate the output from a host country into a larger strategy to meet global or regional competition -- there is evidence of a dynamic "integration effect", which provides newer technology, more rapid technological upgrading, and closer positioning along the frontier of best management practices and highest industry standards, than any other method for the host economy to acquire such benefits. There is evidence of more intensive coaching for suppliers in quality control, managerial efficiency, and marketing than any other means for firms in the local economy to gain these skills.[72]

The transition from the low growth stage to the high growth stage is not automatically monotonic and can exhibit a temporary decline in growth rates. Growth might provisionally go through a transition with positive growth of human capital but is in conclusion trapped in a zero growth stage. Considering development Michal Kejak [73] says that "the economy exhibits

---

[69] Rob, Rafael and Nikolaos Vettas. 2001. "Foreign Direct Investment and Exports with Growing Demand." CEPR Discussion Paper No. 2786.

[70] Elhanan Helpman, Marc J. Melitz, Stephen R. Yeaple, Export versus FDI, 2003, Discussion Paper Number 1998, Harvard Institute of Economic Research, p 29

[71] www.bea.gov Helpman, Elhanan, Marc J. Melitz, and Stephen R.Yeaple (2003), "Exports versus FDI," NBER Working Paper No. 9439. Pol Antras and Elhanan Helpman Global Sourcing, 2003, Discussion Paper Number 2005, Harvard Institute of Economic Research

[72] Theodore H. Moran. 1998. Foreign Direct Investment and Development: The New Policy Agenda for Developing Countries and Economies in Transition. Washington, D.C.: The Institute for International Economics. Wilson Perez Nunez. 1990. Foreign Direct Investment and Industrial Development in Mexico. Paris:OECD

[73] Michal Kejak, Stages of growth in economic development, Journal of Economic Dynamics &Control 27 (2003) 771 –800, p795.

slowly declining growth in physical capital and no growth in human capital, followed by a sudden transition to a sustained or quasi-sustained growth path.".

Contrary to contemporary perceptions about the rapid pace of globalisation, however, the history of the spread of foreign investment in the automotive, petrochemical, and computer/electronics industries shows that international markets have been quite sluggish in reallocating the global and regional sourcing networks of the major international corporations along lines of comparative advantage. Foreign direct investment is most likely to be harmful -- actually damaging -- to the growth and welfare of the developing countries and the economies-in-transition when the investor is sheltered from competition in the domestic market and burdened with high domestic content, mandatory joint venture and technology-sharing requirements. In fact, foreign direct investment typically originates in international industries where there are high barriers to entry and deploys itself in domestic markets in the developing countries and economies-in-transition where there are high degrees of concentration. The key variable is the degree to which the injection of foreign investment into the host economy brings with it increase in competition in the sector or sub-sector where it occurs or a decrease in competition, with particular investors and particular suppliers awarded exclusive domain over the given sector or sub-sector. The most frequently used intervention on the part of host authorities in the developing countries and economies-in-transition -- insisting that foreign investors meet high domestic content requirements in tightly protected markets -- falls into the latter category, of stifling rather than enhancing competition. Except in the largest countries, economies of scale are seldom realised, and there are weak incentives for the foreign firms to upgrade technology, or to maintain highest standards of quality control and improvement of human resources. The imposition of high domestic content requirements in protected markets tends moreover to generate a perverse political economy in which foreign investors themselves frequently join domestic forces in *opposing* further liberalisation of trade and investment. European parent firms and US shun joint venture arrangements where international sourcing, quality control, rapid technological change, product differentiation, and integration with external markets rather than purely domestic sales dictate corporate strategy.[74] Many host governments justify joint venture requirements with arguments that joint ventures achieve greater technology transfer, expanded access to external markets, and more robust backward linkages to the domestic economy than wholly owned subsidiaries. Joint ventures may purchase more inputs from indigenous firms, but their sourcing networks lack most of the technological, managerial, and export marketing spillovers for local suppliers that comes from the more potent relationship with the parent corporation in the case of wholly-owned subsidiaries, described earlier.[75] Indigenous corporate operations that are built via mandatory technology licensing are likely to suffer the same kind of economic disadvantages as joint ventures: lags in technology acquisition, lack of "best management" techniques, powerless penetration of foreign markets, and weak performance in development of a competitive supplier base. In reaction to the globalisation of

---

[74] Paul W. Beamish and Andres Delios. 1997. "Incidence and Propensity of Alliance Formation by U.S., Japanese, and European MNEs." in P. W. Beamish and J. P. Killing, eds., Cooperative strategies: Asian-Pacific perspectives. San Francisco: The New Lexington Press. Shige Makino and Andres Delios. 1996. "Local Knowledge Transfer and Performance: Implications for Alliance Formation in Asia." Journal of International Business Studies. 27:5: 905-927.

[75] E. Mansfield, and A. Romeo. 1980. "Technology Transfer to Overseas Subsidiaries by US-based Firms." Quarterly Journal of Economics. 95:4.

manufacturing activity, developed countries have launched a counter-offensive of their own to capture and hold international corporate operations within their own economies.[76] Many of the most important actions that host countries can take to attract and utilise FDI in their development programs they must initiate on their own -- in particular, improving the micro- and macro-economic functioning of their economies, and strengthening commercial and judicial institutions that provide stability and dependability to all investors, domestic as well as foreign. Rules governing local content, ownership structure, and technology acquisition represent a vast pool of favours to bestow upon rent-seeking constituencies, and the abandonment of public sector regulation in these areas is sure to generate powerful opposition. Export performance requirements that take the form of trade-balancing or foreign exchange-balancing obligations are also subject to elimination under the TRIMs agreement. The consideration of such export performance requirements raises complex strategic considerations. On the one hand, developing countries have sometimes used such requirements to trigger the reorientation of global and regional sourcing strategies on the part of multinational investors. On the other hand, developing countries would benefit from restraining the competition for world scale-sized investment facilities among themselves and between themselves and developed countries. Joint venture and technology-sharing requirements are not included in the illustrative list of the TRIMs Agreement.

5.3 FDI and Competition

The nature of FDI activities is now very different and the process of globalisation has made its impact on the world economy. So, FDI will play a significant role in the transition of these economies. However, in order to maximize the advantages of inward investment it is necessary for the governments of these countries to appraise critically the nature of such investment. The existing domestic industries may have to be restructured to ensure that they are sufficiently competitive to develop the spillovers from the initial investment. The use of joint ventures may well be a way of achieving additional spin-offs for the indigenous industry. This process will be encouraged if foreign-owned firms perceive that such alliances may be formulated with a minimum of bureaucratic procedure. Domestic firms should be encouraged to achieve significant degrees of strategic independence from their foreign partner in order to achieve the maximum possible benefit from the inward investment.

FDI will improve competitiveness and, thus, create employment and increase the welfare of the host nation.[77] This is a result of inward investment increasing the number of entrants in the indigenous industry which forces all competitor firms in the industry to become more competitive by reducing costs and improving efficiency and quality. This should result in lower prices and more efficient levels of consumer service. Benefits may accrue from co-

---

[76] Vijaya Ramachandran. 1993. "Technology Transfer, Firm Ownership, and Investment in Human Capital." The Review of Economics and Statistics. Vol. 75. Nov., pp. 664-70.

[77] Dunning, J.H., " The prospects for foreign direct investment in Central and Eastern Europe", in Buckley, P.J. and Ghauri, P.N. (Eds), The Economics of Change in Eastern and Central Europe: Its Impact on International Business, Academic Press, London, 1994. Giese, A.S., Kahley, W.J. and Riefler, R.F., "Foreign direct investment: motivating factors and economic impact", Regional Science Perspectives, Vol. 20, 1990, pp. 105- 27. Dunning, J.H., "Re-evaluating the benefits of foreign direct investment", Transnational Corporations, Vol. 3 No. 1, 1994, pp. 23-51.

operation as well as competition. Much FDI activity is achieved by way of a joint venture between a foreign company and an indigenous company and this may bring advantages such as risk diversification, capital requirement reductions and lower start-up costs[78]. Indirect impact will manifest itself in the creation of spillovers and linkages – typically in suppliers and customers – whereas the dynamic impact will affect the competitive environment. MNEs choose different entry modes in order to fulfil their international marketing ambitions. Countries are seeking to improve their competitive position by encouraging the flow of inward investment, while firms are pursuing increasingly global strategies, which result in integrated production and marketing activities across international frontiers. Many MNEs are attempting to gain a competitive advantage by acquiring resources and capabilities such as technological know-how, superior organizational and managerial assets, and access to foreign distribution channels and marketing information. FDI is primarily motivated by the availability of lower-cost resources and new markets, the rational response of the MNE is to retain its technological capacity at home and concentrate foreign production on relatively low value-added activities. The risk of operating in a relatively unsophisticated market is high and such risks can be minimized if production is restricted to routinized assembly operations. The majority of product innovation takes place in the core or prosperous regions as opposed to the peripheral or less-prosperous regions. The full benefits of indirect and dynamic effects are only likely to be forthcoming when MNEs set up subsidiaries with more strategic autonomy. This will allow subsidiaries to develop linkages through local procurement activities as they take part in more value-added activities. Only when this autonomy from the parent organization is highly developed is the effect of technology and other asset transfer likely to improve the competitive position of the indigenous economy. Even if linkages are allowed to develop as MNE subsidiaries become more embedded into the host economy, the precise effect on regional development is difficult to calculate. In addition, the role of MNE subsidiaries in the process of regional development is also ambiguous[79]. It is only those subsidiaries, which have substantial levels of strategic autonomy, performing a range of value-added activities, which have the potential to influence local economic development to any great extent[80]. Inward investment is likely to stimulate the production of global competitors in the recipient country[81].

In developed economies, monitoring is expensive relative to capital costs so technologies that involve relatively low monitoring costs are preferred[82]. Concentrated ownership is required to provide shareholders with adequate incentives to engage in active corporate

---

[78] Perlmutter, H.V. and Heenan, D.A.,."Cooperate to compete globally", Harvard Business Review, March-April, 1986, pp. 78-86.

[79] Young, S., Hood, N. and Peters E., "Multinational enterprises and regional economic development", Regional Studies, Vol. 28 No. 7, 1994, pp. 657-77.

[80] Williams, D.A., "Entry mode decisions of multinational enterprises and their impact on the regional economy: a framework for analysis", British Review of Economic Issues, Vol. 17 No. 43, 1995, pp. 27-52.Young, S. and Hood, N., "Designing development after-care programmes for foreign direct investors in the European Union", Transnational Corporations, Vol. 3 No. 2, 1994, pp. 45-72.

[81] United Nations Conference on Trade and Development, Division on Transnational Corporations and Investment, World Investment Report: Transnational Corporations and Competitiveness, United Nations, Geneva and New York, 1995. United Nations Conference on Trade and Development, Division on Transnational Corporations and Investment, World Investment Report: Transnational Corporations and Integrated International Production, United Nations, Geneva and New York, 1993.

[82] Boyd, J,. Smith, B., 1998. The evolution of debt and equity markets in economic development. Economic Theory 12, 519-60.

governance[83] and corporate governance is more effective under concentrated rather than dispersed ownership systems[84] determining the commitment of investors to preserving incentives that encourage managerial investment[85]. Advice to developing countries has been centred on greater market openness and better integration into the global economy. Trade liberalisation can significantly contribute to improve the poverty situation. According to[86] Maurizio Bussolo and Jann Lay "in the case of trade liberalisation, the income channel, i.e. employment status and wage levels, is more important to the poor than the expenditure channel, i.e. the variation in the price of consumption goods". Industries that are dependent on external sources of finance and other stakeholders grow more rapidly in countries with concentrated ownership[87].

What is the relationship between trade, foreign direct investment and the globalisation of production? FDI flows to developing countries, however, tend to be heavily concentrated in some host economies. Enhancing the attractiveness of other developing countries would increase their economic integration and their growth prospects. Developing countries cannot compete with the resources that OECD governments are able to provide for subsidies and tax concessions. Market reforms by non-OECD governments have brought major increases in foreign investment inflows in the 1990s. [88] To what extent do production and affiliate sales in a foreign market replace or help increase exports to the same market? How changes in one quantity affect another quantity? [89] Why a MNE chooses one mode of servicing the foreign market versus the other? Sustainable competitive advantage (SCA)[90] has affirmative effect on cycle time of the worldwide sourcing process and the organization's overall business performance. Cultural manifestations of entrepreneurship, innovativeness, and learning can

---

[83] Huddart, S., 1993. The effect of a large shareholder on corporate value. Management Science 39, 1407-1421. Rajan, R., Zingales, L., 2001. Financial systems, industrial structure, and growth. Oxford Review of Economic Policy 17, 467-482.

[84] La Porta, R., Lopez-de-Silanes, F., Shleifer, A., 2002. Government ownership of banks. Journal of Finance 57, 265-301. Levine, R., 2002. Bank-based or market-based financial systems: which is better? Journal of Financial Intermediation 11, 1-30.

[85] Burkhart, M., Gromb, D., Panunzi, F.,1997. Large shareholders, monitoring and the value of the firm. Quarterly Journal of Economics 112, 693-728.

[86] Maurizio Bussolo and Jann Lay,2003, Globalisation and Poverty Changes in Colombia, no 14 p 38. www.oecd.org

[87] Beck, T., Levine, R., 2002. Industry growth and capital allocation: Does having a market- or bank-based system matter? Journal of Financial Economics 64, 147-180. Beck, T., Levine, R., Loayza, N., 2000. Finance and the sources of growth. Journal of Financial Economics 58, 261-300. Cetorelli, N. Gambera, M., 2001. Banking market structure, financial dependence and growth: International evidence from industry data. Journal of Finance 56, 617-648.

[88] UNCTAD, World Investment Report, 1998 (UN, New York). OECD, 1999. Recent Trends in Foreign Direct Investment (Paris) and Department of Foreign Affairs, Australia, Foreign Direct Investment: The Benefits for Australia (1999).

[89] Graham, E.M., 2000. The relationships between trade and foreign direct investment in the manufacturing sector: empirical results for the United States and Japan. In: Encarnation, D. (Ed.), Does Ownership Matter? Japanese Multinationals in East Asia. Oxford University Press, London. Swedenborg, B., 2000. Determinants and effects of MNE growth: the Swedish case revisited. In: Blomstrom, M., Goldberg, L.S. (Eds.), Topics in Empirical International Economics. University of Chicago Press, Chicago.

[90] Hurley, R. F., and Hult, G. T. M.: Innovation, Market Orientation, and Organizational Learning: An Integration and Empirical Examination. Journal of Marketing 62(3), 42–54 (1998). Hult, G. T. M., Hurley, R. F., Giunipero, L. C., and Nichols, E. L. Jr.: Organizational Learning in Global Purchasing: A Model and Test of Internal Users and Corporate Buyers. Decision Sciences 31(2), (2000). Hult, G. T. M.: Measuring Cycle Time of the Global Procurement Process. Industrial Marketing Management 26(5), 403–412 (1997).

each lead to the firm achieving a competitive advantage. Entrepreneurship involves the intentions and actions of the company performance in a dynamic generative process aimed at new venture- creation. Additionally, entrepreneurial organizations perform better than other organizations and are able to earn larger profits in the short term. Organizations stressing innovativeness, coupled with a suitable entrepreneurial orientation, will be more successful in taking advantage of novel capabilities that may lead to a competitive advantage. Innovativeness is an organizational property that affects the innovation process. Organizations focusing on cycle time reduction aim to condense the time it takes to accomplish procurement processes in a way that reduces costs and/or increases customer service operating behaviours[91]. Smith[92] said that ''as long as the global rate of change continues to accelerate, the competitor who not only recognizes the change but acts on it can achieve a competitive advantage''. MNEs establish their activities abroad in technological areas where they are strong at home[93]. According to Christian Le Bas and Christophe Sierra [94]"the national system of innovation (in particular the system of academic research) should strengthen the technological advantages of local firms and enables them to succeed their location abroad".

A progressive liberalization and deregulation of international trade and investment, and the quick development and diffusion of information and communication technology (IT) have deeply changed the global competitive dynamics, in which MNEs operate. The exploitation of uncertainty through improved operational flexibility, reduced product development and product life cycles, the acquisition of specialized external and a change of market penetration strategies from established to new and unknown markets are factors that influence the actions of MNEs. In fact, MNEs have proliferated as a key organizational innovation in global operations[95]. GPNs change the production and use and increasing mobility of knowledge, with far-reaching implications for an evolutionary theory of economic change. Hence, IT has substantially increased the mobility and dispersion of firm-specific resources and capabilities across national boundaries providing greater scope for cross-border linkages leading to the integration of dispersed specialized clusters.

Is there a transition from multinational enterprises that take advantage of labour cost differentials in different countries to global network enterprises? Global production networks lead to companies that integrate their dispersed supply, knowledge, and customer bases into global (or regional) production networks. According to Dieter Ernst and Linsu Kim [96]"network participation may provide new opportunities for effective knowledge diffusion to local firms and industrial districts in developing countries, *provided* appropriate policies and

[91] G. Tomas M. Hult, O.C. Ferrell, Robert F. Hurley, Global organizational learning effects on cycle time performance, Journal of Business Research 55 (2002) 377– 387

[92] Meyer C. Fast cycle time: how to align purpose, strategy, and structure for speed. New York, NY: Free Press, 1993. p. 11.

[93] Patel, P., Vega, M.,1999. Patterns of internationalisation of corporate technology: location versus home country advantages. Research Policy 28 (2/3), 145–155. Kuemmerle, W.,1999. The drivers of foreign direct investment into research and development: an empirical investigation 30 (1), Research Policy 1–24.

[94] Christian Le Bas, Christophe Sierra, 'Location versus home country advantages' in R&D activities: some further results on multinationals' locational strategies, Research Policy 31 (2002) 589–609, p607.

[95] Borrus, M., Ernst, D., Haggard, S., 2000. (Eds.) International Production Networks in Asia. Rivalry or Riches? Routledge, London.

support institutions are in place that enable local suppliers to exploit the opportunities and pressures that result from network participation". Firm-specific risk refers to operating uncertainties related to labour and employee issues, liability uncertainties associated with detrimental effects of products to users, credit uncertainties arising from inability to collect accounts receivables, reducing the predictability of corporate performance and, so, increase international risk[97].

The competitiveness of the MNE depends on its capacity to make better use of the competencies located in the numerous subsidiaries. The subsidiaries that are important to the MNE employ numerous methods for developing competence. Knowledge, capabilities, and resources have become the central point of behaviour and development in firms. Differences between firms are due to their changing ability to create, exploit, and combine knowledge, skills, and resources. The subsidiary's competence and its use of that competence have been shown to have an influence on the corporate role of the subsidiary. The competitiveness of the local market environment is a significant characteristic of the subsidiary's corporate role. Corporate strategy may clearly identify national markets where the company's presence is crucial, if it is to detect competitive moves and note cutting-edge technology. Competence can be found in several functional areas, such as technology, marketing, human and resource management.[98] It is advantageous for the MNE to establish or acquire subsidiaries in competitive markets, and to integrate these units directly with the rest of the MNE. The dynamism and complexity of the business environment in which the subsidiary is embedded will affect the way its organizational competencies develop. The concentration of companies engaged in comparable or inter-linked activities to a definite geographical region puts pressure on individual companies. Knowledge flows within a cluster of companies operating in a county are intensive, but that knowledge flows to the outside are limited and frequently even distorted[99]. It is crucial for any firm that aims to be a leader in its field to maintain a presence in the leading clusters, where new developments take place. The international competitiveness of a country is the sum of the export performance of all national companies. The foreign activities of companies reduce their dependence on the resources and factors of production available in their home country, and their competitiveness may move independently from the resources shaping the competitiveness of their home country. The competitiveness of countries rests on the quantity and quality of the immobile resources such as climate, land and other natural resources, and most kinds of labour located within them. The competitiveness of companies is based on the kind of assets that are transferable by the firms from country to country within them. In a world that is becoming more and more globalised and integrated, and in which the advantages of companies derive from intangible assets that are apparently not tied to any specific location, home countries continue to exercise a strong influence on the advantages that companies develop. Would the

[96] Dieter Ernst, Linsu Kim, Global production networks, knowledge diffusion, and local capability formation, Research Policy 1419 (2002) 1–13, p12.

[97] Zafar U. Ahmed, Osman Mohamad, Brian Tan, James P. Johnson, International risk perceptions and mode of entry: a case study of Malaysian multinational firms, Journal of Business Research 55 (2002) 805–813

[98] Holm, U., Pedersen, T. (Eds.), (2000) The emergence and impact of MNE centres of excellence - a subsidiary perspective. London: Macmillan.

[99] Malmberg, A., SoKlvell, OG., & Zander, I. (1996). Spatial clustering, local accumulation of knowledge and firm competitiveness. Geografiska Annaler, 78B(2), 85-97.

competitiveness of companies reflect the resources and endowments abundant in their home countries and would grow in the same sectors and industries in which their home country has a comparative advantage? Market-seeking firms typically exported their products before establishing foreign production. Investing companies exported to the target market prior to the investment. Typically a company starts with exports, then establishes marketing and distribution operations and, finally, in some markets, invests in local production facilities. The competitiveness of companies and their home countries are closely linked to each other[100]. On the one hand, companies engage in product or process specialisation in order to utilize international differences in locational comparative advantages and integrate them with other activities performed in another place through intra-firm trade. On the other hand, FDI and trade are flourishing in different activities and industries, suggesting a discrepancy between the competitiveness of companies and their home countries. For instance, according[101] to L. Nachum , G.G. Jones , J.H. Dunning "While the export shares of the country were deteriorating, their MNEs were gaining exports shares, in contrast to our findings, which show that during most of the last century, the competitiveness of the UK and its MNEs moved parallel to each other". Policies intended to advance FDI should not discourage exports and vice versa[102].

Industry clusters are expected to be formed around certain "driver" industries or institutions in which the county has its greatest competitive advantage[103]. The geographic clustering of the many activities of MNEs, and more than ever those relating to knowledge activities, at the present time seems to be a highly energetic and forward-looking phenomenon, mostly driven by innovation and prospective information and technology spillovers, rather than by existing industry linkages[104]. R&D-intensive industries tend to be highly concentrated which has tended to keep on, even in the face of rising' labor and other input costs attributed to economies of agglomeration, but the exact source of these economies is complicated to segregate.

Innovation is not automatically purely a function of R&D, nor is R&D certainly sufficient for the creation of technology-intensive industries and the expensive economic spillovers that result in high value added jobs and exports. Innovation is a combination of factors that have a say to innovation, such as skills, finance, production, user-producer linkages, the capacity of organizations to learn, and multi-layered government policies. There is a need for absorptive capacity which is more than the capacity to master a new technology or innovation. It is the ability to adjust the firm's systems of coordination and organize to contest the new technological opportunities.

---

[100] Pearce, R.D., 1990. The Internationalisation of Research and Development. MacMillan, London.

[101] L. Nachum , G.G. Jones , J.H. Dunning, The international competitiveness of the UK and its multinational enterprises, Structural Change and Economic Dynamics 12 (2001) 277–294. Nachum L., 2001. The impact of home countries on the competitiveness of advertising MNEs. Management International Review, Volume 1. Nachum, L., Dunning, J.H., Jones, G.G., 2000. UK FDI and the comparative advantage of the UK. The World Economy 23 (5), 701–720.

[102] UNCTAD-DTCI, 1996. World Investment Report 1996: Investment, Trade and International Policy arrangements. Geneva, United Nations. UNCTAD-DTCI, 1997. World Investment Report 1997: Transnational Corporations, Market Structure and Competition Policy. Geneva, United Nations.

[103] Hill, E.W., and J.F. Brennan. 2000. A methodology for identifying the drivers of industrial clusters: The foundation of regional competitive advantage. Economic Development Quarterly 14(1): 65-97.

[104] Philip Mccann And Ram Mudambi, The Location Behavior of the Multinational Enterprise: Some Analytical Issues, Growth and Change Vol. 35 No. 4 (Fall 2004), pp. 491-524

Information spillovers in the vibrant MNE fields extend well beyond the dimensions of the individual metropolitan areas. The involvement of MNEs in clusters is not instantly recognizable in that the level of involvement appears to be very sensitive to the kind of the industry structure in which the company operates. The vital justification for the MNE is as a means of internalizing information transactions costs within the individual company, whereas the rationale for industrial clustering is to internalize information transactions costs within the group of clustered companies. Taking into account that prices are high in areas of concentrated activity, locating within a particular cluster can only be gainful to the MNE in situations where the information transactions and internalization requirements of the company can be reconciled with the information transactions quality of the individual cluster. MNEs are often able to hire fitting specialist labor by simply locating within the same broad regional neighbourhood as other companies, rather than within the same urban location. MNE location decisions involve a detailed consideration of the relationship between different types of information internalized and transmitted by the company, the way such information is mediated and transmitted, and the decisive geographical extent over which such information transmission takes place.

MNEs examine their various options and determinants in multinational market competition in order to achieve maximum performance on a global basis. Multinational market competition is a unique case of multipoint competition. Competitive moves in attack and response are the most basic units in any competitive rivalry. Which are the determinants of the particular tactical options for dealing with competitive attack in multiple national markets? The decisive success of any competitive action depends fundamentally on whether that action goes unchallenged or whether the response is delayed, for a company benefits from moves that prevent or delay responses. High visibility, high perceived potential, and high strategic threat provoke rapid responses from incumbent companies. The greater the dependence on a market under attack, the more the respondent will react especially to a price action than other types of competitive moves[105]. It could be said that combination of high visibility and low difficulty is particularly possible to stir up a large number of responses. Multipoint competition refers to situations where companies compete concurrently against the same rivals in multiple product markets, or multiple national markets[106]. A company's action and reaction across a host of markets depend not only on its market overlap with rivals but also on the resemblance between the resource profiles of these multimarket rivals[107]. It could be argued that the significance of company resource and ability in influencing a firm's behaviour in multipoint competition together with a company's resource allocation in multipoint competition can redirect competitors' resource allocation pattern, enhancing the

105 Chen, M.-J., MacMillan, I.C., 1992. Non response and delayed response to competitive moves: the roles of competitor dependence and action irreversibility. Acad Manage J 35, 539–570. Chen, M.-J., Miller, D., 1994. Competitive attack, retaliation and performance: an expectancy-valence framework. Strat Manage J 15, 85–102.

106 Gimeno, J., Chen, M.-J., 1998. The dynamics of competitive positioning: a pair-wise perspective. Acad Manage Proc BPS: O1-O8. Gimeno, J., Woo, C.Y., 1996. Hypercompetition in a multimarket environment: the role of strategic similarity and multimarket contact on competitive de-escalation. Organ Sci 7, 322–341.

107 Baum, J.A.C., Korn, H.J., 1996. Competitive dynamics of interfirm rivalry. Acad Manage J 39 (2), 255–291.

company's own sphere of influence without triggering an all-out war[108]. Moreover, competition among MNEs derives to cross-border coordination of competitive moves by MNEs. Global competitive moves mean sacrificing revenues, profits, or competitive position in specific national markets.

Yip[109] considers "drivers" of global competition—market drivers, cost drivers, government drivers, and competitive drivers—and "levers" of global strategy—market participation, product/service choice, location of value-adding activities, marketing, and competitive moves. Top management team's strategy, globalisation of strategy, corporate ownership of national subsidiaries, intra-MNE information flow, and local market barriers and diversity define the cross-border engagement on multipoint competition. The knowledge of multinational market interdependence will help predict whether MNEs will employ worldwide coordinated moves or not but will not predict whether MNEs will choose either counterattack or total war[110]. Hence, the more markets where rivals encounter each other, the more likely it is for them to be aware of their interdependence across these markets, which means a market overlap. A market overlap is defined as the extent to which a focal MNE's various national markets overlap with those of a global rival[111]. MNEs design their global strategy in such a way as to maximize its overall global performance. Globally coordinated competitive moves assist to amplify the competitive advantages of particular national markets and enhance the MNE's global position.

The ability to diffuse competence beyond its limited context is a key determinant of an organization's competitive advantage and so a MNE must be able to utilize the competencies dispersed in its global organization, it loses much of its competitive advantage[112]. Hence, the corporate role of a multinational subsidiary depends not only upon its absolute level of specialized competence, but also on the extent to which the subsidiary's competence is used in other corporate units[113]. There is a growing tendency for subsidiaries to function as centres of competence or excellence. The importance of the individual subsidiary to the MNE is determined by the subsidiary itself and by corporate top management[114]. The subsidiary has to

---

[108] McGrath, R.G., Chen, M.-J., MacMillan, I.C., 1998. Multimarket maneuvering in uncertain spheres of influence: resource diversion strategies. Acad Manage Rev 23 (4), 724–740. MacMillan, I.C., McCaffery, M.L., Van Wijk, G., 1985. Competitor's responses to easily imitated new products: exploring commercial banking product introductions. Strategic Manage J 6, 75–86.

McGrath, R.G., Chen, M.-J., MacMillan, I.C., 1998. Multimarket maneuvering in uncertain spheres of influence: resource diversion strategies. Acad Manage Rev 23 (4), 724–740.

[109] Yip, G., 1989. Global strategy in a world of nations? Sloan Management Rev 31 (1), 29–41.Yip, G., 1995. Total global strategy: managing for worldwide competitive advantage. Prentice Hall, Englewood, Cliffs, NJ.

[110] Ma, H., 1998. Mutual forbearance in international business. J Int Manage 4 (2), 129–147.

[111] Bailey, E.E., 1997. Integrating policy trends into dynamic advantage. In: Day, G.S., Reibstein, D.J. (Eds.), Wharton on dynamic competitive strategy. John Wiley and Sons, Inc., New York, pp. 76–98.

[112] Forsgren, M., Holm, U., Thilenius, P. (1997) Network infusion in the multinational corporation. In I., BjoKrkman, & M. Forsgren, (Eds.), The nature of the international firm Nordic contributions to international business. Copenhagen: Copenhagen Business School Press.

[113] Forsgren, M., Johanson, J., & Sharma, D. (2000). Development of MNE centres of excellence. In U. Holm, & T. Pedersen (Eds.), The emergence and impact of MNE centres of excellence - a subsidiary perspective.London: Macmillan. Taggart, J. H. (1997). Autonomy and procedural justice: A framework for evaluating subsidiary strategy. Journal of International Business Studies, 28(1), 51-76.

[114] Buckley, P. J., & Casson, M. C. (1998). Models of the multinational enterprise. Journal of International Business Studies, 29(1), 21-44. Fratocchi, L., & Lorenzoni, G. (2000). Mergers and acquisitions as establishment modes for centres of excellence The case of Italian subsidiaries. In U. Holm, & T.

establish business relationships with local counterparts in order to be able to absorb meaningful knowledge from the competitive environment; and second, investment is needed to support the development of new competence and learning. Affiliates operating in the large and worldwide competitive industry clusters of the host country tend to be fundamentally coordinated and integrated with other parts of the parent corporation, principally because parent firms have the incentives to tap into the large pool of technological capabilities generated among the firms constituting the industry cluster. It should be taken into account that technological competencies are time and again generated inside national or provincial innovation systems. [115] Additionally, international trade has grown faster than the global economy, and foreign subsidiaries of MNEs headquartered in various countries now operate in nearly every nation in the world. Although there is variation in the definitions of national competitiveness, most have certain core aspects. These include such concepts as a nation's ability to increase the wealth and welfare of its inhabitants and the ability of its companies to discover and then profit from technologies and products in world markets.[116] The key concept in the national competitiveness definitions untaken here seems to be the ability of the firms within a country to increase their productivity, which leads to the increase of economic benefits by the residents of the country. Efforts toward further holistic improvements of the investment climate of the nation will better serve a country's industrial base than will initiatives directed at aiding any particular industry.[117] With increased industrial globalisation, subsidiaries of foreign firms also play a role in determining a nation's competitiveness, as well as its development. As mentioned above, in Dunning's [118]eclectic paradigm and, generally, in theories of foreign direct investment, nations are considered to hold varying capabilities that lead to country-specific or location advantages and that let firms within those countries to attain competitive advantages based on the resources that are contained in that nation. The industries of some nations seem to dominate their specific global markets and differences among nations contribute to the success or failure of an industry in a nation.

Should a nation be concerned more with the skills of its workers than with the ownership nationality of the firms for which they work? Enhanced productivity is the key means by which the citizens of any region of the world improve their standard of living, regardless of the nation's relative productivity. There is a positive impact of foreign firms on a country's

---

Pedersen (Eds.), The emergence and impact of MNE centres of excellence - a subsidiary perspective. London: Macmillan. Madhok, A. (1997). Cost, value and foreign market entry mode: The transaction and the firm. Strategic Management Journal, 18, 39-61.

[115] Braczyk,H.-J.,Cooke,P.,&Heienreich,M.(Eds.).(1998). Regional innovation systems. London: UCL Press Limited. Dunning,J.H.(1997).Alliance capitalism and global business . London: Routledge. The Economist.(1999).How to merge. The Economist , January 9,19.

[116] Porter defines a nation's competitiveness as depending upon the "capacity of its industry to innovate and upgrade" Porter, M.E., 1990. The competitive advantage of nations. Free Press, New York. P 73. Scott and Lodge define it as "a country's ability to create, produce, distribute, and/or service products in international trade while earning rising returns on its resources" Scott, B.R., Lodge, G.C., 1985. U.S. competitiveness in the world economy. Harvard Business School Press, Boston. P 3. According to Blaine, "a nation's competitiveness refers to its ability to produce and distribute goods and services that can compete in international markets, and which simultaneously increase the real incomes and living standards of its citizens" Blaine, M., 1993. Profitability and competitiveness: lessons from Japanese and American firms in the 1980s. Cal Manage Rev 36(1), 48–74. p 63.

[117] Brewer, T.L., 1993. Government policies, market imperfections, and foreign direct investment. J Int Bus Studies 24(1), 101–120.

[118] Dunning, J.H., 1988. The eclectic paradigm of international production: a restatement and some possible extensions. J Int Bus 19, 1–31.

allocative efficiency or benefits from increases in competition, its level of technical efficiency, and its degree of technology transfer[119]. Furthermore, R&D spillovers from industrial to developing countries occur[120]. Foreign investment may benefit host countries through transfers of technology, stimulation of technology diffusion from new competition, and provision by foreign firms of worker training and management skill development[121]. FDI[122] results in increased host country productivity through technology transfer, but only when the initial level of host industry competition is relatively low. More technology spillovers were evident when there are in existence small technology gaps between the foreign investor and the host economy.[123] For instance, foreign firms locate plants in the United States to gain access to existing technologies, but also spur new technological development within those clusters with which they are involved.[124] Innovation or introduction of something entirely new and unexpected is a non-linear act of unpredictable consequences and cannot be planned. Innovation is usually expensive, risky, disturbing, destabilising and expectant with conflicts and in return, innovation creates a new, normally unknown faculty, which introduces a value diverse from the customary system of social values. The world consists of information just as it contains material and energy. According to Borisz Szanto [125] "There is a race going on between human innovative intelligence and the general regression we are witnessing, causing and participating in. The human being is in a desperate contest with him-self. Actually, this is what the problem of sustainability really means".

The skill and ability of its human resources contributes to its national competitiveness, predominantly with regard to productivity and technological and managerial expertise. As the labour force within a nation becomes more technologically and managerially skilled, it becomes more valuable to the employing firms within the nation as well. As the nation's products become more competitive, the nation's trade balance can be certainly affected, in turn raising the wealth of the nation. Hence, industrialized countries should concentrate on developing those resources that improve the competitiveness of the nation itself rather than on protecting firms that nominally align themselves with the nation but do not operate solely in the home nation's interests[126]. As mentioned above, innovation is a form of knowledge creation in which knowledge is energetically developed to solve defined problems and is important in maintaining a nation's competitiveness, given that competitive advantage is

[119] Caves, R.E., 1974. Multinational firms, competition, and productivity in host country markets. Economica 41,176–193.

[120] Coe, D.T., Helpman, E., Hoffmaister, A.W., 1997. North–south R&D spillovers. Econ J 107, 134–149.

[121] Harrison, A., 1994. The role of multinationals in economic development: the benefits of FDI. Columbia J World Bus 29(4), 6–11.

[122] Chung, W., 1997. Foreign direct investment's effect on host industry mark-up and productivity in the U.S.: the influence of initial host industry competition. Paper presented at the Academy of International Business annual meeting, Monterrey, Mexico.

[123] Kokko, A., 1994. Technology, market characteristics, and spillovers. J Develop Econ 43, 279–293.

[124] Almeida, P., 1996. Knowledge sourcing by foreign multinationals: patent citation analysis in the U.S. semiconductor industry. Strat Manage J 17, 155–165. Cantwell stated that "the use of technology in new environments feeds back into fresh adaptation and (depending on the state of local scientific and technological capability) new innovation" Cantwell, J. 1989. Technological innovation and multinational corporations. Blackwell, Oxford, UK. p 9.

[125] Borisz Szanto, The paradigm of globalism, Technovation 21 (2001) 673–687, p687.

[126] Reich, R.B., 1990. Who is us? Harvard Bus Rev January–February, 53–64.

sustainable only to the extent that cannot be initiated by competitors.[127] The capability to innovate and create new knowledge is a resource or capability that allows competitive advantage to be sustained. Porter argues the innovative capability stems from four different categories of country-level resources, which are the four points of his diamond model: factor conditions, demand conditions, domestic competition, and related and supporting industries. There is a direct relationship between the competitive activities of the firms that comprise a country's industrial force and the country's national competitiveness[128]. Efficiency does not mechanically follow from the acquisition of foreign machinery that uses the new technology and sustained competence depends profoundly on domestic capabilities to generate and manage change in those technologies[129].

Increased globalisation has led to a "borderless world," in which an ever-increasing percentage of a nation's workforce is employed by foreign-owned' companies, foreign subsidiaries have thus become more and more important contributors to a nation's competitiveness by providing product and process technology and technical and managerial skills. Subsidiaries of foreign-owned firms can provide some of the resources that contribute to the competitive advantage of their host nation[130]. Local employees of a foreign subsidiary learn the managerial practices and the technology processes that the foreign parent employs in its operations, as well as its general business practices and strategies. Firm boundaries are permeable to firm-based knowledge and expertise, including management practices. Major inflows of foreign investment generate a great deal of local media and industry attention, much of which is focused on the new technologies and practices employed by the investing firm. Thus, spillovers are likely to occur despite attempts of foreign subsidiaries to protect their valuable stocks of tacit knowledge.

As mentioned above, multipoint competition refers to situations where firms compete concurrently against the same rivals in multiple product markets, multiple geographic markets for the same product, or multiple national markets[131]. To better understand strategic interaction in multipoint competition, firms must be viewed as portfolios of activities rather than competing independently in each industry in which they have operations. Karnani and Wernerfelt[132] suggest that there are essentially four options for a firm under attack in multipoint competition: do nothing, retaliate in the same market where it was attacked, retaliate in other jointly contested markets, and wage total war in all the markets where it encounters the rival that initiates the attack. A firm's resource allocation in multipoint competition can divert competitors' resource allocation pattern, enhancing the firm's own

---

[127] Nonaka, I., 1994. A dynamic theory of organizational knowledge creation. Organ Sci 5, 14–37.

[128] Francis, A., 1992. The process of national industrial regeneration and competitiveness. Strat Manage J 13 (Special Issue), 61–78.

[129] Elias G. Carayannis, John Sagi, Exploiting opportunities of the new economy: developing nations in support of the ICT industry, Technovation 22 (2002) 517–524

[130] Freeman, C., 1995. The "national system of innovation" in historical perspective. Cambridge J Econ 19, 5–24. Mowery, D.C., Oxley, J.P., 1995. Inward technology transfer and competitiveness: the role of national innovation systems. Cambridge J Econ 19, 67–93.

[131] Yip, G., 1995. Total global strategy: managing for worldwide competitive advantage. Prentice Hall, Englewood, Cliffs, NJ.

[132] Karnani, A., Wernerfelt, B., 1985. Multiple point competition. Strat Manage J 6, 87–96. Teece, D.J., Pisano, G., Shuen, A., 1997. Dynamic capabilities and strategic management. Strat Manage J 18, 509–533.

sphere of influence without triggering an all-out war[133]. Hence, MNEs design their global strategy in such a way as to maximize its overall global performance. On the one hand, firms may have comparable internal resources and technological strengths that lend them to similar strategic choices in the marketplace. On the other hand, industries differ among themselves in the manner that they offer market opportunities and impose operational constraints and thereby create greater within-group homogeneity and between-group heterogeneity.

Nations engender competitive advantage through a combination of factor endowments, unique cultural qualities, and deliberate policy options. A country's physical and human resources and political institutions, as well as culturally based characteristics, could provide its firms with superior competitive advantage in comparison with firms from other countries. [134] A country's stock of technology, investment in education, training, and other physical and social infrastructure considerations offer distinct competitive advantages to its MNEs in the international arena. Cultural values and institutional norms of a society influence the institutional process of strategy formulation and implementation by MNEs. The political and regulatory environment of economic activity and the resultant intensity of competition provide distinct competitive advantages to MNEs. A country may spend rare foreign exchange in establishing high-tech industries whereas the educational level of workers would indicate greater opportunities for growth in low-tech industries with higher labor-to-capital ratios[135].

Firm resources and organizational capabilities include all assets, capabilities, organizational processes, firm attributes and knowledge that are controlled by the firm and thereby enable it to conceive and implement a particular strategy, improve operational efficiency, and improve its financial performance. Companies create inter-firm differences and competitive advantage through a combination of their physical and human resources, corporate culture and institutional memory, and managerial characteristics and styles.[136] A MNE's strategic choices and operational modes also may be impacted by a host country's bargaining power emanating from that country's factors endowments, cultural qualities, governmental economic policies, and their relative importance to the MNE in gaining competitive advantages in specific markets. Different countries' bargaining power in the international arena is influenced by both their "country of origin effect" COE-based characteristics and global geopolitical considerations. Countries can manifest their country-based resources only through the operations of multinationals.

International markets, in reality, are a collection of multiple domestic markets each with its own set of structural and institutional rigidities. The implementation of an MNE's global strategy across all markets, however, is affected by the capacity of various host countries to secure for themselves the largest part of gains from the "added value" generated by the MNE

---

133 McGrath, R.G., Chen, M.-J., MacMillan, I.C., 1998. Multimarket maneuvering in uncertain spheres of influence: resource diversion strategies. Acad Manage Rev 23. (4), 724–740. Wind, J., 1997. Preemptive strategies. In: Day, G.S., Reibstein, D.J. (Eds.), Wharton on dynamic competitive strategy. John Wiley and Sons, Inc., New York.

134 Sethi, S.P., Elango, B., 1997. The impact of national characteristics and government policies on the international competitive advantage of multinational corporations. Business and Contemporary World IX, 725–741.

135 Porter, M., 1986. Competition in Global Industries. Harvard Business School Press: Boston. Porter, M., 1990. Competitive Advantage of Nations. Free Press: New York.

136 Grant, R.M., 1991. The resource-based theory of competitive advantage: implication for strategy formulation. California Management Review 33, 114–135.

through its production and distribution activities within a host country's territory, and quite often, beyond that territory[137]. The international competitiveness of a country is the sum of the export performance of all national firms. The international competitiveness of firms and countries alike is based on the location bound resources tied to the home countries. Companies investing overseas have the capacity to avoid unfavourable conditions in their country that reduce the competitiveness of the immobile factors of production located there, and they are able to benefit from more favourable conditions in other locations. As discussed earlier, the competitiveness of countries rests on the quantity and quality of the immobile resources located within them.[138] These include climate, land and other natural resources, and most kinds of labour. The competitiveness of companies is based on the kind of assets that are transferable by the companies from country to country within them, but not from one firm to another, even within countries. The more transferable an attribute is geographically, the less it can be the basis for national competitiveness. The more transferable it is among companies, the less it can be the basis for a company's competitiveness[139]. Traditionally, market-seeking companies typically exported their products before establishing foreign production.

R&D investment plays a fundamental role in a company's future growth. MNEs have a broad market environment and have affiliates located in multiple economies, compared to DCs which operate in one economy, and so providing better diversification opportunities for MNEs. A know-how advantage would enable MNEs to transform the output of R&D into a new form of production at a lower cost than DCs because of economies of scale and to reduce communication costs between R&D, production and marketing. A company's location strategy is determined primarily by the interplay of comparative advantage, barriers to trade, and regional incentives to internalise, and so a company will be multinational when these factors make it best possible to locate different stages of production in various nations. Hence, a company's degree of multinationality plays a role in determining the effect of R&D investment[140]. According to Murali Patibandla And Bent Petersen [141]"The initial stock of human capital leads to entry of transnational corporations (TNC), which triggers a cumulative process of further human capital accumulation through a process of externalities (spillovers) governed by firm-level and market structure dynamics. Spillovers from TNC operations are more effective when TNCs operate at higher end of technology and build backward linkages with local firms and institutions in a developing economy".

The development of modern technologies and the conquest of entrepreneurism have been changing the way of manufacturing production and the pattern of world trading[142]. Characterised by foreign direct investment and international production, industrial

---

[137] Boddewyn, J.J., Brewer, T.L., 1994. International-business political behavior: new theoretical directions. Academy of Management Review 19, 119–143.

[138] Dunning, J.H., 1988. Multinationals, Technology and Competitiveness. Unwin Hyman, London. Dunning, J.H., 1993. Multinational Enterprises and the Global Economy. Addison-Wesley, Wokingham, UK.

[139] Lipsey, R.E., 1995. Competitiveness in a World of MNEs. A Report Prepared for UNCTAD, Division on Transnational Corporations and Investment.

[140] Sung C. Bae , Seungwook Noh, Multinational corporations versus domestic corporations: a comparative study of R&D investment activities, Journal of Multinational Financial Management 11 (2001) 89–104

[141] Murali Patibandla And Bent Petersen, Role of Transnational Corporations in the Evolution of a High-Tech Industry: The Case of India 's Software Industry, World Development ,2002, www.elsevier.com/locate/worlddev

[142] OECD (1992). Globalisation of industrial activities four case studies: Auto parts, chemicals, construction and semiconductors. Paris: OECD.

globalisation integrates the world by the ascending cross-border multinational industrial operations that have made the self- contained and self-sufficient mode of production obsolete. Moreover, industrial globalisation is a procedure linked by interrelated cross-border production, and it enables firms to come into new markets, to capitalise on technological and organisational advantages, and to reduce costs. So, regional co-operation and international splitting up of production have been taking hold in the world economy. For instance, the total global flow of foreign direct investment captured by developing countries increased from 18 per cent in the 1980s to 36 per cent in 1996[143]. The vertically disaggregated network organisation has emerged where approximately all but central co-ordination in the production chain is contracted to independent firms[144]. Jieming Zhu [145] considers that "While new generations of industrial estates are replacing the old ones, and restructuring of industrial space use may be caused by industrial change, cost of industrial space and thus demand – supply equilibriums in the industrial property market are also responsible for the industrial restructuring".

As discussed earlier, differences between firms are due to their varying ability to create, exploit, and combine knowledge, skills, and resources and consequently subsidiaries contribute in terms of the competence, the capabilities, and the knowledge that they possess and develop. The subsidiary management's aptitude should be focused on its competencies to acquire a more important role within the corporation. A subsidiary operates in a business environment that consists of suppliers, competitors, customers, government agencies, and infrastructure, all of which have a possible impact on the development behaviour of the organization. The performance of a firm depends on the dynamism of its environment. Taking into consideration that the industrial cluster is both a result of and a prerequisite for learning, rather than simply a passive surface, clustering is a self-accelerating phenomenon, as new firms seek to establish operations in a region in order to be able to learn from the firms at the competitive edge. Hence, the cluster becomes a dynamic entity with intensive flows of knowledge between the firms. It is fundamental for any firm that aims to be a leader in its field to uphold a presence in the leading clusters, where new developments take place. The fact that a subsidiary is placed in a competitive and dynamic business environment does not automatically lead that subsidiary to acquire cutting-edge knowledge and technology from it. Besides, the development behaviour of the subsidiary is dependent on its embeddedness in the network of local firms, local customers, suppliers, research institutes, and competitors[146].

---

[143] Lo, F.-C.,& Marcotullio, P. J.(2000).Globalisation and urban transformations in the Asia-Pacific region: A review. Urban Studies, 37 (1), 77 –111.

[144] Dicken, P. (1998). Global shift transforming the world economy (3rd ed.). London: Paul Chapman.

[145] Jieming Zhu, Industrial globalisation and its impact on Singapore 's industrial landscape, Habitat International 26 (2002) 177 –190.p 177

[146] Forsgren, M., & Pedersen, T. (1998). Centres of excellence in multinational companies: The case of Denmark. In J. Birkinshaw, & Hood, N. Hood, (Eds.), Multinational corporate evolution and subsidiary development. London: Macmillan. Forsgren, M., Holm, U., Thilenius, P. (1997) Network infusion in the multinational corporation. In I., BjoKrkman, & M. Forsgren, (Eds.), The nature of the international xrm Nordic contributions to international business. Copenhagen: Copenhagen Business School Press. Forsgren, M., Johanson, J., & Sharma, D. (2000). Development of MNE centres of excellence. In U. Holm, & T. Pedersen (Eds.), The emergence and impact of MNE centres of excellence -a subsidiary perspective. London: Macmillan. Forsgren, M., Mathisen, C., & Pedersen, T. (2000). Competence creation and recognition -a case study. In U. Holm, & T. Pedersen (Eds.), The emergence and impact of MNE centres of excellence - a subsidiary perspective. London: Macmillan.

If companies go over the top about an executive's incentive compensation based on annual profitability, under-invested R&D might weaken the subsequent innovative capabilities and accordingly result in poor company functioning. An appropriate level of R&D clustering categorically influences the relationship between innovative capability and company functioning but overcrowded R&D clustering is expected to fabricate a negative relationship between innovative capability and company performance[147]. Integration of equivalent R&D capabilities and innovative efforts help out companies utilize interdependencies across their businesses in order to accomplish synergies. Particularly, technology and knowledge spillover consequence enhances information sharing and technology learning when companies have high R&D staff percentages/or adopt M&A strategies.

As mentioned above, companies with close relationships adapt and modify their resources and routines to each other over time, thus building mutual commitment and trust. The embeddedness in an energetic business environment must be shared with investment in R&D. Patrick Furu [148] presents "the increasing propensity for large multinational firms to acquire companies which they perceive as competent and which are located in markets where the overall level of competition is high". Firm resources, industry structure, and home country factors influence the competitive conduct amongst companies in the international arena[149]. Companies from various countries draw from a different set of factors endowments, cultural traits, and socio-political infrastructure thus giving them exclusive competitive advantages when compared with companies originating in countries that are less welcoming in those areas. A country's homogeneity of workforce, patterns of social harmonization, and emphasis on education can provide that nation's economic institutions with a further productive and disciplined workforce. It should be taken into account that in the international competitive arena, countries can show their country-based resources only through the operations of multinational corporations. A Corporation should take advantage of a particular country's exclusive set of physical resources, human cultural traits, and government's economic policies in a manner that is not available to other MNEs[150].

It should be taken into account that FDI triggers technology spillovers, assists human capital formation, contributes to international trade integration, creates a more competitive business environment and enhances enterprise development contributing to higher economic growth, which is the most potent tool for alleviating poverty in developing countries improving environmental and social conditions in the host country by transferring "cleaner" technologies and leading to more socially responsible corporate policies[151]. Prospective drawbacks embrace a deterioration of the balance of payments as profits are repatriated (albeit often offset by incoming FDI), social disruptions as a result of accelerated

---

[147] Carrincazeaux, C., Lung, Y., Rallet, A., 2001. Proximity and localization of corporate R&D activities. Research Policy 30 (5), 777–789.

[148] Patrick Furu, Drivers of competence development in different types of multinational R&D subsidiaries, Scand. J. Mgmt. 17 (2001) 133-149, p147.

[149] S. Prakash Sethi , B. Elango, The influence of "country of origin" on multinational corporation global strategy: A conceptual framework, Journal of International Management 5 (1999) 285–298.

[150] Sethi, S.P., Elango, B., 1997. The impact of national characteristics and government policies on the international competitive advantage of multinational corporations. Business and Contemporary World IX, 725–741.

[151] OECD Policy Brief: Foreign Direct Investment for Development, Maximising Benefits, Minimising Costs FDI and trade integration, October 2002.

commercialisation in less developed countries, and the effects on competition in national markets and increasing dependence on internationally operating enterprises as representing a loss of political sovereignty. Inward FDI contributes to countries develop their further integration into the global economy by engendering foreign trade flows including the development of international networks of related enterprises and a growing significance of foreign subsidiaries in MNEs' strategies for distribution, sales and marketing. Therefore, a developing country's capacity to attract FDI depends on the entrant's later access to importing and exporting implying that countries looking to attract investors should consider a policy of openness to international trade.

5.4 FDI and Productivity

International trade and strong domestic competition are other factors that seem to have a positive effect on productivity escalation. Foreign investors boost productivity in host countries and FDI is often a vehicle for national investment and technological progress. [152] Vertical production processes are being *fragmente*d, with discrete pieces of these processes being outsourced to countries that have advantages in providing the inputs that fragments use, whether this be unskilled workforce, capital, or cheap energy sources. The costs involved in fragmentation have declined spectacularly, including not only transportation costs, but also the costs of monitoring deliveries and coordination, the costs of delivering information, and the costs involved in dealing in arms-length transactions with foreigners.[153] Greater than before competition associated with the entry of an MNE advances the competence and product quality in national companies, and opens up potential for export.[154] Foreign investment plays a central function in the spreading of gains from innovations, more than ever for developing countries.[155] Additionally, foreign direct investment stimulates growth and has a larger influence than investment by national enterprises.[156] An export position can be established for those products in which the country's comparative productivity is highest, even if this means that the country exports those goods to other nations in which the total level of input productivity is even higher[157]. Thus, Government regulations and taxation can affect the productivity or net returns of inputs[158]. Moreover, developing countries need to

---

[152] De Mello, L.R. (1999)," Foreign Direct Investment-led growth: evidence from time series and panel data" , Oxford Economic Papers 51, 133-151.

[153] Jones, R.W., 2000. Globalization and the Theory of Input Trade. MIT Press, Cambridge, MA. Jones, R.W., Kierzkowski, H., 1990. The role of services in production and international trade: a theoretical framework. In: Jones, R.W., Krueger, A. Eds. , The Political Economy of International Trade. Blackwell, Oxford.

[154] Markusen, J.R. And Venables, A.J. (1999), "Foreign direct investment as a catalyst for industrial development" , European Economic Review, Vol. 43: 335 356.

[155] Ahn, S. And Hemmings, P. (2000), "Policy Influence on Economic Growth in OECD Countries: An Evaluation of the Evidence" , OECD Economics Department Working Paper, no. 246, Paris: OECD.

[156] Borensztein, E., De Gregorio, J. And Lee, L-W (1998), " How does foreign investment affect economic growth" , Journal of International Economics, Vol. 45: 115-135

[157] Donald R. Davis, Technology, unemployment, and relative wages in a global economy, European Economic Review 42 (1998) 1613-1633

[158] Ronald W. Jones, Private interests and government policy in a global world, European Journal of Political Economy Vol. 16 2000 243–256

have reached a certain threshold of development before being able to capture the benefits associated with FDI.[159]

An industry's cumulative productivity can boost all the way through quite a few different mechanisms: from improvements in the productivity in all plants; from increased market shares among plants with comparatively high levels and growth of productivity; or through the opening of plants with high productivity levels and exits of plants with low productivity levels. According to Yumiko Okamoto and Fredrik Sjo¨ Holm[160] "Indonesian productivity growth was not primarily generated through improvements within plants. Instead, increased market shares for plants with high productivity growth and entry of plants with relatively high productivity levels explains most of the productivity growth... foreign plants do not seem to have been acting as particularly strong engines of productivity growth. However, there are sectors where the foreign contribution to productivity growth has been substantial."

On the one hand, investment liberalisation may lead to increased production and consumption of polluting goods or to an expansion in industrial activity. On the other hand, FDI can improve structural efficiencies and make new investments in environmental protection possible. MNEs have a strong incentive to innovate in areas that improve resource efficiency or reduce industrial waste. As mentioned above, FDI by MNEs can also have positive spill over effects on the technological characteristics of national firms since local firms may imitate multinationals' technological practices in order to improve their own production practices. While FDI is an important vehicle for both technological change and diffusion, international capital flows are also an important determinant of the technologies of production. Long-term environmental impacts of international investment will depend in large part on how government environmental policies respond to their pressures and opportunities. Productivity improvements in the high-tech sector depend positively on the skill intensity of the production technique. Productivity improvements are achieved more easily when the intensity of skilled workers is higher, since this favors the informational exchange among skilled workers using a larger stock of knowledge[161].

FDI can impact upon the labour market. Investment and its liberalisation can exacerbate differences in income distribution and inequality that in general result from inadequate national policies regarding wealth distribution. Countries that strengthen their core labour standards can increase economic efficiency by raising skill levels in the work force and by creating an environment,[162] which encourages innovation and higher productivity. International investment can also impact upon the distribution of wealth within and across nations and contribute to poverty alleviation. Policymakers, therefore, need to complement policies stimulating economic growth with policies intended to broaden access to income

---

[159] Saggi, K. (2000), "Trade, foreign direct investment and international technology transfer: a survey" , World Bank, Washington DC.

[160] Yumiko Okamoto And Fredrik Sjo¨ Holm, FDI and the Dynamics of Productivity in Indonesian Manufacturing, The Journal of Development Studies, Vol.41, No.1, January 2005, pp.160 – 182, p 179-80.

[161] Mariassunta Giannetti The effects of integration on regional disparities: Convergence, divergence or both? European Economic Review 46 (2002) 539 –567

[162] Furtado, J.I. Dos R. And Belt, T., with JAMMI, R (eds.) (2000), Economic Development and Environmental Sustainability: Policies and Principles for a Durable Equi-librium, Washington DC: World Bank Institute.

opportunities, and which are needed in order to stimulate welfare gains overall.[163] Much of the overall impact of FDI on sustainable development depends on government policies in the host and the home country, and on the behaviour of the multinational enterprise itself.

As mentioned above, codes of conduct are voluntary expressions of commitment that set forth standards and principles for business conduct covering a broad range of issues and addressing each of the economic, social and environmental "pillars" of the sustainable development agenda[164]and management systems have been developed by firms to implement the strategies and commitments found in corporate codes of conduct. For both developed and developing countries the internationalisation of economic activities poses opportunities and challenges for sustainable development. International investment can stimulate competition, improve resource allocation, and facilitate the international distribution of technology. Indeed, countries with open investment regimes have generally shown higher growth rates than those countries that did not. However, while economic growth has increased over-all world prosperity, inequality between and within both developed and developing countries has increased. MNEs however have generally preferred to reap the scale benefits of standardisation in environmental, health and safety management systems in their foreign affiliates rather than exploiting weaknesses in local legislation. So, MNEs are the main vehicles of FDI, and their behaviour and strategies are crucial in attaining sustainable development. The largest MNEs are increasingly committing themselves to voluntary principles and standards of corporate social responsibility, thereby, contributing to sustainable development. [165] As discussed earlier Globalization raises the question of what initiatives should be undertaken to engender a global economy in which sustainable development is a fact rather than an inaccessible ideal. If sustainable development is to be achieved, the corporations themselves have to take up CSR initiatives. MNEs are leading drivers of globalization and they can be held accountable for the triumph or failure of sustainable development as it relates to persistent economic growth without harm to the environment and exploitation of the human workforce through unsatisfactory labor standards.

A social responsibility policy provides importance as a strategic part of a company's activities for the reason that a company that ignores social and environmental concerns in its conduct will have extensive profit or returns in the sort terms and be content to continue its operations at the status quo, but its actions on the other hand have the upcoming to harmfully affect society and the environment which means that its future profit is diminished when the company does not take a social responsibility approach to the global business environment.

Business functions conducted within a single organisation are no longer carried out and in the context of evolving pattern of cross-border production the vertically disaggregated network organisation has emerged where almost all but central co-ordination in the production chain are contracted to independent companies each of these companies performs

---

163 Ben-David, D., Nordstrom, H. And Winters, A. (1999), " Trade, income disparity and poverty" , WTO special studies 5, Washington: WTO.

164 Kolk, A., Van Tulder, R. And Welters, C. (1999), "International Codes of Conduct and Corporate Social Responsibility: Can Transnational Corporations Regulate Themselves?" , Transnational Corporations, Vol. 8(1): 143-80.

165 OECD (2001), Corporate Responsibility: Private initiatives and public goals, Paris: OECD. RODRIK, D. (1999), "The new global economy and developing countries. Making openness work", ODC Policy essay no. 24, Washington: ODC. UNCTAD (2000), World investment report: Cross-border Mergers and Acquisitions and Development, Geneva: UNCTAD. WORLD BANK (2000), Global Economic Prospects and the Developing Countries, Washington, D.C.

its role within a co-coordinated network. A new form of international division of labour affects both recipient and investor regions and so the formulation of new industrial landscape is the result of interactions between the industrial property market and the industrial restructuring[166]. The allocation of FDI across industrial branches is similarly affected by the dynamics of comparative advantages and price-cost margins play a role in determining (particularly foreign) investment activity. Foreign direct investment – through technology transfers – in turn affects the dynamics of catching-up and hence the dynamics of trade specialization. Information technology facilitates the delivery of many new products and services over electronic networks[167]. Internet retailers have nearly unlimited "virtual inventory" through centralized warehouses and drop-shipping agreements with distributors offering suitable access to a larger selection of products than brick-and-mortar retailers can[168]. For instance, online consumers are effortlessly able to locate, evaluate, order, and receive millions of books that are not available on the shelves of local bookstores[169] and so the benefits of Internet retailing are not fully reflected in lower prices, but rather are due to the new goods and services made readily available to consumers.

The differences between the Southern and the Eastern European countries in terms of gross FDI outflows show that the two groups of countries are still at different stages of their integration process[170]. Decisions of companies to engage in direct investment abroad are driven by factors related to cost advantages, market access, and the maintenance of knowledge assets internally and international investment decisions are guided by the size and the proximity of markets. Brainard[171] argues that multinational activity is determined not by factor endowment differences, but instead by a trade-off between proximity derived from firm-level economies of scale where any type of knowledge capital activity, such as R&D, is transferable to affiliates, thus allowing MNEs to be closer to foreign markets and concentration advantages derived from traditional plant-level economies of scales, which make it more profitable to concentrate production in one location rather than to export. Hence, when proximity advantages outweigh concentration advantages, foreign investment will take place, becoming more likely with higher tangible assets relative to the fixed costs of opening up an affiliate and with higher transport costs[172]. Tariffs have the effect of attracting foreign direct investment to the benefit of consumers in the host country. Countries with large bilateral FDI flows also tend to have large bilateral trade flows. According to Rodney D.

---

166 Jieming Zhu Industrial globalisation and its impact on Singapore 's industrial landscape Habitat International 26 (2002)177 –190

167 Bils, Mark, and Peter J. Klenow. 2001. The acceleration in variety growth. American Economic Review Papers and Proceedings 91(2) 274-280.

168 Brown, Jeffrey R., Austan Goolsbee. 2002. Does the Internet make markets more competitive? Evidence from the life insurance industry. Journal of Political Economy 110(3) 481-507.

169 Lee, Tom S.Y., Ivan Png. 2002. Buyer switching costs: Online vis-à-vis conventional retailing. Working Paper, National University of Singapore, Singapore. (Available at http://www.comp.nus.edu.sg/~ipng/research/books.pdf.)

170 Claudia M. Buch, Robert M. Kokta, and Daniel Piazolo Foreign direct investment in Europe: Is there redirection from the South to the East? Journal of Comparative Economics 31 (2003) 94–109

171 Brainard, S. Lael, 1993. A Simple Theory of Multinational Corporations and Trade with a Trade-off between Proximity and Concentration. NBER Working Paper No. 4269. National Bureau of Economic Research, Cambridge, MA.

172 Kleinert, Joern, 2001. The time pattern of the internationalization of production. German Economic Review 2 (1), 79–98.

Ludema[173] "trade blocs may come in clusters, and there may be a maximum geographic size of an bloc. It is likely that this maximum size would grow as the transport cost falls."

As discussed earlier, the most important source of technology spillovers are "vertical linkages" between MNEs and local suppliers because foreign-owned enterprises offer their suppliers with technical assistance, training and other information to improve the quality of their products assisting local suppliers in purchasing raw materials and intermediate goods and in modernizing or upgrading production facilities. The direct impact on human capital from FDI derives primarily from the fact that MNEs supply more training and other upgrading of human capital than do domestic enterprises but that human capital created spills over to the rest of the host economy is much weaker because the scale of MNE-sponsored training is smaller than that of general (public) education and the advantageous effects of training provided by FDI supplement, but not replace, a generic increase in skill levels. Technologically advanced sectors and host countries are expected to see human capital spillovers and, equally, economies with a high human capital component lend themselves more easily to technology spillovers.

Corporate governance programmes play an important role in economic growth, and the development of equity markets, which enable companies to access financing from a larger pool of investors. So, corporate governance mechanisms facilitate the efficient functioning of capital markets and promote the efficient allocation of resources. This is particularly relevant for international investment given the increase in FDI via mergers and acquisitions. Besides, Bribery and corruption are critical impediments to economic growth. Bribery and corruption distort economic decision-making, and increase transaction costs and uncertainty in the economy. Corruption inflates government expenditure and distorts the composition of this expenditure away from investment in sectors such as health and education towards large public infrastructure projects. Is corruption only a barrier, not a decisive factor, in realizing the full potential of a country's investment? FDI can be negatively affected by corruption if companies find it more and more difficult to perform operations without compromising in some way. Corruption distorts the market by making regulatory controls ineffective and acting as an arbitrary tax on FDI[174]. The impulsiveness in the level of corruption adds to the arbitrariness and is problematical for foreign investment[175]. Under these circumstances, investors will prefer not to invest and will divert the money to a safer investment location. In the long run, the economy and its growth will suffer. Media exposure of corrupt practices increased FDI when investors believed that the government would institute reforms to control corruption.[176] Alternatively, FDI decreased with media exposure when investors felt that the government was unwilling or unable to change the environment for better. The transaction cost and coordination cost variables such as interpersonal relations, information asymmetries,

[173] Rodney D. Ludema, Increasing returns, multinationals and geography of preferential trade agreements, Journal of International Economics 56 (2002) 329–358, p354

[174] Tanzi, V. (1998). Corruption around the world: Causes, consequences, scope, and cures, IMF Working Paper WP/98/63. International Monetary Fund. Gupta, S., Davoodi, H., & Alonso-Terme, R. (1998). Does corruption affect income inequality and poverty? IMF Working Paper. Washington D.C.: International Monetary Fund.

[175] Wei, S. (1997). Why is corruption so much more taxing than tax? Arbitrariness kills, NBER Working Paper 6255. Cambridge, MA: National Bureau of Economic Research. Wei, S. (2000). How taxing is corruption on international investors? The Review of Economics and Statistics, 82(4), 1–12.

[176] Busse, L., Ishikawa, N., Mitra, M., Primmer, D., Surjadinata, K., & Yaveroglu, T. (1996). The perception of corruption: A market discipline approach, Working Paper. Atlanta: Emory University.

language and culture, and the like, are more important than production-related variables in FDI decision[177]. Local investors are better positioned than foreign investors are in managing the transaction and coordination costs because of their experience in the local market. The impact of corruption on local investment is across the board substantially lower than on FDI.

Corruption may have less of significance when all the positive economic and social elements are taken together for a host country[178]. International orientation and political instability of the host country are important determinants of investment[179] and corruption and political instability would be positively correlated[180]. Corrupt countries are more vulnerable to financial crises because they are forced to rely on short-term offshore loans, which flow out much faster then FDI following a shock not mentioning that portfolio investment is also adversely affected by corruption. It could be argued that corruption can be beneficial because it allows firms to get around inefficient regulations such as barriers to import or entry and so promotes competition in the domestic market. The role of corruption in deterring or perverting foreign investment might lead to some agreement on at least minimal rules to protect investors from arbitrary actions by predatory governments and people from human rights or environmental abuses by MNEs that are unregulated by those same governments. Corruption and bribery appear to be widespread features of foreign direct investment activities but institutional inefficiencies such as corruption are detrimental to both FDI and domestic investment. When foreign direct investment suffered from a relative disadvantage in property rights protection, it economized on its physical capital investment and paid its laborers a higher wage premium. Multinational investment specialized in industries in which foreign companies enjoy relative advantages in monitoring costs and so multinationals enjoy managerial advantages in some industries, which correspond to reduced monitoring costs, but suffer from the enforcement disadvantages alluded to above. According to Joshua Aizenman and Mark M. Spiegel[181] "the Corruption term appears to be strongly robust to the inclusion of the conditioning variables, either for FDI as a share of gross-fixed-capital formation or for FDI as a share of private investment."

---

[177] Dunning, J. (1997). Re-evaluating the benefits of foreign direct investment. In J. Dunning (Ed.), Alliance capitalism and global business. London, UK: Routledge.

[178] Drabek, Z., & Payne, W. (1999). The impact of transparency on foreign direct investment, Staff Working Paper ERAD-99-02. Geneva: World Trade Organization. Chen, H., & Chen, T. (1998). Network linkages and location choice in foreign direct investment. Journal of International Business Studies, 29(3), 445–468. Delios, A., & Henisz, W. (2000). Japanese firms' investment strategies in emerging economies. Academy of Management Journal, 43(3), 305–323.

[179] Estrin, S., & Bevan, A. (2000). The determinants of foreign direct investment in transition economies, Discussion Paper 2638. London: Center for Policy Research Publications. Ensign, P. (1996). An examination of foreign direct investment theories and the multinational firm: A business/economics perspective. In M. Green, & R. McNaughton (Eds.), The location of foreign direct investment. Avebury: Aldershot.

[180] Tanzi, V., & Davoodi, H. (1997). Corruption, public investment and growth, IMF Working Paper 97/139. Washington: International Monetary Fund. World Investment Report. (1999). Foreign direct investment and the challenge of development. United Nations: New York and Geneva. Wells, L., & Wint, A. (2000). Marketing a country: promotion as a tool for attracting foreign investment, Occasional Paper No.13. Washington, D.C.: World Bank.

[181] Joshua Aizenman and Mark M. Spiegel, Institutional Efficiency, Monitoring Costs, and the Investment Share of FDI, FRBSF working paper 2003-06 p13.

5.5 FDI and Labour

How the labor market in the home country is affected by outward foreign direct investment (FDI)? In case that there is a big degree of complementarity between activities moved abroad and activities remaining in the home country, it is possible that the firm and the home country workers agree whether it is preferable to undertake FDI. Besides, if there is a big degree of substitutability between activities in foreign affiliates and activities in the home country, it is probable that the firm gains but the workers lose from FDI. Zhao[182] states that FDI gives rise to lower wages, whereas we discover that it depends on the degree of substitutability between activities in the home country and the host country. Is a positive elasticity of substitution between parent employment and employment in foreign affiliates? Brainard and Riker[183] quote cross-elasticities of substitution between labor in parent US firms and foreign affiliates and between labors in various affiliates. A high degree of complementarity between host country activities and home country activities reduces the employment loss in the home country when a company expands activities in the host country, and, if the wage costs in the host country are adequately low, employment in the home country may actually increase. Hence, since the wage is lowest in the multinational case, the firm always prefers to be multinational. According[184] to Mette Yde Skaksen and Jan Rose Sørensen "The higher the degree of substitution between activities in the host country and the home country, the more likely it is that the trade union and the firm disagree whether the firm should become multinational". Moreover, John A. List [185] indicates that stringent environmental regulations do not have a negative impact on FDI inflows.

Countries with a rigid labor market tend to produce comparatively secure goods, at a late stage of their product life cycle. As a result, according to Gilles Saint-Paul [186] in countries with inflexible labor market "their researchers tend to specialize in &...innovation ' which improves existing products, rather than & innovation ' which introduces new products. This is roughly consistent with the observed pattern of R&D in Europe versus the U.S. Employment protection does not necessarily harm the country where it prevails, but typically reduces world welfare and the world number of goods."

Employment in service activities rose in tandem with the exposure of local to foreign competition. It should be taken into account that trade-induced changes in production methods rather than low wage competition, is responsible for an increase in the relative demand for skill. Fragmentation allows sharing of production blocks across various industries and due to indivisibilities and economies of scope horizontal linkages among industries are established as vertical specialization deepens[187]. The scale of production of individual

---

182 Zhao, L., 1998. The impact of foreign direct investment on wages and employment. Oxford Economic Papers 50, 284–301. Zhao, L., 1995. Cross-hauling direct foreign investment and unionized oligopoly. European Economic Review 39, 1237–1253.

183 Brainard, S.L., Riker, D.A., 1997. Are US multinationals exporting US jobs? NBER working paper 5958.

184 Mette Yde Skaksen , Jan Rose Sørensen, Should trade unions appreciate foreign direct investment, Journal of International Economics 55 (2001) 379–390, p389.

185 John A. List, US county-level determinants of inbound FDI: evidence from a two-step modified count data model, International Journal of Industrial Organization 19 (2001) 953–973

186 Gilles Saint-Paul Employment protection international specialization, and innovation, European Economic Review 46 (2002) 375.

187 Jones, Ronald and Henryk Kierzkowski (1999): 'Horizontal Aspects of Vertical Fragmentation', mimeo University of Rochester and Graduate Institute of International Studies.

companies changes endogenously while the production process becomes more fragmented and global sourcing increases. Labor markets segmented by skill level turn out to be crucial for integration-driven fragmentation[188]. Globalization implies a shift in relative labor demand and the relative price of managing more complex production declines endogenously[189].

Most countries have removed their barriers to FDI and have energetically encouraged investment by foreign firms. There may exist backward and forward linkages between foreign affiliates and local firms.[190] Foreign affiliates may increase local firms' productivity and domestic competitors might effectively imitate technological innovations introduced by MNEs. Subsidiaries of foreign firms train local employees who later join local firms or set up their own companies, bringing with them all or part of the technological, marketing, and managerial knowledge that they have acquired. It could be argued that affiliates rely intensively on expatriates, but afterwards they tend to replace them with local workers who have been appropriately trained in the meanwhile[191]. While labor mobility is significant in particular circumstances, mobility is lower for managers employed by MNEs than for those employed by local firms.

MNEs undertake investments and building of higher levels of competences in locations that provide sub-optimal returns but where they have prior experience[192]. The creation of linkages and the internalisation of spillovers from MNE activities still depend on resident absorptive capacity. Co-location of home and foreign companies in intermediate economies has benefits for both groups of companies, and productivity growth in the domestic sector may not mechanically derive from MNE spillovers. Knowledge creation mechanisms of MNE subsidiaries and national companies are independent[193].

The MNE manages to keep the worker only if it offers better conditions than the local firm. Spillovers from foreign direct investment can take two forms. Technological spillovers arise when a trained worker hired by a local firm and pecuniary spillovers arise when the MNE pays the worker a higher wage to prevent him from moving to the local competitor. Technological spillovers do not take place if the joint profit of the MNE and the local firm is highest when the MNE can use the technology as a monopolist. Higher labor mobility and more spillovers arise when the local firm can use the technology in activities that do not compete intensely with the MNE. Additionally, the degree of product market competition affects labor mobility. A low level of ''absorptive capability'' by the local firm, which might be due to technological backwardness, reduces the prospective for FDI generating spillovers.

---

188 OECD (2000): Labour Force Statistics 1978/98, Paris: OECD. Dluhosch, Barbara (2000): Industrial Location and Economic Integration, Cheltenham and Northampton: Edward Elgar.

189 Burda, Michael C. and Barbara Dluhosch (2000): "Cost Competition, Fragmentation, and Globalization," presented at the Delphi 2000 conference "Globalization: Trade, Financial and Political Economy Aspects," Delphi, Greece May 25-27, 2000.

190 Rodriguez-Clare, A., 1996. Multinationals, linkages, and economic development. American Economic Review 86 (4), 851–873.

191 UNLTC, 1993. In: Enderwick, P. (Ed.), Transnational Corporations and Human Resources, Vol. 16. United Nations, Routledge.

192 Hagedoorn, J. and R. Narula, 2001, 'Evolutionary Understanding of Corporate Foreign Investment Behaviour: US Foreign Direct Investment in Europe', in R. Narula (ed.), International Trade and Investment in a Globalising World, New York: Pergamon.

193 Katrak, H., 2002, 'Does Economic Liberalisation Endanger Indigenous Technological Developments? An Analysis of the Indian Experience', Research Policy, Vol.31, pp.19–30.

[194] Moreover, spillovers increase with the degree of absorptive capability of host country firms. A MNE can transfer a superior technology to its foreign affiliate only after having trained a local worker. A MNE might prefer to export rather than to invest, specifically to avoid diffusion of superior technology to the local rival and/ or the payment of rents to the trained worker. [195]

Knowledge of the nature and determinants of foreign plant lifetimes is of great value to host governments and local inward investment agencies[196]. Access to spill over sources, the local incentives, the possibility of achieving substantial cost reductions, and the need to diversify and adapt goods to local tastes and needs in order to compete successfully are fundamental determinants of R&D investment. Obtaining a larger domestic share of knowledge-intensive industries means better jobs and higher wages and therefore they have a stronger impact on national welfare. The cost of R&D activity is modified by government incentives[197].

Companies producing multiple differentiated varieties have an incentive to use trade costs to reduce inter-variety competition. While FDI does move some exports, it also creates some reverse imports[198]. Culture is now seen as a market segment that can be deliberately activated when required by the managers of the macro economy as part of total demand management, and pressed into service to equalize under consumption crises in the economy[199]. On the one hand, one barrier to 'global governance' now remains, and that is local, state, and national restrictions on investment capital. On the other hand, if free trade could be joined with free investment, the objective of total globalisation would ultimately be realized: corporations would be free to move their plants around anywhere in the world, hire the lowest wage labor under conditions most favourable to profit-making and sell their products global. Companies choose to implement projects in more culturally similar states over analogous projects in more distant ones. Cultural distance deters companies from high-commitment entrance all the way through an acquisition and channels them to low-

---

[194] Borensztein, E., De Gregorio, J., Lee, J.W., 1998. How does foreign direct investment affect economic growth? Journal of International Economics 45, 115–135. Horstmann, I.J., Markusen, J.R., 1996. Exploring new markets: direct investment, contractual relations and the multinational enterprise. International Economic Review 37 (1), 1–19. Rodriguez-Clare, A., 1996. Multinationals, linkages, and economic development. American Economic Review 86 (4), 851–873. Siotis, G., 1999. Foreign direct investment strategies and firms' capabilities. Journal of Economics and Management Strategy 8, 251–270.

[195] Acemoglu, D., Pischke, J.S., 1998. Why do firms train? Theory and evidence. Quarterly Journal of Economics 113, 79–119. Blomstrom, M., Kokko, A., 1998. Multinational corporations and spillovers. Journal of Economic Surveys 12 (3), 247–278. Ethier, W.J., Markusen, J.R., 1996. Multinational firms, technology diffusion and trade. Journal of International Economics 41, 1–28. Fosfuri, A., Motta, M., 1999. Multinationals without advantages. Scandinavian Journal of Economics 101 (4), 617–630. Fosfuri, A., Motta, M., Rønde, T., 1998. Foreign direct investments and spillovers through workers' mobility. Universitat Pompeu Fabra, Working Paper No. 248, available on the Internet at http: / / www.econ.upf.es/ cgi-bin / allpapers.

[196] Patrick McCloughan , Ian Stone, Life duration of foreign multinational subsidiaries: Evidence from UK northern manufacturing industry 1970–93, International Journal of Industrial Organization 16 (1998) 719–747

[197] Miller, R.: Global R&D Networks and Large-scale Innovations: The Case of the Automobile Industry, Research Policy 23, 27–46 (1994).

[198] Richard E. Baldwin , Gianmarco I.P. Ottaviano, Multiproduct multinationals and reciprocal FDI dumping, Journal of International Economics 54 (2001) 429–448.

[199] Roby Rajan, Economy and the remembered future, Futures 34 (2002) 47–61

commitment entrance in a greenfield investment or joint venture[200]. On the other hand companies tie together their superior organizational and technological capacities to take advantage of resources or unexploited markets abroad. Moreover, MNEs distinguish and utilize synergies between various types of social capital found in different cultures. Institutional barriers between states produce segmentation gains for companies that use foreign financial markets. Companies in the opening state of foreign expansion keenly choose near and comparable markets. According to Jordan I. Siegel, Amir N. Licht, and Shalom H. Schwartz[201] "cultural distance may also support FDI flows between countries, such that foreignness may in certain circumstances be an asset rather than a liability. Specifically, greater squared distance on harmony is associated positively with the size of FDI flows". Likely profits from foreign entrance have to be drastically higher to rationalize entrance and MNEs enter states lower on impartiality than their home countries, even though the negative effect of squared impartiality distance is more forceful.

In sum, MNEs research activities in foreign centres can be either based in comparable fields to their domestic research, or become more focused in their fields of technological development, according to locally specific knowledge in the host country. The capacity of MNEs to build up integrated technological networks, to coordinate geographically diversified activities, has become an important direction of research in international business. As mentioned above, Horizontal MNEs produce the same product or service with similar factor intensities in various locations. In vertical MNEs the production process is divided into different production stages where the stages use factors of production in dissimilar proportions. The driving force behind the emergence of vertical MNEs is an endeavour to exploit factor price differences across countries. A typical feature of MNEs is that their parents are often companies that make intensive use of knowledge capital. Knowledge capital can be the human capital of the employees, patents, procedures and other proprietary knowledge or marketing assets such as trademarks and reputation[202]. Horizontal MNEs may exist if there are plant-level scale economies in combination with some sort of trade cost. Otherwise production would be concentrated to one single plant serving other locations with exports. Production transfer within horizontal MNEs implies no influence on skill upgrading in the parent firms. Besides, vertical MNEs are encouraged by lower trade costs, but also production transfer within vertical MNEs generates skill improvement in the parent firms in skilled-labor abundant home countries[203]. Increasing labour productivity through downsizing would tend to draw attention to distributive conflict between capital and labour, and trade conflict among nations, specifically because its focus is on market share and the external market, rather than on the internal market[204].

---

[200] Datta DK, Herrmann P, Rasheed A. 2002. Choice of foreign market entry modes: critical review and future directions. In *Advances in International Management*. Hitt MA, Cheng J (eds) JAI Press: Greenwitch, CT; 85-153.

[201] Jordan I. Siegel, Amir N. Licht, and Shalom H. Schwartz, Egalitarianism, Cultural Distance, and FDI: A New Approach, 2006 www.ssrn.com p33.

[202] Slaughter, M, (2000), Production Transfer Within Multinational Enterprises and American Wages. Journal of International Economics, 50, 449-472. Wood, A. (1998), Globalization and the Rise in Labor Market Inequalities. The Economic Journal, 108, 1463-1482.

[203] Blomström, M. (2000), Internationalization and Growth. Evidence From Sweden. Swedish Economic Policy Review, 7, 185-201. Braconier, H. & Ekholm, K. (2000), Swedish Multinationals and Competition from High- and Low-Wage Locations. Review of International Economics, 8, 448-461.

[204] Krugman, P. (1996). Pop Internationalism. Cambridge, MA: MIT Press.

The effect of higher agency costs of debt for MNEs, as a result of international capital and labor market imperfections, complexity of international operations and higher proportions of intangible assets, exceeds the benefits of international diversification and leads to lower debt ratios for MNEs. The consequence of agency costs and international environmental factors such as foreign exchange risk and political risk on the debt policy of an MNE could vary with its diversification strategy. The combination of international and product diversification decreases the operating risk of MNEs. Moreover, the combination of international and product diversification enables MNEs to achieve higher levels of profitability than those of MNEs pursuing a single diversification strategy[205]. According[206] to Imed Eddine Chkir and Jean-Claude Cosset "the effect of agency costs and default risk on the debt ratio of MNEs varies with the diversification regime".

5.6 Information Technology and FDI

The introduction of new information and communication technology (ICT) in the global economy parallels widening and ever increasing asymmetries among countries and even regions within countries. ICT as capital and skilled labour intensive technology brings a radical shift in the production functions of a large array of goods. Moreover, ICT is the result of a bundle of both product and process innovations that apply to a wide variety of activities and mirror the characteristics of the innovating countries and put emphasis on their structural characteristics. Hence, ICT is the result of a sequential stream of introduction of new complementary technologies aligned along a technological path shaped by comparable characteristics in terms of the prevailing output elasticity of production factors[207].

The process of technological convergence that is taking place in the ICT sectors and a key element in the firms' strategies is to endorse the prevailed technology in order to be the window through which the consumers access the market. Securing access to the market can be a way of protecting the distribution of content. The economic impact of an innovation depends on its diffusion- the process of its market adoption favoured by the improvement of the product itself and the manufacture of a set of complementary products, which may originate bandwagon effects and accelerate the diffusion process[208].

Which are the direction of the new technologies introduced and the structural characteristics of the economic systems into which the new technologies are being introduced? What the key role of technological change in assessing the effects in terms of total factor productivity growth? ICT is a superior technology worldwide in a great array of products and factors markets and to the extent to which this new technology is superior and its consequences in terms of productivity growth vary across regions according to their endowments and relative prices. When a new technology is biased, in that it favors the more intensive use of a production factor, the effects in terms of productivity growth will be

---

205 Allen, Linda, Pantzalis, Christos, 1996. Valuation of the flexibility of multinational corporations. Journal of International Business Studies 27(4), 633–653.

206 Imed Eddine Chkir, Jean-Claude Cosset, Diversification strategy and capital structure of multinational corporations, Journal of Multinational Financial Management11 (2001) 17–37, p35.

207 Antonelli, C., 2001. The Microeconomics of Technological Systems. Oxford University Press, Oxford.

208 C. Bore's , C. Saurina , R. Torres, Technological convergence: a strategic perspective, Technovation 23 (2003) 1–13

stronger. The applications of ICT stimulate a systematic growth of total factor productivity and reduction in costs with respect to a great variety of regions and products. Reductions in the costs of the most productive factor have direct effects in terms of a reduction of the production costs, even if are not accounted by total factor productivity measures, have powerful effects upon the competitive advantage on global markets of rival firms based in heterogeneous factors markets. The cost of relative prices of production factors upon the distribution of the actual levels of total factor productivity effects of a given and single new technology, with a wide spectrum of application, is in accordance with its bias. The strong effects of ICT in terms of profitability of adoption and rates of increase of total factor productivity are far from homogenous across countries. Moreover, the increase of total factor productivity differs thoroughly across countries, according to their idiosyncratic characteristics and the specificity of their endowments, with respect to the characteristics of the innovating countries[209]. When a new biased technology is introduced in diverse economic systems with a variety of local factors markets, the effects, in terms of total factor productivity growth, are influenced by the local structure of relative prices. In the international economy the real changes in the general efficiency of agents, in terms of average production costs, depend on both the increase in total factor productivity, brought about by new technologies in terms of bias and shift effects, and upon the changes in production costs brought about by the changes in the structure of the relative prices. In fact ICT has high levels of fungibility as it consists of both product and process innovations where many product innovations in upstream markets stimulate process innovations in downstream industries. In other words, the taking up of a new technological system makes likely a key increase in total factor productivity levels. Companies which are working in different factors markets and in dissimilar products markets can take advantage of ICT[210] engendering major asymmetries and escalating variance in the economic performances of trading partners in the global economy. Hence, the foreword of ICT has momentous effects in terms of a quick reduction of technological variety affecting the source of comparative advantages of countries where most productive inputs are more expensive at least in relative terms engendering new relevant asymmetries among them, not only with respect to the pace of diffusion, but also and principally in terms of the competence of each country to extract appropriate economic benefits from their necessary adoption. Systematic applications of ICT to check and execute market transactions minimize search and comparison costs and increase the scope for the absolute and comparative quality assessment of the products available in the market place. Moreover, transaction costs decline and production processes can be enhanced. The developments of electronic markets makes probable to execute multilateral exchanges with major effects in terms of the number of players in the market place both on the demand and the supply side.

The introduction of ICT is characterized by higher levels of vertical division of labor and specialization with the use of highly qualified knowledge intensive business services relevant

---

[209] Freeman, C., Louca, F., 2001. As Time Goes By: From Industrial Revolution to Information Revolution. Oxford University Press, Oxford.

[210] Jorgenson, D.W., Stiroh, K.J., 2000. Raising the speed limit: U.S. economic growth in the information age. Brookings Papers on Economic Activity 1, 125–211. Ruttan, V.W., 2001. Technology Growth and Development. An Induced Innovation Perspective. Oxford University Press, Oxford. Schreyer, P., 2001. Information and communication technology and the measurement of volume output and final demand. Economics of Innovation and New Technology 10, 339–376.

in the new service industries where skilled labor intensity is very high and exhibits well defined features in terms of formal training and academic background. The new knowledge-intensive-business service industries are global in character with a direct access to international markets characterized by the pervasive use of advanced communications and information processing services as key intermediary inputs[211]. The interaction between technological complementarities and technological convergences and the strategies of companies, exposed both to constant cross-entry from nearby markets and adjacent technologies, has provided significant insight both on the understanding of the generation of the new technological system and to rapid and systemic technological changes characterized by high levels of interdependence in the production and use of new products and processes[212]. Moreover, the introduction of the new technology parallels an increased segmentation in the labor markets with higher demand levels for skilled labor and a rapid shift away from unskilled labor coincided with an increased variance in wage levels. Wages for skilled labor have increased far above the average rates on increase in wage levels and reductions in wages for unskilled labor have been noticed. There is a fall in the demand for labor with low levels of formal training and the steep increase in the demand for labor with high levels of formal skills. The skill-biased-technological-change is not exogenous, but the intentional result of the introduction of innovations, which make use of the most abundant local factor and the skill bias takes place because the new technology requires high levels of formal learning based upon academic training. The introduction of ICT acts as an authoritative factor towards increased segmentation and asymmetries of the labor markets within the economy of advanced countries, well ahead in the process of introduction and adoption[213]. Additionally, ICT requires specific innovations that consist in the elaboration of specific applications and in the usage of new intermediary inputs and of course new capital goods. The digital divide is rising with growing effects in terms of total factor productivity differentials and average production costs and so diminishing opportunities for expansion in the global economy and recombination of external and domestic technological knowledge in order to apply the general knowledge available to the local structure of endowments and the consequent introduction of contingent technologies is stronger and stronger[214]. Countries differ extensively in terms of their ability to take advantage of the new general purpose' technology and the integration of the economics of innovation and the economics of technical change play an essential role to recognize the systemic characteristics of the new technology in the global economy.

The introduction of a new pervasive technology, able to activate a widespread convergence of dissimilar technologies towards a single dominant design is at the same time the cause of a general opportunity for development in the global economy and yet the cause of widening gaps and asymmetries across countries and the circulation of such a pervasive and superior technology in fact reduces the technological variety upon which the competitive position of countries with different economic structures and relative factors prices could rest.

---

[211] Abbate, J., 1999. Inventing the Internet. MIT Press, Cambridge.

[212] Shapiro, C., Varian, H., 1999. Information Rules. Harvard Business School Press, Boston.

[213] Quah, D., 2001. The weightless economy in economic development. In: Pohjola, M. (Ed.), Information Technology Productivity, and Economic Growth: International Evidence and Implications for Economic Development. Oxford University Press, Oxford. Ruttan, V.W., 2001. Technology Growth and Development. An Induced Innovation Perspective. Oxford University Press, Oxford.

[214] Mansell, R., 2001. Digital opportunities and the missing link for developing countries. Oxford Review of Economic Policy 17, 282–295.

The introduction of ICT is the result of thorough new generic knowledge and information and the in depth understanding of the idiosyncratic features of the local production process so as to specify the preeminent applications of the new external knowledge to the characteristics of the production process resulting the generation of new innovations and the adoption of new capital goods and intermediary production factors that include a drastic reorganization of the vertical division of labour within companies and across industries. The vertical disintegration of large manufacturing corporations and the change towards a digital economy are corresponding aspects of the generalized introduction of ICT in the economic system. High levels of fungibility of ICT are key input to a technology strategy at a company level and a technology policy at a country level. According to Cristiano Antonelli [215]"the complexity of the new system and the tight fabric of requirements in terms of complementarity, interoperability and interdependence among the different technological components, changes in the structure of the technological system are difficult and can take place only in a long stretch of time. As such the introduction of incremental and biased technological changes in following countries in order to increase the local fitness to the domestic endowments of production factors, seems most difficult".

Although it is a realistic assumption that MNEs have superior firm-specific assets, the assets they transfer to specific host countries are not always those that the latter seek or are able to take on board.

MNE competitive advantages derive first from technology knowledge, capabilities or machinery and equipment, secondly superior intra-firm hierarchies within and across national borders and thirdly is multinationality itself. MNEs gain from their superior knowledge of markets and internal governance of transactions and accordingly MNEs may have analogous technologies to national counterparts but still they out compete them.

Absorptive capacity is significant for development for the reason that it allows national actors to confine knowledge that exists in a different place. Where absorptive capacity is lacking in national companies, they may, instead of reaping technological benefits from FDI, be 'crowded out[216]'. Capabilities in the host country context matter for the magnitude and intensity of technological upgrading and accordingly FDI in activities that correspond to the comparative advantage of the host country provides superior linkages. Wider technology gaps between national and foreign-owned activities tend to lead to less backward linkages and to lower technological substance in the inputs sourced locally.

A minimum level of scientific and technical knowledge is required to use innovation because below this level, the cost of adoption can be unaffordable and subsequently there is a need for a minimum threshold of absorptive capacity is indispensable for FDI to have a say to higher productivity growth[217].

The successful use of information technology (IT) develops a company's performance and competitive position but any performance advantage granted by IT is short lived because

---

215 Cristiano Antonelli, The digital divide: understanding the economics of new information and communication technology in the global economy, Information Economics and Policy 1 (2002) at 24. www.elsevier.com/ locate / econbase.

216 Agosin, M. and R. Mayer, 2000, 'Foreign Investment in Developing Countries: Does it Crowd in Domestic Investment?', UNCTAD Discussion Papers No. 146.

217 Narula, R., 2003, Globalisation and Technology, Cambridge: Polity Press. Narula, R., 2004, 'Understanding Absorptive Capacities in an Innovation Systems Context: Consequences for Economic and Employment Growth', MERIT Research Memorandum 2004-003.

computer-based information systems (IS) are with no trouble replicated[218]. Competitors will try to neutralize the competitive advantage of the successful users by copying and possibly improving the IT used.[219] According to Sambamurthy[220] "Overall there is a growing realization that firms can sustain strategic IT innovation and differentiate business success only by developing superior capabilities for enterprise IT management and use". Generic lead-time affecting how long a firm has before competitors can respond with a similar application, competitive asymmetry referring to competitors' ability to replicate the IT application, and pre-emption potential referring to the ability of first movers to effectively pre-empt retaliation by followers are the primary factors that contribute to sustaining an IT-enabled competitive advantage[221]. Capabilities, a unique type of organizationally embedded, non-transferable, firm-specific resource, mirror a company's ability to merge resources that the organization can muster in ways that promote superior performance in spite of the opposition stemming from the competition and circumstances improving the productivity of the other resources possessed by the company.[222]An IT enabled strategy is a corporate strategy that uses IT at its core to maintain and permit major economic activities performed by the company gaining a competitive advantage over their direct competitors[223]. Sustainability is attributed to certain IT resources and capabilities that are difficult to imitate gaining a sustained competitive advantage through barriers to entry, switching costs, and mobility barriers, including managerial IT skills-management's ability to conceive, develop, and exploit IT applications, technical IT skills-skills referring to the expertise needed to build and use IT applications, and IT infrastructure-a complex combination of technology and personnel. Flourishing development of IS applications requires teams rather than individuals and building IT teams that will be receptive to new technology is a long-term investment; teams are less mobile than individuals, and team-embodied knowledge decays at a slower rate as it passes to new generations of team members. According[224] to Bruce Dehning and Theophanis Stratopoulos "successful users of IT whose accomplishments are widely recognized by their peers do indeed have a shorter duration of competitive advantage."

---

[218] Stratopoulos, T., Dehning, B., 2000. Does successful investment in information technology solve the productivity paradox? Information and Management 38 (2), 103–117.

[219] Bharadwaj, A., 2000. A resource-based perspective on information technology capability and firm performance: an empirical investigation. MIS Quarterly 24 (1), 169–196.

[220] Sambamurthy, V., 2000. Business strategy in hypercompetitive environments: rethinking the logic of IT differentiation. In: Zmud, R.W., (Ed.), Framing the Domains of IT Management, Pinnaflex Educational Resources, Cincinnati, OH, pp. 245–261, p246.

[221] Feeny, D., Ives, B., 1990. In search of sustainability: reaping long-term advantage from investment in information technology. Journal of Management Information Systems 7 (1), 27–46.

[222] Makadok, R., 2001. Toward a synthesis of the resource-based and dynamic-capability views of rent creation. Strategic Management Journal 22 (5), 387–401.

[223] Barua, A., Mukhopadhyay, T., 2000. Information technology and business performance: past, present and future. In: Zmud, R.W., (Ed.), Framing the Domains of IT Management, Pinnaflex Educational Resources, Cincinnati, OH, pp. 65–84. Barua, A., Kriebel, C., Mukhopadhyay, T., 1995. Information technology and business value: an analytical and empirical investigation. Information Systems Research 6 (1), 3–23.

[224] Bruce Dehning, Theophanis Stratopoulos, Determinants of a sustainable competitive advantage due to an IT-enabled strategy, Journal of Strategic Information Systems 12 (2003) 7–28

5.7 EU AND FDI

The European Union was set up half a century ago with the express purpose of achieving deep economic integration. The European countries have attained a level of economic integration that provides considerable static gains from trade and momentous dynamic gains from increased market competition. Moreover, the European Union is both the largest 'home' and the largest 'host' region, accounting for about 40% of global flows; the United States, with about a quarter of world FDI flows, is the largest single host nation and the largest single home nation for FDI[225]. MNEs are one of the main conduits through which investment is channelled and their evolution has reflected broader developments in OECD economies. Although large multinationals continue to dominate international investment, numerous smaller firms now play a more visible role on the international scene. MNEs are an integral part of the international economy, as agents for beneficial investment flows and for diffusion of technology and as an important source of tax revenues. Since the mid 1970s have been seen as crucial allies in achieving the goals of EU industrial policy and the Commission has adopted a flexible approach to their behaviour. The removal of tariffs and barriers to trade and investment may be expected to result in decreased horizontal integration. Companies producing substantially identical products in plants in different countries of the bloc should be stimulated to remove duplication if costs differ or economies of scale are significant and to concentrate their activities by divestment on fewer countries and plants. The opportunity that integration affords for a better international division of labour may be expected to stimulate increased vertical integration and perhaps component specialization by MNEs seeking lower costs and scale economies. It should be taken into account that MNEs firstly entered EU as replicas of their parent companies to specialize in particular products and processes for all markets in the region and to trade these products across national boundaries.[226] For instance Ford-Europe was set up specifically to integrate and co-ordinate the company's motor vehicle production on a European basis and represented the globalisation of its product and marketing strategies. European headquartered MNEs have sought to rationalize their European investment and production, often stimulated by competition from US MNEs and Japanese competition.[227] Intra-EU defensive investment can be expected to fall.

Market size and market growth have been shown to be important determinants in the attraction of FDI. Increased market size favours geographically dispersed FDI, whilst economic integration via better market accessibility is more likely to lead to intra-regional platform FDI. Third country firms will invest inside the customs union and supply the other union members by exporting from the plant located inside the union. Economic integration will lead to centralisation of FDI by third country firms inside the customs union. Furthermore, firms originating from the customs union may be induced to switch from intra-regional FDI to intra-regional exporting.[228] For instance, Svensson[229] considers that Swedish

---

225 UNCTAD, 1997. World Investment Report, UNCTAD, Geneva. Dunning, J., 1981. International Production and the Multinational Enterprise. George Allen and Unwin, London.

226 UNCTAD 1992, Transnational Corporations As Engines of Growth. UN, New York.

227 J Stoford, C Fuller "Globalisation frustrated: The case of white goods" 1991 Strategic Management Journal 473.

228 Motta, Massimo and Norman, George (1996): Does Economic Integration Cause Foreign Direct Investment?, in International Economic Review, Vol. 37, No. 4, pp.757-783. OECD (1996): International Direct Investment Statistics Yearbook 1996, (OECD: Paris).

MNEs' affiliates in the EU are more export orientated than their affiliates in other parts of the world, and that their exports to third countries have a strong effect of replacing parent exports to third countries. Increased regional integration can lead to increased intra-regional FDI flows[230]. If European integration significantly reduces trade costs, then vertical MNEs are expected to concentrate their activities further. Forces leading to more concentration of activity are economies of scale and vertical integration between parent and subsidiary. [231] Single product firms have to choose to either save on trade costs or to exploit scale economies. FDI does not fully displace exports since the overseas factory buys intermediate goods from the home-based factory and intermediate goods are responsible for the complementarity of trade and FDI (US-Japan trade and investment in cars and car parts). According to Baldwin[232] enterprises simultaneously engage in intraindustry FDI and intraindustry trade in a manner that leads to similarity in the trade and FDI patterns. FDI displaces some exports but it increases reverse imports.

Towards the end of the 1980s, Foreign Direct Investment (FDI) flows to the European Union (EU) increased dramatically[233]. Most of these FDI flows came from third countries such as the USA and Japan.[234] The geographical concentration of the activities of MNEs serves as a good indication of the presence and importance of forces leading towards agglomeration or dispersion of industrial activity. MNEs have an inherent ability to move production between different locations and need to possess three advantages, namely ownership, localisation and internalisation advantages. Ownership advantages are associated with intangible assets, firm specific knowledge, patents and trademarks, which are internationally mobile and would allow the firm to efficiently spread production abroad. Ownership advantages are captured by the idea of introducing firm-specific fixed costs that do not have to be incurred again when setting up a new plant abroad. Research & Development (R&D) expenditure is a common measure to proxy for the importance of firm specific assets.[235] According to Joseph Zeira [236]"growth rates do not rise unboundedly with the size of the economy, and also the relation between the growth rate and the size of the R&D sector is not simplistically positive."

---

[229] Svensson, Roger (1996): Effects of Overseas Production on Home Country Exports: Evidence Based on Swedish Multinationals, in Weltwirtschaftliches Archiv, Vol. 132, No. 2, pp. 304-329.

[230] Sanna-Randaccio, Francesca (1996): New Protectionism and Multinational Companies, in Journal of International Economics, Vol. 41, pp. 29-51.

[231] Aristotelous, Kyriacos and Fountas, Stilianos (1996): An Empirical Analysis of Inward Foreign Direct Investment Flows in the EU with Emphasis on the Market Enlargement Hypothesis, in Journal of Common Market Studies, Vol. 34, pp. 571-583. Brainard, Lael. S. (1997): An Empirical Assessment of the Proximity-Concentration Trade-off Between Multinational Sales and Trade, in American Economic Review, Vol. 87, No. 4, pp. 520-544. Dunning, John H. (1981): Explaining the International Direct Investment Position of Countries: Towards a Dynamic and Developmental Approach, in Weltwirtschaftliches Archiv, Vol. 117, pp. 30-64.

[232] E Baldwin, O Ottaviano, Multiproduct Multinationals and reciprocal FDI dumping, NBEr Working paper 6483 1998.

[233] Eurostat (1995): European Union Direct Investments 1984:93, (Luxemburg: Eurostat).

[234] Dunning, John H. (1997): The European Internal Market Programme and Inbound Foreign Direct Investment, Part I, in Journal of Common Market Studies, Vol. 35, No. 1, pp. 1-30. Dunning, John H. (1997): The European Internal Market Programme and Inbound Foreign Direct Investment, Part II, in Journal of Common Market Studies, Vol. 35, No. 2, pp. 189-222.

[235] Caves, Richard (1996): Multinational Enterprise and Economic Analysis; 2nd edition, (Cam-bridge: Cambridge University Press)

[236] Joseph Zeira, Innovation, Patent Races, and Endogenous Growth, November 2002, RWP02-047 p25.

As firm specific assets give rise to both ownership advantages and internalisation advantages, which is due to its joint input, public goods character, it is also possible to use this measure as a proxy for the importance of transaction costs. Segmentation of countries into nationally confined markets will result in dispersion of multinational activity. Economic integration is modelled via better market accessibility and not via an increase in market size. Market size and market growth have been shown to be important determinants in the attraction of FDI. Increased market size favours geographically dispersed FDI, whilst economic integration via better market accessibility is more likely to lead to intra-regional platform FDI. Third country firms will invest inside the customs union and supply the other union members by exporting from the plant located inside the union. Economic integration will lead to centralisation of FDI by third country firms inside the customs union. Furthermore, firms originating from the customs union may be induced to switch from intra-regional FDI to intra-regional exporting.[237] For instance, Svensson[238] considers that Swedish MNEs' affiliates in the EU are more export orientated than their affiliates in other parts of the world, and that their exports to third countries have a strong effect of replacing parent exports to third countries. Increased regional integration can lead to increased intra-regional FDI flows[239].

The centralisation at headquarters of MNEs has opened the road to financial disintermediation. Centralized cash management centres, netting cash flows and pooling cash balances have been arisen in Europe performing a series of functions related to working capital and accordingly speeding up collections, discreetly managing payments[240]. Current accounts and deposits may be managed with not as much of lending and borrowing requests, while liquidity shortages and surpluses may be limited by overprotective cash levels. According to *Wim Wester man* and *Henk von Eije*[241], "in the after math of liberalisation and deregulation of financial markets, as well as the lessening of currency volatility and the introduction of the euro, transaction and bankruptcy costs for multinationals have been reduced."

Centralisation and disintermediation cause further benefits for the reason that they strengthen corporate head quarters. Centralisation and disintermediation brings forward a mixture of advantages such as cash balances, cash flows and risk exposures turn down reducing financing costs, concentrating financing gives rise to triumphant interest rate reduction. The services of banks in transferring cash will be reduced, management becomes easier and less costly which means that treasury personnel at a choice of levels will be reduced and over all leading and lagging of intra- company cash flows will be traced and controlled more straightforwardly. Thus, it becomes probable to supervise and reconcile accounts for a large province attaining higher level of security of cash flows. On the other hand, a centralised cash management system goes along with rising regulative, administrative

---

[237] Motta, Massimo and Norman, George (1996): Does Economic Integration Cause Foreign Direct Investment?, in International Economic Review, Vol. 37, No. 4, pp.757-783. OECD (1996): International Direct Investment Statistics Yearbook 1996, (OECD: Paris).

[238] Svensson, Roger (1996): Effects of Overseas Production on Home Country Exports: Evi-dence Based on Swedish Multinationals, in Weltwirtschaftliches Archiv, Vol. 132, No. 2, pp. 304-329.

[239] Sanna-Randaccio, Francesca (1996): New Protectionism and Multinational Companies, in Journal of International Economics, Vol. 41, pp. 29-51.

[240] ECB (2002) Structural analysis of the EU banking sector: Year 2001, European Central Bank, November.

[241] Wim Wester man and Henk von Eije , Multinational Cash Management in Europe Towards Centralisation and Disintermediation: The Philips Case, Managerial Finance Volume 31 Number 10 2005, 65 at71.

and information costs demanding an exceedingly formalised and upgraded cash balance control system that may be contrary to the corporate decentralisation philosophy[242]. Internalizing and re-organising cash balances and flows may bother relationships between subsidiaries and their resident banks.

If the production costs were the same in both countries, firms would always want to locate near the larger market, thus minimising transport costs. Both economies of scale and transport costs give rise to the incentive to locate production where the relative demand is highest. It exists a tension between the proportion of labour that is mobile between locations and the transport costs that have to be incurred to reach remote customers. Larger levels of economies of scale have the effect of facilitating the sustainability of the core-periphery pattern. Therefore, the agglomeration forces are larger for industries with large economies of scale. Vertical multinationals are commonly associated with exploiting country differences in relative factor endowments, which is in stark contrast to horizontal multinationals. Multinationals arise so as to exploit differences in factor prices. Multinationals exploit these factor price differences in fragmenting production geographically.[243] Allowing multinationals to enter increases the factor price equalisation set, as demand for capital and labour are increased in the capital and labour abundant countries, respectively. If European integration significantly reduces trade costs, then vertical MNEs are expected to concentrate their activities further. Forces leading to more concentration of activity are economies of scale and vertical integration between parent and subsidiary. [244]

Horizontal multinationals tend to arise if countries are similar in relative and absolute factor endowments, and if trade costs are medium to high, while vertical multinationals arise mainly if countries are very different with respect to their relative factor endowments and if trade costs between countries are low[245]. Vertical multinationals draw part of the skilled labour requirement from the host country. Firms have to trade off the benefits of proximity to customers with the concentration of production at a single plant. Proximity to customers saves transport costs, while concentration of production allows the firm to reap the benefits of plant-level economies of scale. Thus, Horizontal multinationals cannot arise if transport costs are assumed to be negligible.[246] This is due to the fact that, by establishing a manufacturing plant abroad, the horizontal multinational has to incur fixed plant set up costs without being able to save on transport costs from doing so. If factor prices are virtually equalised, vertical multinationals cannot be supported due to the cost disadvantage of splitting headquarter

---

[242] Eije, H. von & W. Wester man (2002) "Multinational cash management and conglomerate discounts in the euro zone", International Business Review, Number 4, pp. 453- 464.

[243] Helpman, Elhanan and Krugman, Paul (1985): Market Structure and Foreign Trade: In-creasing Returns, Imperfect Competition, and the International Economy, (Cambridge Mass.: MIT Press).

[244] Aristotelous, Kyriacos and Fountas, Stilianos (1996): An Empirical Analysis of Inward Foreign Direct Investment Flows in the EU with Emphasis on the Market Enlargement Hypothesis, in Journal of Common Market Studies, Vol. 34, pp. 571-583. Brainard, Lael. S. (1997): An Empirical Assessment of the Proximity-Concentration Trade-off Between Multinational Sales and Trade, in American Economic Review, Vol. 87, No. 4, pp. 520-544. Dunning, John H. (1981): Explaining the International Direct Investment Position of Countries: Towards a Dynamic and Developmental Approach, in Weltwirtschaftliches Ar-chiv, Vol. 117, pp. 30-64.

[245] Markusen, J. R., Venables, A. J., Konan; D. E. and Zhang, K. H. (1996). A Unified Treatment of Horizontal Direct Investment, Vertical Direct Investment, and the Pattern of Trade in Goods and Services, NBER Working Paper Series, No. 5696.

[246] Ekholm, K. (1998). Proximity Advantages, Scale Economies, and the Location of Production, In (eds. Braunerhjelm, P. and Ekholm K.). The Geography of Multinational Firms, Boston: Kluwer Academic.

services and production. [247] The share of the net outward foreign production to total foreign production is positively increasing in absolute capital per capita differences, and particularly in human capital differences. Horizontal multinationals have the tendency of reducing trade volumes between countries. Investment liberalisation may lead to increases in trade flows. Increases in trade flows are especially likely if one country is small and skilled labour abundant, whilst the other country is large and unskilled labour abundant.

Investment liberalisation has the effect of relaxing constraints in both the small and large country and lead to relocation of headquarter services to the small skilled labour abundant country. Small countries have difficulties in attracting vertically integrated multinationals, as transport costs have to be incurred for a large share of finished products when shipping them back to the home country. Horizontal multinationals tend to emerge due to market proximity considerations, which have to be traded off against concentration of production. Vertical multinationals fragment production into geographically separate stages to exploit factor price, and thus relative factor endowment differences or technologies. Vertical multinationals engage in intra-firm trade, and therefore tend to emerge if transport costs are low and relative factor endowment differences are large.[248] The internationalisation of research and technology is one key constituent of the globalisation of trade and business, with potentially major impacts on patterns of economic development and public policies worldwide. The promotion of research and technology by the state is always based on premises on the behaviour of enterprises performing R&D. The attractiveness of the European Union is determined by dynamic efficiency, the ability to support learning processes in complex system innovations, and the interaction of specific institutions firms, R&D institutes, universities, and policy administration. Modern methods of networking and coordination and business approaches to international R&D management clearly show how strongly innovation processes are influenced by non-technical determinants. Extra -European collaboration and mobility and intra-European technology-related cooperation is needed in order to achieve development of R&D. According to Frieder Meyer-Krahmer [249] and Guido Reger "the integration of different policy areas and the use of indirect policy measures (e.g., competition, standards, or labor market defragmentation) towards a European innovation policy should be at the top of the policy agenda". Horizontally and vertically integrated multinationals emerge with regard to firm and plant-level economies of scale, host country market size, trade costs and relative factor endowments and factor prices.[250] Vertically integrated multinationals can compensate the cost penalty of producing below minimum scale of production, as they fragment the production process geographically, and thereby not only are able to exploit differences in relative factor endowments but also relative factor prices.

---

[247] Zhang, K. H. and Markusen, J. R. (1996): Vertical Multinationals and Host Country Characteristics, NBER Working Paper Series, No. 6203.

[248] Brainard, L. S. (1997). An Empirical Assessment of the Proximity-Concentration Trade-off Between Multinational Sales and Trade, American Economic Review, Vol. 87, No. 4, pp. 520-544.

[249] Frieder Meyer-Krahmer, Guido Reger, New perspectives on the innovation strategies of multinational enterprises: lessons for technology policy in Europe, Research Policy 28 1999 751–776, p774.

[250] Andersson, T., Fredriksson, T. and Svensson, R. (1996). Multinational Restructuring, Internationalization and Small Economies: The Swedish Case. London: Routledge. Markusen, J. R. and Venables A. J. (1998). Multinational Firms and New Trade Theory, Journal International Economics, Vol. 46, pp. 183-203.

Are trade and FDI complements rather than substitutes? While FDI does displace some exports, it also creates a number of reverse imports[251]. Multinationals must have some sort of advantage over local firms. FDI does not completely displace exports since the overseas factory buys intermediate goods from the home-based factory. For instance, intermediate goods are indeed responsible for the complementarity of trade and FDI in the case of US–Japanese trade and investment in cars and car parts[252]. Firms producing multiple differentiated varieties have an incentive to use trade costs to reduce inter-variety competition. Countries separated by low transport costs are more likely to be capable of maintaining a free trade agreement than countries separated by high transport costs[253]. The cost of transporting goods across distance is one component of the cost of delivering a product to a foreign market[254]. European companies have a high percentage of revenues being international and also have a longer history of moving managers around the world[255]. National history has affected the general order of entry into international markets and European MNEs were the first to internationalise[256]. European MNEs built up overseas subsidiaries that enjoy a large degree of autonomy[257]. Thus, European MNEs have limited ability to switch from the direction of local autonomy towards global integration. Bartlett and Ghoshal[258] state that American MNEs stress formalization of structure and process while European MNEs place greater importance on socialization.

The dismantling of barriers to the movement of goods, capital and labor within Europe led to a rapid increase in cross-border trade and higher levels of intra-European foreign direct investment that has intensified the trend toward regional integration. A growing emphasis on regionalization as the route to globalisation for many MNEs is observed and international

---

251 Baldwin, R.E., Ottaviano, G.I.P., 1998. Multiproduct multinationals and reciprocal FDI dumping, NBER Working Paper 6483, March 1998.

252 Horstmann, I., Markusen, J., 1987. Strategic investments and the development of multinationals. International Economic Review 28, 109–121.

253 Maggi, G., 1999. The role of multilateral institutions in international trade cooperation. American Economic Review 89 (1), 190–214. Markusen, J.R., 1995. The boundaries of multinational enterprises and the theory of international trade. Journal of Economic Perspectives 9 (2), 169–189. Markusen, J.R., Venables, A.J., 1998. Multinational firms and the new trade theory. Journal of International Economics 46, 183–203. Motta, M., 1992. Multinational firms and the tariff-jumping argument: a game-theoretic analysis with some unconventional conclusions. European Economic Review 36, 1557–1571.Bagwell, K., Staiger, R., 1999. An economic theory of GATT. American Economic Review 89 (1), 215–248. Lowe, J., & Taylor, P. (1998). R&D and technology purchase through licence agreements: Complementary assets. R&D Management, 28(4), 263–278.

254 Brecher, R.A., Diaz Alejandro, C., 1997. Tariffs, foreign capital and immiserizing growth. Journal of International Economics 7, 317–322. Caves, R., 1996. In: Multinational Enterprise and Economic Analysis, 2nd Edition. Cambridge University Press, New York. Smith, A., 1987. Strategic investment, multinational corporations and trade policy. European Economic Review 31, 89–96.

255 Hugh Scullion, Chris Brewster The Management of Expatriates: Messages from Europe? Journal of World Business / 36(4) / 346–365.

256 Yip, G. (1997). A borderless world: Issues and evidence. In: I. Islam & W. Sheperd, (Eds.), Current Issues in International Business. Cheltenham, UK: Edward Elgar Press. 87–107.

257 Dowling, P. J., Welch, D. E., & Schuler, R. S. (1999). International human resource management: Managing people in an international context, 3rd ed., Cincinatti, OH : South Western College Publishing, ITP.

258 Bartlett, C. A., & Ghoshal, S. (1989). Managing across borders: The transnational solution, Boston, MA: Harvard Business School Press Scullion, H., & Starkey, K. (2000). In search of the changing role of the corporate human resource function in the international firm. International Journal of Human Resource Management, 11(6): 1061–1081.

corporations more and more treat the European market as a single entity and seek to integrate production, marketing, and human resource strategies at the European regional level. The Single European Market facilitated a rapid growth in the number of large cross-border mergers and acquisitions that ever more became the most important foreign market entry strategy for many larger European companies in the late 1980s and 1990s[259].

The elimination of internal barriers to trade and capital mobility during the single market programme has been accompanied by a rapid growth in multinational activity in the European Union (EU) both by European and non-European firms, inspiring research into the policies available to national governments to affect location decisions and the potential benefits of inward investment[260]. The taking away of barriers to trade and capital mobility within the European Union has changed the locational advantages of member states and the Union as a whole. According to Ray Barrell and Nigel Pain [261]FDI has risen significantly in all the major European economies.

Europe has consistently under-performed compared to US and unless the EU improves its competitive position, it will be unable to sustain its social and political objectives[262]. The growth of the digital economy can be explained by reference to characteristics such as the rapid and cost-effective exchange of information, the expansion of markets for various types of products, the deregulation of product and labour markets, and the increased flow of financial assets around the world. Knowledge, competence, and intellectual property are the most significant elements of the digital economy and have a distinctive geography established in regional clusters of innovation, technology, and human and social capital. The essence of the digital economy, and what makes it a very real phenomenon which has deeply affected rates of labour productivity, innovation and economic growth, are the unique ways in which knowledge is created and disseminated between constituent actors, and the accompanying changes to the organization of companies, industries and regions.

Digitalization of EU's economy will be boosted by the formation of learning environments that bring together in virtual spaces the intellectual potential of European industry[263].

In the United States, the growth rate of labour productivity fell from 3.3% in 2000 to 1.9% in 2001 and labour productivity experienced by the EU in 2001 was +0.4%[264]. The growth performance of the U.S. economy has been attributed to the enhanced capital

---

[259] Bonache, J., & Brewster, C. (2001). Knowledge transfer and the management of expatriation. Thunderbird International Business Review, 43(1): 145–168. Forster, N. (2000). The myth of the international manager. International Journal of Human Resource Management, (1): 126–142.

[260] Barrell, R., Pain, N., 1997. Foreign direct investment, technological change and economic growth within Europe. Economic Journal 107, 1770-1786. Barrell, R., Pain, N., 1998. Real exchange rates, agglomerations and irreversibilities: Macroeconomic policy and FDI in EMU. Oxford Review of Economic Policy 14 (3).

[261] Ray Barrell, Nigel Pain, Domestic institutions, agglomerations and foreign direct investment in Europe, European Economic Review 43 (1999) 925-934.

[262] Teece, D. J. 2000. Managing Intellectual Capital. Oxford: Oxford University Press.

[263] Porter, M.E. 2000. Locations, clusters and Company Strategy. In The Oxford Handbook of Economic Geography edited by G.L. Clark, M.P. Feldman and M.S. Gertler. Oxford: Oxford University Press.

[264] WITSA (2002), Digital Planet, Volume 3, March. Nordhaus, W.D. (2001), Productivity growth and the new economy, NBER Working Paper, #8096. Jalava, J., and M.Pohjola (2001), Economic growth in the New Economy, UNU/WIDER, Discussion Paper 2001/5, May. Jorgenson, D.W., and K.J. Stiroh (2000), Raising the speed limit: U.S. economic growth in the information age, Brookings Papers on Economic Activity, 125-235

accumulation and the acceleration in the pace of technical change enabled by the production and diffusion of information technology. The introduction of computers must occur in parallel with wide-ranging organizational changes in the modes of production in order to propel productivity growth[265]. If the costs of adjusting to a new technology are significant, along the time interval between their introduction and their effective adoption, productivity growth will suffer an underperformance and so the productivity-enhancing effects of the ICT acceleration of the late 1990s are still to be seen in Europe[266].

The forces of economic globalisation propelling international migration not only control labour demand in receiving countries, but also adjust productive structures, consumption patterns and cultural values in societies of origin. Transnational migrant networks, operating across national borders and connecting people who live in divergent localities, generate an assortment of kinds of cross-border, trans-local flows which are now facilitated by the near-instantaneous character of communication: from the physical movement of migrants between countries of origin and destination to the movement of remittances, information, commodities and values. The globalisation of capitalism creates the surroundings for the 'transnationalisation of labour', which, at a first stage, can be observed in the structures and processes of modern-day international migration.

Globalisation increases competition among private economic agents, but also among nation states' governments induced competition among governments is the increased mobility of capital, labour, households, and consumers with governments compete more energetically for mobile factors and tax bases[267]. Will globalisation give rise to predatory competition between the governments of the European nation states? It could be said that globalisation puts significant constraints on the political leverage of European nation states. The success of European economic integration calls for a deep rethinking of the future political order in Europe. Should a European constitution restrict horizontal and vertical governmental competition? The EU needs strong horizontal and vertical governmental competition in order to achieve economic integration stimulating political innovation and entrepreneurship. It is essential to observe that the processes of innovation and competition reinforce each other: on the one hand innovation gives rise to competition, on the other hand competition drives entrepreneurial behaviour and so a political order attempting to promote innovation needs to take advantage of all possibilities to stir competition[268]. Hence, globalisation provides the European Union with the innovation incentives indispensable for regaining a leading position in the global economic and political arena.

FDI into Europe is market-seeking horizontal investment but the arrangement of FDI activities across countries varies significantly with a set of host-country policies and characteristics and manufacturing accounts for less than half of all European FDI. According to Matthew J. Slaughter[269] "different affiliates have different degrees of vertical links to their

---

[265] Solow, R.M. (1957), Technical change and the aggregate production function, Review of Economics and Statistics, August, 312-320. Solow, R.M. (1987), We'd better watch out, New York Review of Books, July 12, 36

[266] Schreyer, P. (2002), Computer price indices and international growth and productivity comparisons, The Review of Income and Wealth, 15-32

[267] Schulze, G. and H. Ursprung (1999). 'Globalization of the Economy and the Nation State.' World Economy, 22: 295-352.

[268] Vaubel, R. (1999). 'Enforcing Competition Among Governments: Theory and Application to the European Union'. Constitutional Political Economy, 10: 327-338.

[269] Matthew J. Slaughter, Host-Country Determinants of U.S. Foreign Direct Investment into Europe, p21.

U.S. parents through cross-border outsourcing and also different degrees of external orientation in terms of domestic sales versus exports. All of this suggests that government policy may play an important role in shaping the com-position of inward FDI flows, above and beyond their overall level." The creation of a global core-periphery situation is a necessary condition for the growth take-off. The recent decades of international integration have lowered the cost of trading ideas more than they have lowered the cost of trading goods and integration can be the key to southern industrialization.[270]

The EU has been slow to adapt to information and communication technologies and the fragmentation of the innovation process. Education and skills help to raise the competitiveness of enterprises and the EU's unfortunate performance in this field may be due in part to the broad mismatch of human resources to market needs. The weak productivity growth in the European Union is predominantly sensitive in the services sector. The emergence of new technologies has not led to noteworthy productivity gains, while in the USA productivity in this sector accelerated from 1.3 % in the period 1990-95 to 3.1 % in the period 1995-99, as against a growth rate of 0.1% to 0.3% in the EU. The productivity gains in the USA are largely in the wholesale and retail trade sector and the progress recorded in the EU found primarily in the telecommunications and transport sectors[271]. European SMEs need to take advantage of new economic opportunities and the GoDigital initiatives aim first of all to make optimum use at Community level of the programmes, which finance them[272].

The processes of globalization are the driving force of the newly emerging world order. Globalization" implies a never ending expansion of market economy and market based culture, science and technology driven increases in global interdependence and cooperation for the sake of new economic and cultural opportunities increasing the cross-border flows of goods, services and capital and it means an likewise increase in cross-border exchange of knowledge. Does "globalization" mean the end of politics and the end of the established nation-state and globalization has unleashed forces which undermine all known notions of territorially based loyalty and power? Does economic globalisation foster transnational systems of governance that are seen to threaten nationally based systems of democracy? While globalization was induced by the market and through technological achievements, the European integration was based and remains based on the assumption that politics shall bring nations and states together. Globalization and European integration have become parallel processes. The EUs political economy will undergo nonstop challenges because of the implications and consequences globalization. Moreover, the more the EU develops as a global economic and political actor, the more it will be confronted with the hopes and interests of developing countries who want a fair share in the overall pursuit of globalization. It could be argued that economic globalisation[273] creates problems for national democracy because

---

[270] Richard E. Baldwin Philippe Martin Gianmarco I. P. Ottaviano, Global Income Divergence, Trade, and Industrialization: The Geography of Growth Take-Offs Journal of Economic Growth, 6: 5–37 (March 2001).

[271] European competitiveness in 2002 www.europa.eu.int

[272] http://europa.eu.int/comm/enterprise/ict/policy/godigital.htm

[273] Laxer, Gordon 1995. 'Social Solidarity, Democracy and Global Capitalism' Canadian Review of Sociology and Anthropology 32(3): 287-313. Laxer defines globalisation as: "the norms, institutions, and laws that supports global capital accumulation along neo-liberal principles." Clarkson, Steven 1999. 'The Global-Continental-National Dynamic: Some Hypotheses on Comparative Continentalism' in Stuart Nagel ed. Global Public Policy: Among and Within Nations. New York: St Martin's Press. "Under globalism, states are: oriented less to internal demands, focused on maximizing exports, freeing

decisions are more and more made in contexts well beyond national control, and the range of policy options available to national decision-makers is significantly narrowed having companies evade national jurisdictional control and taxation, transnational networks, committees, special agencies, and other bodies make decisions and regulations with profound consequences for social interests - beyond popular control and sanction which means that global private regimes ever more create law without any legal and political authorization. Hence, the core elements of liberal *government* as sovereignty is disjointed and as critical conditions for competent governance are no longer subject to national control. States[274] are more and more have supplanted by networks and other arrangements associated with transnational governance. Does globalism challenge democratic assumptions about the sovereignty of states and national citizenry? E-government has the prospective to transform profoundly people's perceptions of civil and political interactions with their governments. Unlike e-commerce, e-government services must be accessible to all. So, e-government provides communication, transaction and integration of administrative services.

the flow of capital and enshrining transnational corporate rights as 'national treatment', and locked into neo-liberal principles ... by international agreements and institutions".

274 Weber, [1948] 1991. Essays in Sociology1991: 78 The state is "a human community that (successfully) claims the monopoly of the legitimate use of physical force within a given territory".

Chapter 6

GLOBALIZATION, MNE AND FINANCE

6.1 GLOBALISATION

Globalization is the phenomenon of improved integration of the world economy as evidenced by the growth of international trade and factor mobility. In countries such as US, Japan and European Union there are locational changes in production owed to changes in comparative advantage as a result of factor changes due to induced accumulation, plus economies of scale. Chemical and metallurgical, whose manufacture is characterized by the need for large plants to enjoy economies of scale, access to raw materials and efficient transport facilities are moved into new locations. Unskilled labor is bound to be the losing party when international trade is on the rise, and production is relocated abroad to cheaper sources of supply for labor and intermediates. The nation state is affected in various ways by the increased power of markets. There is a need for not excessive reliance on debt finance and bank intermediation but trying to offer similar opportunities for equity financing and so achieving a better balance between debt and equity and improving risk-sharing and reducing the impact of financial crises[1].

Globalization is characterized by the increase of MNEs, by an increased role for international financial institutions, and by explosion of multilateral agreements and arrangements[2]. Despite the fact that international financial institutions and MNEs are the engines of economic globalization, powerful states remain the vital drivers. State decisions dictate economic policies in weaker countries providing their MNEs with momentous financial and political backing that permit MNEs to organize resources and markets in countries in which they function or where their goods are sold. Home states have to employ due diligence in regulating the activities of MNEs where the home state exercises influential control over the capacity of MNEs to function in an unregulated manner abroad. It is argued that there is a decline of the nation State accompanied by the rise of MNEs as powerful

---

[1] Sassen, S., 1998. Globalization and its Discontents, New York: The New Press. Sidelsky, R., 2001. "The World on a String", The New York Review of Books, Vol.XLVIII, No.4, March 8.Simon Teitel "Globalization and its Disconnects",2001, ICER working paper, Turin.

[2] Beth Lyon, *Discourse in Development: A Post-Colonial "Agenda" for the United Nations Committee on Economic, Social and Cultural Rights*, 10 AM. U.J. GENDER SOC. POL'Y & L. 535, 556 (2002).

actors[3]. This author thinks that state power is not declined but it has taken another form over economic development in globalisation and MNEs play the game on behalf of powerful governments of states controlled by unknown networks. MNEs have a colossal influence on the production, trade, processing, marketing, and retailing of food determining the types of food produced, the technologies related with that production, and the prices at which such resources are offered. Additionally, MNEs shift the focus away from meeting the desires and requests of the local people towards profit-maximization. On the other hand, people can force by their preference which has to be formulated according to their healthy diet and not the MNEs marketing campaign to produce the goods necessary for the good health of people and the protection of the environment which means that people cannot move their own fault for MNEs' bad behaviour to MNEs management. As mentioned earlier, international legal accountability for MNEs remains fictional but legal regulation of domestic corporate activity is becoming usual and laws do not apply to the extraterritorial operations of MNEs[4]. MNEs have to respect economic, social and cultural rights, including "the rights to development, adequate food and drinking water,"[5] and to "refrain from actions which obstruct or impede the realization of those rights[6]" but the nonbinding of Norms is an essential problem.

Travel and communication, finance and trade, sporting competitions, the professions, insurance, and even popular music, are no longer confined by the domestic frontiers of any single country: rather, they operate on a multinational or transnational scale. So globalisation, as a process, is by now a historical fact, which enriches the interactions of people in a lot of different countries: they meet, swap goods and ideas and borrow or buy resources. Many of the functions traditionally performed by governments are being disaggregated and privatised. The Westphalian view was simple: each country was separated from its neighbours by frontiers: interaction took place at or across the frontiers. On a post-Westphalian view, there are no such separations: interactions take place within different "trans-national" networks.

Three primary factors have affected the process of economic globalisation and are likely to continue driving it in the future. First, improvements in the technology of transportation and communication have reduced the costs of transporting goods, services, and factors of production and of communicating cost-effectively useful knowledge and technology. Second, the tastes of individuals and societies have generally, but not universally, favoured taking advantage of the opportunities provided by declining costs of transportation and communication through increasing economic integration. Third, public policies have significantly influenced the character and pace of economic integration, although not always in the direction of increasing economic integration. Characterised by foreign direct investment and transnational production, industrial globalisation integrates the world by the ascending cross-border multi-national industrial operations, which have made the self-

---

[3] Menno T. Kamminga, Holding Multinational Corporations Accountable for Human Rights Abuses: A Challenge for the EC, in The EU and Human Rights 553 (Philip Alston ed., 1999).

[4] David Kinley, *Human Rights as Legally Binding or Merely Relevant? in* Commercial Law And Human Rights 25 (Stephen Bottomley & David Kinley eds., 2002) (legal regulation of corporate activity affecting human rights can be found in areas such as criminal law, and in antidiscrimination, health, work safety, environmental protection, and labor rights laws).

[5] Norms on the Responsibilities of Transnational Corporations and Other Business Enterprises with Regard to Human Rights, U.N. Subcomm'n on the Promotion and Protection of Hum. Rts., 55th Sess., U.N. Doc. E/CN.4/Sub.2/2003/12/Rev. 2 (26 Aug. 2003). ¶ 1.

[6] *Id.*, ¶ 12.

contained and self-sufficient mode of production obsolete[7]. Regional co-operation and international division of production have been taking hold in the world economy and so new linkages between sectors and regions are being created and industrial production and decision-making are increasingly becoming global in scope. Industrial globalisation is a process linked by interconnected cross-border production, and it enables companies to enter into new markets, to capitalise on technological and organisational advantages, and to reduce costs. New patterns of industrial linkages such as relocating plants to foreign countries and cross-border subcontracting are replacing a production process that was customarily organised within the national boundary. The total global flow of foreign direct investment captured by developing countries increased from 18 per cent in the 1980s to 36 percent in 1996[8].

Have MNEs become too big and are supplanting government authority through the process of globalisation? It could be said that non-governmental organizations, environmental groups, consumer groups and trade unions consider that MNEs have somehow become too big and are supplanting government authority through the process of globalisation. On the other hand, multinationals circumvent ineffective and inefficient governments in providing essential services to the communities in which they function, including education and health care. Are MNEs, by their global reach, eluding national regulatory controls and influence? Does globalisation result in lower environmental and labor standards? Non-governmental organizations, environmental groups, consumer groups, trade unions and their supporters argue that MNEs, by their global reach, are eluding national regulatory controls and influence and assert the right to impose restrictions on corporate actions, as well as a right to monitor and judge corporate behaviour. It is a fact that MNEs have helped raise living standards around the world and have acted as engines of development and growth through the economic activity they generate, their transfer of technology and skills, and improved labor, health, safety and environmental conditions. MNEs can apply higher environmental and labor standards than those required by the host government or followed by local companies. Corporate responsibility initiatives may be used to communicate a company's involvement with the communities in which it operates, in which case local or national frameworks may be best suited.

Globalisation refers primarily to the progressive elimination of barriers to trade and investment and unprecedented international mobility of capital. P Hirst and G Thompson[9] identify that globalisation is "large and growing flows of trade and capital investment between countries". Globalisation also refers to the rapidly improved communications systems (information and transportation), which have served to reduce distances between different countries and regions, bringing not only a greater exchange of goods and services but also more exchanges between people and information from different countries. A fundamental part of the economic globalisation agenda has been the establishment of regional trading blocs. These include the European Union, the North American Free Trade Agreement (NAFTA), the ASEAN Free Trade Area (AFTA), the Commonwealth of Independent States (CIS), MERCOSUR, the Andean Pact, the Caribbean Common Market (CARICOM), the

---

[7] OECD (1992).Globalisation of industrial activities four case studies: Auto parts, chemicals, construction and semiconductors .Paris : OECD.

[8] Lo, F.-C.,& Marcotullio, P.J.(2000).Globalisation and urban transformations in the Asia-Pacific region: A review. Urban Studies ,37 (1),77 –111.

[9] P Hirst, G Thompson "Globalisation:Ten frequently asked questions" 1996 Soroundings Vol 4, 47-66, p48.

Central American Common Market (CACM), the Gulf Cooperation Council (GCC) and the Asia Pacific Economic Cooperation (APEC). The establishment of the World Trade Organization brought sustainability on the global market economy and its rules. Globalisation however has done little to reduce the gap that exists between rich and poor countries, or between the wealthy and the poor within countries. Moreover, globalisation is radically altering the role of the nation state. The economic choices that *all* governments can make regarding their own level of involvement in the economy and their own monetary and fiscal policies are limited by international factors over which they have no control. This author considers that countries not only can have a say in the process of globalisation and shape its form but also the process itself is based on international principles that have been formed during the development of capitalism taking into consideration the needs and principles of economic development. Economic decisions about investment, intellectual property, technical standards and new social programs are substantially moving from individual governments to supranational public bureaucracies and large private enterprises. NGOs are part of the globalisation process demanding accountability from international institutions, which are having such a profound effect on people's lives.[10]The ILO is the main international body dealing with the development of common standards for the protection of workers' rights. Economic development and human rights are some of the central concerns of the ILO.[11] The increased openness and reliance of developing countries on foreign direct investment has meant more industries being established in cities, while rural areas are left out of the development priorities. The result of rapid urbanization has been the uprooting of many villagers, disruption of the sense of community belonging, and social and environmental degradation. The lack of basic infrastructure leads to precarious working conditions and inadequate inspection in the newly constructed factories. MNEs seek to ensure the highest rate of return on their capital by enhancing labour productivity. In a given manufacturing sector, the cost of raw material and technology being more or less the same, MNEs or their sub-contractors will go for the lowest labour cost possible, relocating their plants according to changing wage levels. Workers are then literally forced to compete with each other. The ones accepting the lower wages and the least enjoyment of their basic rights are the ones who will keep their jobs. It could be argued that frequent relocation of important sources of employment endangers the already fragile economic viability of the less developed societies, while contributing to the rise of unemployment and precarious employment in highly industrialized ones. Furthermore, the resulting flexibility of the labour market based on weak or non-existent labour rights allows for all kinds of employment situations including the growth of the informal sector economy. The sub-contracting chain includes the extensive use of home workers, who are generally paid by piecework, not at the minimum hourly wage level. A sub-contracting factory of a transnational company will in turn sub-contract to one or many of its own workers, who in turn sub-contract in their family or community. At each

---

[10] Ian Robinson, "Globalization and Democracy," Dissent, Summer 1995Dietrich Rueschemeyer, Evelyne Huber Stephens and John D. Stephens, Capitalist Development and Democracy, Chicago, University of Chicago Press, 1992.

[11] See Martin Rudner, "APEC: The Challenges of Asia Pacific Economic Cooperation" in Modern Asian Studies, 29, 2 (1995) p. 403.Leary, Virginia A., "Lessons from the Experience of the International Labour Organisation", in ALSTON, Philip (ed.) The United Nations and Human Rights: A Critical Appraisal, Oxford, Clarendon Press, 1992Trade Unions in the Asia-Pacific Region: Characteristics,

level of the sub-contracting lies the vulnerability of the worker, isolated, with no access to labour laws and no guarantee of future work.[12]

The business of global governance is set to become one of the key international policy issues of the twenty-first century. The governance of global business is one of the most difficult action points in this agenda. Economic globalisation – the linked processes of trade and investment liberalization, sustainability and deregulation – has brought huge increases in movements of capital, goods and services. Multinationals are the vehicles for much of this globalized economic activity, and in turn, foreign direct investment by multinational corporations accounts for an increasing proportion of global economic activity. [13] Multinational enterprises have the option of taking advantage of lower environment or social standards or weak systems of governance in developing countries. It is argued that economic power brings political power and that the world is witnessing increasing power imbalances between multinationals – particularly large ones – and nations, with governance mechanisms at every level struggling to keep up[14]. The mechanisms of national policy and intergovernmental cooperation are poorly suited to governing multinationals in a way that matches the reality of transnationally coordinated economic networks. National governments are tied to domestic policy constituents and constrained by the need not to impinge on other countries' sovereignty. It could be said that since MNEs, by their very nature, are able to coordinate above and beyond the boundaries of territorial sovereignty, an internationally coordinated approach may be the most appropriate way to ensure that regulation, whether 'soft' or 'hard', is capable of providing an effective normative framework for multinational corporate activity.[15] Codes of conduct may themselves be understood as an evolutionary step along the way to legally binding standards that carry the support of a responsible majority while ensuring censure and accountability of wrongdoing companies. Furthermore, globalisation, a fundamental process of change that is transforming the world economy, widening and intensifying international linkages in trade and finance. It is being driven by a near-universal push toward trade and capital market liberalization, increasing internationalisation of corporate production and distribution strategies, and technological change that is fast eroding barriers to the international tradability of goods and services and the mobility of capital.

Markets for merchandise trade are expanding, more and more services are becoming tradable, and capital is flowing in increasingly diverse ways across countries and regions in search of profitable investments. Alongside the new opportunities in trade and external finance offered by globalisation have come new challenges of economic management in an increasingly open, integrated, and competitive global economy. Globalisation is having the effect of "endogenizing" policy reform in developing countries. Greater integration into the

---

Problems and Trends of Development, ICFTU/APRO Regional Coordination Conference, Singapore, March 8 to 11, 1994,

[12] Commission on Global Governance, Our Global Neighbourhood, New York, Oxford University Press, Inc. 1995.

[13] Foreign Direct Investment and the Challenge of Development, United Nations, New York and Geneva, 1999. ECON Centre for Economic Analysis and Fridtjof Nansen Institute, Petro-states – Predatory or Developmental?, ECON-Report no. 62/2000, FNI Report no. 11/2000, October 2000.

[14] Joshua Karliner 's book, The Corporate Planet: Ecology and Politics in the Age of Globalization , Sierra Club Books, San Francisco, 1997.

[15] Phillip I. Blumberg The Multinational Challenge to Corporation Law, Oxford University Press, Oxford, 1993. *http://www.grisnet.it/filb/tribu%20eng.html.*

world economy raises the payoffs to increased competitiveness but also compounds the losses from failure to act. Additionally, global integration permits a country to seize the opportunities presented by an unsustainability external environment, notably the importation of new technology, the more efficient allocation of productive resources, and the reduced cost of capital. Thus, increased integration has a substantial impact on domestic growth and living standards. It could be argued that the increasing integration of developing countries into the global economy represents a major—perhaps the most important—opportunity for raising the welfare of both developing and industrial countries over the long term. Gains to industrial countries from increased trade integration with developing countries are potentially larger than the gains from additional integration among industrial countries, as the cost-price differences between developing and industrial countries can be more than twice as large overall as those between industrial countries. Industrial countries also stand to gain from increased financial integration with developing countries. Additionally, increased foreign direct investment allows firms in industrial countries to reap the benefits of specialization in production and distribution on a global scale. In portfolio investment, emerging markets provide an outlet offering higher returns and risk diversification for the savings of the aging populations of industrial countries.

At present, there is the beginning of an antiglobalist coalition, based on hostility to immigration, a belief in capital controls, and skepticism about global trade. Global flows threaten hope about income and wealth distribution. The mobility of labor and goods undermines the incomes of the less skilled and the under-privileged. It could be said that mobility of labor helps less developed countries and less skilled workforce. Hence, the antiglobalist coalition might be against the interests of the workers. A growing industrial working class wanted to use political power to change economic relations. International competition is a threat, as imports or immigrants may cut wages for less skilled workers. The fear of lowered wages plays into a broader coalition based on umbrella anti-globalisation resentments directed against MNEs and international financial institutions.[16]

In today's unpredictable and hyper-competitive global markets, achieving and sustaining competitive advantage necessitate not only the creation of superior customer value but also the continuous pursuit of operational effectiveness. Synergy[17] is supposed to lead to a competitive advantage as two or more units of a company share know-how or resources, coordinate strategies, and pool negotiation power. Thus, capturing cross-business synergies is an essential part of corporate strategy. As competition is growing more intense, firms look for synergies in their overall global purchasing effort across business units. Synergy initiatives

---

[16] Adam Przeworski, Democracy and Development: Political Institutions and Material Well-being in the World (Cambridge: Cambridge University Press, 2000). Charles P. Kindleberger, The World in Depression (Boston: Little Brown, 1973).

[17] Global purchasing synergies can be divided into three categories • Economies of information and learning: sharing all available purchasing knowledge on suppliers, new technologies, markets, internal users, applications, the prevention of mutually incompatible negotiating strategies, the prevention of affiliates from depriving one another of the limited available resources in times of scarcity, etc. • Economies of process: establishing a common way of working thereby showing worldwide one line of con-duct to suppliers, benchmarking procedures and results, and joint training and development • Economies of scale: pooling volumes to enforce purchasing power, reducing the number of global suppliers, standardization and synchronizing requirements.

often fall short of management's expectations and might even distract managerial attention.[18] Hayes[19] argues that a "coordinated global sourcing for competitive advantage" is a logical extension of respectively domestic and foreign sourcing. Cultural differences and local market conditions might further prevent companies from realizing global efficiencies. Can globalisation be achieved without the expansion of MNEs and their activities? Mobility of labor and capital, transfer of technology and innovation, advanced technology and evolvement of cyberspace have been achieved by the development and expansion of MNEs and their role in international trade. Application of advanced technology in production and management of MNEs led to the evolvement of e-commerce and consequently to digital economy. Does globalisation associate with progress, prosperity and peace? Globalisation necessitates the creation of a new paradigm of social and political enquiry and is associated with technological revolutions in transport, communications and the data processing deriving to centrality of manufacturing industry in a global economy deriving to a digital economy.

Have globalization promoted by the international financial institutions (IFIs) adverse consequences for the vast majority of people in third world countries? Globalization can intensify inequalities both within and between states and that it further undermines the precarious position of the poorest and most vulnerable, the vast majority of whom live in third world countries[20]. The Copenhagen Declaration on Social Development[21] reiterates that globalization "opens new opportunities for sustained economic growth and development of the world economy, particularly in developing countries." So, it could be said that globalization, whatever negative effects it may have, is nevertheless essential for development and there is need to mitigate their negative effects. Human rights should attempt to adjust the outcomes of globalization rather than determine the manner in which globalization occurs in the first place avoiding the promotion of the market to become an end in itself rather than a means of promoting human welfare and social goals.

6.2 Globalisation and Integration

The developing countries are active participants, as both agents and beneficiaries of globalisation. Alongside the new opportunities in trade and external finance offered by globalisation have come new challenges of economic management in an ever more open, integrated, and competitive global economy. There is a need to maintain the confidence of markets, both national and, increasingly, international. The pace of integration among developing countries, however, has been uneven. Commodity dependence has been a feature

---

[18] Goold, M., and Campbell, A.: Desperately Seeking Synergy. Harvard Business Review 76(5), 131–143 (1998). Quelch, J.A., and Hoff, E.J.: Customizing Global Marketing, in Transnational Management, C. Bartlett, and S. Ghoshal eds., Irwin, Chicago, IL, 1995, pp 638–649. Quelch and Hoff suggest five approaches ranging from very low to extreme centralization. These are: (1) information sharing among local executives (stimulating word-of-mouth); (2) friendly persuasion by headquarters; (3) global coordination, whereby headquarters has a structured role in both decision making and performance evaluation (often using a matrix or team approach); (4) "stamped and approved," (i.e., a properly managed approval system); and (5) directing or "doing it the headquarter's way."

[19] Hayes, H.M., Jenster, P.V., and Aaby, N.E.: Business Marketing: A Global Perspective. Irwin, Chicago, 1996, pp 88–89.

[20] Nancy Birdsall, Life is Unfair: Inequality in the World, 111 FOREIGN POl'Y 76

[21] Copenhagen Declaration on Social Development art. 14 *http://www.un.org/esa/socdev/wssdco-2.htm.*

of most of the countries that have lagged in global integration. Successful commodity exporters maintained macroeconomic stability and a climate that encouraged investment. The abolition of public sector monopolies in production and marketing produced large efficiency gains. Technology was upgraded by fostering market incentives in the private sector and by the removal of regulatory barriers, particularly to foreign firms. The strong integrators were able to increase productivity in traditional commodity sectors and considerably expand production in non-traditional commodities. Gains to industrial countries from increased trade integration with developing countries are larger than the gains from additional integration among industrial countries, as the cost-price differences between developing and developed countries can be more than twice as large overall as those between industrial countries. These gains arise from increased market size, competition, and technology spillovers. For a successful transition, much will depend on industrial country policies for mitigating the social costs of adjustment and facilitating the reallocation of resources toward activities that will be spurred by integration. According to Dani Rodrik [22]"there is inadequate appreciation of the fact that economic globalization is necessarily limited by the scope of desirable institutional diversity at the national level. Under current political configurations and economic realities, deep integration is a utopia."

Economic engagement with the rest of the world has played a key part in the U.S. economic revival. America's increasing economic interdependence with the rest of the world, known as "globalisation," has come under attack. A broad consensus appears to exist that governments should strive to improve the stability of the world economy and to advance living standards. But the consensus breaks down over how to do so. The challenge of globalisation cannot be avoided. It should be taken into consideration that meeting globalization through unilateralism or one worldism are likely both to destabilize the world economy and slow improvements in living standards at home and abroad. Instead the embracement of the opportunities that globalisation affords, ease the anxieties it generates, and reform and strengthen the international economic institutions created to promote both global economic stability and growth. Globalisation, and in particular the move by many developing and emerging economies in recent years to seek more actively to attract foreign direct investment, is raising policy makers' concern that intensifying global competition among governments to attract FDI may have undesirable effects. As barriers to international investment have fallen over the last two decades, the significance of competition for FDI has increased. Many of the governments that are most successful in attracting FDI are also among those that best meet the requirements for good governance. Furthermore, competition for FDI among sub-national governments has been "activitated" by privatisation and liberalisation of trade and investment policies. International regional-integration agreements can be a powerful policy tool both for attracting FDI and for enhancing co-operation among governments to limit the potential negative effects of policy competition. B.E. Tonn, E. Ogle[23] say that "If current globalisation trends continue unabated, globalisation may result in a future world characterized by satiated consumers whose every desire is met by a totally efficient but completely impersonal economic system. In this world, people do not depend directly upon face-to-face interaction for their economic well being". Hence, the global economy has to be

[22] Dani Rodrik, Feasible Globalizations, July 2002, RWP02-029 p24.

[23] B.E. Tonn, E. Ogle, A vision for communities in the 21st century: back to the future, Futures 34 (2002) 717–734, at 717.

more efficient than regional or local economies, because of the principle of comparative advantage and larger economic entities, the transnational corporations, will benefit from economies of scale and scope.

Globalisation today goes well beyond the economic dimensions and has spread through political, cultural, environmental and even security influences. In other words globalisation is increasing integration of the global economy through product and factor markets by way of trade, direct investment and financial flows, greatly aided by deregulation of markets and the liberalisation of trade and capital movements. Linkages with companies in other countries, probably through networks of business relationships, help small and medium-sized businesses, which are addressing international markets to overcome hurdles of market and cultural differences and the more essential the international linkages between companies, the more that strategy formation involves negotiation, agreement and exchange between business leaders from various national cultural values and traditions[24]. Successful cross-border alliances involve basic behavioural and cognitive learning, and the formation of appropriate trust, power, co-operation and social relationships on an international scale. The main ``spheres of influence" affecting business leaders' ways of thinking are their individual personalities, their core beliefs, and their early industrial experiences[25]. The increasing integration of global markets means that relations among cultures have increased and will do so gradually more in the future imposing uniformity. On the other hand it could be argued that globalisation rather enhancing cultural diversity through various manifestations of localisation, and with new technologies, video, radio, TV and predominantly the cyber-world, helping to empower minorities and maintain threatened identities. Globalisation cannot be reversed and technological change will continue to be rapid and this will stimulate further the interconnecting process of global communication and global governance. Moreover, they are not reversible other aspects of globalisation such as the global dimensions of environmental issues such as global warming. Export-led growth and the opening of domestic markets to competition have facilitated rapid growth and economic development globally. Losers at the country level include those countries with weak institutions unable to control the structural adjustment and social change that benefiting from globalisation requires. Certainly, globalisation redefines what constitutes an effective and efficient government system in an increasingly interdependent and interconnected world.

It could be said that globalisation is multidimensional, with such distinctive features as advances in new technology, in particular information and communications technology, cheaper and quicker transport, trade liberalisation, the increase in financial flows and the growth in the size and power of MNEs. Additionally, globalisation is not a homogeneous phenomenon and it should be taken into consideration that in globalisation an underground economy is proceeding apace, taking advantage of a technology initially developed for service to humanity and there is traffic of illegal drugs, terrorism, the illegal trade of small arms, missile parts, and components of weapons of mass destruction, and the laundering of money generated by these reprehensible activities. Moreover, there is a global crime economy, which cannot be broken by one state alone, or even by a group of states requiring

---

[24] Doz, Y.L. (1996), ``The evolution of cooperation in strategic alliances: initial conditions or learning processes?", Strategic Management Journal, Vol. 17, Special Summer Issue, pp. 55-83.

[25] Ghauri, P.N. and Prasad, B. (Eds) (1995), International Business Management: A Reader, Dryden Press, London.

global awareness, global commitment, and global action. In fact there is a need to strengthen the role of the United Nations and the global action of the United Nations reinforces the sovereignty of states preventing the fragmentation of states and societies enhancing economic cooperation, through the development of regionalism, and through efforts at the democratisation of the international environment[26].

6.3 The Evolvement of FDI, MNE and Globalization

The world economy has internationalised in its basic dynamics, it is dominated by uncontrollable market forces, and it has as its principal economic actors and major agents of change truly MNEs, that owe allegiance to no nation state and locate wherever in the globe market advantage dictates. The greater part of social life determined by global processes in which national economies and national borders are dissolving. Central to this perception is the notion of a rapid and recent process of economic globalisation. Are most companies nationally based and trade multinationally on the strength of a major national location of production and sales? Is there a tendency towards the growth of truly international companies? Is capital mobility producing a massive shift of investment and employment from the advanced to the developing countries? Is FDI highly concentrated among the advanced industrial economies? Are trade, investment and financial flows concentrated in the triad of Europe, Japan and North America? On the one hand, divergent interests of the great powers and the economic doctrines prevalent among their elites limit global markets. On the other hand, globalisation in its radical sense should be taken to mean the development of a new economic structure, and not just conjuctural change toward greater international trade and investment within an existing set of economic relations. In sum, the post 1960s era was one of the emergence of MNE activity on the one hand and the rapid growth of international trade on the other. It is the development of international manufacturing as the industrial revolution took hold that presents the closest precursor to the modern day MNE. The exploration and development of minerals and other raw material products attracted large amounts of FDI. Furthermore, FDI is concentrated in the advance industrial states and a small number of rapidly developing industrial economies. Free trade in combination with the management of investment offers the best prospect for promoting growth through fairer redistribution. As mentioned earlier, protectionism will do little in the long turn to promote growth in either rich or poor countries and will fail to control the consequences of flows of FDI and would enhance the tendency to trade through investment. Economies may have internationalised to a considerable degree, but wealth and output remain local and extremely unevenly distributed. There is a national sectoral trade specialization and diversity rather than a homogenisation of inter-country trade. [27]

The relationship between growth in output and growth in trade is a central one for international economies analysis. Does globalisation register a quantitative change in the extent and scope of migration rather than a feature of a potentially different socio-economic order? A world market for labour just does not exist in the same way as it does for goods and

---

26 Boutros Boutros-Ghali, Globalisation Trends: Considerations And The Role Of Theunited Nations, 1996 Journal Of International Affairs,Volume INo2.

27 Archibugi D, J Michie " The globalisation of technology" 19 Cambridge Journal Of Economics 121. Archibugi D, M Pianta " The Technological specialization of advanced countries" 1992 Kluwer.

services. Most labour markets continue to be nationally regulated and accessible only marginally to outsiders, whether legal or illegal migrants or professional manpower. Moving goods and services is easier than moving labour. Even a rapid and sustained expansion of the world economy is unlikely to significantly reduce the multiple barriers to the movement of labour. The benefits of cheap labour are unlikely to dominate all the strategies of firms for whom R&D costs or marketing costs are as significant or more so than labour costs, or those of firms for whose quality of the final product is a primary concern. Low wages alone are unlikely to be decisive in the location of production. The widespread adoption of flexibly specialized production strategies in many industrial sectors favours broadly skilled and well-educated labour. Extra- regional migration of all kinds is a small percentage of global labour movements. The supposed era of globalisation has not seen the rise of a new unregulated and internationalised market in Labour migration. The advantage of the economies of scale, the consumer needs in different countries and the right use of gained experience in global and local markets to strengthen the recourse base of the firm as a whole are the elements that lead to a successful manage of the cross border value-adding activities.[28] Governments can create asset endowment advantages such as infrastructure provision and the generation of a highly skilled labour force rather than simply rely on natural ones.[29] Small and medium MNEs are important in the case of new innovative technologies. Their technological transfer can be in labour intensive form appropriate to the circumstances of the specific economy and country. SMEs' FDI is directed towards the advanced countries. North America, Europe and Japan dominate as both the originators and the destination for international investment. In 1990s Japan remained a net exporter of FDI and the US was a net importer of FDI. There is a lack of integration in FDI flows and a grouping of the states where FDI is directed, which show a geographical and regional discreteness in the relationships between countries. Multilateral trade integration is lower than is integration in the case of FDI despite that it remains very geographically discrete in the case of investment. Protectionism is lower in the field of investment than in the field of trade. Investment is the driving force of international integration. Geographical distance is less of an inhibitor to FDI that it is to trade because transactions costs are lower with respect to the FDI. National endowment advantages in respect to FDI are less specific than they are with respect to trade. The factors for a successful FDI are more widely distributed geographically and not concentrated as in trade. There is a geographical concentration of FDI in the big three and a few other states. Moreover, there is an increase flow of FDI to developing countries such as China and the rapidly growing East Asia countries and a few in Latin America.

Asian countries have managed rapid industrialization because their authoritarian regimes have used their control of political power to promote public investment in education, housing and infrastructure. Growth and continued foreign direct investment depend on political stability. Economic modernization is bringing social dislocation, with predictions of large-scale unemployment. Rapid population growth affects both the prospects for political stability and sustained high rates of economic growth in developing countries. National integrity has been sustained by a strongly protectionist regime and strong state intervention and regulation.

---

[28] C Bartlett, S Choshal " Managing across borders-The transnational solution," 1989 Harvard Business School Press.

[29] M Porter 'Competitive advantage of nations" 1990 Macmillan.

The very high ratio countries are vulnerable since they have become almost totally dependent upon their "international competitiveness" for the prosperity of their citizens.[30]

The heavily export oriented economies can easily become trade policy hostages to countries such as the triad group. Will low wages confer a significant competitive advantage leading to a large-scale shift of output and employment from the developed to the developing world? The massive influx[31] of foreign capital opened Latin American states to violent externally generated shocks that their socio-political systems and means of economic governance were unable to master in the early 1980s. Heavy dependence on foreign loans led to subsequent high inflation and to deflationary policies imposed on local governments by the international financial system. The more open a developing country is to FDI and the more dependent its modernization is on foreign capital sources, the more likely its growth is to be driven by exogenous forces by cycles of demand in the developed world, and by fluctuations in the supply of capital and the cost of borrowing. Investment levels fluctuate with international conditions. National policies will return to solicit foreign capital and MNE investment. Moreover, the level of FDI in the developing world is tied to the economic cycle in the advanced countries with depressions in the first world stimulating a flow of capital to key developing countries.

Dominant problems of economic governance now lie in the international domain. Wealth and output remain local and extremely unevenly distributed. Can FDI be governed? The emergence of distinct regional patterns of FDI distribution is one noticeable development. The formation of EU and NAFTA are two main examples, while Ford has developed a genuine network of integrated sourcing, production and marketing exclusively in EU, it has decided to adopt a global strategy of producing a single different model in its various manufacturing environments and then selling these world-wide. There is an emergence of regionally based trading and investment blocs together with the emergence of the specific contradictory interests attaching to them. There is a development of different forms of collaborative arrangement between firms and national subsidiaries of the same firm. Ohmae[32] describes the emergence of "stateless" corporations and he argues that macroeconomic and industrial policy intervention by national governments distorts the rational process of resource allocation by corporate decisions and consumer choices on a global scale. What is the role of Cyberspace? Is the era of effective national economies and state policies over? Countries vary considerably in the effectiveness of their economies in delivering FDI advantages to MNE firms, which cannot be ignored. Advantages are not merely associated with the cost of labour. A high level of telecommunications and electronic technology, logistics and use of cyberspace will play a role in delivering FDI advantages by a country not only to MNE but also to e-MNE. Successful MNEs are those that can tap into the specific advantages offered by different countries. Moreover, firms also need national legal and commercial policy provisions to protect their investments. Strategic alliances of MNEs are creating an extremely uneven international market place, which is being duplicated in many other manufacturing and service sectors. Does the globalised economy exist and work on an oligopolistic way

---

[30] G Thompson "Comment on the crisis of cost recovery and the waste of the industrialized nation" 1995 Competition and change Vol 1 October No1.

[31] A Singh "Asian economic success and Latin American failure in 1980s" Vol 17 International Review of Applied Economics P 267-89

[32] K . Ohmae "The rise of the region state" 1993 Foreign Affairs p 78. K Ohmae "The borderless world" 1990 London Collins. K Ohmae "Putting global logic first" 1995 Harvard Business Review p 119.

rather than according to the dictates of a perfectly competitive model? MNE deploy all manner of business strategies to exclude some competing players from their networks whilst locking others firmly into them. There are still massive and important national differences in the attractiveness of locations for investment. There is a considerable difference in the effectiveness of the economies of different countries in delivering FDI advantages to MNE firms, which cannot be ignored. Furthermore, there is a difference in the performance of basic economic functions and productive tasks by various countries. The success of MNE FDI is depended on its adaptation into the particular institutionalised national environments of business and innovation into which it settles. MNE are networks of semi-autonomous units and so the strategies of successful companies must allow flexibility in accordance with the specific national environments. Is globalisation threatening biodiversity as global economic pressures beat efforts to protect the earth's tropical rainforests, wetlands, coastal regions, forests, and wilderness areas? Globalisation seems to threatening biodiversity but this should be avoided immediately[33].

Does globalisation compel countries, industries and companies to converge towards a single, most efficient or adaptive, pattern? Companies do not incline towards a supposedly universal model of economic success in order to cope with globalization. Counties and companies leverage their unique economic, political and social advantages in the global marketplace. Is globalization possible without development? Economic development is about finding feasible, tolerable, and economically workable combinations of domestic and foreign resources to promote growth. Globalization is not only the result of an intensification of long-standing trends such as increasing cross-border flows of goods, money and people, and a growing mutual awareness and interdependence among social, economic and political units in the world, but also the very context in which development has taken place during the post World War II period. Governments and countries can and do exercise choice in the global economy following their political and ideological instincts and preferences, and they try to strike a balance among competing claims and pressures. Does globalization produce homogeneity or diversity in the world? Globalisation multiplies the chances of linkage and the possibilities for exchange and actors become less bound by location finding it easier to develop their own identity. The enhanced possibilities for networking in a global world makes it easier for companies and labor unions to bypass brokers, to look around by themselves, adopting the patterns of economic action and organizational form that they find most appealing and so leading to diversity rather than homogeneity.

6.4 Globalisation and FDI

The notion of sustainable development presents a challenge for policy makers and goes beyond the traditional concerns for economic growth. Globalisation, in economic terms, can be thought of as a process in which business decisions, production processes and markets gradually come to exhibit more "global" characteristics and less " national" ones. Globalisation is characterised by structural reforms – especially trade and investment liberalisation – and increased trade and international investment flows. International trade and

[33] C. Soudien, Education in the network age: globalisation, development and the World Bank, International Journal of Educational Development 22 (2002) 439–450.

investment promote growth, alter the composition and geographical distribution of economic activities, stimulate competition and facilitate the international diffusion of technologies. Depending on the circumstances, trade and investment can have significant effects, both positive and negative, for sustainable development. Because of the long-term focus inherent to the notion of sustainability, the most important influence of investment may well be its indirect influence on environmental and social performance, both nationally and globally. The growth in international investment also means that a country's sustainable development outlook is increasingly influenced by MNEs. Not only is foreign direct investment becoming more important for developing countries in relation to GDP, it is also overshadowing other capital flows such as official development assistance (ODA) or export credits. In recent years, an increasingly large part of FDI flows have been through mergers and acquisitions (M&As). The value of cross-border M&As rose by 88% over 2004, to $716 billion, and the number of deals rose by 20%, to 6,134. A recent aspect of the current M&A boom is escalating investment by collective investment funds, primarily private equity and related funds[34]. The geographical composition of FDI has changed over time and the most remarkable long-term development being the continual growth of developing Asia as a source of FDI. MNEs from developing and transition economies have become central investors in many LDCs. A number of MNEs from developing and transition economies have risen to principal worldwide positions in industries such as automotives, chemicals, electronics, shipping, information technology services and construction. Companies reply in a straight line to international competition or opportunities by utilizing their active competitive advantages to set up affiliates abroad (*"asset exploiting")*. Other companies opt for an *"asset augmenting"* strategy in order to advance their competitiveness by exploiting their limited competitive advantages to obtain created assets such as technology, brands, distribution networks, R&D expertise that are not available in the home economy. The utilization of foreign intermediate goods in final output production gives companies entrée to new technology enhancing growth by facilitating learning about products and replication of the technologies developed in other countries.

Foreign direct investment flows from OECD countries are also more and more oriented towards the services sector. The improvement in the investment climate in the 1990s was influenced in part by the recognition of the benefits of FDI. The 1990s also witness the removal of domestic impediments through widespread regulatory reform and privatisation. The countries that adhere to the OECD Declaration on International Investment and Multinational Enterprises have also undertaken a political commitment to provide national treatment for established foreign controlled enterprises, to avoid conflicting requirements on those enterprises and to work together to improve the investment climate. Bilateral investment treaties (BITs)[35] have become an increasingly important vehicle for promoting and protecting investment flows by providing legal security to foreign investors and their investments. The privatisation movement was in large part induced by dissatisfaction with the performance of state-owned enterprises, and the increased capital investment needed to upgrade infrastructure, especially in the public utility sector. The privatisation process needs to be open and transparent and allow foreign participation in a non-discriminatory manner. Subsidies for R&D activities are meant to reap the maximum benefits associated with the activities of MNEs such as knowledge, management skills, and technological advantages.

---

[34] UNCTAD, *World Investment Report 2006*

[35] P. Muchlinski, Multinational enterprises and the law, 1995 Blackwell.

Many countries remain reluctant to undertake legal commitments to liberalisation, even where they are actively encouraging FDI. In order to maintain national control over the economy, restrictions on foreign ownership provide an important barrier to entry and prevent the market for corporate control from functioning efficiently. Restrictions include reciprocity and discretionary liberalisation. Though these barriers to FDI are being reduced, many exceptions for 'strategic sectors' exist. A lack of political and economic stability and predictability can act as a barrier to investment, as can a lack of transparency of regulations, corruption, weak protection of intellectual property rights, and arbitrary application of regulations and laws. Open markets allow resources to be used more efficiently and productively may provide countries with technology, not locally available, and by helping firms to tap into world markets increasing their sales potential and realising economies of scale. Efficiency, in turn, contributes to economic growth and rising incomes. Liberalisation can also benefit citizens in tangible ways, through lower prices and greater product diversity, and an increase in the purchasing power of their wages. Benefits associated with the inflow of FDI include an increase in the production base, the introduction of new skills and technologies and the creation of employment. MNEs are a powerful and effective means to disseminate technology from developed to developing countries, and are often the only source of new and innovative technologies that are usually not available through the market.

Many states are centralizing institutions and strengthening regulations for facilitating international transactions in financial assets. On the one hand, the state is apparently being constrained and weakened in exercising its economic and political authority. On the other hand, the nation-state is being strengthened in certain respects in so far as it suits MNEs' interests in trade, investment and finance. The current process of globalisation is shifting the balance from the internal to the external market. Do nation-states help in setting up an international regime of trade, finance and technology transfer in the name of globalisation, more in the interest of multinational corporations who are accountable at best only to the narrow sectional interest of their managers and shareholders? Is economic nationalism degenerating into mere competition among nation-states? The notion of competition applies to companies, not to nation-states and the most important objective of competition is to increase productivity. Increased productivity of one nation need not by any means imply decreased productivity of another. The rights, which the nationals of a particular territory enjoy is determined by the sovereign state according to the principle of 'self-determination of a people'. Increasing specialization in production and exchange, the growth of trade and commerce, and the spread of a commercial society, weaken many earlier social bonds and norms, while creating new commercially-oriented norms that contributes to the development of economic nationalism, that is, a process of convergence of 'norms' dominated by their economic content. The current experiences of the collapse of centrally planned economic system strengthened the faith in the market as the only viable alternative. The state depends to a large extent on the market forces in matters of international trade, investment and finance, it tries either to adapt or mould market forces to its advantage. It should be taken into consideration that the state, if it is a weak player in the international economic scene, rely more on the internal rather than on the external market. If the size of the domestic market and economic activity decline as foreign producers take over a larger share of the market, the level of consumers' welfare within the nation-state may decline due to lower employment. Since one country's export surplus is another country's import surplus in the global balance of trade, this straight away points to a source of conflict of interests among the trading nations.

Higher demand can cause output to expand with the price level comparatively stable in situations of substantial unemployment or excess capacity. The effectiveness of the price mechanism would require the assumption of full employment, or at least the implicit assumption that output is constrained by supply, and not by demand so that the effect of higher demand would be felt on higher price and not on higher output level. Moreover, the price mechanism would fail to do its job if the trade elasticities are adequately low. Economic models were constructed to demonstrate that the economic policies of the state would necessarily be ineffective in the long run to reduce unemployment below its 'natural rate'. With increased relative importance of the external compared to the internal market under globalisation, policies aimed at promoting aggregate demand through 'high wage' policies are less likely to be effective. Attracting direct foreign investments of the corporations assumes a special significance for improving the trade performance of nations.

FDI has undertaken by large MNEs located in a handful of countries into a global phenomenon. MNEs still dominate global flows in value terms, but they are increasingly only one part of an expanding universe of firms investing abroad. Many MNEs are small or medium-sized companies originating from countries which were formerly principally hosts to foreign investors, including some non-OECD countries. The expansion of international direct investment is part of a long-term trend towards increasing economic integration of the world economy. The nature of multinationality is varying, as the activities of foreign affiliates have become more integrated with the parent and with other affiliates. FDI is a means by which the world economy becomes more integrated and multinational enterprises lower the transactions costs involved in international business and assist to channel goods, services, capital, labour and technology worldwide.

Globalization has caused spatial allocation of FDI across regions. Capital incorporates technological progress and increase of physical capital generates a process of sustainable growth. Poor regions are deemed to lag behind except they succeed to raise their technology level and move thus to a higher growth level. Even regions with analogous features come out to have distinct production structures. Regions are possible to differentiate into a rich 'core' and a poor 'periphery', creating virtuous cycles for valuable regions and vicious cycles for the less profitable ones. Globalization forces outline a borderless world where the transfer of capital, goods, services and people is straightforwardly taking place, it is remarkable that some regions are more advantageous in hosting foreign operations and for that reason acquire the benefits associated with these. The increased competitiveness and desires of the investor induces national suppliers to move forwards their operations and work well in order to meet their customer's needs. Rich countries strengthen their advancement constantly, whilst poor regions deemed to lag behind except they succeed in raising their technology level and break away from the poverty 'trap' moving to a higher growth level. Free trade and factor mobility produce a growth bonus to both rich and poor countries. Factor mobility induces human capital to flow to states with higher wages. Consecutively, the inflow of human capital in a county increases its stock of knowledge, creating as a result knowledge spillovers. FDI constitutes a vibrant practice that evolves over time following economic, political and technological changes. To that extent globalization and technological developments alter without doubt the comparative advantage of countries and regions, consequently, bring an endless relocation of international production. According to Constantina Kottaridi and

Dimitrios D. Thomakos[36] "as globalization forces intensify and the flow of people, capital, knowledge etc. is becoming easier and faster, there is a possibility that production would tend to concentrate in large markets benefiting the host milieus and creating virtuous cycles." Information and competition export spillovers are differ according to whether the contact home companies have with foreign multinationals is horizontal or vertical. Export oriented foreign companies are more expected to be the source of export spillovers than host market oriented foreign affiliates. Foreign occurrence leads to information spillovers which reduces the sunk-costs of exporting for national companies. There is policy competition between governments to attract FDI because there are direct effects stemming from increases in the demand for labour, R&D expenditure, additionally to injection of supplementary capital in the host economy. The prospect for certain spillovers arises for the reason that multinationals find it not easy to protect a leakage of their firm specific asset to other companies in the host country. The failure of MNEs to shield the asset is due to labour mobility between companies, but also to buyer-supplier linkages between home and foreign companies. The enticement for foreign affiliates to distribute general technical knowledge with companies in upstream and downstream sectors with which they have business linkages have consequences on both the quantity and quality of the inputs supplied. According to Richard Kneller and Mauro Pisu[37] "the export decision of domestic firms does not seem to be affected by contacts they may have with multinational enterprises. Except for backward spillovers (which are positive and significant) we did not find any evidence of forward and horizontal spillovers. On the contrary, the decision concerning how much to export appears to be influenced by the presence of foreign multinationals in the same, upstream and downstream industries. In addition, intra-industry (i.e. horizontal) spillovers seem to depend on the export orientation of foreign firms. Both export oriented and domestic market oriented multinationals appear to generate positive and significant export spillovers, but those from former are stronger." Vertical linkages among companies are central for the phenomenon of export spillovers. Governments take on export sponsorship activities ranging from financing trade fairs, all the way through providing information about foreign markets to export credit insurance. The grounds of all initiatives are founded on the belief that exports supply certainly to economic development and productivity.

The modern MNE embodies a sizeable quantity of intra-firm transactions of both tangible and intangible nature and as a result more opportunities for transfer pricing[38]. Developing and transition economies play a more and more principal part as a source of global FDI flows. The quick industrialization in economies like China and India has led to policy-induced efforts to concentrate overseas investments on securing access to primary resources, while oil-producing states have seen their investment rank strengthened all the way through higher oil revenues and robust growth rates. Distinctive company-level competences and globalized

---

[36] Constantina Kottaridi, Dimitrios D. Thomakos, Global FDI Convergence Patterns? Evidence from International Comparisons, 2005, *www.ssrn.com*, p14.

[37] Richard Kneller and Mauro Pisu, Industrial Linkages And Export Spillovers From Fdi, Research Paper 2005/20, p22.

[38] Desai, M.A., C.F. Foley and J.R. Hines (2006). "Taxation and multinational activity: new evidence, new interpretations", *Survey of Current Business*, 88(2), pp. 16-22. Eden, L. (2005). "Went for cost, priced at cost? An economic approach to the transfer pricing of offshored business services", *Transnational Corporations*, 14(2), pp. 1-52.

aggressive postures offer MNEs extensive bargaining strength[39]. MNEs boost the development of local companies all the way through creating backward and forward linkages facilitating local companies to diminish costs by increasing the scale of production[40].

The expansion of FDI flows has been driven by several inter-related factors such as rapid technological change, trade and investment liberalisation at a national, regional and global level, privatisation, deregulation, demonopolisation and the turn in emphasis by companies away from product diversification towards a more balanced geographical distribution of production and sales. Governments try to increase their attractiveness to foreign direct investors by liberalisation and reform. The upward trend in FDI flows can be interrupted temporarily by a decline in global growth. Economic growth influences both the "supply" and "demand" for FDI. A noteworthy share of FDI among OECD countries represents acquisitions of local firms by foreign investors. FDI facilitates the international transfer of capital, technology, and goods and services because such transfers are apparently easier between the parent and its affiliates than they are among unconnected companies. FDI through M&As can bring about efficiency gains through economies of scale and scope. Technology transfers incline to be greater when the foreign affiliate faces severe competition in the local market[41]. Multinational enterprises invest abroad for market access, not in the narrow sense of avoiding tariff barriers, but rather in order to limit the distance between buyer and seller in a world where there are important information costs that rise with distance. The composition of international capital flow changed markedly in the 1990s. Portfolio inflows to emerging markets stretched from a mere trickle in 1990 to a peak of $51 billion in 1993, external finance shifted from a reliance on official flows to borrowing on private markets and the share of FDI increased from less than 20 percent of total inflows in 1985 to over half of all inflows in 1998[42]. Capital market liberalization allows for greater risk sharing for immobile factors of production and consequently reduces the risk premium associated with specialization Leslie Hull, Linda L. Tesar [43] think that "the opening of capital markets has led to increased volatility and exchange rate pressures for many developing countries. This has led to a debate over the desirability of various types of capital controls."

The recent surge in patenting in the United States was most likely explained by changes in the management of innovative activities and the growth of venture capital is one such management change. According to Samuel Kortum and Josh Lerner[44] while the ratio of venture capital to R&D averaged less than 3% from 1983–1992 venture capital may have accounted for 8% of industrial innovations in that period. The past two decades, FDI grew

---

[39] Robert Pearce, Globalization and development: an international business strategy approach, *Transnational Corporations,* Vol. 15, No. 1 (April 2006) p39.

[40] Frances Ruane and Ali ugur, Export platform FDI and dualistic development, *Transnational Corporations,* Vol. 15, No. 1 (April 2006) p75.

[41] Foreign Direct Investment and Economic Development: Lessons from Six Emerging Economies, OECD, Paris, 1998.

[42] Aizenman, Joshua, (1999), "Çapital Controls and Financial Crisis," NBER Working Paper #7398. Global Development Finance, The World Bank, Washington, D.C., various issues. Edwards, Sebastian (1999), "How Effective Are Capital Controls?" NBER Working Paper # 7413. Emerging Stock Market Factbook, International Finance Corporation, Washington, D.C., various issues.

[43] Leslie Hull, Linda L. Tesar, Risk, Specialization and the Composition of International Capital Flows, April 2000 p24.

[44] Samuel Kortum and Josh Lerner, Assessing the contribution of venture capital to innovation, RAND Journal of Economics , Vol. 31, No. 4, Winter 2000 pp. 674–692.

faster than world GDP becoming a large component of all forms of foreign capital flows. Foreign direct investors pick the high productivity firms in transition economics and labor productivity improves faster over time and faster with age in foreign owned establishments. The abundance of intangible capital in specialized industries in the source countries is positively correlated with FDI flows to the host countries[45].

European integration has played an important role in FDI trends in Europe, encouraging investment by companies from outside of the region, promoting consolidation of European industry and serving to shape the geographical pattern of production by both European and non-European companies in Europe[46]. Global competition and the resulting cost pressures have impelled companies to look for a broader international division of labour encompassing developing countries. Intra-OECD FDI flows dominate global flows in value terms. Companies are driven to invest abroad first and foremost for market proximity, and the rising share of developing countries in the world economy will imply a growing interest of OECD investors in locating within these dynamic regions. Market size is the main determinant of the global distribution of FDI flows, so it is not surprising that host developing countries receive such a small share of global direct investment. The benefits of proximity between producers and consumers or even among producers themselves are part of the issue of agglomeration in the world economy that is as much a characteristic of national economies as of the global one. Companies invest abroad not only in search of new markets but also to seek out more competent locations in which to manufacture a given good or service. FDI promotes a more efficient distribution of economic activities worldwide to the benefit of all. The investment motive is the strategy of acquiring a rival foreign firm through FDI in order to enhance economies of scale for the combined firm at a global level. Mergers are also used frequently as a means of rapid access to a foreign market. In a global economy, investors seek out not only locations with the lowest unit labour costs, but also those where environmental or social regulations are most lax or where fiscal policies are least burdensome. Hence, FDI and globalisation more generally will lead to a race to the bottom with governments lowering standards in order to attract FDI. It could be said that FDI stimulates economic growth, but also reacts to economic growth and progress of transformation[47]. Growth is generated by FDI through imported means of investment, new technologies and capabilities transferred by foreign multinationals and international networking. Moran[48]states that: "Direct evidence is not promising on the use of joint ventures to try to enhance technology transfer, penetrate international markets, or even expand and strengthen backward linkage to the domestic economy". Additionally Mansfield and Romero[49] find that parent firms transfer technology to wholly-owned subsidiaries in developing countries one-third faster, on average, than to joint ventures or licensees.

---

45 A Mody, A Razin and E Sadka, The role of information in driving DFI flows: Host-country transparency and source-country specialisation , IMF Working Paper WP/03/148

46 "M&A records on both sides of the Atlantic", Financial Times, 1 January 2000.

47 Hunya, Gábor (1998), "Recent developments of FDI and privatisation", The Vienna Institute Monthly Report, 5, pp. 1-7.

48 Moran, Theodore, Foreign Direct Investment and Development: The New Policy Agenda for Developing Countries and Economies in Transition, Institute for International Economics, Washington, December 1998, p 121.

49 Mansfield, Edwin, and Anthony Romero, "Technology transfer to overseas subsidiaries by US-based firms", Quarterly Journal of Economics 95, no. 4, December 1980.

International direct investment is more and more recognised as an engine of economic growth and a powerful force for global integration. As mentioned above, foreign direct investment is defined as capital invested for the purpose of acquiring a long-term interest in an enterprise and of exerting a degree of influence on that enterprise's operations. Direct investment differs from portfolio investment in that it involves control of the asset in question, while portfolio investors are passive investors, motivated only by the rate of return on the asset. In addition to job creation and technology transfer, governments became more helpful to the beneficial effects of foreign companies' presence on domestic competition, productivity and competitiveness. The internationalisation of the world economy and the emergence of new markets encouraged the removal of obstacles to outward direct investment so that domestic companies could take better advantage of growth potential abroad.

Increasing global competition in product and service markets, incentives to reduce costs and produce more effectively, systematic efforts to increase output and diversify exports as well as the role of new technologies in reducing communication and transport costs all promote global capital flows. External liberalisation, including removal of barriers to FDI via establishment or acquisition, brings the extra benefits of improved access to world capital markets and the prospective to increase the efficiency of the domestic financial sector through inward and outward financial-sector investment, together with equity participation and establishment in the financial sector. Governments have been pursuing comprehensive policies aimed at enhancing efficiency, through deregulation and structural reform, partly to inject more competition into the economy. Rationalisation to achieve greater productivity and efficiency is partially reflected in mergers, acquisitions and strategic alliances, aimed at developing highly competitive entities with strategic positions in their own industry frequently on a global basis. Foreign direct investment influences growth by contributing new capital and technology. Open trade policies contribute to the attractiveness of each country as a location for MNE production by allowing firms to make use of cheaper inputs from abroad. Globalisation is one of the most important forces driving the restructuring of the world economy[50]. New trends in investment, trade and collaboration between firms have immensely changed the scope of world business and extended the role of foreign companies in national economies. Companies are engaging in cross-border activities across the whole spectrum of their development, production, supply, marketing and financing activities enabling them to expand and achieve greater global effectiveness. It should be taken into consideration that companies transfer their production to other countries more readily than their R&D and other strategic operations, which they tend to centralise in the home country. Foreign companies invest extensively in R&D in some countries where R&D efforts of domestic companies are weak and where market access is valuable to them.

Certain economies with larger domestic markets are able to attract investors by closing off their market to imports. MNEs and joint ventures can play a critical role in the expansion of technologically sophisticated manufactured exports, given the particular technological advantages they possess. Foreign affiliates rely for their technology on the parent company, although the share of foreign affiliates in overall research and development (R&D) has tended to rise over time. When a company shifts production abroad, it is assumed to have a direct effect on domestic employment in that part and an indirect effect on relative wages in the home country through the increased imports that flow from affiliates in lower wage locations.

[50] Globalisation of Industry: Overview and Sector Reports, OECD, 1996.

MNE motives for investment abroad are to gain more effective access to local or regional markets in which the affiliate is located. Globalisation affords higher incomes at an aggregate level, it will affect production and consumption in each country and hence will have indirect income effects on the demand for labour, including for unskilled workers[51]. Foreign investment enhances the level of competition in domestic markets and so economic competence to the benefit of the host country. By bringing new players able to challenge market positions of previously established enterprises, foreign investments and mergers and acquisitions provide incentives for domestic enterprises to adjust in order to remain competitive. Is anti-competitive practice an inherent or exclusive behaviour of foreign investors? National competition authorities using their enforcement powers can control abuse of a dominant position by any company, foreign or domestic.

Better international capital mobility improves global resource allocation by directing world savings to its most productive uses, allows recipient countries to sustain stable levels of investment and consumption in spite of fluctuations in their income, and sends important signals to host countries concerning the sustainability of their policies. Economic policies that do not distort the flow of capital into particular areas allow the host economy to sustain higher growth rates than would otherwise have been possible. Capital controls impose a cost on the domestic economy through the inefficiencies that they engender. As globalisation has moved forward, labour unions fear that multinational enterprises can undermine labour regulations and social protections developed over decades in many OECD countries by moving production facilities into locations with less labour-friendly policies. MNEs are at the forefront of the globalisation process and the problems of controlling them are one of the central concerns and by their very nature these enterprises' operations straddle a variety of social, economic and regulatory contexts. Moreover, Sally[52] says that MNEs are "embedded in networks of relations with a number of important external actors, not only governments. These networks manifest marked differences between nations and regions, with differential implications for production and managerial relations within the firm, public policy choices and the constellation of MNE-government relationships".

FDI - investment by foreign companies in overseas subsidiaries or joint ventures - has a usual reliance on natural resource use and extraction, particularly agriculture, mineral and fuel production and so the poorest countries still receive an uneven amount of investment flows into their natural resource sectors[53]. Additionally, FDI is an increasingly powerful stimulant to economic growth and therefore of growing importance to global environment protection[54]. Moreover, globalisation refers to the increasing similarity in consumption patterns and income levels across countries and the concurrent rise in cross-border activities of firms from

---

[51] The World in 2020: Towards a New Global Age: Challenges and Opportunities, OECD, 1997.

[52] Sally, Razeen (1994) "Multinational enterprises, political economy and institutional theory: domestic imbeddedness in the context of internationalisaiton" Review of International Political Economy Spring. Volume 1, Number 1.

[53] Jenkins,R (1999), Environmental regulation and international competitiveness – a framework for analysis, Paper presented at a conference on Environmental Regulations, Globalisation of Production and Technological Change, University of East Anglia, 1-2 July 1999. Jha, V. (1998), Environmental Regulation, Finance and MNE's, Paper presented at the Trade, Investment and Environment Conference, Chatham House, London 29-30th October 1998.

[54] OECD, Open Markets Matter: the Benefits of Trade and Investment Liberalisation, OECD, 1998, Paris.

these countries[55]. Globalisation is associated primarily with the industrialized countries of the Triad (Europe, North America and Japan)[56] and its effects diverge across industries and are predominantly acute in sectors, which are capital and knowledge intensive, as well as those that depend on new and fast-evolving technologies. Companies doing more R&D through collaboration, they are doing so with overseas partners, and often, in foreign locations[57].

Strategic alliances emerged as an organizational design enabling companies to deal with the increasing complexity of building new sources of competitive advantage in order to compete in the global market. The formation of strategic alliances combines competition and cooperation to create a collaborative strategy. Alliances create synergies between resources enhancing or reshaping competition within the market. In exchange alliance companies cooperate in some way to achieve their respective objectives. In integration alliance resources are integrated within a certain organization designed by the partners to perform prescribed functions, which serve a common purpose for the partners, although the partners' ultimate goals will remain distinct. Integration alliances lead to a partial incorporation of the partner's activities into the firm's own organisation. Partners have more control in integration alliances than in exchange alliances. Exchange alliances allow the partners to focus on their core competence whilst outsourcing those activities regarded as being of secondary importance. In contrast, integration alliances allow the partners to realise synergies by placing distinctive resources into one organisation. Strategic alliances refer to inter-firm cooperative agreements that are intended to affect the long-term product market positioning of at least one partner. Cooperative agreements indent either to a cost economizing to minimize net costs or a strategic motivation to enhance the value of the firm's assets. Companies from the Triad (Europe, North America and Japan) are engaged in cross-border economic activity in order to survive and so adopt policies that maximize their presence in not just those locations, which are their primary markets, but also all those locations where their competitors are operating. Net-work-like behaviour of MNE activity is driven in part by the fact that there are still distinct differences in the resources available in various countries. Strategic technology partnering is fundamentally a firm-level phenomenon. Enhancing competitiveness and value of the firm in a more long-term horizon motivate the growth of strategic alliances, rather than improving short-term cost efficiencies as a result of globalisation[58]. The tendency to use equity agreements is associated with industry-specific differences, rather than country-specific differences. According to Rajneesh Narula[59] and John Hagedoorn "the increasing similarity of technologies across countries and cross-fertilization of technology between sectors, coupled with the increasing costs and risks associated with innovation, has led to firms utilizing STP as a *first-best* option".

---

[55] Dunning, J.H., Narula, R., 1998. Developing countries versus multinationals in a globalising world: the dangers of falling behind. In: Buckley, P., Ghauri, P. (Eds.), Multinational Enterprises and Emerging Markets. Dryden Press, London.

[56] Knickerbocker, F., 1973. Oligopolistic Reaction and the Multinational Enterprise. Harvard University Press, Cambridge, MA. Knickerbocker stated that companies sometimes simply establish themselves in some markets simply because their competitors have done so.

[57] Hagedoorn, J., 1996. Trends and patterns in strategic technology partnering since the early seventies. Review of Industrial Organization 11, 601–616.

[58] Inkpen, P., Beamish, P., 1997. Knowledge, bargaining power, and the instability of international joint ventures. Academy of Management Review 22, 177–202.

[59] Rajneesh Narula ,John Hagedoorn, Innovating through strategic alliances: moving towards international partnerships and contractual agreements, Technovation 19 (1999) 283–294, p292.

6.5 GLOBALISATION AND DEVELOPMENT

Is globalisation impossible without development? Globalisation is not only the result of an amplification of long-standing trends- such as increasing cross-border flows of goods, money and people, and a rising mutual awareness and interdependence among social, economic and political units in the world-but also the very context in which development has taken place during the post World War II period. Comte, Saint-Simon, Spencer, Marx, Durkheim, Weber and Parsons developed theories to understand the changes induced by industrialization, and could be regarded as pioneering theorists of globalisation[60]. Capitalistic development created oppressive relationships between developed and underdeveloped countries as first-world multinational corporations sought to exploit their oligopolistic advantages in developing countries. Location matters in a global world because it shapes the very ability, tendency and desire of actors to network and therefore social, cultural, political and even geopolitical conditions smooth the progress of various types of relationships, e.g. vertical, horizontal, cooperative, competitive, domestic or cross-border. Established social organizational patterns or ideologies have fostered relationships between certain categories of domestic and foreign actors allowing foreign actors unrestricted access to the country. For instance, a vertical pattern of social organization facilitates producer-driven linkages fostering large-scale, capital-intensive activities by local firms, while a horizontal pattern allow buyer-driven linkages leading to flexible, knowledge-intensive activities[61]. Mauro F Guillén refers that [62]"a global world is more unpredictable and ambiguous than the modern world of the recent past. But it allows individuals and organizations to grow out of the straightjackets of location and the modern nation-state, to express them in a more boundless way, to pursue their identities without having to conform to a dominant model or paradigm. The task of an institutional theory of development is precisely to provide an understanding of how difference empowers and enriches without denying the unity and mutual awareness that globalisation entails".

If countries at first have different levels of productivity in the high-tech sector, their comparative performance depends on the strength of knowledge spillovers. If these are low, the high-tech sector expands faster in the originally more productive country and countries do not converge, but regions become more similar in the less productive country, which gradually loses its high-tech sector. Moreover, the amplification of knowledge spillovers, due to more cross-country interaction, drastically alters these growth paths. In sum, stronger knowledge spillovers bring convergence across regions that can competitively produce the high-tech good and brings convergence across countries since the high-tech sector becomes an increasing share of total output. Speciality causes divergence in per capita income, because endogenous productivity improvements have an effect on primarily the production of the high-tech sector and because after integration countries normally specialize in the sector in

---

[60] Albrow, Martin. 1997. The Global Age. Stanford, CA: Stanford University Press.

[61] Berger, Suzanne. 1996. "Introduction." National Diversity and Global Capitalism. Ed. Suzanne Berger and Ronald Dore. Ithaca, NY: Cornell University Press. Pp. 1-25. Biggart, Nicole Woolsey and Marco Orrú. 1997. "Societal Strategic Advantage: Institutional Structure and Path Dependence in the Automotive and Electronics Industries of East Asia." State, Market and Organizational Form. Ed. Ayse Bugra and Behlul Usdiken. Berlin: Walter de Gruyter. Pp. 201-239.

[62] Mauro F Guillén, Diversity In Glob Alization, Organizational Change in Argentina, South Korea and Spain, January 2 0 0 0, Paper Number 6, P 21. Unpublished by Mauro F. Guillén

which they have a comparative advantage[63]. Young[64] shows that free trade increases the growth rate of the developed countries and lowers that of the less developed countries. Mariassunta Giannetti [65] found that "in regions that already have a small high-tech sector an industrial policy which fosters employment in the growing sector is welfare-reducing, if knowledge spillovers are strong. However, regions completely specialized in traditional sectors may still benefit from attempts to increase the productivity of the more technologically advanced sectors, as, for instance, the Welsh development agency did in Wales by offering highly professional public services to new firms, or in Ireland where industrial policy contributed to the recent sustained growth phase by increasing services and research infrastructure. In fact, by favouring the development of a small high-tech sector in laggard regions these policies can have dramatic effects, because they enable the poorest regions to benefit from international knowledge spillovers". Additionally Gilles Saint-Paul [66] considers that "the pattern of comparative advantage induced by employment protection tends to bias the research effort to secondary innovations that improve on existing products rather than take the risk of creating new ones. In an open economy, the high - firing cost country will imitate more than the low firing cost country, and more than if it were closed. It may even fully specialize in secondary innovation, which cannot happen if it were closed. Invention is more sensitive to firing costs in the open than in the closed economy. Firing costs reduce the total number of goods available in the world economy and reduce welfare if secondary innovation does not enhance efficiency by too much". It is difficult to explain the positive correlation between agglomeration and productivity because productivity is high because of agglomeration effects and agglomeration is a consequence, not a cause, of high productivity. Antonio Ciccone [67] shows that productivity gains in dense regions are to a certain extent realized through a change in industry structure.

Long-term improvement in production (technological progress) is the essence of industrialization, the main source of the wealth of the advanced capitalist nations, and the origin of favourable wages compared with the poorer regions of the earth. High productivity is an indispensable but not sufficient condition for good wage. Productivity only delivers good wages if the working class has the ability to extract a good price for its labouring power, a fair share of the social product. Supply and demand conditions may be more or less favourable to workers and wages. Globalisation could further impoverish countries with predominantly unfavourable initial conditions and child labour is likely to rise where the share of educated workers is very low[68]. Besides, the net effects of globalisation are vague for developing countries, but child labour is more likely to fall. Capital flows are worldwide,

---

63 Goodfriend, M.,McDermott,J.,1998.Industrial development and the convergence question. American Economic Review 88,1277–1289.

64 Young,A.,1991.Learning by doing and the dynamic effects of international trade.Quarterly Journal of Economics 106,369–406.

65 Mariassunta Giannetti, The effects of integration on regional disparities: Convergence, divergence or both? European Economic Review 46 (2002) 539–567, p560

66 Gilles Saint-Paul, Employment protection, international specialization, and innovation, European Economic Review 46 (2002) 375–395, p369.

67 Antonio Ciccone, Agglomeration effects in Europe, European Economic Review 46 (2002) 213-227.

68 Balland, J.M. and A. Robinson (2000), "Is Child Labor Inefficient?", Journal of Political Economy 108, 663-679. Cigno, A., Rosati, F.C. and Z. Tzannatos (2002), Handbook of Child Labor, The World Bank, Washington D.C.

competition is global, manufacturing is universal, and labor migration is global.[69] Geography still matters extremely in the course of capitalist development. Globalisation has not eroded all shores on which home difference and competitive advantage are anchored. Internal flows of goods within multinationals do not eliminate the spatial division of labor; they merely alter its organizational form. The specific qualities that confer productive competence and competitive advantage remain anchored to localities in a variety of ways. The demise of the nation-state in the face of capital money capital is vastly more mobile than it was a generation ago, thanks to an electronic and institutional revolution in finance, and it puts the monetary policy of every country in jeopardy to the forces of the market and financial speculation.

Economic territorialization – meaning greater internal integration than global exposure – has the effect of binding together the fate of capital and labor within a single country or place, and differentiating it from those beyond the pale. Is industrial location driven merely by the cost of labor and employers will move away from high wage areas to places where lower wages prevail? Most of the world's industry is found in the advanced capitalist countries where costs, including wages, are generally the highest, not the lowest. It could be said that a global economy is still a geographically concentrated economy[70]. As mentioned above, the private sector and MNEs in particular, play an important role in the economic development strategies of less developed countries (LDCs). The failure of import substitution policies and the demise of central planning accompanying the collapse of communism, have led many LDC governments to adopt more liberal economic development policies that emphasize export-led growth, the attraction of FDI and the use of markets to determine resource allocation. MNEs are more and more attracted to LDCs due to the presence of some of the world's fastest- growing consumer markets; the potential for some of the world's most important unexplored natural resources. There is recognition that for the sustainable development of LDCs, economic growth needs to be accompanied by greater environmental protection and social equity. [71] The objective of sustainable development can be seen as one of balancing gains or losses in different types of capital such that there is a net overall increase[72]. Within MNEs some characteristics (culture and politics) are not necessarily homogenous since the organization itself has to work across many geographic and cultural boundaries; corporate policies do not necessarily translate into uniform practices across all operations. As globalisation has facilitated time-space compression, economies more and more compete at all levels including that of attracting foreign investors and advances in communication and transportation have created new opportunities placing LDCs on the menu of choice in spite of the somewhat higher degree of political risk. Regulation plays a role in

---

[69] Dicken, P., 1998. Global Shift: Transforming the World Economy, 3rd ed. Guilford Press, New York.

[70] Wade, R., 1990. Governing the Market: Economic Theory and the Role of Government in East Asian Industrialization. Princeton University Press, Princeton.

[71] -Productive capital comprises a country's stock of financial resources, plant, equipment, infrastructure and other productive resources. -Human capital comprises a country's stock of investment in the education, health, and nutrition of individuals.- Social capital comprises a country's stock of social institutions, both formal and informal, that facilitate the functioning of society.- Natural capital comprises a country's stock of environmentally provided assets, notably its stock of physical, biophysical and natural reserves. Serageldin, I. (1996). Sustainability as opportunity and the problem of social capital. The Brown Journal of World Affairs, 3(2), 187-203. OECD (1992). The OECD guidelines for multinational enterprises. Paris, France: OECD.

[72] Munasinghe, M. (1993). Environmental economics and sustainable development. World Bank environment paper No. 3. Washington, DC: The World Bank.

persuading or dissuading MNEs' investment decisions through consequential cost implications. Market imperfections provide opportunities for technologically superior MNEs to extend their reach overseas and internalise additional productive activities rather than buying-in from external providers.

Growth generates high employment and labor demand in the long run, and sufficient returns to pay good wages and so a high wage economy is a product of development, not a barrier to it[73]. The companies that perform well over time do so principally by keeping on top of technical change, product marketing, and organizational improvements. Labour's remuneration and competition between groups of workers are mediated by the performance of nations, regions, sectors and firms. It is the high-productivity, high-wage economies that engage in most of world trade and international competition. Manufacturing is the part of the economy most exposed to international competition by virtue of the nature of its products. Rising productivity is central to long-term economic growth, which tends to concentrate in the most favoured places in the global system.

The distribution of the social product depends on the bargaining power of labor and capital. Accumulation is the main driving force of the world economy, along with its correlates, capital-capital competition and capital-labor exploitation. The global effect of lower profit rates was weaker performance in the key indicators of economic growth. Weakening capital accumulation caused a productivity slowdown and wage stagnation. It could be said that the real drag on the world economy is overcapacity - too many factories - rather than too few customers. [74]

Is it profitable for a country to concentrate production in one sector, or in one location? The degree of sectorial relocation realized, has depended significantly on the costs of relocating factors across sectors. The long-term unemployment rate is a proxy for measuring the cost of relocating labor in a country. [75]In many mature industrial markets, foreign market entry through foreign direct investment (FDI)[76] is considered a primary source of future sales and profit growth[77]. The multinational enterprise (MNE) must decide between an expansion strategy[78] of expanding its main line of business (LOB) into the new market and a product

[73] Romer, P., 1996. Why indeed in America. Theory, history and the origins of modern economic growth. American Economic Review 86 (2), 202-206. Webber, M., Rigby, D., 1996. The Golden Age Illusion. Guilford, New York. Storper, M., 1997. The Regional World: Territorial Development in a Global Economy. Guilford Press, New York.

[74] Cox, K. (Ed.), 1997. Spaces of Globalization: Reasserting the Power of the Local. Guilford Press, New York. O'Brien, R., 1992. Global Financial Integration: The End of Geography. Pinter, London.

[75] Baldwin, R., 2001. The core-periphery model with forward-looking expectations. Regional Science and Urban Economics 31 (1), 21–49. Ottaviano, G.I.P., 1999. Integration, geography and the burden of history. Regional Science and Urban Economics 29, 245–256. Lazear, E.P., 1990. Job security provisions and employment. Quarterly Journal of Economics 105 (3), 699–726. Krugman, P., 1998. Space: the final frontier. Journal of Economic Perspectives 12, 161–174.

[76] Shaver, J. M. (1998). Accounting for endogeneity when assessing strategy performance: Does entry mode choice affect FDI survival? Management Science, 44(4), 571–585.

[77] Forsgren, M., Mathisen, C., & Pedersen, T. (2000). Competence creation and recognition: A case study. In U. Holm, & T. Pedersen (Eds.), The emergence and impact of MNE centres of excellence (pp.167–181). London: Macmillan.

[78] Hitt, M. A., Hoskisson, R. E., & Kim, H. (1997). International diversification: Effects on innovation and firm performance in product-diversified firms. Academy of Management Journal, 40(4), 767–798.

diversification strategy of producing products in a secondary or new LOB[79]. Firms should strive to integrate their international diversification[80] and product diversification strategies in order to achieve synergies and optimal performance[81].

As discussed earlier, the activities of MNEs are important both for the technological development and international competitiveness of small open economies. Possession of firm-specific advantages is generally argued to be required before a firm is able to enter foreign markets. Firm-specific advantages (superior technology, human capital, or product differentiation) increase the market concentration and can be derived from factors that create barriers to entry for recent competitors. When a firm expands sales, at home or abroad, the R&D-created knowledge will be utilized more widely, leading to a better rate of return on each dollar spent on R&D. Technological opportunity and appropriability conditions influence a firm's R&D-decision and refers to that the cost and possibilities for technological advance may differ between industries. Appropriability conditions concerns the issue to what extent a firm can appropriate the returns from its R&D expenditures. Foreign markets can be served either through exports from the parent company or by production in foreign affiliates. For MNEs in small countries, there is less scope to finance R&D investments by sales in the home market alone[82]. Manufacturing firms from small countries have limited growth opportunities in their home markets, and hence are more dependent on foreign sales[83].

The global dispersion of R&D has been driven by companies' needs to get hold of new knowledge and capabilities, and to multiply access to unique human resources. The proliferation of national innovation systems and knowledge centres at a mixture of locations throughout the world has strengthened the incentives for multinationals to go for global knowledge sourcing. A subsidiary's capacity to acquire access to local knowledge sources is dependent upon its embeddedness in the host country context and the social relations of technological innovation. There is a sound effect of national innovation systems on the technological and innovation activities of MNEs. The role of the central R&D unit shifts from a control centre to a group with rights and duties identical to those of the dispersed units and accordingly overseas R&D units take on a strategic responsibility affecting the whole company enjoying a high degree of autonomy and play idiosyncratic roles in knowledge creation through their extensive external networks.

The production in the firm can be split into a number of activities, and the firm has the opportunity to become multinational and move one of the activities to the host country. In the host country, the firm has to bargain over the wage rate with a local trade union. If the activities kept in the home country are adequately corresponding to the activities moved to the host country, the workers in the home country keep a sound bargaining position relative to the firm. FDI gives rise to lower wages dependent on the degree of substitutability between

79 Cantwell, J. A., & Mudambi, R. (2000). The location of MNE R&D activity: The role of investment incentives. Management International Review, 40(1), 127–148. Caves, R. E. (1996). Multinational enterprise and economic analysis (2nd ed.). Cambridge: Cambridge University Press.

80 Kim, D. J., & Kogut, B. (1996). Technological platforms and diversification. Organization Science, 7(3), 283–301.

81 Busija, E. C., O'Neill, H. M., & Zeithaml, C. P. (1997). Diversification strategy, entry mode, and performance: Evidence of choice and constraints. Strategic Management Journal, 18(4), 321–327.

82 Vernon, R., 1966. International investment and international trade in the product cycle. Quarterly Journal of Economics 80, 190–207.

83 Cohen, W.M., Klepper, S., 1996. A reprise of size and R&D. Economic Journal 106 (437), 925–951.

activities in the home country and the host country[84]. According to Brainard and Riker[85] there is a positive elasticity of substitution between parent employment and employment in foreign affiliates but it is comparatively small. FDI gives rise to an increase in the wage of skilled workers in the skilled labor abundant country. Employment in the home country decreases, but the higher wage may compensate for the employment loss[86].

The quick growth of global markets has been accompanied by a world-wide increase of inequality and environmental degradation. Can the process of globalisation jeopardise the social and environmental sustainability[87] of development? Sustainable development should be considered as the development that gives "equal opportunities" to all generations. So, both inequality and environmental degradation violate the underlying equity principle of giving every agent the same opportunities. Increasing level of inequality and environmental degradation is a matter of concern also for economic reasons, since both have potential adverse consequences on the performance of an economy[88]. High levels of inequality cause social and political tensions that frequently have negative effects on income growth[89]. Moreover, poverty enhances the negative effects of inequality on economic growth. Environmental degradation has adverse effects on production by increasing workers' health problems and so reducing their productivity[90]. Additionally, ecological degradation reduces land productivity in the long run. So, there is a need for reforming the process of globalisation in the direction of its long-run sustainability integrating in a more satisfactory way the conditions of environmental sustainability with those of social sustainability.

6.6 Globalisation, Law and Economy

It has become clear in recent times that markets do not emerge full blown when old-style regulations are removed. In fact, new rules are often necessary. It is important to emphasize that deregulation of and delegations to the market do not take place in a vacuum[91]. Markets

---

[84] Naylor, R., Santoni, M., 1998. Wage bargaining and foreign direct investment. Working paper, University of Warwick.

[85] Brainard, S.L., Riker, D.A., 1997. Are US multinationals exporting US jobs? NBER working paper 5958.

[86] Markusen, J.R., Venables, A.J., 1997. The role of multinational firms in the wage-gap debate. Review of International Economics 5, 435–451. Slaughter, M.J., 2000. Production transfer within multinational enterprises and American wages. Journal of International Economics 50, 449–472. Zhao, L., 1995. Cross-hauling direct foreign investment and unionised oligopoly. European Economic Review 39, 1237–1253. Zhao, L., 1998. The impact of foreign direct investment on wages and employment. Oxford Economic Papers 50, 284–301.

[87] WCED (The World Commission on Environment and Development), 1987. Our common future. Oxford University Press p.43. Brundtland Commission: "Sustainable development is development that meets the needs of the present without compromising the ability of future generations to meet their own needs".

[88] Vercelli, S., 2001. New globalization and sustainability. Quaderni del Dipartimento di Economia Politica, No.329, Università di Siena.

[89] Benhabib, J., Rustichini, A., 1996. Social conflict and growth. Journal of Economic Growth, 1 (1): 129-146. Alesina, A., Perotti, R., 1996. Income distribution, political instability and investment. European Economic Review, 81 (5): 1170-1189.

[90] Lindert, P.H., Williamson, J.G., 2001. Does globalization make the world more unequal? Paper presented at the NBER conference on Globalization in historical perspectives, Santa Barbara, US, May 3-6 2001.

[91] "Social systems cannot exist in splendid isolation from their environment. This point is conceded even by ardent proponents of regime specialization. . . . Similarly, legal subsystems coexisting in isolation from

need to be understood as part of a major reconceptualization of the country, as it comes to terms not only with universal competition but with the fact that it must deal with issues, technologies, and players whose problems, influence, and power do not map onto its own territory or political geography. Globalisation of markets involves the growing interdependency among the economies of the world; multinational nature of sourcing, investment activities, trading, and manufacturing; escalating occurrence of cross-border financing and dealings; and heightened intensity of competition among a larger number of players. The creation of new products and development of new technologies also contributes to the globalisation of markets. The globalisation of markets has led to the formation of irreversible economic linkages among countries. This phenomenon has been fuelled by developments in transportation and communication technologies, widen of economic growth and wealth around the world, the loosening of barriers to trade, and the formation of regional economic blocs. It has also shifted the focus away from the nation-state, and more toward industry and the individual company. Processes of globalisation and internationalisation as well as strong countervailing forces of old and new nationalisms are but three major facets of this new complexity. It seems that globalisation as distinct from internationalisation denotes a process of denationalisation of clusters of political, economic and social activities. Internationalisation refers to cooperative activities of national actors, public or private, on a level beyond the nation-state but in the last resort under its control. In the world of the vertically integrated firm as in the world of socialism, economic relationships are determined by internal command. Besides, globalisation here refers to a worldwide increase of legal protection against the ill effects of technical, economic, and social devices too complex, distant, or powerful to make individual self-protection possible. The most recent manifestation of this movement is the outburst of environmental protection law that is partially fuelled by a concern with nature itself but tends to achieve its maximum impetus when that concern is coupled with putative injury to individuals from pollutants. On the one hand, a MNE operating in many nations and integrating its activities globally is an example of globalisation. On the other hand, a MNE pursuing a strategy of maximising the interests of each corporate entity within the MNE and within the national boundaries in which it operates could be viewed as an example of internationalisation. Government policy is now influenced and dictated by the free and substantial flow of capital worldwide. The main areas of change in the international financial markets have been the international financial system; advances in information technology and telecommunications; the rise of global business strategies and the MNE; new political and economic structures; new political imperatives, such as economic liberalization, privatisation and deregulation; and the rise of the institutional investor; The process of harmonization will add to the erosion of national sovereignty brought about by globalisation. According to Yadong Luo[92] "Increased globalization, adaptation requirements, and global competition all increase an MNE's environmental and operational complexity. Heightened complexity increases information processing and agency demands, and MNEs manage such demands by instituting more efficient governance arrangements. Meanwhile, information processing and agency demands are partly determined by an MNE's international

---

the remaining bulk of international law are inconceivable. There will always be some degree of interaction, at least at the level of interpretation." Bruno Simma and Dirk Pulkowski, *Of Planets and the Universe: Self-Contained Regimes in International Law,* 17 EUR. J. INT'L L. 483, 492 (2006).

[92] Yadong Luo, How does globalization affect corporate governance and accountability? A perspective from MNEs, Journal of International Management 11 (2005) 19– 41 p37.

experience; such demands may become even stronger if the firm has little global experience. Globalization scale, adaptation requirements, foreign competition, and international experience are hence proposed to affect information processing and agency requirements, and, in turn, governance and accountability."

Together, these changes have formed a trend towards international financial integration. National sovereignty is further eroded by the restrictions on policy, which the global financial markets have imposed; Countries with an open market approach to regulation and harmonized rules are more probable to flourish in the global economy as capital, both human and financial, more and more ignores national boundaries. Globalisation is an important emerging business mandate applicable to virtually all businesses. It is an Information Economy, as opposed to an Industrial Economy, business concept[93]. Modern communications tolerate businesses to operate in multiple countries with diverse shapes and forms of organization and control. They make it possible to send information to any part of an organization instantly, enabling every part to know what every other part--and the organization as a whole--is doing all the time. In the first place international trade law establishes the idea that public intervention to regulate trade is exceptional, while entirely free private trade is the norm. The rise of multinationals has impacted on the strategies and decision-making processes of the managers of such corporations. The interests of the multinational group as a whole need to be reconciled with the individual interests of each associate corporation. In other words, there is a need to integrate the decision-making process across affiliates. Treaty-based rules against tariffs and quotas, procedures for mitigating swings in commodity prices, and provisions managing exchange rate fluctuations are all presented as exceptional measures which in normal circumstances characterized by stable and *self*-regulating trade, commodity exchange, and currency convertibility would not be required. The EU puts forward as the normal premises of political life that administration is supplementary to politics; technical expertise is the servant of public decision-making; and executive power is subject to the popular will. Free movement of workers, goods, and capital, freedom of establishment, and freedom to provide services, all depend on an extensive regulatory framework, implemented through compulsory harmonization of national law, EU legal regimes, and common policies. In the EU the technocratic character of the political regime has reached the point where concern is voiced about the "democratic deficit."[94]

First, according to neo-liberal economic theory, the globalisation of economic markets will reduce inequality; second, the creation of international institutions will increase incentives for cooperation; and third, globalisation brings with it ideological convergence. There is a tendency to liberalize or deregulate, thereby adopting rules and regulations designed largely to introduce competition into markets once dominated by State monopolies. Because of the liberating effects of technology and the free flow of capital around the world, private decisions involving finance, production, and investment can occur increasingly free of direct State involvement. It should be taken into account that the fall of communism led many politicians and academics to argue that there is no alternative to the neo-liberal values

---

93 Bruce A. Markell, A View from the Field: Some Observations on the Effect of International Commercial Law Reform Efforts on the Rule of Law, 6 IND. J. GLOBAL LEGAL STUD. 497 (1999).

94 D. Federico Mancini & David T. Keeling, Democracy and the European Court of Justice, 57 MOD. L. REV. 175 (1994); Karlheinz Neunreither, The Democratic Deficit of the European Union: Towards Closer Cooperation Between the European Parliament and the National Parliaments, 29 GOV'T & OPP'N 299 (1994).

associated with privatisation, low taxation, open markets, and a minimalist conception of government. Has not globalisation transcended the complex relationship between the universal and the particular that has framed international politics since at least the Westphalian settlement in the mid-seventeenth century? As Ian Clark says, "globalisation needs also to be understood as a number of changes within the state, and not simply as a range of external forces set against it."[95] Hence, markets are largely concentrated in a denationalised way. The investment necessary to build or expand a manufacturing or distribution facility freely flows across national borders. The financing for this investment is created increasingly without regard to any single place and by a worldwide financial industry located in various interconnected worldwide cities. The end result of the new networks of finance, investment, and production is that they help to create relatively integrated markets for the goods produced, and they produce new and numerous sets of relationships or economic networks that transcend the geography of countries. MNEs move their production activities from location to location around the world, often loosely affiliating with various independent contractors to obtain the services or materials they need. They seek out the most cost-effective relationships as possible in what are usually the long value chains connected with the production and marketing of goods and services. MNEs may locate research and development in one country, component assembly in another, final assembly in yet another country, and distribution networks in still another. They also decide how much to customize globally conceived products for local markets.

Businesses finance their growth and expansion through international capital markets. As such, they are able to take advantage of varying interest rates and currency markets by tapping a variety of funding sources. As transactions get international character, they have a sweeping impact on firm performance and industry structure. On one hand, global linkages may shorten product life cycles, create intense price pressures, outdate technology or design, or simply cause sales and profitability declines. On the other hand, global exchange may lead to new growth opportunities, new sources of know-how and production inputs, new product ideas, or partnerships, which cause new sources of competitive advantage. Entire industries, if caught unprepared, can be lost to competitors due to the realities of global competition. For instance, in the United States, it is observed the decline of industries such as steel, textiles, shoes, tires, and electronics. To that extent globalization of markets causes the individual firm to understand and operate within a more complex political, legal-regulatory, and cultural framework. While the transactions are essentially the same, the context is quite different, and often, overwhelming for managers. To operate effectively in less familiar environments, managers must develop a sufficient understanding of the government sector, regulatory framework, and the cultural characteristics of the markets where they wish to carry out business.

Privatisation, like nationalization before it, is a macroeconomic policy whose parameters are determined by political considerations. For the implementing government, the primary determinants of the decision to privatise include the following: sustainability of monetary policies, capital and employment needs, and pressures from external financial institutions and foreign governments. For the investor, the economic terms of the transaction are primary. The weight assigned these considerations may be influenced by the rule of law criterion. An investor's calculation of the potential returns on an investment made in a privatised entity will

[95] Ian Clark, Globalization And International Relations Theory (1999), at 52

likely reflect a rule of law premium or discount. The rule of law does not depend for its legitimacy on the automatic application of specified doctrines, or on the existence of equal and like bargaining powers among the parties. Thus, since one of the motivations for privatisation frequently is to bring forth financial inflows from foreign investors, a privatising government is likely to adopt those measures that foreign owners of capital would deem as consistent with the rule of law. For the privatising government, the consequences of the perceptions held by the investor and the international financial institutions are real, but they alone do not determine privatisation policies. The results were "mixed economies" in which the State, for a variety of reasons, acquired outright ownership in certain industries, while heavily regulating others. In other words, the so-called "natural monopolies" and "national security enterprises" were acquired by governments to save employment in failing industries, for national security purposes, to protect the "national patrimony" from foreign ownership, or as sources of patronage. Typical nationalization was the product of extended bargaining between the national government and the foreign concession holder. For multinational companies, economic interests were secured by pre-existing arrangements, notably previous contracts. Can the collapse of the State interventionist model evident in the privatisation movement be attributed simply to the legal reasons? The existence of formal institutions may be necessary to the idea of the rule of law in the foreign investment sphere, but they are hardly sufficient. On the one hand, globalisation of markets is best reflected in the "internationalisation" of business transactions. On the other hand, competition for customers and markets has intensified significantly as a result of globalisation. Nowadays, business activity flows freely to places best equipped to perform it most cost-effectively and efficiently. Whereas only a handful of MNEs dominated international trade a couple of decades ago, today companies from all parts of the world are participating in worldwide business. The types of international business transactions have proliferated. In the past, much of international business activity was in the form of export-import and foreign direct investment. Nowadays, transactions are varied and more complex: contract manufacturing, franchise operations, turnkey construction, technology transfers, international strategic alliances, and more. Technology spreads freely and quickly between markets and players. Technological leadership does not provide a monopolistic advantage for very long. Companies must capitalize on their discoveries rapidly, before others match them. Borrowing-financing activity has become worldwide as well. Businesses finance their growth and expansion through international capital markets. As such, they are able to take advantage of varying interest rates and currency markets by tapping a variety of funding sources. As transactions get international character, they have a sweeping impact on firm performance and industry structure. On one hand, global linkages may shorten product life cycles, create intense price pressures, outdate technology or design, or simply cause sales and profitability declines. On the other hand, global exchange may lead to new growth opportunities, new sources of know-how and production inputs, new product ideas, or partnerships, which cause new sources of competitive advantage. Entire industries, if caught unprepared, can be lost to competitors due to the realities of global competition. For instance, in the United States, it is observed the decline of industries such as steel, textiles, shoes, tires, and electronics. To that extent globalisation of markets causes the individual firm to understand and operate within a more complex political, legal-regulatory, and cultural framework. While the transactions are essentially the same, the context is quite different, and often, overwhelming for managers. To operate effectively in less familiar environments, managers must develop a sufficient understanding of the government sector, regulatory framework, and the cultural characteristics of the markets where they wish to carry out business.

Globalization integrates labor markets around the world and creates a growing reciprocal dependence of national economies through: superior telecommunications and international transportation systems; government policies that endorse trade liberalization; and corporate strategies of buying and selling around the world through exports and relocation of production to low-cost production places. It could be argued that the significance of globalization rests in the way the global economy alters the production of goods and assets around the world. The structural changes resulting from globalization lead in more flexible labor markets and, thus, a more flexible work force with reduced labor regulations and costs. In order to achieve greater competitiveness on a global scale, and in response to the need for greater mobility, the deregulation of labor markets has been a strategic mechanism.

A convergence had taken place throughout the Western economies in the way that the model of "managed capitalism" was developing and all countries were converging toward economies dominated by a handful of powerful enterprises, guarded only by the countervailing powers of the state and workers[96]. While globalization is a multidimensional phenomenon encompassing a broad spectrum of economic and social dimensions, almost all measures of trade, foreign direct investment and integration indicate a sharp increase in recent years. The emergence of the entrepreneurial economy is a response to the advent of low-cost but highly skilled competition in Central and Eastern Europe as well as Asia and the telecommunications and microprocessor revolution that has reduced the cost of shifting standardized economic activity out of high-cost locations, such as Europe and into lower-cost locations worldwide. As a result, the comparative advantage of high-wage countries is no longer compatible with common economic activity, which can be easily transferred to lower-cost regions outside Western Europe. Thus, maintenance of high wages requires knowledge-based economic activity that cannot be easily diffused across geographic space.

Production in the managed economy results from the inputs of land, labor and capital but the standardization of products and production reduces the importance of regional-specific characteristics and idiosyncrasies. While traditional inputs (land, labor and capital) still play a role, knowledge has emerged as the most important factor of production in the entrepreneurial economy and it cannot be costlessly transferred across geographic space. Taking into account that knowledge spillovers tend to be geographically bounded within the region where the new economic knowledge was created, geography plays a more important role in that knowledge tends to be developed in the contexts of localized production networks embedded in innovative clusters[97]. Thus, the geographic extent of knowledge spillovers is limited. Besides, investment in R&D by private corporations and universities spills over for economic exploitation by third-party firms[98].

The global experience of the devastating effects of modern warfare, including the first uses of atomic weapons, induced the international community to rethink the century-old

---

[96] Galbraith, John K., 1956, American Capitalism: The New Industrial State, Boston: Houghton Mifflin. Servan-Schreiber, Jean-Jacques, 1968, The American Challenge, London: Hamish Hamilton.

[97] Audretsch, David B. and Maryann P. Feldman, 1996, "R&D Spillovers and the Geography of Innovation and Production," American Economic Review, 86(3), June, 630-640. Audretsch, David B. and Paula E. Stephan, 1996, "Company-Scientist Locational Links: The Case of Biotechnology," American Economic Review, 86(3), June, 641-652.

[98] Jaffe, Adam B., 1989, "Real Effects of Academic Research," American Economic Review, 79(5), 957-970.

concept of state sovereignty. The international community began to realize that international peace and security had become not only an international responsibility, but also a universal or global responsibility and they limited the principle of state sovereignty accordingly. The international community is gradually recognizing the existential threats to the survival of Earth posed by the escalating destruction of the human environment. Ozone layer depletion, water pollution, global warming, soil and groundwater pollution, and vast land areas radiated by nuclear waste have reached dimensions that go beyond the capabilities of not only individual states but also regional organizations to cope with these threats. The above problems create global threats. The close interrelation of environmental destruction and underdevelopment adds to the worldwide scope of these problems. The rapid advancement of air traffic has brought the economic community closer together than ever before. But much more importantly, the telecommunications revolution has truly globalized international markets, particularly financial markets. The movement of capital, once a matter of weeks or days occurs in a matter of seconds these days. A national decision on interest rates in many cases immediately affects trade policies worldwide. This decisive acceleration of market transactions does not only amount to quantitative time savings; it is in fact changing the market and the agents' behaviour qualitatively. A third factor contributing to the globalisation of markets, closely linked to the high international mobility of capital, goods, and services, is constituted by the emergence of MNEs. For instance, the process of globalisation within the framework of the EC shows that both the mechanisms of a free market and the instruments of central regulation, backed by central enforcement authorities (Commission and Court), have been applied. Under the EU or supranational model, the effect of globalizing lawmaking is an immediate one, in line with a monistic approach to the relationship between international/supranational and national law. The principle of the supremacy of EU law means that national law is set aside or, in the case of Directives national lawmaking is prearranged by the compulsory goals set by the Directives. There is, with regard to the goals, no room for discretion on the part of the national lawmakers. The immediate effect of the supranational law as the globalizing agent is independent of the sovereign will of the Member States and is backed up by the enforcement powers of the ECJ.

6.7 Globalisation and Marketing

Business and marketing are inseparable concepts and the customer becomes the way to increase growth and profits. Brands compose some of the most valuable assets owned by a company[99]. Improved technology is seen to be the primary force in creating standardized consumer markets. International marketing has become a vital function for any large corporation's handling of the impacts of globalization. Core values are the values that are primarily part of an organization in such a way that they will not be compromised such as safety, which Volvo would never trade off. Marketing has focused on a short-term analysis of identifying mark sales and market share. Intangible assets have neither a physical nor a financial form and so this makes them difficult to measure. Besides, intangibles can have a huge impact on shareholder value. It has to be taken into consideration that in some sectors,

[99] Rao, V. R., M. K. Agarwal, and D. Dahlhoff. 2004. "How is Manifest Branding Strategy Related to the Intangible Value of a Corporation? Journal of Marketing 68 (October): 126-141.

enterprise marketing plays a very small role because intangible assets have less impact on shareholder value in industries that are exceptionally dependent on tangible assets[100]. In software, semiconductors, and electro-medical apparatus intangible values is driven by patents, while intangibles in candy and household commodities are driven more by brands. Enterprise marketing works only if we achieve an important connection between sales revenues and selling, general and administrative expenses. There is a relation between marketing and finance by linking the profit and cost per market share point to earnings and shareholder value and so management has to boost the price of their stock by increasing (or decreasing) spending on enterprise marketing funds. Marketers should make a great contribution to financial measures regarding the capability-building and brand-building activities that the marketing department is expected to bring to the corporate agenda. Profit cannot be maximized by financial management[101] alone but marketing and corporate finance have to work together in globalization in order to maximize returns. Maximizing returns on company marketing increases earnings and add to shareholder value.

The international marketing refers to an enterprise operating in more than one country whose marketing strategy in each is being chosen deliberately from being very diverse to being standardized between countries. Besides, global marketing is a form of international marketing that has standardized its marketing strategy between the world's countries. It should be taken into account that international marketing approaches are based on culture-sensitive adaptation as each new foreign market is entered. Comprehensive standardization of marketing mixes is not feasible because the differences in language, cultural features, Regulations governing marketing, retail structure and topography are great. Global marketing is the attempt to standardize all elements of marketing mix. There is a strong desire on the part of companies to maximize the benefits from standardization through globalisation capturing economies of scale, reduced working capital requirements such as logistics and administration costs, reduced unit cost of products and services, reduced marketing expense such as advertising, promotion and research. Under a global mandate, a company will assign the entire world market to a single unit and no longer subdivides market responsibility by country or region. The collective share of global businesses in the value of world trade will continue to grow. The feasibility of international standardization and the degree of it depends on the type of product or service. Very large companies such as Coca-Cola, IBM, Ford, and Ferrero consider global strategies and deliberately adopted a global marketing strategy for specific products. Global brands have adapted global marketing mixes[102].

6.8 Financial Globalization

Globalization brings a reduction in the barriers—whether technological or legislative—to economic exchanges between countries. Has globalization caused erosion or destruction of the ability of individual national governments to pursue distinct social objectives?

[100] Foster, B. P., R. Fletcher, and W. D. Stout. 2003. "Valuing Intangible Assets." The CPA Journal 73 (October): 50-54.

[101] Sutton, D. and T. Klein. 2003. Enterprise Marketing Management: The New Science of Marketing. John Wiley & Sons, Inc.

[102] J Kapferer, Strategic Brand Management, 1992, Kogan Press, London. T Levitt, The globalisation of Markets, 1983 Harvard Business Review 92.

Historically, the gold standard period (1880-1914) saw a key wave of financial globalization, as cross-border capital flows surged, incorporating countries in the center and the periphery into a worldwide network of finance and investment. A slow reconstruction of the world financial system took place during the Bretton Woods era (1945-1971), although national financial markets remained deeply regulated and controls were characteristically imposed on capital flows. The beginning of a new wave of international financial integration placed in 1970s, reflecting the dismantling of capital controls, de-regulation in national financial systems, and revolutionary technological innovations (not just in information and telecommunications but also in financial product engineering). Globalisation waves (1870-1914, 1960-present) were driven by radical changes in technical and policy barriers to international transactions but the recent globalisation is shaped by radical reduction in communications cost.

Does the rapid globalisation of financial markets takes humanity into uncharted territory? Worldwide finance grows more intricate every year as new sophisticated financial instruments appear continuously. Is massive international lending a new phenomenon? The gold standard allowed huge flows of capital to search the world for the highest return permitting rapid growth and so fostering international trade making gold standard look like the golden age of the international monetary system[103]. Capital mobility is today very high for short-term instruments but not for long-term capital movements. Besides, at the end of the 19th century more important was the long-term than the short-term capital flows. Currency and financial crises are symptoms of financial globalisation, not mentioning the impact on exchange rate management and so there is a need to choose between floating exchange rates which mean instability and joining a monetary union with the loss of sovereignty.

The finance allocation is effective when the alternative with the highest value is chosen. Existing value is viewed as the current value of claims on future cash flows. Consequently financial decisions concern the evaluation and valuation of future cash flow streams. The existing value must be guarded and protected against influences that may eat away existing value[104]. The globalization of finance has accelerated over the last few years and the portfolio diversification of investors has changed[105]. In accordance with Sylvain Champonnois[106] view "financial integration leads to a reorganization of production that generates an increase in aggregate investment and the exit of the least productive firms".

Financial globalization refers to the process by which financial markets of various countries of the globe are integrated as one. A country can pursue only two out of the three policy objectives: free capital mobility, a fixed nominal exchange rate, and an autonomous monetary policy. International capital mobility has prevailed in periods of political support either for subordinating monetary policy to exchange rate stability (as in the gold standard), or for giving up exchange rate stability so as to enable monetary policy to pursue domestic objectives (as in the post-Bretton Woods era). Besides, when countries attempted at the same

---

103 Cairncross, F 1997, The death of distance, Orion, London. R Baldwin, P Martin, Two waves of Globalisation, 1999 WP 6904. Eichengreen, B 1996, Globalising Capital, Princeton University Press.

104 Zopounidis, C., 1999, "Multicriteria Decision Aid in Financial Management", *European Journal of Operational Research* 119, pp. 404-415

105 Forbes, K. (2005): \The Microeconomic Evidence of Capital Controls: No Free Lunch," *NBER* Working Paper No. 11372.

106 Sylvain Champonnois, The Impact Of Financial Integration On Investment And External Financing, 2006 *www.ssrn.com p10.*

time to target their exchange rates and use monetary policy in pursuit of domestic objectives, they had to impose controls to curtail capital movements. According to Augusto de la Torre[107] "Although financial globalization alone cannot explain the frequency and severity of financial crises, its post-Bretton Woods incarnation has been associated with a rising incidence of twin (currency and banking) crises, and even triple (currency, banking, and debt) crises such as the recent ones in Ecuador and Argentina…the successes and failures experienced by countries as they integrate into international financial markets can be linked to the nature of interactions between three elements: (1) money, particularly in its role as store of value; (2) nominal (asset and factor price) flexibility; and (3) the quality of contractual and regulatory institutions." It seems that the integration of the national financial systems from middle-income countries into the world's financial markets has not led to the materialisation of a truly counter-cyclical monetary policy, consumption smoothing, deepening and diversification of their national financial markets, evident reduction in the cost of capital, and important availability of long-duration financial contracts denominated in the national currency. International currency, flexible exchange rate, and sound institutions are considered as a benchmark that defines conditions under which countries can integrate effectively into the world financial markets. In contrast, weak currency, fear of floating, and weak institutions are experiences of developing countries as they integrate into international financial markets.

Are financial markets, both national and international, perfect? Finance is subject to problems like incomplete markets, asymmetric information, bubbles, moral hazard, and contagion. There is a need to prevent financial instability by controlling financial flows that were solely speculative in nature, and to ensure that potential expansion of aggregate expenditure in the productive aspect of the economy was not constrained by inadequate financial flows which means that the introduction of regulations within national boundaries taking the form of preventing financial flows that are mainly geared for speculative activity is necessary. In other words regulations must bring financial stability and promote governments' economic and social objectives. The productive sectors must neither constrained by the price of finance nor by inadequate financial flows. The ceiling on interest rates can be introduced in order to ensure that borrowers are not constrained by the price, and specialized banks are developed to guarantee that the lenders' lack of knowledge does not prevent the financial flows to specific sectors. It could be argued that interest rates play a central linking and causal role amongst savings, investment and growth and government intervention might either distorts or de-emphasizes the role of interest rates, which produces lower savings and consequently lower growth rates than otherwise.

Can interest rate liberalization generate competition in the market? Government intervention in the determination of the price of the currency causes a distortion in the allocation of exports and imports and so bringing a discrepancy between them[108]. It is said that if the currency is allowed to float then the mechanism of its appreciation and depreciation will eventually bring a balance between exports and imports. Philip Arestis and Santonu Basu[109] argue that "it is the flexibility of interest rate movements that would bring the lending

[107] Augusto de la Torre, Eduardo Levy Yeyati, and Sergio L. Schmukler Financial Globalization: Unequal Blessings 2002 *www.ssrn.com*

[108] Cordon, W.M. 1981. Inflation Exchange Rates and the World Economy Lectures on The International Monetary Economics, Second Edition, Oxford: Clarendon Press.

[109] Philip Arestis and Santonu Basu, Financial Globalization: Some Conceptual Problems, The Levy Economics Institute of Bard College and London South Bank University p 6.

and borrowing countries into one market, thereby integrating all the financial markets across the globe." The loan market operates under conditions of uncertainty which means that interest rate variation alone cannot clear this market and interest rates by themselves cannot bring lending and borrowing countries into one market. Any country wanting to borrow from the international financial markets would have to meet the credit standard requirements which are appropriate for these markets. It should be taken into account that countries whose currencies are either not recognized or have a low degree of recognition in international financial markets, would have very limited access to international financial markets, basically because of their very small export sector and since they can only accumulate internationally recognized means of payment. Countries with low export potential have lower access to international financial markets than otherwise. Although the current free movement of financial capital may have opened up the likelihood for the emergence of integrated financial markets, it has also introduced the seeds for inequality in the world economy, and has increased the rate of financial crises. Financial globalization will develop a global institution that can play the central coordinating role[110]. This author considers that IMF should take new responsibilities and contribute to the harmonious financial development in a digital and global world. It is argued that a single currency will allow the global financial market to develop uniform credit standard requirements and in the absence of the latter, this process will cause periodical financial crises and will further intensify the unequal distribution of income and wealth, which immediately contravenes the true meaning of the word globalization[111]. To that extent this author considers that the interplay of values among strong currencies is a dynamic factor for the move of capital creating development opportunities worldwide.

The fitting fiscal strategy vary across countries, depending on the quantity of their revenues, the level and composition of their expenditures, their stage of indebtedness, their endowments of public capital, their fiscal institutions, and a range of other country specific elements. The determination to invest is guided by the return determined by the marginal productivity of public capital dependent on the government's capacity to choose suitable projects and the availability of infrastructure services and the cost of investment[112].

Financial globalization is a free movement of finance across national boundaries without facing any restrictions but financial liberalization is not alone sufficient condition for financial globalization. Moreover, financial globalization means that lending and borrowing countries should be merged into one market. Greenspan[113] suggests that "A clear benefit of financial globalization is that, to the extent that it reduces home bias, savings will be better directed to the most promising investments in the world, increasing global economic growth and prosperity. However, so long as risk aversion exists and trust is enhanced by local

---

[110] Eichengreen, B. and Bordo, M.D. 2002. "Crises Now and Then: What Lessons From the Last Era of Financial Globalization?" NBER Working Paper No. 8716. Dawson, T. C. 2003. "Globalization,the Transition Economies, and the IMF." Remarks to the IMF Seminar for Parliamentarians from Transition Economies, Vienna, 14 March.

[111] Arestis, P. and Demetriades, P. 1997. "Financial Development and Economic Growth: Assessing the Evidence." Economic Journal 107: 783-799.

[112] Buiter, W., and C. Grafe (2004): "Patching up the Pact: Suggestions for EnhancingFiscal Sustainability and Macroeconomic Stability in an Enlarged European Union," *The Economics of Transition* 12 (1), pp. 67 - 102. Harris, Clive (2003): "Private participation in infrastructure in developing countries: Trends, impacts, and policy lessons." World Bank Working Paper No. 5.

[113] Greenspan, A. 2003. "Global Finance: Is It Slowing?" Presented at the Banque de France International Symposium on Monetary Policy, Economic Cycle, and Financial Dynamics. 7 March, Paris: France p3.

familiarity, we cannot expect that home bias will fully dissipate". This author considers that financial globalisation allows a better environment where capital will be moved around the world with less possible barriers where productivity will bring higher profit and so financial globalisation means growth of developing economies as global savings are resourcefully directed to capital accumulation in developing countries where the marginal product of capital is highest. Integration requires individual countries to have the capability to attract financial capital, which is independent of external barriers, which is determined by the internal state of the economies of the countries concerned and the future opportunities these economies can offer[114]. Developed and newly-formed countries undertake various measures in order to prevent financial instability by controlling financial flows that are purely speculative in nature ensuring that possible expansion in aggregate expenditure in the productive aspect of the economy is not constrained by inadequacies in the financial flow.

Government intervention in the foreign exchange market determines the price of currency and could cause a great deal of distortion in the allocation of exports and imports[115]. The existence of different currencies with different degrees of convertibility in the international markets causes a problem in introducing uniform credit standard across the globe and domestic borrowers are required to have an international marketable asset in order to meet international credit standard requirements against which they can obtain loans. According to Philip Arestis and Santonu Basu[116] "Financial liberalization alone does not constitute financial globalization. The process of financial globalization can only be completed if a global financial institution is developed and created that can play a central coordinating and regulatory role. Alongside such an international institution is the requirement for an international single currency, which does not depend on any national currency. Such a currency will allow the global financial market to develop uniform credit standard requirements." Additionally Prasad, E., K. Rogoff, S-J Wei and M. A. Kose [117] consider that "unresolved tension between having good institutions in place before undertaking capital market liberalization and the notion that such liberalization can itself help import best practices and provide an impetus to improve domestic institutions. Such questions can best be addressed only in the context of country-specific circumstances and institutional features". Hence, it could be said that financial free flow between countries is a by-product of financial liberalization which is part of financial globalization. Financial markets and institutions have a positive and significant effect over long-run growth. The export sector of the developing countries is a proxy to credit standard, which also acts as the vital means to repay the loan and any negative performance of this sector produces difficulties in recouping the loan, which in turn brings periodic financial crisis. According to Matías Braun and Borja Larrain[118] "if financial conditions play an important role on aggregate cyclical behavior, one

[114] Kose, M. A., E. S. Prasad and M. E. Terrones. 2003. "Financial Integration and Macroeconomic Volatility." IMF Working Paper, WP/03/50, March.

[115] Cordon, W. M. 1981. Inflation Exchange Rates and the World Economy Lectures on the International Monetary Economics, 2nd Edition, Oxford: Clarendon Press.

[116] Philip Arestis, and Santonu Basu, Financial Globalization and Regulation Working Paper No. 397 p15.

[117] Prasad, E., K. Rogoff, S-J. Wei and M. A. Kose. 2003. "Effects of Financial Globalization on Developing Countries: Some Empirical Evidence." Mimeo, 17 March, Washington D.C.: International Monetary Fund p5.

[118] Matías Braun and Borja Larrain, Finance and the Business Cycle: International, Inter-Industry Evidence, March 4, 2004, p2. p29 "The financial mechanism is asymmetric over the cycle, stronger during downturns than in booms, and especially strong when recessions are accompanied by credit crunches."

expects the response to negative shocks to depend on the agent's reliance on financial markets." Financial development allows companies to grow faster by supplying more external funds; the effect being predominantly strong among companies or industries that normally need more external funds to finance their investments. When investment is principally financed with internal funds, worsening conditions should not have as large an impact as when external funds account for the bulk of financing and if financial markets are imperfect, the differential impact should be stronger when financing frictions are more dominant.

Services provided by financial institutions such as mobilisation of savings, evaluation of projects, management of risks are critical for technological innovation and economic growth[119]. Financial intermediaries can race with domestic companies, which could lead to a credit crisis that lowers investment and productivity. Economic growth induces an opening out of the financial system while the lack of financial growth is a sign of the lack of demand for financial services[120]. Moreover, economic growth demands various new financial services and these are met from the financial side. Channelling sparse resources from savers to investors the financial sector brings actual growth. On the other hand, ceilings on interest rates and directed credit programmes are hampering financial development and in that way reducing rates of capital increase and productivity growth[121]. Advanced degree of financial openness brings high growth rate of a country. The development of banks and stock markets has a certain effect on growth.

Financial services industries have undergone numerous changes in latest decades including consolidation within and across markets, better cross-border financial services provision, the appearance of new financial products and the use of new distribution channels, including e-finance triggered by regulatory changes such as liberalization and by technological advances. Technological progress immediately raises per capita income and a country specializes in the production of goods and services in which it has a comparative advantage increasing productivity growth. According to Anastasia Guscina[122] "changes in labor's share during the preglobalization era are mostly driven by productivity increases and, to a lesser extent, by trade. During the postglobalization era, changes in labor's share of the national income have been equally driven by productivity and openness to trade". Global competition keeps inflation in control, and free capital flows keep interest rates low. While an open economy spurs innovation, globalization permits a further allocation of resources globally and, so, increases the volume of the national income. As a rule central deregulation has been the removal of barriers between commodities, markets and countries. The elimination of barriers of entry and the exclusion of product restrictions has led to new competition in financial services industries. Cross-border banking and internationalization of financial services has been widespread in developing countries. Waves of merger and acquisitions in banks and other financial services providers took advantage of larger markets

---

119 Beck, Thorsten, Ross Levine and Norman Loayza, 2000,'Finance and the source of growth,' Journal of Financial Economics, 58: 261-300. Bekaert, Geert and Christian Lundblad, 2005, 'Does financial liberalization spur growth,' Journal of Financial Economics, 77: 3-55.

120 Chanda, Areendam, 2005, 'The influence of capital controls on long-run growth: where and how much?,' Journal of Development Economics, 77 : 441-466.

121 Durham, J. Benson, 2004,'Absorptive capacity and the effects of foreign direct investment and equity foreign portfolio investment on economic growth,' European Economic Review, 48: 285-306. Eicher, Theo and Leslie Hull, 2004, 'Financial liberalization, openness and convergence,' Journal of International Trade & Economic Development, 13(4): 443-459.

122 *Anastasia Guscina,* Effects of Globalization on Labor's Share in National Income, WP/06/294 p24.

reaping economies of scale advantages[123]. Several emerging markets have seen fast sizeable foreign entry in their banking systems.

Companies in emerging markets are engaged in activities far from the technological frontier innovating not just through first inventions but also by adopting new ways of production, new goods and new forms of organization. The outwardly financed percentage of a company's investment expenditures is related to company's innovation. Financial liberalization boosts economic development by getting better distribution of resources and the investment rate. It has to be taken into consideration that suppliers of capital have a distinctive capacity in many occasions to associate with the most skilled and flourishing entrepreneurs. Financing from foreign banks has a sound influence than financing from resident banks, both in promoting hub innovation of introducing new goods lines and technologies as well as other innovative performance related to opening a new factory, establishing foreign JV and new licensing agreements. Condensed entrée to peripheral finance is associated with lower growth rates. Financial development adds to economic development all the way through more resourceful source allocation rather than through increases in the level of investment or savings recruitment. Innovation responses to a mobile economic environment are the main driver of the development process, understanding the contacts between finance and company innovation is a vital stride in identifying the channels through which financial advance contributes to economic growth. According to Meghana Ayyagari Asli Demirgüç-Kunt and Vojislav Maksimovic[124] "the more innovative firms are younger but larger, and are exporting firms characterized by private ownership, highly educated managers with midlevel managerial experience, and access to external finance. By contrast, firms that do not innovate much are typically state owned firms who do not have foreign competitors. Identity of the controlling shareholder seems to be particularly important for the introduction of new technology and those private firms whose controlling shareholder is a financial institution, tend to be the least innovative".

6.9 MNE, Law and Finance

Horizontal FDI is characterised by a duplication of investment on the domestic and the foreign market which means that the foreign plant produces for the foreign market. Vertical FDI, by contrast, involves the allocation of different stages of production across various countries depending on relative factors prices and final output is then sent back to the home country or it is sold on third markets. Companies invest abroad when the gains from lower variable transportation (or information) costs are higher than the additional fixed costs involved. Firms[125] choose their most favourable strategy after the observation of a random productivity coefficient. Domestic companies would first export and then set up affiliates

[123] Stijn Claessens, Current Challenges in Financial Regulation, WPS4103

[124] Meghana Ayyagari, Asli Demirgüç-Kunt, Vojislav Maksimovic, Firm Innovation in Emerging Markets, 2007 WPS4157 p26. Thomas M. McDonnell et al., *Human Rights and Non-State Actors*, 11 Pace Int'l L. Rev. 205 (1999).

[125] Helpman, E., M. J. Melitz, and S.R. Yeaple (2003). Export versus FDI. National Bureau of Economic Research. NBER Working Paper 9439. Cambridge, MA. Buch, C.M., and A. Lipponer (2004). Clustering or competition? The foreign investment behaviour of German banks. Discussion Paper 06/2004, Economic Research Centre, Deutsche Bundesbank.

abroad if transportation costs fall. As companies engage in FDI, trade in intermediate and final goods and in headquarter services between the parent company and the foreign affiliate increases and the use of intermediate goods and fragmentation of the production process are channels through which complementarity between FDI and trade can arise. According to G. Buch, Alexander Lipponer[126] "banks substitute FDI and cross border services in the sense that they do not invest their capital in these countries but still provide some cross-border services. Overall, our results point towards complementarity rather than substitutionality between FDI and cross-border financial services. These two forms of entering a foreign market share many common determinants, and banks provide more services to countries in which they have also large foreign direct investments (and *vice versa*)." The combination between domestic and headquarters-country borrowing depends on the relative creditor -friendliness of the legal systems and the most advantageous mixture of domestic-country and headquarters-country financing depends on the financial health of the company because claim enforceability is optimistically related both to creditor-friendliness and to balance between the size of claims in the headquarters and domestic-country capital markets. MNEs diminish the credit spread on their debt by equating the marginal enforceability of debt claims in different capital markets leading to internal most advantageous mixes between subsidiary borrowing and borrowing at the parent level.

Technology spillovers from MNEs and the associated increase in productivity enable host country firms to produce at a lower average cost for a given level of production, which increases their price-cost-margins. R&D, human capital accumulation and spillovers are determinants of long-run economic growth and FDI is a mechanism of technology diffusion across countries than international trade[127]. This author believes that the effect of FDI on host economy growth depends on the human capital, measured by level of education, in the host economy and so FDI contributes to economic growth according to absorptive capacity of the host economy. Foreign companies producing at lower marginal costs than domestic companies have a reason to increase output and attract demand away from domestic companies causing host country rivals to cut production which, if they face fixed costs of production, will raise their average cost and, consequently, reduce their probability of survival. The high-level structure of the MNE does not mean that there is no need for country-level management and so it has to find its way back into the organisation chart at an operational level by developing the appropriate management systems. FDI makes major contributions to the economic development of emerging markets, emerging markets play a crucial role in the global strategies of MNEs, and so MNE and local policy makers have a common interest in encouraging foreign investment. In fact, MNEs balance localization and standardization viewing global strategy in focusing on similarities across countries, and the potential for the scale economies that such commonalities unlock, as their primary source of

---

[126] Claudia M. Buch, Alexander Lipponer, FDI versus cross-border financial services: The globalisation of German banks, Discussion Paper Series 1: Studies of the Economic Research Centre No 05/2004,p36, p15 "(i) Firms with a low productivity level service only the domestic market since their expected profits from exports or FDI are negative, (ii) firms at an intermediate level of productivity export, and (iii) only the highly productive firms engage in FDI."

[127] Blomström, M., and A. Kokko, 2002. FDI and Human Capital: A Research Agenda, Technical Paper no. 195, OECD Development Centre, Paris: OECD, August. Klaus E. Meyer, FDI Spillovers in Emerging Markets: A Literature Review and New Perspectives, 2003, DRC Working Papers, No. 15.

added value. Correctly choosing how much to adapt a business model is important for extracting value from international operations.

Financial strategies involving factors such as debt/equity swaps or equity-listings in foreign equity markets affect the company's relative cost and accessibility of capital, and motivate a company's engagement in FDI. In other words, a company′s financial strength affects its ability to engage in FDI. The ability for a company to make the most of its competitive advantage through FDI depends on discovering product, locational or financial market imperfections that encourage FDI. Finance-specific factors are recognized as control variables or locational advantages to be dealt with by reactive financial strategies. Companies must be able to gain and retain their present access to foreign investors. According to Lars Oxelheim, Trond Randøy and Arthur Stonehill[128] "First, we suggest that a firm is more likely to engage in FDI when it has access to competitively priced equity. Second, we hypothesize that a firm is more likely to engage in FDI when the firm is cross-listed in a prestigious capital market. Third, we suggest that a firm is more likely to engage in FDI when it is following globally recognized accounting and disclosure standards. Fourth, we hypothesize that a firm is more likely to undertake FDI after it has retained as advisors one of the prominent international banking institutions. Fifth, we suggest that a firm is more likely to engage in FDI when it enjoys a strong investment grade credit rating. Sixth, we hypothesize that a firm is more likely to engage in FDI when the firm is able to negotiate reduced taxation and/or to attract subsidies for financing it. Seventh, we suggest that a firm is more likely to engage in FDI when the firm is able to reduce financial monitoring costs through such an investment. Finally, we hypothesize that a firm is more likely to engage in FDI when this enables the firm to reduce financial and operating exposures." Foreign companies face additional costs, arising from their unfamiliarity with and lack of roots in a foreign environment. There are advantages gained by indigenous companies due to their easier access to local information and knowledge, and higher transaction and information costs incurred by foreign companies. The characteristics of companies themselves create the advantages of a location and the size of MNEs is regarded as a key factor affecting the nature of their international activity and their ability to own and control resources on a global scale.

Venture capital is used to finance companies with the potential and ambition to grow rapidly that may be unable to obtain bank finance because of the high risk they present. Venture capital involves the supply of equity finance—so the investor shares in the benefits of high growth—alongside 'hands-on' governance so as to aid in bringing about the success of such companies. 'Start-up' companies developing new technologies do not generate steady cash flows which can be used to make interest payments on debt and their cash flows are *negative*, with large sums being spent in order first to develop a product and second to grow the market leading to a long lag-time before any repayment to investors can be made. The worth of a start-up company inhere in the ideas—the 'human capital' of the entrepreneur, and their opportunities for growth, which are not amenable to enforcement by an investor rather than liquid assets. Finance is not advanced all at once, but rather is 'staged' and so finance may not be available, or only on significantly more expensive terms which means that if performance targets are not met in the interim the venture capitalist control rights over the

---

[128] Lars Oxelheim, Trond Randøy and Arthur Stonehill, On the Treatment of Finance-Specific Factors Within the OLI Paradigm, Working Paper No. 554, 2001, p26.

decision whether or not to continue the project[129]. Venture capitalists naturally take preferred shares, usually convertible on demand into ordinary shares, whereas the entrepreneur takes 'plain' ordinary shares[130].

Law affects the incentives of marginal investors and entrepreneurs, in that way affecting the aggregate levels of venture capital investment in a country. A series of different regulatory provisions have an impact on the incentives of investors to supply, or of entrepreneurs to demand, venture capital finance. Globalisation brings harmonization and law reform seeking to stimulate the supply of domestic venture capital will make less of a difference to overall levels of investment than efforts to stimulate demand.

Risk management was implemented on an uncoordinated basis across various units of a company and the primary focus was to minimize costs. Besides, nowadays risk management involves a broader view of a company addressing short term and long term exposures encompassing financial and operational hedges and so reducing risk while placing a company in a position to benefit from opportunities arising from exchange rate changes. A company relies on operational adjustments in sourcing, utilizing different plant locations and pricing. It should be taken into account that exchange rates influence MNEs' current and future cash flows and so stock prices. The structure of the foreign currency cash flows of a company depends on the company's competitive position in the industry in which it operates. Companies use a combination of production and marketing strategies across a company's operating units to manage long term exposure, whereas foreign exchange derivatives are more often used to manage short term exposure. A company's ability to implement operational hedges is measured by examining the network structure of its foreign operations. A MNE's network has to do with the various foreign countries in which operations are conducted and the concentration of operations in different locations. Foreign exchange exposure is a vital source of risk for MNE and they effectively manage this exposure by utilizing financial hedges and operational strategies to achieve an optimal hedging outcome[131].

MNEs operate in the interstices between national systems, pursuing advantage by maneuvering across boundaries as separate legal entities, headquarters and subsidiaries, under unified managerial control and the different legal entities that comprise the multinational operate under different legal systems[132]. Legal systems reveal significant cross-sectional differences that wield substantial predictive power for national financial structures and legal-system variables are determinant of a multinational's subsidiary/home country borrowing mix, even after controlling for other effects such as taxes[133]. When the multinational becomes financially distressed, these differences between legal systems generate differences in the bargaining power of national and headquarters-country creditors which means that if creditor protection is weak, borrowers capture most of the surplus from flourishing restructuring, and the shortfall between promised and received payments is large. According to Thomas H.

---

[129] Corcoran, E. (2002), 'Digital Diaspora; From the Internet wreckage, the Spirit of Silicon Valley Emerges', 169(4) Forbes

[130] Cumming, D.J. (2002), 'Contracts and Exits in Venture Capital Finance', working paper, University of Alberta School of Business.

[131] D Carter, C Pantzalis, B simkins,, Asymmetric exposure to foreign-exchange risk: Financial and real option hedges implemented by US multinational corporations, 2 003.

[132] Hansmann, H. and R. Kraakman, O., 2000, The essential role of organizational law Yale Law Review 110, 387-440.

[133] Desai, M., 1998, A multinational perspective on capital structure choice and internal capital markets, working paper, Harvard University.

Noe[134] "The exact mix of financing chosen depends on the creditor friendliness of the headquarters and host countries, the going-concern versus liquidation value of the firm, the total external financing needs of the firm, and the distribution of operating cash flows. Testable comparative statics are then derived which link multinational capital structure, multinational debt renegotiation strategy, security allocation, and the impact of currency risk, to these variables." Moreover, the multinational can purposefully exploit conflicts of interest between headquarters-country and domestic creditors by using the claims of one country's creditors as a wedge to force concessions from the other country's creditors creating valuable renegotiation options for the distressed multinational. Furthermore, the capacity to renegotiate ex post, because it weakens the relationship between company performance and stockholder payoffs produces agency costs, which means that agency costs are borne by the shareholders of the multinational which attempt to curtail agency costs by minimizing financial shortfalls, and so the credit spreads, associated with its capital structure.

Capital structure choice of foreign affiliates is predominantly essential for MNEs because the capital markets diverge among states concerning the degree of development and so MNEs have to maximize its consolidated company value under such difference raising capital in a state where capital cost is low, and optimally assign the means to the companies that provide it with the highest price. The country-of-origin of foreign subsidiaries influences the corporate structures and financing patterns of the foreign companies. For instance, Japanese MNEs allocated finances effectively by utilizing internal capital markets to the same degree as U.S. MNEs did relying on financing from their parent affiliates and Japanese banks. The corporate finance of foreign affiliates of Japanese MNEs was analogous to that in Japan2. Therefore, foreign affiliates of Japanese MNEs were bare higher risk of the scarcity of finances when the Japanese banks could not supply enough credit capacity[135]. The foreign subsidiaries are able to adjust themselves to the host countries' financial environment but the extent to which they differ is according to their country-of-origin. Japanese foreign affiliates rely less on financial institutions and capital market of the host country coming across a problem in procuring enough amounts of local currency. According to Takeshi Yamamoto, Yasuhiro Yonezawa, Hiroshi Yamaguchi and Tomoshige Nambu[136] "financing of foreign affiliates is by far lagged behind that of the Japanese companies. It is understandable that the asymmetry of information is higher in foreign countries than in Japan. But foreign affiliates of U.S. multinationals have far advanced financing strategy in terms of diversification of the source of funds, by including local financing as options from the beginning. Such practice should also be inevitable for the Japanese multinationals to manage their risk effectively".

It is worth mentioning that finance has various effects on growth in different countries, time periods or stages of development and according to Levine, Loayza, and Beck[137] the effect declines as the level of financial development increases and the structure of financial

---

134 Thomas H. Noe, Legal-system arbitrage and the theory of multinational finance, Working Paper 2003, p64.

135 Banga. R., 2002, Corporate Financial Structures and Financial Performance of Japanese, US and Indian Firms in the Indian Manufacturing, *Journal of International Economic Studies*, No.16.

136 Takeshi Yamamoto, Yasuhiro Yonezawa, Hiroshi Yamaguchi and Tomoshige Nambu, Capital Structure Choice of the Foreign Affiliates of Japanese Multinational Firms: Characteristics and Problems, www.ssrn.com p14-15.

137 LEVINE, ROSS, NORMAN LOAYZA, AND THORSTEN BECK, "Financial Intermediation and Growth: Causality and Causes," Journal of Monetary Economics, 2000, 46(1), 31-77.

markets changes as a country becomes more developed. Increased availability of financial instruments and institutions reduces transaction and information costs in an economy helping economic agents hedge, trade, and pool risk raising investment and economic growth. The financial sector has to develop to a certain minimum size before adequate funds can be pooled together to finance larger projects. According to Felix Rioja and Neven Valev[138] "In the low region (countries with very low levels of financial development), additional improvements in financial markets have an uncertain effect on growth. In the intermediate region, financial development has a large, positive effect on growth. Finally, in the high region, additional financial improvements have a positive, but smaller effect on growth...the effect of finance on growth is not uniformly positive and even when positive its size differs. Our results suggest that financial development exerts a strong positive effect on economic growth *only* once it has reached a certain size threshold, i.e., in what we call the "middle" region. In the "low" region (below this threshold), the effect is uncertain as different empirical measures of bank-based financial development suggest a zero effect or a positive effect. At the other end, in the "high" region, the growth effect of financial development declines once it reaches very high levels." It could be said that financial intermediaries mitigate risk by holding diversified portfolios shifting towards more high-return projects and so contributing to economic growth and the scale of risk diversification and the resulting positive effect on growth increase as the size of the financial system grows from low to high levels[139]. Development in the financial sector produces sound results only if the regulatory and supervisory authorities have enough expertise to manage that growth. Furthermore, Rousseau and Wachtel[140] consider that the outcome of finance on growth is drastically reduced in high inflation environments, which is more common in lower income countries with less developed financial markets. High inflation leads to underdeveloped financial systems and consequently to a collapse of the finance growth nexus. Levine and Zervos[141] specify that market-based external financing becomes more and more central as the financial system evolves. The effect of financial development (bank and stock market measures) on growth is positive, it is difficult to evaluate if a bank-based or a market-based financial system produces stronger effects and their contributing analogy depends on the specific characteristics of every financial market. Access to credit is necessary for development and growth and asymmetric information between borrowers and lenders results in unproductive allocation of credit and credit rationing. According to Inessa Love and Nataliya Mylenko[142] "the existence of private credit registries is associated with lower financing constraints and higher share of bank borrowing in firm's financing structure, while public credit registries do not seem to have significant effect on availability of financing." This author considers that an effective law is resulting in effective private credit registries and an effective legal system for the operation of credit markets as a whole and credit registries in particular is necessary for less financing constraints

138 Felix Rioja and Neven Valev, Does One Size Fit All? : A Re-examination of the Finance and Growth Relationship, 2003, http://ssrn.com/abstract=438262 p1,3.

139 Berthelemy, Jean-Claude And Varoudakis, Aritomene. "Economic Growth, Convergence Clubs, and the Role of Financial Development," Oxford Economic Papers, Apr 1996, 48(2), pp. 300-28.

140 Rousseau, Peter And Paul Wachtel, "Inflation Thresholds and the Finance-Growth Nexus," 2002 Journal of International Money and Finance, 21, pp. 777-793.

141 Levine, Ross and Sara Zervos, "Stock Markets, Banks, and Economic Growth," American Economic Review, 1998, 88(3), 537-58.

142 Inessa Love and Nataliya Mylenko, Credit Reporting And Financing Constraints, World Bank Policy Research Working Paper 3142, October 2003, p22.

which means more effective allocation of credit translated into higher productivity and so growth.

Banks and stock market development enhance economic growth and financial institutions are central for company and industrial expansion[143]. A legal system where private property rights are enforced, support private contractual arrangements, and protect the legal right of investors, means that savers are prepared to finance companies and financial markets flourish. Besides, legal institutions that neither support private property rights nor assist private contracting hamper corporate finance and so inhibit financial development. This author considers that successful investor protection facilitates efficient corporate financing leading towards growth-enhancing financial development. Legal institutions influence corporate finance and consequently the financial development of a country. For instance, a country's contract, company, and bankruptcy, and securities laws, and the enforcement of these laws primarily determine the rights of securities holders and the operation of financial systems and so have the environment where finance occurs. If managers and controlling shareholder are in a position to expropriate minority shareholders and creditors and legal institutions play a central role in determining the degree of expropriation which in turn adds to the financial development or negates the relation of finance-growth nexus. Moreover, cross-country differences in (i) contract, company, bankruptcy, and securities laws, (ii) the legal systems' emphasis on private property rights, and (iii) the effectiveness of enforcement affect the degree of expropriation and so the confidence with which people purchase securities and participate in financial markets and so harmonisation of the way of working of financial markets is imminent. Easterbrook and Fischel[144] stress that successful legal institutions allow knowledgeable and experienced financial market participants to design sophisticated private contracts to ameliorate complex agency problems. To that extent, Posner[145] considers that legal systems that accept case law and judicial discretion are more responsive to changing financial conditions than legal systems that adhere firmly to formalistic procedures and that rely more strictly on judgments based closely on statutory law.

Sharpe ratios converge to competence following liberalization not because the level of growth is enhanced, but rather because instability converges fast to its efficient level. Branching restrictions is a limit to the scope of banks from an effective diversification standpoint. Sectoral shares of output converge notably faster towards their efficient levels after bank branching deregulation. The efficient frontier implies efficient patterns of specialization rather than ones that merely average investments across all sectors. The central outcome of branching deregulation that affects effectiveness of capital allocation is the appearance of larger, better-diversified banks, rather than merely an increase in the number of banks or branches operating in a state. Investments in high risk, high return technologies are attained only after suitably high levels of diversification have been reached. To that extent financial development has imperative consequences for the specialization of investment in a

[143] Demirgüç-Kunt, A., Maksimovic, V., 1998. Law, finance, and firm growth. Journal of Finance 53, 2107-2137. Demirgüç-Kunt, A., Maksimovic, V., 2002. Funding growth in bank-based and market-based financial systems: Evidence from firm level data. Journal of Financial Economics 65, 337-363.

[144] Easterbrook, R., Fischel, D., 1991. The economic structure of corporate law. Cambridge, MA: Harvard University Press.

[145] Posner, R.A., 1973. Economic Analysis of the Law. Boston, MA: Little-Brown, 1973. Thorsten Beck and Ross Levine, Legal Institutions and Financial Development, World Bank Policy Research Working Paper 3136, September 2003.

manner that depends on the variance-covariance properties of investment returns. Access to finance affects specialization patterns. Sectors with large liquidity needs have greater unpredictability of output escalation and lower output growth in underdeveloped financial markets. According to Viral V. Acharya, Jean Imbs and Jason Sturgess[146] "finance (and in particular banking deregulations) have an effect on aggregate economic growth. We find that the share of fast-growing, volatile sectors in the overall (state) economies actually increases with liberalization. High growth industries effectively become more important in liberalized states. Our conclusions are strongest in industries that are populated by young, small and financially constrained firms, and they are indeed often absent from the complementary samples."

Convergence of financial regulation across jurisdictions has been considered as a precondition of market integration and the relationship between financial integration and regulatory harmonization has changed as a result of the accelerating pace of financial globalization. Should regulatory developments be left to market forces alone? It is worth mentioning that coordination failures associated with market-led initiatives produce negative systemic externalities, attracting capital toward less regulated systems and institutions or generating forms of competition in laxity that undermines financial stability. The cost of financial regulation and supervision should not be too high. Countries with better legal systems, favorable conditions for foreign investment and investor protection, generate larger growth effects[147]. According to Aliber[148] financial integration was the result of increased provision of foreign financial services associated with the trade of goods rather than an independent phenomenon. Additionally, financial integration takes place separately from the level of economic integration. The growth of capital movements, related to technological developments and to current and capital account liberalization, brought forward the fact that financial integration is less dependent on other aspects of economic integration than in the past. Scott[149] points out that harmonization of regulatory systems is not an easy process at the best of times and often proves illusory where distorted by asymmetries in size and influence. Different legal traditions and to deal with the specific needs of financial systems of different size and complexity brings forward the need for different regulatory reforms in order to improve the effectiveness of the standards and codes approach as a whole. According to Cally Jordan and Giovanni Majnoni[150] "The process of financial globalization has shifted the balance of power from governments to markets and has made the traditional solution, - resort to international treaties - less viable. Historic references are often lacking and new institutional solutions are being tested through a process of trial and error. The dissemination of international codes and standards supported by IFIs represents an innovative and constructive effort in coordinating national regulatory dynamics. It combines some of the key features of the most successful episodes of regulatory harmonization - minimum

---

146 Viral V. Acharya, Jean Imbs and Jason Sturgess, Finance and Efficiency: Do Bank Branching Regulations Matter?, Research Paper Series N°06 – 36,SFI.

147 Wurgler, J., 2000, Financial Markets and the Allocation of Capital, Journal of Financial Economics 58, 187-214.

148 Aliber, Robert, (1984), "International Banking: a Survey", Journal of Money, Credit and Banking, pp. 661-695, November.

149 Scott, Hal. S. (2000), "Internationalization of Primary Public Securities Markets", Law and Contemporary Problems, pp. 71-104. vol. 63, n.3.

150 Cally Jordan and Giovanni Majnoni, Financial Regulatory Harmonization and the Globalization of Finance, World Bank Policy Research Working Paper 2919, October 2002, p25.

harmonization and reputationally induced discipline – and represents, with all its limitations, a structured approach to the problems raised by the globalization of capital markets." Equity market liberalization by allowing foreign investors to transact in local securities and vice versa increases economic growth. Moreover, Laurence Ball, N. Gregory Mankiw and Ricardo Reis[151] consider that "When the economy is hit by shocks to aggregate demand or productivity, strict price level targeting is optimal: policymakers should return the price level to a predetermined path as quickly as possible. However, if there are persistent shocks to firms' markups, the optimal rule allows temporary deviations from the long-run price target."

Financial markets and financial intermediaries play a vital role by mobilizing savings, allocating credit, and facilitating the hedging, pooling and pricing of risks. The need for financing depends on the type of activity companies engage in and a well-functioning financial sector has positive effects on a country's aggregate growth opportunities[152]. Industries dependent on external financing grow faster in countries with well-developed financial systems and well-developed financial intermediaries and markets have a constructive outcome on the content of external financing in net trade. Differences between countries in their domestic institutions of credit contract enforcement give rise to comparative advantage taking into account that financial markets and intermediaries are factors in the production of goods and services. According to Svaleryd and Vlachos[153] there is considerable relation between the degree of financial development and comprehensive openness to trade. Financial markets shape industry specialization patterns and so international competitiveness. Financial services are difficult to trade geographically even within a country but geography is still of significance for financing[154] and how internationally mobile financial capital is put to use depends on the immobile institutional features of a society. When financial markets work without hostility, the supply of external financing will be very elastic and differences in the real use of external financing in such an economy will reflect differences in demand for this type of funding. Taking into consideration that the legal system protecting creditors and minority shareholders against expropriation by majority shareholders and managers is key to the working of the financial system, markets and banks are complements rather than substitutes and it is the effectiveness of the financial sector as a whole that is of significance[155]. It could be argued that operative corporate governance constitutes a better staring point for cross-country comparisons of financial systems than the bank versus market framework. MNEs are insensitive to local financing conditions and to the extent that MNEs increase their share of international trade, local financial markets wield a continuously smaller impact on the pattern of production and trade. Financial markets solve information

---

[151] Laurence Ball, N. Gregory Mankiw and Ricardo Reis, Monetary Policy for Inattentive Economies Discussion Paper Number 1997, 2003 p1, *http://post.economics.harvard.edu/hier/2003papers/2003list.html*

[152] Levine, R., N. Loayza, and T. Beck (2000), "Financial Intermediation and Growth:Causality and Causes", Journal of Monetary Economics, 46, 31-77.

[153] Svaleryd, H. and J. Vlachos (2001), "Markets for Risk and Openness to Trade: How are they Related?", Journal of International Economics 253.

[154] Pagano, M., O. Randl, A. Röell, J. and J. Zechner (2001) "What Makes Stock- Exchanges Succeed? Evidence from Cross-Listing Decisions", European Economic Review, 45, 770-782.

[155] La Porta, R., F. Lopez-de-Silanes, A. Schleifer, and R. Vishny (2000), "Investor Protection and Corporate Governance", Journal of Financial Economics, 58, 3-27.

problems in the market place affecting the choice of technology and so the financial system affects R&D[156].

Which are the growth effects of international financial liberalization and integration? Rodrik[157]considers that no effect of liberalized capital accounts, either on the per capita GDP growth rate or the investment to GDP ratio. There is an increase in stock prices and investments after stock market liberalization[158] and the cost of capital is after stock market liberalization[159]. FDI reduces, and capital account restrictions increase firms' financing constraints and international financial integration affects growth by enhancing the performance of the domestic financial sector. Financial development adds to the ability to allocate the capital to producers in the economy. The influence of financial liberalization on growth depends on the level of financial development in a country because developed economies are better able to make productive use of new capital inflows than are emerging market economies. According to Jonas Vlachos and Daniel Waldenström[160] "industries highly dependent on external financing do not experience a higher growth in value added among countries with liberalized capital accounts or equity markets. The same result holds for countries more integrated with the international capital market in terms of actual capital flows and stocks." Financial liberalization stimulates company creation, which increases competition and production and accelerated company growth is vital for a functioning creative and sustained long run economic development[161]. Financial variables affect future inflation primarily via their effect on aggregate demand and real money balances have a straight effect on aggregate demand because they affect a wide range of yields and relative prices, which are relevant for aggregate demand, and also via real balance effects. Instability in the money demand function has made the growth of monetary aggregates an unpredictable variable of monetary policy and of future inflationary pressures in many countries[162]. Aggregate demand responds to the expected long-term real interest rate, which can be proxied by the short-term nominal rate.[163] Price stability produces stable macroeconomic conditions and higher inflation and surging asset prices are both counteracted by higher interest rates and

---

[156] Carlin, W. and C. Mayer (1999), "Finance, Investment and Growth", CEPR Discussion Paper #2233.

[157] Rodrik, Dani (1998) "Who Needs Capital-Account Convertibility?" in "Should the IMF pursue Capital-Account Convertibility?", Essays in International Finance, 207, Princeton University.

[158] Henry, Peter Blair (2000) "Stock Market Liberalization, Economic Reform, and Emerging Market Equity Prices", Journal of Finance, 55:2, 529-564. Henry, Peter Blair (2000) "Do Stock Market Liberalizations Cause Investment Booms?", Journal of Financial Economics, 58:1-2, 301-334

[159] Bekaert, Geert and Campbell Harvey (2000) "Foreign Speculators and Emerging Equity Markets", Journal of Finance, 55:2, 565-613. Bekaert, Geert, Campbell Harvey and Christian Lundblad (2000) "Emerging Equity Markets and Economic Development", Journal of Development Economics, 66, 465-504. Bekaert, Geert, Campbell Harvey and Christian Lundblad (2001) "Does financial liberalization spur economic growth?", NBER WP #8245.

[160] Jonas Vlachos and Daniel Waldenström, International Financial Liberalization and Industry Growth, 2002-11-14, SSE/EFI Working Paper Series in Economics and Finance No. 513 p16.

[161] Arteta, Carlos, Barry Eichengreen and Charles Wyplosz (2001), "When Does Capital Account Liberalization Help More Than It Hurts?", NBER WP #8414.

[162] Bernanke, B., M. Gertler and S Gilchrist, (1998), 'The Financial Accelerator in a Quantitative Business Cycle Framework', NBER WP 6455. Ball, L., (1998), 'Policy Rules for Open Economies', NBER Working Paper No. 6760

[163] Rudebusch, G. and L. Svensson, (1999), 'Policy Rules for Inflation Targeting', in: J. B. Taylor (ed.), Monetary Policy Rules, University of Chicago Press for NBER. Wright, S., (1998), 'Monetary Policy, Nominal Interest Rates, and Long-Horizon Inflation Uncertainty', University of Cambridge, DAE Working Paper No. 9820

so price stability and financial stability are conflicting goals of monetary policy as economic theory suggests that both price shocks and interest rate shocks are two essential forces that produce financial trouble[164]. Financial distress is directly related to macroeconomic developments and financial stability is an additional channel of the monetary transmission mechanism. Important role played by credit expansions, price shocks and interest rate shocks in explaining increases in financial distress. High real interest rates, high inflation and rapid credit growth are important leading indicators of banking crises leading to financial distress[165]. According to Helena Svaleryd and Jonas Vlachos[166] the degree of integration on international financial markets has an independent, positive, effect on openness to trade. Agell[167] considers that the recent trend towards globalization of economic activity leads to a greater exposure to risk, and so greater demand for risk-reducing reforms, while at the same time reducing the scope for government interventions more than ever through taxation and labor-market regulations. This author believes that domestic asset markets and the integration of international asset markets assist liberal trade policies and advanced domestic and international financial markets lessen some negative effects of globalization. Financial liberalization not only brings more funds to capital-poor states, but also improves corporate governance[168].

Are financial markets efficient and rational? The industrial economy with factories producing commodities changes into a service economy where networks provide financial and other services. Money management more and more dominates real management and simply two percent of currencies flooding across the world are in essence real trade which means that great amounts of rapid financial capital transgressing geographical and temporal boarders establish a virtual level of business. Monetary products are basis for the value of financial derivatives. The liberalisation of financial systems in recent decades appears to have increased the frequency and scope of financial cycles[169] and the relationship between credit and asset prices lies at the heart of financial cycles. High credit growth have a direct and indirect effect on asset prices and credit expansions fuel aggregate demand and tend to generate an upswing in economic activity and so higher asset values strengthen the net worth of agents and their borrowing capacity by increasing the value of collateral. According to *Jan Hansen*[170] financial cycles amplify, and are amplified by, the business cycle, meaning that financial and real developments are mutually reinforcing. Rapid credit growth, rapid increases

---

[164] Allen, F. och D. Gale, (1999), "Bubbles, Crises, and Policy," Oxford Review of Economic Policy, 15, 9–18. Allen, F. och D. Gale, (2000), "Bubbles and Crises," Economic Journal, 110, 236–255.

[165] Bell, J. och D. Pain, (2000), "Leading Indicator Models of Banking Crises — A Critical Review," Financial Stability Review, 9, 113–129. Daltung, S., (2001), "The Relationship Between Price Stability and Financial Stability," Sveriges Riksbank Economic Review, 2001:4, 5–27. Goodfriend, M., (2001), "Financial Stability, Deflation, and Monetary Policy," Bank of Japan, Monetary and Economic Studies, Special Edition, 19, S143–176.

[166] Helena Svaleryd and Jonas Vlachos, Does Financial Development Lead to Trade Liberalization?, 2000 09 10 working paper.

[167] Agell, J. [1999], "On the benefits from rigid labor markets: Norms, Market Failures, and Social Insurance", Economic Journal, 109, F143-F164.

[168] Stulz, René, 2005, The limits of financial globalization, Journal of Finance 60, 1595-1638.

[169] Borio, C., C. Furfine and P. Lowe, (2001), "Procyclicality of the Financial System and Financial Stability: Issues and Policy Options" in Marrying the Macro- and Micro-Prudential Dimensions of Financial Stability, BIS Papers No. 1.

[170] Jan Hansen, Financial Cycles and Bankruptcies in the Nordic Countries, AUGUST 2003, Sveriges Riksbank Working Paper Series 149.

in asset prices or an investment boom, by itself, does not pose threat to the stability of the financial system but it is the combination of these events that increases the probability of problems. Rapid credit growth, rapid increases in asset prices and, in some cases, high levels of investment should not occur concurrently and so the system cannot absorb the sudden changes[171]. Fiscal policy and the inflow of foreign capital keep down interest rates and the cost of capital contributing to the high level of investment. The use of IT by large service industries such as wholesale and retail trade, finance and business services increases labor productivity growth than the economy as a whole.

The monetary policy is predominantly vital since the central bank has a natural role in ensuring financial stability and has virtually always been involved in financial stability, directly or indirectly[172]. Financial crisis exist when financial markets are unable to effectively channel funds to those who have the most productive investment opportunities. Low growth or recessions have been found to increase the likelihood of a banking crisis. Too high real interest rates (either external or domestic), large capital inflows but also capital flight, predominantly in the case of emerging countries, and shocks to inflation or to the price level enhance the likelihood of a banking crisis. Besides, inflation is related to the way monetary policy is conducted, in so far as monetary policy aims at price stability. In fact, disproportionate credit growth and low levels of liquidity in the banking system increases the probability of banking crises[173].

Central bank independence and authorization to restrain inflation are important institutional devices to ensure price stability. Money demand is stable in the long run in countries having experienced systemic banking and banking crises do not automatically lead to substantial changes in the monetary policy design[174]. Capital inflows add to over-borrowing and increase credit risk leading to currency mismatches if foreign capital flows are converted into domestic-currency denominated loans. The monetary policy objectives and strategies are the key tools the central bank has to perform its functions influencing financial stability, directly or indirectly and if the central bank plan leads to a too lax monetary policy, inflation will be more volatile. A very tight monetary policy leading to very low inflation levels and, thereby, very low interest rates, makes cash holdings more attractive than interest-bearing bank deposits and so causing financial instability. If a tight monetary policy does not bring down inflation and real interest rates remain high, financial stability is at risk. Domaç and Martinez Peria[175] consider that fixed exchange rate regimes, and unreservedly an exchange rate-based monetary strategy, are preferred to reduce the probability of banking crises among developing countries. A high degree of central bank independence fostering price stability contributes to financial stability.

---

[171] Borio, C. and P. Lowe, (2002), "Asset Prices, Financial and Monetary Stability: Exploring the Nexus", BIS Working Paper No. 114.

[172] Schinasi, G. J. (2003). Responsibility of central banks for stability in financial markets, IMF Working Paper 03/121.

[173] Gourinchas , P. O., R. Valdés, And O. Landarretche (2001). «Lending booms: Latin America and the world», Economía, Vol. 1(2).

[174] García Herrero, A. (1997). Monetary impact of a banking crisis and the conduct of monetary policy, IMF Working Paper 97/124. Martínez Peria, M. S. (2000). The impact of banking crises on money demand and price stability, The World Bank Working Paper n.º 2305.

[175] Domaç, I. And M. S. Martínez Peria (2000). Banking crises and exchange rate regimes: is there a link?, The World Bank Working Paper n.º 2489.

A mixture of improved information technology and financial innovations such as derivatives contracts has in most developed countries reduced the proportion which interest income contributes to financial GDP[176] contributing to financial conglomeration, involving the creation of entities which combine banking, insurance and other financial services under one umbrella. European conglomeration has been motivated by significant cost advantages arising from economies of scale and scope in insurance sales and underwriting. Banks have combined with life insurance firms to form companies which have generated a return on sales and on capital of 20 to 30 percent[177].

Financial structure is unrelated to the level and growth rate of economic development. Stock markets permit investors to hold diverse views about investments, whereas banks can exploit economies in acquiring information about companies. Banks exploit economies of scale in collecting information about more traditional investments. According to Dewatripont and Maskin[178] decentralized financial systems with many small banks impose tighter budget constraints than centralized systems with a small number of banks and financial systems with many small banks foster industries with short-term projects whereas industries with longer term investments fare better in systems with a few large banks. Corporate governance is effective under concentrated rather than dispersed ownership systems but active corporate governance by large shareholders should not create interference in activities that are best delegated to managers. Burkhart, Gromb, and Panunzi[179] consider that ownership concentration determines the commitment of investors to preserving incentives that encourage managerial investment. Financial and ownership systems are associated with various types of corporate activities and investments. Securities markets consent to diverse views amongst investors about, for example, new technologies, while more traditional investments benefit from the economies of monitoring banks provide. Concentration of credit markets in fragmented banking systems and credit markets are associated with high-risk R&D investments, and concentrated credit markets are associated with long-term investments in more mature industries. Levine and Zervos[180] regard that the size of the banking sector and the extent of stock market activity are related to future economic growth. Industries dependent on external finance grow faster in the presence of a concentrated banking system[181]. It should be taken into account that financial development based on an efficient legal system according to the circumstances and conditions and phase of development of a country rather than financial structure influence growth. According to Wendy Carlin and Colin Mayer[182] "there is a link between financial systems and types of activities in advanced

---

176 Allen, F. And A. M. Santomero, 2001, "What Do Financial Intermediaries Do?", Journal of Banking and Finance, 25, pp. 271 — 294.

177 Lown, C. S., C. L. Osler, P. E. Strahan And A. Sufi, 2000, "The Changing Landscape of the Financial Services Industry: What Lies Ahead?", Federal Reserve Bank of New York Economic Policy Review, 6, pp. 39 — 55.

178 Dewatripont, M., Maskin, E., 1995. Credit efficiency in centralized and decentralized economies. Review of Economic Studies 62, 541-555.

179 Burkhart, M., Gromb, D., Panunzi, F.,1997. Large shareholders, monitoring and the value of the firm. Quarterly Journal of Economics 112, 693-728.

180 Levine, R., Zervos., S., 1998. Stock markets, banks and economic growth. American Economic Review 88, 537-58.

181 Cetorelli, N. Gambera, M., 2001. Banking market structure, financial dependence and growth: International evidence from industry data. Journal of Finance 56, 617-648.

182 Wendy Carlin and Colin Mayer, Finance, investment, and growth, 2002 Working paper University of Oxford p25.

economies... For example, the relevance of ownership concentration and the concentration of banking systems could be quite different for countries in early and late stages of development." Financial development measured by the size and depth of banking sectors and securities markets promotes economic growth.

Do institutional differences in financial systems, ownership structure and legal systems create a form of comparative rather than absolute advantage? Different forms of economic activity have different characteristics associated with them that make the provision of particular types of finance or particular forms of governance arrangements desirable because activities differ in their degree of uncertainty or in the extent to which cooperation from stakeholders in the company (employees and suppliers) is required for successful performance. Stock market liquidity and banking development are both definitely correlated with contemporary and future rates of economic growth. Financial development is relevant to industries that are dependent on external finance and that these industries grow fastest in countries with well-developed financial systems. There is a strong relation between economic growth in various industries and countries and the interaction of financial development of countries and the financial dependence of industries. Hence, financial development has influence on the rate of economic growth by reducing the cost of external finance to financially dependent companies as they are most of the big companies and stock market turnover and the size of the banking system are definitely related to excess growth. Wendy Carlin and Colin Mayer[183] consider that international comparisons of financial and corporate systems in developed countries do not reveal clear effects of financial or corporate structures on economic performance. This author thinks that there is not automatically a dominant financial and corporate system that is appropriate to all economies or all industries within an economy which means that financial and corporate systems should be adjusted to the type of economy and stage of development in order to achieve the best results.

Legal codes, contract enforcement mechanisms, and information disclosure systems affect financial development and economic growth. Moreover, diverse legal traditions underline the comparative rights of individual investors vis-a-vis the state, with principal ramifications for financial development. Furthermore, political differences shaped the formation of many legal traditions. State control produced legal behaviour that focus more on the power of the State and less on the rights of individual investors. Legal behaviour differs in terms of their abilities to adjust to changing conditions. When a group gains power, it will outline policies and institutions to its own advantage. Differences in state power in conjunction with the interests of the elite establish a financial development to their advantage. Whereas law play a technical role, centralized and powerful political systems are more likely to impede financial development than competitive and open political systems. States that adapt a transplanted law to native conditions have a probability of constructing a flourishing legal system. According to Thorsten Beck, Asli Demirgüç-Kunt and Ross Levine[184] "there is an independent link between legal origin and financial institutions beyond our proxies of political power. This finding is consistent with the dynamic law and finance's emphasis that

---

[183] Wendy Carlin and Colin Mayer, How Do Financial Systems Affect Economic Performance? 1999 Working Paper p24.

[184] Thorsten Beck, Asli Demirgüç-Kunt and Ross Levine, Law, Politics, and Finance, 2001 *www.ssrn.com* p38.

the adaptability and flexibility of legal systems importantly influences financial development."

The foremost role attributed to law is that it empowers creditors to put into effect their contracts. Thus, effective legal institutions diminish the risk of lending by mitigating both moral risk as well as undesirable selection problems, in so doing increasing lenders' willingness to lend effecting capital mobility in the economy which in turn leads to financial development. Rainer Haselmann, Katharina Pistor and Vikrant Vig[185] argue "that new entrants, in particular foreign banks, benefit more from legal change by expanding their lending volume to a greater extent than do incumbent domestic banks. Finally, our findings offer some important insights into the dynamics of how law affects financial development. We find that law affects financial development through both an increase in the number of banks in an economy as well as increased lending volume per bank."

There are differences in the degree of investor protection across countries and that these differences are correlated with both the development of capital markets and the ownership structure of companies. Better legal protection for investors and stricter law enforcement reduce the risk of expropriation by managers and controlling shareholders and so more effective legal protection and stricter enforcement enable companies to raise more external capital, and so enhance the growth of capital markets[186].

Differences in business environment justify much of the discrepancy across countries in companies' financial policies and performance. Additionally differences in legal and financial systems make clear much of the variation across countries in companies' financial policies and performance. Anti-competitive regulations such as entry barriers lead to slower expansion in reputable companies. Corruption is more damaging than taxation for the reason that of the uncertainty and secrecy that accompanies bribery payments. Political instability and exchange rate unpredictability have a more indirect force on sales growth by affecting the type of financing accessible to companies[187].

Exchange rate depreciations raise the leverage of companies that have borrowed foreign currency denominated debt, constraining their capability to obtain new equity or to modify their capital structure. Meghana Ayyagari Asli Demirgüç-Kunt and Vojislav Maksimovic[188] state "the importance of macroeconomic policies in influencing growth at the firm level as indicated by the correlation between high interest rates and banks' lack of money to lend variables. Furthermore, the high interest rates variable is also correlated with high collateral and paperwork requirements, the need for special connections with banks and unavailability of long term loans. These results suggest that bureaucracy and corruption in banking, greater

---

185 Rainer Haselmann, Katharina Pistor and Vikrant Vig, How Law Affects Lending, 2006 *www.ssrn.com* p35.

186 Gilson, Ronald J. (2000), "Globalizing Corporate Governance: Convergence of Form or Function," Working Paper No. 192, Stanford Law School. Pagano, Marco, and Paolo F. Volpin (2000), "The Political Economy of Corporate Governance," CSEF Working Paper no. 29, *www.dise.unisa.it/WP/wp29.pdf*, and CEPR Discussion Paper no. 2682, www.cepr.org/pubs/dps/DP2682.asp.

187 Beck, T., Demirgüç-Kunt, A., Maksimovic, V., 2005. Financial and Legal Constraints to Firm Growth: Does Firm Size Matter. Journal of Finance 60(1), 137-177.

188 Meghana Ayyagari Asli Demirgüç-Kunt Vojislav Maksimovic, How Important Are Financing Constraints? The role of finance in the business environment, World Bank Policy Research Working Paper 3820, January 2006 p29.

collateral requirements and lack of long term loans are common in high interest rate environments."

6.10 Monetary Policy and Financial Markets

Monetary growth in excess of increases in the public's demand for money balances will finally decrease the purchasing power of money or, equivalently, raise the general price level. Monetary developments should not be ignored since they offer a further source of information which can help improve the robustness of monetary policy decisions. As Milton Friedman[189] said monetary dynamics are central to understanding the inflation process. Money and credit play vital role if imperfections in the financial sector such as borrowing and liquidity constraints permit changes in the structure of balance sheets to affect yields and spreads in a manner that is relevant for inter-temporal economic behaviour, such as pricing, consumption, saving and investment decisions. Monetary aggregates are playing an active role in the transmission mechanism of monetary policy. The stability of the relationship between the money stock and the price level is evaluated in the context of a money demand equation, which relates money to prices and other key macroeconomic variables such as real income and interest rates. A monetary policy should respond to monetary developments - in addition to the fundamental shocks which hit the economy from time to time - helping to rule out destabilising explosive paths for inflation expectations. Monetary developments include information about the state of the economy which - irrespective of whether money plays an active role in the transmission mechanism of monetary policy - should be integrated into the policymaking process[190]. A credible monetary policy contributes to reducing uncertainty and so risk premiums and ultimately increases the growth potential and consequently asset prices[191]. It should be taken into account that financial markets still suffer from information imperfections and asymmetries and there is concern about corporate earnings disclosure and accounting standards illustrating how difficult it is for creditors to assess not only businesses' financial statements but also the real value of their assets as well as the nature and degree of the risk associated with their capital projects. Macroeconomic changes show that the growing weight of financial factors in the economy's dynamics may have a destabilising effect. Central banks cannot justify a noteworthy interest rate increase in order to ensure financial stability in the absence of price pressures. The central bank should not focus excessively on financial factors when conducting its monetary policy leading to a probably dangerous asymmetrical reaction from the central bank creating a moral hazard for economic agents[192].

---

[189] Friedman, M and A Schwartz (1963): A monetary history of the United States, 1867-1960, Princeton University Press, Princeton, New Jersey.

[190] Borio, C and P Lowe (2002): "Asset prices, financial and monetary stability: exploring the nexus", BIS Working Papers, no 114, July. Brand, C, D Gerdesmeier and B Roffia (2002): "The derivation of the reference value for monetary growth", ECB Occasional Paper, no 2.

[191] Norman, B, M Sebastia-Barriel and O Weeken (2002): "Equity wealth and consumption – the experience of Germany, France and Italy in an international context", Bank of England Quarterly Bulletin, spring, pp 78-85. Peersman, G and F Smets (2001): "The monetary transmission mechanism in the euro area: more evidence from VAR analysis", ECB Working Paper, no 114, December.

[192] Angeloni, I, A Kashyap, B Mojon and D Terlizzese (2002): "Monetary transmission in the euro area: where do we stand?", ECB Working Paper, no 114, January.

The global shift of financial markets from what has been called a government-led to a market-led financial system was largely complete by 1990s, sustained by the ascendancy of free market philosophy, the recognition of the costs of financial repression, and technological innovation with financial deepening within individual countries and tighter links across countries. A central bank can do is to foster a macroeconomic environment of low and stable inflation and sustainable economic growth[193]. A liberalised financial system can more easily accommodate, and reinforce, fluctuations in economic activity. Central banks can alter monetary policy to preclude or mitigate the consequences of financial instability for the economy and in case that such instability slides into crisis, they can employ their basic tools (through provision of reserves via open market operations and direct lending to depository institutions via a lender of last resort or discount window function, lowering policy interest rates to provide a boost to the economy) to lessen liquidity pressures and to bolster public confidence. Financial markets are dynamic and the incorporation of IT and the constant interplay of the forces of competition, deregulation, and globalisation imply that some companies will fail over time through a process of economic change in which more competent business models displace the status quo. In today's globally integrated financial markets, it is more significant than ever for central banks and other financial authorities to share information, to communicate about crisis prevention measures, and to recognise a common interest in effective crisis management actions[194].

Monetary policy is based in many countries on targeting of a key interest rate and the amount of money in existence arises from the interaction of the private sector and the banks on the basis of the demand to hold money and the willingness of banks to provide loans. The "new consensus,"[195] theory treats money as endogenously created, though the terminology of endogeneity is seldom used and the stock of money is a "residual" based on the demand for money. It should be taken into account that monetary policy has become closely linked with the targeting of the rate of inflation. Besides, the Keynesian[196] view of endogenous money pays a great deal of attention to the process by which loans and deposits are created and destroyed. The accessibility to loans permits the expansion of investment, which leads to a corresponding increase of savings and to an expansion of bank deposits, which may later be extinguished as and when loans are paid off. According to Philip Arestis and Malcolm Sawyer[197] "Fiscal policy to regulate aggregate demand is paramount, along with monetary policy to control the exchange rate. In addition, credit controls may be used in a supportive manner as necessary, but we are not convinced by their effectiveness."

Monetary transmission refers to the process through which changes in monetary variables such as money supply, interest rates, exchange rates and credit are transmitted into the real

193 Brousseau, V and C Detken (2001): "Monetary policy and fears of financial instability", ECB Working Paper, no 89. Borio, C and P Lowe (2002): "Asset prices, financial and monetary stability: exploring the nexus", BIS Working Papers, no 114. Borio, C, B English and A Filardo (2003): "A tale of two perspectives: old or new challenges for monetary policy?", BIS Working Papers, no 127.

194 Bordo, M and O Jeanne (2002): "Monetary policy and asset prices: does 'benign neglect' make sense? ", International Finance, 5(2), pp 139-64.

195 Meyer, L. H. 2001. "Does Money Matter?" Federal Reserve Bank of St. Louis Review 83(5): 1-15.

196 Keynes, J. M. 1930. Treatise on Money, London: Macmillan (page references refer to The Collected Writings of John Maynard Keynes, Vol. V. London: Macmillan). Lavoie, M. 2000. "A Post Keynesian View of Interest Rate Parity Theorems." Journal of Post Keynesian Economics 23(1): 163-179.

197 Philip Arestis and Malcolm Sawyer, The Nature and Role of Monetary Policy When Money IS Endogenous, *www.ssrn.com* p29

economic activity[198]. The task of fiscal and structural policies is to enhance the growth potential of the economy, while monetary policy contributes to long-run growth only by maintaining price stability over the medium term. Monetary policy actions affect real variables only in the short run, whereas in the long run the effect of monetary policy on real output, employment and real interest rates cease to exist due to the so-called neutrality of money. Monetary policy actions affect the external finance premium through bank lending and balance sheet channels. A rise in the money supply leads to extreme holdings of money increasing demand for goods raising their prices and the general price level rises due to higher inflationary expectations because they affect asset prices and price setting in product and labour markets which means that the higher monetary growth is associated with higher inflation, leading to lower purchasing power of money and so neutralising economic growth in real terms. Investment patterns look for first and primary to equate the marginal product of capital across sectors. Capital allocation is not entirely driven by the need to equate marginal returns across sectors, but also by a portfolio reason given an exogenous structure of returns.

The premier return investments are new technologies investors are unfamiliar with. Financial systems often fail to advance flows of capital to high-productivity investments and new technologies. Capital allocation is driven by connections more than by market mechanisms and information on future expected returns. Investors are hesitant to obtain information because the available information is vague, fallacious or costly. Financiers choose to fund entrepreneurs whom they are already familiar with because of geographical closeness or personal connections[199]. The detection of distant investment opportunities is critical for achieving an effective capital allocation. Information significantly affects financiers' returns and entrepreneurial rents and so financiers have partial investment opportunities if they do not get hold of information, and will end up funding even low-productivity projects.

Interest rate and exchange rate movements are affect directly the components of aggregate demand, which in turn is considered to determine output in the short term under fixed prices and changes in exchange rates influence the real economy due to their effect on net exports through import and export prices[200].

The flow of resources into the liberalizing countries would reduce their cost of capital, increase investment, and raise output[201]. Besides, capital account liberalization invites speculative hot money flows, increases the chance of financial crises, and brings no discernible economic benefits and capital markets may even be detrimental to economic development[202]. Liberalization of portfolio equity flows has been associated with booming stock markets, greater capital investment, and faster economic growth. Shleifer and

---

198 Fase, M.M.G. – de Bondt, G.J. (2000) Institutional Environment and Monetary Transmission in the Euro-Area: a Cross-Country View. Revue De La Banque / Bank- En Financiewezen 2–3, 149–155.

199 Almeida, Heitor and Daniel Wolfenzon 2005, The effect of external finance on the equilibrium allocation of capital, Journal of Financial Economics 75, 133-164

200 Angeloni, I. – Kashyap, A. – Mojon, B. – Terlizzese, D. (2002) Monetary Transmission in the Euro Area: Where Do We Stand? ECB Working Paper 114. Hanna Putkuri, Cross-country asymmetries in euro area monetary transmission: the role of national financial systems, Bank of Finland Discussion Papers 15/2003.

201 Summers, Lawrence H. 2000. "International Financial Crises: Causes, Prevention, and Cures." American Economic Review 90 (2): 1–16.

202 Stiglitz, Joseph. 2002. Globalization and Its Discontents. W.W. Norton.

Wolfenzon[203] consider that weaker investor protection reduces the marginal product of capital and eliminates the incentive for capital to flow from rich to poor countries which means that stock market liberalization is a necessary but not sufficient condition for increased access to global equity capital.

Balance sheet variables, principally cash flow and net worth, affect investment and the financial accelerator aggregates these balance sheet effects to produce business cycle dynamics. Falling asset values harm borrowers' balance sheets to the point of interrupting the intermediation of credit, which in turn exacerbates macroeconomic conditions.[204] According to Goetz von Peter[205] financial instability is possible once banks become capital-constrained, loan losses can be a decisive macroeconomic quantity and self-fulfilling capital crunches and banking crises are likely when loan losses force a credit contraction that feeds back onto asset prices. Moreover, an asset price decline causes default among leveraged companies, and banks suffer loan losses and their size determines whether a capital crunch, financial instability, or a banking crisis occurs.

How quickly monetary policy actions impact on inflation? The transmission lag depends on a large number of individual factors, together with the degree of financial liberalisation, an economy's degree of openness and the composition of the private sector's asset holdings. According to Milton Friedman[206] the policy transmission lag will vary over time as economic behaviour and policy regimes change. The central bank's capacity to control output and inflation deteriorates when it underestimates the transmission lag. Moreover, Yuong Ha[207] regards that "rules with larger response coefficients and shorter target horizons still produced lower overall inflation variability." The central bank lowers interest rates in a deep recession to stimulate the economy. Monetary policy only regulates the borrowing of a domestic agent from a domestic lender but monetary policy is ineffective in foreign investors because it does not alter the international collateral of the country. Financial markets are characterised by imperfections arising from information asymmetries between borrowers and lenders. Banks specialise in extending credit to borrowers that cannot obtain other types of credit. Monetary policy affects the level of investment and consumer spending by indicating changes in the cost of capital and yield on savings. Monetary policy can be effective through the credit channel and the interest rate channel concurrently. Banks as financial intermediaries are special in gathering and distilling information enabling them to make loans to borrowers at more favourable terms. Monetary policy affects the lending behaviour of small banks with less liquid balance sheets. Banks base their loan supply on their credit margin and their capital position decreasing their loan supply gradually after a restrictive shift in monetary policy[208].

---

[203] Shleifer, Andrei, and Daniel Wolfenzon. 2002. "Investor Protection and Equity Markets." Journal of Financial Economics 66 (1, October): 3–27.

[204] Hubbard, Glenn, (1998),"Capital-Market Imperfections and Investment", Journal of Economic Literature; Vol. 36, March 1998, p. 193-225. Hubbard, Glenn; Kenneth Kuttner and Darius Palia (2002) "Are there Bank Effects in Borrowers' Cost of Funds? Evidence from a Matched Sample of Borrowers and Banks", Journal of Business, Vol. 75(4), p. 559-81.

[205] Goetz von Peter, A Unified Approach to Credit Crunches, Financial Instability, and Banking Crises, 2003 Working Paper Columbia University.

[206] Friedman, M (1961): "The lag in effect of monetary policy" Journal of Political Economy, 69, 447-66.

[207] Yuong Ha, Uncertainty about the Length of the Monetary Policy Transmission Lag: Implications for Monetary Policy, DP2000/01, p20 Reserve Bank of New Zealand.

[208] Oliver Huslewing, Bank Behaviour, Interest Rate Targeting and Monetary policy transmission, 2003 WEP No 43.

Money stock and taxes in accordance with Sargent and Wallace[209] are substitutes in the backing of government debt and monetary and fiscal policies are linked via a budget constraint. Can Fiscal and monetary policy be coordinated under an independent authority? Fiscal policy hampers the effective control of the money supply by requiring excessive revenue because monetary policy must control the money stock. Public sector budget constraint is the key equation linking the joint feasible sequences of monetary and fiscal variables through time and a deficit been plugged by suitable monetary policy. Interest rate has to be consistent with the way the central bank acts in practice. Macroeconomic stability has to do with fiscal policy than monetary policy because monetary policy no longer controls inflation. According to J Chadha and C Nolan[210] "monetary and fiscal policy may not be coordinated at the business cycle frequencies, with the implication that output and employment may be more volatile than necessary". It should be taken into account that by increasing the money supply available for transactions when the transactions demand is high and by providing monetary support in the future when needed, the monetary authority keeps the price level stable, and so limiting depositor incentives to withdraw, and as a result limiting both nominal interest rates and future real repayment obligations of banks[211]. Monetary policy affects bank loan supply, which in turn has an independent and considerable effect on aggregate economic activity. Moreover, monetary policy has effects on bank loan supply and it worth mentioning that it has greater effect on banks at times when their balance sheets look worse[212]. Increase in the money supply increases financial liquidity alleviating the real liquidity demands on banks, which then allows them to fund more long-term projects to fruition. According to D Diamond and R G. Rajan [213] "repayments on bank loans are determined by the underlying value of collateral, so they are effectively real even if denominated in nominal quantities. Of course, if the required nominal repayment on a bank loan is small relative to the underlying collateral, then the bank loan is effectively denominated in nominal terms. This is likely to be the case in cyclical upturns. So a fruitful extension would be to see how the value of a bank's loan portfolio responds to changes in monetary policy, and how this affects credit. One conjecture is that this will depend on the phase of the business cycle."

6.11 Globalisation and Finance

Globalization is a process which partly involves redefining time and space changing financial flows, trade in services and outsourcing of production. Globalization is a process which inevitably means that nationality becomes increasingly irrelevant. Globalisation implies the progressive integration of world markets induced by the liberalisation of international trade in goods, services and productive factors. FDI has led to the emergence of

209 Sargent J, N Wallace, Some Unpleasant Monetarist Arithmetic, FRBMQR, Vol 5, No3, pp1-17.

210 J Chadha and C Nolan, On the Interaction of Monetary and Fiscal Policy, 2003, DAE Working Paper No 0303 p 57.

211 Champ, Bruce, Bruce Smith, and Stephen Williamson, 1996. .Currency Elasticity and Banking Panics: Theory and Evidence,. Canadian Journal of Economics 29, 828-864.

212 Kashyap, Anil K.; Stein, Jeremy C. "What Do a Million Observations on Banks Say about the Transmission of Monetary Policy?" American Economic Review v90, n3 (June 2000): 407-28.

213 Douglas W. Diamond Raghuram G. Rajan, Money in a Theory of Banking, 2003 NBER p40.

MNEs on a quite unprecedented scale. Globalization raises insecurity, but also seems to provide workers and firms with better incentives and more opportunities. Companies, facing more competition from abroad should invest more in training and human capital, in order to innovate and differentiate their products, and save profit margins /market shares. If workers have limited access to credit markets, when facing higher real income uncertainty should invest in training, effort and productivity in order self insure and raise the probability of a promotion[214]. Employees of import-competing, exporting and foreign-owned companies profit from more involvement in training programs; employees of exporting companies also benefit from more rapid careers. Employees of companies subject to foreign competition face more uncertainty in their earning stream and employment prospects but their career is faster and/or their capacity to upgrade their skills is higher than employees of companies shielded from foreign competition[215]. As market size grows, workers benefit from higher real wages and better employment opportunities because trade integration brings higher growth via technology transfers, knowledge spillovers and scale economies, influencing exporting and productivity levels and growth rates[216]. The rapid increase in cross-border economic, social, technological and cultural exchange might become destructive. It could be said that globalization is not only the result of an escalation of longstanding trends such as increasing cross-border flows of goods, money and people, and a growing mutual awareness and interdependence among social, economic and political units worldwide, but also the background in which development takes place. Economic development based on effective combinations of domestic and foreign resources to sponsor growth. Does globalization mean development? In fact, globalization and development are processes of catching up exhibiting certain patterns of convergence, including the growth of large enterprises in industries similar to those found in the advanced countries. Globalization brings convergent and homogenizing effects upon developing and developed countries. According to Mauro F. Guillén[217] "Globalization is neither to be opposed as a menace nor to be celebrated as a panacea; it is to be engaged: comprised, located, given form."

Moreover, globalization brings the gradual integration of economies and societies driven by novel technologies, new economic interaction and interrelation among the national and international policies of various actors such as governments, international organizations, business, labour and civil society. Economic operators no longer work within one national system. It could be argued that enhance in cross-border business doings created a rise in the prevalence of overlapping regulatory jurisdiction[218]. According to Bernhard G. Gunter and Rolph van der Hoeven[219] "though globalization had often not produced the benefits that were promised, the issue is not whether globalization can be a force for good which benefits the

---

214 Becker, S. and A. Ichino (2002), Estimation of average treatment effects based on propensity scores, the Stata Journal, 2, 358-377 Besley, T. and R.Burgess (2002), Can Labor Regulation Hinder Economic Performance? Evidence from India, CEPR Discussion Paper #3260, March

215 Manasse P. and A.Turrini (2002)"Trade, Wages and Superstars", Journal of International Economics, 54(1),97-118

216 Wood, A. (1998), Globalisation and the Rise in Labor Market Inequalities, Economic Journal, 1463-1482

217 Mauro F. Guillén, Diversity In Globalization Organizational Change in Argentina, South Korea and Spain Discussants: Evelyne Huber and Michael Mosher JANUARY 2 0 0 0, PAPER NUMBER 6 p 25.

218 Hannah L. Buxbaum, *Conflict of Economic Laws: From Sovereignty to Substance*, 42 VA. J. INT'L L. 931, 935-936 (2002)

219 Bernhard G. Gunter and Rolph van der Hoeven, The social dimension of globalization: a review of the literature, 2004 Working Paper No. 24 p25.

poor of the world (which it can of course be), but that globalization needs to be managed in the right way and too often it has not been".

Globalisation refers to the increasing integration of domestic and international financial markets, as well as the increasing international presence of major banks and other financial intermediaries and consolidation refers to the growing size and cross-sectoral scope of financial institutions. Consolidation and concentration in the financial services industry has been raised particularly in the origination of syndicated loans and in derivatives markets. Globalisation has encouraged changes in the activities of the IMF and there is a shift in emphasis away from the problems of individual countries to concerns about contagion and systemic problems in international financial markets. It could be argued that interactions between the effects of consolidation and the problems arising from marketisation and globalisation give further grounds for more extensive use of public safety net instruments. Large companies are protected by the diversity of their income streams, and are more able to afford and expected to use the most sophisticated risk management systems available. Large financial institutions are now very active, indeed often dominant, players in a number of financial markets and they rely on the markets and the markets rely on them[220]. Recently the global financial system has changed deeply and technological improvements and deregulation have increased competition in the financial services industry. There is pressure by marketisation (greater reliance on market-based financing), globalisation (the internationalisation of financial markets) and consolidation (cross-sectoral and more highly concentrated provision of financial services on financial institutions to keep up rates of return contributing to their greater willingness to take on risks[221]. Marketisation has encouraged the use of generalised injections of liquidity when financial disruptions threaten[222]. Globalisation has implications for the generalised injection of liquidity in the face of financial difficulties inducing national monetary authorities to react to international as opposed to solely domestic objectives. According to William R White[223] "to the extent there has been growing recourse to the use of safety net instruments, the question of moral hazard takes on greater importance. The risk is that measures taken to deal with short-term problems in the financial system may inadvertently make problems more difficult to deal with over time."

The last twenty years there is an increase in the income gap between the advanced nations and all other developing and transitional countries, as well as a worrying reversal in many nations of past trends towards lower domestic inequality. Is possible to separate the effects of globalisation from those of domestic liberalisation? The rise in foreign investments of the 1990s often consisted in the acquisition by multinational firms of state-owned enterprises and would not have taken place without their prior privatisation and the parallel liberalisation of the labour market that allowed large job cuts in privatised firms. Similarly, the surge in short-term portfolio flows of the 1990s would not have happened without the

---

220 Maclachlan, F C (2001): "Market discipline in bank regulation: panacea or paradox?", The Independent Review, vol VI, no 2, Fall, pp 227-34. McDonnell, W (2003): "Managing risk: practical lessons from recent "failures" of EU insurers", Occasional Paper, 20, UK Financial Services Authority.

221 Kane, Edward J (2001): "Financial safety nets: reconstructing and modelling a policymaking metaphor", NBER Working Paper Series, 8224, April.

222 Padoa-Schioppa, T (2002): "Central banks and financial stability: exploring an intermediate land", speech given at the 2nd ECB Central Banking Conference, Frankfurt, 24-25 October.

223 William R White, Are changes in financial structure extending safety nets? BIS Working Papers No 145, p31.

liberalisation of the domestic financial markets during the 1980s. Liberalisation improves global income distribution because of the equalisation of factor prices across nations and the convergence of the income per capita of poorer countries with those of the advanced nations.

Trade flows are more and more being governed by the international law of the WTO, and capital flows are regulated by the international "soft" law according to Eatwell and Taylor[224]. Significant cost reduction of transportation and communication and the reduction of artificial barriers to the flows of goods, services, capital, knowledge, and people across borders are the results of globalisation. Stiglitz[225] considers that globalization is driven by MNEs, and governed by the IMF, the World Bank, and the WTO. In other words, globalization brings trade liberalization, financial liberalization, outsourcing of production, and the increased harmonization of economic institutions and regulatory framework worldwide. Financial liberalization is one of the most important aspects of globalization involving both short-term capital flows and FDI. Additionally, liberalization of short-term capital flows minimizes risks and maximizes profits for the investors in the financial markets. Liberalization of short-term capital flows has its negative impact on investment and production because the fast and large profits that short-term capital convey in a rather short period of time by moving globally between financial markets reduces the supply of funds available for direct investment. Obstfeld[226] observes that the increase in profits achieved by the globalization of production does not translate into increased investment in production but a good part of these profits finds its way to financial markets abroad. The collapse of the Bretton Woods system of fixed exchange rates, the liberalization of domestic capital markets, liberalization of international capital flows, and the very rapid development of information and communication technology have contributed to financial market integration. Financial globalization is illustrated by the fact that trading in the global foreign exchange market has far outpaced the growth in international trade in goods and services. Additionally, foreign exchange is increasingly being treated as an asset or a commodity, not just as a means of payments with a parallel increase in the use of derivatives in foreign exchange markets. Changes in global conditions such as the decline in nominal interest rates gave a spur to capital flows to emerging markets. According to Gouda Abdel-Khalek[227] "structural changes in international financial markets in the 1990s have influenced both the scale and composition of capital flows to emerging markets. The growing importance of portfolio flows (both bonds and equities) has reflected the extended role of such financial innovations as securitization." Unchecked massive and sudden movements of capital into and out of emerging market economies seriously undermine a small open economy.

The accessibility of financial instruments and institutions reduces transaction and information costs in an economy raising investment and economic growth. According to Acemoglu, Aghion, and Zilibotti[228] a developing country that is behind the technological

---

224 Eatwe ll, John and Lance Taylor, eds., 2002, International Capital Markets: Systems in Transition. Oxford: Oxford U. Press.

225 Stiglitz, Joseph, 2003, Globalization and Its Discontents. New York: W.W. Norton & Company.

226 Obstfeld, Maurice, 1998, "The global Capital Market: Benefactor or Menace?," Journal of Economic Perspectives, 12(4). Fall.

227 Gouda Abdel-Khalek, Bad Policies or Systemic Dysfunction? The Perils of Financial Globalization A South View, USC Center for Law, Economics & Organization, Research Paper No. C03-18, p20.

228 Acemoglu, D., P. Aghion, and F. Zilibotti "Distance to Frontier, Selection, and Economic Growth." NBER Working Paper # 9066, 2002.

frontier will follow a capital accumulation growth strategy ("investment-based growth"). Lending decisions improve over time as lenders acquire project specific information by making investment decisions which means more efficient allocation of funds that go to the most productive companies, in developed economies. Finance has a constructive influence on productivity growth primarily in more developed economies and On the contrary, in less developed economies, the effect of finance on output growth occurs above all through capital accumulation and not productivity. Kalemli-Ozcan, Sorensen and Yosha[229]consider that there is a notably positive relationship between specialization and risk-sharing and financial integration should affect negatively cycles' synchronization, via its effect on specialization. The contribution of productivity to economic growth increases substantially after carefully accounting for human capital. According to Felix Rioja and Neven Valev [230] "the strong contribution of financial development to productivity growth does not occur until a country has reached a certain income level, roughly in the range that defines our middle-income group. Until then, most of the effect occurs through capital accumulation."

Qualitative changes have shaped the internationalisation of the banking industry and banks are more and more providing non-trade-related financial services across borders, and they often do so through affiliates in foreign markets. For instance, German financial institutions accounted for 9% of cross-border acquisitions of financial institutions that took place in OECD countries between 1985 and 2002, and Germany reported about 10% of international bank lending in the 1990s[231]. Openness to goods trade results in high degrees of specialization as financial liberalizations result in specialization do and both trading in goods and in financial assets, in turn, potentially affect the cross-country synchronization of business cycles[232]. Heathcote and Perri[233] regard that the U.S. business cycle has become more and more distinctive over the past thirty years, and relate this to the increasing share of international assets held in the U.S. Capital flows are correlated internationally, and that financial integration tends to synchronize business cycles. A limited ability to borrow and lend internationally hampers the transfer of resources across countries and increase GDP correlations but when investors have imperfect information or face liquidity constraints, limiting capital flows actually decrease GDP correlations. Frankel and Rose[234]estimate a strong and positive relationship between trade and cycle synchronization, taking specific care of the endogeneity of trade to the business cycle with suitable instrumentation. Moreover,

[229] Kalemli-Ozcan, Sebnem Sorensen, Bent and Yosha, Oved (2001), Economic Integration, Industrial Specialization and the Asymmetry of Macroeconomic Fluctuations, Journal of International Economics, 55, pp.107-137.

[230] Felix Rioja and Neven Valev, Finance and the Sources of Growth at Various Stages of Economic Development, http://ssrn.com/abstract=438261, p20.

[231] Berger, A., C.M. Buch, G. DeLong, and R. DeYoung (2003). Exporting Financial Institutions Management via Foreign Direct Investment Mergers and Acquisitions. Journal of International Money and Finance, 230.

[232] Ambler, Steve, Cardia, Emmanuela and Zimmermann, Christian (2002), International Transmission of the Business Cycle in a Multi-Sector Model, European Economic Review, 46, pp. 273-300. Saint-Paul, Gilles (1992), Technological Choice, Financial Markets and Economic Development, European Economic Review, 36, pp. 763-781.

[233] Heathcote, Jonathan and Perri, Fabrizio (2002), Financial Autarky and International Business Cycles, Journal of Monetary Economics, 49(3), pp. 601-627. Heathcote, Jonathan and Perri, Fabrizio (2002), Financial Globalization and Real Regionalization, NBER Working Paper No 9292.

[234] Frankel, Jeffrey and Rose, Andrew (1998), The Endogeneity of the Optimum Currency Area Criteria, Economic Journal, Vol. 108, No. 449, 1009-1025.

Jean Imbs[235] regards that "Patterns of specialization have a sizeable direct effect on business cycles correlation, as two economies with a similar economic structure are significantly more correlated ceteris paribus. This is shown to happen mostly because economies grow through evolving stages of diversification, and in spite of the specialization effects induced by financial integration. Finally, business cycles in financially integrated regions are significantly more synchronized, ceteris paribus. This remains true even though financial integration tends to result in more specialized economies and less synchronized cycles as a consequence." Hence, financial integration means another pattern of business cycles which could be argued might be integrated by achieving a synchronization causing problems when a whole area is in the same phase of down fall of a business cycle not mentioning the effects of globalisation and the emergence of e-finance and e-commerce.

The significance of efficient financial markets is in allowing those that want to obtain capital from different sources at reasonable rates. Finance is vital for a strong entrepreneurship and subsequently constraints on finance have an impact. Financial intermediaries mobilise scarce savings, evaluate research projects, managing risk by evaluating future cashflow and facilite transactions. Finance holds back the opening out of markets along both supply and demand lines via its influence on the growth of fixed-cost investments such as infrastructure. The development of an efficient infrastructure is correlated with trade development and infrastructures are constructed using both public finance and private enterprise under public regulations. Financial constraints deriving from imperfections in financial markets are a result of both information asymmetry and the politico-institutional environment. Costs to the attainment of information mean that information-efficient markets are impractical. According to Mariassunta Giannetti and Xiaoyun Yu[236] "markets in which financiers acquire information and fund distant investment opportunities are unnecessary for reaching an efficient capital allocation at early stages of development. As the economy accumulates capital, acquisition of information on distant investment opportunities becomes crucial for achieving an efficient capital allocation. Nevertheless, entrepreneurs may not have an incentive to favor higher disclosure or stricter listing standards because they enjoy higher rents when financiers only have information on a limited sets of investment opportunities."

A loss of investor confidence, collapse of exchange rates, the insolvency of many leading local companies and financial institutions, runs on banks and secondary financial institutions by panicked depositors, a considerable contraction of the domestic economy and spiralling unemployment characterized the Asian financial crisis. The crisis unfavourably affected the economies of the neighboring countries of the region and influenced their economic policies, as neighboring countries took measures calculated to avoid a repetition of the crisis countries' experience. The Asian financial crisis brought changes to the crisis countries in their political, economic and social lives. The crisis was generally viewed as a consequence of political and bureaucratic support of favored corporate groups and the continuing availability of credit from banks and other financial institutions to such groups irrespective of credit fundamentals. The individual characteristics of the crisis, however, were structural microeconomic problems in the financial sector and the corporate sector and financial institutions both banks and

---

[235] Jean Imbs, Trade, Finance, Specialization and Synchronization, 2003, London Business School and CEPR p28.

[236] Mariassunta Giannetti, Xiaoyun Yu, Favoritism or Markets in Capital Allocation?, Working Paper N°. 153/2007, p26.

secondary financial institutions were revealed to be fragile, under-capitalized, under supervised and poorly managed. It is argued that the Asian crisis was mainly a crisis of corporate indebtedness and financial institution indebtedness, rather than a crisis of public sector indebtedness. Financial sector restructuring – rehabilitating, recapitalizing and reforming – each of the crisis country's banks and other financial institutions was the principal focus of the structural reforms in each country's IMF program. In other words there was a need for broadly based reform process, reshaping and updating the corporate form to the requirements of a globalized marketplace and globalized capital markets. The IMF program placed corporate governance reforms during the crisis onto a reform basis, involving financial sector restructuring, corporate debt restructuring and other economic reforms[237].

Enterprises globalizing their operations and the associated capital flows have become key players of the world economy and cross-border conduct and capital flows span institutional settings with shifting investor protections and levels of capital market expansion. MNEs' activity and FDI arise endogenously in settings characterized by financial differences. Liberalization has a large consequence on multinational affiliate activity in states with vulnerable investor protections because, in those states, ownership restrictions limit MNEs doings the most. MNEs doings and capital flows react to heterogeneity in institutional settings. Vulnerable financial institutions lessen the scale of MNE' activity but at the same time enhance the dependence on capital flows from the parent. Heterogeneity in right to use capital interrelate with MNEs production decisions. The decisive limitation in the exploitation of technology by MNEs is the character of capital market development and investor protections in host countries. According to Pol Antràs, Mihir A. Desai, and C. Fritz Foley[238] "Entrepreneurs must raise capital to fund projects, and external investors are aware of the possibility that these entrepreneurs might behave opportunistically. Inventors can alleviate financial frictions because they have a comparative advantage in monitoring entrepreneurs. Multinational activity and capital flows arise endogenously to ensure that monitoring occurs. External investors demand higher levels of multinational parent firm financial participation in countries with weak investor protections". Moreover, according to Bettina Hagmayr, Peter Haiss And Kjell Sümegi[239] "segments of financial markets that include public finance (especially bond markets) contributed to economic development, whereas private credit and stock market capitalization had no significant influence on growth". Increases in international inflows lead to lower cost of capital and inflation rates in receiving states. Peter Groznik[240] finds 'evidence that not only do labor and capital move in the same direction, but also that labor leads capital, if capital is defined as foreign direct investment".

---

[237] "Asia and the IMF," Remarks by Stanley Fischer, First Deputy Managing Director, International Monetary Fund at the Institute of Policy Studies, Singapore, June 1, 2001 (available at *http://www.imf.org/external/np/speeches/ 2001/060101.htm*).

[238] Pol Antràs, Mihir A. Desai, and C. Fritz Foley, Multinational Firms, FDI Flows and Imperfect Capital Markets, 2007 www.ssrn.com p29.

[239] Bettina Hagmayr, Peter Haiss And Kjell Sümegi , Financial Sector Development and Economic Growth – Evidence for Southeastern Europe, 2007 *www.ssrn.com* p 20.

[240] Peter Groznik, Immigration and International Financial Flows, *www.ssrn.com* P22-23.

6.12 Finance and Dollarization

Is official dollarization the best path towards stability? Dollarization entails two potentially large benefits for emerging economies by eliminating price and wealth distortions induced by the lack of credibility of stabilization policies and by improving the efficiency of financial markets by weakening informational or institutional frictions driving credit constraints. Domestic financial underdevelopment affects foreign lending supply and as financial development falls, foreign lenders find that it is less profitable to lend to companies with poor collateral and their entry into domestic financial markets is cut back which means that when interacted with a thin-market supply externality, this withdrawal raises the risks that the fewer suppliers are exposed to and so can feedback into higher lending and insurance premia. Moreover, excessive dollarization of private liabilities has played a vital role in recent emerging market crises. By dismantling exchange rate and monetary policy, a dollarized economy is left with only two options after an exogenous shock. It could stick to the previously determined priorities that have structured the patterns of demand, employment, income, and distribution, while leaving to supply and demand for bonds the task of financial consolidation. The alternative is adjusting to the shock by tightening the fiscal stance, thus achieving financial consolidation, disregarding whether the structural patterns of demand would be altered, perhaps irreversibly. Domestic financial underdevelopment shrinks the size of the effective international liquidity market motivating intervention to manage the international liquidity of a country[241].

The cost of insurance against exchange risk goes up with exchange rate volatility. Floating exchange rate regimes promote deposit dollarization more strongly than they encourage credit dollarization and so currency mismatches in financial intermediation are more severe under exchange rate flexibility[242]. Goldstein[243] has blamed fixed exchange rates for recent financial meltdowns and recommends floating. It should be taken into account that hedging opportunities with foreigners are limited because they are unwilling to sell dollars forward in exchange for domestic currency. Eichengreen and Hausman[244] support that exchange rate volatility increases the cost of hedging and consequently floating regimes increase the amount of unhedged dollar debt. Floating exchange rates exacerbate bank currency mismatch in emerging markets. According to Adam Honig[245] "the exchange rate regime is not an important determinant of unofficial dollarization, having a marginal impact at best and an insignificant effect in most specifications." It could be argued that sound policy and good governance can reverse the dollarization process and building a strong policy stimulates growth of domestic capital markets so that less foreign borrowing is needed.

---

[241] R Caballero, Dollarization of Liabilities, MIT Working paper 00-14.

[242] Catão, Luis and Marco Terrones (2000), "Determinants of Dollarization: The Banking Side," International Monetary Fund Working Paper 00/146, (August).

[243] Goldstein, M. (1999), "Safeguarding prosperity in a global financial system: The future international financial architecture report of an independent task force," Washington, DC: Institute for International Economics for the Council on Foreign Relations.

[244] Eichengreen, B., and R. Hausmann (1999),"Exchange Rates and Financial Fragility," NBER Working Paper 7418.

[245] Adam Honig, Dollarization, Exchange Rate Regimes And Government Myopia, 2003 Working paper, p27 Columbia University

Contagion is a significant increase in cross market linkages after a shock to a country and cross market linkages measured by correlation in asset returns or the transmission of volatility in asset returns. Predictability of currency crises involves monitoring the evolution of several indicators in various countries that tend to exceed a given threshold during the period preceding a crisis in a specific country. If the exchange rate is allowed to float, domestic investors recoil from foreign-exchange denominated debts because they will face a larger *currency* risk than under fix. According to Guillermo A. Calvo and Carmen M. Reinhart[246] "a country cannot have a currency crisis if it does not have a domestic currency in the first place; firms, banks, and households are immune to currency mismatches if all assets and liabilities are denominated in the same currency." Partial dollarization increases the cost of exchange rate volatility which, in turn, induces the central bank to intervene in the foreign exchange markets to avert fluctuations in the nominal exchange rate. Fear of floating arises from domestic companies' use of imported raw materials driving authorities to adopt additional measures, like controls on capital mobility. In fact, fear of floating induces more liability dollarization, creating a vicious circle from which it is difficult to exit. A better resource allocation framework created by a liberal financial system should be safeguarded against negative spillovers and international crises contagion by means of sound domestic policies. Trade liberalization stimulates industry fragmentation increasing trade. In Europe a more liberal product market regulation positively affected per capita growth.

Developing countries gradually removed barriers on international movements of capital maintained fixed or quasi-fixed the international value of their currencies, with the aim of stimulating commodity trade and of fighting high inflation. Milton Friedman[247]and Harry Johnson[248] argued that under clean floating a country recover its monetary policy autonomy; after an adverse demand shock, spontaneous currency depreciation help it to restore export competitiveness without implementing a hurting adjustment in prices. Besides, developing countries export only a narrow range of commodities characterized by volatile international prices, and so their nominal exchange rate might be subject to "excessive" volatility. Developing countries have difficulty in implementing complex monetary policy needed to control inflation. For this reason, exchange rate volatility is translated into price volatility, a situation that can prove to be exceptionally detrimental for somewhat poor countries[249]. If companies issue momentous dollars debts while their assets are denominated in the local currency, depreciation is particularly dangerous putting additional strain on the debt service[250]. In fact, depreciation erodes companies' net worth putting a brake on investment, which in turn depresses global demand. According to Damien Besancenot and Radu Vranceanu[251] "If both fixed and flexible exchange rate regimes come with major shortcomings in a context of large capital mobility, policymakers might re-consider this

[246] Guillermo A. Calvo and Carmen M. Reinhart , Reflections on Dollarization, 2000 NBER WP. p1

[247] Friedman, Milton, 1953, Essays in Positive Economics, University of Chicago Press, Chicago.

[248] Johnson, Harry G., 1969, The case for flexible exchange rates, 1969, Federal Reserve Bank of St. Louis Review, June, pp. 12-24.

[249] Fischer, Stanley, 2001, Exchange rate regimes: Is the bi-polar view correct?, Journal of Economic Perspectives, 15, 2, pp. 3-24. Edwards, Sebastian, 2002, The great exchange rate debate after Argentina, NBER Working Paper 9257, October.

[250] Calvo, Guillermo A. and Carmen M. Reinhart, 2002, Fear of Floating, Quarterly Journal of Economics, 67, 2, pp. 379-408.

[251] Damien Besancenot, Radu Vranceanu, Financial Instability under Floating Exchange Rates, March 2003, DR 03011, p19.

fundamental option. More in detail, governments in developing countries may impose some limits on the foreign currency denominated liabilities of firms belonging to the non-tradable sector. In the aggregate, country risk evaluation should take into account dollar debt as compared to the degree of trade openness, for instance, such as proxied by the foreign debt to exports ratio." In reality, governments in developing countries did not let the international value of their currency vary too much and even those governments which declare to operate flexible exchange rates regimes limit exchange rate fluctuations through direct central bank intervention or by interest rate manoeuvring.

6.13 Finance and EU

In the last two decades Europe has experienced a spectacular expansion of financial markets, particularly of arm's length financial markets. It should be taken into consideration that arm's-length financing delivers better results when markets and companies are bigger, when companies are more formally organized, when there is better legal enforcement and transparency, and when innovation tends to be more revolutionary. Besides, relationship-based systems perform better when markets and companies are smaller, when legal protection is weaker, when there is little transparency, and when innovation is incremental, rather than revolutionary providing better forms of insurance, but it does that at the cost of reducing access to financing and curtailing future opportunities relying on implicit or explicit government guarantees.

The process of integration, both monetary integration at the European level and financial integration at the worldwide level, and the revolutionary nature of innovation have supported the expansion of arm's length financing in Europe. In Europe the dominance of a few large banks facilitated the creation of a political coalition between more interventionist governments and the banking system. Neither the European bank-centered system nor the American market-based one is the natural outcome of market forces but the result of political choices. According to Rajan and Zingales[252] the collapse of the Bretton Woods System and the integration of national financial markets, weakened the political opposition to financial markets, leading to their expansion throughout the world and particularly in Europe. Integration opened up national intermediaries to foreign competition, which, being foreign, could not be controlled through the political process which means that external competition limited the capacity of incumbents to impede the development of arm's-length markets. It should be taken into account that arm's length markets need a good legal, regulatory, and monitoring infrastructure to work accurately and the ability of a country's economy to take advantage of arm's length markets depends upon its industrial structure. Moreover, there is an increased role of markets appreciated by looking at growing importance of corporate debt issues growing from 13% of GDP to 17% of GDP and international corporate debt growing from 2.4% of GDP to 6% of GDP[253]. Markets are replacing banks in many of the traditional roles performed by the latter for instance in securitization, where traditional loan and mortgages are sold as securities. Relationship-based financing ensures a return to the

---

252 Rajan R. G., and Zingales, L. (2003), 'The Great Reversals: The Politics of Financial Development in the 20th Century,' Journal of Financial Economics, 350.Rajan R. G., and Zingales, L. (2003), Saving Capitalism from the Capitalists Crown Books, Random House, New York, NY.

253 Bottazzi, L. and M. Da Rin, (2002) "European Venture Capital" Economic Policy April, p. 231-269

financier by granting some form of power over the company being financed serving as the sole lender, supplier, or customer and so attempting to secure returns on investment by retaining some kind of monopoly over the company he/she finances. Besides, in arm's-length financing, the financier is principally or solely protected by explicit contracts and the company will be able to tap a wider circle of potential lenders because there will be more widespread financial information about it and so the loan will be contracted for a particular period, and the interest rate will be a competitive one that will compensate the lender for time and the risk of that specific loan. Venture capital financing is much relationship-based, even though it is typically not done by banks, and is found mainly in market-based economies and multiple banking relationships diminish the power of each individual bank, leading to a system that has many aspects of an arm's length one[254]. It could be said that the problem of misallocation of resources due to the lack of price signals in the relationship-based system is severe, because it lacks a self-activating mechanism to correct it. Besides, the arm's-length transactions that prevail in market-based economies have the beneficial effect of making prices more informative. In a relationship-based system the financier's information is private particularly when the projects being financed consist of intangible assets such as intellectual property and so the initial financier appropriates a greater share of the return to new technologies[255]. The arm's length system permits more flexibility in explicit contracts allowing the system to absorb adverse shocks. Companies avoid becoming dependent on a single bank when they have high market to book ratios, because they fear the bank may have too much power to extract rents and direct strategies. Financing in an arm's-length system has higher fixed costs, but enjoys better economy of scale. Arm's length financing relies profoundly on legal protection and judicial enforcement, while relationship financing is principally self-enforcing, requiring just the protection of the most basic property rights. In fact, relationship-based system perform better when markets and companies are smaller, when legal protection is weaker, when there is little transparency, and when innovation is mainly incremental, rather than revolutionary and so relationship-based systems work best in the early stages of industrialization where the companies to be financed are physical asset intensive, where the legal system is ineffective, and where skill-based or idea-based industries are of limited import which means that they work best in small, homogenous, closed economies. Besides, arm's-length financing works better when markets and companies are bigger, when companies are more formally organized, in the presence of better legal enforcement and transparency, and when innovation tends to be more revolutionary and so as economies develop and focus more on knowledge-intensive industries arm's-length markets can function successfully and aid the process of economic growth. A more efficient financial system facilitates entry, and so leads to lower profits for incumbent companies while financial development aids the entry of new companies, so enhancing competition. Financial development not only introduces competition, which puts pressure on the incumbent financial institution's profitability and its relationships, it also makes the financier's skills – his human capital -- redundant. Financially developed markets have greater availability of derivatives contracts, more liquid derivatives markets, and less severe currency restrictions influencing

254 Hoshi, T., Kashyap, A., and Scharfstein, D. (1990), 'The Role of Banks in Reducing the Costs of Financial Distress in Japan,' Journal of Financial Economics, 27, 67-88.

255 Hellwig, M, 2000. On the economics and politics of corporate finance and corporate control. In: Vives, X. (Ed.), Corporate Governance: Theoretical and Empirical Perspectives. Cambridge University Press, Cambridge, pp. 95-136.

the corporate hedging decision to the extent that these factors affect the incentives and the capacity of companies to hedge foreign exchange risk. Moreover, financial liberalization leads to a greater degree of integration with global markets making the national markets more susceptible to global shocks and to financial crises and companies are progressively exposed to global economic fluctuations which means that financial liberalization provides incentives for companies to mitigate currency risk through hedging[256]. According to Ugur Lel[257] "the degree of financial market development increases the likelihood of hedging. We also find that firms located in floating exchange regimes are more likely to engage in hedging. This suggests that exchange regimes are important to the firm's decision to hedge currency risk."

The creation of a common market for good and services magnified the effect of a surge in international trade and not only did the increase in the size of the market improve the effectiveness of an arm's length system, it also changed the underlying political economy making more discrete, and so more politically visible, the choice of the level of openness to trade and capital movements which means that the European Union made it also more difficult for particular interest groups to lobby for individual protections. The benefits of an arm's length system have been increased by the process of European integration, culminated with the introduction of the Euro and so while the process of international integration has removed many barriers to entry, enhancing both national and international competition, the introduction of the Euro has removed many of the remaining economic and psychological barriers which means that European countries now face a large integrated market, where information can travel freely as can competition. Moreover, Rajan and Zingales[258] consider that physical capital is becoming less important, while human capital is taking the center stage and relationship based systems find it hard to finance human capital companies, particularly when these human capital-intensive firms are involved in disruptive innovation which means that the relative benefit of an arm's length system may grow as companies change their nature. While free movement of goods and capital is essential to keep in check the local vested interests who want to repress finance and in particular arm's length finance, the political consensus in favor of free trade and free capital movement is eroding, under the effect of international crises and the anti-globalization movement[259] It should be taken into account that a reversal in financial development is made possible by the new intellectual climate triggered by the fall out of the Internet bubble and by the highly publicized corporate scandals in the United States, all of which creates an anti-market political climate and when coupled with the increasing willingness of politicians to sacrifice free trade for political expediency, the political climate does not look good for the opening out of markets. According to Raghuram G. Rajan and Luigi Zingales[260] "Enlargement will increase economic

---

[256] Mehrez, Gil, and Daniel Kaufman, 1999, Transparency, liberalization, and financial crisis, World Bank Policy Research Working paper No. 2286.

[257] Ugur Lel, Currency Risk Management, Corporate Governance, and Financial Market Development, 2003 Indiana University Working paper, p36.

[258] Rajan R., and Zingales, L. (2001) "The Influence of the Financial Revolution on the Nature of Firms" American Economic Review (2001), 91: 206-212. Rajan R., and Zingales, L. (2001) "Financial Systems, Industrial Structure, and Growth," Oxford Review of Economic Policy, 2001 17: 467-482. Rajan, R., Zingales, L., (2001) The firm as a dedicated hierarchy: a theory of the origins and growth of firms. Quarterly Journal of Economics 116, 805-852.

[259] Stiglitz, J. E., 2002. Globalization and Its Discontents. W. W. Norton, New York

[260] Raghuram G. Rajan and Luigi Zingales, Banks and Markets: The Changing Character Of European Finance, 2003 2nd ECB Central Banking Conference, p58.

competition, reducing the resistance to financial markets. At the same time, the introduction of new divergent interests inside the European Union will make coordination and lobbying more difficult, reducing the political threats to markets. By contrast, further steps toward political integration will reduce political competition and strengthen the central authority, increasing the return to lobbying at the central level. Both these effects will tend to reduce the political support for markets…it should promote structural reforms in Southern European countries, in order to reduce the distributional effects of an expansion of arm's length markets." In fact, the completion of the economic integration and the beginning of the political integration will lead to a shift in the pro-market stand of the European Union.

The field of finance is concerned with decisions with respect to the efficient allocation of scarce capital resources over competing alternatives and the allocation is effective when the alternative with the highest value is chosen. According to Article 2 in the Treaty, broader aims of the European Community comprise the promotion of a harmonious, balanced and sustainable development of economic activities, a higher level of employment and social protection, equality between men and women, sustainable and non-inflationary growth, a higher degree of competitiveness and convergence of economic performance, a high level of protection and improvement of the quality of the environment, the raising of the standard of living and quality of life, and economic and social cohesion and solidarity among the Member States. Regardless of common monetary policy actions, the mechanisms through which the actions are transmitted into the real economy and the extent to which they affect output and prices fluctuate from one country to another, and even over time within the same country and different economic and financial structures respond asymmetrically to monetary policy shocks of a given size. The primary objective of the ESCB and its monetary policy is to maintain price stability but price stability is to be maintained particularly over the medium term, since short-term volatility in prices cannot be controlled by means of monetary policy and excessive short-term inference might cause unnecessary, self-sustaining volatility into the real economy. Taking into account that a considerable amount of inflation has to be accepted in some countries in order to avoid the risk of pushing others into deflation, national inflation rates vary across countries due to differences in productivity and growth and also depending on in which point the countries are in their inflation cycles and so it can be difficult for the monetary authorities to assess the appropriate stance of the common monetary policy. Monetary authorities follow inflationary expectations constantly, since they can be seen as a prediction for future inflation and inflationary expectations affect pricing decisions and consequently actual future inflation, it is central that the expectations match the central bank's inflation target. Moreover, inflationary expectations are based on the prospect of future economic developments and the future course of monetary policy but they are influenced by announcements and implementation of the current monetary policy, if the public considers the central bank credible. The Eurosystem[261] (the ECB and the NCBs carry out the tasks of the ESCB within the euro area) has available three types of monetary policy instruments; it executes open market operations, offers standing facilities and requires minimum reserves. Open market operations are conducted in financial markets, typically in the money market, by the national central banks on the initiative of the ECB for the purposes of steering interest rates, managing the liquidity situation in the market and signalling the stance of the current monetary policy. Since the ECB has a monopoly over the issuance of base money, it

[261] European Central Bank (2001), The Monetary Policy of the ECB.

influences the overall conditions in the money market and it is the key ECB interest rate, since changes in it signal the stance of the ECB's monetary policy and affect short-term interest rates in the euro area money market. Monetary tightening raises not only money market rates but characteristically also long-term interest rates but less than the short ones which means that a rise in the official central bank rate not only raises the yield curve but also makes the curve flatter by narrowing the spread between short- and long-term interest rates[262]. The more credible is monetary policy, the less long-term interest rates should rise due to a rise in the central bank rate but if the rise in the policy rate is considered unsatisfactory to control the future inflation, the yield curve becomes steeper as long-term interest rates rise more than the short ones. Minimum reserve system aims at stabilising money market interest rates and creating or enlarging a structural liquidity shortage contributing to the capacity of the Eurosystem to operate effectively.

Centralised monetary policy in the ECB was linked to a decentralised fiscal policy in which individual countries retain the authority for taxation and expenditure. The most significant components of the SGP are that governments accept a 3% budget deficit maximum --except under very specific circumstances of negative growth (the excessive deficit procedure), and a balanced budget over the cycle and within the foreseeable future. When the budget deficit of an EMU member-state reaches 3%, the Commission reports on the member-state's transgression, Ecofin evaluates the Commission's report and issues a warning. If no corrective action is taken, the member-state is provisionally fined (up to 0.5% of its GDP). The SGP stipulates that government budgets have to be balanced both over the cycle and within foreseeable future and a balanced budget offers states more freedom for a fiscal stimulus when growth slows without breaching the SGP. It could be said that SGP is essential in order for the EU to avoid being stuck in a deflationary system within which individual member-states are bearing the costs of adjustment[263]. It seems that as long as member-states contribute to the target of low aggregate EMU-wide inflation, either by pursuing explicitly dis-inflationary policies or by not adopting policies that incite inflation, the SGP is interpreted very liberally, both by Ecofin and by the ECB. Monetary stability, expressed as low inflation, is a public good, of which all EMU members benefit in the form of low interest rates) and so a framework of sanctions and incentives is required that imposes individual compliance with the collective targets which means that the policies of individual member-states are harmonious with a low collective inflation goal[264]. Inflationary fiscal policies by individual member states are sanctioned by the group as a whole, while non-inflationary fiscal policies are left in relative peace and the SGP/BEPG framework is not just a narrow instrument to control overly expansive fiscal policies, but also an indirect sanctioning mechanism for Ecofin in its derived goal of containing inflation. Hence, fiscal policies that do not endanger the ECB's low inflation target are left untouched.

During the first few years of EMU, economic performance differed notably among Member States and differences in growth performance boil down to dissimilar supply

[262] Estrella, A. – Miskin, F.S. (1997) The Predictive Power of the Term Structure of Interest Rates in Europe and the United States: Implications for the European Central Bank. European Economic Review 41, 1375–1401.

[263] Schelkle, W. (2002), Disciplining Device or Insurance Arrangement? Two Approaches to the Political Economy of EMU Policy Coordination. LSE, European Institute working paper 2002-01.

[264] Gatti Donatella, Van Wijnbergen Christa (2002), "Coordinating Fiscal Authorities in the Euro-zone: A Key Role for the ECB." Oxford Economic Papers 54(1): 56-71.

conditions but these do not hamper the well-functioning of the monetary union. The more flexible prices and wages are, the smaller will be the volatility in output. Both real and nominal wages are quite rigid across most European countries, albeit with notable differences and apart from labour market regulation and the social security system, the degree of wage rigidity depends *inter alia* on the level of centralisation of wage bargaining. Downward nominal wage rigidity is explained by the institutional feature of European labour markets: nominal wages are a part of a contract, either a collective agreement or an individual employment contract. The degree of centralisation of wage bargaining is a key factor in the macroeconomic effects of economic shocks, as a high level of centralisation enables the internalisation of the adverse effects of real wage rises. Higher inflation in a cyclically advanced country implies lower real interest rates and profit margins are inflated due to demand pressures if the cycle is exacerbated by an undervalued real exchange rate. Investment opportunities in a period of overheating seem more optimistic, and in a period of overcooling more dark and producers assess their profit prospects too positively, based on actual price developments of their products and information failures with respect to the state of the economy. People over-invest at low interest rates in good times, underestimating a potential build-up of macro-economic imbalances leading to low investment growth in periods of economic overcooling.

Chapter 7

DIGITAL ECONOMY, MNE AND E-COMMERCE

7.1 "DIGITAL ECONOMY"

At the beginning of the 21st century, a global/new/digital economy has emerged that ties together all parts of the world and impacts almost every community. A homogeneous global culture is emerging based on American popular culture and the English language, but in the not too distant future, Chinese will challenge English as the dominant language on the Internet. The global economy is competitive spurring innovation and benefits consumers worldwide. Moreover, the global economy is bound to be more efficient than a set of regional or local economies and countries will only produce goods and services, which they are best at producing and second because larger economic entities, MNEs, will benefit from economies of scale and scope. International diversification is one means by which companies can leverage underutilized intangible resources. Global alliances are a means to achieve international development not only because they allow companies to again access to several markets at the same time but also because they make it possible to enhance their own international competitiveness through the use of their partners' resources. Globalization is threatening biodiversity regardless that global economic pressures overwhelm efforts to protect the earth's tropical rainforests, coastal regions, forests, wetlands, and wilderness areas but countries and states within countries should not be in a race to environmental oblivion in order to attract MNE investments and jobs. Consequently, global competition among localities for new business units promotes a downward spiral of reduced tax revenue and decreasing environmental standards and so the local costs of globalization exceed the benefits. Information technology has to a large extent increased the pace of the globalization process. A globalization of the human lookout is needed to guarantee the journey of earth-life through time and space[1].

New/Digital Economy is being driven by innovations in technology and by the evolution of new forms of work organization in the background of increased globalization. Companies are increasing their capital investments mainly in information-technology software and hardware. Companies are adopting "knowledge-based" work processes in which an escalating

---

[1] B.E. Tonn , E. Ogle, A vision for communities in the 21st century: back to the future, Futures 34 (2002) 717–734

percentage of non-managerial workers are involved in problem solving and identifying opportunities for innovation and growth. Companies re-engineer their workplaces to fit in more high functioning practices experience higher productivity[2]. The adoption of a sound system of new human resource management practices such as flexible job definitions, cross-training, and work teams, in conjunction with extensive reliance on incentive pay, results in significantly higher levels of productivity than more traditional human resource management practices. The establishment practices encourage workers to think and cooperate in order to improve the production process increasing company productivity. Essential factors such as adoption of a new technology-driven marketing channel increase uncertainty in product markets, rather than market microstructure variables and inadequacy lead to increased volatility[3]. Companies making strategic IT investments that are transformative in nature help more than companies making investments in IT for automation. Changes in technological regimes shift companies from stable business environments into more unstable, uncertain ones, creating a noteworthy influence on both real activities within the companies as well as on their stock market performance. The taking on eCommerce by a traditional company is associated with a higher demand ambiguity and this increase in demand ambiguity leads to an increase in company-specific stock volatility. A key strategy in developing knowledge industries is to generate a capacity to analyse an organisation's current knowledge-processing environment. The low marginal cost characteristics of information commodities and services make it appealing to create dedicated distribution channels for information transfer. The influence of cyberspace and computer networks however has created a new type of market failure driven by technology and high-risk network externalities. Networks no longer belong to a single company and strategy goes beyond the effective use of network structure and the appropriate allocation of cost. Partnership between companies has become mandatory for intra-network compatibility. The essence of the knowledge management challenge lies in creating a balance of knowledge supply and demand. New competitors with new knowledge make cross-competition more possible in new/digital economy. Companies need to focus their strategic investments and their management interest on those knowledge-intensive activities that develop the basis for sustainable competitive advantage[4]. Moreover, the triumph of companies hinges on the conventional flow of products to the supply channels, and the flow of information from the company to the consumer, via channels such as cyberspace. Interconnectivity allows consumers to use and link products, giving rise to virtual networks of customers. New economy markets specialising in the production of knowledge with costs for companies in terms of outsourcing of activities and for approaches focused not only to their own knowledge base but also to the getting hold of of knowledge from outside[5]. The exploitation of technology to focus on constant innovation and continue to offer customized tailor-made and personalized service to consumers are considered indispensable tools to stay competitive in eCommerce. Speed, quality, use of logistics and e-logistics and

---

[2] Mazzucato M., 2002. The PC Industry: New economy or early life-cycle? Review of Economic Dynamics, 5, 318-345.

[3] Sambamurthy, V., Bharadwaj, A., Grover, V. 2003. Shaping Agility Through Digital Options: Reconceptualizing the role of IT in Contemporary Firms MIS Quarterly 27, 2, 237-264.

[4] Shapiro C, Varian H (1999) Information Rules: A Strategic Guide to the Network Economy, p 2. Boston, MA: Harvard Business School Press.

[5] Geoffrion, A. M., R. Krishnan. 2003. E-Business and management science (Part 1 of 2). Management Sci. 49 (10) 1275-1286.

responsiveness of eCommerce companies are key competitive factors that are compulsory if companies wish to sustain their consumer base in a competitive environment in which consumers have easy access to information for comparison shopping.

The determinants of industrial country interest rates in an era of global capital mobility reflect a fundamentally diverse relationship between the traditional variables including fiscal imbalances and interest rates. Greenspan[6]argued "whatever those forces [underlying low U.S.long-term rates] are, they are surely global, because the decline in long-term interest rates in the past year is even more pronounced in major foreign financial markets than in the United States." Distance accumulation by non-G-7 central banks has to a large extent depressed long-term interest rates in the big industrial countries—regardless the potentially offsetting effect of a decline in the fiscal positions of most G-7 economies. States that have budgetary difficulties even in the present lowrate environment are expected to experience even greater difficulties when rates rise[7]. The long-run real interest rates are determined by ex ante levels of saving and investment. Industrial states nominal rates have been on a downward trend due to globalization and the increasing integration of developing countries into the world economy have contributed to flatten industrial countries' Phillips curves[8]. Low real rates echo a net underperformance of planned investment over planned saving. The integration of markets in the world economy depresses not only inflation prospect but also real interest rates[9].

The digital economy can be described as a global business environment in which the electronic exchange of goods and services, ideas and capital drive value creation. Financial institutions create digitally linked horizontal and vertical communities and new technologies are driving transaction friction out of the supply chain, making it more cost-effective to conduct commerce outside the traditional firm optimizing their cost-income ratio through the intelligent use of sourced services and must be flexible in meeting increasing consumer demands, or they risk losing their entire business. Product and service information and the resulting data generated from digital transactions are exceptionally marketable and precious products by themselves. Virtualization is not just about how organizations behave but it is also very much about the changing face of the workplace. In the networked/digital economy, enterprise will become more and more transparent to all their take-holder.

Knowledge management and data mining allow enterprises to attain a higher level of customer intimacy, turning information and knowledge into currency. It should be taken into account that knowledge can therefore be defined as the asset of an individual or group that allow them to formulate the right goal and to embark on the right actions to accomplish that goal in a given situation. Today, markets are global, competition is global, capital is global and Information and Communication Technology has played a noteworthy part in the development of globalization. The World Trade Organization and the Organization for

---

6 Greenspan, Alan, 2005, testimony before the Committee on Banking, Housing, and Urban Affairs, U.S. Senate, February 16. Greenspan, Alan 2005, testimony before the Committee on Financial Services, U.S. House of Representatives, July 20.

7 Warnock, Francis E., and Veronica Cacdac Warnock, 2005, "International Capital Flows and U.S. Interest Rates," International Finance Discussion Paper No. 840 (Washington: Board of Governors of the Federal Reserve System).

8 Hauner, David, Manmohan S. Kumar, 2005, "Financial Globalization and Fiscal Performance in Emerging Markets," IMF Working Paper 05/212

9 Catão, Luis, and George A. (Sandy) Mackenzie, 2006, "Perspectives on Low Global Interest Rates," IMF Working Paper 06/76.

Economic Co-operation and Development have created the environment where global trade is gradually more possible.

Cyberspace is both an effect and a cause of the new economy. Is there a transition of global economy to electronic commerce? Companies have to master the use of information technology, and e-commerce not only to better manage their own affairs but also to compete and thrive in the emerging digital economy. Management of internal change will be a key factor in success of companies in the electronic commerce. The new economy is shaped not only by the development and diffusion of computer hardware and software, but also by much cheaper and rapidly increasing electronic connectivity helping to level the playing field among large and small firms in business-to-business e-commerce and making it easier and cheaper for all businesses to transact business and exchange information. Companies are moving their supply networks and sales channels online, and participating in new online marketplaces intensifying their use of networked systems to expand internal business processes--to coordinate product design, administer inventory, develop customer service, and diminish administrative and managerial costs. Moreover, companies are participating in and developing online marketplace and escalating their use of networked systems to advance a host of business processes and new products and services are formed and incorporated into the networked world.

Information technology facilitates the distribution of many new products and services over electronic networks. Cyberspace retailers present expedient access to a larger selection of products than brick-and-mortar retailers can. Gains in all product categories increases as more consumers gain access to the cyberspace channel and as new technologies such as print-on-demand, digital content delivery, mobility services, and broadband access further diminish consumer search and transactions costs. Cyberspace has allowed *brick-and mortar* consumers to locate and evaluate goods they would not have been able to find otherwise. Moreover, cyberspace has led to a net increase in special order sales through the physical channel as well.

While the managed economy depended upon continuity, the entrepreneurial economy thrives on change. In the managed economy, the traditional factors of land, labor and capital are predominant as sources of comparative advantage, which means that geography provides a platform to combine mobile capital with (immobile) lower-cost labor and mass production where abundance of capital determined the comparative advantage[10]. The entrepreneurial economy is based less on the traditional inputs of land, labor and capital, and more on the input of knowledge. Knowledge as an input into economic activity is essentially different from land, labor and capital characterized by high uncertainty, high asymmetries across people and is costly to transact. Thus, in the entrepreneurial economy the comparative advantage is based on innovative activity and knowledge spillovers that cannot be simply diffused across geographic space with local characteristics and regional idiosyncrasies providing a rich source of new knowledge in the entrepreneurial economy[11]. It could be argued that globalization has shifted the comparative advantage of high-cost locations towards economic activity that cannot be costlessly diffused across geographic space and

---

[10] Chandler Alfred D. jr, 1977, The Visible Hand: The Managerial Revolution in American Business, Cambridge: Harvard University Press. Chandler, Alfred, 1990, Scale and Scope: The Dynamics of Industrial Capitalism, Cambridge: Harvard University Press.

[11] Kindleberger, Charles P. and David B. Audretsch (eds.), 1983, The Multinational Corporation, Cambridge: MIT Press.

taking into account that the formation and spillover of tacit knowledge is a localized phenomenon, local proximity and regions have emerged as an important locus of economic activity. Information generated by R&D in mature industries can be transferred to lower-cost locations for economic commercialization. Besides, the knowledge resulting from R&D in newly emerging industries cannot be effortlessly transferred to lower-cost locations for economic commercialization.

The process of creating diverse ideas and selecting across these diverse ideas is critical in both the managed and entrepreneurial economies. While in the managed economy, research activities are organized and scheduled in departments devoted towards novel products and services, in the entrepreneurial economy the selection between viable and non-viable ideas is the result of the market process and not restricted to internal decisions imposed by decision-making hierarchies and the commercialization of ideas takes the form of new firms. In the entrepreneurial economy, motivating employees to take part in the creation together with commercialization of new ideas add more than in merely controlling and regulating their behavior. The new legal forms of employment practices and contracts, such as part-time workers, temporary workers, contract workers, consultants, characterize the injection of entrepreneurial forces in the labor market[12].

Specialization of industry activities is associated with lower transactions costs and consequently greater efficiency, but a diversity of activities facilitates the exchange of new ideas and so greater innovative activity and efficiency. Spillovers are an important source of knowledge generating innovative activity. A world of homogeneous economic agents promotes diffusion but not innovation. An increased specialization of a specific industry facilitates knowledge spillovers across firms because all workers are engaged in the same activity. The exchange of complementary knowledge across diverse MNEs yields a greater return on new economic knowledge and the variety of industries within a geographic region promotes knowledge externalities and eventually innovative activity and economic growth. Diversity is more conducive to knowledge spillovers and finally innovative activity and subsequent growth than is specialization[13]. Globalization has shifted the comparative advantage of high-cost locations to knowledge-based activities, and in particular search activities, which cannot be costlessly transferred around the globe.

Integration in Europe has been formulated in terms of lower costs resulting from a greater exploitation of scale economies. Diversity, not convergence, generates innovation and growth. David B. Audretsch and A. Roy Thurik[14] say that the major economic benefits of European Integration will come not through economies of scale, but rather through economies of diversity.

In the managed economy competition and co-operation are viewed as being substitutes because firms are vertically integrated and compete mainly in product markets and co-

[12] Paque, Karl-Heinz, 1998, "Structural Unemployment in Europe: A Bird's-Eye View," in John T. Addison and Paul J.J. Welfens (eds.), Labor Markets and Social Security: Wage Costs, Social Security, Financing and Labor Market Reforms in Europe, Berlin: Springer Verlag, 17-44.

[13] Feldman, Maryann P. and David B. Audretsch, 1999, "Innovation in Cities: Science-Based Diversity, Specialization and Localized Competition," European Economic Review, 43, 409-429. Feldman, Maryann P., 1996, The Geography of Innovation, Boston/ Dordrecht: Kluwer Academic Publishers.

[14] David B. Audretsch and A. Roy Thurik, What's New about the New Economy? Sources of Growth in the Managed and Entrepreneurial Economies, 2000 Erasmus Research Institute Of Management, Ers-2000-45-Str

operation between firms in the product market reduces the number of competitors and lessens the degree of competition. Besides, in the entrepreneurial economy firms are vertically independent and specialized in the product market and co-operation among independent firms replaces internal transactions within a large vertically integrated corporation. So, co-operation between different companies generates the spillover of knowledge and new ideas. The relative innovative advantage between newly established enterprises and incumbent companies depends upon the source of information generating innovative activity. If information based on non-transferable experience in the market is a significant input in generating innovative activity, then incumbent companies will tend to have the innovative advantage over new companies. Distinctive feature of "new economy" firms is their aggressive reliance on the use of equity grants (stock options and restricted stock) as integral components of their compensation packages for executive and non-executive employees providing a larger proportion of compensation in the form of equity grants, and are more likely to use broad-based stock option programs that cover employees throughout the organization.[15]

Cyberspace can improve the productivity by lowering prices and search costs[16]. The Internet is especially useful in reducing international communication and searching costs and makes entry into several markets easier by lowering entry costs. Both lower search costs and lower entry barriers result in a greater market competition, and productivity can be improved by intensified competition. Second, cyberspace use can cut the cost of holding inventories by allowing large suppliers to bypass retailers and contact customers directly contributing to the improvement of productivity. Lastly, cyberspace usage can improve the transparency of the host countries and make it comfortable to do business. For example, the effects of corruption in a country can be reduced by the extensive use of cyberspace and make the economy more efficient and thus improve the productivity indirectly. Consequently, it is very natural that international direct investors may prefer to invest in a country with a well-established cyberspace infrastructure. International direct investors may well choose the country with more cyberspace availability. Development of cyberspace in a host country induces inward FDI significantly. While changing the geographical distances between the two countries is impossible, cyberspace usage can play an equivalent role to the narrowing the geographical distances between two countries in inducing FDI. The progress of the Internet will contribute to the worldwide increase in cross-border FDI and will be one of main driving forces in expediting the integration of the world economy and thus enhancing the welfare of the human beings. When markets are optimal, prices equal the full reproduction costs of goods, and control over goods is decentralized to encourage repeated, arms-length transactions based on the best available information and comparison-shopping.

Cyberspace will be used in ways that will transform existing relationships such as those between buyers and sellers, workers and owners, and suppliers and assemblers. In the process there will be vital changes in institutions such as manufacturing firms, service providers, and retailers. There is a distinction between two types of dot com companies - digital and

---

[15] Anderson, M., Banker, R., Ravindran, S., 2000. Executive compensation in the information technology industry. Management Science 46, 530-547. Baker, G., 1992. Incentive contracts and performance measurement. Journal of Political Economy 100, 598-614. Prendergast, C., 2000. What trade-off of risk and incentives?. American Economic Review 90, 421-425.

[16] Sichel, D. E. (1999, April). Computers and aggregate economic growth: An update. Business Economics, 18–24.

physical. Digital dot coms are cyberspace based companies such as Yahoo, Ebay and America Online, whose products and services are digital in nature and are delivered directly over cyberspace. By contrast, the physical dot coms sell physical products, books, CDs, toys that are shipped to consumers. Information Technology (IT) capital such as computer hardware, software and networking equipment contributes drastically to financial performance measures for the digital dot coms. However, the IT contribution for physical dot coms is less significant because physical dot coms, beyond the digital customer interface, are not deeply different from traditional business operations. Physical dot coms hold and manage inventory, and handle packaging and shipping processes by themselves, citing customer service excellence as the primary reason. By contrast, the digital products companies manage content inventory in a straight line through their Web sites and related applications. Physical dot coms need to adopt more digitization in their extended value chain in order to function as virtual organizations, whose heart competency is customer relationship and knowledge. Digital and physical dot coms respectively contribute to spectacular growth of online commerce activity.

The power of cyberspace is its simplicity; it is a medium for connections and is able to transmit anything digitised allowing the instantaneous exchange of information in digital form among an unlimited number of nodes. The information content of the cyberspace is entirely dephysicalized or dematerialised and reduced in its physical essence to the most abstract possible formulation: 1s and 0s carried by laser light, electrons, or electromagnetic waves. Multi-platform accessible standards, hypertext, and dematerialization are forcing and combining with an amazing increase in the capacity of global telecommunications systems to swiftly reduce the costs of communicating digital data. The flexibility of cyberspace allows it to be used for a large number of activities with differing real world manifestations. Activities as diverse as booking airline flights, purchasing items, playing games, viewing pictures, listening to music, or accessing public information, many of which previously were intermediated by human operators are being transferred to cyberspace.

E-commerce has the largest impact on standardized products that are cheap to transport and relatively easy to sell on-line. If there are large potential cost savings from selling on-line, on-line sales are likely to be large. A fall in transport costs may have large impact both on prices and the volume of e-commerce. The growth of e-commerce may create economies of scale in transports that cause costs to fall. Cyberspace is an important part of the ongoing transformation of the global economy to a form in which materiality becomes subordinate to information and knowledge creation representing the formation of an entirely novel economic space. By connecting computers cyberspace allows direct access to processes and procedures that were previously matched in the back offices and data processing centres of government and corporations, while also creating utterly new sources of information.

E-commerce represents a flood of new market opportunities but it should be taken into consideration the comparatively broad extent of electronic interchange that already exists between a range of supply chains from raw materials production down to retail sale businesses in highly developed economies such as the US, Japan or Europe. Is electronic commerce an evolutionary transformation, a further, undoubtedly more ubiquitous, efficiency- improving factor in a long series of improvements in logistics and wholesale and retail trade activities, from bar coding, EDI to e-commerce? The Internet provides an immeasurable array of new information and communication access opportunities[17]. The emergence of the notion of an Information Society means that the ease of communication and access to information and data are not just fundamental ingredients of economic activity in the production, distribution and consumption, increasingly of digital goods and services but also of leisure, of social interaction and democratic expression. Advancing technology and changing business organizations transform economies and societies. Information technologies, data communication and data processing technologies are tools to manoeuvre, arrange, transmit, and store information in digital form. Moreover, the Digital economy refers to changes in business organization, market structures, government regulations, and human experience as it is about new technology. Is digital economy becoming global? The Digital economy is generating considerable and unforeseen increases in productivity that have motored our recent surge in economic growth and that have enlarged the margin for monetary policy. The economic transformation is about structural transformation and developments that carry interference and alteration. So, the information technology revolution is transforming economy. The technological explosion of the invention of the semiconductor and following productivity gains in making semiconductors has produced and will produce a spectacular advance in information-processing power. The explosion in computing power had as result that the Digital economy has emerged earlier, diffused more rapidly and more widely throughout the economy than prior technological revolutions[18]. Productivity growth and technological change in the main sectors of the information-processing revolution have been enormous. Some technological changes do not just intensify productivity in one sector but give all economic sectors new "tools" and open new potential for economic organization across the board. The transition to a Digital economy based on the emergence of patently new forms of business organization and work. It should be taken into consideration that sweeping technological developments and applications from semiconductors through the personal computer and the cyberspace were developed and commercialised by start-ups, not by established organizations.

Quantitative and qualitative changes in the employment market were the first indication of a shifting economic system by the usage of Cyberspace. There is a structural change in terms of greater competitiveness, economic growth, and in due course increased employment demands a loss, or at least an apparent loss of particular other economic policy goals. The costs of economic restructuring are vast and encompass practically every dimension of economic life. Changes go together with knowledge based activity and knowledge based activity results in innovations that are more drastic and less incremental[19]. In fact knowledge is developed in the contexts of localized production networks embedded in innovative clusters. It has to be taken into account that globalization has not had symmetric impacts on knowledge and information but it has made it likely to convey information costlessly across geographic area. Alteration in the prices of knowledge and information has triggered a change in comparative advantage. Resident characteristics and regional idiosyncrasies are lees

---

[17] OECD, 1998. The Competitive Dynamics of Internet-Based Electronic Commerce. Paris.

[18] Paul A. David (1991), "Computer and Dynamo: The Productivity Paradox in a Not-too-Distant Mirror," Technology and Productivity: The Challenge for Economic Policy (Paris: OECD), pp. 315-347. Carl Shapiro and Hal Varian (1998), Information Rules: A Strategic Guide to the Network Economy (Boston: Harvard Business School Press), p. 9.

[19] Christensen, Clatton M., 2000, The Inventor's Dilemma: When New Technologies Cause Great Firms to Fail, New York: Harper Collins.

relevant as a knowledge source and as a result as a source of competitive advantage[20]. Globalization has shifted the comparative advantage of high-cost locations to knowledge-based activities and especially in search conduct which cannot be costlessly transferred around the world. Knowledge as an input into economic activity is characterized by high uncertainty, high asymmetries across sectors and is costly to transact.

Does the new/digital economy contribute to economic growth in developing countries? The contribution of the digital economy to economic growth in developing countries has been minimal when viewed from a macroeconomic perspective and the traditional economy will for long be the primary force behind economic growth in transition economies. At present the impact of the digital economy on the worldwide economy has so far been quite limited, particularly in terms of its geographical reach. Besides, the acceleration in productivity and output growth could allow transition economies to shorten the process of their catching-up with developed countries. Pohjola [21]shows that the relative contribution of IT to GDP growth in developing countries was less than 2% (China, India, Argentina, Chile, Brazil, Thailand, Venezuela) compared to more than 10% in the US, Finland, Canada, Sweden, and UK[22]. In transition countries there is relatively small value of IT investments. Developing countries, as opposed to developed countries, have not been able to profitably use ICT products and services due to the lack of complimentary investments in infrastructure, human capital, R&D and so on. Thus, returns on investments in basic infrastructure (drinking water, primary schools, irrigation) are very likely to be more productive than high-technology investments and so the technological gap could also widen between more or less developed transition economies. In the shorter run, it appears that traditional accumulation of physical and human capital matters more than technological progress. A significant portion of the growth resurgence of the U.S. economy after 1995 is attributed to advances in IT[23]. The levels of IT investment by businesses during the last half of the 1990's contribute to a large extent to increased labor productivity growth[24]. Moreover, price decline has stimulated the deployment of IT equipment and software by the IT-using industries[25].

The social benefits of an information-commodity need to exceed its high fixed costs to make its production desirable. The marginal production costs of information-commodities are low and its digital character allows for a multiplication and distribution at virtually no costs, for instance by means of the cyberspace without any capacity constraints. Taking into account that the new/digital economy offers possibilities for product differentiation that were traditionally less readily available, producers of information-commodities will try to differentiate their product from the ones of their competitors maintaining and enforcing their monopoly positions.

---

[20] Audretsch, David B. and A. Roy Thurik, 2000, Capitalism and Democracy in the 21st Century: from the Managed to the Entrepreneurial Economy, Journal of Evolutionary Economics, 10(1), 17-34.

[21] Pohjola, M. (ed.). 2001, 'Information Technology, Productivity, and Economic Growth". Oxford University Press, pp. 11-12.

[22] World Economic Forum. 2001. 'Global Competitiveness Report 2001-2002', pp. 21. Downloaded from http://www.cid.harvard.edu/cr/pdf/GCR0102%20Exec%20Summary.pdf

[23] Jorgenson, Dale W. (2002), Economic Growth in the Information Age, Cambridge, The MIT Press.

[24] Economic Research Institute, Economic Planning Agency (2000), "The Effect of Information and Technology on Productivity: In Search of Japan's 'New Economy' (in Japanese)." Seisaku Koka Repoto (Report on Policies and Effects), No. 4, October 2000.

[25] Dale W. Jorgenson and Kazuyuki Motohashi, Economic Growth of Japan and the United States in the Information Age, RIETI Discussion Paper Series 03-E-015, July 2003

Moreover, investment in physical capital expands and renews the existing capital stock and enables new technologies to enter the production process[26]. However, the IT revolution contributes to productivity and output growth on a microeconomic level in certain industries (retail, financial services, transportation) and specific enterprises. Productivity improvements at the company and industry level driven by information technology are expected in medium and long-term to contribute to acceleration in aggregate growth[27]. Additionally, the potential of the Internet revolution allows for faster diffusion and adaptability of innovations, and as a result higher value of international R&D spillovers. Nonetheless, digital economy represents a momentous potential for less developed and transition economies to achieve long-term growth, sustained and fast socio-economic development, and catch-up with developed countries[28]. Different speeds of adoption of technological innovations resulting from the different quality of institutional infrastructure are expected to contribute – along with the traditional 'old' economy – to diverging rates of economic growth and consequently add to the growing income polarization among the less developed and transition economies[29]. The digital/new economy is construed as a superior economic structure perpetuated by innovations in information and communications technologies, which -- while impacting all sectors of the economy – accelerates productivity and economic growth. New technologies of production and distribution, which have a qualitative influence on ways of doing business and productivity improvements in the ICT sector alone complemented by cyclical effects of higher investments have transformed traditional economy into digital economy. It could be said that the digital economy is a multipart of new economic phenomena and interdependent processes based on ICT products and services, which permeate the whole economy and bring new ways of doing business.

There is a connection between human resource management systems and business performance measured by labor productivity. Organizational capital includes workforce training, employee right to be heard, and work design. The degree of control a company has over assets such the design of production processes, human capital, and organizational capital varies along with the capability of a company to "sell" these assets. Employer provided training is an important component of workplace organization and organizational capital. Workplace training is a decision undertaken by the worker and the company investing in additional skills training[30]. Organizational capital interacts with human capital and the capability of a company to embark on organizational change. As employee voice increases, companies are able to use the knowledge of non-managerial workers. The use of cross-functional production processes lead to more flexible allocation and reallocation of labor in the company. For instance, new technologies reduce the cost of cross communication. Monitoring technologies can be used to shrink the number of supervisors required in the

---

[26] Zinnes, C., Eilat, Y. and Jeffrey Sachs. 2001. 'Benchmarking Competitiveness in Transition Economies'. Economics of Transition, Volume 9 (2) 2001, 315-353.

[27] Bassanini, A., Scarpetta, S., and I. Visco. 2000. 'Knowledge, Technology and Economic Growth: Recent Evidence from OECD Countries'. Paris: OECD, Economics Department Working Papers, No. 259.

[28] Bassanini, A., Scarpetta, S., and P. Hemmings. 2001. 'Economic Growth: The Role of Policies and Institutions. Panel Date Evidence from OECD Countries'. Paris: OECD, Economics Department Working Papers, No. 283.

[29] Kolodko, G.W. 2001. 'The 'New Economy' and the Old Problems. Prospects for Fast Growth in Post-Socialist Countries. Zagreb International Review of Economics & Business, Vol. 4, No. 2, pp. 71-90.

[30] Black, Sandra E. and Lisa M. Lynch. 2004. "What's Driving the New Economy: The Benefits of Workplace Innovation," The Economic Journal, vol. 114, February, pp. F97-F116.

production process. The acceptance of a sound system of new human resource management practices such as cross-training and work teams, along with broad reliance on incentive pay, results in significantly higher levels of productivity than more conventional human resource management practices[31].

Companies in knowledge intensive industries have employed mergers and acquisitions, joint ventures and strategic alliances to get hold of knowledge/ technology[32]. Supremacy over knowledge accrues from having way in to knowledge and ownership of knowledge. Way in to knowledge implies getting to know the elaborate details required to make the most of the knowledge for production. It has to be taken into account that choosing access and ownership reduces the misrepresentation between agents' privately optimal and socially most favourable investments engendering first best incentives in various industries. Possession of knowledge confers the legal right to make lasting decisions about the employment of the knowledge at the same time as access to knowledge represents the needed expertise that lends substance to such a right. According to Krishnamurthy Subramanian[33] "optimally choosing access and ownership reduces the distortion between agent's privately optimal and socially optimal investments and can generate the first best. The theory predicts that when knowledge of both firms becomes easier to replicate, they will provide less access to each other through less integration. In contrast, the firm whose knowledge is easier to replicate will acquire one whose knowledge is difficult to replicate to prevent inefficient investment by the latter."

The rapid technological advance makes it possible that the share of ICT industries in gross domestic product increases while ICT prices decline. The trade of ICT products, intermediate goods, and components has quickly increased as a consequence of the new production modes and distribution systems. According to Matti Pohjola [34] "A thriving New Economy requires a high degree of diversity in institutions, investments and forms of control". Clustering does not necessarily obey national borders. The productivity gains not only reflect increased investment in ICT, but also corresponding innovations in business organization and strategy[35]. In accordance with H. Koski , P. Rouvinen, and P. Yla-Anttila [36]"availability of high-skilled labour is indeed one of the key reasons for a firm to locate within a cluster of similar businesses, and that the high-IT industries are *not* directly comparable to the ICT sector, not least because the latter is largely comprised of manufacturing-related activities". Moreover, according to Inge Ivarsson and Jan-Erik Vahlne [37] "A logistic regression analysis showed that coordination and integration of technology in MNEs is positively correlated with the length of time the a affiliates have been a part of the

[31] Sandra E. Black,Lisa M. Lynch, Measuring Organizational Capital in the New Economy, 2005 IZA DP No. 1524

[32] Baker, George and Thomas N. Hubbard. 2004. "Contractibility and Asset Ownership: On-Board Computers and Governance in US Trucking," Quarterly Journal of Economics, 119(4), 1443 - 1479.

[33] Krishnamurthy Subramanian, Firm Boundaries in the New Economy: Theory and Evidence, 2005 www.ssrn.com p31.

[34] Matti Pohjola, The New Economy: facts, impacts and policies, Information Economics and Policy 14 (2002) 133–144, p144.

[35] Jukka Jalava , Matti Pohjola, Economic growth in the New Economy: evidence from advanced economies, Information Economics and Policy 14 (2002) 189–210

[36] H. Koski , P. Rouvinen, P. Yla-Anttila, ICT clusters in Europe The great central banana and the small Nordic potato, Information Economics and Policy 14 (2002) 145–165, p157.

[37] Inge Ivarsson , Jan-Erik Vahlne, Technology integration through international acquisitions: the case of foreign manufacturing MNEs in Sweden, Scand.J.Mgmt.18 (2002)1-27, p1.

parent corporation, while dynamic technological integration was positively correlated with affiliates operating in competitive Swedish industry clusters".

The growth of the digital economy is expected to depend on growth of discretionary time and integration of digital technology into new forms of socializing, transacting, and spending time. Internet has enabled globally available discussion forums that appeal to a large number of diverse participants. The most important characteristic of the new digital economy may be the increasing dependence of revenue on personal habits and norms rather than on the characteristics and values of products. Services compete in a much broader field of human interactions and the major challenge of the new economy is getting persons to pay for new digital services needing to create new payment habits and norms in a commercially driven environment. The key fundamentals of the new/digital economy include an innovative information technology service sector that is organized in network firms of organization, rather than traditional firms or markets, high rates of economic growth and share prices on stock markets in America have plummeted, leading to a medium-term volatility in share prices unprecedented in the second half of the last century. Especially, Internet service providers are amongst the companies with the highest volatility in stock market capitalization. If a company is tied into its network of customers and suppliers and sustain a course of innovation that maintains its position within existing markets and technologies, then it is likely not to undertake radical innovation and will be blindsided by breakthrough technologies[38]. Start-ups have been the drivers of much of the radical innovation in the transition to a Digital economy. Fundamental production innovations that meant that lower cost could also bring higher quality forced American and European producers to reorganize deeply their production and business practices. The market advantages of many innovations are vanished if the innovating company cannot also be world-class producers, or at least have close access to world-class production. Leading companies lower their costs by concentrating on what they did best, and contracting to buy the rest from producers with a firm-specific advantage in productivity or a nation-specific factor cost-based comparative advantage. The aptitude to use modern data communications networks to transmit information allows client firms to state in great detail what they want their contractors to do. There is a shift from a market dominated by integrated producers to one in which companies situated anywhere in the disintegrated value chain can potentially control the evolution of key standards and in that way define the terms of competition — not just of their specific sector, but critically in final product markets as well. As discussed earlier, globalisation presses the sense of international forces sweeping past the capacity of nations to respond, channel, or control. The Internet multiplies connections, generating an apparently placeless cyberspace. The rapid development of a broad network creates great gains for each participant, generating new markets and opportunities for companies, and new possibilities for consumers. The global information economy and society is a network that crosses borders in a world organized into nation-states creating a role for national governments. The principal task of a global information processing is to assure a sufficient agreement on standards to permit the operation of global networks and to assure markets for equipment, tools, and applications open.

[38] Katie Hafner (1996), Where Wizards Stay Up Late: The Origins of the Internet, New York: Simon and Schuster. Michael Hiltzik (1999), Dealers of Lightning: Xerox PARC and the Dawn of the Computer Age, New York: Harper Business.

The digital economy company is characterized by its high reliance on intangible assets for generating wealth creation with an increased value of human capital relative to other more tangible assets. The organizational[39] architecture of a company consists of three complementary components: performance measurement, incentive compensation or rewards, and the allocation of decision rights and according[40] to Elizabeth Demers, Margaret Shackell, Sally K. Widener "a firm's performance measurement, rewards, and delegation decisions are complementary components of an integrated system of control, with the implication that modifications to one element of the system should be accompanied by alterations and rebalancings in the other components of the firm's holistic architecture." Furthermore, the New/digital Economy has accelerated productivity growth, making the economy more resilient and flexible, with less volatile growth rates and fewer and milder recessions, thereby improving living standards. Technological change has accelerated not only the pace of innovation but also the pace at which new products gain widespread use and produce significant sales. Supply chain management, just-in-time inventory, rapid production and delivery systems are now proven business practices given momentum by new information technology. Better inventory management has been responsible for the decline in the volatility of GDP growth. Productivity growth has increased in recent years, with the rate about 1 percentage point higher in the post-1994 period than in 1973–94. Information technologies have changed where we work, how we work and what kind of work we do. The declining of stock prices and the rising corporate shutdowns among Internet-related firms shows that the New Economy has negative aspects as well. Thus, business cycles are not dead and never will be but the new technology should allow firms to better use information, thereby reducing output volatility and the rate and harshness of recessions[41]. New information technology has increased competition and reduced profit margins and in a world of fierce competition, fast-moving information and low barriers to entry means that a dominant market position can evaporate quickly. Manufacturing remains important and is being re-invented through cyberspace[42].

If new, more powerful electronic commerce technologies are developed and marketed then many transacting parties may find their access to global markets conditioned by their ability to conform their business behavior to the norms embodied in the technology. Cyberspace processes must be standardized and businesses should be able to use software agents to seek out new trading partners on the Internet, to do background checks on prospective trading partners, to negotiate contracts, and in transactions involving digital media, to perform the contract online. Governments could direct investments in electronic

---

[39] Nagar, V. 2002. Delegation and Incentive Compensation. Accounting Review, 77(2): 379-395. Brickley, J. A., Smith, C. W., and Zimmerman, J. L. 2000. Managerial Economics and Organizational Architecture (2nd ed.). Boston: Irwin/McGraw-Hill.

[40] Elizabeth Demers, Margaret Shackell, Sally K. Widener, 2002, Complementarities in Organizational Design: Empirical Evidence from the New Economy, The Bradley Policy Research Center, Working Paper No. FR 03-01, p37.

[41] Dale W. Jorgenson and Kevin J. Stiroh, "Raising the Speed Limit: U.S. Economic Growth in the Information Age," Brookings Papers on Economic Activity, 2000, pp. 125–211.

[42] Andrew Odlyzko, "Internet Growth: Myth and Reality, Use and Abuse,"iMP: The Magazine on Information Impacts, November 2000. Evan F. Koenig, "Productivity, the Stock Market and Monetary Policy in the New Economy," Federal Reserve Bank of Dallas Southwest Economy, January/February 2000, pp. 6–12. Owen Irvine and Scott Schuh, "Inventory Investment and Output Volatility," Federal Reserve Bank of Boston Working Paper no. 02-6, December 2002.

commerce technologies for use by public sector organizations in their procurement functions in order to encourage the development of technologies that meet public policy objectives and regulators and courts should make out ways to manage the interface between law and technical norms that preserve the effectiveness of legal institutions while harnessing the power of technological innovation for the public interest.

Virtual stores are being created with virtual inventories far larger than any physically existing store and their products available are fully computerized, the customer rapidly pinpoints the exact product desired by using specially tailored database query software. These products can be drop-shipped from a production or distribution node to anywhere in the world using the various courier services that are now on-line. Cyberspace eases many market entry barriers because of minimal start-up costs, thereby radically accelerating the realization of an idea and allowing flourishing ventures to grow exponentially. Commercial content providers required to find ways to catch the attention of people to their site, either by providing striking content for them to consume or some service or product they desire to use or buy, or by creating a system for purchasing non-Internet particular products that offers something conventional retail channels do not. So, Commercial publishers desiring to be successful on cyberspace have to offer more to customers than that which is customarily available in print or from some other media. The speed at which businesses can be established on cyberspace places a great deal of emphasis on being the first in a specific market category. Cyberspace is establishing a completely new retailing channel that is already affecting traditional retail industry. Building successful cyberspace retail web sites is extensively more complex than merely moving a catalog online creating a feeling that it is the place to go to buy something.[43] Goods and services in the digital economy typically are not rival, excludable, or transparent. In the absence of rivalry, excludability, and transparency, policy makers will not be able to replicate the ideal market of neo-classical economics through the design of a legal and regulatory framework.

Digital networks and e-commerce strategies are transforming the organization and practice of economic activity. The powerful communications instruments of the digital technology will produce a single global market. Regionally and nationally based lead users, or their regionally specific needs, may drive distinctive lines of technology development in which local firms may have an advantage. Differences in policy may also profoundly affect the development of technology, markets, and products. The regulation of telecommunications and other networks will considerably influence the organization of the electronic economy with respect to worldwide access, competition, and network technologies and architectures. As the digital economy becomes a larger and more essential structural feature of national economies will become vital to understand the political, economic, and regulatory conflicts that unavoidably accompany significant technological transformations. The rise of cyberspace and e-commerce concern the reform and creation of legal rules to govern and regulate market transactions in cyberspace. Furthermore, the expansion of cyberspace and e-commerce departs from the usual pattern of economic change and policy response. Cyberspace and e-commerce are global and international phenomena and so the regulatory

[43] Bransten, Lisa. 1998. "There's More to E-Commerce Than Just the Lowest Prices." Wall Street Journal Interactive Edition, http://interactive.wsj.com. Davis, Stan and Christopher Meyer. 1998. Blur: The Speed of Change in the Connected Economy (Reading, Mass: Addison-Wesley). Reuters. 1998. "E-commerce a boon to consumers," ABC News-Reuters (July 5), *http://www.abcnews.com/sections/tech/DailyNews/neteconomics980705.html*

and governance response must also be international in scope and character. Competition policy and antitrust enforcement remain vital to the maintenance of an energetic digital economy. The cyber world is intertwined with our traditional world. Will we have a cyber world free of regulation? New rules require that the political bargains among different interests and objectives that defined the current policies be renegotiated. Digital economy creates new products and transforms conventional industries with the new ways it transforms storage, search, diffusion, and indeed production of ideas and information. Given the escalating pace of innovation that rests on new ideas and the importance of information based products, the question of intellectual property becomes central. Cyberspace is no longer a free zone it is a focus for difficult policy-making including not only narrowly technical problems but also through the narrowly legal into fundamental questions of how to organize markets and society[44].

Cyberspace enables companies to reduce the costs of carrying inventory, obtaining and managing necessary supplies, and dealing with customers allowing consumers greater choice in products and services as well as the ability to find the least expensive and most suitable products and services. E-commerce technologies appear to be driving changes among traditional intermediaries such as wholesalers, travel agents, or shippers that add value between the production of a good or service and its sale to the final consumer creating efficiencies by eliminating the need for intermediaries. Manufacturers and service providers would begin selling directly to the customer and "middlemen" would disappear some intermediaries would exhibit in finding new ways to add value in an online world. Hence, instead of vanishing, traditional intermediaries are adapting to exploit new possibilities as providers of logistical, financial, and information services.

Increased employment together with low inflation and growth in productivity resulting in GDP growth over a long period is relating to the spread of the use of the Information and Communications Technologies. The new/digital economy is defined as one based on knowledge and information, relying on sub sectors such as entirely digital goods and services and mixed goods that is, physical goods that are sold through the Internet. The development of an interconnected, interdependent economy, with a network structure and tremendous flexibility of ICT and capacity for transformation permit the increasing convergence of specific technologies into a highly integrated system. Cyberspace is an open web based on open standards that allow any computer on the net to connect, through the same protocols permitting the interaction of different computer platforms and simplifying the exchange of information, multiplying the possibilities of links between the different agents operating in the electronic marketplace. The emergence of new agents, processes, business relations and patterns of communication and organization are typical features of the electronic marketplace. New markets are opening up for traditional products, new information-based products and new delivery channels, thereby making it easier to adapt to individual consumer preferences. Knowledge-based digital products share with knowledge itself the common features of infinite supply and non-rivalry, which mean that they will never run out and can be used repeatedly by numerous users bringing forward the need to regulate intellectual property

[44] G Zekos "Personal Jurisdiction and applicable law in Cyberspace transactions" 2000 Journal of World Intellectual Property 977, No6. G Zekos "Issues of Intellectual Property in Cyberspace" 2002 Journal of World Intellectual Property 233. G Zekos "Legal Problems in Cyberspace" 2002 Managerial Law 45, Number 5. G Zekos, Cyberspace Sovereignty and Jurisdiction, *2005 The ICFAI Journal Of Cyber Law No 1 p 31-59 www.icfaipress.org*

rights. Consumer behaviour differs between the virtual market and the physical world, the quantity and quality of the information that is handled, accessed and processed through a network in which time and space take on a new meaning. The use of ICT brings changes to the business environment, where transaction costs decrease, production factors become less expensive, lesser quantities of stocks are needed, and time to market is reduced. For instance, transformations resulting from technological and organisational changes and their combined effects have influenced the role of governments and the design of government policy. The information age is giving rise to processes of severe social exclusion, both in developing countries and in poorer, depressed areas of the developed world and so alongside the acceleration of the globalisation process, apparent in growing mobility among the factors of production, brings changes in the world of finance and trade, liberalisation of the flow of capital goods and services, the role of direct investment and transfer of technology. The goods and services associated with the digital economy are going through major technological changes and quality improvements that are not reflected in price levels or in quality indices. New products and services are emerging complicating the measuring process in the services sector. The new environment of the electronic marketplace favours changes in market structure and competitive strategies as well as speeding up convergence in technologies, infrastructure, markets and products. Is the new economy focused on sustainability and stability? Businesses no longer essentially have a nationality and know no borders and faced with a New World economic order driven by global ideas of vast corporate empires, compliant governments, a globalized consumer monoculture and a unanimous ideological commitment to corporate libertarianism[45]. In market mechanism the only variable that matters is the competitive pricing to quality ratio[46] and so the concept of competition means everything. Globalization undermines national policy autonomy. The multinational enterprise takes on many national identities, while it is maintaining local sales facilities and production in individual countries. The MNE organizes its operations around vertically integrated supplier networks and outsources its production to other firms in the network

The extensive use of microelectronics and computer based networks as information and communication technologies have enabled knowledge to become the 'key' economic engine[47] but evidence from traditional trade and foreign direct investment flow data show no increase in globalisation. Microelectronic technological revolution is the route by which capitalism has evolved from the mass production manufacturing base to the new information and knowledge base.[48] Global access clustered around new ICT has led to an increased rate of innovation consequent on reduce of information handling and processing costs. Additionally, higher innovation rate under ICT, introduces a requirement for shorter payback periods on investment commitments compared to manufacturing investment where the nature and extent

---

[45] Korten, David, 1995, When Corporations Rule the World,. Earthscan Publications Ltd. London.

[46] Fuller, Donald A., 1999. Sustainable Marketing. Managerial-Ecological Issues. Sage Publications, Thousand Oaks, London, New Delhi p31. Fouler writes about competition: "This is accomplished through the market mechanism, which allows customers to make informed choices (market transactions) after considering the various competitive offerings"

[47] Soete, L. (1999) "The New Economy: A European Perspective", paper presented to the European Socio-Economic Research Conference, Brussels, 28-30 April. p. 3 The "...new intangible features of international transactions appear to form the essence of what the 'new' economy is all about." Thurow, L.C. (1999) Building Wealth: The New Rules for Individuals, Companies and Nations in a Knowledge-Based Economy, New York: Harpercollins.

[48] Lavoie, M. (1992) Foundations of Post-Keynesian Economic Analysis, Aldershot: Edward Elgar.

innovation involves a longer time horizon. Keynes[49] said that waves of investment expenditure are stimulated by new technology. Moreover, radical innovation generates structural change, powerful burst in economic growth and strong susceptibility to cyclical downturn.[50] Global operations and international strategic alliances are integral components of organizational strategy. Strategic alliances can better meet the needs of global products and customers. Operating internationally brings to the company the benefits of access to new markets and raw materials and the prospect to include and improve knowledge derived from the best possible operations worldwide. IT is essential to this strategic choice because it makes globalisation possible by providing a co-ordination mechanism for geographically disseminated activities and reshapes individual organizations into global co-operatives by providing a coalition mechanism.

E-commerce represents a flood of new market opportunities but it should be taken into consideration the comparatively broad extent of electronic interchange that already exists between a range of supply chains from raw materials production down to retail sale businesses in highly developed economies such as the US, Japan or Europe. Is electronic commerce an evolutionary transformation, a further, undoubtedly more ubiquitous, efficiency- improving factor in a long series of improvements in logistics and wholesale and retail trade activities, from bar coding, EDI to e-commerce? The long-term growth impact of electronic commerce is more significant given the greater opportunities for replacement of physical commerce for electronic commerce. Greater market transparency allowing consumers to identify products at lowest price versus possible social and cultural needs for shopping is likely to differ across various product categories. The Internet provides an immeasurable array of new information and communication access opportunities[51]. The emergence of the notion of an Information Society means that the ease of communication and access to information and data are not just fundamental ingredients of economic activity in the production, distribution and consumption, increasingly of digital goods and services but also of leisure, of social interaction and democratic expression. Advancing technology and changing business organizations transform economies and societies. Information technologies, data communication and data processing technologies are tools to manoeuvre, arrange, transmit, and store information in digital form. Moreover, the Digital economy refers to changes in business organization, market structures, government regulations, and human experience as it is about new technology. Is digital economy becoming global? The Digital economy is generating considerable and unforeseen increases in productivity that have motored our recent surge in economic growth and that have enlarged the margin for monetary policy. The economic transformation is about structural transformation and developments that carry interference and alteration. So, the information technology revolution is transforming economy. The technological explosion of the invention of the semiconductor and following productivity gains in making semiconductors has produced and will produce a spectacular advance in information-processing power. The explosion in computing power had as result

---

[49] Keynes, J.M. (1930) A Treatise on Money, London: Macmillan.

[50] Kalecki, M. (1954) Theory of Economic Dynamics, London: Allen & Unwin. Courvisanos, J. (1996) Investment Cycles in Capitalist Economies: A Behavioural Kaleckian Contribution, Cheltenham: Edward Elgar. Hollanders, H., Soete, L. and ter Weel, B. (1999) "Trends in Growth Convergence and Divergence and Changes in Technological Access and Capabilities", MERIT Research Memorandum 99-019, Maastricht: Maastricht University.

[51] OECD, 1998. The Competitive Dynamics of Internet-Based Electronic Commerce. Paris.

that the Digital economy has emerged earlier, diffused more rapidly and more widely throughout the economy than prior technological revolutions[52]. Productivity growth and technological change in the main sectors of the information-processing revolution have been enormous. Some technological changes do not just intensify productivity in one sector but give all economic sectors new "tools" and open new potential for economic organization across the board. The transition to a Digital economy based on the emergence of patently new forms of business organization and work. It should be taken into consideration that sweeping technological developments and applications from semiconductors through the personal computer and the cyberspace were developed and commercialised by start-ups, not by established organizations. Entrepreneurial companies have spotted new opportunities and have taken risks to build on new applications of information technology. Companies in a broad range of sectors have forcefully and productively pursued innovation to defend and expand their market positions. Established companies are compelled, re-created and re-organized themselves to respond to competitive pressures and opportunities that define the new economic landscape. Developing countries are struggling to determine how they can benefit from the emerging digital economy, given the condition of their electric and telephonic infrastructure. The World Wide Web is getting entangled in the webs of law, custom, and commerce and cyberspace is no longer a policy-free zone.

Changes in the powers and capabilities made available by modern information technologies are redefining competent business practices, and sustainable market structures. The activities that belong inside a firm and which can be purchased from outside are redefined together with changing business models and market structures. The on-going innovations in business strategy and organization lead to efforts to resolve real problems or take advantage of real opportunities. Changes due to electronic technology and digital economy amount to the creation of a considerably new business system—a system with two differentiating features: constant on-going innovation, and speed to market. It should be taken into account that big established firms are slow in fully developing and commercialising technologies that interrupt their existing markets and procedures. Large companies are not eager to contemplate the risky development of a new technology and characteristically they will doubt the feasibility, the reliability, and the marketability of the potential technology. For instance, Microsoft[53] came late to the web browser, web server, and web development tools.

The significant manage differences not only between old and new economy firms but also between various types of New Economy firms. There is a fast changing control structure in new than old economy firms. Central control structures in old economy firms are concentrated and slowly evolving. Principal control structures of New Economy firms change quickly between entrepreneurs and diverse investor groups as the production process and financing needs of firms amend. Firms are concentrated in R&D intensive sectors of the economy. Martin Zagler [54] found that "productivity gains are no longer realized within but between service firms, as the increase in variety increases value-added per employee. Whilst

[52] Paul A. David (1991), "Computer and Dynamo: The Productivity Paradox in a Not-too-Distant Mirror," Technology and Productivity: The Challenge for Economic Policy (Paris: OECD), pp. 315-347. Carl Shapiro and Hal Varian (1998), Information Rules: A Strategic Guide to the Network Economy (Boston: Harvard Business School Press), p. 9.

[53] Charles Ferguson (1999), High Stakes, No Prisoners (New York: Times Books).

[54] Martin Zagler, Services, innovation and the new economy, Structural Change and Economic Dynamics, www.elsevier.com/locate/econbase, *http://www.wu-wien.ac.at/vw1/ zagler/*

service innovators, such as the information technology manufacturers, get ever more productive, individual service firms will exhibit low productivity". E-commerce has the potential to revolutionize customer relationship management (CRM). Moreover, Information technology and the global availability of products have resulted in distributor alliances with their source manufacturers, with their industrial customers, and with other distributors[55]. Vital to the competitive advantage of distributors is the capability to constantly provide added value, both to manufacturers and to customers. According to Susan M. Mudambi and Raj Aggarwal [56]"as the e-commerce marketplace continues to evolve, the systems are likely to become more manageable, efficient, and profitable. That will reward the surviving firms in the marketing channel". For higher skilled workers, the new economy offers strong demand and high wages. IT allows greater flexibility in working arrangements. Hence, labor markets in the new economy provide workers with both opportunities and challenges. IT producers are leaders in the world economy and US remain the world's largest exporter of IT goods[57]. As a result of the globalisation of production, internal transfers between accounting units of a single enterprise may become international transactions affecting national trade balance. According to the 2002 report on digital economy US industries are continuing to benefit from past and current investments in IT equipment, software and services realizing the benefits of the new economy.

The rapid technological advance makes it possible that the share of ICT industries in gross domestic product increases while ICT prices decline. The trade of ICT products, intermediate goods, and components has quickly increased as a consequence of the new production modes and distribution systems. According to Matti Pohjola [58] "A thriving New Economy requires a high degree of diversity in institutions, investments and forms of control". Clustering does not necessarily obey national borders. The productivity gains not only reflect increased investment in ICT, but also corresponding innovations in business organization and strategy[59]. In accordance with H. Koski , P. Rouvinen, and P. Yla-Anttila [60]"availability of high-skilled labour is indeed one of the key reasons for a firm to locate within a cluster of similar businesses, and that the high-IT industries are *not* directly comparable to the ICT sector, not least because the latter is largely comprised of manufacturing-related activities". Moreover, according to Inge Ivarsson and Jan-Erik Vahlne [61] "A logistic regression analysis showed that coordination and integration of technology in MNEs is positively correlated with the length of time the a affiliates have been a part of the parent corporation, while dynamic technological integration was positively correlated with affiliates operating in competitive Swedish industry clusters".

---

[55] Syverson N. E-commerce: what does it mean for you? http:// www.Manufacturing.Net, June, 2000.

[56] Susan M. Mudambi, Raj Aggarwal, Industrial distributors Can they survive in the new economy?, Industrial Marketing Management 31 (2002) 1– 9, p8.

[57] *www.bea.gov*

[58] Matti Pohjola, The New Economy: facts, impacts and policies, Information Economics and Policy 14 (2002) 133–144, p144.

[59] Jukka Jalava, Matti Pohjola, Economic growth in the New Economy: evidence from advanced economies, Information Economics and Policy 14 (2002) 189–210

[60] H. Koski, P. Rouvinen, P. Yla-Anttila, ICT clusters in Europe The great central banana and the small Nordic potato, Information Economics and Policy 14 (2002) 145–165, p157.

[61] Inge Ivarsson, Jan-Erik Vahlne, Technology integration through international acquisitions: the case of foreign manufacturing MNEs in Sweden, Scand.J.Mgmt.18 (2002)1-27, p1.

The key fundamentals of the new/digital economy include an innovative information technology service sector that is organized in network firms of organization, rather than traditional firms or markets, high rates of economic growth and share prices on stock markets in America have plummeted, leading to a medium-term volatility in share prices unprecedented in the second half of the last century. Especially, Internet service providers are amongst the companies with the highest volatility in stock market capitalization. If a company is tied into its network of customers and suppliers and sustain a course of innovation that maintains its position within existing markets and technologies, then it is likely not to undertake radical innovation and will be blindsided by breakthrough technologies[62]. Start-ups have been the drivers of much of the radical innovation in the transition to a Digital economy. Fundamental production innovations that meant that lower cost could also bring higher quality forced American and European producers to reorganize deeply their production and business practices. The market advantages of many innovations are vanished if the innovating company cannot also be world-class producers, or at least have close access to world-class production. Leading companies lower their costs by concentrating on what they did best, and contracting to buy the rest from producers with a firm-specific advantage in productivity or a nation-specific factor cost-based comparative advantage. The aptitude to use modern data communications networks to transmit information allows client firms to state in great detail what they want their contractors to do. There is a shift from a market dominated by integrated producers to one in which companies situated anywhere in the disintegrated value chain can potentially control the evolution of key standards and in that way define the terms of competition — not just of their specific sector, but critically in final product markets as well. As discussed earlier, globalisation presses the sense of international forces sweeping past the capacity of nations to respond, channel, or control. The Internet multiplies connections, generating an apparently placeless cyberspace. The rapid development of a broad network creates great gains for each participant, generating new markets and opportunities for companies, and new possibilities for consumers. The global information economy and society is a network that crosses borders in a world organized into nation-states creating a role for national governments. The principal task of a global information processing is to assure a sufficient agreement on standards to permit the operation of global networks and to assure markets for equipment, tools, and applications open.

Cyberspace explosion is boosted by the deregulation of the telecommunication networks and of major telecommunications user industries such as finance and airlines. The development and deployment of advanced information technology need a well-trained workforce because without that, the ability to use and develop the Digital economy will be limited. The cyber world is intertwined with our traditional world. Will we have a cyber world free of regulation? New rules require that the political bargains among different interests and objectives that defined the current policies be renegotiated. Digital economy creates new products and transforms conventional industries with the new ways it transforms storage, search, diffusion, and indeed production of ideas and information. Given the escalating pace of innovation that rests on new ideas and the importance of information based products, the question of intellectual property becomes central. Cyberspace is no longer a free

[62] Katie Hafner (1996), Where Wizards Stay Up Late: The Origins of the Internet, New York: Simon and Schuster. Michael Hiltzik (1999), Dealers of Lightning: Xerox PARC and the Dawn of the Computer Age, New York: HarperBusiness.

zone it is a focus for difficult policy making including not only narrowly technical problems but also through the narrowly legal into fundamental questions of how to organize markets and society.

While the benefits of free capital mobility are widely believed to be significant, the recent volatility of flows to emerging markets and the associated costs has raised questions about the desirability of unrestrained capital movements to these economies. Given the potential benefits of international integration, emerging market economies should aim at progressive liberalisation of capital account transactions over time[63]. Large-scale capital inflows have a tendency to reverse themselves if they unsettle the macroeconomic environment. The Digital economy has brought about tools for thought, tools that transform every sector of the economy and there is a shift in the very terms and dynamics of market competition. Stephen Cohen, Brad DeLong and John Zysman have stated that the new technologies "do not just amplify productivity in one sector but give all economic sectors new 'tools.' They are tools for thought that amplify brainpower in the way the technologies of the Industrial Revolution amplified muscle power." [64] Digital economy based on the intersection of the technological advances of processing and bandwidth with the business process innovations rests primarily on business applications and business reorganization. Research problems cannot be so isolated nor causal relationships plainly specified.

The new digital economy rests on advanced data networks and is facilitated by new software tools and especially the alteration of network communications underpins and expresses the evolving e-commerce. Hence, the Internet surpasses any preceding communications technology in diffusion speed by accomplishing the same penetration in less than 7 years[65]. Cyberspace could be primarily deployed over the older, existing infrastructure for voice communication, telephones. The Internet system that allowed and facilitated the new e-business strategies is in turn being shaped by the emergence of e-business including a more advanced technology. The network revolution was generated by intense and increasingly international competition. It is productivity, not technology per se, that eventually determines what people are paid, the types of skills and training required. The companies will test the transformative capacity of the new digital technologies firstly. Regionally based lead users, with regionally precise market needs and operating in dissimilar policy environments, will drive distinctive lines of technology development in which local companies may have competitive advantages. The Internet is by all accounts one of the most important innovations of the late twentieth century. As yet the Internet's impact on the economies of developed countries is not obvious, and the economic implications for developing countries are even more unclear. The Internet dramatically lowers barriers to cross-border trade. Increased trade with less-developed countries making intensive use of low-skilled labor in their exports displaces less-skilled labor-intensive production in the

---

[63] Eichengreen, B. and P. Masson with H. Bredenkamp, B. Johnston, J. Hamann, E. Jadresic and I. Ötker (1998), "Exit Strategies - Policy Options for Countries Seeking Greater Exchange Rate Flexibility", IMF Occasional Paper No. 168, Washington DC. Eichengreen, B. and M. Mussa with G. Dell'Ariccia, E. Detragiache, G.M. Milesi-Ferretti and A. Tweedie (1998), "Capital Account Liberalization, Theoretical and Practical Aspects", IMF Occasional Paper No. 172, Washington DC.

[64] Stephen Cohen, Bradford De Long and John Zysman (2000), Tools for Thought: What is New and Important about the "Digital economy"?, Berkeley Roundtable on the International Economy (BRIE) Working Paper 138. pp. 2, 5.

[65] Steven Weber (1997), "The End of the Business Cycle?," Foreign Affairs (July/August, 1997), pp. 65-82.

developed countries and thereby reduces the demand for low-skilled labor in these countries[66]. In accordance with the emerging digital economy report issued by the department of commerce[67] of US the rate of increase in gross product originating per worker (GPO/W) has been extraordinarily rapid by the use of advanced IT. So, small firms are competing globally and multinationals are expanding their global operations influencing employment demand, wages and skill requirements.

OECD[68] Consumer Protection Guidelines for E-Commerce represent an international consensus that there is a framework of core principles that should govern the relationship between buyers and sellers in cyberspace. Consumers should not be disadvantaged when transacting business online rather than offline. Guideline's call for international law enforcement cooperation and effective law enforcement in the global context requires cooperation with counterparts around the world. E-business security breaches in the banking and utilities sectors have damaged consumers' confidence in making transactions over the Internet. Companies must provide their customers with a secure framework for E-business. Using a WAP-enabled mobile phone, people can bank, shop, send E-mails, book tickets, pay bills and stock trade which means that M-commerce can be viewed as the natural development of E-commerce. M-commerce will be much more pervasive than E-commerce as we know it today. Co-operation among certification authorities, mobile operators, systems integrators and device manufacturers are needed to ensure that mobile security is implemented properly, and that various implementations will be able interact. Uniform standards need to be established and adhered to.

Software products, such as operating systems, libraries, and development tools are designed and developed for an international environment working in environments that have very different linguistic, cultural, and presentation requirements which means that these globally distributed computing environments must support location-based changes in numeric values, time, date, monetary format, message representation, and codeset encoding schemes in other words needing a *globalized* software. You accomplish software globalization by addressing necessities for both *internationalization* providing software portable between regions in which various spoken languages and customs are used and *localizatio*n creating locale-specific versions, or *package*s, of the locale-dependent pieces including the translation of text such as labels in the user interface and online help[69].

Application Service Providers (ASPs) are companies that provide other companies with leased IT applications, infrastructure and support applications and with an ASP solution, the ownership of the servers and the delivery of services becomes the accountability of the ASP service provider with the dealer paying monthly fee without facing the prospect of huge upfront Dealer Management System (DMS) server investments and periodic server upgrades allowing the top management of dealership to focus on the business of selling and servicing, not managing the next backup of the in-store server and the service provider becomes responsible for the IT administration –and assumes the risk of doing the job right[70]by building a reliable and robust infrastructure that can handle hundreds —if not thousands — of users concurrently.

---

[66] Brenton, P. & Pelkmans, J. (eds), (1999), Global Trade and European Workers, London: Macmillan.
[67] *www.ecommerce.gov* Chapter III, p8.
[68] *www.oecd.org*
[69] See BEA Systems, Inc. *www.bea.com*

7.2 E-COMMERCE

The applications of electronic transmissions are just beginning to be felt and the breadth and depth of what lies ahead is only beginning to be fathomed. Even our notions of sovereignty and governance could be profoundly affected. Electronic commerce should remain market-driven so that many of today's difficult problems can be overcome through the competitive interplay of market forces. Moreover, Electronic Commerce refers generally to all forms of transactions relating to commercial activities, involving both organisations and individuals that are based upon the processing and transmission of digitised data, including text, sound and visual images. Firms engage in Electronic Commerce in order to achieve better management of commercial transactions and to increase business efficiency. In today's globalising economic environment the most important incentive is the opportunity to create whole new business areas for information and knowledge-based "intangible" products. Cyberspace is a major catalyst in the diffusion of Electronic Commerce into an increasing number of economic spheres, and is rapidly harmonizing the general environment in which electronic transactions of all kinds take place. Governments must act in concert with each other, and with private sector users and suppliers of Electronic Commerce facilities, to create a commercial environment that is responsive to technical change. Electronic Commerce is part of an evolving approach to business and administration that could eventually involve the application of information and communication technologies to an enormous range of production and distribution processes on a global scale. Electronic services infrastructures like telecommunications, television and data networking, as well as the regulatory regimes that effect them, must converge in order to reflect the rapid convergence of networking technologies employed in Electronic Commerce applications. Governments should evaluate current competition policies to ensure that they do not impede orderly development of the information and communication infrastructure. National data protection laws should be harmonized early in order to prevent situations that could destroy public confidence in Electronic Commerce where privacy and confidentiality implications are concerned. Harmonization should not, however, be promoted in a way that would inhibit the legitimate use of databases. So, governments should not act to restrict transborder data flows unduly, but should act multilaterally to minimise the possibility of abuse in the utilisation of customer information when databases are transported from one jurisdiction to another. Electronic Commerce cannot function on its own. Costly and inefficient systems for the physical transportation of goods could slow down the development of the electronic marketplace. Governments have a major role to play in ensuring that physical transportation infrastructures are developed in coherent, co-ordinated ways, such that they complement the transaction efficiencies generated by Electronic Commerce and do not interfere with speedy process. As mentioned above, an internationally clarified legal environment must be supported by international agreement on policing and enforcement. Electronic Commerce is part of an evolving approach to business that could eventually involve the application of information and communication technologies to the production and distribution of goods and services on a global scale. Moreover, Electronic Commerce interacts not only with electronic distribution systems, as in electronic publishing or financial services applications, but also with the physical infrastructure for the distribution of manufactured products.

---

[70] See *www.eds.com* , *www.atkearney.com*

Most Electronic Commerce occurs on a business-to-business level, although substantial activity also occurs at a business-to-government level in connection with public procurement, and with administrative functions like customs. At present, Electronic Commerce at the business-to-individual and individual-to-individual levels, and at the government-to-individual level in the delivery of government services, occurs on a comparatively small scale. Even though much electronic business will continue to be transacted in domestic markets, Electronic Commerce is difficult to contain within geographically defined trade areas and frontier-based regulatory and administrative regimes. Electronic Commerce facilitates the globalisation of business by providing more economical access to isolated markets, and by supporting novel opportunities for firms to increase economies of scale and scope by distributing their production and distribution assets internationally. For non-electronic transactions in a "material" product environment, the source of a product, the locations of its suppliers and distributors, and the respective responsibilities and liabilities of the buyer and seller can be verified relatively easily. On the other hand, intangible transactions blur many of the existing distinctions between domestic and foreign business, and between on-shore and off-shore transactions. The location at which a transaction actually takes place, and hence the jurisdictions to which it may be subject is very difficult to define. Ultimately, the Internet may become but one part of a much broader evolution in electronic communications, but it has already established the first basic networking paradigm that could eventually allow Electronic Commerce facilities to be extended throughout the entire spectrum of commercial activity. An important aspect of Internet evolution for Electronic Commerce purposes will be the development of managed network facilities to bridge the gap that currently exists between the largely unmanaged public Internet domain, and the rapid proliferation of private corporate Internets. Are we entering the era of the virtual enterprise in which maximum flexibility in the organisational and even physical distribution of business resources is facilitated by ICT? Electronic Commerce applications can contribute to increased responsiveness, flexibility, efficiency and accountability in business structures. Moreover, many of the most promising new business areas are intangible in nature – defined by the exchange of information and knowledge, rather than by the exchange of physical objects. Tele-shopping, home banking and on-line information services are facets of Electronic Commerce, but so is corporate and inter-corporate supply-chain management.

E-commerce provides a mechanism to allow a larger share of the labor element in transactions to be delivered at any location with access to international electronic communication offering effectiveness gains without the more destabilizing prospect of physical migration and its attendant increases in family attenuation and cultural tensions. Moreover, e-commerce facilitates mobile, long-distance, or anonymous transactions when the seller may be outside the territorial power of the taxing government and so buyers may not have to pay sales tax on goods purchased from a seller in a different tax jurisdiction, putting non-e-commerce companies at a disadvantage and reducing overall tax revenues. For income taxes, most international tax mechanisms give priority to the *source* state and so in e-commerce, technology can make it difficult or confusing to identify sources. Destination becomes a tricky concept when the particular product or service being sold or licensed will be "used" in multiple jurisdictions by the buyer. The technologies that generate e-commerce have challenged existing mechanisms with transactions that cannot readily be identified under existing definitions in the treaty networks, nor in the domestic statutory provisions for sales and income taxation. If e-commerce not taxed without fail with other forms of commerce, market distortion and subsequent inefficient allocation of resources would arise. At present it has proved technically and administratively complex to impose a consistent pattern of taxation covering e-commerce. It could be argued that favoring e-commerce over other commerce may lead to short-term market distortion and incompetence, but that has been perceived as a rational price to achieve longer-term objectives[71]. A state where technical expertise and an established technology base has created an early lead in e-commerce expanding its share of a market and in international trade, e-commerce provides a major opportunity for enhancing overall productivity. Governments should not use domestic laws, tariffs, and regulations on e-commerce as a means to minimize competition from foreign, online interests or the efficiencies of e-commerce will be severely undermined. It should be taken into account that technology that gives consumers better control over their personal information reduces the need for government controls on data privacy.

The goal of Electronic Commerce is the creation of a new kind of commercial environment in an electronic setting. So, Electronic Commerce may create many new employment opportunities, but it may also facilitate the international mobility of enterprises. By opening channels of communication, exchanging and selecting information, e-commerce is allowing companies to reconsider which functions they have to perform "in house" and which are have to be provided by others. Markets involve multifaceted interactions between precise business/organisational factors, and general economic, social and political factors. Companies are learning to identify the new consumer communities that are emerging in cyberspace environment, and to evaluate their product and service needs. Firms and organisations can construct a variety of communications capabilities behind protective "firewalls". Substantial numbers of consumers now make electronic purchases of information and entertainment products like books and Compact Disks, and service products like airline tickets – some of them products that could soon migrate entirely to an electronic format. The huge capacity of facilities like the Internet requires the development of Electronic Commerce applications that allow buyers to locate products and information about products quickly and easily, and to conduct transactions in a simple and straightforward manner. Electronic Commerce has not emerged all at once in a standardized form but it progress differently according to the requirements of particular industries. Moreover, e-commerce capabilities are giving birth to new classes of business intermediaries and activities such as aggregators, auctions, and exchanges. Electronic networking minimises many of the economic impacts of time and distance. The promise of Electronic Commerce is that transaction costs can be constrained to the minimum that is appropriate to each type of transaction. The documentation for many kinds of complex technological systems can run into millions of printed pages. Distributing this information electronically not only facilitates more efficient storage and retrieval, but also helps ensure that operators of these systems always access the most up-to-date manuals, thus increasing their margins of safety and reliability. Firms deploy

---

71 The European Commission, Taxation Policy of the European Union (2000) at *http://europa.eu.int/comm/taxation_customs/publications/taxation/tax_brochure.htm* ("Tax policy is a symbol of national sovereignty and part of a country's overall economic policy, helping finance public spending and redistribute income. In the European Union, responsibility for tax policy mainly lies with the Member States, that may delegate some of it from central to regional or local level, depending on the constitutional or administrative structure of government."). Taxing Digital Downloads, 3 E - COMMERCE L. REV. 29 (2001) ("the EU is proposing that the company will be required to file a

ICT as part of programmes to support and/or promote organisational and process change in order better to meet the challenges of what they see as an increasingly global business environment. Electronic links are deployed in the insurance industry more to link remote operatives to home offices, than to link customers to firms. Additionally, Electronic Commerce generates transaction information that can be captured and archived immediately in a form that permits sophisticated processing and quick distribution. The development and creative use of customer information databases has assumed greater than before importance in the operations and strategies of firms. In the insurance industry, Electronic Commerce is being used with corporate customers in a risk management role. Hence, Electronic Commerce links set up initially on an inter-firm basis soon develop interfaces with a greater variety of uses and users. Electronic Commerce links established in one sector (shipping and forwarding) can migrate into other sectors (like retailing and manufacturing). In the transport industry, intangible support services like dispatch, routing and reservation systems are being developed into products in their own right, so creating new revenue producing business areas. In the business strategies of individual firms, these Electronic Commerce business dimensions will tend to be balanced according to the nature of the product or service concerned. For instance, automobile manufacturers who now use electronic networks above all to support production and maintenance supply chains, and to communicate with franchised dealers, could finally use Electronic Commerce to sell their products directly to individual consumers, perhaps employing virtual showrooms to illustrate a range of design options.

Card technology has undergone substantial evolution, and present applications include the whole thing from the now ever-present credit card to advanced "smart-card" applications that could support an array of commercial and non-commercial functions. Smart cards offer an interim solution to a number of the problems of making consumer transactions more secure in an electronic environment. Problems like reducing transaction costs cannot be addressed by technology alone. The degree of integration achieved can vary according to the type of enterprise, market or product involved, or according to the size and business scope of firms. Nevertheless, the economies of an Electronic Commerce strategy can be achieved only if there is logical harmonization of business process integration between transacting firms. Firms can integrate internal processes with a range of resources that are shared with suppliers and product development partners. Commerce depends on confidence. For the electronic market place to thrive in both its customer and enterprise dimensions, buyers and sellers alike must have the level of confidence in the outcome of Electronic Commerce as they have in more traditional kinds of transactions. The non-territorial and intangible nature of Electronic Commerce calls into question the competence of existing law enforcement mechanisms that are still geared to tangible products and national legislation. A globalised electronic market-place could allow a prospective buyer to locate the lowest available price for a given product anywhere in the world, and to locate it swiftly. Provided that ordering, payment and delivery structures also are existed the customer could obtain the product at the lowest world price, and so circumventing the conditions in his own local market, save for taxes and delivery costs. All payment systems involve costs that need to be recovered in some way if the system is to be sustainable. As Electronic Commerce payment needs become more diverse and sophisticated, new methods will be essential to meet the costs of payment systems. If

monthly report in the chosen country, but pay taxes based upon the country of each customer's purchases. The VAT would then be redistributed to the relevant country.").

cyberspace vendors will be free to operate and generate revenue without incurring obligations to collect sales or use taxes from their customers, states will lose an increasing percentage of their tax[72] base as more business is conducted over cyberspace. So, changes must be made to existing tax laws to put up the complexities introduced by the emerging e-commerce industry together an economic presence of on line stores or e-MNEs within a state in the electronic commerce context is needed[73]. Emerging technologies and e-commerce may force states to redefine the types of commodities subject to sales taxes[74]. In 2000, retail e-commerce sales were estimated at $25.8 billion, comprising almost 1% of total retail sales.[75] Digital money with its benefits of privacy, anonymity, low transaction costs and the satisfaction of heterogeneous demands will be a solemn runner for current money in the future. The increase in the demand for digital money will have an impact on economic policies, either monetary or fiscal. The impact on fiscal policy is linked to the capacity of the government to tax transactions done with digital money, especially anonymous transactions.[76]

Advances in information technology also influence the structure of (financial) markets, the (financial) behaviour of economic agents and the types of (financial) products traded; that is the entire monetary transmission mechanism enabling the creation of new clearing mechanisms which can compete with the central banking settlement systems[77]. Workflow Management Systems (WFMSs) are used to coordinate the business processes of organizations and thus they represent one of the key components of e-commerce and one of the key aspects is that of developing appropriate access control mechanisms for workflow applications.[78] New business processes and models are devised due to inherent driving forces obtained from various e-commerce technologies in the effort to reduce the costs and obtain better customer-centricity in the organization and to boost the overall productivity[79].

---

[72] Peter Cobb, Transcript: Taxing E-Commerce: The Landscape of Internet Taxation, 21 U. PA. J. INT'L ECON. L. 659, 659 (2000), Robert MacMillan, Sen. Graham Stresses Need for Net Sales Tax, Newsbytes, at http://newsbytes.com/news/01/163092.html (Mar. 13, 2001).

[73] R. Todd Ervin, State Taxation of Financial Institutions: Will Physical Presence or Economic Presence Win the Day?, 19 Va. Tax Rev. 515, 523 n. 30 (2000) Annette Nellen, Overview to E-Commerce Taxation Guide to Understanding the Current Discussions and Debates at *http://www.cob.sjsu.edu/facstaff/nellen_a/* (Dec. 2000).

[74] Jeremy Holmes, Taxing Electronic Commerce: Adapting to a New Age, at *http://internetlaw.pf.com/subscribers/html/NewOverview.asp*

[75] National Governors' Association Online, Overview of Sales and Use Taxes and Electronic Commerce, at *http://www.nga.org/nga/legislativeUpdate/1,1169,C_ISSUE_BRIEF^D_1248,00.html* U.S. Census Bureau, United States Dept. Of Commerce News, at http://www.census.gov/mrts/www/current.html

[76] Intertrade (1999). Digital Money Online. *URL:www.intertrade.com/library/DigitalMoneyOnline/dmo/dmo_c.html*. Berentsen, A. (1998). Monetary Policy Implications of Digital Money.Internation Review of Social Science (Kyklos), Vol.51, 1: 89-117. Bern. Digital Money, Liquidity, and Monetary Policy, First Monday *http://www.firstmonday.dk/issues/issue2_7/berentsen/index.html,*

[77] King, M. (1999), 'Challenges for monetary policy: new and old' In: Federal Reserve Bank of Kansas City, New Challenges for Monetary Policy, pp. 11-59.

[78] Ghosh, A., "E-commerce Security, Weak Links, Best Defenses," John Wiley, NY, 1998. Bhavani Thuraisingham, Chris Clifton, Amar Gupta, Elisa Bertino, Elena Ferrari, (2002) Directions for Web and E-Commerce Applications Security, MIT Sloan School of Management Working Paper 4259-02

[79] McCall T, 2000,"Gartner Group Forecasts worldwide business-to-business to reach $7.29 trillion in 2004", online, available at *http://www.gartner5.gartnerweb.com/public/ststic/aboutgg/pressrel/pr012600c.html*

15. McCall T, 2000"Gartner Group Says business-to-business e-commerce transactions becoming more global", online, Gartner Group, available at *http://www.gartner5.gartnerweb.com/public/ststic/aboutgg/pressrel/pr021600.html*

The informational problem about the new technology and the threat of imitation from the licensee are two important concerns in case of technology transfer[80]. While it is regularly problematical for a licensee to get all information about the new technology from the patent disclosures, it may not also be possible for the licenser to convey all the good things of its new technology forming an asymmetric information problem under technology transfer and creates the possibility of opportunism on the part of the licenser. On the other hand, technology transfer may encourage imitation from the licensee depending on the type of patent protection extended by a particular country.

In an electronic environment, commercial firms have an awareness of the need to be able to protect trademarks and commercial information held in databases. New challenges exist for the enforcement function of the IPR system, as electronically distributed information is very much prone to casual and undetectable copying and re-distribution. IPR policies will have to be synchronised with encryption policies. The security of the networks themselves must be ensured. This involves quality of service provisions to ensure that network facilities for Electronic Commerce are forceful and available as needed, and that unauthorised access to networks is minimised. The most central goal of any security scheme is to protect the truthfulness of transaction related information. Cryptography has been used to encode information to conceal secret messages from unauthorised parties and, as such, it has customarily been important for military and national security use. Cryptography uses an algorithm to transform data in order to render it incomprehensible to anyone who does not have the cryptographic "key" needed for decryption of the data. Open networks like the Internet provide much less security than "dedicated" network links. This limits Internet use in commercial situations even though it may offer distinct economic advantages to buyers and sellers in terms of flexibility of use and access charges. The developing information infrastructure is an environment for all kinds of computer-related crime, including fraud and privacy infringement, thus prompting demands for effective data security measures. Governments have a direct stake in Electronic Commerce by virtue of the fact that in almost every country, the public sector is the largest single procurer of goods and services. As governments seek to increase their own implementations of Electronic Commerce solutions, they become subject to the same kinds of pressures for organisational and managerial' change as do private firms. The private sector is making growing demands for the simplification of interactions with government agencies, and the harmonization of transaction procedures. On the other hand, the procurement power of governments places them in especially strong positions to influence the development of new commercial technologies and practices. Hence, Electronic Commerce provides governments with the opportunity to re-examine the established underpinnings of policies for trade and commerce. Many major kinds of strategic decisions about the national and international provision of network services now reside almost exclusively with the private sector. As discussed earlier, the existing codes of conduct are too diverse, there is too little background literature and too little is known about their effectiveness. The best way to proceed could lie in complementary and mutually reinforcing efforts by governments, companies and other stakeholders in a spirit of shared responsibility and partnership.

---

[80] Gallini, N. T. and B. D. Wright, 1990, 'Technology Transfer under Asymmetric Information', RAND Journal of Economics 21: 147 - 60.

Have the existing WTO-Treaties extensively contributed to the development of E-Commerce? Compared to the situation before E-Commerce, electronic trade provides firms of the developing nations with less cost-intensive means to set up efficient global marketing and open international distribution channels[81]. The principle of territoriality appears to be carried forward in TRIPS, since Article 16 of TRIPS allows countries to premise protection for all but well-known marks upon domestic registration.[82] Enforcement-based territoriality is premised on the need to enforce rights in some particular forum against a perceived violation. According to Doris Estelle Long [83] "Dogmatic territoriality" has to give way to unitorriality if the commercial and economic benefits of these new twenty-first century markets are to be entirely realized. In other words dogmatic territoriality ignores reality because international products cannot be located at a specific place on the globe[84]. Harmonization of trademark law could be achieved by abandoning territorial justifications of sovereignty.[85] The communication services that provide access to E-Commerce fall under the GATS and the execution of an electronic transaction necessitates infrastructure services whose liberalisation evenly falls under the GATS[86]. Finally online commerce mainly takes place in services and the liberalisation of content-services is a crucial prerequisite for the exploitation of E-Potential[87]. So, a new liberalisation round within the GATS framework would create new business opportunities for E-Commerce.

Rayport and Jaworski[88]define e-commerce as ''technology mediated exchanges between parties (individuals, organizations or both)as well as the electronically based intra-or interorganizational activities that facilitate such exchanges.'' Schneider and Perry[89]state that a good definition of electronic commerce ''would mention the use of electronic data transmission to implement or enhance any business process ''. Hence, electronic commerce involves the use of information technology to improve communications and transactions with a company 's stakeholders including activities such as establishing a web page to facilitate those communications and involving the development of an information system to enable trading to take place[90]. It should be taken into account that e-commerce projects are not just an issue for the IT department, but a change affecting the company as a whole and business processes have to be transformed, new systems have to be interfaced back to, or replace, legacy systems, and international time differences in various instances force a company to operate extended and more flexible working hours to satisfy new customers and guarantee

---

81 Alliance for Global Business 1999: A Global Action Plan for Electronic Commerce.,*http://www.giic.org/focus/ecommerce/agbecplan.html*. Aronson J. 2000: After Seattle: Trade Negotiations and the New Economy. In Regulating the global Information Society, ed. Marsden, C. London: Routledge.

82 33 ILM 81

83 Doris Estelle Long "Unitorrial" Marks and the Global Economy, 2002 JMLSR 35

84 M Leaffer, The new world of international trademark law, 1998 Marq IPLR 1.

85 K Port, trademark harmonization norms, names & nonsense, 1998 Marq IPLR 33.

86 Drake W and Nicolaidis K. 1999: Global Electronic Commerce and the GATS: The "Millennium Round" and Beyond. In GATS 2000: New Directions in Services Trade Liberalisation, ed. Sauvé, P. and Stern, R. Washington: Brookings Institution Press.

87 GBDe. 2000: Electronic Commerce and the WTO. Global Business Dialogue on Electronic Commerce, *www.GBDe.org/media/papers/GBDe_wto.html.*

88 Rayport,J.F.,& Jaworski,B.J.(2001) .E-commerce Singapore: McGraw-Hill.

89 Schneider,G.P., & Perry,J.T.(2000).Electronic commerce Course Technology-ITP , Canada.

90 Tom Addison , E-commerce project development risks: evidence from a Delphi survey, International Journal of Information Management 23 (2003) 25 –40

web site credibility[91]. The cyberspace influences new directions in business processes, new job titles begin to emerge and supply chains transform[92]. Web-based payment systems do not yet enjoy the trust and security of well-entrenched traditional payment systems, and the development of digital certificates and security protocols is relatively new and maybe not absolutely secure. Hence, the accuracy and security, in the web environment, of data, systems and equivalents to cash, should not be worse than that offered with conventional systems and procedures. Many businesses in order to be successful in the world of e-business, they need to be able to satisfy the needs of their existing and potential customers, as well as to improve their loyalty towards their enterprise[93]. Companies should consider VCs (a group of people who communicate with each other via electronic media) as a new market place since their members are current or future customers learning more about the needs of their customers, they will strengthen their relationships customizing their services.

UK and US retailers perceive little threat or impact from e-commerce taking into account that fulfilment and security issues are barriers to e-commerce growth indicating that their retail space needs will remain the same or increase in the short term, despite of the threat e-commerce and entertainment is a central strategy if shopping centers are to remain viable[94].

7.3 E-COMMERCE AND INTERNET

Cyberspace is governed by non-state organizations that have a State-like monopoly on serving public interests but lack adequate public accountability provisions. With the rising number of Internet connections world-wide, the demand for additional TLDs will continue to increase[95]. Additionally, the general accessibility of techniques to set up root server systems and to register domain names establishes competition between DNS services providers. As information processing tools like cyberspace becomes progressively widespread, and increasingly indispensable to the conducting of business, the capacity of governments to limit their spread and use without bearing formidable economic costs will be much less. In reality the entity that holds the electronic means via which cyberspace is practically in existence dictates the rules and its usage[96]. The Internet has made communication and research easier

---

91 Scott,G.,& Walter,Z.(2001).Management issues in web systems development. Working paper, University of Connecticut, April. Watson,R.T ., Berthon, P ,Pitt,L .F.,& Zinkhan, G.M.(2000).Electronic commerce Florida: Dryden Press.

92 Rothaermel,F.T.,& Sugiyama,S.(2001).Virtual Internet communities and commercial success: Individual and community-level theory grounded in the atypical case of timezone.com. Journal of Management 27 297 –312. Siu,W.(2002).Marketing activities and performance: A comparison of the internet-based and traditional small firms in Taiwan, Industrial Marketing Management 31 177 –188.

93 Kardaras,D.,& Papathanassiou,E.(2000).The development of B2C E-commerce in Greece. Internet Research: Electronic Networking Applications and Policy 10 4), 284 –295. Dimitris Kardaras, Bill Karakostas ,Eleutherios Papathanassiou, The potential of virtual communities in the insurance industry in the UK and Greece, International Journal of Information Management 23 (2003)41 –53

94 Elaine M. Worzala and Anne M. McCarthy, Tim Dixon and Andrew Marston, E-commerce and retail property in the UK and USA, Journal of Property Investment & Finance, Vol. 20 No. 2, 2002, 142.

95 WGIG report June 2005, at *http://www.wgig.org/docs/WGIGREPORT.pdf.*

96 G Zekos "Internet or Electronic Technology: A Threat to State Sovereignty" 1999 JILT, *http://www.law.warwick.ac.uk/jilt/99-3/zekos.html*

than ever, coherent environment in which to operate[97]. There is an inherent tension between various nations attempting to regulate the activities of sellers and consumers of goods and content because without coordinating such regulatory activities, there is no coherent environment in which to operate running the risk of undermining both consumer confidence and the predictability that companies need in order to execute business plans and so buyers and sellers will stop engaging in cross-border transactions.

The increased transparency that is made possible by the Internet makes incompetent markets more efficient and companies are expected to use the Internet to alter existing industry structures and business processes, to improve company information, redefine their information with clients, leverage global resources, and pioneer new business models streamlining their supply chain, and eliminate inefficiencies with increased automation. Goldman Sachs[98] estimates that using the Internet will reduce purchasing costs in several industries by more than 20%, so reducing the total cost of doing business by as much as 12.5%. The Internet provides managers with information on transportation, inventory, purchasing, customer service, production scheduling, order processing, and vendor operations and enable them to improve the profitability of the supply chains[99].

The collection of networks, computers, and information tools that has emerged in the last decade represents a new leading economic sector. The emergence of a digital economy represents the creation of a new set of general tools that is vitally transforming every sector of the economy. Stephen Cohen, Brad DeLong and John Zysman[100] have stated that the new technologies "do not just amplify productivity in one sector but give all economic sectors new tools. They are tools for thought that amplify brainpower in the way the technologies of the Industrial Revolution amplified muscle power." The digital economy, the intersection of the technological advances of processing and bandwidth with the business process innovations, rests mainly on business applications and business reorganization.[101] Consumer applications that are closely entangled with social and community evolutions will become the drivers that induce the ongoing progression of technical innovation. The alteration of network communications underpins and expresses the evolving e-commerce. The new Internet-based economy grew extremely fast in comparison with previous communications and transportation technologies.[102] Furthermore, the new technological system, the cyberspace system for linking and addressing computers, could be primarily deployed over the older, existing infrastructure for voice communication, telephones.[103] The Internet system that allowed and facilitated the new e-business strategies is now in turn being shaped by the

---

97 Georgios I Zekos, Business Methods and Software Patenting, 2006 Hertfordshire Law Journal 4(2), 24-35 ISSN 1479-4195 Online / ISSN 1479-4209 CDRom

98 Ackerman E. To B2B or not to B2B? US News & World Rep 2000;128:36 (Feb.7)

99 Lancioni R, Smith M, Oliva T. The role of the Internet in supply chain management. Ind Mark Manage 2000;29:45 – 56.

100 Stephen Cohen, Bradford De Long and John Zysman (2000), Tools for Thought: What is New and Important about the "Digital economy"?, Berkeley Roundtable on the International Economy (BRIE) Working Paper 138. pp. 2, 5.

101 John Naughton (1999), A Brief History of the Future: the Origins and Destiny of the Internet (London: Weidenfeld & Nicolson);

102 Stephen Cohen and Gary Fields (1999), "Social Capital and Capital Gains, or Virtual Bowling in Silicon Valley" California Management Review Vol. 41, No. 2. Steven Weber (1997), "The End of the Business Cycle?" Foreign Affairs (July/August).

103 *http://www.usic.org.*

emergence of e-business. Both regions (North (the developed countries) and South (the developing countries)) can gain from an agreement that requires the South to harmonize its IPR standards with those of the North, and the North to liberalize its traditional goods market.

The IT revolution has been driven largely by private creativity and entrepreneurial courage. The diffusion of information technology and the Internet have continued to expand opportunities for all Americans to communicate, shop, and learn. Despite the recession, businesses continued through 2001 to build stocks of IT capital. Moreover, due to some extent to continuing IT innovation and deployment, inflation has remained low, and productivity growth, breaking the pattern of every recession since 1950, has been positive in recent days, the economy has shown welcome signs of imminent recovery. Additionally, IT innovation is driven by the demand for improved technologies in the using industries in order to improve their productivity and be ahead of other competitive companies outsourcing parts of the value chain extending the benefits of comparative advantage. Thus, using the improvements in computing and communication technologies companies achieve substantial downsizing. The rapid grow of venture capital has contributed to the changes in organisation and facilitating an increase in small firm R&D. Advance in IT operating in an environment of globalization, intense competition and sound monetary and fiscal policy spurred improved economic performance in the 1990s, rapid growth in the high-tech sector and the declining in capital goods prices increased the rate of productivity growth[104].

The Internet is giving consumers more power in the marketplace by making information on the prices and qualities of a wide range of goods and services more accessible. Consequently, price competition may be significantly enhanced by the ability of buyers to search for alternative suppliers of goods and services on the Internet. The direct contributions of high-tech products—such as computers, software, and telecommunications— to real GDP growth in 1995–2000 are averaged 29 percent or 1.20 percent point of the 4.1 percent growth in real GDP[105].

Cyberspace provides new ways to trade goods and services by separating the physical and information flows connected with each transaction and the choice between an Internet-based transaction or marketplace and a physical one depends on the transaction costs of each of the two alternatives. The key consequence of cyberspace and other New Economy innovations is to change the costs (and benefits) of transacting. Cyberspace improves efficiencies by reducing the costs involved in an existing business process and reduces transaction costs by making a marketplace more efficient. Cyberspace reduces a buyer's cost of finding a product or a supplier because it is less expensive to search for products and compare prices, product characteristics, and better information about buyers and sellers over the Internet than it is to read catalogs and make phone calls. It could be argued that conducting the transaction over the Internet may increase these transaction costs, due to the buyers' inability to physically inspect the merchandise object of the exchange[106]. The

---

104 M Baily, Labor productivity: Structural change and cyclical dynamics, 2001 Review of Economics and Statistics 420.

105 J. Steven Landefeld and Barbara M. Fraumeni, Measuring the New Economy, Survey of Current Business 27. Nordhaus, William D. 2001, "Productivity Growth and the New Economy." Working paper no. W8096, National Bureau of Economic Research, Cambridge, MA, January 2001.

106 Ofek, Eli and Matthew Richardson, 2001, "Dotcom mania: The rise and fall of internet stock prices," NBER Working Paper #8630. Demers and Lev, 2000, A rude awakening: Internet shakeout in 2000, Working paper, NYU. Steven N. Kaplan, Valuation and New Economy Firms, First Draft: April 2002

information technology, the Internet, and other related technology have generated and will continue to produce substantial improvements in productivity regardless a short-term drawbacks.

Within the e-commerce environment there are a number of sub-environments such as business to business (B2B), electronic data interchange (EDI) through formal information systems (IS) and local and wide area networks (LANs and WANs) using either bespoke protocols or generic protocols such as UN/EDIFACT (United Nations Electronic Data Interchange for Finance, Administration, Commerce and Transport); B2B via the Internet through modems and personal computers; and business to consumer (B2C) via cyberspace[107]. The improvements in data processing and communication speed make possible manipulation of multimedia data at a usable rate. In the physical world in the late twentieth century, economies have globalised and societies have become multicultural and companies today have to respond to these challenges and effective launch into the digital economy of the this millennium[108].

The infrastructure of the digital economy, the innovations and the evolving networks themselves have been developed and deployed by private companies in competitive markets. In fact, the network revolution was generated by user-defined needs, private provision, and intense and gradually more international competition.[109] Business to business (B2B) and business to consumer (B2C) projects have induced the development of a new data communications infrastructure. On the one hand, complex reorganization impacts levels of productivity. On the other hand, it is productivity that eventually determines what people are paid, the types of skills and training required. Companies will adjust to the new productivity dynamics and terms of competition and it is subsequently on the level of the firm that the transformative capacity of the new digital technologies will be emerged. There is a shift in emphasis and focus from issues of scale to scope, from the economies of production to the economics of networks and standards.[110]

As business-to-business (B2B) commerce shifts to the Internet and secure business intranets, markets will move to perfect competition delivering peak performance. By improving the flow, accuracy and timeliness of information, secure Internet-enabled systems provide greater transparency and effectiveness at all points along the supply chain. The Internet is a continuation of technological improvements delivering information faster and cheaper, reducing search and transaction costs in online markets and improving the management of transporting and inventorying products. B2B electronic commerce (e-commerce) boosts productivity and reduces costs. The part of B2B e-commerce that grows faster is electronic marketplaces (e-marketplaces), which use vast amounts of information and bring together multiple sellers and buyers on-line. The Internet reduces costs by increasing access to information and so better-informed market participants and supply-chain managers

---

[107] G. Duffy and B.G. Dale, E-commerce processes: a study of criticality, Industrial Management & Data Systems 102/8 [2002] 432-441.

[108] Morris, M. (1998), "Marketing in the Internet culture", *http://www.sun.com/960101/columns/mary-morris.960101.html*

[109] David Bach (2000), "International Cooperation and the Logic of Networks: Europe and the Global System for Mobile Communications (GSM)" BRIE Working Paper 139.

[110] Carl Shapiro and Hal Varian (1999), Information rules: a strategic guide to the network economy (Boston: Harvard Business School Press). Marc A. Smith and Peter Kollock, eds. (1999), Communities in Cyberspace (New York: Routledge).

can ensure that resources are allocated to their most productive use. It is less expensive to search for products and compare prices through e-market-places than to hunt through catalogs and make phone calls. Both private networks and industry-established online exchanges can help participants better manage production schedules and inventory levels. Market transaction costs fall with the maturation of B2B e-commerce resulting in more independent entities along the supply chain because firms in the supply chain will specialize in doing what they do best outsourcing the management of internal activities relying on coordination through markets and less reliance on vertical integration. The Internet improves supply chain efficiency and management by lowering required inventory levels, reducing transportation costs eliminating order and delivery lead times and so participants throughout the supply chain can share information about forecasted demand, delivery schedules and cargo capacities as well as inventory levels, availability and locations in real time, allowing processes to be redesigned and automated. Supply chain management innovations were already in progress before the Internet's explosive growth, as companies developed their own internal networks (that is, intranets) for sharing information. Despite the collapse of many dot-coms, efficiency improvements and cost savings already achieved through B2B e-commerce have led to higher productivity growth, lower costs and reduced pricing power allowing the U.S. economy to grow faster without inflationary pressures[111].

Globalisation becomes a matter of playing out on a large stage nationally rooted innovations.[112] Will the powerful communications instruments of the digital technology produce a single global market and similar business models under the governance of convergent, apparently neo-liberal regulatory regimes? Can the Internet exist apart from and independent of the rest of the economy and society? Anyway, the cyber world is entangled with the traditional world[113]. Competition policy, taxation, intellectual property rights, and privacy are issues that have to be decided by the international society in order to achieve convergence and efficiency. What is the influence that the shifting locus of transaction has on government revenue streams and their capacity to deliver services to their community? Information technology is penetrating each aspect of business, the economy and society as a whole. Understanding the way technological, organizational and political-legal changes cooperate in shaping a future characterized by ever-present digital networks connecting countless nodes globally will be essential for our understanding of political economy, whether national, comparative or international, and for our understanding of society as a whole.[114]

Since the configuration of the information infrastructure has a robust impact on both the global economy and world politics, the rise of open source software is something that is best seen in a broader light, giving consideration to implications beyond the software industry. Digital economy, open source software is an interesting social phenomenon with broader

---

[111] Fraumeni, Barbara M. (2001), "E-Commerce: Measurement and Measurement Issues," American Economic Review 91 (May): 318–22. Baily, Martin Neil, and Robert Z. Lawrence (2001), "Do We Have a New E-conomy?" American Economic Review 91 (May): 308–12.

[112] James P. Womack, Daniel T. Jones and Daniel Roos (1991), The Machine that changed the World (New York: Harper Perennial). Michael Borrus and John Zysman (1997), "Globalization with Borders: The Rise of Wintelism as the Future of Global Competition," Industry and Innovation Vol.4, No. 2 (December). Marc A. Smith and Peter Kollock (1999), eds., Communities in Cyberspace (London: Routledge), p. 230. Steven Weber (2000), "The Political Economy of Open Source," BRIE Working Paper 140.

[113] Lawrence Lessig (1999), Code and Other Laws of Cyberspace (New York: Basic Books).

[114] *http://www.shop.org.*

economic implications. Open source software presents a collective action problem, since there are no apparent individual incentives for participation. The Internet will be used in ways that will change existing relationships such as those between buyers and sellers, workers and owners.

The power of the Internet is its simplicity; it is just a medium for connections and is able to transmit anything digitised. Internet allows the instantaneous exchange of information in digital form among an unrestricted number of nodes.[115] The protocols used to transmit data across the Internet are standardized and readable by an array of computing platforms. Activities as varied as booking airline flights, purchasing objects, playing games, viewing pictures, listening to music, or accessing public information, many of which previously were intermediated by human operators are being transferred to the Internet. The Internet is a key aspect of the in progress renovation of the global economy to a form in which materiality becomes subordinate to information and knowledge creation. It is an interactive communications medium through which the user accesses information that would have formerly taken much time and physical effort to find. Cyberspace is significant because the user has the sensation of travelling, though in reality the user is just electronically reaching out and retrieving data to be visualized on a computer monitor. In this course the costs of information search drop noticeably. Virtual stores are being created with virtual inventories far larger than any physically existing store, which means that e-MNE can be established in this basis. Cyberspace eases many market entry barriers because of minimal start-up costs, thereby radically accelerating the realization of an idea and allowing successful ventures to grow exponentially. Hence, cyberspace represents a powerful dematerialization.[116] A leader must match their environmental and organisational settings, suggesting that the different situational context of e-business will dictate a distinctive set of leadership characteristics. Information technology and project management skills, the ability to exploit technology and an aptitude for risk-taking are characteristics of a leader in e-business[117].

It is no longer essential to disseminate information in the physical medium of paper, floppy disks, or CDs. Such flexibility and ease of use accelerates information flow and communication, facilitating new knowledge creation and modern forms of social production. Commercial content providers must find ways to attract people to their site, either by providing appealing content for them to use or some service or product they want to use or buy, or by creating a system for purchasing non-Internet particular products that offers something conventional retail channels do not. The convenience and availability of information are key advantages. The generalization of the Internet and its numerous protocols creates the prospect of developing one language for all interfirm data communications. With the computerization of the entire logistics and distribution functions of an increasing number of companies, the stage is set to use the Internet to interconnect companies and eliminate the human and paper intermediates. The establishment of global freight delivery firms simplifies logistic significantly, again decreasing temporal and cost distance. Cyberspace reduces

---

[115] Bianco, Anthony. 1997. Virtual bookstores start to get real." Business Week Online (October 27), *http://www.businessweek.com.* Bransten, Lisa. 1998. "There's More to E-Commerce Than Just the Lowest Prices." Wall Street Journal Interactive Edition, http://interactive.wsj.com

[116] Hauben, Michael and Ronda Hauben. 1998. Netizens: On the History and Impact of Usenet and the Internet *http://www.columbia.edu/~rh120/*

[117] Penny Horner-Long, Richard Schoenberg, Does e-Business Require Different Leadership Characteristics? An Empirical Investigation, European Management Journal Vol. 20, No. 6, pp. 611–619, 2002.

physical and bureaucratic hindrance by radically reducing the significance of location and the number of procedural steps requiring the direct intervention of firm operatives. Hence, cyberspace replaces physical space with a virtual space within which all places are basically the same.[118]

When designing network protocols, engineers must consider the interoperability implications at the application layer and the difficulty with designing interconnection agreements is that applications on the Internet are dynamic—new applications are constantly being developed[119]. Productivity growth matters to policymakers and to all participants in the economy. Heavy investment in computer and telecommunications technology in the 1990s accounted for as much as a half of all plant and equipment investment in recent years played a significant role in the recent productivity surge[120]. The macroeconomic conditions of the late 1990s, tight labor markets, low inflation, and fierce global competition, encouraged firms to use new technologies as a way of economizing on labor while surviving in an intensely competitive marketplace. But the real power of cyberspace will be felt in the existing economy, which will make increasing use of cyberspace to deliver benefits to consumers.

Separating the potential impact of the Internet on productivity is important because even a few tenths of a percent impact on the growth rate could represent a noteworthy portion of any permanent surge in productivity that is maintained in the future. The Internet can increase productivity growth in a variety of ways, including:

- Extensively reducing the cost of many transactions needed to produce and distribute goods and services;
- Escalating management efficiency
- Rising competition, making prices more transparent, and broadening markets for buyers and sellers;
- Increasing the effectiveness of marketing and pricing;
- Growing consumer choice, convenience and satisfaction in a range of ways.

Internet can transmit information promptly, conveniently, and inexpensively. Using Internet technology, many firms, especially those in data-intensive industries such as financial services and medical care, can reduce their cost of production. For instance, the prospective for transactions cost savings from transition to the Internet is particularly high in the health care sector, because it is so large, so information-intensive, and so dependent on paper records. The Internet offers great potential in the area of managing medical records, not only for cutting costs, but also for improving the quality and effectiveness of care. Providers would then be able to access the patient's full medical history quickly and enter their own observations and treatments. The Internet has precipitated a split between the relationship-dependent services of investment advising and portfolio management and the standardized service of stock trading. The Internet has massive potential for dispensing information to citizens less expensively and more accurately than telephone inquiries. The use of the Internet

---

[118] Davis, Stan and Christopher Meyer. 1998. Blur: The Speed of Change in the Connected Economy (Reading, Mass: Addison-Wesley).

[119] Farrell, J. and G. Saloner (1985). "Standardization, Compatibility, and Innovation." Rand Journal of Economics, 16, Spring. Katz, M. L. and C. Shapiro (1985). "Network Externalities, Competition, and Compatibility." American Economic Review, 75.

as a management tool may have significant potential for improving efficiency in many sectors of the economy and may cause momentous restructuring of those sectors in the process. One of the features of the Internet revolution is the prospective to make the whole economic system, nationally and internationally, more competitive. So, the results should be lower profit margins, more efficient production, and greater consumer satisfaction. The growing transparency of prices and the widening reach of markets provided by the Internet are likely to be a continuing global force for better efficiency. The Internet is lowering barriers to competition by increasing the likelihood that a company anywhere in the world that develops a better product can win bids, sell products, and compel other competitors to improve their productivity.

Will Internet produce acceleration in the growth? The Internet makes an identifiable contribution to productivity growth. Large and medium-sized businesses are using the Internet to some extent, although not necessarily extensively or effectively. Competition should supply a positive countervailing force, provided that markets are not unduly constrained by anticompetitive practices, and that the antitrust laws are enforced. Cyberspace plays an important role in fuelling the growth of electronic commerce. Developments in global network technologies and graphic-based Internet applications make transmission of all kinds of digitised data fast, cheap and simple, at a time when public consumption of computer technologies is increasing. Electronic commerce has expanded from business-to-business transactions between known parties to a complex web of commercial activities, which can involve vast numbers of individuals, many of whom may never meet. Because electronic commerce provides a deeply new way of conducting commercial transactions, it has potentially far-reaching economic and social implications for many facets of life, including, the nature of work, the role of governments, and even the environment. The interest in electronic commerce's economic impact is linked to the underlying fact that it shrinks the economic distance between producers and consumers.

Consumers can go directly to producers without the need for traditional retailers, wholesalers and, in the case of intangibles, distributors. It could be said that electronic commerce succeeds in moving economic activity closer to some of the ideals of perfect competition: low transaction costs, low barriers to entry, and improved access to information for the consumer. It may considerably lower prices while improving quality. Because it is a new way of conducting business, it may be a momentous source of new products, jobs, and economic growth. Consumer sales today are dominated by services and intangibles: travel and ticketing services, software, entertainment and financial services. This makes instinctive sense, given the convenience of electronic commerce for products that cannot be physically examined or those that consumers already purchase distantly. More generally, the digital nature of e-commerce successfully standardises transactions, making the information contained in them a commodity in its own right and very much increasing opportunities for storing, searching and manipulating it. Dependence on self-regulation, entrepreneurial ingenuity, and the power of technology have fostered the development of the Internet, and it has defied predictions about its capacity to scale up to serve user demand. However, it may be necessary to place self-regulatory approaches within a legal framework to ensure enforcement and implementation. As forms of communication become more and more digital allowing the development and integration of generic networks able to provide and support all types of

[120] Robert Litan and William Niskanen (1997), Going Digital, Brookings Publications.

applications, including entertainment, voice telephony, and electronic commerce will be key to expanding network capacity. Policies to promote electronic commerce must be directed towards developing and implementing reliable technologies and policies, scheduling to avoid and react to failures, gaining public support for and confidence in their use, developing restore mechanisms to reduce the occurrence of problem transactions and resolve those that occur, and developing law enforcement mechanisms to reply to those who seek to misuse the technologies. Governments should implement technology-neutral policies, so as not to limit electronic commerce or create regulations that will hamper electronic business transactions. The magnitude of information systems for society and the global economy is escalating as the value and quantity of data transmitted and stored on those systems increases. At the same time, systems and data are more and more vulnerable to unlawful access and use, misappropriation, alteration, and destruction. Cryptography is one of the most important technological tools in an information security system, as it can ensure both the confidentiality and the integrity of data. The worldwide interconnection of computer systems has made security an international problem. Security of information systems depends not only on the hardware and software used, but also on superior managerial, organisational and operational procedures. Global electronic commerce highlights the substance of common standards and procedures for security techniques.

Cyberspace is one of the factors that should be considered in productivity growth[121]. There is an increasing and significant impact of the Internet on bilateral trade flows from 1997 to 2007 which keep on growing. Cyberspace lowers prices by lowering search costs, reducing international communication and searching costs, making entry into several markets easier by lowering entry costs and Business-to-consumer (B2C), business-to-business (B2B), and business-to-government (B2G) are excellent examples. Both lower search costs and lower entry barriers result in a greater market competition, and productivity is improved by intensified competition and cutting the cost of holding inventories by allowing large suppliers to bypass retailers and contact customers directly contributes to the improvement of productivity. Cyberspace usage expands the transparency of the host countries and makes it comfortable to do business[122]. Additionally, cyberspace usage plays an equivalent role to the narrowing the geographical distances between two countries in inducing FDI. The advancement of the cyberspace will contribute to the worldwide increase in cross-border FDI and it will be one of key driving forces in expediting the integration of the world economy and so enhancing the welfare of the human beings[123]. International direct investors choose the country with more cyberspace availability assuming high productivity inducing inward FDI significantly.

As discussed earlier, explosion in B2B Internet business is fueling the rise of digital economy and companies must commit to full participation in the new electronic global marketplace seizing their opportunities in this explosive business environment. Companies must commit fully to cyberspace business, understand the digital infrastructure required to participate develop, and execute a coherent plan of action and their Web strategy should be

---

[121] Freund, C., & Weinhold, D. (2000, December). On the effect of the Internet on International trade (International Finance Discussion Papers). Board of Governors of the Federal Reserve System.

[122] Changkyu Choi, Does the Internet stimulate inward foreign direct investment? Journal of Policy Modeling 5304 (2002) 1–8

[123] Sichel, D. E. (1999, April). Computers and aggregate economic growth: An update. Business Economics, 18–24.

suitable to their size and scope and adapted to their competitive situation, industry focus, and available resources. Many companies, unwilling or not capable to initiate the deep change that the new business climate requires, have so far made only minor technical changes that hardly touch their culture or business processes have not made the investment in strategy, people and money needed to carry on in the B2B eCommerce world. Online markets, also known as B2B marketplaces, permit participants to access various mechanisms to buy and sell almost anything, from services to direct materials. B2B marketplaces are redefining how companies interact with each other. Furthermore, B2B marketplaces have the potential to drive the B2B eCommerce revolution uniting member companies in seamless trading communities of common business interest maximizing speed and efficiency and offering buyers and sellers exceptionally powerful forums to diminish transaction costs, enhance sales and distribution processes, deliver and consume value-added services, and streamline customer management. One of the key factors in building a successful B2B marketplace is to focus on meeting all the buying needs of the target user and the capacity of marketplaces to interoperate extends the idea of liquidity and network effect by joining more buyers with more suppliers, but does not sacrifice the aptitude of each marketplace to be highly specific to the supply-chain node or target buyer group it serves.

Every market represents a complex assembly of buyers and suppliers united by complicated lines of power and dependency but the B2B marketplace minimizes inefficiencies by tightening the relationship between supplier and buyer, promoting price discovery and spend aggregation, slashing supply chain costs, and increasing the reach of suppliers. Additionally, B2B marketplaces must provide access to services ranging from baseline interoperability and directory services to specialty services such as online payment, logistics and dynamic trade. It should be taken into account that without enough buyers and suppliers on the network, or enough total purchase volume, the marketplace cannot capitalize on its potential for efficiency. Moreover, the B2B marketplace platform should facilitate complex business rules, workflow, and relationships, and allow for integration with custom and third-party commerce modules. Hence, companies can use B2B marketplaces to reinforce their existing trade relationships, discover and develop new ones, and support faster and more competent trading[124] enabling various companies to locate trading partners dynamically completing transactions swiftly, securely and efficiently, without the need for any central aggregator or facilitator[125].

7.4 LOGISTICS IN GLOBALISATION AND E-COMMERCE

Logistics was defined as a function that was minimizing total distribution costs and logistics costs or maximizing profits, while achieving desired levels of service performance. To that extent logistics is directing towards maximizing local flexibility inside the company and customer service issues. In other words logistics has been implemented as a part of the strategic level decision-making process. Logistics is the science dealing with the planning,

---

[124] *www.ariba.com*, Porter, M. (2001), ``Strategy and the Internet'', Harvard Business Review, March. ``the greatest threat to an established company lies in either failing to deploy the Internet or failing to deploy it strategically''.

[125] Mark Lunn, Using business models and revenue streams for digital marketplace success, Information Management & Computer Security 10/1 [2002] 20-27.

organisation, control and automation of the material and information flow. So, the logistics combine, machines, information technology; and factory organisation and economy. Jules Dupuit[126] firstly introduced the concept of logistics and compared road transport with transport over water in order to identify the most optimal way of transporting goods from origin to destination. Modern logistics incorporates information technology, generating the definition that "modern logistics is the movement and storage of goods, together with associated information flows, from the beginning to the end of the supply chain"[127].

What is e-logistics? E-logistics are designed to fit into the new, electronic economy and the cyberspace transactions. Globalisation is one of the most important forces driving the restructuring of the world economy[128]. New trends in investment, trade and collaboration between firms have immensely changed the scope of world business and extended the role of foreign companies in national economies. Globalisation, in economic terms, can be thought of as a process in which business decisions, production processes and markets gradually come to exhibit more "global" characteristics and less " national" ones. Globalisation is characterised by structural reforms – especially trade and investment liberalisation – and increased trade and international investment flows. International trade and investment promote growth, alter the composition and geographical distribution of economic activities, stimulate competition and facilitate the international diffusion of technologies. . P Hirst and G Thompson[129] identify that globalisation is "large and growing flows of trade and capital investment between countries". Globalisation also refers to the rapidly improved communications systems (information and transportation), which have served to reduce distances between different countries and regions, bringing not only a greater exchange of goods and services but also more exchanges between people and information from different countries.

The essential task of logistics is to create a flexible and coherent production system that spans the globally dispersed set of production resources and logistics is not merely a set of shipping and delivery transaction that can be made paperless. Only by linking all logistics activities directly to the organisation's strategic plan can logistics manager work effectively to support their organisation's strategy for achieving competitive advantage. The cost of information was one of the few business costs to reduce during the 1980's. The revolution in information technology provides the opportunity for logistics to utilise transaction based and decision support systems as a source of competitive differentiation and increased market share. Management of inbound raw materials utilising electronic data interchange (EDI) between the organisation and key suppliers can provide substantial cost savings.

Due to the complexity of logistics, it is nowadays almost inconceivable to manage the logistics operation without the support of computers and management information systems. Computer hardware and software provide a solid basis for computer systems to be used in logistics. Electronic data interchange is currently one of the most important subjects in the area of computer applications in logistics. The use of EDI in logistics applications mainly concerns the electronic interchange of trading documents such as purchase orders,

[126] See Dupuit Jules (1952) "On the measurement of the utility of public work" reprinted in International Economic Papers No2 translated from French by Barback R , Macmillan Press London.

[127] Cooper, Brown, Peters " European Logistics: Markets, Management and Strategy " 1994 Blackwell Publishers

[128] Globalisation of Industry: Overview and Sector Reports, OECD, 1996.

[129] P Hirst, G Thompson "Globalisation:Ten frequently asked questions" 1996 Soroundings Vol 4, 47-66, p48.

acknowledgements, letters of credit, bills of lading, and invoices. The advantages of EDI are identified at the operational level (increased productivity, cost reductions), the technical level (improved customer service) and the strategic level (using JIT- suppliers, repositioning on the market). EDI have significant implications regarding the firm's behaviour and its organisational structure. It is achieved internal efficiency of the firm and its competitive position by speeding up its response to customer service. There are some problems related to the interconnectivity of EDI systems of different companies. The differences are related to: data structure, operating system, transmission services, organisation of data and organisational differences between companies. Thus, there is a need to agree upon all that issues. The system provider defines the message format and all participants have to apply the same message format. The same rule applies if the data have to be sent according to legal regulations.

There is a time gap between the production of the goods and their consumption. The time gap between consumer and producer arises when goods are not produced at the same time, as the consumer requires them. The warehousing process bridges this gap. The second is the geographical gap, which is covered by transportation. Most companies are not able to give a clear insight into there logistical costs. Logistical costs are generated in several departments of the company and are allocated to other cost components in corporate accounting. According to measures 2,3% and 3% of the companies' total turnover are respectively warehousing costs and transportation costs[130]. Can we isolate transport as an independent activity from the logistical system? Transport is part of the logistical system, which makes it complex to separate transport as an independent activity. The logistical structure determines the points in space and the patterns of trading links, which pairs of points in space are connected and in which direction. Decisions on product design affect transport through the complexity of the product, and packaging of goods. Concepts of logistic organisation including distance, speed, frequency and point in time do not translate purely into consequences for transport logistical chain. Transport is a required precondition of economic growth and of extended logistical reach and transport is inevitable consequence of the development[131].

Significant advances in operations and logistics software tools, along with the growth of third party logistics services, have enabled MNEs to more efficiently segment their production globally, while at the same time reducing inventory and shipping times and so reducing governance costs. With reliable single sources for nearly all out-bound logistics services, MNEs have achieved both cost and time savings[132].

Management of inbound raw materials utilising EDI between the organisation and key suppliers can provide substantial cost savings. Logistics manage the interrelationship of all the factors, which affect the flow of both information and goods necessary to fill orders. Strategic planning forces management to reconcile two contradictory tasks: long term planning with short-term responsiveness to customers. The principles of logistics excellence are the following: 1. Link logistics to corporate strategy. 2. Organise comprehensively. 3.

[130] A T Kearny "Value Added Logistics" 1993 Amsterdam.

[131] Lise Drewes Nielsen , Per Homann Jespersen, Tina Petersen, Leif Gjesing Hansen, Freight transport growth —a theoretical and methodological framework, European Journal of Operational Research 144 (2003) 295 –305 *www.elsevier.com/locate/dsw*

[132] S Feinberg, M Keane, Accounting for growth of MNC-based trade using a structural model of US MNCs, 2003 SSRN-ID3741103.

Use the power of information. Successful logistics departments take full advantage of information and information processing technology. Electronic data interchange links with customers. Creative use of computer-based models can yield cost service improvements, which bolster competitive advantage. 4. Emphasise human resources. 5. Form strategic alliances. 6. Focus on financial performance. 7. Target optimum service levels. 8. Manage the details. 9. Leveraging logistics volumes. 10. Measure the react to performance.

Customer order satisfaction and product processes increasingly often take place not within a single company, but cross company borders with the result that the enterprise executing the engineering processes is virtual. Suitable methodologies of product modelling, engineering data management, and project management must be identified and combined as a unified whole. Moreover, the central element of the global logistic design and controlling system is the assessment of what kind of logistic tasks have to be solved in autonomic way by virtual co-operating companies and what kind of tasks belongs to the capability of the virtual logistic centre. Efficient software tools must be used in order to follow the internal and external material flow. The development of just-in-time (JIT) concept has been set by the automotive industry. Logistics is the integrating element of the globalised production, especially of the virtual factories. The production can be fully automated, but other areas might demand a lower grade of automation. L. Cser, J. Cselenyi, M. Geiger, M.Mantyla, and A.S. Korhonen[133] specify that "Virtual factory is a product of globalisation in production as well as a new type of task sharing among the manufacturers, and between the manufacturer and customer". Production networks perform as one factory, independent of borders and geographic distances and logistics play an important role in the production of a virtual factory. IT of production networks of virtual factories is much higher than those in the traditional one-site factories. At present logistics has been expanding increasingly from the traditional material flow towards the chain connecting the network of production, sales, and maintenance and recycling.

Computer and information systems technologies have brought forward the use of Internet, e-commerce, and virtual reality/manufacturing[134]. Computers and information systems have become so much a part of every business's core that other areas of the business are now designed around it. Developments and growth in IT have impacted manufacturing activities concerning their capacity utilization, inventory turnover and quality, price reduction, market share and return on assets together with the use of computer-integrated manufacturing, and virtual manufacturing. The early twentieth century was an era of global integration, marked by extraordinary flows of goods, capital, and people. When economies generate rising returns in one sector within a state, that state is ready for 'industrial clustering', which would increase its productivity and wages. Specialization and the speed of relocation of factors depends on the costs of relocating factors, on comparative advantages and market rigidities and comparative advantages contribute to lock a country in its existing

---

[133] L. Cser , J. Cselenyi, M. Geiger, M.Mantyla, A.S. Korhonen, Logistics from IMS towards virtual factory, Journal of Materials Processing Technology 103 (2000) 6-13.

[134] O.Felix Offodile ,Layek L.Abdel-Malek, The virtual manufacturing paradigm: The impact of IT/IS outsourcing on manufacturing strategy, Int.J.Production Economics 75 (2002)147 –159. Fujita, M., Krugman, P., Venables, A.J., 1999. The Spatial Economy. MIT Press, Cambridge, London.

specialization pattern slowing relocation of factors.[135] Mobility of the highly skilled may necessitate harmonization or coordination between the countries' policies.

What is the relationship between the regional and global economy and the urban social and physical environment? The globalisation of communication by satellite is inevitable and is the result of the spread of medium- power telecommunication satellites as support for international television broadcasting. In economic terms globalisation of communication represents high stakes since it is well known that an investment in the global audiovisual market or its content has become a rare and in demand resource. Satellite television without frontiers can be of tremendous use for governmental communication, so much so that the satellite has become a privileged instrument of international state politics. Globalisation is likely to manifest itself in the dynamics of financial indices of stock markets in different countries.[136] Not only does globalisation increasingly impact the social stability of cities, however, it is also important to environmental conditions[137]. Globalisation not only drives contemporary development[138]but also is a long-term process that can be shaped by its own internal contradictions along with a host of other factors[139].

The increasing globalisation of computer hardware and software production coupled with active government encouragement of inward investment within the context of the single European Market. If technological convergence is a strong factor in determining sectoral ownership patterns, then one may conclude that acquisition and setting up of subsidiaries is apart of a wider search for technology on the part of large international firms. The main difference between national and international firms may well be in the degree of global integration they offer, and industrial policy may trade off increased market power for a few firms in exchange for wider global integration. Technological convergence is defined as the process by which two hitherto different industrial sectors come to share a common knowledge and technological base. Hence, technological convergence is a concept that is used to link industrial sectors that may seem unrelated in consumption terms, because of the cohesion in their technological bases. In order to establish an international information system to facilitate transfer of data across borders, MNEs must take into consideration that they are operating within and among different sovereignties, under different social, economic, cultural, and legal climates, with people of different value systems, and in national markets varying in structure, population, and area. Trans-border data flow (TDF) restrictions significantly increase IS costs and influence MIS decisions overseas[140].

---

135 Baldwin, R., 2001. The core-periphery model with forward-looking expectations. Regional Science and Urban Economics 31 (1), 21–49. Ottaviano, G.I.P., 1999. Integration, geography and the burden of history. Regional Science and Urban Economics 29, 245–256.

136 Sergei Maslov, Measures of globalization based on cross-correlations of world financial indices, Physica A 301 (2001)397 –406

137 McGranahan,G.,Songsore,J.,&Kjellen,M.(1999).Sustainability, Poverty and urban environmental transitions. In D.Satterthwaite (Ed.), Sustainable cities (pp.107 –130). London: Earthscan. Douglass, M., & Ooi, G.-L.(1999).Industrializing cities and the environment in Pacific Asia: Towards a policy framework and agenda for action. at *http://www.usaep.org/policy/framing1.html.*

138 Held,D.,McGrew,A.,Goldblatt,D.,&Perraton,J.(1999).Global transformations, politics, economics and culture . Stanford : Stanford University Press.

139 Peter J.Marcotullio, Asian urban sustainability in the era of globalization, Habitat International 25 (2001)577 –598

140 Vincent S. Lai, Steven Floyd, The impact of transborder data flow restrictions on international information systems management, Decision Support Systems 22 1998 121–134

Has technological convergence meant a convergence of product markets? Digitalisation is gradually replacing earlier mechanical technologies and involves the hardware sector more than the software sector, since a lot of it involves using the microprocessor. With multimedia revolution all forms of media are now accessible to the computer user, such as graphics, newspapers, audio information or complex combinations of these. Technological convergence has implied rapid redefinition of industry boundaries. In order to utilize the full range of implications that technological changes may have for firm growth, firms must possess a wider range of competencies in generic technologies than that which their production requires. Convergence has created problems of technological access and of market access. Companies may overcome the shortcomings in their internal competencies by entering into alliances of various kinds such as joint ventures and technology collaborations, mergers and acquisitions with other firms having a complementary range of competencies. Acquiring subsidiary companies or setting up independent subsidiaries may be another mechanism to overcome the shortcomings in the internal competencies of companies. A Firm must find a kind of coherence between its own activities and the activities of the acquired/merged firm. Companies that retained a stronger focus on particular product markets appear to perform better[141]. Product market access has various costs not all of which are technological. Has collaborative behaviour between companies changed the existing technology structures of the collaborating firms very much? High-technology companies are less likely to enter into equity-based relationships for purposes of access to technology[142]. What is the impact of technological change, technological convergence and consequently increased competition on the processes of globalisation? It is obvious that the degree of multinationality is notably associated with a company's increase of its technological advantages from foreign sources. Globalisation processes have been investigated under the purview of processes of internationalisation of capital and foreign direct investment.

According to Cantwell[143] technology leaders are pace-setters in the globalisation of technology, through"...the development of international intra-firm networks to exploit the locationally differentiated potential of foreign centres of excellence". MNEs enhance systems of innovation through selective specialisation. Firms internationalise in order to gain market share and develop control over major foreign markets. Choice of national location within the EU also reflects such factors as government policies and financial incentives to locate in less developed or industrially declining regions[144]. Production inter-nationalisation is associated with the maturity stage of innovation development, in which standardisation of production and increasing price competition forces relocation to low production cost countries[145]. Location decisions have frequently been a function not of labour costs alone, but

---

141 Gamberdella, A., Torrisi, S., 1996. Does technological convergence imply a convergence in product markets? Mimeo. IEFE, Bocconi University, Milan.

142 Hagedoorn, J., 1993. Understanding the rationale of strategic technology partnering: interorganizational modes of cooperation and sectoral differences. Strategic Management Journal 14, 371–385.

143 Cantwell, J., 1995. The globalisation of technology: what remains of the product cycle model? Cambridge Journal of Economics 19, 155–174. p. 157.

144 Stone, I., Peck, F., 1996. The foreign-owned manufacturing sector in the UK peripheral regions, 1978–1993: restructuring and comparative performance. Regional Studies 30 (1), 55–68.

145 Frobel, F., Heinrichs, J., Kreye, O., 1979. The New International Division of Labour. Cambridge University Press, Cambridge.

also of the quality of infrastructure and of agglomeration economies[146]. According[147] to Suma Athreye and David Keeble long-term problems of finance for computer sector firms, together with market access and profitability considerations for parent firms, may explain the large presence of subsidiary firms in this sector.

The global information society brought the development of telecommunications so that not only can data from large knowledge bases be exchanged rapidly, but also complex systems can be run remotely. The explosive growth of the Internet has enabled complex telemedicine applications including remote in vivo diagnostic analysis as well as teleconsultation[148]. As mentioned above, the firm-specific knowledge is a part of the fixed costs and the transfer of the knowledge to other plants implies that the production is subject to increasing returns to scale. Strength, broaden product diversification by expanding product lines or achieving scale economies, high costs of research and development, capital or equipment can be shared with other firms, therefore, the risk will be reduced and the cost burden of a firm is lowered are factors that allow the firms to prefer joint ventures. FDI, either establishing wholly-owned subsidiaries or joint ventures allows a firm to cut cost of production and then an MNE is able to earn more from foreign expansion.

Which are the conditions under which firm-specific knowledge and plant-specific knowledge will persuade a MNE to integrate horizontally into a foreign country through both wholly-owned subsidiaries and joint ventures? Cultural considerations may be central in an MNE's choice between acquiring a wholly-owned subsidiary or entering into a joint venture with an established domestic firm, in the partnering process. Either way, the foreign partner brings with it plant-specific knowledge. Establishing a joint venture is a choice as long as the cooperation cost can be covered by the gain of joint contribution from the parent firms. Leung[149] considers that the learning and growth matters are important in the decision making of an MNE A MNE operates both joint ventures and wholly-owned enterprises in a foreign country if the technology advantage over the native competitors is larger and the local firms' plant-specific knowledge is further valuable[150].

In the process of globalisation the ability of MNEs to develop integrated technological networks, to coordinate geographically diversified activities, has become the rule. The product cycle model[151] shows the international technology flows, which are seen as running from creation in one location, through transfer to a firm or affiliate in another location, to diffusion to a wider variety of firms in the host country. MNEs will have a valuable source of

---

146 O'Connor, D., 1985. Global trends in electronics: implications for developing countries. Mimeo. World Bank, Washington, DC.

147 Suma Athreye , David Keeble, Technological convergence, globalisation and ownership in the UK computer industry, Technovation 20 (2000) 227–245

148 Michael Rigby, The management and policy challenges of the globalisation effect of informatics and telemedicine, Health Policy 46 (1999) 97–103.

149 W.-F. Leung, A model of coexistence of international joint ventures and foreign wholly-owned subsidiaries, Japan and the World Economy 10 (1998) 233-252.

150 Horstmann, I.J., Markusen, J.R., 1987. Strategic investments and the development of multinationals, International Economic Review 28, 109-121. Horstmann, I.J., Markusen, J.R., 1987. Licensing versus direct investment: A model of internalization by the multinational enterprise, Canadian Journal of Economics 3, 464-481. Horstmann, I.J., Markusen, J.R., 1989. Firm-specific assets and the gains from direct foreign investment. Economica, 56, 41-48.

151 Vernon, R., 1966. International investment and international trade in the product cycle. Quarterly Journal of Economics 80, 190–207. Vernon, R., 1979. The product cycle hypothesis in the new international environment. Oxford Bulletin of Economics and Statistics 41, 255–267.

competitive advantage by locating in the technological centres of excellence to get hold of access to differentiated streams of new knowledge. The 'new' technologies are complex because of the complex nature of contemporary technological interdependencies. A company is obliged to broaden its technological activity through an international strategy if it wants to improve technological development even in its own immediate primary field of interest. The technological specialisation of each company within its field is intimately related to the pattern of its corporate technological competence.

A company may choose to concentrate its efforts on each area of activity in particular international locations rather than others. Globalisation tends to increase national differentiation and technological specialisation. Have countries tended to narrow their technological specialisation and become focused on areas of chronological competitive advantage? Globalisation makes the understanding of locational specificity further significant, and the nation state remains a potent force in the competitive advantage of nations. According[152] to John Cantwell, and Odile Janne "leading multinational firms from the major European centres in their industry tend to carry out technological activity abroad which is relatively differentiated from their domestic technological strengths'. European firms are stirring towards international strategies for technological development to engender geographically dispersed but complementary streams of innovation through the construction of international research networks in Europe[153].

Shorter product life cycles, fragmented markets, more demanding customers, consolidation and mergers of companies together with rapid advances in technology' processes always presenting a dynamic competitive situation are other factors which further deter the global competitiveness of a company. Manufacturing and operations excellence are essential factors for profitability, and globalisation is a critical component of the firm's competitive strategy[154]. Finally, lobalisation means moving production facilities around to benefit from the skilled executives or the cheapest labor to position a firm competitively against its competition.

Does e-commerce represent nothing new for how goods are being handled and moved in economy and society? Is e-commerce more than just a tool for optimizing goods flows? E-commerce is an essential element of a lately emerging 'sphere of circulation', the system of information, finance and goods flows that is both a fundament and an outcome of the network economy[155]. What is the typical empirical pattern by which commercial firms translate Internet technology into private value and, more broadly, into sustained economic growth? Doing business electronically over the cyberspace has increased exposure to unfair market practises, insecure means of payment, loss of privacy and lack of enforceable remedies. E-

152 John Cantwell , Odile Janne, Technological globalisation and innovative centres: the role of corporate technological leadership and locational hierarchy, Research Policy 28 1999 119–144. Patel, P., 1995. Localised production of technology for global markets. Cambridge Journal of Economics 19, 141–153.

153 Freeman, C., 1995. The 'national system of innovation' in historical perspective. Cambridge Journal of Economics 19, 5–24. Zander, I., 1995. Technological Diversification in the Multinational Corporation—Historical Evolution and Future Prospects. In: Schiattarella, R. Ed., New Challenges For Europe and International Business. Confindustria, Rome.

154 S. Nahmias, Production and Operations Analysis, 3rd ed., Irwin, Homewood, IL, 1997. J.T. Harvey, S.F. Quinn, Expectations and rational expectations in the foreign exchange market, Journal of Economic Issues 31 (2) (1997) 615-622.

155 Castells M. The rise of the network society. In: The Information Age: Economy, Society, and Culture, vol.1. Oxford, UK: Blackwell, 1996.

commerce is defined as any actions undertaken by business, which requires a commercial transaction to be carried out over a network such as the Internet. E-presence starts with one-way information about the enterprise, its products and services. Furthermore, E-commerce offers benefits to both seller and buyer. The seller can create a global presence and therefore reducing costs, increasing competition and allowing the ability to customise products. E-commerce has the ability to eliminate the time span between ordering, delivery, invoicing and payment by using the World Wide Web[156]. The new developments of economy forced logistics to respond to changing customer requirements and deal with freedom of choice, discontinuity, flexibility, and economies of scope. The advent of digital economy has triggered the emergence of e-logistics to deal with speed, flexibility, connectivity, interactivity and electronic products. The competitive advantage is embedded in knowledge and competence and a company must improve and adapt physical flows according customer's demands. Hence, traditional logistics must be combined with process management and use of cyberspace. Process management requires understanding and acceptance of what has to be done, why and how. Every company competes in two markets: the marketplace, in which resources and products exist physically and the market-space, which is a virtual world of electronic commerce in which the main object of transaction is information. The market space involves the company, its partners, and its customers and provides the opportunities for developing communication interactions, including customer surveys and information exchange on such things as product warranty and service capabilities.

The emergence of the global economy and intensified competition have led many companies to be aware of the importance of managing their supply chains for fast product introduction and service innovations to the markets and in order to improve competitiveness, many of them have embraced supply chain management (SCM) to enhance organizational effectiveness and achieve such organizational goals as improved customer value, better utilization of resources, and increased profitability[157]. SCM is concerned with managing the upstream and downstream relationships with suppliers and customers to deliver superior customer value at the least cost to the chain as a whole and implementing SCM requires both ''inter-functional ''and ''partnership ''perspectives avoiding inward-looking and self-focused attitudes in the management approach[158]. The management of a supply chain encompasses customer values and costs to customers that together emphasize the significance of getting goods/services to customers at the right time, in the right place, in the right quantities, under the right conditions, and at the lowest possible costs. Low cost is reflected in the costs of the product/service to the customers achieving a competitive advantage by striving for excellence in both service and cost leadership[159]. In the context of SCM, the focus of performance measurement should be not only on process operations within the organizational boundaries of a company, but also requires an understanding of the performance prospect of other member companies in the supply chain, backward from the suppliers and forward to the

[156] *G Zekos "Legal Problems in Cyberspace" 2002 Managerial Law 45, Number 5.*

[157] Lee, H.L.;2000. Creating value through supply chain integration. Supply Chain Management Review 4 (4), 30 –36. Lee, H.L.,Billington, C.,1992.Managing supply chain inventory: pitfalls and opportunities. Sloan Management Review 33 (3),65 –73.

[158] Holmberg, S., 2000. A systems perspective on supply chain measurements. International Journal of Physical Distribution and Logistics Management 30 (10), 847 –868.

[159] Dreyer, D.E., 2000. Performance measurement: a practitioner's perspective. Supply Chain Management Review 4 (4), 30 –36.

customers being the key to its effective implementation[160]. It is important to measure performance for the effective management of a supply chain and to that extent Harrington[161] refers that "If you cannot measure it, you cannot control it. If you cannot control it, you cannot manage it. If you cannot manage it, you cannot improve it". Besides, companies involved in various parts of the supply chain are likely to work to improve performance in those areas within their interest but they need a complete overview of their supply chain activities and full appreciation of the impact of their performance on other member companies in the supply chain. There is a need of integrating the internal functions within a company and effectively linking them with the external operations of member companies in the chain and a correct performance measurement is contributing to successful SCM implementation. According to Mentzer and Konrad [162] performance measurement is the effectiveness and efficiency in accomplishing a given task in relation to how well a goal is met meaning the extent to which goals are accomplished and they may include lead-time, stock-out probability, fill rate, inventory costs and operating costs. The goal of a transport logistics service provider is to satisfy the customers (both upstream and downstream) in the chain with greater effectiveness and efficiency than the competitors. Moreover, SCP in transport logistics should encompass not only operations efficiency parameters, but also measures of service effectiveness to meet the goals of all shipper, service provider and consignee and not be centered only on individual functional areas, but rather on the various parties involved in the transport logistics processes and the overall SCP. Lai, Ngai and Cheng[163] present practitioners with a 26-item measurement instrument for evaluating SCP in transport logistics suggesting that all 26 measurement items are critical attributes of SCP in transport logistics. Thus, e-logistics deliver solutions that are built on virtual integration and information and communication technology enabling the optimization of customer's value.

The model (SCOR)[164] developed by the Supply Chain Council provides a useful framework viewing activities in the supply chain as a series of interlocking inter-organizational processes with each individual organization comprising four components: plan, source, make, and deliver. Moreover, the SCOR model provides an indication as to how effective a company uses resources in creating customer value. Furthermore, SCOR not only identifies both the effectiveness and efficiency aspects of performance, but also recognizes that there can be internal as well as customer-related reasons for performance measurement.

The physical distribution (PD) sector comprises the entire system of goods handling and goods movement. Is PD influenced by e-commerce? Would the electronic transfer of information through a logistics system lead to more competent transport operations by cutting out 'unnecessary' transactions, by avoiding redundant traffic flows and by eliminating under-utilised infrastructure? An optimised logistics system would lead to more efficient transport

---

160 Frohlich, M.T., Westbrook, R., 2001. Arcs of integration: an international study of supply chain strategies. Journal of Operations Management 19 (2), 185 –200.

161 Harrington, H.J.,1991. Business process improvement: the breakthrough strategy for total quality, productivity, and competitiveness. McGraw-Hill, New York.

162 Mentzer, J.T., Konrad, B.P.,1991. An efficiency/effectiveness approach to logistics performance analysis. Journal of Business Logistics 12 (1), 33 –62.

163 Kee-hung Lai, E.W.T.Ngai, T.C.E.Cheng, Measures for evaluating supply chain performance in transport logistics, Transportation Research Part E 38 (2002) 439 –456.

164 Stewart, G.,1995. Supply chain performance benchmarking study reveals keys to supply chain excellence. Logistics Information Management 8 (2),38 –44.

operations[165] and electronic exchange would make the logistics market transparent allowing for optimal organisation[166] and allocation of transport services. The goods distribution system in industrialised countries has been undergoing profound changes over the last two decades and the introduction of supply chain management and its integrated approach to corporate re-organisation has vitally changed the entire system of goods processing. A PD comprises all functions of movement and handling of goods, above all transportation services (trucking, freight rail, air freight, inland water ways, marine shipping, and pipelines), logistics and warehousing service such as consignment, storage, inventory management, packaging, wholesale and mainly retail as well. PD gets the right assortment of raw materials and finished products to the right location in a proficient manner timely to marketing and manufacturing requirements. One of the primary changes associated with electronic commerce in terms of logistics is the process of disintermediation, leading to a reduced number of members in the distribution channel, compared with traditional supply chains. Features like electronic data interchange (EDI), the automatisation of product flow in dedicated warehouses and distribution centers (DCs), or the recent computer-based tracking-and-tracing systems (which offer on-line insight into the status of your shipment via the web) are primary sources of enormous productivity gains over the last two decades. Global Positioning Systems (GPS) allow for identification and both well-organized and flexible routing of vehicles in a way that was not known before. The material foundation for the contemporary 'network economy' is based both on modern logistics and on traditional asphalt and concrete. Cyberspace functions as a main platform for information exchanges, transforming them into market transactions. Business customers can speed up the entire ordering process, receive delivery faster, and are able to follow the status of their order on-line. Companies experience greater market transparency (offers, prices) and are able to increase their purchasing power, in order to achieve overall cost reduction. Does on-line retail mean that a product is being delivered directly either from the manufacturer or distributed out of a dedicated DC to the final consumer? It is unclear how many agents are financially involved in the transactions, nor how many operate within the physical transfer[167]. It should be taken into account that electronic commerce is certainly not only a matter of virtual information flows but also has a material goods movement dimension. Competition drives service level and time requirements, and in order to fulfill these needs, a certain transport and environmental expense is generated. Due to integrated data transfer and information management, flexible distribution and e-commerce would permit the processing and shipping only those materials that have been ordered. Air transport is critical for the sustainability of the entire transport system and e-commerce as a major customer of airfreight is also expected to increase (even indirectly) the pressure on airports for further growth and further expansion. E-commerce by airfreight will be associated with future air traffic growth and related problems. Moreover, e-commerce is the increasing need for trans-shipment points, such as warehouses and DCs operated in order to control the more complex, mass-customised freight flows without increased logistics costs. Furthermore, the new technology enables continual

[165] Meyer MD. Delivering The Future: E-Freight. Provided by the Foundation for Intermodal Research and Education, Greenbelt, MD 20770, USA (on the web: http://intermodal.org/FIRE/meyerpaper.html).

[166] Song J, Regan A. Transition or transformation? Emerging freight transportation intermediaries. Transportation Research Record 2001;1763:1-5.

[167] Reynolds J. E-commerce- a critical review. International Journal of Retail and Distribution Management 2000; 28(10):417-44.

movements of products in the supply chain, which means that traditional storage space must start housing activities that involve more horizontal movement rather than vertical stacking. New Economy by modernising production and distribution facilities more and more will cluster around major airfreight hubs and logistics drive distribution facilities to strategic locations, often closer to customers[168] and so the new DCs, designed for rapid material flow, are more and more being established at strategic, time- and space-sensitive locations. New warehouses, DCs and logistics facilities are moving at the edge of the agglomeration and the demand for developed land for distribution purposes is likely to increase. Taking into account that not all goods can be electronic, the economic success and logistics efficiency of e-commerce are challenged by the costly frictions of physical space. According to Markus Hesse[169] "Possible contributions of e-commerce to a more efficient and sustainable distribution system very much depend on particular regional circumstances, such as consumer habits, certain delivery modes and the important question of population density."

Horizontal logistics concern relations between parties within a group of companies at the same level in a supply chain, while vertical logistics concern relations between companies at different levels in the supply chain. Electronic commerce is one of several marketing channels, including the use of the Internet to support inter-organizational processes such as marketing, ordering and related service activities. [170]

Logistics is referred to as a non-homogenous part of the supply chain that involves several participants at different levels[171]. A logistics platform is a homogenous and controlled part of a logistics system by one actor in the supply chain affected by marketing channel strategy and should as such support the strategy across and within business units. MNEs outsource the operation of logistics to transport and logistics providers taking over a large variety of services such as transportation, warehousing, warehousing services, pick and pack, packing, statistics and many other value added services. Recently companies prefer to use a third party logistic provider in order to manage different parts of their strategic plan of development or even a part of their logistic schedule. A third part logistics provider (TPL) is defined as the services offered by a middleman in the logistics channel that has specialized in providing, by contract, for a given period, all or a substantial number of the logistics activities for other companies. A logistics partnership is defined as a long-term formal or informal relationship between shippers and logistics providers to render all or an extensive amount of logistics activities for the shipper. It should be taken into account that the way the logistics firms manage to organize and choose their customers as well as combine their different logistics solutions is vital not only for their own but often also their customers′ and sometimes even for their customers′ customer survival. There is economic, physical, technological, and legal knowledge exchange between firms, but also a social exchange where trust and communication are vital for the use of TPL. Awareness, formation, closer cooperation, extension and maintenance and then finally looser cooperation and dissolution

---

168 Kirschbraun T, Bomba T. The New Economy. Effects on corporate real estate strategies. In: Jones Lang LaSalle: Property Futures. Occupier Strategies in the New Economy: Chicago, London 16, 2000.

169 Markus Hesse, Shipping news: the implications of electronic commerce for logistics and freight transport, Resources, Conservation and Recycling 36 (2002) 211/-240, at 234.

170 European Commission, 1998. An Introduction to Electronic Commerce. *http://europa.eu.int/ISPO/ecommerce*.

171 Lambert,D.,Cooper,M.,2000.Issues in supply chain management. Industrial Marketing Management 29,65 –83.

are stages of a professional relation between a customer and a TPL which means that changes of increasing integration and commitment seem to take place in logistics alliances[172] between the TPL and its customers[173]. The logistics strategy and marketing of the customers will be of importance for what type of demands the customer set on TPL[174].

An important aspect of logistics in general, and therefore of the logistics platform, is the need for flexibility[175] in order to support the marketing strategy in the long and short-term perspective. Hence, logistics need to be flexible in the short term to offer operational opportunities, and flexible in the long term to apply to new marketing channel positions. Examples of logistics flexibility types needed in the short and long term are volume flexibility, time-based flexibility and flexibility in products and services. There is an interaction between marketing and logistics, horizontally and vertically in the supply chain. The possibility of adapting to changes in the environment concerns the possibility of choosing different lines of action in terms of disintermediation, multiple marketing channels, composite supply chain channels and/or multiple logistics channels, ordering channels or distribution flows[176].

The distinctive feature of an Electronic Marketplace is that it brings multiple buyers and sellers together (in a ''virtual ''sense) in one central market space enabling them to buy and sell from each other at a dynamic price, which is determined in accordance with the rules of the exchange. Co-operative supply chains aim to reduce the number of suppliers and form long-term strategic alliances that lock in suppliers and lockout competition, while EMs promote competition and permit buyers to search for appropriate suppliers and support ''transaction-based '' partnering. Supply chain management needs to manage the organizational complexity of adopting a dynamic mix and emphasis between content, context and infrastructure. Internet commerce does not eliminate the need of physical logistics systems; in fact, it even increases their importance. The flow of information between the supply chain partners can be efficiently managed over cyberspace, reducing the costs and increasing the speed and the quality of data transfer. On the other hand, the EM should organise a complementary physical logistics system in order to distribute material products to its clients. Hence, the EM[177] must decide to create its own physical assets in order to provide a

---

172 Kyle, P., H.Singh & H. Perlmutter (2000) "Learning and Protection of Proprietary Assets in Strategic Alliances: Building Relational Capital". Strategic Management Journal, 21: 217-237

173 Bagchi, P.K. & H.Virum (1998) "Logistical Alliances: Trends and Prospects in Integrated Europe". Journal of Business Logistics, Vol 19 No 1 (pp 191- 213)

174 Hertz, S., (1996). "The Dynamics of International Strategic Alliances -A Study of Freight Transport Companies." In: International Studies of Mangement and Organisation, Vol. 26, No 2, pp. 104-130Lieb, R.C. & H.L. Randall, 1996. "A comparison of the Use of Third Party Logistics Services by Large American Manfacturers, 1991, 1994 and 1995." In: Business Logistics Vol 17, No 1

175 Upton,D.M.,1994.The Management of Manufacturing Flexibility. California Management Review, Winter, pp. 72 –89. Flexibility is here defined as ''the ability to change or react with little penalty in time, effort, cost or performance ''

176 Niklas Aldin, Fredrik Stahre, Electronic commerce, marketing channels and logistics platforms —a wholesaler perspective, European Journal of Operational Research 144 (2003) 270 –279 *www.elsevier.com/locate/dsw*.

177 Martin Grieger, Electronic marketplaces: A literature review and a call for supply chain management research, European Journal of Operational Research 144 (2003) 280–294 *www.elsevier.com/locate/dsw*

consistent quality of product delivery. Finally, different electronic marketplaces require supply chain management[178].

7.5 E-Commerce and Industrial Distributors

E-commerce has the prospective to transform customer relationship management. Is there room in this revolution for the middleman? Are still distributors parts of a logistics plan? A distributor is a company that serves as a conduit between manufacturers of a product and the business users of a product. Distributors gained power and authority in the 1980s, as they functioned as the manufacturer's sales arm, and as manufacturers more and more relied on distributors to transfer to them knowledge of customer needs and market trends. Customers can bypass intermediaries and order a wide range of goods and services direct from the manufacturer. It must be recognized that industrial distributors are still very much around. E-commerce and globalization have squeezed out weaker competitors and pressured distributors to develop. Distributors must react to demands for improved services and investments, all the while experiencing and expecting reduced profit margins. Distributors deal with more than one manufacturer and with multiple customers and manage relationships with other distributors. Information technology and the global accessibility of products have resulted in distributor alliances with their source manufacturers, with their industrial customers, and with other distributors. Therefore, the distributor needs to uphold electronic links with the manufacturer, the customer, other third party or intermediary partners, and each of their web sites[179]. Manufacturers have utilized distributors in order to expand their operational efficiency, under the supposition that distributors could perform tasks at a lower per unit cost than the manufacturer could. Distributors are credited with reducing the number of contacts manufacturers have with other companies to a manageable number. Reducing the number of business contacts used to be seen as a fundamental, constructive role of intermediaries. A well-maintained buyer–supplier relationship decreases many transaction costs and increases competitiveness and distributors can possess important competitive advantages. Thus, the distributor's traditional logistics role of handling the physical goods may not be sufficient for continuing competitive advantage[180].

Information technology facilitates the entry of new competitors, who offer customers information and transaction assistance and some power is shifting away from distributors, and towards manufacturers and customers. Distribution changes are both evolutionary (motivated by the drive to reduce inefficiencies), and revolutionary (driven by redefining distributor role, scope, and relationships). Sourcing and procurement are strategically significant to business. Electronic technology facilitates efforts to outsource, reduce the number of suppliers, adopt just-in-time procedures, and raise quality and service standards for their suppliers. The capacity to offer cutting edge technical assistance can be a key competitive advantage for

---

[178] Christopher, M. (1998) Logistics and Supply Chain Mangement - Strategies for Reducing Cost and Improving Services. London, U.K. Financial Times/ Pitman Pbl.

[179] Lancioni RA, Smith MF, Oliva TA, The role of the Internet in supply chain management, Ind Mark Manage 2000;29:45 –56. Cort SG. Industrial distribution: how goods will go to market in the electronic marketplace. Bus Econ 1999; 34(1):53 – 55.

[180] Lancioni RA. New developments in supply chain management for the millenium. Ind Mark Manage 2000;29:1 –6.

manufacturers and distributors. Moreover, market knowledge is important, including knowledge of the major trends in the environment, knowledge of customer needs and past behavior, and knowledge of competitor strategy and activity, especially in technological areas. Technology-driven links and networks using cyberspace seem to downplay the role of interpersonal trust and directly affect the traditional role of the industrial salesperson emphasizing impersonal efficiency. The decision to use a distributor depends to some degree on the prospect of cost reduction, both in the short term and the long term, and the expected impact on business growth together with their ability to develop sources of added value[181]. Hence, distributors need to add value, communicate their added value, and protect their sources of value. Distributors need to examine their relative position as a provider of the key value sources of customer relationship management, production and operations management, and knowledge management in a digitized business world[182]. In other words, industrial distributors have to develop proactive and effective strategies to enhance their viability embracing e-commerce. Finally, distributors must compete more efficiently and valuably, given the changing business environment of the electronic economy.

In the electronic era a company must move beyond the replacement of paper-based transactions or e-logistics and to create an intelligent logistics environment that spans the company. Hence, the transformation from e-logistics to intelligent logistics is driven by an increase in the complexity of the logistics processes needed to support new production strategies organised around speed and time-definite delivery. The supply chain dimension of e-business is in principal neglected and inadequately managed, while the mal-performance of logistics is presently hampering turnover and revenues of e-commerce applications in a severe way. If basic operational performance is not even assured, more advanced approaches of e-business will not take off, since the support for concepts in the physical domain is inadequate. The implementation of cyberspace is changing the structure of the classical distribution channel, encouraging an increased specialization of the physical delivery functions.

7.6 Characteristics of Digital Economy

Increased employment together with low inflation and growth in productivity resulting in GDP growth over a long period is relating to the spread of the use of the ICT. The new/digital economy is defined as one based on knowledge and information, relying on sub sectors such as entirely digital goods and services and mixed goods that is, physical goods that are sold through the Internet. The development of an interconnected, interdependent economy, with a network structure and tremendous flexibility of ICT and capacity for transformation permit the increasing convergence of specific technologies into a highly integrated system. Internet is an open web based on open standards that allow any computer on the net to connect, through the same protocols permitting the interaction of different computer platforms and simplifying the exchange of information, multiplying the possibilities of links between the different agents operating in the electronic marketplace. The emergence of new agents, processes, business relations and patterns of communication and organization are typical

[181] Anderson JC, Narus JA. A model of distributor firm and manufacturer firm working partnerships. J Mark 1990; 54(1):42 – 58. Ghosh S. Making business sense of the internet. Harv Bus Rev 1998;76 (March–April).

[182] Frazier GL. Organizing and managing channels of distribution. J Acad Mark Sci 2000; 27(2):226 – 240.

features of the electronic marketplace. New markets are opening up for traditional products, new information-based products and new delivery channels, thereby making it easier to adapt to individual consumer preferences. Knowledge-based digital products share with knowledge itself the common features of infinite supply and non-rivalry, which mean that they will never run out and can be used repeatedly by numerous users bringing forward the need to regulate intellectual property rights. Consumer behaviour differs between the virtual market and the physical world, the quantity and quality of the information that is handled, accessed and processed through a network in which time and space take on a new meaning. The use of ICT brings changes to the business environment, where transaction costs decrease, production factors become less expensive, lesser quantities of stocks are needed, and time to market is reduced. For instance, transformations resulting from technological and organisational changes and their combined effects have influenced the role of governments and the design of government policy. The information age is giving rise to processes of severe social exclusion, both in developing countries and in poorer, depressed areas of the developed world and so alongside the acceleration of the globalisation process, apparent in growing mobility among the factors of production, brings changes in the world of finance and trade, liberalisation of the flow of capital goods and services, the role of direct investment and transfer of technology. The goods and services associated with the digital economy are going through major technological changes and quality improvements that are not reflected in price levels or in quality indices. New products and services are emerging complicating the measuring process in the services sector. The new environment of the electronic marketplace favours changes in market structure and competitive strategies as well as speeding up convergence in technologies, infrastructure, markets and products.

The manufacturing industry is changing and the increasing emphasis is on electronic business (e-business). E-business technologies are meant to help adopters to reach new customers more efficiently and effectively. Moreover, E-business technologies, the latest development in ICTs have potentials to benefits not only producers but also users of services and products. Conduct variables such as skill intensity of firms, investment on R&D, wage rates are principal factors that are expected to have bearings on the adoption of e-business. Higher remuneration is a major incentive for the workforce to create and adopt innovations effectively and efficiently. Many firms adopt e-business because of low coordination costs. Additionally, E-business transforms the exchange of goods, services, information, and knowledge through the use of ICTs. Hence, E-business has the potential to redefine the existing business infrastructure organisations and to re-evaluate the way in which they do business.

The full economic impact of information technology cannot yet be precisely evaluated but its impact is significant[183]. Businesses in practically every sector of the economy are beginning to use the Internet to cut the cost of purchasing, manage supplier relationships, streamline logistics and inventory, plan production, and reach new and existing customers more effectively. Cost savings, increased consumer choice and superior consumer convenience are driving growth in the sale of physical goods and in the digital delivery of goods and services via cyberspace. A global digital network using new packet switching technology combines the power of remarkable innovations in computing and communication.

183 Goff, Leslie. "Online computer store forecasts growth." Interactive Age Digital. 1997. *http://techweb.cmp.com/ia/iad_web/networth/ccstudy/necx.html*

Cyberspace ties together the computing power on desks, in factories and in offices around the world through a high-speed communications infrastructure. For instance, software programs, newspapers, and music CDs no longer need to be packaged and delivered to stores, homes or news kiosks. Airline tickets and securities transactions, consulting services, entertainment, banking and insurance, education over cyberspace already occur in large numbers. Reducing inventory levels means that existing manufacturing capacity is more resourcefully utilized. More efficient production can reduce or eliminate the need for further investments in plant and equipment. Cycle time is the total time it takes to build a product and electronic commerce allows "cycle times" to be shortened, allowing more to be produced for the same or lower costs. Companies by establishing electronic links with their large suppliers and customers enable them to transmit and receive purchase orders, invoices and shipping notifications with much shorter lead times than previously. Cyberspace permits even further reductions by broadening the network of businesses connected electronically and by facilitating collaboration on projects across work teams and geographical locations. Sharing information electronically allows different members of a group to work on projects together. Before the use of EDI, automotive companies communicated production requirements and schedules to their suppliers by phone, fax or mail. This meant time-consuming manual data entry, photocopying and information hand-offs from one supplier to another. Cyberspace can make traditional sales organizations, layered distribution channels, catalog sales and advertising more efficient[184]. Direct marketing online can shorten repurchase cycles and increase the ability to sell additional items.

Financial institutions venturing on cyberspace have had to figure out how to deal with the increased risk of operating in this electronic environment because the lack of face-to-face contact and the failure to utilize magnetic-stripped cards with secure ATM networks make it difficult to authenticate instructions from customers. Many financial institutions have responded by modifying their operation of account agreements to shift such risks onto their customers[185]. E-commerce facilitates cyberspace anonymous transactions (electronically conveyed services and digitized products) when the seller may be outside the territorial power of the taxing government or when the destination of goods and services can be masked. So, buyers may not have to pay sales tax on goods purchased from a seller in a different tax jurisdiction, putting non-e-commerce merchants at a disadvantage and reducing overall tax revenues.[186] Most countries claim some degree of tax jurisdiction on income and transactions with foreign aspects under their own domestic tax laws that may tax income received by residents from foreign sources, or income remitted abroad from domestic sources. Cross-border sales are regularly subject to customs duties or registration fees in the state where

---

[184] "Internet Shopping." Ernst & Young, LLP. January 1998.

[185] Alan Gahtan and Jeff Graham, Financial Services in an Electronic Age: Some Emerging Legal Issues, 1997 Cyberlaw Encyclopedia *www.gahtan.com*

[186] Reuven S. Avi-Yonah, International Taxation of Electronic Commerce, 52 T AX L.REV. 507 (1997); Organisation for Economic Co-operation and Development (OECD), Electronic Commerce: The Challenges to Tax Authorities and Tax Payers (1997), available at *http://www.oecd.org//daf/fa/e_com/turku_e.pdf.* David R. Tillinghast, The Impact of the Internet on the Taxation of Informational Transactions, 50 BULL. I NT'L FISC. DOC. 524 (1996) ("When an enterprise provides me with information, is it selling me property (the paper on which statistics are recorded)? Is it providing a service (because it has gathered the information for me)? Or am I paying for the use of intellectual property (because the provider has developed a unique composition).").

goods are used.[187] The extension of tax jurisdiction to digitally-delivered products was broadly opposed[188]. Besides, according to Sarah W. Salter[189] "reliance on sales taxes under more uniform tax rules is likely to become intense". The application of existing taxation on commerce conducted over cyberspace should be consistent with the established principles of international taxation, should be neutral with respect to other forms of commerce, should avoid inconsistent national tax jurisdictions and double taxation, and should be simple to administer and easy to understand.

Paul Miller and James Wilsdon [190] consider that despite the death of the dot-coms, there's no doubt that the digital revolution is reshaping the way we do business and communicate to each other. By contrast, this author thinks that the dot-coms need restructuring and new ways of doing business. The defining characteristic of the digital economy is not technology but innovation developing exclusively new ways to deal with old problems. E-commerce should be a vehicle for revitalising marginalized areas and communities by transforming existing social, environmental and economic maps. It is important to know that many times even if the initial contact with an individual or organisation is electronic it usually turns into a face-to-face relationship. Cyberspace can be used as the ideal tool for creating more inclusive, accountable models of business. Moreover, Dot-coms, dot-orgs and dot-govs need to work together to embed sustainability in every area of the digital economy.

Progress exists within a certain techno-economic paradigm, but occurs within a framework defined by a set of foundation technologies and modes of organizing economic activity. So, innovation occurs as the core technologies become more and more enveloping and affect ever-wider realms of production and distribution. Moreover, the materialization of a new core technology requires, and creates the prospect for, an entire new set of small and incremental innovations that allow the widespread usage of the new core technologies. It could be said that the procedure of materialization of a new techno-economic paradigm results from the interaction of the technological, economic, institutional, and social spheres. The capacity to constantly produce skills and ideas accumulating knowledge through learning is the crucial driver of economy long-run prospects. P. Conceicao, D. Gibson, M. Heitor,

---

187 George Zodrow, Notes: Efficiency and the Choice of Tax Base, available at *http://www.owlnet.rice.edu/~econ483/notes/NotesEff.pdf* The European Commission, Taxation Policy of the European Union (2000) at *http://europa.eu.int/comm/taxation_customs/publications /taxation/tax_brochure.htm* ("Tax policy is a symbol of national sovereignty and part of a country's overall economic policy, helping finance public spending and redistribute income. In the European Union, responsibility for tax policy mainly lies with the Member States, that may delegate some of it from central to regional or local level, depending on the constitutional or administrative structure of government.").

188 Backing Sought for Offshore Tax Initiative, N.Y. TIMES, June 14, 2001, at C4 (OECD-US negotiations to set guidelines for disclosure of information and other measures to reduce tax evasion by use of tax havens). Taxing Digital Downloads, 3 E -COMMERCE L. REV. 29 (2001) ("the EU is proposing that the company will be required to file a monthly report in the chosen country, but pay taxes based upon the country of each customer's purchases. The VAT would then be redistributed to the relevant country.").

189 Sarah W. Salter, E-Commerce and International Taxation, 2002 NEW ENG. JOURNAL OF INT'L & COMP. LAW 5, at 17.

190 Paul Miller and James Wilsdon, Digital Futures — An Agenda for a Sustainable Digital Economy, *www.corporate-env-strategy.com*, Sustainable Digital Economy.

And G. Sirilli [191] estimate that by 2001, e-commerce in the United States will be almost 60% of a combined 354.5 billion U.S. dollars total Internet-related market. The accomplishment of regional economic development based on new information technologies results from a combination of efforts from the private and the public sector.

Firms offer their products and services through the digital channel alone and give life to virtual companies such as Amazon.com and Ebay.com. The appeal of doing business on cyberspace comes from the possibility of contacting consumers and producers in a highly flexible way. e-Commerce is increasingly only a first step within a wider goal of digitalisation of the firm 's entire frontline and back-office applications. The way from e-commerce to an enriched e-business perspective suggests a change not only in the way outputs are sold (e-commerce), but also in a redefinition of offer types and procurement practices together with a one-to-one consolidation of the links with the target customers or suppliers. For instance, the application of e-commerce solutions on airlines have had a considerable positive impact on containing carriers 'costs by smoothing their dependence on computer reservation system (CRS[192]) interfaces and on travel agents 'commercial practices. David Jarach[193] considers that "Today, Internet potentially permits carriers to get significant economic and competitive benefits beyond those simply coming from e-commerce. A wider e-business perspective may assure a one-to-one relationship with target customers, with a consequential fine-tuning of a firm 's system offer".

Digital economy is being shaped not only by the development and diffusion of computer hardware and software, but also by much cheaper and increasing electronic connectivity. Cyberspace is helping to level the playing field among large and small firms in business-to-business e-commerce. In the past, larger companies had more and more used private networks to carry out electronic commerce, but high costs kept the resulting efficiencies out of reach for most small businesses. The Internet has altered this equation by making it easier and cheaper for all businesses to transact business and exchange information. Corporations are expanding their use of networked systems to improve internal business processes--to coordinate product design, manage inventory, improve customer service, and reduce administrative and managerial costs. IT has not only propelled faster growth during this expansion, but it will have a tendency to dampen the next business cycle downturn. Productivity gains come not only from deploying innovative technologies that enable workers to process information faster but also companies intent on taking advantage of innovative new technologies often have to rethink the way they operate and reorganize their operations, which can produce a round of organizational innovation. Moreover, companies have discovered that the new technologies can be used to develop and produce new goods or services for themselves, producing yet another round of innovation. The synergistic convergence of dramatic increases in computer power, an explosion in connectivity, and increasingly powerful new software in technology have produced sharp declines in the prices of computer processing, data storage and retrieval, and communications, that are in turn

---

[191] Pedro Conceicao, David V. Gibson, Manuel V. Heitor, And Giorgio Sirilli, Beyond the Digital Economy: A Perspective on Innovation for the Learning Society, Technological Forecasting and Social Change 67, 115–142 (2001)

[192] Frances Slack, Jennifer Rowley, Kiosks 21:a new role for information kiosks? International Journal of Information Management 22 (2002) 67 –83.

[193] David Jarach, The digitalisation of market relationships in the airline business: the impact and prospects of e-business, Journal of Air Transport Management 8 (2002) 115 –120, p115.

driving both the surge in Internet activity and the increases in business investment in IT hardware and software. The Internet is both an effect and a cause of the digital economy. It is, in part, a product of the powerful technological and economic changes that are shaping a new epoch of economic experience. However, cyberspace and related networking technologies are progressively more the digital economy's medium. As cyberspace gains popularity, its technological specifications have become a default standard, encouraging new hardware and software innovations that use Internet technology as a platform.

A large part of the growth in the emerging digital Economy will come at the expense of the physical economy through a substitution effect. However, the convenience, flexibility and efficiency gained by doing business through cyberspace are noteworthy, which should eventually be reflected in the value added in the digital economy. Furthermore, new demand is being created by cyberspace. For instance, dynamic pricing is being used to match supply and demand (airlines, hotels); buyers and sellers now have direct or electronically intermediated access to each other worldwide, which often results in transactions that would not have occurred otherwise. What the characteristics of company who add the most value in this digital economy? Cyberspace Infrastructure layer consists of the telecommunications companies, Internet Service Providers, Internet backbone carriers, "last stage" access companies and manufacturers of end-user networking equipment all of which is a prerequisite for the Web and the proliferation of Internet based electronic commerce.

Cyberspace Applications Infrastructure includes software products and services necessary to assist Web transactions and transaction intermediaries. In addition to the software products that help facilitate Web transactions, this layer of the digital Economy includes the consultants and service companies that design, build and maintain all types of Web sites, from portals to full E-commerce sites. A distinct type of company does not directly generating revenues from transactions but their Web-based business generates revenues through advertising, membership subscription fees, and commissions. Some of them are purely Web content providers while others are market makers or market intermediaries. This is a significant group of companies that is expected to have a significant impact over time on the competence and performance of electronic markets. New developments in the Internet industry may put an end to the frustration of waiting for a Web site to load and open a world of new opportunities. Broadband will transform the Internet, as a new wave of high-speed. Cyberspace users will generate an entire new set of opportunities for all Internet companies. Moreover, cyberspace is fundamentally changing business models, strategies, and processes, and is also creating new opportunities for the small and big companies.

There are two types of "dot com" companies: digital and physical. Digital dot coms are Internet based companies such as Yahoo, and America Online, whose products and services are entirely digitised in nature, and which are delivered directly over the Internet. By contrast, the physical dot coms sell physical products such as books, CDs, jewelry, and toys that are shipped to consumers. Of course, the level of digitisation of business models, strategies and processes is superior in digital product companies than in Internet based companies selling physical goods. While the Internet and electronic commerce applications are available to both types of companies, electronic retailers (e-tailers) of physical products often build warehouses and are subject to many of the physical constraints of bricks-and-mortar companies. By contrast, due to the very nature of their business, most of the business processes and delivery mechanisms of digital dot coms are implemented online. The physical dot coms undergo the lack of complementary digitisation in their value chain. That is, while a physical dot com may have digitised its interactions with customers, its value chain partners may not have yet embraced the use of cyberspace for their operations. However, the benefits of electronic commerce will not be harvested until all value chain partners enter the digital economy. Further, the ability of a digital dot com to differentiate itself from its competitors directly depends on being able to translate innovative business strategies into online capabilities. The most significant distinctions between a digital and a physical dot com involves the degree to which business strategies, processes and relationships can be digitised and the type of inputs used by each company. In other words, the business model of a digital products company is reflected in its IT applications. Any business strategy in the digital products world is immediately translated into systems capabilities. By contrast, the differentiation strategies of a physical products company on the Internet are frequently implemented offline, and may have little to do with IT. So, there is a need to deal with warehouses and inventory in order to provide fast delivery of goods to the customers. E-tailer companies have to maintain merchandise inventory, and handle packaging and shipping processes by themselves, citing customer service excellence as the primary reason. Besides, the digital products companies manage content inventory in a straight line through their Web sites and related applications. The digital products companies, cost of sales consists of Internet connection, Web hosting, telecommunications, Web site infrastructure and development, networking, computer hardware, software development, payroll for Web site operation, and digital content provided by other companies. The cost of sales of the majority physical dot coms consists of the cost of merchandise sold and inbound/outbound shipping. A digital products company can expand by creating more content alliances and by escalating and enhancing its Web presence. By contrast, an e-tailer has to undertake a complex and often labor intensive expansion program to increase the volume of business. As digitisation of business processes becomes more widespread throughout the value chain, the role of IT capital in the production process even for the physical dot coms will change. Physical dot coms and their trading partners must install new business models, redesign business processes including interaction with customers, order taking, coordination in fulfilment and delivery, and quality control. Hence, each aspect of the business other than the actual physical production and delivery must be digitised. Even the product itself may be digitised whenever possible, as witnessed in the online music and entertainment industry. Companies need to form new alliances and partnerships to facilitate this move towards digitisation. Barua, Whinston and Yin[194] consider that "businesses will realize the Internet's maximum benefits when all players in the physical economy adopt the Internet in every aspect of their business. Today a relatively small percentage of US businesses actually use the Internet to sell products and services, while a vast majority continue to operate in the physical world, doing business as usual."

If the spreading out in e-commerce continues at a rapid pace, as is expected, then in four to five years from now, e-commerce transactions between businesses (B2B) and between businesses and consumers (B2C) will account for about 5 per cent of inter-company transactions and retail sales correspondingly[195]. The structure of cyberspace and low cost of using it permit the interconnection of new and existing information and communication technologies, and offers businesses and consumers a new and powerful information system and a new form of communication, making possible for buyers and sellers to come together in

---

[194] *www.internetindicators.com*

[195] Goldman Sachs (2000), "The shocking economic effect of B2B", Global Economics Paper, No. 37.

more efficient ways, creating new marketplaces and opportunities for the reorganisation of economic processes, and altering the way products are customised, disseminated and exchanged and how businesses and consumers consume products[196]. Productivity and economic growth will rise as a result of more efficient management of supply and distribution, lower transaction costs, low barriers to entry and better access to information[197]. The development of cyberspace and e-commerce will modify the cyclicality of economies and how payments are made, changing the setting and operation of monetary policy and the cyclical[198] characteristics of economies may change to the extent that e-commerce facilitates more efficient stock management, leading to inferior inventories as a ratio of sales and perhaps modifying the stock building cycle. To that extent Friedman[199]said that cyberspace related technologies could increase the speed of financial operations, raising the issue as to how interest rates should be set and whether the short end of interest setting needs to become shorter.

As discussed earlier, GDP estimates are used to calculate the growth rates of global and national GDPs. Since the industrial revolution the growth rate of the global economy has been comparatively fast with increasing availability of material goods, services, and wealth which based on increases in capital stock, knowledge, science and technology, population, innovation, the supply of resources, better management practices, and improved productivity. The central issue for the global economy in the determination of optimal economic growth is the rate at which the global community should save, invest, and consume out of the global income so that the global economy grows at the maximum growth rate over a time horizon[200]. Globalisation characterizes international economic relations and the nature of trade is changing, with intermediate goods and goods in process becoming more prominent. Vertical production processes are being split, with separate pieces of these processes being outsourced to countries that have specific advantages in providing the inputs that such fragments use intensively, whether this be unskilled labor, skills, capital, or cheap energy sources and the costs of fragmentation have declined considerably, including not only transportation costs, but also the costs of conveying information, the costs of monitoring deliveries and coordination, and the costs involved in dealing in arms-length transactions with foreigners[201].

The virtual organisation is a set of co-operating (legally) independent organisations, which to the outside world offer a set of services and functionality as if they were one organisation. The characteristic is that no single company has the overall decision authority that decisions will have to be reached in consultation and between independent entities. Tools to explore, optimise and make use of business process frameworks are key to management of these virtual organisations. Amazon is selling books over the Internet and is a company created for and because of the development of e-commerce. Apart from a small number of companies that can only exist because of the invention of Electronic Commerce, the majority

[196] Lee, H. (1997), Do electronic marketplaces lower the price of goods? Communications of the ACM. Volume 41, Number 12.

[197] European Central Bank (1999), The Effects of Technology on the EU Banking Systems.

[198] Mcguckin, R.H. And K. Stiroh (1999), "Theory and history behind business cycles: are the 1990s the onset of a golden age?" Journal of Economic Perspectives, Vol. 13, No. 2, Spring.

[199] Friedman, B. (1999), "The future of monetary policy: the central bank as an army with only a signal corps?", International Finance (2:3), pp 321- 338.

[200] S.M.N. Islam, Optimal multiregional global economic growth: Formulation of an optimal growth program, growth prospects, and convergence, Journal of Policy Modeling 23 (2001) 753–774.

of companies should view Electronic Commerce as one instrument in a range of thousands of equipments that may, or may not, be applicable to their business. Their decision must be made in the light of their global business strategy and not because it is the latest thing to employ a particular technology.

Is there a transition of global economy to electronic commerce? Companies have to master the use of information technology, and e-commerce not only to better manage their own affairs but also to compete and thrive in the emerging digital economy. Competency in e-commerce will become precondition to survival any sector of commerce. Electronic commerce carries an underlying promise of being a great equalizer exposing small enterprises to a number of original and cost-effective ways to advance their goods and services on a global level. Additionally, electronic Commerce scenery is changing quickly and the continuous motion makes it exceptionally difficult for a business to completely embrace and engage in commerce on-line but once the technology and standards mature, electronic commerce is certain to produce remarkable results. Companies can sell products and services more easily and as a result, buyers and suppliers can conduct their activities more effectively. It could be said that numerous businesses have at first established a Web presence more for image-building reasons than for financial reward enhancing their company's image, and distributing prices and product information. The initial costs and infrastructure concerns are considerable enough to discourage many companies from making a transition from using Web as a marketing tool to fully embracing E-commerce. A number of companies are not prepared for the complexities in business-to-consumer E-commerce and there is a need for efficient logistics on the back end. Management of internal change will be a key factor in success of companies in the electronic commerce. Cyberspace transactions have a spectacular impact on traditional ways of doing business, bringing producers and consumers closer blurring the lines between manufacturer and retailer, and entirely eradicating many of the costs encountered until now. Internet service providers and E-commerce companies will need a set of technologies and integration capabilities that will help them offer reliable and predictable service to users. Until the problem of security is wholly solved, companies and consumers will be apprehensive about performing financial or other confidential transactions on-line and reluctant to use cyberspace and public networks for conducting business and so cyberspace transactions must be completely reliable and secure.

The spread of ICT and the process of globalisation have brought a superior business competitiveness due to the growth of various market segments and to the subsequent high demand for hi-technological products. Small companies, in order to respond to the quick diversification of markets, need large investments in resources for technology development. Besides, SMEs are in principle quite adaptable to changes, since they have an inherent capability to drive re-organisational processes or to readapt their productive performances they often lack the scale and resources to conduct research, development and training in-house that in a straight line reflects in their capability to improve their competitiveness.

All copyrighted works can be digitised and, once put on the Net, copying tends to be unproblematic, costless, extensive and immediate. While right holders want to fight against piracy and optimise their revenues with usage control, the consumer expects that digital technology will bring an added value in terms of usage and quality of information. A balance between owners' concerns and consumers' expectations must be found to ensure mutual trust.

---

[201] Jones, R.W., 2000. Globalization and the Theory of Input Trade. MIT Press, Cambridge, MA.

At the same time, co-existence between commercial and non-commercial communication must be ensured. Technological mechanisms are being developed and implemented to prevent unauthorised use of digital copyrighted information, but such mechanisms must comply with the legal environment in which they will function. For instance, the diversity of the legal environments makes it difficult to implement such applications at a global level. As mentioned above, cyberspace has no international regulatory body to resolve disputes. Instead, disputes have to be resolved by reference to the national laws of the territories where the electronic commerce takes place.

Despite the slowdown of dot.coms the Internet is continuing to grow strongly and Internet connections, the number of secure servers (which are needed for E-commerce transactions), Internet traffic and the volume of electronic commerce have all grown unabated, even as the NASDAQ and other stock market indicators have fallen back from a peak in the spring of 2000. The danger of a widening gap between countries that take advantage of ICT and those that do not is popularly known as the "digital divide".

As stated above, in a globalised economy a lot of the issues correlated to corporate accountability stem from the emergence of the multinational enterprise. The capacity of the MNEs to assign resources across borders, to take no notice of national boundaries in producing and selling their goods has had a positive effect on investment, in both OECD and developing economies. Nevertheless, MNEs in the absence of global regulation have been perceived as using their role of "regulatory arbitrage" between national regulatory systems to avoid national requirements; or using their power to shift resources in a way that might unjustifiably damage some economies in which they operate in. In other words, MNEs are at once global and local citizens and are increasingly expected to act as such by the key constituencies they depend on. The Guidelines are the only comprehensive, multilaterally endorsed code of conduct for MNEs. First adopted in 1976, the revisions have updated the recommendations, which now cover areas such as corporate responsibility including labour relations, environment, information disclosure, anti-corruption and consumer protection. Although the Guidelines are not legally binding, adhering governments are dedicated to promoting their observance. The institutionalisation of today's market economies is characteristic of modern days. Corporate governance becomes an issue of systemic stability in the financial markets. The OECD Principles cover five main areas: the rights of shareholders and their protection; the equitable treatment of all categories of shareholders; the role of employees and other stakeholders; timely disclosure and transparency of corporate structures and operations; and the responsibilities of the board towards the company and shareholders. The Principles would have remained a dead letter if the international community that helped produce them did not take steps for their implementation. The OECD and the World Bank put together a far-reaching global co-operation framework and on June 16 1999, the OECD Secretary General and the President of the World Bank signed a Memorandum of Understanding to this effect The OECD Principles of Corporate Governance are the starting point and reference of this partnership.

It could be said that nowadays the term "New/digital Economy" signifies a non-inflationary growth model based both on heavy investment in new information and communications technologies (ICTs) and on reforming the economy around these new technologies[202]. The Internet is clearly a vital component of the new economy. At present the digital economy has proven to be less destructive than had been thought. For instance, in the automobile sector, on-line sales have not replaced dealer sales but informational visits to Internet sites precede and encourage visits to dealer showrooms, where the actual sales still take place. The digital economy is a structural development because the dissemination of ICTs will have a long-term effect on the economic behaviour of producers and consumers across all sectors of the economy, and in trade and investment. The digital economy should not be confined just to e-business and e-commerce. The tangible goods will continue to be produced in factories probably with a further use of logistics and e-logistics. It should be taken into account that the development of digital economy do not mean that all tangible goods will be transformed into digital ones but the prevailing element is the digitisation all the other aspects that can be digitised. The connotation of the digital economy cannot be gauged from start-ups, but rather from the transformations observed in the more traditional sectors of the economy[203]. The digital economy means better integration in the world economy, through trade in ICTs[204] and the ensuing repercussions for development.

7.7 Digital Economy and Globalisation

The growing importance of the global information technology effect is robust across different specifications, notably for equal-versus value- weighting. Digital economy is raising the profile of industry sectors in portfolio diversification strategies[205]. Does globalisation increases the need for governmental intervention while, at the same time, it reduces its capacity to intervention? If globalisation reduces tax revenue and the governments' ability to have tax systems that are progressive and equitable, the governments will lose a major instrument for promoting social protection. Moreover, globalisation is likely to reduce the ability of individual governments to impose regulations and so globalisation has increased of the likelihood of financial crises. Hence, if globalisation increases financial instability, it increases the need for the government to pursue a greater stabilizing role in the economy than in the past. Additionally, globalisation tends to raise the share of trade in gross domestic products and to expose inefficient industries of sectors to greater foreign competition. In other word, globalisation and cyberspace provide much more timely information of prices and other relevant variables thus increasing competition. With globalisation financial capital and high skilled individuals become much more mobile because their options expand to other countries. The loss of skilled labour force and the outflow of financial capital can leave a negative effect on the growth rate and on the tax revenue of a country. In sum, globalisation brings strong pressures on the international community to level the international field in which individuals and enterprises operate. Digital economy is affecting not only the

---

[202] OECD (2000) A New Economy? The Changing Role of Innovation and Information Technology in Growth, OECD, Paris.

[203] Gordon, R.J. (2000) "Does the 'New Economy' Measure up to the Great Inventions of the Past?", NBER Working Paper, No. 7833, NBER, Cambridge, MA, August.

[204] Morgan Stanley Dean Witter (2001) Technology, Media and Telecommunications (TMT) Database, (*http://www.msdw.com*).

[205] Cavalgia, S "The increasing importance of industry factors" 2000 Financial Analysts Journal, September 41-54.

information and communication technologies (ICT) sector but also the whole economic structure. Besides, some industries are closer to the epicentre, and are by now transformed by the digitisation of business processes and products. European industry and policy-makers is to exploit specific European dynamics in order to ensure lasting growth, competitiveness and employment in the digital economy. The digital economy has been characterized by the combination of three phenomena:

- Faster growth, with low inflation;
- Strong job creation and declining unemployment;
- Increased productivity.

Traditional economic patterns have been altered by the wide adoption of ICTs, resulting in a reduction in structural and cyclical unemployment, low inflation and a smoother business cycle. The ICT industry that is characterized by its global reach, rapid technological cycles and high investment in R&D, is a strong contributor itself to overall productivity and GDP growth. EU[206]companies focus on cost-saving and productivity-enhancing applications, looking for immediate results rather than exploring new markets and developing new activities. In the digital economy, companies use technology to innovate and deliver improved or novel goods and services. Labour productivity and total productivity have been increased by the combination of ICT investment and organizational change. Hence, to accomplish full benefits of the digital economy, ICT investments must be complemented by organizational change. Is digital economy the product of a "financial revolution", rather than a technological revolution? The generalization of digital economy processes in online brokerage or electronic markets mobilises new sources of capital, facilitating in turn risk-taking, and more innovation. It is in the business to business (B2B) area that the most significant changes are taking place. E-business is developing not only in the area of services such as travel and financial services, but also in the area of tangible goods such as apparel, publishing and food. Borders between B2B and B2C activities are disappearing, which means that Internet retailers have to "source" and extend upstream into supply chain activities. Many B2B companies are tempted to maximize their supply chain investments by extending "downstream" to reach the final consumers. Many businesses introduce the combination of an online and physical presence. Retailers shift part of their activities online, adding new distribution channels, often by creating a "web-page" and improving their Internet skills for a fraction of their former value. The degree of reorganization of distribution channels is an imperative measure of change in the digital economy. Existing intermediaries such as traditional brokers are displaced by online brokers and logistics firms engaging in software design together with e-business brokerage emerge. Hence, E-business is challenging the status quo, and there is a need for a new legal and regulatory framework.

As discussed earlier, virtual enterprises are emerging in many sectors such as construction projects, ICT, consumer electronics, and car manufacturing. Can virtual enterprises be developed into e-MNEs? Virtual enterprises go much beyond electronic trading and imply complex production and value creation processes and so traditional MNEs can be transformed into e-MNEs. The move from traditional electronic data interchange (EDI), to

[206] Patrick Vittet-Philippe, Europe In The Digital Economy: Challenges For Eu Enterprises And Policies, Computer Law & Security Report Vol. 18 no. 1 2002.

new Internet business applications is deemed to result in further cost savings. Joint product development emerges and companies collaborate to create value with partners worldwide.

The digital economy is generating new challenges for competition rules. Market definition is made more complex, market data is often hard to find, products and services are technically complex and fast-changing that means the need for the definition of the relevant market. Market dominance, information transparency leading to collusion, information transparency leading to insider advantage, joint purchasing and joint selling in cyberspace are matters that must be defined. Digital economy is dependent on efficient logistics, which play an important role in increasing the efficiency of supply chains, and in implementing new e-marketplaces and new forms of collaborative commerce. Logistics have a powerful force in the digital economy not only as a facilitator for other businesses, but also as a pioneer of the digital economy itself. Global logistics firms have moved into the management area and e-business services activities incorporate not only added functionalities, such as parcel tracking, tax collection, automated calculation of costs, but also the provision of one-stop-shop for e-business needs, such as market advice and provision of e-business systems. Competent logistics should reduce environmental and energy impact of developing e-business trade.

The globalisation of companies, markets and technologies, has considerably affected the role of the nation state and its capacity to act in technology policy. International trade and investment have expanded in recent years in tandem with the number and capitalization of multinational firms. Has markets and technologies, the very capacity of the nation state to promote and to control the creation, distribution and utilization of advanced technologies been declining due to the globalisation of companies? There is a growing asymmetry between the limited, territorially-based scope of the state's jurisdiction and the global, borderless range of action of companies. According to Edgar Grande [207]"public R&D policy both on the national and on the supranational level has been confronted with an intensifying strategic dilemma: policy strategies which have been feasible within the existing institutional structures turned out to be under-complex and, hence, inadequate to improve industrial competitiveness in the IT sector; however, more adequate, comprehensive innovation policy strategies tended to be over-complex and overstrained the state's institutional capability, in particular its capacity for horizontal and vertical policy coordination.". Internet should be developed into a network with end-to-end protections[208].

Spatial fragmentation[209] does not automatically lead to multinationality, since it may be accompanied by organisational fragmentation, the contracting of activities to outside firms. It could be said that fragmentation of production is one expression of globalisation of the world economy. Fragmentation may lead to the development of "vertical" MNEs, in which all activities of a particular type are concentrated in a single location; in consequence, instead of undertaking all production in a single country, fragmentation results in downstream production being undertaken in one country, and upstream production in another. Alternatively, fragmentation may cause the development of "horizontal" MNEs, in which at

---

[207] Edgar Grande, The erosion of state capacity and the European innovation policy dilemma: A comparison of German and EU information technology policies" Research Policy 30 (2001) 905–921, p916.

[208] Steve Mott, The second generation of digital commerce solutions, Computer Networks 32 (2000) 669-683.

[209] Magnus Blomstrom, Fredrik Sjoholm, Technology transfer and spillovers: Does local participation with multinationals matter?, European Economic Review 43 (1999) 915-923.

least some of the Firms' activities are replicated in two places. According to Anthony[210] J. Venables "fragmentation does not necessarily lead to increased trade volumes, or to international convergence of factor prices. Its effects depend on the relative factor intensities of different stages of the production process."

Transportation costs induce plants to locate nearer to their inputs and close to their customers[211]. Technical progress is propelled not only by innovations but also by experience in producing with a certain technology. The value of clustering is especially great in the early stage of development of a new technology. The need to cluster near other firms diminishes over time. Production scatters not only due to the rising factor prices within agglomeration centers but also because consumers are decentralized. Industries became more localized as regions became more specialized. According to Audretsch and Feldman[212]while the marginal cost of transferring information across geographic space has been made invariant by the telecommunications revolution, the marginal cost of transferring knowledge, principally tacit knowledge, is rising with distance. Moreover, according to Laura Bottazzi [213]"A decline in transportation costs, an increase in the rate of innovation or an increase in the technology gap, all factors that promote specialization and lengthen the industry life cycle increase trade and growth". If we arrange regions in a technological space, only R&D in those regions which are technologically closest has an impact of innovation. Bottazzi and Peri[214] have considered in "geographical" space as well as in "technological" space, the extent of the externalities generated from the stock of technological knowledge of European regions.

The changes in the structure of retailing and industrial structure, in general, have been enormous over the last two centuries. Aggregate demand is generated from explicit aggregation of heterogeneous individuals. According to Simon P. Anderson and Andre de Palma [215]"a higher taste for variety breaks down the localization of competition in the spatial market and brings firms into market contact with other firms beyond their nearest neighbours. The consequent higher degree of contact engenders more competition for consumers farther away, and thence lower prices". Moreover, Walz[216] considers that trade liberalisation is shown to lead to agglomeration and faster growth. Technological change, when it materializes in the creation of new goods and new firms, has an impact on the extent and the direction of foreign direct investment and capital flows. In accordance with Philippe Martin and Gianmarco I.P. Ottaviano [217] "industrial concentration fosters growth due to the local spillovers. If the R&D sector also uses the differentiated goods, then an increase in growth

---

[210] Anthony J. Venables, Fragmentation and multinational production, European Economic Review 43 (1999) 935-945, p944.

[211] Marshall,A.,1920.Principles of Economics .Macmillan, London.

[212] Audretsch,D.,Feldman,M.,1996.R&D spillovers and the geography of innovation and production. American Economic Review 86,641-652.

[213] Laura Bottazzi, Globalization and local proximity in innovation: A dynamic process, European Economic Review 45 (2001)731-741, p740.

[214] Bottazzi,L.,Peri,G.,2000.Innovation and spillovers: Evidence from European regions. Mimeo.

[215] Simon P. Anderson , Andre de Palma, From local to global competition, European Economic Review 44 (2000) 423-448, p424.

[216] Walz, U., 1996. Transport costs, intermediate goods, and localized growth. Regional Science and Urban Economics 26, 671-695.

[217] Philippe Martin, Gianmarco I.P. Ottaviano, Growing locations: Industry location in a model of endogenous growth, European Economic Review 43 (1999) 281-302, p300.

will increase the market size of the innovative location and lead to industrial relocation to that location".

International trade and investment now play a greater role in each country's economic policy than 15–20 years ago. The globalisation of business has been based on the revolution in information and communication technology and helped by the rapid improvement in the quality and sharp decline in the prices of ICT equipment and software, the convergence in communication and computing technologies and the swift growth in network computing. The Internet is integrating markets and linking together people across all kinds of traditional boundaries. Baily and Lawrence[218] held that IT innovation has been driven by the demand for superior technologies in the using industries and that in the United States competition in the service industries, often on a global scale, has encouraged them to seek out innovative technologies to increase their own productivity. The fast technological advance makes it possible that the share of ICT industries in gross domestic product increases while ICT prices decline. Increasing returns, knowledge spillovers and skill complementarities drive economic growth and development, increase the spatial agglomeration of production and generate income differentials between people. Two-thirds of the recent improvement in labour productivity can be attributed to ICT[219]. On the one hand, ICT innovations have been driven by the demand for improved technologies in the using industries. On the other hand, the productivity gains do not only echo increased investment in ICT but also corresponding innovations in business organization and strategy. Technological knowledge leaks from one firm to another and companies may also benefit from sharing an intermediate input or from sharing access to a common pool of skilled labour[220]. The location of production diminishes in importance in a global digital economy where the costs of transportation and information are declining. The comparative advantage of a location does not any longer depend as much as it used to on some important endowment like the availability of cheap labour or the existence of an intermediate product. High IT clusters persist not because they are technology intensive per se, but because they rely on highly skilled labour. Global technical progress never raises the relative wage of the unskilled. According to Donald R. Davis[221] "the qualitative change in equilibrium relative wages does depend on whether the technical progress is global or local, and if the latter, in which country it is localized. However, it does not depend on the factor bias of the technical change".

As increased size and complexity threaten to upset the equilibrium between the limited information-processing capacities of the MNE HQ and the increasing information-processing requirements facing the HQ decentralization reduces the information-processing requirements facing the HQ and maintains the equilibrium between information-processing capacities and needs. Companies don't abandon states of equilibrium unless they can no longer cope successfully with their environments[222]. Hence, MNEs need to change their strategies and

---

[218] Baily, M.N., Lawrence, R.Z., 2001. Do we have a new digital economy. National Bureau of Economic Research, Cambridge, MA, Working paper no. 8243.

[219] Pohjola, M. (Ed.), 2001. Information Technology, Productivity, and Economic Growth. Oxford University Press, Oxford.

[220] Quah, D., 2001. ICT clusters in development: theory and evidence. European Investment Bank Papers 6, 85–100.

[221] Donald R. Davis, Technology, unemployment, and relative wages in a global economy, European Economic Review 42 (1998) 1613-1633.

[222] Romanelli, E., Tushman, M.L., 1994. Organizational transformation as punctuated equilibrium: an empirical test. Acad Manage J 37 (5), 1141–1166.

organizational designs as they develop, so that at each stage of development they retain some balance or equilibrium between the MNE's organizational design and its strategy and environment. It should be taken into consideration that MNEs from time to time ignored structure and used more informal and personal means of coordination to develop and apply new ideas that otherwise lay outside of the dominant strategy and were not supported by the formal structure and organizational design. Failures are widespread in a global framework due to restrictions on capital flows, double taxation, legal framework, inadequate ICT infrastructure and failure to use logistics effectively and consequently MNEs arrange an internal market with networking to avoid unnecessary transaction costs. Through networking and internal control MNEs protect and retain control of their tangible and intangible assets in other words their intellectual property, while at the same time, deserve an economic rent on these assets. Services are intangible in nature, whose quality cannot be judged prior to consumption, increasing the information asymmetry. The demands of the MNE need to be balanced in equilibrium with the demands of other institutions in a wider social context. Finally, William G. Egelhoff[223] says that "insights can be reconciled by using a framework that generally confines the flexible, change-oriented perspective of transnationalism and heterarchy to a micro level domain and the equilibrium-seeking perspective of structural contingency theory to a macro level domain".

[223] William G. Egelhoff, Organizational equilibrium and organizational change: two different perspectives of the multinational enterprise, Journal of International Management 5 (1999) 15–33, p32, at 15 "the new change-oriented models are most applicable at the micro levels of MNEs, while traditional equilibrium models are more applicable at the macro levels".

CONCLUSION

Since the 1970s, international and supranational organizations have urged MNEs to adopt voluntary codes of conduct. The *Norms* point to potential far reaching changes in global consensus with significant ramifications for corporate law. First, the *Norms* considerably alter the framework of the debate about corporate social responsibility seen them as social, political, and economic actors, but constraints on action against shareholders, and especially corporate shareholders effectively disregarded for virtually all purposes. Second, MNEs are enlisted as agents of international law implementation, even against states that have either refused to ratify certain international instruments or that have objected to the gloss advanced by international institutions implementing international law standards through private law. International human rights and other norm standards are incorporated in the contractual relations to whom MNEs are parties. It could be argued that MNEs are used as a means of end-running states, and in the process create a basis for the articulation of customary international law principles that will apply to states. Third, the *Norms* largely alter the balance of power over corporate governance between inside stakeholders (shareholders, lenders) and outside stakeholders (community, society, the state) by providing a substantial role for NGOs to monitor the conformity of MNEs with the requirements of the *Norms*.

Consequently, the Norms symbolize a deep shift in responsibility for protecting human rights--from governments to private actors, including MNEs— successfully privatizing the enforcement of human rights laws[1]. The proposed norms are said to be "non-voluntary" meaning obligatory but it is entirely uncertain who would have the responsibility for enforcing their implementation. The norms create a new international legal framework, cutting across virtually every area of business operation, with companies, rather than the governments that negotiated them, responsible for implementing international treaties and conventions creating conflict on legal requirements for companies operating around the world and so diverting attention from efforts to expand the capacity of national governments to implement and enforce existing human rights laws. The obligations of corporations are no greater than those of other non-state actors engaged in business. The Norms appear to contemplate the direct imposition of international legal obligations on private Corporations and their adoption would represent a remarkable shift in how international law regulates non-state actors. If international legal norms were extended to corporations and backed by effective enforcement mechanisms, states would lose control over compliance with the

[1] United States Council for International Business, UN to Review Proposed Code on Human Rights for Business, Mar. 5, 2004, at *http:// www.uscib.org/index.asp?documentID=2846*.

norms. If not accompanied by an effective enforcement mechanism, the norms would probably be widely disregarded.

It is worth mentioning that the state itself is gradually more delegating authority to private actors who exist in a shadowy world of quasi-public/quasi-private authority[2]. It could be argued that international law lost its privileged place as the principal conceptual framework for understanding the cross-border development of norms by the introduction of universal human rights standards, the recognition of interdependence among nation-states and the development of international courts and institutions. The present world order is characterized by a complicated mix of cross-border dealings between individuals and/or public entities and many transactions take place within loose regulatory schemes provided by international networks of public agencies, or by horizontal clusters of transnational market actors. A state-centred democracy can be defended against globalisation otherwise a global state has to reproduce the classical ordering forms of the nation state on a global scale.

A body of law emerges from globalization processes in multiple sectors of civil society independently of the laws of the nation-states[3]. Private law performs a state-breaking function and de-emphasizes the 'vertical' subordination of citizens to their sovereigns, and points at 'horizontal' relations between equally situated market actors. Post-national institutions such as EU differ severely from national governments and need not even be identified by geographical borders and there is no doubt that such institutions constrain the political will of state sovereigns[4].

States no longer dominate the international landscape, as international organizations and private actors such as MNEs and NGOs exercise increasing influence in the creation, implementation, and enforcement of international norms[5]. It has to be taken into consideration

---

[2] P.W. Singer, War, Profits, and the Vacuum of Law: Privatized Military Firms and International Law, 42 Colum. J. Transnat'l L. 521 (2004). Jody Freeman, Extending Public Law Norms Through Privatization, 116 Harv. L. Rev. 1285 (2003); Gillian E. Metzger, Privatization as Delegation, 103 COLUM. L. REV. 1367 (2003).

[3] Sol Picciotto, Introduction: Reconceptualizing Regulation in the Era of Globalization, in New Directions In Regulatory Theory 1-11 (Sol Picciotto & David Campbell eds., Blackwell, Oxford, 2002).

[4] Laurence R. Helfer & Anne-Marie Slaughter, Toward a Theory of Effective Supranational Adjudication, 107 Yale L.J. 273 (1997). Daryl J. Levinson, Framing Transactions in Constitutional Law, 111 Yale L.J. 1311, 1313 (2002) ("Common-law rules and adjudication are structured around discrete transactions between strangers. The prevailing, classically liberal, model of tort, contract, and property cases features atomistic individuals who interact only at the point of a discontinuous event, sharply limited in space and time.")

[5] Steve Charnovitz, Opening the WTO to NonGovernmental Interests, 24 Fordham Int'l L. J. 173, 210–11 (2000) (noting developing country fears that NGO participation in the WTO may diminish their sovereignty, and discussing how sovereignty can be challenged by NGOs); Philip R. Trimble, Globalization, International Institutions and the Erosion of National Sovereignty and Democracy, 95 Mich. L. Rev. 1944, 1946 (1997) ("The new conditions loosely associated under the platitudinous rubric of 'globalism' pose new and quite visible challenges to national sovereignty . . . ."); at 1946 ("In the past, international law concerned itself mostly with states and official intergovernmental relations. Now it increasingly concerns itself with private personae, including multinational corporations, as well as governments, and it deals with subjects that traditionally were treated as purely domestic matters."); Stephen D. Krasner, Sovereignty: Organized Hypocrisy 3 (1999) ("Analysts have argued that sovereignty is being eroded by one aspect of the contemporary international system, globalization, and others that it is being sustained . . . .").at 12 ("The inability to regulate the flow of goods, persons, pollutants, diseases, and ideas across territorial boundaries has been described as a loss of sovereignty."); Leo Gross, The Peace of Westphalia 1648–1948, in Essays on International Law and Organization 3 (A. Rubin ed., 1993) (articulating the notion of a Westphalian legal order based on "states exercising untrammeled sovereignty over certain territories and subordinated to no earthly

that state making power is today not as much of obvious, but no less effective than it ever was. The fact that in international law diplomacy, raw politics, and states' self interest dominate the scene of intergovernmental relations has given place to growing emphasis on the role of international courts and tribunals[6]. On the other hand, it could be said that international law over the last half century supports investors and encourages investment by weakening state power and authority[7].

Public international law has imposed substantial limitations upon the freedom of states but it does not take away their legal status as sovereign entities as long as the essence of state functions is retained and so states still have international legal personality[8]. The general consent of states creating rules of general application remains the operating principle of the international legal order and so by treaty or by practice it is states whose conduct determines the rules of international law. Modern states recognize the capacity of other actors to have rights and duties on the international plane, a status that, while definitely not equal to states, is adequate for those actors to participate in the formation, implementation, and even the enforcement of international law. The international sovereignty of states remains fundamentally unchanged and the international legal personality of states is untrammeled. States not only continue to have the authority to create, implement, and enforce international law, they also have the authority to determine who else may participate in that process. International law remains both the subject and master of states and the system maintains its legitimacy with respect to its existing actors—states.

International human rights law aims principally to protect individuals and groups from abusive action by states and state agents. Globalization has led to the emergence of powerful non-state actors such as MNEs who have resources sometimes greater than those of many states. The international legal personality of inter-governmental organizations is seen to carry with it the obligation to conform to general international law norms, above and beyond the requirements of the constituting charters or constitutions of the organizations. Globalization

authority"); Kanishka Jayasuriya, Globalization, Law and the Transformation of Sovereignty: The Emergence of Global Regulatory Governance, 6 Ind. J. Global Legal Stud. 425, 425 (1999) (arguing that sovereignty is being transformed since the concept of it as "exclusive territorial jurisdiction—given the shorthand term 'Westphalian' . . . is no longer theoretically or empirically serviceable in the face of the internationalization of economic and social activity").Jack Goldsmith, Sovereignty, International Relations Theory, and International Law: Sovereignty: Organized Hypocrisy, 52 Stan. L. Rev. 959, 959 (2000) (noting conventional wisdom that sovereignty in the sense of a nation's exclusive and absolute power within its territory "appears to have diminished significantly in the past half century as a result of economic globalization, transportation and communications advances, the rise of nongovernmental organizations (NGOs), and the spread of international human rights law"); Kal Raustiala, Sovereignty and Multilateralism, 1 Chi. J. Int'l L. 401, 418–19 (2000) ("We are increasingly choosing to regulate at the international level. . . . Sovereignty traditionally conceived will necessarily be compromised . . . .");

6 Anne-Marie Slaughter, A Global Community of Courts, 44 Harv. Int'l L.J. 191 (2003). Bernardo M. Cremades & Steven L. Plehn, The New Lex Mercatoria and the Harmonization of the Laws of International Commercial Transactions, 2 B.U. Int'l L.J. 317, 319-20 (1984) (explaining that "[a]s the modern nation-state developed during the 16th century, rulers of sovereign states began to regard the autonomous Lex Mercatoria as an external threat to internal cohesiveness.... Merchant courts were merged into national court systems [, and] the innovations of the Lex Mercatoria... were assimilated into national law.")

7 Tai-Heng Cheng, Power, Authority and International Investment Law, 20 Am. U. Int'l L. Rev. 465, (2005),

8 Alexander Orakhelashvili, The Position of the Individual in International Law, 31 Cal. W. Int'l L.J. 241, 252 (2001) ("[T]he distinction between the nature of legal capacity of State and international organizations on the one hand, and individuals on the other, is apparent. The individual does not have any legal capacity under general international law.").

has created centers of power that are alongside, even in competition with the power of states. Accountability for human rights violations and prevention of future ones must today and in the future take into account these non-state actors: the media, corporations, and international organizations such as the WTO and the World Bank imposing increased international obligations on non-state actors through multilateral mechanisms. Thus, even though states will retain the primary responsibility for ensuring the promotion and protection of human rights, non-state actors will be held accountable when they undermine state efforts to do so or are complicit in violations undertaken by the state. Globalization and the emergence of worldwide norms in some realms, such as human rights, may be creating a limited global community[9].

States base their opposition to the *Norms* on opposition to making transnational corporations both a subject and a source of international law. States are reluctant to acknowledge the effectiveness of law in the absence of a sovereign. The *Norms* point to the advancement of significant changes in global thinking about corporations and the character and source of their regulation, which together will have noteworthy ramifications for national laws. The ideas the *Norms* embody, supported by important sectors of civil society and the international law establishment demonstrate the development in fact of a mechanics of interplay between national, international, public, and private law systems in allocating and competing for regulatory power. The regularization and institutionalization of these mechanics evidence transnational law coming into its own as a separate field of power.

MNEs are key actors within the world economy alongside the states. Is there currently a legal personality for MNEs in international law? Law reflects moral connections and it is not static which means that its content is shaped according to new situations and demands. In many situations MNEs have already been acceded as subjects of international law –Iran versus US claims tribunal 198110. There is a tendency to admit MNEs as actors in international law. It could be said that MNEs are not in position to freely decide if they accept their responsibilities according to international law and especially in the human right field. There is a need for more transparency in MNEs actions. MNEs are key actores in globalization and they have a duty to act in conformity with international law. This author thinks that there is a need in distinguishing between the MNE as an economic entity and so allowing the national law of establishment, the private international law and the international commercial law to deal with the economic matters and the MNE as a whole unit (parent company with all subsidiaries regardless its separate establishment in various states under national laws) an international social policy actor in globalization whose actions affect the global world. The latter characteristic of MNEs need to be dealt effectively in an international level by attributing international law legal personality to MNEs for specific purposes such as human right, crimes against humanity and environmental protection. Thus, the answer to our question is the attribution and confirmation of an international law legal personality for MNEs and for specific purposes such as global protection of human rights, crimes against humanity and environment protection. In other words MNEs to be considered as functional state actors for the specific purposes of protection against global level of abuses against human rights, crimes against humanity and environment protection. Private law cannot solve

[9] Oona A. Hathaway, Do Human Rights Treaties Make a Difference?, 111 Yale L.J. 1935, 2005 (2002) (arguing that human rights treaties have an "expressive function" that supports worldwide norms).

[10] ECJ case 4/73 WvG judgment of 14 May 1974.

matters of public international law and so the efforts to solve problems with a mixture of private law in an international cover allow MNEs to remain unregulated regarding major and global abuses against humanity and environment. A MNE cannot be transformed into a state because its main substance and role are the maximization of the profits of its shareholders.

The declaration by UN of an international law legal personality of the MNE (functional state actor) as a whole unit for the specific purposes of abuses in an international and global scale of human rights, crimes against humanity and environment protection will make MNEs subjects of international law with direct rights and duties. The establishment of a specific department within the ICJ which should have jurisdiction to deal with abuses *of* human rights, crimes against humanity and environment protection in an international and global scale committed by MNEs which could be the international enforcement mechanism against MNEs *functional state actors*. MNEs will not be able to circumvent national laws by spreading the abuses on human rights, crimes against humanity and environmental protection across various jurisdictions because the spreading of abuses by the MNE as a Unit will mean global abuse corresponding to the MNE's international legal personality for the specific purposes and consequently the MNE accountable before the ICJ as *a functional state actor.* NGO, MNEs and states can take a MNE before the ICJ for the specific matters for which a MNE has been attributed with an international legal personality. States should acknowledge the effectiveness of law in the global sovereign regarding the function of MNEs as global social actors and for abuses considering human rights, crimes against humanity and environment protection in a global scale rather than as economic entities.

Globalisation is disruptive and in places where the adjustment mechanisms are imperfect or non-existent because challenges protected niches, and established patterns of activity. Moreover, globalisation does not mean that the rich get richer and the poor get poorer. It could be said that those who argue against globalisation are denying the 1.5 billion people who live in absolute poverty the means of escape. Is the role of multinationals exploitative, environmentally damaging, hostile to human rights and democracy, and divisive, destroying established communities? Global corporations have a key role to play in issues ranging from human rights to environmental policies[11]. Particularly, corporations can be most valuable in helping the poor by investing in local and global communities on a long-term basis rather than by acting as charities or aid agencies.

Technological war is also the feature of today's world in the middle of a never experienced, relatively high fraternity, and broad co-operation. Norms of ethics are to be adjusted to the phenomenon of globalisation. The successful implementation of new and innovative Information Technology (IT) and Information Systems (IS) by enterprises requires the development of strategic implementation plans prior to IT/IS project commencement[12]. So, embracing innovative IT/IS applications such as e-commerce and e-conferencing must be the result of an analysis of the market in order to make the best of the use. The sweeping reductions in barriers to international trade have opened the door for export-led growth. Global economic integration is not a new phenomenon. Some communication and trade took place between distant civilizations even in ancient times. Globalization creates, through

[11] John Browne, The Role of Multinational Corporations in Economic & Social Development of Poor Countries: Leading Toward a Better World? *www.corporate-env-strategy.com* Corporations and Development

export-led expansion, the prospective of quick output growth, increasing national wealth and contributing to develop living standards in developing countries. Moreover, globalization allows the access to a wide variety of consumption goods, new technologies and knowledge to ideas and international best practices in different fields. Globalization has its limits, however. Considerations of time and distance, cultural differences between countries, and differences in government regulation all have combined to maintain the unique identities of national economies.

Do we live in a homogeneous world economy? It could be said that despite the trends toward globalization, we do not live in a seamless, homogeneous world economy. Global political action seems to be needed to avert deterioration in the global environment and to prevent unsustainability of development. The most evident changes implied by the increasing globalisation of innovation and technology are the tougher and increased competition and the greater collaboration between actors, both across and within national boundaries. The advantages, just as the costs, of these tendencies can be substantial, leading to a higher risk of `winners and losers'. It should be taken into account that acquisition or imitation of foreign products, technologies or foreign social models to local conditions with all their specificities is not a warranty of success. In a more interdependent and inter-linked world economy any unfavourable worldwide or regional shock, for instance the Asian crisis of 1997-98, is fast propagated to other economies. Economies that depend a great deal on a few main commodities as their main source of export earnings and fiscal revenues can be hit hard by these shocks. Highly integrated financial markets incline to convey global, regional or local shocks much more fast than in past decades when financial markets were less integrated. Uncertainty and volatility penalize capital formation with undesirable effects on economic growth. Additionally, portfolio shifts affect exchange rates, interest rates and economic activity. Thus, globalization is regularly associated with increased instability of output and employment affecting job security. Flexibility in labor markets required to compete effectively, in international markets, tends to erode long-term work. Furthermore, globalization tends to transmit the cultural patterns of large countries to the rest of the world through imitation of consumption patterns leading to homogenization of values, thereby reducing cultural diversity and national identities.

Global economic integration, domestic deregulation and the evolution of IT have stimulated MNEs to globalise their market positioning options in the past 5 years[13]. MNEs must develop a global network of relationships that can be restructured quickly to provide support for effective management of risk engendered by ubiquitous factors of globalisation, such as fluctuations in exchange rate, accelerating technology transfers, increased intervention of third party supranational entities, technological developments and the shift from economies of scale to economies of scope.

The private sector must bear a larger responsibility for the outcomes of in crisis management and must share the responsibility and the costs when the international flow of capital fails to deliver positive results. Many problems on the global economic scene, including the post socialist theatre, have evolved because of the lack of coordination between institutions dealing with particular aspects of international and global economic activities.

[12] Rodney A. Stewart, Sherif Mohamed, Raul Daet, Strategic implementation of IT/IS projects in construction: a case study, Automation in Construction 11 (2002) 681– 694.

[13] H Paul "Creating a global mindcest" 2000 Thunderbird IBR 187-200.

Some of the transition countries are on the path toward a full-fledged market economy, while others are attempting to reform their existing economic systems. The transfer of new technologies from advanced economies to catching up countries contributes significantly to the growing competitiveness of all emerging markets. If macroeconomic fundamentals are sound and financial stabilization is accomplished and if the political institutions perform well, then technology transfer brings about a major acceleration of the rate of growth. Technology transfer is raising the level of labor skills faster than its costs. Production located in less developed countries by developed countries will grow faster than the global average. Net transfer of resources from western to eastern-Europe has worked as a catalyst of growth. Financial liberalisation has less effect on firms from countries with more developed domestic financial systems. The international financial institutions have a crucial role in ensuring that globalisation occurs in an orderly fashion. Merely liberalisation does not drive the economy to over borrowing. Short-term debt maturity can play a crucial role in financial crises. Foreign investors with inferior information are willing to lend only short term[14]. Capital market integration is another feature of globalisation that has expanded substantially in recent years. Capital inflows contribute to growth by stimulating investment and promoting financial development[15]. Global inequality has two dimensions: inequality across and within countries[16]. Globalisation[17] may be associated with increased inequality and volatility, which may justify strengthening domestic safety nets and financial supervision and regulation and enhancing international economic policy coordination.

Volatility in financial markets seems to bring the volatility of economic activity. Recent international financial crises are the result of vulnerabilities related to financial sector weaknesses, overvalued exchange rates and unsustainable fiscal positions. The IT has strengthened real and financial linkages across countries[18]. Liberalisation should be accompanied by strengthened prudential regulation to prevent maturity mismatches. Countries with more developed domestic markets should be less concerned about opening their financial systems[19].

Flows of FDI into OECD countries declined more steeply in 2001 than in any previously recorded year, according to data from the OECD[20]. The economies of the euro area show considerable convergence of investment rates, accompanied by convergence of economic conditions such as profitability and interest rates, which are the result of both deeper market integration and a more harmonised institutional framework. M&A activities reflecting the longer-term strategic objectives of companies have dominated FDI flows in recent years.

---

[14] G Kolodko "Globalisation and catching up: From recession to growth in transition ecopnomies" 2000 IMF Working paper wp/00/100 p1 "As structural reforms and gradual institution building have taken hold, the post-socialist economies have started to recover, with some leading countries building momentum toward faster growth".

[15] D Dollar, A Kraay " Growth is good for the poor" 2001 World Bank Policy Research Paper N0- 2587.

[16] P Lindert, J Williamson "Does globalisation make the world more unequal?" 2001 NBER Working paper 8228.

[17] JA Scholte "Globalisation-A critical introduction" 2000 St Martin's Press Inc.

[18] F Mishkin "Financial policies and the prevention of financial crises in emerging market countries" 2001 NBER Working paper 8087.

[19] A Lehman "FDI in emerging markets" IMF Working paper wp/02/47 p 24 "US data show returns on total foreign direct investment capital in emerging markets in the order of 15 to 20 percent. The high returns of fereign affiliates are explained in part through access to intangible assets- technology, managerial know-how, and international marketing- that explain the international expansion of multinationals".

[20] EIS Europe Information Service "Montly report on Europe", June 2002.

Political and regulatory risk in the host country need to be compensated for though higher returns on domestic sales[21]. Easier imitation can increase growth by increasing the proportion of industries in which the more intense neck-and-neck competition takes place. Modern economies are based more on knowledge than previous ones, which were based on resources. The capacity to access information and to transfer it cheaply and instantaneously to people is the advantage rather than merely classical resources without underestimating their value. In accordance with M Harvey and M Novicevic[22] "the sharing of knowledge throughout the organisation dissolves the foundation of global ignorance and provides the awareness about global hyper competitiveness that is absent in the organisation".

The implementation of just in time systems and business process reengineering have achieved huge savings for supply chains and so firms managed to reduce costs associated with production, inventory, transportation and administration. For instance, local decision-making within the supply chain can be harmful if it is not linked to global evaluation of the performance. MNEs have shown a tendency to internationalise an increasing proportion of their R&D. Countries hosting high-technology productive investments of MNEs are not necessarily important hosts of their R&D investments. Local technological capability plays an important role in attracting MNE investments in R&D. Major motivation of overseas R&D investments is to utilize technological resources available in different countries and to internalise the spillovers from R&D done by national firms. For developing countries, strength of intellectual property protection does not contribute for R&D investments[23]. MNEs tend to widen the gap between technologically richer and technologically poorer nations by concentrating their R&D investments in the countries already ahead in this respect. Firms' long-term performance has been concluded to be a direct result of effective planning and control. Centralised planning and decentralised operations constitute a common means for running a worldwide business. If a host country prefers to generate the highest tax revenue it should impose no governmental restrictions to a MNE. If a host country prefers to maximise its national welfare it should impose reasonable restrictions such as setting ceilings on ownership and royalty fees. How the intangibility and perishability of services affect entry mode choice? Does the electronic form of MNE change the entry-modes? Companies change from one entry-mode to another while remaining in the same location. Maximal firm performance is the ultimate goal of international entry and can be achieved accordingly by estimating the relevant factors influencing the profits of a company. MNEs goals are to maximise earnings, minimize taxes, maintain stable growth, and keep risk within prudent limits. Hence, MNEs overall goal is to maximize the stock market value of the enterprise's common stock.. E-MNEs will use the entry-modes used by traditional MNEs in order to deal with their tangible goods and entry-modes suitable for their intangible goods and services such as delivering their products via a central electronic store using cyberspace transactions. Companies engaged in electronic business transformation must make synergistic investments and commit resources not only in information technology, but also must align processes and

---

[21] R Lipsey "FDI in three financial crises" 2001 NBER Working paper N0 8084.

[22] M Harvey, M Novicevic "The hypercompetitive global marketplace: The importance of intuition and creativity in expatriate managers" 2002 Journal of World Business 127-138, p136.

[23] N Kumar "Intellectual property protection, market orientation and location of overseas R&D activities by Multinational Enterprises", 1996 World Development 673-688.

customer and supplier readiness to capitalize on the benefits[24]. E-business involve the total digitisation of value chains and business processes and serving traditional organizations create new value and reach up to that time unattained heights of operational and financial excellence. For instance, Cisco Systems and Dell Computer report in excess of 250% return on invested capital, and over $650,000 in revenue per employee[25]. There are momentous financial payoffs from e-business initiatives; however, firms must focus their efforts on exact areas to take in such gains[26]. The global community needs to develop is a forceful and adaptable environmental management system to meet the challenge posed by MNEs posing criminal sanctions and civil liability against them[27].

Globalisation cannot be reversed and technological change will continue to be rapid and this will stimulate further the interconnecting process of global communication and global governance. Moreover, they are not reversible other aspects of globalisation such as the global dimensions of environmental issues such as global warming. Export-led growth and the opening of domestic markets to competition have facilitated rapid growth and economic development globally. Losers at the country level include those countries with weak institutions unable to control the structural adjustment and social change that benefiting from globalisation requires. Certainly, globalisation redefines what constitutes an effective and efficient government system in an increasingly interdependent and interconnected world. A nation's per capita income can rise on a sustained basis only if its workers are provided with a steadily rising stock of physical, human and/or knowledge capital. Accordingly, European integration will affect the growth rate only to the extent that it affects the rate of accumulation of physical, human and knowledge capital. ICT remains a major positive dynamic force in OECD economies. Additionally, ICT has fostered networking, which has enabled informal learning and interdisciplinary co-operation between companies, as well as more outsourcing. To reinforce innovation, policy needs to give better priority to fundamental research, improve the effectiveness of public R&D funding and support the flow of knowledge between science and industry.

The competitive strategies of MNEs are determined by regional, country, industry, firm, business unit and organizational task level. A MNE can become a leader ("flagship firm") by providing strategic leadership to partners such as key suppliers, customers and the non-business infrastructure. The existence of a leader company pulls the network together and provides leadership for the strategic management of the network as a whole. Big companies, such as Chrysler, follow close collaborative relationships with its key suppliers. The French telecom is a leader company and its role is to provide the vision and direction for the

---

24 C. Murphy and C.T. Heun, "E-Business Helps Companies Weather Economic Chill," InformationWeek, January 29, 2001. J. Berry, "Why Companies Fall Short In E-business," InternetWeek, *http://www.techweb.com/wire/finance/story/INV20000417S0006.* P. Seybold, "Customers.com," 1998, Crown Business: New York. E. Berkman, "Clicklayer," CIO Magazine, February 1, 2001, *http://www.cio.com/archive/020101/officedepot_content.html.* TechWeb News, "Dell Applies Direct Model to Suppliers, Too," *http://www.techweb.com/wire/story/TWB20000811S0016.*

25 A. Barua, J. Pinnell, J. Shutter, A. B. Whinston, and B. Wilson, "Internet Economy Indicators: Wave IV," http://www.internetindicators.com. A. Barua, J. Pinnell, J. Shutter, A. B. Whinston, and B. Wilson, "Internet Economy Indicators: Wave III," *http://www.internetindicators.com.*

26 T. Wilson, "Nike Model Shows Web's Limitations," InternetWeek, December 3, 1999, *http://www.internetwk.com/story/INW19991203S0004.*

27 Michael Anderson, Transnational Corporations and Environmental Damage: Is Tort Law the Answer? 2002 Washburn Law Journal 399.

technological choices and commercial initiatives for the system. The vertical keiretsu can be seen as flagship models, where they band formidable global competitive positions and differ from the traditional Japanese keiretsu[28]. Companies in order to avoid a clash between global economic interests and local interests must know how to be responsible to the needs of the countries where they operate even as they globalise. IT and telecommunications in the MNE can be used for defensive and offensive strategies in its effort to reduce response time to important external events in the globalisation era. Management of the transition to a global information system based on new opportunities in telecommunications can be done by electronic gateways to customers and developing international technology linkages enabling the MNE to become a virtual global enterprise.

Globalisation leads to economic integration and has taken world politics away from the state-centric, sovereignty-based model of governance. Is globalisation a post-colonial imperialism of the transformed colonial powers over the rest of the world? Decolonisation gives the less developed countries more opportunities for development and self-determination in world affairs. Global governance institutions have promoted human rights. Globalisation leads to increases of interaction and independence between people in different countries. Globality describes circumstances where territorial space is substantially transcended and in global transactions place is not territorially fixed territorial distance is covered in effectively no time, and territorial boundaries present no particular impediment. Additionally, globality is evident in social activity through global consciousness and distance and borders are irrelevant. Communications networks, road links, railways, and air and shipping lanes are territorial. Moreover, territorial borders continue to exert considerable influence on flows of merchandise trade, investment and migration, and so lots of commodities remain bound to particular territorial markets. Many production processes are still linked to specific places and limited to single countries. Hence, globalisation is not antithetical to territoriality. The world is faced with a solemn "global governance gap" and in order to make globalisation sustainable there is a need for a much better balance between global market forces on the one hand and global governance and political institutions on the other. So, enhancing good governance throughout the developing and the developed world and at a global level is a vital precedence[29].

---

[28] A Rugman, J Dcruz "The theory of the flagship firm" ,1997 European Management Journal N.4 403-12.

[29] A Sustainable Europe for a Better World: A European Union Strategy for Sustainable Development COM(2001) 264, Commission Of The European Communities Communication From The Commission To The European Parliament, The Council, The Economic And Social Committee And The Committee Of The Regions Towards a global partnership for sustainable development Brussels, 13.2.2002 COM(2002) 82 final

INDEX

B

C

D

E

F

G

J

K

L

M

N

O

P

Q

R

S

T

U

V

W

Y

Z